THE GLORY AND THE DREAM

THE GLORY AND THE DREAM

THE HISTORY OF CELTIC F.C.

1887–1986

Tom Campbell & Pat Woods

MAINSTREAM
PUBLISHING

First published in 1986 by
MAINSTREAM PUBLISHING COMPANY (EDINBURGH) LTD.
7 Albany Street
Edinburgh EH1 3UG

British Library Cataloguing in Publication Data

Campbell, Tom
    The glory and the dream : the history
    of Celtic F.C. 1887-1986.
    1. Glasgow Celtic Football Club——History
    I. Title   II. Woods, Pat
796.334′63′0941443   GV943.6.G64

ISBN 1-85158-054-9

Typeset by Pulse Origination, Edinburgh.
Printed by Billings & Son, Worcester.

To John Campbell and James Woods,
and to Susan and Rosalind.

ACKNOWLEDGEMENTS

The authors wish to acknowledge their indebtedness to the many people who helped, encouraged and advised in the course of writing and researching this book.

Our thanks are extended (alphabetically) to Jim Gillespie, Kevin McCarra and Bill Murray for reading drafts of the manuscript and for their comments and suggestions for improvement.

We also appreciate the contribution of the following in providing information, photographs, advice or general assistance: Archie Baird, Sir Matt Busby, Daniel Cairns, Tom Cockburn, Tom Collin, Willie Cowan, Bob Crampsey, Pat Crerand, Cyril George, Hugh Keevins, Charlie Morgan, John Motson, Jack Murray, George Oliver, John Rowlinson, George Sheridan, Jack Webster and posthumously, George Paterson.

Lastly, we would like to thank Richard Jackson and Jerry Stubbings of the Ottawa Board of Education for their help in explaining the mystery of word-processing . . . and the staff of the Glasgow Room of the Mitchell Library for their unfailing patience and professionalism.

Front Cover: Celtic players celebrate the Scottish Cup final victory at Hampden, 1985 *(George Ashton)*
Inset: Postcard of Celtic player wearing the striped jersey which was the club's regular strip until 1903-04, when the famous hoops were introduced. One of a series of postcards from the Jack Murray collection on view at the exhibition, 'Scottish football: a history' (researched by Kevin McCarra) held at the Third Eye Centre, Glasgow, in 1983. *(Reproductions distributed by the Third Eye Centre).*

Back: Billy McNeill leads out Celtic for the European Cup final in Lisbon, 1967.

Contents

THE HISTORY

Brother Walfrid

1

JOINER, TAILOR, SOLDIER, PRIEST . . .

THE two men were so intent on their conversation that they were
oblivious to the darkening gloom of the December evening and the sight
of gas-lighters scurrying down side streets that seemed to stretch away
endlessly; the horse-drawn bus, the pride of Glasgow's expanding fleet,
lumbered and jolted along behind the two powerful Clydesdales at a
steady walking pace but the men, one burly and broad in the shoulders
and the other neat and dapper, ignored the passing scene of 'the second
city'. They were discussing the plight of yet another Irish family in
Glasgow; straight off the boat, penniless, and crowded into a couple of
bare rooms in a damp tenement on a mean street. John Glass had already
noted the man's name, and agreed to meet him to find him a job if
possible, even a short-term one as a labourer.

Listening to the conversation from the bench behind, Brother Walfrid,
an alert man in his mid-forties and dressed in a well-worn, almost shabby,
overcoat, felt in his pocket for a notebook as he reminded himself that he
had promised to visit the Granite Warehouse, the large retail store at the
corner of the Trongate and Stockwell Street, and attempt once again to
find places for two of the lads at the Literary Society who desperately
needed work.

Not for the first time he studied the other two, and thought almost
ruefully of the sequence of events that had brought them together. He had
no doubt about their worth. John Glass was a joiner, a man with many
contacts in all the building trades, a strongly built man of Donegal stock
recognised as a leader in the Irish community, a meticulous, careful man
but with the human touch, naturally dignified. He could charm the birds
down from the trees if he wanted to. The other, Pat Welsh, was a master
tailor with premises on fashionable Buchanan Street, a prospering
business, a lovely wife and a fine family, although he didn't speak much
about his days in Ireland and there were rumours that . . . well,
sometimes it's wiser not to delve too deeply into a man's past.

"Now, Pat, is this boy the right type for us?" John Glass had addressed

11

the question to Pat Welsh and waited sober-faced for an answer.

The tailor considered his words carefully before replying, "He's highly thought of as a footballer, and they tell me he's very fast — in fact he runs as a harrier. He trained as a teacher in London, a very articulate fellow; he's been playing with Third Lanark but he's free to join us if he wants to."

"And the family? A good Catholic family, is it?"

Again Welsh pondered, but his words were emphatic, "A fine family. I've known Thomas Maley for twenty years and he's an army man — used to be a sergeant with the North British Fusiliers and went all round the world with them. He has four sons, you know. Charles, his oldest, is a priest, and was born in the West Indies; Tom, the one we'll see tonight, was born in Portsmouth; Willie's training to be a chartered accountant and he was born in the army barracks at Newry; and young Alec was born here, in Cathcart village."

Brother Walfrid broke his uncharacteristic silence. "That's the tragedy of Ireland, isn't it now? Four fine Irish boys, and only the one born in Ireland. It's a queer world this, and the three of us, a tailor, a joiner, and a Marist Brother, going out to Cathcart to sign up a footballer — and not one of us knows a thing about the game."

Pat Welsh sighed in agreement, but John Glass was quick to sense and dispel the momentary shadow. "We're doing the right thing, never fear; not only this lad tonight, but the whole project, the whole endeavour."

Brother Walfrid smiled and spoke briskly, this time with all the enthusiasm and authority that ten years as Headmaster of Sacred Heart School had instilled in him. "You're perfectly right, John. God works in mysterious ways, and if it's up to us to form a football club so that our children can get food and clothing, then that's exactly what we'll do."

The three men lapsed into a thoughtful silence, as the omnibus lurched its way through the city.

Brother Walfrid, as he had been doing all too frequently, was thinking of money and the need to keep the Poor Children's Dinner Table afloat; for some years the Saint Vincent de Paul Society had struggled manfully, but with the growing numbers and recent increases in unemployment its resources were stretched to breaking point. For him the saving of the Poor Children's Table was a matter of body and soul: the families in the east end parishes, and in particular the children, were the victims of degrading poverty, and hunger was a constant factor in their lives. There had been a growth in the number of Protestant soup kitchens and Brother Walfrid, born as Andrew Kerins in Ballymote, County Sligo, had the Irishman's distrust of charity dispensed by the British; it could well be the means of Catholics slipping away and becoming Protestants by default.

John Glass sat upright on the hard, uncomfortable bench and thought back to the tumultuous meeting at St. Mary's Hall a little more than a

*month ago on 6 November, 1887, when a new 'football and athletic club'
was formed, and he again considered the implications of what he had seen
and heard. Clearly, charity and the children, would benefit, but would
there not be another and more far-reaching advantage for the Catholic
community? The Irish were looked down upon by the native Scots,
despised for their lack of education, loathed for their religion, and
distrusted as probable scab labour; cruel jokes and cartoons were
common, reflecting such a weight of hatred and resentment that many
Irishmen were already thinking of themselves as second-rate. A club such
as he envisioned could change that. An established team, successful on
the field and with compact, neat premises, would be a boost to the
community's morale, a source of legitimate pride, and a symbol of Irish
accomplishment.*

*Pat Welsh's thoughts were different. He was thinking not of the future
but of an event that had taken place twenty years earlier in Dublin at the
Pigeon House Fort on the Liffey when he first met Sergeant Thomas
Maley of the North British Fusiliers. He still remembered the iron grip of
the stocky sergeant, and his steady eyes fixed upon his face; he knew that
the game was up — as a suspected Fenian and an enemy of the British, he
could expect little mercy throughout their interrogations or in jail. He had
to admit to the soldier that he had come to the docks hoping to board one
of the boats heading for Glasgow. With senses sharpened by panic, he
was aware that the sergeant's voice retained the accent of a County Clare
upbringing and, encouraged by a silence that might be interpreted as
sympathy, he poured out his troubles as one Irishman to another. Maley
interrupted the story finally to ask, "What will you do in Glasgow?" and it
was a question that had to be answered. He had expressed haltingly the
aspirations of all emigrants: a fresh start, a new life away from 'the
troubles' . . . and as he stumbled on he was realising that perhaps the
politics of violence was not the solution, that a trade and respectability
would give him a voice that might be heard. Again Maley stopped him,
"My lad, I don't know, I just don't know; but, if I were to let you go here
and now, would I have your assurance that you'll go to Glasgow and
keep out of trouble?"*

*Now twenty years later, here he was on his way to see the old sergeant
again. In gratitude he had kept in touch with the Maleys over the years,
even finding accommodation for them when they arrived in Scotland after
the soldier's honourable discharge from the army. That gesture of
kindness to the desperate young Fenian would have got Thomas Maley a
court-martial had it been discovered, he thought . . .*

* * *

A novelist, writing a work of fiction, might be tempted to open his
account of the founding of the Celtic Football Club with the above; and

such a dramatisation would be true to the spirit of the founders and their times, but it would not be literally true. Truth, however, can be stranger than fiction and, as the authors suspected and have verified by their research, the history of one of the world's great football clubs needs no embellishment from fiction.

A deputation representing Celtic's first committee did visit the Cathcart home of Thomas Maley in December 1887, hoping to persuade his son Tom to join the newly formed club. As a student in London Tom had played for Caledonians, and in Scotland he had played for Hibs, Partick Thistle and had joined Third Lanark, in those days a force in the game. The visitors comprised the president of the club, John Glass, Brother Walfrid, a Marist Brother who held no official position with the club but who was an 'honorary member' of every committee, and Pat Welsh, who had been asked to accompany the other two because he was a family friend of the Maleys. They were greeted warmly by Thomas Maley and another son, Willie, a well-built youth getting a reputation for himself as a sprinter with Clydesdale Harriers. Tom was out, courting his wife-to-be, and Willie promised to relay the invitation to attend the next committee meeting.

It was a pleasant visit and during the conversation Brother Walfrid found himself becoming more and more impressed with the young man's maturity and poise; noting his athletic bearing and acting on an impulse, he added, "Why don't you come along as well?"

Nobody present could have realised that the casual invitation was perhaps the most important in Celtic's history. Along with his brother, Willie joined the club as a player and soon as a committee man. He later took on the added responsibility of match secretary and, despite his youth, was so competent in the task that he was appointed Celtic's first manager and was destined to fill that position until 1940. He must be regarded as the central figure in the club's first fifty years and perhaps in its entire history.

Where did that chain of events have its start? Was it in Brother Walfrid's invitation? Or did it really start when an otherwise exemplary sergeant in the British Army was touched enough by the distress of a fellow Irishman to risk his career in an act of kindness?

2

CATHOLIC AND IRISH

CELTIC Football Club arose out of the needs, physical and emotional, of a whole community in Glasgow: the club's revenues were designed to alleviate the worst effects of chronic poverty among the city's Catholics, and its anticipated success was calculated to engender a feeling of pride within an Irish community suffering from persecution and cultural alienation.

In order to suggest the nature and extent of the hostility that the Irish faced in Scotland, it is essential to examine the historical context. Ireland and Scotland are a mere stone's throw apart in geographical terms, and that seems an apt description of the relationship that the two nations have 'enjoyed'.

For more than a century before 1887 there had been migrations of agricultural workers from Ireland, workers who stayed for the summer and the harvest before returning home; in the second half of the 19th century many stayed longer and signed on for the duration of such massive industrial projects as the Loch Katrine Reservoir. This semi-permanent labour force was barely tolerated, and frequent clashes broke out between the native Scottish labourers and the newcomers. After 1840 the cyclical pattern changed with a dramatic increase in the numbers emigrating from Ireland; a series of failures in the potato crop culminated in the famine known as 'the Great Hunger', and the resultant unemployment in an agricultural economy was followed by heartless evictions that forced tens of thousands into permanent exile. Those who could afford it sailed for the United States far away from the unvarying backdrop of political unrest, but many crossed the Irish Sea bound for the industrial slums of Liverpool, Manchester and Glasgow. The fare from the Irish ports to the Clyde varied between 4d and 6d, but it was a miserable crossing within the crowded holds of the paddle-steamers, packed in along with the cattle. Jobless, impoverished, and often hungry, they arrived in Glasgow set apart from the native Scots by

15

accent and clothing, but there were the even more damning differences of nationality and religion.

The Scots greeted them with a resentment that often erupted into open hostility, and that was scarcely surprising. Struggling for survival themselves, they regarded the Irish as an economic threat. The Irish were considered scab labour, being willing in their desperation to accept lower wages and miserable working conditions without protest. Unscrupulous employers used the threat 'to bring in the Irish' as a tool to hamstring the emerging trade unions, and that caused further resentment. Scottish civic authorities blanched at the intolerable strain the flood of immigrants imposed on the existing resources. There was a lack of decent housing, schools and hospitals for the newcomers who crowded into the cities looking for mainly unskilled work; medical officers feared outbreaks of cholera and other communicable diseases. Old prejudices emerged from the tensions: the Irish were dirty and feckless; they were ignorant, drunken, violent, and even depraved . . . it was recalled that Burke and Hare, the infamous Edinburgh 'body snatchers', were Irish and former navvies on the Union Canal.

The question of religion caused most animosity. After the Reformation no country in Europe was more Protestant than Scotland. Pervaded with the grim enthusiasm that sometimes animates Calvinism, the Scots had removed all vestiges of 'Popery': in 1790, for example, there were 43 anti-Catholic societies flourishing in Glasgow at a period when only 39 Catholics were living in the city. It was basically a clash between two philosophies; of all the branches of Christianity, Presbyterianism and Catholicism are perhaps the least compatible in doctrine and when the practitioners of both religions held to the hard line as they did in Victorian times there was bound to be suspicion and friction in daily social life. Middle-class Scots, the elders or 'the Holy Willies', disapproved of the more tolerant Catholic attitude towards drinking, and they were scandalised on Sundays when Catholics after attending Mass would set out to enjoy the rest of the Sabbath. Even the lowliest Scot, a citizen of one of the most literate nations in Europe, was unable to understand the lack of motivation 'to get on' within the Irish working class and to improve their station through education. Scots were united in despising the Irish for their apparent subservience to the parish priest.

Alienated from the Scots by nationality, religion, politics, customs and status, the Irish were the victims of cultural apartheid, and it was as much for consolation as survival that they huddled into self-contained ghettoes to become 'a community within a community'. The principal consolations were offered by the common religion and a sense of nationalism, tinged and illuminated with the flicker of wit and laughter, but for many there was the darker comfort of 'the drink'. By 1887,

16

however, the grim lot of all workers in industrial Scotland had improved marginally, and within the Irish community there was some hope for the future as a middle class had started to evolve from the general drabness. Glasgow Celtic was formed to provide some of this community's still unanswered needs. From the start Celtic was an Irish and Catholic club, and made no attempt to disguise the associations; indeed, it frequently drew attention to its origins as a matter of pride.

It was manifestly clear that Celtic was a Catholic club. Founded largely through the determination of a Marist Brother, its first patron was Charles Eyre, 'His Grace the Archbishop'. Its revenues were earmarked for Catholic charities, its players, officials, members, and committee men were overwhelmingly Catholic, as were the vast majority of its supporters.

While his principal reason for founding a football club was to raise money to help feed and clothe the poor of the east end parishes, Brother Walfrid had other concerns. He was haunted by the fear that the Protestant soup-kitchens recently set up in Glasgow to combat distress might be the means of luring Catholics into apostasy; he was equally worried about the danger to the faith of young Catholics when they first started work and associated with Protestants. Thus, the circular of January 1888, distributed to raise funds, stressed the Catholic aspect and contained a paragraph that reflected Brother Walfrid's thinking: "Again there is also the desire to have a large recreation ground where our Catholic young men will be able to enjoy the various sports which will build them up physically, and we feel sure we will have many supporters with us in this laudable object." The *Glasgow Observer* noted with approval "the clusters of clergy" present at the opening games on the first ground in May 1888: Hibs against Cowlairs, and Celtic against Rangers three weeks later. Many contemporary cartoons, in the Catholic as well as the secular press, included sympathetic caricatures of priests among the crowds at Celtic games. Indeed, up to the present time the club continues the admirable tradition of admitting clergymen of any denomination into the ground free of charge; it would be safe to assume, however, that most of those clerics are Catholic.

In their coverage of football the Catholic newspapers concentrated on Celtic, and were unashamed apologists or propagandists for the club, whether in the *Glasgow Examiner* or the *Glasgow Observer*. Among their columnists in later years were John H. McLaughlin, the chairman of the club, and Tom Maley, a former player and committee member. For many years a regular weekly column under the *nom de plume* 'Man In The Know' appeared, written by writers deservedly anonymous and notorious for an outrageous bias in favour of Celtic.

Celtic's association with Catholicism had its lighter moments. One member of a Celtic committee, Ned McGinn, was so delighted at

Celtic's winning the three major trophies (the Scottish, Glasgow, and Charity cups) that he wired Rome in 1892: "We've won the three cups, Your Holiness." He was incensed at not receiving a reply, and it was with difficulty that his fellow members in the Home Government branch of the Irish National League restrained him from moving a vote of censure on the Pontiff.

Although Celtic was a Catholic club, and started off in imitation of Edinburgh Hibs and its sectarian policy, the team, the most visible element in the organisation, has not been exclusively Catholic and this practice stems from the earliest days. One of Celtic's first goalkeepers, the unfortunately named Duff, was an Orangeman who was replaced only after a cavalier performance in a friendly against Dumbarton, lost by 8-0 at Celtic Park on New Year's Day 1892. In 1895 a resolution was placed before the committee that no more than three Protestants be selected for the side, but this proposal was rejected and a counter-resolution was approved authorising the club to sign and field as many non-Catholics as it wanted. A similar attempt was made in 1897 to have future teams composed only "of the right sort" but the directors, with commendable firmness, squashed the misguided effort.

At the time of Celtic's founding the words 'Catholic' and 'Irish' were interchangeable in the West of Scotland, and the club acknowledged its Irish roots just as openly and proudly. Brother Walfrid was born in Ballymote, County Sligo, and one of the club's original patrons was Michael Davitt, the celebrated Irish patriot; all the founders were expatriate Irishmen or of Irish stock and the new club's support was drawn largely from the swelling Irish community in Glasgow. The donations to charity frequently included some to exclusively Irish causes such as the Evicted Tenants' Fund.

If, as Catholics, the members were concerned about the plight of local charities, as Irishmen they were obsessed with that perennial question of Irish politics, Home Rule. It need hardly be said that the various organisations mentioned here worked within the political framework and were as legitimate in their aspirations and methods as, for example, the Scottish Nationalist Party of today. John Glass, the president of the club from its inception until the change to a limited liability company in 1897, and a director from then until his death, was an outstanding figure in nationalist circles; he was prominent in the Catholic Union and was a founder of the O'Connell branch of the Irish National Foresters, as well as treasurer of the Home Government branch of the United Irish League. As with Bob Kelly in more recent times his interest and association with Celtic was a daily and all-absorbing one, but his obituary in 1906 appeared in the political rather than in the sports pages. William McKillop, of Antrim stock although born in Ayrshire, started in business as a licensed grocer with his brother John after moving to

Glasgow; with expansion his interests switched to restaurants, culminating in the ownership of the palatial Grosvenor. In public life he was the most visible of Celtic's membership, entering politics as MP for North Sligo, holding the constituency for eight years before winning in South Armagh in 1908, the year prior to his death. Many others in Celtic's early committees were involved actively in the discussions, debates and meetings of the period and their presence was noted approvingly by the Catholic press. In 1896 John Glass and William McKillop were part of an enthusiastic audience in the Grand National Halls to celebrate St Patrick's Day with speeches about Home Rule and the release of Irish political prisoners; those same committee men, along with Tom Colgan, attended another meeting later in the year advocating similar causes under the auspices of the Glasgow Amnesty Association, the Young Ireland Society, and the Irish National League. In the early 1900s the club was represented conspicuously if informally at various functions by players and directors; among those identified were Barney Battles, John Campbell, Sandy McMahon and William McKillop, James Grant, Tom Colgan and James Kelly.

The *Glasgow Observer* reported in June 1910: "Mr William Maley, secretary of the Celtic Football Club, gave a political address in Partick on Sunday last under the auspices of the United Irish League. Although the Maley family are best known by reason of their football fame, the various members of it have always taken a keen interest in politics. Mr T. Maley is a constant figure on the Nationalist platforms, and Mr Alex Maley took a prominent part some years ago in the affairs of the Pollokshaws branch of the United Irish League, while Father Charles O'Malley[1] of Ayr has never suffered his political sympathies to be secreted on the shady side of the bushel." The Irish connection was a recurring *leitmotif* in the Celtic meetings. John H. McLaughlin, secretary at the time, railed against the ground's owner in 1891: "Being an Irish club it is but natural that we should have a greedy landlord, and we have one who is working hard to take a high place among the rack renters in Ireland." The reports of that particular half-yearly meeting indicate an upsurge in Irish feelings among the members. Thomas Flood stated: "Celtic's success was welcomed by our countrymen all over Great Britain who take a deep interest in the working of our club. Irishmen in Scotland in past years have been made little of because we have very few of our numbers in business or in positions of responsibility, but we have lately demonstrated that not only in commercial life can we be successful, but we have proved the possession on our part of an amount of pluck and perseverance by which we have risen to the top of the ladder in the football world. The Celtic team is the pride of the Irish race in England, Ireland, and Scotland . . .". Stephen Henry added his comments: "We have in the splendid report submitted by our secretary,

Mr McLaughlin, a proof of the ability of Irishmen to manage any concern in which we take an interest . . . I have no fear but that the interest of the club, the fair fame of our nationality, and the exposition of genuine football will be the first consideration of our players."

Irish politicians saw the advantage in linking themselves with Celtic. Michael Davitt, a former Fenian and founder of the National Land League, visited Celtic Park in his role as 'patron of the club'. In March 1892 he laid the first sod at the new Celtic Park, a piece of turf specially transported from Donegal; the sod containing shamrocks was stolen shortly afterwards, and the action provoked an outbreak of poetry in which the thief was memorably vilified:

> Again I say, "May Heaven blight
> That envious, soulless knave;
> May all his sunshine be like night,
> And the sod rest heavy on his grave."

Throughout his speech Davitt referred to the club as 'Keltic', the correct pronunciation but one that caused much amusement for the crowd, to the patriot's bafflement. He was not the only politician to visit Celtic Park; T. D. Sullivan, an MP best known as the composer of the song *God Save Ireland* that served as an Irish national anthem for almost fifty years, was fêted by the club and cheered by the players in November 1892, returning the hospitality by making a speech and singing a verse of his song.

Ironically, the sport that was attracting so much attention and enthusiasm among the expatriate Irishmen in Glasgow was in the process of being banned from Irish soil as 'unIrish' by a motion of the Gaelic Athletic Association in 1892. Perhaps this was the clearest indication of all that the Irish in Scotland were about to go their own way and that the original ties with Ireland were weakening.

Notes
1   Charles reverted to the original family name, presumably to stress his Irish background and convictions.

3

THE START

'The birth of Celtic', as seen by the artist of The Celtic Story *in the* Scottish Daily Express, *21 January, 1961.*

ONE of the most tragic manifestations of the poverty was the harmful effects upon the children, many of whom lacked the necessities of food and clothing. As the Headmaster of Sacred Heart School since 1874 Brother Walfrid could see the consequences at first hand, and had organised a Poor Children's Dinner Table where children (and some old people) were provided with one warm and substantial meal each day. To salvage self-respect a penny was charged for those who could afford it. The Marist Brother was aided in his efforts by the members of the Saint Vincent de Paul Society, but there were so many pressing claims that funds were always low. Brother Walfrid was an energetic man and a born organiser; besides his clerical and educational duties, he ran youth football teams, initiated and chaired a Literary Society for the school-leavers in the parish, and was noted for his determination and success in pursuing employers on behalf of his young people. Shrewdly he observed the interest in the growing sport of football among the working-class, and with the Saint Vincent de Paul Society he had been involved in arranging exhibition games in aid of charity; several games were played at Clyde's ground, Barrowfield, in Bridgeton, including a match between Dundee Harp and Clyde.

The Irish community in Glasgow took a great interest in Edinburgh Hibs, formed in 1875 by the Irish-born Canon Edward Hannan and run

21

as a strictly Catholic organisation. It was laid down in its constitution that the players had to be practising Catholics, as one found to his cost when he was dropped for not attending Mass regularly. In the early days the club faced difficulties, being refused admission to the Edinburgh Association because "they were not a Scottish club" and having their entry money returned from the SFA. Eventually, they were accepted grudgingly, and went on to defeat Dumbarton in the Scottish Cup final in February, 1887, to the delight of the Irish in the West of Scotland who attended the match in large numbers. It was regarded as a victory for the Irish and when the team returned to Edinburgh later that night they were greeted with a huge banner that proclaimed "God Save Ireland". The team and its officials were late in returning to the capital, however, because immediately after the game they had been fêted by throngs of admirers at St Mary's Hall, East Rose Street (now Forbes Street) in the Calton district of Glasgow's east end. At the reception John McFadden, Hibs' secretary, responded to the toasts and congratulations with a speech in which he traced the history of his club from its Catholic origins, stressed its continuing commitment to Irish causes, gave an account of obstacles overcome, and urged the Catholics of the West of Scotland, and in particular those in Glasgow, "to go and do likewise" (in the words of Tom Maley, recollecting the event in the *Glasgow Observer* of 16 April, 1910). The attentive listeners included Brother Walfrid and his assistant Brother Dorotheus, John Glass, Dr John Conway, William McKillop, James McKay, John O'Hara, Pat Welsh and James Quillan, and all were to be associated directly with the founding of Celtic.

These men were soon to be given ample proof of the potential of football for generating money as Hibs accepted an invitation to contest the East End Charity Cup with Renton, when the proceeds went to the Poor Children's Dinner Table and local charities. It was a crowd-pleasing fixture with the Scottish Cup holders from the East competing against the Glasgow Charity Cup winners from the West, and a crowd estimated at 12,000 — larger than the crowd that had seen Hibs beat Dumbarton — attended the challenge match at Barrowfield Park (on French Street in Bridgeton), loaned free of charge by Clyde; the game ended in a draw, and Renton won the replay held three months later in August, 1887, at the same ground, when another large crowd of 4,000 saw Neil McCallum, a reserve player, score five of Renton's six goals. Less than a year later the same player would earn football immortality by scoring Celtic's first-ever goal, in the friendly against Rangers.

The challenge thrown out by Mr McFadden was taken up by the three east end parishes of St Mary's, St Andrew's and St Alphonsus. Representatives from the three parishes held several stormy, inconclusive meetings before the St Mary's members took the initiative. From the start this parish, or its representatives such as John Glass, James McKay, Hugh Darroch, John O'Hara, and John H. McLaughlin, had been the strongest advocates. This enthusiasm was scarcely surprising because St Mary's parish was one of the most enterprising in the city. It had set up a parish library, established a Penny Savings Bank, and founded a Total Abstinence Society. This latter organisation met on Saturday nights for tea and a sing-song, a counter attraction to the temptations of the pubs; at a later date when the League of the Cross, a Catholic temperance society, was introduced into Scotland, St Mary's branch became one of the most flourishing in the country.

This initiative on the part of the parish seems to have taken root in September 1887. The annual *Celtic Football Guide* regularly stated in the early decades of this century that the club was founded in September 1887, and the evidence points to this month being the decisive moment when the enthusiasts made up their minds that "it was time Glasgow had an Irish club". Thus, a club was formally constituted at a meeting chaired by John Glass and held in St Mary's Hall on 6 November, 1887, a Sunday; the new club, named Celtic in deference to Brother Walfrid's wishes after a lengthy debate, applied to join the Glasgow and Scottish Football Associations the following year and was admitted to the latter at a committee meeting on 21 August, 1888. Joining the SFA the same day were the following: Champfleurie (Edinburghshire), Adventurers (Edinburgh), Balaclava Rangers (Oban), Temperance Athletic (Glasgow), Leith Harp (Edinburgh), Whifflet Shamrock (Lanarkshire) and Britannia (Auchinleck).

Only a week after that first meeting the club leased six acres of vacant ground, bounded on its west side by Janefield Cemetery and on its east by Dalmarnock Street (now Springfield Road); the site, to judge by a contemporary map, appeared to encompass roughly the waste ground now bounded by the cemetery's east wall, Malcolm Street, Janefield Street and Springfield Road. Apparently, Celtic was not the first club to play on the site which, according to 'Old International' writing only a few years later, ". . . long anterior to their [Celtic's] existence served as a playing pitch for, I think, the Oxford, away back in the 70s — and this fact also served as an inducement to open proceedings at Parkhead." (*25 Years' Football*, 1896). Little is known of the Oxford except that it was a nomadic club throughout a short-lived existence and played at times at Crosshill and at Copland Road, a road on which the present ground of Rangers is located. Survival was precarious for football clubs then, as witnessed by the disappearance of the above-named clubs who joined the SFA on the same day as Celtic. Similarly, Celtic's initial success enabled the club to avoid the fate of earlier ones in Parkhead. Blackfriars and Our Boys, both of whom played in the vicinity of Belvidere Hospital in London Road, and who had been founded in the

1870s did not outlast the decade; the same fate had befallen Albatross who played at Helenvale Park, a ground that still exists, in the late 1870s.

Celtic's first match vs Rangers at Celtic Park, on 28 May, 1888, as seen by the artist of the Scottish Daily Express, *27 January, 1961.*

Two other household names in Scotland were to be associated with the district: Beardmore's Forge, a world-famous giant in Scottish industry (but now defunct), and Barr's, the aerated water manufacturers and producers of 'Irn Bru', Scotland's 'other' national drink.[1] In 1887 Parkhead and its environs were in the throes of industrialisation, as chemical works, railways and iron foundries altered the near-rural complexion of the district. In the early part of the century it was the last stopping place of the London mail-coaches on their way to the Saracen's Head Inn in the Gallowgate and it still retained vestiges in its cottages of what had once been a village of hand-loom weavers; the village had been absorbed into the expanding city of Glasgow in 1846, and by that time 'the dark Satanic mills' of the Industrial Revolution had broken the weavers' traditional and independent means of livelihood. The girls were forced to serve in the mechanised mills, and the young men in Beardmore's. Writing in the *Glasgow Eastern Standard* in late 1923, John Wheatley claimed that: "[Parkhead] was a child of James Watt. Had steam power not been discovered the handloom weavers might still be busy in Westmuir Street . . . and cabbages might still be growing in Celtic Park." So, remarkably, a relatively unimportant district on the fringes of Glasgow was to achieve fame throughout Scotland and further abroad by serving as home to three 'institutions'.

The annual rent was fixed at £50 and soon a throng of voluntary workers was swarming over the site every night of the week. Within six months a transformation had occurred, and the first game at Celtic Park was held. Edinburgh Hibernians and Cowlairs played an exhibition that ended 0-0 before a crowd of 5,000, but on that May evening the spectators admired the stadium more. By modern standards it was small and primitive, but it evoked only compliments. There was an open-air stand, and a rough mound around a narrow track provided a basic terracing; the more athletic of the spectators obtained a better view by climbing up on the wall of the cemetery. There were nine admission gates making access relatively easy and the price of admission was 6d (2.5p), with women allowed in free. The playing field was level, 110 yards long and 66 wide; the pavilion was located under the stand and contained a referee's room, an office, and a trainer's room as well as dressing rooms with baths and showers for both teams.

The bare, vacant site had been leased on 13 November, 1887, and the first game was played on 8 May, 1888. Only three months after that opening a member of Hibs' committee was moved to write about the impression it had made on him: ". . . was struck at the manner in which the formation of the new club has been taken in hand, and at the evidence of wealth with which the appearance of everything impressed a beholder. It certainly made a brave show: the spacious grounds, commodious stand, and the white flag with green crossbar flying triumphantly above."

Celtic soon had trouble with the landlord; the owner was concerned about the changes being made on his property, and moved to halt the first game by interdicting the ground, but the committee called his bluff with a threat of court action. That was an early indication of the first committee's hardheaded and aggressive approach.

One persistent discrepancy about the founding should be cleared up and, as it involves an unconscious slight to hundreds of unsung volunteers, the time has surely come to correct the situation. It concerns the date of the founding of the club. Any uninformed visitor to Celtic Park today who glances at the neon letters on the stand would have to assume that the club was founded in 1888; however, he would be wrong, because the Celtic Football Club was formed in November, 1887. The confusion is understandable, arising from the fact that the club played its first game in May, 1888, a friendly against Rangers, and that its first regular season was 1888-89. The evidence, however, in favour of the earlier date is overwhelming.

The *Scottish Umpire* in its issue of 29 November, 1887, stated it clearly enough: "We learn that the efforts which have lately been made to organise in Glasgow a first-class football club have been successfully consummated by the formation of the 'Glasgow Celtic Football and Athletic Club' under influential auspices. They have secured a ground in the east end and which they mean to put in fine order. We wish the Celts all success."

In January, 1888, a circular, asking for financial support, was distributed and read in part: "The above club was formed in November, 1887, by a number of the Catholics in the east end of the city. . . . We have already several of the leading Catholic football players of the West of Scotland on our membership list." The circular went on to list the subscriptions received; by that date, in January, there were 45 names, including that of 'His Grace the Archbishop' who led the list with a donation of 20/- (£1).

The *Glasgow Observer*, a Catholic newspaper catering to the Irish immigrant community, took a keen interest in Celtic's progress, and periodically printed articles about the club's early days. A special Athletic Supplement to the 5 June, 1897, issue contained a contribution by 'An Old Member' which stated: "So, it came about that on the 6th November, 1887, the Celtic FC was formally constituted in the hall of the St Mary's branch of the St Vincent de Paul Society, East Rose Street. No time was lost in getting to work and a week later, November 13th, ground was leased in Dalmarnock Street, Parkhead."

The *Evening Times* of 16 April, 1904, endorsed this account of how the new club was 'launched' on "a Sunday afternoon in the month of November, 1887" and listed the office-bearers, chosen clearly as a steering committee: "President, Mr John Glass; vice-president, Mr James Quillan; treasurer, Mr James McKay; secretary, Mr John O'Hara . . .". Significantly, Celtic chairman Tom White is specific about this date in his brief history of the club published in the *Glasgow Eastern Standard* of 3 and 10 March, 1923 (penned six years before records were destroyed in the fire that gutted the pavilion in 1929).[2]

The date of the club's founding is beyond dispute, but apart from the matter of historical accuracy there is another merit in asserting 6 November, 1887, as the founding date. When the first side trooped from the pavilion on the evening of 28 May, 1888, dressed in their first strip of a white shirt with a green collar and a Celtic cross on the right breast, that was not the start of Celtic. Rather, that moment was the culmination of months of herculean labour and dedication. Think of how much had been accomplished. A club had been discussed, formed and organised; there was a written constitution, an elected committee, an established membership and a lengthy subscription list; a lease had been taken out on a vacant site and by May it had been transformed into a compact, enclosed ground — a feat achieved through the efforts of many voluntary workers, labouring on winter nights after long hours put in at their regular work. It is time that those efforts made on the club's behalf were honoured by official recognition of the earlier date as that of the club's founding.

Notes
1   Mr R. F. Barr of the firm was one of the subscribers who responded to the January 1888 circular.
2   Pat Woods wrote a two-part article ("1887 and All That") for *The Celtic View* in February 1983 and provided detailed supporting evidence for November 1887 as the founding date; no one, from the general readership or from within Celtic Park, contested the evidence or the claim.

4

GENTLEMEN . . . AND PLAYERS

IN the early months of 1888 Celtic were in the strangest position for a football organisation. There was unprecedented activity behind the scenes, but the club had not fielded a team in a game, friendly or competitive. The original committee, an unwieldy group of about twenty men most of whom had never seen a football match, agreed eventually that the growth of the club should be revolutionary rather than evolutionary as was the case with other clubs. Novices though they were they sensed the need to field an attractive side from the beginning; they wanted and needed to be successful immediately, and because of their enthusiasm and pragmatism the success in the first season was no accident nor should it be thought surprising.

There was no shortage of players; offers to play for the new club poured in from all over the country, and the members spent many winter nights reading letters, studying lists of names and trying to make decisions. The Maley brothers, Tom and Willie, having agreed to join the club, added expertise to the committee; more than adequate players themselves, both had leadership qualities. Tom was initially the more valuable, having retained his contacts with Edinburgh Hibernian for whom he had played recently, and he was able to persuade some of them to consider joining Celtic. In private, though, the brothers had some doubts about the new club's prospects of survival, as Tom indicated in a column years later for a newspaper: "[Celtic] would follow the various Hibs, Shamrocks, Harps, and Emmets that had for but a brief season or very little more lingered a weary existence . . .". But they underestimated, if only for a short time, the drive and business sense of the founders.

It took little to convince the committee that an established team was imperative, but John Glass next set out to persuade the others that the best way to attract good players would be by signing the most outstanding footballer in the country, James Kelly of Renton. Kelly was an attacking centre-half and an internationalist, but he seemed happy at

27

Renton, the self-proclaimed 'champions of the world' after their victory over West Bromwich Albion in 1888 when each was its country's cup winner, and had little desire to move. With the legalisation of professionalism in England in 1885 it was just a matter of time until that team disintegrated; as an 'amateur' Kelly was free to play where he liked, and both Hibs and Celtic entertained hopes of landing him. He turned out for Hibs, helping them beat their Edinburgh rivals, Hearts, and was coaxed shortly afterwards into appearing for Celtic in their first game, a friendly against Rangers. Celtic had used the compelling argument that his presence would swell the gate and that charity would benefit. He played and scored a goal in the 5-2 win but was reluctant to commit himself further. Celtic delegated several committee men to work on him, but it was John Glass who finally convinced him after a lengthy courtship. The critical date for an anxious Celtic committee was 1 September, 1888, when Celtic were due to meet Shettleston in the Scottish Cup. Before the League was formed the clubs played friendly games and only cup-ties were considered official; it was recognised that players who turned out in those cup-ties belonged to that club. Thus, although Celtic had played eight games in August with Kelly as their centre-half, both Renton and Hibs intensified their efforts to sign him. To Celtic's relief he played and led the side to a 5-1 cup-tie win.

James Kelly was the most important signing; Celtic captured the finest centre-half in Scotland and an inspiring presence on the field, but even more importantly the new club gained instant credibility. Such was his reputation that his astonished landlady in Glasgow reported that "he took his food like an ordinary man". If Edinburgh Hibs were disappointed at the loss of Kelly, within weeks they were to be devastated by it; after Kelly's decision six of their players, most admittedly from the West of Scotland, finally defected to the Glasgow 'upstarts'. They were Michael Dunbar, Paddy Gallagher, John Coleman, Mike McKeown, and both Jimmy McLaren and Willie Groves who had played in the 1887 final against Dumbarton. Celtic claimed that the players, concerned about Hibs' currently precarious finances, had in effect approached them rather than the newcomers 'tapping' established players, but the animosity lingered for years in Edinburgh.

Scottish football was supposed to be amateur, but with the exception of Queen's Park every club made under-the-counter payments to its players because that was the only way to prevent them from going to England. From the start Celtic was the most open and professional of the 'amateur' clubs, recognising that working-class lads had to be paid, and that every player had his price. A reputable English newspaper, the *Athletic News*, was to state in September, 1889, that Celtic had donated £421 to charity, but indicated that the captain, James Kelly, formerly a young joiner in Renton, had bought a public house for £650; it posed the obvious and legitimate question: "Where had the money come from?" Despite originating in the public schools, being codified in the universities, and retaining an upper-class cachet, football had become the truly popular sport, the game of the people. A vast social gulf now separated the legislators from the players and the majority of spectators: the legislators were middle-class Victorians, nominally imbued with an amateur ideal as were the newspapers who reported the games; most of the players were apprentices or relatively unskilled labourers and it was ludicrous to expect them to devote so much time to the sport without compensation. The result was widespread hypocrisy; players were paid at a scale a little higher than working wages, but the clubs had to disguise the payments.

The SFA, the guardians of amateurism and the status quo, arranged for a Professional Committee to investigate any suspected transgressions and sensing rightly that the formation of the Scottish League with its regular schedule in 1890 would be the means of professionalism being adopted the committee set to work with a will. The SFA had its problems. One club, when asked to present its accounts for inspection, blandly stated that it was unable to comply "because the books had been burned in a fire". Edinburgh Hibs' books were checked, and the intriguing fact emerged that, although the club had employed three different secretary-treasurers during the period in question, all the entries were in the same handwriting. The chief result of the SFA's zeal was to raise the level of the clubs' books, normally the most prosaic of documents, into the realm of imaginative literature. However, at least two clubs, Cowlairs and St. Bernard's, were caught and suspended, while a third, Renton, was expelled from the new Scottish League after only five games for playing against the suspended St. Bernard's, though both were later reinstated.

The most common method of avoiding detection was by 'skimming' money off the top: the clubs would fake gate receipts, agreeing between themselves about the amount so that their records would match, and players were paid out of the unrecorded proceeds. The clubs were allowed to pay 'broken-time', a form of compensation for wages lost at work while playing or training for important games. Of course there was flagrant abuse of the practice. Queen of the South Wanderers were convicted of making broken-time payments to two players who were unemployed at the time. In 1887 Vale of Leven, anxious to find grounds for a protest against Hibs who had beaten them in the Scottish Cup, hired a detective to investigate and his report concentrated on Willie Groves,[1] an apprentice stonemason earning between 7/6d (37.5p) and 10/- (50p) a week; this player was given 3/6d (17.5p)[2] for one morning off work and later £1 for three days. The most farcical situation arose at Celtic Park in 1891 after the return of Dan Doyle and others from

England when the regular players threatened to strike if their wages were not raised to parity with the newcomers — and this was while they were classed as amateurs. After the Scottish Cup victory in 1892, the year before legalised professionalism came to Scotland, Celtic paid a bonus of £3, and a new suit, for each player.

During the period of the 'paid amateur' Celtic had been the most aggressive in recruiting players, and had won no friends. Hibs were the hardest hit, and there was trouble on and off the field whenever the sides met in Celtic's early seasons; Queen's Park disapproved most strongly of Celtic's practices and their matches were hard-fought, determined battles that came to symbolise the struggle between the old and new orders in the game; other clubs who had lost players to the upstarts harboured grudges. Even Willie Maley, that most ardent of apologists, had to admit: "Celtic were reared on breaches of the professional law, but charity covereth a multitude of sins."

Some of Celtic's recruiting had a touch of piracy about it. Jerry Reynolds, a splendid full-back and the pillar of Carfin Shamrock's defence, had been in Celtic's mind for some time, and when they found themselves short of a defender on the eve of an important tie with Queen's Park in 1889, John Glass and another committee man made their way after midnight to the mining village, leaving horse and cab on the outskirts to make their entry as silent as possible. Finding his house in the colliers' row, they roused him from bed and, standing in the doorway speaking in urgent whispers, persuaded the sleepy Reynolds to get dressed and leave that moment for Glasgow. The three men tip-toed through the darkened village to the waiting cab and escaped to Glasgow. According to local sources Celtic's poaching was bitterly resented and the animosity lingered on for almost half a century. The famous Dan Doyle was captured from Everton with whom he was a great favourite. The English club made strenuous efforts to recover him and were confident that their offer of £5 a week and the managership of a public house in Liverpool would lure him south again; to their surprise Doyle turned down the terms, being satisfied with his life in Glasgow as an 'amateur' and comfortable as the owner of a pub that he had presumably purchased on his savings from wages of £2 a week . . . "How can an amateur club like Celtic outbid a very wealthy professional team in Everton? It is far easier to comprehend the weaving of one of Mr. Gladstone's speeches than the exact process by which the Celtic can induce a Scot well paid in England to return to his native land and yet keep within the rules of the Scottish Association. That Doyle now proposed to cross the border to play for an amateur club like the Celtic imposed too great a strain on the credulity." (*Scottish Referee*: 3 August, 1891).

Celtic proved equally determined to retain players against the temptations of English clubs. Sheffield Wednesday were interested in John Madden and Alec Brady, managing to get them to Yorkshire where they played in a midweek trial and delighted their prospective employers. For safety Wednesday split them up, Brady being lodged in Boston and Madden in Sheffield, but Celtic's network was equal to the task. John Glass and another committee man travelled south, were able to contact Madden, and 'persuaded' him to return to Celtic Park. An agent for the Sheffield side recalled that: "I would be the last to introduce any element of theology, but I may say you had to be specially careful if you ever ventured to do any spying on the ground of a club which was run under the auspices of Roman Catholics. They always seemed to have bands of supporters who were especially alert and eager." (*The Romance of the Wednesday*: R.A. Sparling, 1926.) The person who informed Celtic of the players' whereabouts was a local priest.

Nottingham Forest were interested in Neil McCallum and arranged by letter to meet him near Celtic Park after a match. Suspicious about the letter, McCallum's landlord opened it and handed it over to John Glass for action. When the agent turned up for the rendezvous he was met, not by the player, but by some Celtic members and an indignant crowd of sympathisers who had to be dissuaded from tarring-and-feathering the wretch. The English club, however, were able later to entice him to sign along with the talented Sandy McMahon, and Celtic again made successful attempts to recover their property.[3]

In 1888 the Scottish game was in danger of becoming moribund. Queen's Park, once the undisputed leaders in the sport, were withdrawing slightly from the creeping professionalism that surrounded them; Hibs and Hearts waged a dreary internecine war in Edinburgh; Rangers were a moderate force at the time; Dumbarton, Vale of Leven and Renton were the outstanding teams, but their rivalry was local in nature and their prospects for expansion were limited because of their rural location. Until 1890 there was no Scottish League, and many players had begun the trek south for money. The only answer the legislators provided was censure and criticism.

Celtic's founding and immediate success changed Scottish football. The club could rely on the loyal support of a captive audience, but crowds everywhere flocked to see the team that was challenging the established sides. Interest was revived throughout Scotland, and it was no coincidence that the first boom in attendances came in the late 1880s and early 1890s, attributable directly to the new and enterprising club, dubbed "novelty purveyors to the millions", whose advent was the most significant factor in the development, if not transformation, of football into a mass spectator sport in Scotland. Indeed, in 1890, when the young club defied the SFA's amateur tenets by playing 'Old

Renton' (an aggregation composed mainly of ex-Renton stars now playing professionally in England) in a benefit match for Renton's Jimmy McCall, the press hinted that the authorities were reluctant to impose the most severe penalties because Celtic were doing more for the game than any other club.

In the matter of professionalism Celtic clearly were flouting the rules of the SFA with impunity, and their success pointed the way for others; with such widespread disregard for the rules it was futile to punish the transgressors — a reaction analogous to rearranging the deckchairs in the *Titanic* after the collision. Celtic led the fight to have professionalism made legal and had in John H. McLaughlin a fiery and eloquent spokesman in the SFA councils where he stressed the inevitability of the situation: "You might as well attempt to stop the flow of Niagara with a kitchen chair as to endeavour to stem the tide of professionalism." He pointed out the advantages for the clubs: "With veiled professionalism players are masters of the clubs, and can go and debauch themselves without being called to account. Under the new system the clubs will be masters of the players, and the standard of play will rise." McLaughlin was right in his claims and eventually he was able to convince a majority of his fellow legislators in 1893 to adopt professionalism (eight years after the change in England), and Scottish football was to change dramatically.

Notes
1 Willie Groves was one of Celtic's earliest signings.
2 Nostalgia has a compelling claim with pounds, shillings and pence, but for the sake of a modern generation, the decimal equivalents are provided.
3 See profile of Sandy McMahon.

5

FOOTBALL . . . AT LAST

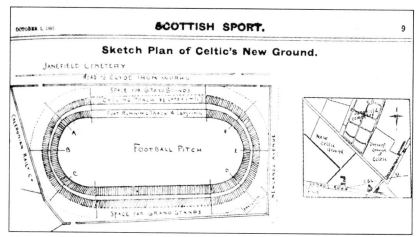

Sketch Plan of Celtic's New Ground.

The site of Celtic's first ground is on the right-hand side of this Scottish Sport *drawing, 2 October, 1891. NB — Dalmarnock Road should be Dalmarnock Street.*

THE social and political aspects of a club's founding and early days may be of engrossing interest to the historian, but most general readers are more interested in the football (and, it must be confessed, so are the authors). Celtic's claim to an honourable place in the history of the sport must lie ultimately in the calibre and performances of the teams that the club has fielded throughout its hundred years. It is time to turn to those early seasons and examine them from a football perspective.

Celtic played their first match on their own ground on 28 May, 1888, a Monday evening, and the first opponents were the well-established Rangers. Nobody among the 2,000 spectators present could ever have imagined that this 'friendly' marked the start of the most bitter and vigorously contested rivalry in all sport. Celtic's side consisted of: Dolan (Drumpellier), Pearson (Carfin Shamrock), McLaughlin (Govan Whitefield), Maley W. (Cathcart), Kelly (Renton), Murray (Cambuslang

Hibs), McCallum (Renton), Maley T. (Cathcart), Madden (Dumbarton), Dunbar (Edinburgh Hibs), Gorevin (Govan Whitefield). Rangers fielded some regulars in their side, but more members of their reserve team known as the Swifts, and the result was an emphatic 5-2 win for Celtic, to the delight of the crowd. Neil McCallum had the distinction of scoring Celtic's first goal.

After the game the officials of the two clubs and the members of the teams, a group of about 70 in all, were conveyed to St Mary's Hall where they had supper, were entertained with a concert, and participated in several toasts; a contemporary account stated that "the proceedings were of the happiest character". In view of subsequent happenings it may be surprising to record that the early relationships with Rangers were very friendly. John H. McLaughlin, a Celtic stalwart in committees and after 1897 the club's first chairman, was a talented musician and played the organ, as well as accompanying the Rangers Glee Club on the piano for several years, and a newspaper account four years later attests to the enduring friendship between the clubs: "Financially Dumbarton or Queen's Park might have pleased treasurer Maley better, but for a genuine good match the Light Blues are favourites with the Parkhead crowd." (*Scottish Sport*: 29 January, 1892.)

A couple of weeks after the Rangers game the second fixture was played against Dundee Harp and the visitors, assured of a warm welcome because of their Irish sympathies, attracted a crowd of 6,000; Celtic won this match 1-0. Two other friendlies followed: a 3-3 draw with Mossend Swifts, and a 4-3 loss to Clyde — the first defeat. These games were important because they established credibility and were a useful preparation for Celtic's first season of 1888-89. In those days there was no Scottish League, and the season consisted of friendly games and various cup tournaments.

The first competition entered was the Exhibition Cup and Celtic opened with a 1-1 draw with Abercorn, a Paisley side; there remains a minor mystery here because no record exists of any replay although Celtic advanced to knock out the formidable Dumbarton by 3-1 and Partick Thistle 1-0 before falling to Cowlairs in the final by 2-0. There was some talk among Celtic partisans about Cowlairs fielding a side that had been strengthened by recruits from other clubs and, at the dinner given after the final, John Glass responded to the toast to the losers by commenting on the hostile reception his club had received from some of the spectators: "Let them scoff and jeer. Celtic will yet win to their proper position by their merits and those who scoff today will one day have to applaud." In the Glasgow Cup Celtic made splendid progress, thrashing Shettleston 11-2 at Parkhead and Rangers 6-1 at Ibrox before losing to the powerful Queen's Park by 2-0 at Celtic Park.

The Scottish Cup, a tournament to be associated indelibly with Celtic, provided the excitement of the season. In September Celtic defeated Shettleston 5-1 and gained revenge on Cowlairs by toying with them 8-0 (Willie Maley always recalled that match as much for the manner of winning as the retribution, claiming that for the first time "the side struck up what is now a traditional Celtic game of accurate short passing"). In October they knocked out Albion Rovers 4-1, and in November beat St. Bernard's in Edinburgh by the same score. Then came the first controversy. Drawn at home against Clyde, Celtic lost 1-0 on a waterlogged pitch and the match was played in murky light for the last ten minutes. Willie Maley in his capacity as match secretary initiated a protest against the conditions, indicating that Clyde had contributed to the situation by turning up late. Celtic won the protest, but Clyde appealed and at a heated SFA meeting described Celtic's case as "a tissue of falsehoods". However, Celtic's evidence was supported by the referee, who added that the game had been delayed for some minutes when three Clyde players had to change and remove illegal bars from their boots. Maley testified that he had delayed his protest until later in the evening to prevent any ill-feeling at the social after the match; since the basis of the protest was the poor conditions he had the backing of the rules which allowed him to lodge it the same day rather than before or during the match which was the normal procedure. Clyde's appeal was dismissed by only one vote, and the cup-tie was ordered to be replayed. The visitors were so incensed that they refused to strip in the Celtic pavilion, turning up at the ground already dressed for the game, and predictably Celtic won easily by 9-2.

Two difficult away games followed: a narrow 2-1 win over East Stirlingshire at Falkirk, and a convincing 4-1 victory against Dumbarton at Boghead. Thus the new club was a talking-point in its first season, having fought its way through to the 1889 final of the Scottish Cup. Because of astute recruiting it was not surprising, but it was a major accomplishment nevertheless. Although the opponents were the redoubtable Third Lanark, Celtic were fancied to cause an upset.

Even more controversy surrounded this game because in those days the finals were played in winter, usually in February, and the weather was often a major factor. Celtic's first appearance was fated to be remembered as 'the snow final'. On the morning of the match snow had been falling steadily, but the referee and the umpires, after inspecting the Hampden pitch, discussed the options and declared it playable. In the hour before the kick-off the weather turned worse, and officials of both clubs began to negotiate in the pavilion; a protest against the conditions was drawn up by a solicitor on behalf of both and signed by the captains prior to being handed to the referee for him to convey to the SFA. Little thought was given to informing the spectators that the game was to be played as a friendly, although those spectators had paid double the regular admission fee and contributed more than £920, the largest gate ever taken at a Scottish ground until that time. Third Lanark, nicknamed 'the Warriors' because of their military associations, won the friendly convincingly by 3-0, but a week later had a much harder task, struggling to a 2-1 win in the real final for their first Scottish Cup.

The limited schedule of cup-ties was augmented by friendly games against local teams and sadly their names now evoke only fading memories: Abercorn, Cowlairs, Dundee Harp, Northern, Renton and Third Lanark. More interesting to the spectators was the regular appearance of top English clubs at Celtic Park: Preston North End, Bolton Wanderers, Mitchell's St George, and Corinthians and the club paid return visits to England, including games in London, Bolton, Burnley and Newcastle; in April Celtic played two games in Belfast winning both, against Distillery (1-0) and United Belfast (5-2).

It was a highly successful season: as promised, Celtic fielded a fine team and, although including several star players, the emphasis was on teamwork. The members could take genuine pride in the organisation and running of the club, and after all the expenses were met there were substantial donations to charity — a total of £421 16s 9d (£421.84). The impact of the new club could be judged from this excerpt from a later newspaper: "Football was given a new lease of life. The eastern club brought a new following to the game; thousands who had never previously given a thought to football rallied to the new club." (*The Bulletin*: 19 May, 1917.)

The Scottish Cup has provided excitement and controversy from its earliest days and Celtic more than any other club was to provide the lion's share. This was the case even in the first decade. In Celtic's second season the club was drawn at home against Queen's Park, and it was a memorable clash. All ten entrances to the ground were jammed with thronging spectators, the touchlines were almost obscured by the encroaching spectators, and the opposition, the darlings of the sporting press, was unable to find a way into the ground, until a Celtic official thought of smuggling the visitors along a back passage through neighbouring gardens. Celtic's ambition to end Hampden's "invulnerable dominion" was thwarted by a disallowed goal and frequent crowd invasions provoked by overcrowding (0-0). The replay was ordered to be played at Hampden Park, and the SFA raised the admission to one shilling in a bid to keep the crowd down or to attract a 'better' class of spectator. Queen's Park won 2-1 after a hard-fought match, the winning goal coming only four minutes from the end. The 'gates' were substantial and an indication of the drawing power of the new club: £453 in the first match at 6d (2.5p) a head, and £564 for the replay at one shilling (5p). The team experienced an adventurous, roller-coaster ride through the competition in 1890-91. Rangers visited Celtic Park in the first round, where they lost to a spectacular goal: "When Groves scored the goal, T. Maley, who was umpiring,[1] waved his flag in jubilation. The Rangers' players stared in blank amazement, the Celtic players shook hands effusively, the stands rose bareheaded to a man cheering vociferously, the crowds lining the railing did much the same thing, and the noise that little manoeuvre of Groves evoked could have been heard at Ibrox Park; it rose and swelled into one ground-note of triumph that bore in its tone the delighted response of ten thousand thankful hearts." (*Scottish Sport*: 9 September, 1890.) Surprisingly Celtic were held to a 2-2 draw at Celtic Park by Carfin Shamrock (perhaps still smarting from the hijacking of Reynolds) before winning 3-1 in the replay; a convincing away win by 6-2 over Wishaw Thistle was followed by a visit to Dundee to defeat Our Boys, a quaint but popular name among clubs at the time.

The controversy arose over the tie with Royal Albert (named after Queen Victoria's husband) at Larkhall where some supporters invaded the pitch near the end to halt the game with Celtic leading 4-0. Neither club applied to have the tie replayed, and the referee's testimony stated that the home team's fans had staged the break-in "to give their team another chance", but the SFA ordered a replay at neutral Ibrox; the *Scottish Referee* criticised the decision stating that it had punished the wrong team and that the decision was "a dangerous evil leading to scheming and forced riots". At any rate Celtic won the replay 2-0 and advanced to the quarter-final against Dumbarton. The 'Sons' were a powerful squad, especially at home, and their pitch had gained the significant ephithet of 'fatal Boghead'. It was no real surprise that Celtic were eliminated on a frozen, bumpy pitch by 3-0.

The next season (1891-92) was the first great one in the club's history. Not only did it win the Scottish Cup but it also captured two other trophies, the Glasgow Cup and the Charity Cup. At the time the two Glasgow tournaments had considerable status in Scotland, combining with the Scottish Cup in what was known as 'the big three', so much so that Ned McGinn sent his telegram to the Vatican to inform the Pope of the feat. In the Glasgow Cup Celtic defeated Clyde 7-1 at Cathkin, and in the Charity Cup beat Rangers by 2-0 at Hampden. However, as always, the main interest was in the Scottish Cup. Celtic reached the final by defeating Rangers at Parkhead 5-3 in the semi-final, and Queen's Park disposed of Renton 2-0 in a replay at Hampden, after an exciting first game at Renton's Tontine Park when the grandstand collapsed. The teams, the most attractive and best supported in Glasgow, made a popular final and it was expected that a capacity crowd of 36,000 would attend at Ibrox. There was the added excitement of a thinly disguised rivalry between the clubs. Queen's Park, as the representatives of pure amateurism, and Celtic, as the flagbearers for the new reality in the game, had engaged in fierce battles sometimes ending with ill-feeling and fighting in the dressing rooms afterwards. Queen's Park still retained the psychological advantage of never having lost to Celtic. Shortly before the kick-off thousands, impatient at the delays at the turnstiles, rushed the gates, forcing their way in free and it was estimated that 40,000 watched the final. The authorities had little experience and no expertise in crowd control, although they had hired 150 policemen, including four on horseback (a novelty at the time), to handle the crowd. The terracings were of wooden construction with no crush barriers to prevent swaying, and only a rope separated the closest spectators from the pitch; during this final the crowd encroached upon the field several times, causing delays although there was no real danger to the players nor malice in the crowd's intentions.

The field was slippery, and it was an evenly contested match with Queen's Park having slightly the better of the exchanges, but it was Celtic who scored the only goal after 60 minutes when Campbell netted. However, nothing was at stake, as representatives of the clubs and the SFA had met during the first half to consider the scenes and the outcome was predictable. One newspaper expressed it succinctly: "Owing to the encroachment of the spectators, it was agreed in the first half that a friendly game only be played, and at a meeting of the SFA committee at night it was decided that the tie replay on 9th April, and that the gate money be doubled." Some comments might be made about the arrangements. The delay of almost a month was to allow Rangers more time to construct additional stands or terracings. The decision to double the admission price offers more than one interpretation — it may simply have been a move to profit unduly through another enormous gate, or, as some suggested, it was an effort to restrict the crowd for the replay. At any rate a smaller and more manageable crowd of 22,000 turned up for the final.

After 20 minutes Queen's Park opened the scoring and held on till half-time despite Celtic's increasing pressure, but in the second half Celtic were relentless and the amateurs had to yield. The incomparable left wing of McMahon and Campbell was in devastating form. Campbell equalised in 50 minutes and shortly after he put Celtic ahead following a neat bout of passing with his partner that split the defence; not to be outdone McMahon scored two, one with a long dribble through the Queen's Park defence and his second from a header in the last minute. Celtic's other goal, their fourth, was a deflection from a free kick by a defender past his own keeper. The 5-1 rout was a triumph for Celtic, but a sobering experience for Queen's Park; the amateur side found they could not match the professionals in pace and fitness, nor despite their traditional enthusiasm could they cope with the competitive edge their opponents had cultivated in the recently formed Scottish League which Queen's Park had chosen to shun.

It was brilliant football on the field, and celebrations in the streets: "Even the women lent a hand, and helped in no small measure to make the rejoicings hearty. But it was when the boys came marching home from the aristocratic Ibrox that the fun began in earnest . . . Bands? you ought to have seen them. They perambulated the whole district until well on in the evening . . . Truly the East End was a perfect turmoil until the very early hours of the Sunday, and many of the crowd won't be able to get over the rejoicing racket for days to come" (*Scottish Referee*: 11 April, 1892).

Two years earlier the Scottish League had come into existence, as the inevitable forerunner of professionalism. Along with Celtic the following clubs took part: Abercorn, Cambuslang, Cowlairs, Dumbarton, Hearts, Rangers, Renton, St Mirren, Third Lanark and Vale of Leven. The new competition had its teething problems. A prolonged period of bad weather led to a backlog of fixtures. Originally eleven teams registered for the tournament and that meant one club was always idle, and at the end there was no outright champion: Dumbarton and Rangers finished level on points, and a deciding game resulted in a 2-2 draw. One club was disqualified and three others had points deducted for irregularities. Renton, still a force in Scottish football, were disqualified after five games and had their record expunged for playing a game against St. Bernard's, a club under suspension, while Celtic, Cowlairs and Third Lanark all had four points deducted for fielding ineligible players (Celtic's being Bell, a goalkeeper). Celtic finished a respectable third, and improved to second place the next season (1891-92), finishing behind the powerful Dumbarton. On New Year's Day a memorable friendly took place at Celtic Park between Celtic and Dumbarton when it was claimed that for the first time in Scotland goalnets were used, and Dumbarton celebrated by winning 8-0, a result that caused the club to start looking for another kèeper, whom it found in Cullen of Benburb. Sportswriters had hinted that too many Celtic players had overindulged the festivities.

The following season's Scottish Cup final again featured Celtic and Queen's Park and once more there was controversy; fortunately these recurring wrangles were to hasten the evolution of the sport. On 25 February, 1893, a bitterly cold day, a crowd of 25,000 turned up at Ibrox, having paid double the usual price to see . . . not the Scottish Cup final, but yet another friendly game. The newspapers were becoming more critical of these arrangements: "During the night a keen frost set in, and on inspection of the ground before the match it was declared unplayable, and only a friendly game took place. The secret was well kept, however, and even at the finish the majority of the crowd were of the opinion that it was a tie." Of the previous five finals this was the third to be played under such circumstances and, as all three had affected Celtic, many began to wonder if the popularity of Celtic at the turnstiles was a factor. The following attendance figures might suggest this was the case:

1889 Celtic vs Third Lanark 18,000[2]
      Celtic vs Third Lanark 18,000.
1890 Queen's Park vs Vale of Leven 10,000.
      Queen's Park vs Vale of Leven 14,000.
1891 Hearts vs Dumbarton 10,836.
1892 Celtic vs Queen's Park 40,000[2]
      Celtic vs Queen's Park 22,000
1893 Celtic vs Queen's Park 25,000[2]
      Celtic vs Queen's Park 22,000

Queen's Park, after the defeat of the previous year, were given little chance but, as they have done so often throughout their history, proved their resilience. Celtic won the friendly 1-0, Towie scoring the only goal in 60 minutes, but it was vastly different in the replay held two weeks later. Queen's Park pressed furiously from the start and Sellar scored in ten minutes after Cullen had parried a shot. Twenty minutes later he scored again, this time a hotly disputed goal, and before the interval Maley had to retire briefly to have stitches for a mouth injury. One Queen's Park historian described the Celtic spirit in the second half: "Argue as they might, Celtic went in at half-time two goals down and with three men limping, which may have had something to do with what an evening paper described as the 'excellence of the QP charging'. From who knows where, the battered Celtic side found new stomach for the fight, cut the lead and came very close to taking matters to a third game." (*The Game for the Game's Sake*: R.A. Crampsey, 1967.) Blessington revived hopes by scoring in 54 minutes with a header. In the last ten minutes Doyle moved up from his spot at full-back to centre in a spirited bid to equalise, but the amateur side held on for their tenth (and last) Scottish Cup triumph.

The advisability of continuing to play the final in mid-winter was debated, and rightly only two years later this tradition was dropped. There was also criticism that the SFA had got into the habit of doubling the admission price depending on the popularity of the finalists, and a swelling chorus of disapproval was raised about the practice of substituting friendlies for cup finals, an action that came close to fraud . . . and in this 1893 final controversy surrounded the second goal for Queen's Park, a dispute that concerned the use of goalnets. Celtic had wished to use them, but the tradition-bound amateurs objected on the grounds that their players were not accustomed to them, and thus the final was played

Celtic's 6-3 victory over Queen's Park in the Glasgow Cup Final, November 1895, as sketched in the Evening Times.

without nets; inevitably there was doubt about the legality of a goal, and the Celtic players were adamant that the ball had not passed between the posts and that the use of nets would have resolved the matter in their favour.

Celtic did receive some consolation as they won the championship in the third year of the competition, and retained the Charity Cup by beating Rangers 5-0 in the final. In the following season (1893-94) they duplicated this performance by retaining the championship and beating Queen's Park 2-1 in the Charity Cup, but they were disappointed in the final of the Scottish Cup, losing deservedly, albeit injury-hit, to Rangers by 3-1 in the first 'Old Firm' final. Rangers' superior stamina in the gruelling conditions was the deciding factor.

In the 1890s the league championship was not considered the premier tournament, and Celtic felt their first flags were little more than consolation prizes for failure in the cup. In 1894-95 Celtic slipped in the league, finishing second behind a very strong Hearts side that beat them twice, by 2-0 at Parkhead and 4-0 at Tynecastle; however, there was the consolation of beating Rangers 2-0 in the Glasgow Cup final despite playing the second half with ten men, McMahon having to retire with a knee injury, and again retaining the Charity Cup by thrashing Rangers 4-0.

Queen's Park, although still remaining aloof from league play, featured prominently in 1895-96. Celtic were victorious over them in two finals, by 2-1 in the Charity Cup which they now had won for the fifth year in succession, and in the Glasgow Cup by 6-3, a memorable win after being 3-1 down at the interval. However, Queen's Park exacted the full measure of revenge by beating Celtic 4-2 in the Scottish Cup at Parkhead. Once again there was the satisfaction of another championship, the club's third. This was a year for high scoring, with Celtic's forwards frequently on the rampage — in a 6-2 win over Rangers, a 7-0 rout of Third Lanark, and an almost embarrassing humiliation of Dundee by 11-0, a victory that still stands as the club's record win in major competitions.

Success on the field was becoming commonplace, but the tension and the squabbles within the committee continued to divide the club. During 1896-97, the year the club finally became a limited liability company, the situation at last appeared to affect the performance of the team. For the first time in its history the club went through a season without gaining an honour.[3] The administrators of the club were too preoccupied with committee politics to deal decisively with the trouble manifesting itself in dissension among the players and in poor morale. From being league champions Celtic slipped to fourth place and were never in contention throughout the campaign. Before one important league match against Hibernian at Parkhead three valuable players, Meechan, Battles and Divers, refused to strip and play unless the club removed the reporter of the *Scottish Referee* from the press box because they felt that his criticism had been unfair. The players overreacted, as the comments appear to be valid and typical of the period: "[Some of Celtic's players] are often guilty of unnecessary charging and the stupidity of their conduct is heightened by the fact that in ability they have no need to adopt such tactics" (16 November, 1896). In a later issue Battles was advised "to try a little less pugilism and a little more football" (23 November, 1896). The disgruntled players chose to deliver their ultimatum only half an hour before the kick-off, and Celtic's officials rightly refused to yield to it, suggesting that they discuss it after the game, but the players were adamant; the travelling reserve was promoted for the match, and Willie Maley, although he had retired as a player by that time, stripped and turned out for the team, who played a man short for most of the first half until another reserve player arrived from Hampden Park to help salvage a 1-1 draw. For a later fixture against Hearts in Edinburgh Celtic turned up a man short and were forced to borrow Turner of Liverpool FC, an intended spectator. Over-confidence was a factor in the shock 1-0 defeat at Celtic Park by Dundee, when the visitors atoned for the previous season's 11-0 thrashing . . . and after five successful campaigns in the Charity Cup, Celtic finally lost, by 4-1 to Rangers, but one newspaper complained that "Celtic were poorly shod for the conditions".

The gravest disappointment came in the Scottish Cup with an easy looking first tie against non-league Arthurlie at Barrhead. In a sensational result (even more surprising than Rangers' defeat at Berwick in 1967) Arthurlie beat the favourites 4-2 on a bumpy pitch. The circumstances were as disturbing as the result because the team that took the field to represent Celtic bore little resemblance to the club's recognised best: the three players who had 'gone on strike' were serving a club suspension and could not be considered, Doyle had been chosen to play but he neglected to turn up and other players were absent through injury. Club officials were not amused and their reaction was immediate. Doyle was fined £5, a hefty sum, for his cavalier attitude; two forwards, Madden and Morrison, had given wretched performances and had their wages reduced; within weeks of the upset four players had left Celtic Park — King and McIlvenny being released outright, while Morrison and Meechan were transferred to English clubs. The newspapers speculated on the internal squabbles at Celtic Park: "There is a pretty widespread feeling that all is not well at Parkhead . . . a superabundance of unpatriotic apathy which is doing even more to degrade the club than any multiplicity of misfortune." (*Scottish Sport*: 15 January, 1897.)

These drastic measures indicated that Celtic, barely ten years in existence but already established as one of the great British clubs, was not prepared to tolerate failure.

Notes
1   Tom Maley, Willie's brother, was acting as Celtic's umpire. In those days there were no neutral linesmen, each side having its own umpire, while the referee was regarded as the final court of appeal.
2   'Final' played as a friendly.
3   Celtic won the North-Eastern Cup, a local competition, in the first season of the club's history, beating Cowlairs 6-1 in the final at Barrowfield. The competition did not carry the same prestige as the Glasgow Cup or the Glasgow Charity Cup. Celtic retained the trophy in 1889-90.

6

THE LURE OF PROFITS

THE success that the original members must have prayed for spelled the end of the idealistic motives for which the club was founded. From the outset Celtic was one of the best-supported sides in Britain; this support came predictably from the Irish community responding with enthusiasm and pride to the team's success. Crowds flocked to see the new side: more than 16,000 turned up on New Year's Day in 1889 to see them play Corinthians, and 25,000 saw them face Queen's Park on 7 September of the same year in the Scottish Cup. The primary aims, the distribution of funds to local Catholic charities and a fostering of pride within Glasgow's Irish community, were being realised but change was inevitable and natural.

Celtic, founded as a charitable trust with a local mandate, soon outgrew the circumstances of its birth and emerged as a leader of the sport within Britain. The club, as it had promised to do, fielded a strong side in the first season and reached the final of the Scottish Cup to face the redoubtable Third Lanark; within a few years Celtic established itself as a dynamic organisation with a stadium, facilities and players superior to almost every other club. Its enthusiasm and drive was revitalising the sport with a massive increase in public interest, and the initiatives proposed by Celtic's determined committee men forced changes upon the organisation of Scottish football. John H. McLaughlin, Celtic's representative on SFA councils, deserved much of the credit for the progress and was recognised as the driving force behind two football landmarks, namely the founding of the Scottish League in 1890 and the legalisation of professionalism in 1893. Football now had a structure and a regular competitive schedule, the standard of play was about to rise, and there was a chance of keeping Scottish players in Scotland. Almost every club in Scotland had to reorganise to deal with the changes and Celtic's preparation was superior to its rivals.

The ambition of the committee was expressed most visibly in the development of the stadium.[1] Celtic continued to have trouble with the landlord and when he tried to raise the annual rent from £50 to £450 in 1891 it was time to move from the original ground. When the committee made its decision the only advantage to their choice seemed to be that it involved a flitting of a mere two hundred yards. The site looked impossible: an old, disused brickfield with a gaping hole, a quarry more than 40 feet deep and half-filled with water. Courageously Celtic took a ten-year lease on the property and their regular army of volunteers set to work. The first task was to fill the hole, and a few weeks before the start of the new season a newspaper could report: ". . . yet there it stands today, the playing pitch looking as if the turf had existed there for many years" (*Scottish Sport*: 22 July, 1892). The stand, pavilion and terracings were equally impressive, so that it was little wonder that one journalist described his feelings as "like leaving the graveyard [Janefield] to enter Paradise". To this day Celtic Park is often called 'Paradise'.

The water-filled quarry had been transformed and the enterprising committee men saw the opportunity of profits to be made in renting the ground and started to bid for the international matches; the club hosted the four internationals between 1894 and 1900 against England, and set new standards of excellence for the fixture. To land the 1894 match improvements to the ground were required and Celtic repaired the roof of the stand after a winter storm had blown it away, supplied additional seating, redrained and returfed the playing surface and provided more space and better facilities for the press. Although touted as capable of holding 50,000 spectators, Celtic Park was uncomfortably packed with the 46,000 who paid £2,650 to see Scotland and England settle for a 2-2 draw, the attendance and gate receipts both establishing records. Yet only two years later the ground held 57,000 who crammed in to see the same fixture, marshalled by a hundred policemen assisted by soldiers from Maryhill Barracks.

In 1895 the Scottish Cyclists' Union offered Celtic £500 to use the stadium and track for three days to hold the World Cycling Championship; in the latter quarter of the century cycling was a most popular sport and Celtic had catered to the craze by building an outer track round the running track. However, the offer was conditional upon further renovations being made and when these were effected the World Championship of 1897 was held at Celtic Park on the cement track now banked to a height of seven feet and adjusted for lapping requirements (3½ laps to the mile). Held for the first and only time in Scotland, the event was a spectacular success, but by then Celtic had changed drastically.

There had been a continuing debate within the membership about the best way to meet the original purposes of the club and the discussions frequently erupted into rows marked by the heat and passion perhaps inevitable in an Irish organisation. A majority among the ordinary

RECORDS, BEGONE!

CELTIC SPORTS!

RECORD ENTRIES

WILL ENSURE

RECORD SPORT,

AND RECORD SPORT WILL ENSURE

RECORD TIMES

*At CELTIC PARK, TO-MORROW, at Three
o'clock, and MONDAY Evening at 6.30.*

MULLEN (the Irish Champion and Conqueror of Crossland)
is a certain starter, and will race against DUFFUS and
ROBERTSON.

KILLACKY will ride in the B races without fail.

JAMES M'LAREN will go for record.

MULLEN (the Irish Champion) and DUFFUS and ROBERTSON
(the Scottish Champions) will run against "Father Time"
and A. D. M'FARLANE, the cyclist.

Champion MALEY will toe the line against AULD, COONEY,
WILSON, HUNTER, and others in a special sprint.

NOVELTIES! NOVELTIES! NOVELTIES!

COME IN YOUR THOUSANDS!

THERE'S ROOM FOR ALL!

THE ADMISSION IS ONLY SIXPENCE, AND SIXPENCE EXTRA FOR GRAND STANDS.

Advert for the annual Celtic sports meeting in Scottish Sport, *7 August, 1896.*

46

founding members were pleased and satisfied with the contributions to local Catholic charities, but while their view was admirable it was limited; against them a smaller coterie emerged, a hard-working and ambitious group who could see the possibilities for the club and themselves. Those tensions surfaced at AGMs and half-yearly meetings with fiery exchanges, charges and countercharges, contested votes and recounts, amendments and points of order. Members formed into cliques and voting blocs, and feelings were intense within the factions.

Tensions reached crisis proportions in the summer of 1889 when a dissident group, unhappy with the direction in which they sensed the club was moving, made serious attempts to set up a rival team in Glasgow to carry out the original aims. They held a meeting in Bridgeton described by their detractors as 'a hole-in-the-wall' affair, but it was attended by some Celtic members who took an active part in the discussions. Several options were evaluated: the possibility of taking over the running of Celtic by means of a *coup d'état* or an open break with Celtic followed by the formation of a new senior club, perhaps in combination with Benburb, or an offer for Edinburgh Hibernians to move to Glasgow.

The dissidents accepted the reality that they could not assume control of Celtic from within, and they were thwarted by Celtic's adroit politicians from using the junior club Benburb as a base. Celtic had a traditional relationship with Benburb, a friendship they strengthened by promising to open the Govan club's ground in August, and they continued to use the junior club as a nursery to the benefit of both organisations. The third option was an intriguing one and negotiations started with Edinburgh Hibs to consider a move to Glasgow; this was a proposal that Hibs took seriously because they had many admirers in the West of Scotland and they were still bitterly resentful at Celtic's raiding of their players. The prospect was tempting, but in the end they decided to remain in the capital.

Thus the faction was forced to form a new club from scratch. Securing a trim ground at Oatlands on the opposite bank of the Clyde from Flesher's Haugh, they were accepted by the SFA and the Glasgow Association as members under the appellation 'Glasgow Hibernian', the name Brother Walfrid had opposed so strenously in favour of 'Celtic'. Drawn against Thistle, a Bridgeton side, in the Scottish Cup of 1889 they fielded a useful eleven that included two members of Hibs' 1887 team, but they lost 3-1, a defeat due mainly to goalkeeping errors; two weeks later Queen's Park thrashed them 4-0 in the Glasgow Cup before a respectable crowd of 4,000.

During its short life Glasgow Hibernian was plagued with problems, and by Christmas as many as ten players had defected; and it was revealed later that goalkeeper Tobin, a star for Edinburgh Hibs in 1887, had been acting as a recruiting agent for English clubs. Their financial plight was so desperate that the trainer, Paddy Cannon, donated a trophy won by him as a professional runner for a competition in aid of the club. Although Hibernian received 20% of the gate receipts from the tournament, which was won by Dumbarton who beat Thistle 6-1 in the final, it still was a surprise when the club reappeared for the 1890-91 season. After dismissal from the Scottish Cup by Wishaw Thistle and from the Glasgow Cup by Summerton Athletic, they found it difficult to carry on; against Dundee Wanderers at Morgan Park they were unable to muster a full team, and there were rumours that the club's books were being examined by the SFA. The last mention of Glasgow Hibernian was in an SFA report of April 1891 stating briefly that they had become defunct of their own accord.

Celtic found it easy to withstand the threat posed by its hapless rivals, but inside the club an intense and prolonged battle for control raged on. In simplistic terms it was a struggle between the idealists and the opportunists, and with the team's success on the field being reflected at the turnstiles the result was inevitable. The most successful and profitable football club in the country could scarcely continue to be run by enthusiastic amateurs no matter how well intentioned or skilled in other fields, and it was naïve to expect that such an organisation, forced by circumstances and ambition to expand and to assume a leading role in council chambers, could remain simply as a charitable trust. At the 1891 AGM Dr Conway, a much-loved medical practitioner, an original member and the honorary president, spoke out against the increasing practice of paying officials of the club, declaring that "it is creating a bad precedent to pay men who at the last general meeting were elected to do the work for nothing" and his motion was seconded by John H. McLaughlin, later a strong advocate of the change to 'a business concern'. Significantly perhaps, J. M. Nelis was appointed honorary president in Dr Conway's place at that same meeting — an indication of the changing times.

The idealists may have been taken by surprise at the impact Celtic had made in Scottish football and the money generated by that success. Many of the founders argued passionately against expansion and change, but it was a losing cause. Their concept of the club was a narrow one; it was to be local, with facilities for Catholic youths to train and exercise, and it was to be confined to Catholic interests — charities, members, committee men and players. On the other hand, the men who were emerging as Celtic's leaders ("the real managers of the club", in Willie Maley's phrase) were a new breed of Irishmen; level-headed, aggressive in business and astute in politics, they saw clearly enough that any expansion of the club meant a dilution of the original aims, but they were prepared to accept that in the name of progress. As a Scottish club, a member of the SFA and the newly formed Scottish League, Celtic could scarcely continue as an Irish and sectarian club; as an expanding organisation with legitimate and increasing expenses it could not continue as a mere charitable trust. The ties that had bound the Irish with Scotland were fraying with each generation, and Celtic's future had to lie in identification with the larger community.

The men who engineered the gradual transition of the club from a charitable trust to a limited company were realists above all; Irish and Catholic to a man, and capable of appealing to those traditional loyalties, they still had an eye for the main chance and were prepared to wait patiently for the right opportunity. They had risen to prominence and power in the club by dint of merit and hard work, and within a few years of its founding they were running a football club that was a model for the times. A widening gulf appeared between them and many of the more typical founder-members, and the schism could be seen clearly at the AGMs and half-yearly meetings, increasingly becoming forums for censure and praise or acclaim or recrimination. At one meeting the election of nine members to a committee took more than two hours to complete, and the assembly passed the intervening time in an impromptu concert.

The opportunists gained the upper hand in 1892 when Brother Walfrid was transferred to London. With the move the club lost a source of inspiration and its unswerving primary interest in charity. Although the Marist Brother held no official position of power, his influence was far-reaching and extended into every committee and meeting. Reluctantly perhaps, he had accepted the initial expansion of the club with its attendant expenses, but as the pragmatic manager of a poor parish he had respected the efficiency and zeal of the early committees; while he was there Celtic was steered in accordance with its founding principles. His transfer left a moral vacuum, and the space was soon filled with capable men of a practical bent, motivated in a variety of personal ways, but who shared a common and understandable interest in profitability.

The treasurer's report in the year after Walfrid's departure showed the first indication of a new trend; there were donations for several charities, but nothing for the Poor Children's Dinner Table. It was clear that the committee was trying to put some distance between itself and the original obligations of the club, as this became a practice that was pursued for a number of years. The rank-and-file members were dismayed, but the committee members were not deterred. They pointed out the extent of the legitimate expenses involved in running the organisation and that the club was technically in debt; they gave the impression that charity would benefit considerably after the debts were cleared.

The most obvious expense was the ground; the necessary move to the present site in 1892, as well as the subsequent building and expansion of the stadium, cost vast sums. Originally the ground was leased for a period of ten years from the owner, Sir William Hozier, but the committee moved to purchase it outright only five years later for £10,000. Another considerable outlay was in players' wages, even in the 'amateur' days. With Celtic deciding to field a competitive team from the start, there was pressure to sign established players. Men such as Kelly (Renton), Groves, McMahon and McLaren (Hibernian), Doyle (Everton) and Reynolds (Carfin Shamrock) signed on, but they expected, and got, high wages and 'perks'. When Doyle arrived, the 'amateur' players threatened to strike unless their wages were raised, and the committee agreed partially to the demands by giving a regular wage of £2 a week, with bonuses for important matches. Soon the bonus system was in operation for all games and by 1894-95 it had been established at 10/- (50p) for a win and 5/- (25p) a draw for league fixtures. While these wages were above the average for working men in the 1890s, several Celtic players, including Kelly and Doyle, were affluent enough to open and operate public houses, fairly conclusive evidence of substantial signing-on incentives.

Accusations were made that some officials had profited unduly as a result of their association with the club and questions were raised about honoraria or outright gifts of money for past services. At the AGM of 1894 the treasurer reported with pride that the club had spent over £1,000 in ground improvements and had reduced the debt by £236, but the meeting was unwilling to approve any further donation to charity that year, although it voted an honorarium of £100 for the treasurer. At the AGM of 1895 it was noted that two players who had played as amateurs, James Kelly and Willie Maley, had each been awarded £100 for turning professional and another player was given £10, while only £91 was distributed to charity. In 1896 the treasurer could report that £1,156 had been spent on further alterations to the ground and the debt had been reduced by £761; at the same meeting it was agreed to award the treasurer, McKay, and the match secretary, Maley, the sum of £75 each but, although the Saint Vincent de Paul Society requested help for the Poor Children's Dinner Table, that appeal was turned down. . .

In most organisations such changes of direction would have been effected with little fuss, but within Celtic's membership there was a real crisis of conscience. Thus the process, inevitable in its outcome, was prolonged and agonizing. The simmering feuds among the factions were given an airing in a court case. John H. McLaughlin, the leader in the movement towards the creation of a limited liability company, was intolerant of opposition and went on record as describing the opponents as 'corner boys and loafers', but when one of those members, Frank Havelin, a labourer, answered in kind, McLaughlin initiated a court action for slander, claiming £100 in damages. It was an unworthy act, petty and vindictive, as the sum would represent almost two years' wages for Havelin and it seemed calculated to silence opposition through coercion. Fortunately, the sheriff dismissed the claim, observing pointedly that it should never have been raised in the first place and awarded the costs to Havelin. Ironically, Havelin was soon afterwards elected as a committee member and served alongside McLaughlin in the last year before the club became a company.

By 1892 the composition of the committee was generally static, being confined to the business and professional class who alone had the leisure time, education and expertise to offer the expanding club; they also had money to lend in emergencies, at a healthy 5% rate of interest. Happy with the *status quo*, the treasurer proposed that the membership be limited to 200 and that no new members be accepted, and his motion passed for 1892-93.

In 1893 the issue of the club's future was raised finally in the open when John H. McLaughlin and Joseph Shaughnessy proposed the motion that read in part: "that we re-elect the present committee en bloc, and take steps immediately to form the club into a limited liability company". The battle lines were drawn between the advocates of the scheme and those who resented the club's being turned into "a mere business". The debate was fierce, and it was disclosed in answer to a question that the vote in committee prior to the general meeting had been 11 to 4 in favour. At the end of a long session, the meeting lasting past midnight, the proposal was turned down by the membership, the vote being 86 to 31; the committee was not discouraged, feeling it was only a temporary setback to their ambitions.

A year later, in 1894, one member, concerned about the path the club was pursuing, proposed a heartfelt motion: ". . . that the Celtic Football Club take on 200 new members at 10/- (50p) each, and that the money so obtained be handed over immediately to those charities, namely St Mary's Dinner Table, the Sacred Heart, Bridgeton, and St Michael's, Parkhead, for which purpose the Celtic club was started". Significantly, this motion, which would have resulted in an infusion of new members and an immediate donation of £100 to charity at no cost to the membership nor at any increase in the club's liabilities, was rejected. Its supporters talked defiantly of forming another football club, but too many difficulties lay in the way.

The committee called a special meeting in April 1895 to discuss and approve a new constitution and rules drawn up by its members. The committee was to be expanded and was to retire annually but was eligible for re-election; any new members were to pay an entrance fee of 7/6d (37.5p) besides the annual subscription of of 5/- (25p). Another rule was proposed, that members of the club should be required to pay their share of the liabilities and debts on a proportionate basis *as and when the committee decided*, but this measure was rejected emphatically, the general membership seeing that the change strengthened only the power of the committee and the moneyed members.

In December 1895, at the half-yearly meeting, the committee again invited the membership to debate and vote on the advantages of forming a limited liability company. Tom Maley objected to the question being raised at such a meeting, and suggested that an AGM or an extraordinary meeting called for that purpose with sufficient advance notice would be a more appropriate forum. Unlike his brother, Tom appeared to have lost some favour at this time with the committee, although he remained highly visible and was popular with the ordinary members because he frequently castigated the committee for the neglect of the Poor Children's Table. The committee expressed surprise at Maley's objection, and proceeded to play their most important card — the conditional offer of £500 by the Scottish Cyclists' Union for three days' use of Celtic Park in July 1987. A subcommittee appointed by the club to negotiate with the SCU eventually reported back; the cost of changing the track to have it conform to international standards would be £900, and as the cyclists had promised £500, this would mean an increase in the club's liabilities of £400. The politicians on the committee used the report as a lever. They indicated that they were not prepared to sanction any alterations unless the club proceeded in the undertaking as a limited liability company . . . and the membership accepted that position on 4 March 1897, at a meeting in the same St Mary's Hall where the club had been founded for charity less than ten years previously.

The change had been inevitable, but in no other footballing organisation could such a normal transition have caused such genuine turmoil.

Notes
1   See chapter 'The Stadium'.

7

FIN DE SIECLE

SOME historians claim to have noted a phenomenon known as 'fin de siecle' anxiety. Apparently, as a century draws to a close a collective mood of disillusion and depression grips much of the population, an awareness that another era has come to an end without the promise being fulfilled or much sign of improvement. It was a bit like that for Celtic in the last years of the nineteenth century: although the club had reorganised itself into a limited liability company with a board of directors and the team had established itself as one of the best in the country . . . although the premises were touted as the most up-to-date anywhere and the followers were considered among the most loyal . . . something seemed missing.

Some considered the change a mixed blessing; the club was making progress, but at what cost? For years Celtic committees — a fortunate, if unruly, blend of pragmatists and idealists — had run an organisation that was a model for the period, but the times were changing. In July 1897, when presenting the Charity Cup to Rangers, Colonel Merry of the organising committee stated at the banquet: "Football is no longer a pastime; rather, it has become a huge, commercial undertaking." As a business the club was now a victim of its own momentum, fated to succeed only by progressing and expanding, or doomed to fail by inertia and stagnation. During this period the club as an organisation improved markedly, but not without further soul searching among the more idealistic members.

The first major step forward was to appoint Willie Maley as secretary-manager and his tenure started on 23 June, 1897, with a salary of £150 a year; at the meeting that approved the appointment he was given a further honorarium of £40 (as was James McKay, the treasurer) for past services, and his efforts on the club's behalf during the 'strike' were noted and appreciated. Although still young for the position, Maley was an excellent appointment; he was an enthusiastic player at right-half and at times outstanding, having been capped for Scotland, but his greater contribution was to come in the new role that soon expanded into an all-encompassing one. His ability was soon recognised: "He lives for the club and as long as its interests move smoothly he is happy; but when they don't go with as much rhythm as he would like, Mr Maley never allows his temper to be ruffled. An ideal secretary in every way, the Celts are indeed fortunate that they have such a gentleman as Mr Maley to look after the affairs of the club." (*Scottish Sport*: 10 August, 1900.) Maley was a rare find for a football club, having an old head on young shoulders. His early training was as a chartered accountant, a career he abandoned to devote more time to the club as it expanded; apparently, when he was a trainee with an established firm in the city, his employers called him into the office and requested him to give up appearing for Celtic as a professional, but Maley continued to play, for a while using the name 'Montgomery', his mother's maiden name. Always aware of business opportunities, while acting as match-secretary he opened a sports outfitters on the Gallowgate and landed some lucrative contracts, supplying Scottish teams with 'caps' and strips; later he was to operate the Bank Restaurant, a famous rendezvous for sportsmen, but despite these interests he put in a full day at Celtic Park and made himself responsible for every detail of the running of the club.

Although largely forgotten now, the annual Celtic Sports was considered one of the premier meetings in Britain, attracting athletes from England and overseas as well as Scottish talent. Maley was the driving force behind their success, showing considerable ingenuity in persuading athletes to appear, organisation in arranging the programme, and energy in supervising all the details. His interest in athletics was an absorbing one, and in 1896 he won the 100 yards event at the Scottish Amateur championships, a distinction he shares with Olympic heroes Eric Liddell and Allan Wells. Young, energetic and practical he was to play an increasingly important part in making the club one of the most renowned in Britain.

Doubts were expressed in the *Glasgow Observer* about the altruism of the directors: "Though the vast majority of the old members are not at all satisfied with the selection, they have only themselves to blame, as in handing over the club to a few moneyed individuals they cut a rod to beat themselves and must endure their whipping with the best grace they can muster." The new board of directors had an ominously early skirmish with the brake-clubs, the forerunners of modern supporters' clubs. Originally they were affiliated to local parishes, their members also belonging to the Catholic temperance society known as the League of the Cross, and by 1895 fourteen parishes, led by St Mary's, Calton, boasted 20 brakes which attended home games, driving up to the ground on four-in-hand wagons decorated with bunting and carrying as many as 25 persons, some of whom held aloft the club banner depicting

WILLIAM MALEY

(Celtic F.C.)

HOSIER. HATTER. GLOVER
AND
ATHLETIC OUTFITTER.

155 GALLOWGATE, GLASGOW.

SPLENDID SELECTION ALWAYS ON HAND OF

Hats, Hosiery, Gloves, and all kinds of General Outfits.

ATHLETIC OUTFITS A SPECIALTY.

Willie Maley using his footballing name to business advantage. Advert in the SFA Annual 1894/95.

their favourite player. Any surplus funds at the end of the season, from annual concerts, picnics or other social gatherings, would be handed over to charity. Usually the 'brakes' purchased season tickets for the members in quantity and in 1896 they thought they had been promised a reduction; however, with the forming of the new company in 1897 the Board did not feel obliged to honour this commitment and unpleasantness broke out between the brakes and the club. This was doubly unfortunate because the brake clubs represented the cream of the support and deserved preferential treatment; and it seemed that a more mercenary element was taking over the club. Some felt that a natural antipathy existed between the League of the Cross and the directors over the question of drink; one member of a brake-club, noting the preponderance of liquor interests on the new Board, wittily described it as "one Glass among six publicans". The directors, sensing accurately that any protest or boycott would be short-lived, held out, and flatly denied that such an agreement had been reached. The crisis escalated briefly and resolved the issue of the ultimate authority at Parkhead. The brake-clubs discussed vaguely among themselves the possibility of forming another "new Irish football club in Glasgow", but it did not go beyond talk; the brake-clubs also discussed their dissatisfaction with the number of non-Catholics now appearing for Celtic and advocated "players of the right sort from stem to stern". Fortunately, neither proposal gained much currency, and the debate died down, but Celtic's captive columnist in the *Glasgow Observer* had the last word, gibing that "a body which can go in for gaily caparisoned steeds and expensive banners would surely be able to pay full price for their season tickets, but apparently such is not the case".

The club showed financial acumen in other ways: the World Championship in cycling held at the ground in 1897 was a tremendous success despite forebodings that such a 'meet' could not be held in Scotland, and two other cycling events in the same year produced a further profit of £410 for the club; in December 1897 the directors purchased Celtic Park from the landlord when the current lease still had four years to run, and one of them, James Grant, erected a new double-decker stand as a private speculation; in 1898 Celtic and Rangers competed for the honour of hosting the international against England and Celtic was again given the preference (and the opportunity of profit). But sadly the original purpose of the generation of money was largely forgotten, as in 1898, when the club's revenues totalled £16,267 (a record for a British club) and a dividend of 20% was declared, no donations were made to charitable causes.

On the field Celtic attained reasonable success, but a feeling of disappointment prevailed over the period. The club still tended to buy its best players rather than develop them and with such star-laden line-ups should have done better. In 1897-98, however, Celtic won the league championship for the fourth time and went through the 18-game schedule without a defeat, conceding only 13 goals — a clear indication that the tightening up after Arthurlie was having an effect. The loss of only 13 goals was a remarkable feat, particularly in a league noted for high scoring, and the defensive strength was a major factor in achieving a four-point advantage over the runners-up, Rangers, in a season marked by trouble at the Celtic-Rangers game at Parkhead in January 1898 when 50,000 attended a closely contested match; the crowd frequently encroached upon the pitch, and the small contingent of 40 policemen hired was unable to handle the invasions, the game being abandoned after 60 minutes. The newspapers criticised Celtic for the lack of crowd control: "Until they have added considerably to their accommodation, and they should be at the job at once, the Celtic directors in their own interests should see on such special occasions that they do not take in one copper more than they have accommodation for. It is not good business, and it constitutes at least an excuse for breaking-in." (*Scottish Sport*: 4 January, 1898.) Celtic's chairman took a more predictable tack, preferring to blame the fans and "the idiotic and stubborn portion of the spectators in their selfish endeavour to see the game at closer quarters". The authorities were united in their condemnation of the spectators, described in an editorial as comprising "the very scum of the city, drunken and brutal in their behaviour and language . . . an exhibition of low, unredeemed humanity". Interestingly, Robert Campbell, a recruiting sergeant from the Gallowgate, sued Celtic for £3 in damages as compensation for injuries sustained at the match, but the sheriff dismissed the claim. The real controversy, however, broke out not over the field invasion, nor about the dangers posed by crowded terracings, but concerning the distribution of the gate receipts. Rangers claimed that even prior to the official stopping of the match, representatives of both clubs had agreed that the game would be considered a friendly; accordingly, the gate should be split equally. Once more the word of the Celtic directorate was called into question, as Celtic denied making such a deal. Despite Rangers' claim and a suggestion from J. J. Bentley, the president of the English League, that the gate at the replay be divided equitably, Celtic kept their 'legal' 80% of the original receipts and 66% at the rematch.

In 1898-99, the following season, came the second 'Old Firm' final of the Scottish Cup, with the following teams facing each other before 25,000 at Hampden.

> *Celtic:* McArthur, Welford, Storrier, Battles, Marshall, King, Hodge, Campbell, Divers, McMahon, Bell.
> *Rangers:* Dickie, Smith N., Crawford, Gibson, Neill, Mitchell, Campbell, McPherson, Hamilton, Miller, Smith A.

By all accounts it was a sporting encounter, unlike some later matches between the clubs that have marred the occasion. Despite an injury to Bell, an internationalist bought from Everton earlier in the season, Celtic had slightly more of the play and stout defence rarely allowed Rangers near McArthur. With the score 0-0 at half-time Celtic pressed and McMahon, a deadly and brave header of the ball, rose to connect with a corner in 57 minutes; after 75 minutes Hodge added the second from an allegedly offside position, but Rangers' appeals were dismissed by the referee, Mr T. Robertson (Queen's Park). Rangers, holders of the trophy for the past two years, fought hard but Celtic retained the two-goal advantage till the end.

Celtic matched Rangers' feat by retaining the cup in 1899-1900. The club fielded the same forward line but made changes in defence: McArthur, Storrier, Battles, Russell, Marshall, Orr. Queen's Park in their last Scottish Cup final, in April 1900 at the new Ibrox Park, played the legendary R. S. McColl at centre-forward, but were very much the underdogs against a Celtic team that had thrashed Rangers 4-0 in a replayed semi-final. Despite that, they put up a good fight and took an early lead. Celtic asserted themselves, with McMahon leading the way. He equalised with a shot from the wing and a few minutes later, although surrounded by defenders, headed on Bell's corner for Divers to score easily to give Celtic a 2-1 advantage that was increased to 3-1 before half-time. Queen's Park fought bravely in the second half but it was slack covering in Celtic's defence that helped them tie the score; again Celtic increased the tempo to score a late winner through Bell.

Celtic's 'money players' frequently lacked consistency in the league, but could raise their game for the big occasion (or bonus) and the directors were beginning to question the policy of buying ready-made players: "Perhaps the greatest fault in past Celtic management has been the unwillingness of the officials to give young players a chance. They loved a player with a reputation . . . and in fact engaged players whose only claim to recognition was their past, very much past, reputations." (*Glasgow Observer*: 5 January, 1901.)

Certainly the previous policy had been practised assiduously. Celtic fielded teams that were all-star sides, composed of players bought from other clubs in Scotland and a contingent from England anxious to return to Scotland with the recognition of professionalism in 1893 or, prior to that date, as 'amateurs' — players such as Doyle and Brady from Everton, and Welford from Aston Villa.[1] Although the practice had proved successful on the field and profitable at the turnstiles, the individualism of such players was now being viewed as a liability in a more commercially orientated sport where success was more than ever dependent on team building. Certainly, the club's practice throughout its first decade had helped to acquire an unrivalled reputation for colour

A portrait of Dan Doyle taken in 1895/96.

and entertainment, but perhaps the club was running out of luck or judgement in its more recent purchases; the comparative failure of forwards Bell, signed from Everton in 1898 and who left in 1900, and McDermott, bought from Dundee in 1901-02 and who departed the next season, were cited as evidence that the policy did not guarantee success. It was a haphazard approach, conducive neither to consistency nor to *esprit de corps*; such players often brought with them a tarnished disposition towards the sport in addition to their skill on the field.

The career of Dan Doyle, one of the greatest full backs of the last century, illustrates the pitfalls and the advantages of the policy. Doyle was an unashamed football 'soldier of fortune' and played for many clubs: Rawyard Juniors, Slamannan Barnsmuir, Broxburn Shamrock, Hibernian, East Stirlingshire, Newcastle East End, Grimsby Town, Bolton Wanderers, Everton and finally Celtic. Doyle was a handsome figure and newspapers of the period frequently compared his athletic figure to that of a Greek god; he could tackle robustly, but with sound judgement and was celebrated for his long clearances and for placing free kicks into the heart of opponents' defences. He was an inspiring figure, capable of rallying his mates with spirited example, but he did present problems because of his maverick reputation, exemplified with a story about his appearance for Scotland against England at Liverpool in 1895: ". . . Scotland misplaced their captain, Doyle, then a Celtic stalwart, who travelled down with the team and promptly disappeared. He was missed at breakfast and a frantic search of the city found no trace, and at lunch the Scots decided substitute Foyers would play. But within an hour of the match Doyle reappeared beaming, with the explanation that he had spent the night with some of the cronies of his former playing days with Everton. It says much for his personality that no one dared break the news that he had already been replaced . . . and says a lot for his play that he was chosen to captain Scotland twice more against England." (*England v Scotland*: Brian James, 1969.) Everton were furious at losing him to Celtic as an 'amateur' and fought strenuously to recover him, and it was said that Doyle had asked for the Mersey Docks as his share in any transfer back to Liverpool. When with Celtic he was fined several times for breaches of discipline, most notably for missing the Arthurlie cup tie, but he claimed that most of those fines had been rescinded later. His happy-go-lucky demeanour, his humour, his aggressive play, his good looks, his skill — all made him the idol of the supporters, but he always posed a potential disciplinary problem for the club's officials.

Increasingly the new business-like Board was becoming wary of such expensive personality players: ". . . lavishly treated by directors and well looked after by the manager. I may add that the management intends dealing firmly with all and sundry, and will stand no nonsense."

(*Glasgow Observer*: 16 December 1899.) The chairman in his football column for the *Glasgow Examiner* on the same day complained about lack of heart and stated that stringent measures would be taken against certain players.

Clearly, a new determined mood was apparent at Parkhead, and Willie Maley's advocacy of a youth policy was no longer falling on deaf ears.

Notes
1   When Celtic obtained the services of Campbell, Welford and Reynolds in 1897, and Fisher in 1898, from Aston Villa, England's most prestigious club, the Birmingham *Sports Argus* newspaper lamented 'When is this migration of Villa players to the crack Celtic club going to cease?' (quoted in *Scottish Sport*: 16 September, 1898). Welford was an all-rounder, having played cricket for Warwickshire, and is still the only Englishman to have won an F.A. Cup winners medal (with Villa in 1895) and a Scottish Cup winners medal (with Celtic in 1899).

8

RIVALRY

IT was a frustrating time to be a Celtic supporter as the Board worked out its new policy. The team still contained a number of veterans, including such players as McMahon and Campbell, besides Battles who had returned from England, and a number of promising recruits such as Quinn and McMenemy. By most standards it was an acceptable team, but the Board and supporters were growing impatient. Between 1900 and 1903 Celtic appeared in six finals and lost them all: in the Charity Cup Third Lanark romped to a 3-0 win in 1901, and in the following year Hibernian, the Scottish Cup holders, thrashed Celtic 6-2, the Edinburgh team having been invited to swell the receipts for the Ibrox Disaster Fund; in the Glasgow Cup of 1901 Celtic scratched rather than replay Rangers at Ibrox, and next year lost 3-0 to Thirds; in the Scottish Cup Celtic lost in successive finals to the Edinburgh sides, Hearts and Hibernian.

In April 1901 Celtic faced a strong Hearts team at Ibrox before a smallish crowd of 12,000, kept down by the cold, stormy weather. Hearts used the right tactics for the conditions, being direct and economical in their long passing, while Celtic persisted in their traditional intricate short passing that frequently got bogged down. However, the contrast made it an enthralling final. Hearts led 3-1 shortly after the interval, but Celtic fought back. McOustra scored following a Battles' free kick, and with only a few minutes left McMahon from a corner inevitably headed in the equaliser. The celebrations were short-lived as Hearts, the better team on the day, broke away to score the winner after an uncharacteristic fumble by Dan McArthur, a brave and acrobatic keeper for Celtic.

A year later, in April 1902, Celtic lost another Scottish Cup final despite the advantage of playing at Parkhead, the change in stadium being due to the disaster at Ibrox, the original venue. Hibernian were much the superior side as Celtic never settled. The only goal was scored by McGeachan who stationed himself at the post to net after a corner, and the Celtic marking was so slack that the player had time to back-heel the ball into the net.

Similar frustration was building up in the league where Celtic finished runners-up in consecutive championships. The loss of the title to Rangers in 1902, the Light Blues' fourth in a row, was a bitter blow. With five matches left, Celtic led Rangers by five points, but lost successive games to Hearts by 2-1 and Queen's Park by 3-2; in both games Celtic's traditional close game was criticised as contributing to the upsets and, after another point was dropped in a draw with Hibs, the Ne'erday fixture would virtually decide the title winners. Celtic had home advantage, but it turned out to be a most controversial match. McMahon gave Celtic an early lead, but Rangers led 3-1 at half-time despite furious Celtic protests about two of the goals: an indirect free kick that entered the Celtic net allegedly untouched by any player, and a shot by Campbell after he handled the ball, ". . . but the referee would have none of it. Immediately he was surrounded by expostulating Celts and, under the impression that McMahon had attempted to trip him, ordered the famous Celt off." Marshall reduced the margin to one goal in an exciting second half and, while Celtic pressed for the equaliser, Rangers broke away to score a fourth goal that Celtic claimed was offside, the game ending in some confusion. Celtic's chairman, John McLaughlin, registered a protest on the grounds that short time had been played and in respect of statements made to the newspapers by the referee, Mr Nisbet of Edinburgh. McMahon escaped further punishment after the referee both failed to post his report to the SFA within the required time and refused to answer questions put to him by that body. Given such incompetence, Celtic's sense of injustice seems justifiable, although the protest was to no avail. Willie Maley was unrestrained in his comments: ". . . would have been champions but for the vile treatment we received at the hands of the referee on New Year's Day, when the Rangers were practically given the game."

Shortly after the turn of the century, by 1903, the increasing rivalry of Celtic and Rangers took on new dimensions. Celtic, who burst upon Scottish football and revived it at a time when Rangers were a mediocre outfit, at first rarely concerned themselves with matches against the Light Blues, having established an early supremacy. However, Rangers had recovered in football and fiscal strength to emerge as Celtic's leading rival for the honours. The clubs had started the most intriguing of all sporting rivalries, based on three potentially explosive ingredients: football, profit and nationalism.

On the field the quest for football glory was a deadlock: both clubs had won the championship four times, although Rangers had shared another title with Dumbarton; Rangers had won the cup four times to Celtic's three, but the Celtic partisans pointed out that Rangers were fifteen years older than Celtic and thus had more opportunities to gain that trophy. In the Glasgow tournaments it was much the same story: Celtic had won the Charity Cup seven times to Rangers' three, and Rangers claimed seven Glasgow Cups to Celtic's four, but again it was indicated that Rangers had entered more times for the latter tournament. It was clear that the two clubs had started to dominate Scottish football, although Queen's Park still held a commanding lead in Scottish Cups with ten victories and eight successes in the Charity Cup. The matches between the two were attracting large crowds and the contrast in style was an added feature: Celtic favoured a close-passing game, marked by clever touches from individuals with flair and colour; Rangers stressed enthusiasm and industry, characterised by energy and effort. Whatever the merits of the approaches the competition was razor-keen and unrelenting.

In the boardrooms equally fierce skirmishing was taking place, but for profits. Football had become a business and the two clubs were in the forefront. Celtic signalled the new direction in the sport by becoming a limited liability company in 1897, Rangers followed suit two years later, and the changes were extremely profitable for both organisations. The progress was best seen in the expansion of the stadiums, improvements designed to cater for the increasing crowds that watched them, but more importantly to land the financial plum of staging the internationals, especially the one against England. The SFA chose Ibrox for the 1892 fixture, but Celtic Park for the matches held between 1894 and 1904 — with the exception of the ill-fated one of 1902 — and from 1906 till the present time have chosen the new Hampden Park. The negotiations between the clubs and the SFA for the business were intense and complicated, and it was a mark of the acumen of Celtic's Board that the club was given the preference so often. Both clubs could rely on revenue from loyal supporters: Celtic's from a captive audience within the Irish community and Rangers' from a populace eager to fix on a side capable of beating the upstarts from Glasgow's east end. No other clubs in Scotland could attract such followings, and it was support that grew with success and the tension of the rivalry. This rivalry and the profits to be derived from it was the cause of the clubs being linked in the ambiguous sobriquet the 'Old Firm', a description half distasteful and half admiring, as many unsympathetic cartoons in the papers showed the club treasurers bearing bulging money-bags to the bank.

The clubs were more than football and business rivals; they represented two different cultures and ways of life within Glasgow. Celtic represented initially the Irish (and Catholic) element, while Rangers had come more and more to represent the Scottish (and Protestant). Celtic's origin had been nationalistic and religious, designed to cash in on the growing interest in football; and Rangers' earlier start had been athletic and sporting. The further development was a fascinating one: the immediately successful Celtic evolved into a more Scottish club without sacrificing its residual loyalties, and the once moderate Rangers became the standard-bearers of a restrictive nationalism. The original animosity was understandable: the Celtic support revelled in the triumphs of the team, compensating as they did for the daily troubles in a harsh life amid uncongenial surroundings; the neutral Scottish enthusiast understandably resented the nationalist undertones of Celtic's achievements and looked around for a more representative team to cheer for against 'the Irishmen'. The rivalry was threefold: on the field the players fought it out for supremacy; in the boardrooms the directors squabbled for profits; and on the terracings the supporters separated under the banners of religion and nationalism — a division to be widened rather than closed in the future.

Disputes, foreshadowed by the 1898 episode when Rangers suspected they had been cheated out of gate money, set the tone. Celtic were disappointed that Ibrox was chosen in preference to Celtic Park in 1902 and, after the disaster at the match that caused 25 deaths when the wooden terracings collapsed under the weight of an excited crowd, the *Glasgow Observer*, so often a mouthpiece for the club, could not resist commenting that "Celtic's splendidly equipped ground, which has stood the test of previous record crowds" had been rejected, hinting that Ibrox was unsafe by quoting from another source: "Catastrophe, vaguely apprehended, spoken of last week in whispers as a possibility, has unfortunately taken place, and the International Football Association match at Ibrox Park has been marked by an appalling disaster." Celtic had been fortunate in avoiding a similar mishap, as several complaints were made about the terracing conditions at the 1894 and 1896 internationals; it was not surprising that a disaster should occur somewhere, as crowds grew in size and stadiums expanded on a trial-and-error basis.

Another flare-up took place over the venue for a Glasgow Cup final between the clubs in 1901 when Ibrox was chosen and the game ended in a draw; Celtic wanted the replay held at Parkhead, but Rangers felt the final should be completed at the original venue. When the Glasgow FA sided with Rangers, Celtic withdrew from the competition rather than play again at Ibrox. In the same year the clubs disagreed about the Glasgow Exhibition Trophy, originally won by Rangers but gained by Celtic when Rangers were forced to stage a competition to help the Disaster Fund. Rangers expected that the winners would return the trophy to them afterwards, or put it up for annual competition, but the Celtic Board considered it to be its property, won in open competition, and the resulting coolness lasted for some years over the matter.

Progress within football was not uniform, however. As the clubs expanded and profits grew, the security of the players, always precarious, remained shaky. The club was now 16 years old, but already some of its former players had died young and in unfortunate circumstances. Dunning, an early goalkeeper, died of 'consumption' (a euphemism for tuberculosis) in 1902, as had Peter Dowds, the club's most famous all-rounder; the *Glasgow Observer* of 31 October, 1903, wrote of the death of Mick McKeown, a popular full-back who had been given a handsome signing-on bonus: ". . . drinking the very dregs of human misery . . . once in a very comfortable way of business in Glasgow but apparently did not take account, in his hour of prosperity, of the rainy day". Even more sad was the later acount of the death of Willie Groves. His health had broken down in the mid-1890s after the failure of his business and, unable to find work, he had become destitute, living as a recluse 'on the parish' in Northampton where he "lingered for some years rather than lived" — a pathetic end for a man described in his playing days as ". . . tall, sinewy and graceful on the ball, his work was beautifully close, artful and deceptive. He was a picturesque figure, a sort of Romeo in the sport with his raven locks and classic-cut features. His career in all its varied spheres is one of the most romantic, and his personality will long remain as one of the most unique in British football." (*Glasgow Observer*: 17 February, 1908.)

Still, football was for the young and healthy: Celtic continued the new policy of fielding even younger sides and every indication was that success was imminent. In 1902 when Rangers put up the Glasgow Exhibition Trophy for competition to help the Ibrox Disaster Fund,[1] Celtic won it, defeating Rangers 3-2 in the final after extra time, and at the end of the next season won the Charity Cup with an exhilarating display.

The stage was being readied to receive a splendid Celtic team — a team recalled with awe for decades as "the greatest".

Notes
1   See Chapter 'The trophy room'.

9

ASCENDANCY

A PRESIDENT of the United States, ruminating on the effects of a controversial decision, was moved to comment that success has many fathers while failure is an orphan. There was no shortage of claimants for the credit to be derived from Celtic's remarkable run of success after 1904. The directors felt that by putting the affairs of the club "on a sound, business-like footing" they had made the renaissance possible; the secretary-manager felt that by signing on and training juniors he had made the major contribution; the players, at a time when tactics and coaching were largely unknown, must have felt that they had something to do with it.

The Board contained former players such as James Kelly and Michael Dunbar who dispensed practical advice, often at the training sessions. These directors helped the manager in selecting the team and, given Maley's reputation as a martinet, it is surprising to realise that he was not wholly responsible for the team selection. Contemporary evidence suggests that it was an amicable arrangement and, as the other members of the Board confined themselves to the business side of the club with conspicuous success, it was a *modus operandi* that worked for the benefit of both team and club. Maley had emerged as an indispensable presence at Celtic Park, but he had to face up to a difficult situation. Only an average player himself, he had to deal with the star players signed from English clubs and as a young man he felt some uneasiness in the role. Thus, it was not surprising that he became the leading advocate of a youth policy by which home-grown products could be "selected, pruned and shaped as the club desired"; as manager he could advise, lead and, if necessary, bully to produce results.

Some juniors, who would have been outstanding in any era, were being signed and had appeared for the first team. Jimmy Quinn was signed from Smithston Albion in January 1901, although he was reluctant at first, feeling that he should remain with the juniors. A young inside-forward, Jimmy McMenemy, enrolled from Rutherglen

Glencairn with a reputation for clever play; he was joined some months later by his team-mate, centre-forward Alec Bennett, who had a fine understanding with him. The junior internationalist keeper, Davy Adams, was signed from Dunipace and two other youthful players returned from England, one being Peter Somers, back at his old club after a brief transfer to Blackburn Rovers, and the other an Ayrshire lad, Jim Young ('Sunny Jim'), a strapping half-back from Bristol Rovers. A year later Alec McNair, a promising forward from Stenhousemuir, joined Celtic and as a defender became the classic poacher turned gamekeeper. The policy was acknowledged in the *Scottish Referee* of 8 August, 1902: "In previous years we have been accustomed to announce important captures from some English club or other, but this season there are none; and here we think the directors have given further proof of their wisdom. It is to junior talent they now direct their attention . . .".

But the transition was slow and painful. Maley described 1902-03 as "the most disheartening season in the club's history and the worst in terms of results", and even 'Man in the Know', the most partisan of all Celtic sympathisers, showed signs of the frustration: "We get too much football in Scotland. Indeed most sensible people are thoroughly sick of the game with its crude, bestial methods, its blatant partisanship, its strenuous nerve-wracking noise, and the oozing vulgarity of its unwashed votaries."

The Charity Cup in May, 1903, afforded the first sign of the breakthrough, Celtic coasting to a 5-2 win over St. Mirren at Cathkin Park with the new recruit Alec Bennett scoring three times and renewing a profitable partnership with his former junior colleague Jimmy McMenemy; after Willie Maley, acting as Celtic's linesman, had complained of being pelted by missiles the referee "advanced to the ropes to deliver a pacificatory harangue". Less than a year later 'Man in the Know', was exultant in the wake of a Scottish Cup victory over Rangers: ". . . the Ibrox ancients could not stand the pace of the young, fast, eager Celtic pack . . . a complete justification of the Celtic directors in their drastic removal of 'has-beens' and 'back-numbers' to make way for young, fresh, crusty players" (*Glasgow Observer*: 23 April, 1904).

It was a splendid occasion, this first Scottish Cup final to be played at the present Hampden Park before a crowd of 65,000, attracted by the 'Old Firm' clash and a sharp reduction in the price of admission.

Celtic: Adams, McLeod, Orr, Young, Loney, Hay, Muir, McMenemy, Quinn, Somers, Hamilton.

Rangers: Watson, Smith N., Drummond, Henderson, Stark, Robertson, Walker, Speedie, Mackie, Donnachie, Smith A.

CELTS' GREAT CUP TRIUMPH,

DUNDEE BADLY BEATEN AT PARKHEAD.

QUINN BREAKS THROUGH AND SCORES

MUIR SCORES FIRST

BENNET LEADS THE ATTACK

M'FARLANES DESPERATE TRY

W.D.

Celtic's 5-0 rout of Dundee in the Scottish Cup quarter-final at Parkhead as seen by the Glasgow Observer, *12 March, 1904.*

Celtic started brightly, but Rangers broke away to score through Speedie, and the same player scored another only a minute later. Celtic fought back furiously. Quinn burst through to pull one back and before half-time he scored the equaliser with a typically unsaveable shot. The younger, fresher Celts pressed throughout the second half and Quinn accomplished the rare feat of a hat-trick in a Scottish Cup final with the winning goal about ten minutes from the end. Maley's faith in the young man from Croy was completely justified. Earlier in his career some of the directors had questioned his ability as Maley experimented with him, sometimes playing him on the left wing as well as on the right. To replace the 'injured' Bennett, Maley had chosen him for centre-forward in the final despite the doubts of his directors.[1]

A glorious chapter had opened in the book of Scottish football . . . and Maley, now being recognised as a manager pointed out with pride that 'his' team had cost less than £200, mostly paid out in signing-on fees to juniors.

In 1904-05, the start of the great run, the main rivals were Rangers. The Ibrox club was shading off from its peak while Celtic were reaching for eminence, and thus the competition between them was intense. Celtic won the Glasgow Cup early in the season, getting past Queen's Park and Partick Thistle before scraping through against Rangers by 2-1. Davy Adams in goal played heroically in the first half to keep Rangers' advantage down to a single goal, and the young Celtic side again was stronger in the second half, doing enough to eke out a narrow win before 65,000. Rangers claimed ample revenge in the Scottish Cup, beating Celtic 2-0 in a tumultuous semi-final at Parkhead.

Having beaten Rangers twice already that season, Celtic were established as clear favourites, especially when Rangers were forced to field some less experienced players because of injuries to regulars, but Rangers battled furiously to hold Celtic to 0-0 at half-time. Just before the interval McLeod, Celtic's full-back, pulled a thigh muscle and had to retire. Heartened by this and growing in confidence as the tie went on, Rangers struck for two goals, but Celtic fought back in the rain before a most controversial incident occurred. Quinn, chasing every ball and harrying the Rangers' defence, was tackled by Craig, who held him by the legs when the ball broke loose; Quinn struggled to free himself by lashing out at Craig with his feet, and the referee immediately ordered him off. Subsequent histories differ on this point. James E. Handley's *The Celtic Story* describes the scenes: "To some of the crowd, miserable in the pouring rain and irritated by the tactics on the field, this was too strong a provocation to be taken calmly. Some 150 of them, chiefly boys, ran on to the pitch and remained there apparently with the intention of forcing a replay. The game was abandoned, but the Celtic officials immediately offered to cede the tie, a gesture which was confirmed by the SFA when Rangers officially claimed it." But Willie Allison's *Rangers — The New Era* takes a different view: "Some rowdies invaded the field, and the players were forced to seek the pavilion's shelter. When the tumult had quietened, the referee asked the players to resume, but this was the second time they had been forced to quit. We were ready to go out, but Celtic had had enough; Mr J. H. McLaughlin, on behalf of Celtic, intimated that his club withdrew from the tie."

The sequel was a sensational one. The referee's report, apparently relayed to the clubs' officials shortly after the match, indicated that Quinn had kicked Craig and stamped on his face; some Celts visited Craig's home later that night to see for themselves and Craig contradicted the report in a statement and acted as a witness for Quinn when the case was heard. But the SFA backed the referee, as commonsense would indicate it had to, and suspended Quinn; the four-week suspension was harsh, however, given the doubts about the evidence presented and Celtic appealed on Quinn's behalf. The appeal was turned down, and understandably perhaps the SFA's resolve had been stiffened by the crowd's break-in. At the same time Celtic initiated a court action for libel against a Glasgow newspaper that had accused Quinn of "violent play" and got a judgement in their favour, but only for one shilling (5p) damages and no costs — a Pyrrhic victory.

However, Celtic triumphed in the league for their first championship since 1898, but only by the closest of margins. Celtic and Rangers finished level in points after the scheduled 26 games and, fortunately for Celtic, neither goal average nor goal difference was then an acceptable method of deciding the outcome, because Rangers' was much superior (83-28 as against Celtic's 68-31). The practice was to hold a play-off game, as had been done between Dumbarton and Rangers in the first league season, and the 'Old Firm' met at Hampden Park on 8 May, 1905, to determine the title; after a close, hard-fought battle Celtic won 2-1 to start off the run of six successive league flags.

Rangers went into a decline for the next few seasons and only rarely challenged for the league; in 1905-06 Celtic easily won the title by a six-point margin over Hearts and as comfortably in 1906-07 by seven over Dundee with a points total of 55 for the new 34-game schedule, and held off free-scoring Falkirk in 1907-08 by four points, equalling the points total of the previous season.

By now Celtic's team was being thought of as an exceptional one, and like all truly great sides it played as a unit over an extended period with the minimal number of changes, long enough to be evaluated fairly. The regular team was as follows: Adams; Watson, Orr; McNair, Loney, Hay; Bennett, McMenemy, Quinn, Somers, Hamilton. The only other players who participated meaningfully in the run were McLeod, who was the regular left-back in 1905-06, and Young, who established himself in the side at right-half in 1906-07, allowing McNair to revert to right-back and replace Watson.

CELTIC FOOTBALL CLUB, 1905-06
Back row: R Davies (Trainer), R G Campbell, D McLeod, H Watson, D Hamilton, A McNair, A Wilson, E Garry, J McCourt, D Adams. Front row: J Young, J Hay, A Bennett, J McMenemy, W Loney, J Quinn, P Somers, W McNair.

The defence was sound: in goal Adams was a substantial figure and capable of maintaining his concentration while relatively idle; Watson, Orr, and McLeod were dependable full-backs in the hard-tackling style of the period the latter two players gaining caps for Scotland; at right-half Alec McNair played a studious game as befits a player who had started off as an inside-forward (with Stenhousemuir) and rarely wasted a ball while providing reliable service to his forwards; at centre-half Willie Loney was consistent and often under-rated, but he was a difficult man to get round and dominated his area of the field. Jimmy Hay, the left-half, was the captain and highly competent, his clever positional and tactical sense compensating for a lack of pace. He was recognised as 'the General', even in a side that included Jimmy McMenemy, nicknamed 'Napoleon'.

Many supporters consider the forward line to be the most balanced in the club's history, and it is a view to be given serious consideration. The right wing consisted of Alec Bennett and Jimmy McMenemy. Bennett was a fast, tricky winger, courageous and full of running, a goalscorer and a fine crosser of the ball, while McMenemy was the personification of the Scottish inside-forward, masterly at passing and controlling the direction and tempo of the game, and another regular scorer once he heeded his chairman's advice "to pass the ball inside the post". The left

72

wing consisted of Peter Somers and Davy Hamilton and again the balance was there; Somers was a deceptively frail player, but another 'fetch-and-carry' inside-forward in the Scottish tradition, spreading the play around and probing for weaknesses, while his partner Hamilton was a spirited winger, full of trickery and noted for his crosses. And at centre-forward was one of the legendary figures in Celtic's history, Jimmy Quinn, a fearless striker with head and foot, an intense, passionate leader and a prolific scorer. If any criticism could be made of the combination it would be that too often the lead-up work of the others was designed to spring Quinn loose, and when the dashing leader was off because of injury the total effectiveness was reduced more than it should have been.

In 1906-07 Celtic finally accomplished 'the double' by winning the league and cup in the same season, the first time ever in Scottish football. The club, operating throughout this era with a small squad and without a reserve team, got help from an unexpected source. Playing in a benefit game, Adams cut his hand on a goalpost at Ibrox and Rangers loaned Celtic their reserve keeper while Adams was off. Tom Sinclair compiled a remarkable record that season: he played ten matches for Celtic and did not give up a goal in his first nine, and while he conceded two in the last game Celtic still won 3-2 in the Glasgow Cup final against Third Lanark; after he returned to Ibrox he played for the reserves and won a medal in the Second Eleven Cup to add to the Glasgow Cup medal gained with Celtic; and before the season's end he was transferred to Newcastle United where he won an English League championship award.

Quinn was again in trouble this season: playing against Rangers at Parkhead he was sent off 'for kicking Hendry in the face'. Quinn claimed that he had started towards Hendry to avenge an earlier foul on a smaller Celtic forward, but had jumped over the fallen Ranger without harming him; the club again fought on Quinn's behalf, making the weak defence that another Celt had struck Hendry in the face, but the SFA suspended Quinn for two months. The *Glasgow Star and Examiner*, whose chairman was Tom White, a Celtic director, organised a subscription list for the player and donations poured in, reaching a total of more than £250 — a handsome compensation for the punishment. It should be acknowledged that the affair did not show Celtic in a good light, and the response of the supporters, players and directors to the fund indicated a knee-jerk loyalty to causes other than the administration of justice; this appeal to 'patriotism' (which recalls Dr Johnson's definition as "the last refuge of a scoundrel") has been used too often over the years by the club to distract attention from lapses in behaviour.

Celtic were supreme in the league because of methodical play and consistency, but the players could be knocked off-stride in cup-ties and the triumph in 1907 was a reward for temperament. It took three games to get by Morton, and another three to defeat Hibs but little trouble to eliminate Rangers 3-0 at Ibrox. These teams lined up for the final at Hampden on 20 April:

Celtic: Adams, McLeod, Orr, Young, McNair, Hay, Bennett, McMenemy, Quinn, Somers, Templeton.

Hearts: Allan, Reid, Collins, Philip, McLaren, Henderson, Bauchop, Walker, Axford, Yates, Wombwell.

The holders, Hearts, were desperate to retain their crown but faced a Celtic side approaching its peak. Both teams went out for goals and play was bright and keenly contested in the first half which ended 0-0. The turning point came with a disputed penalty for Celtic that Orr converted after 55 minutes. Within a few minutes Somers had added two more goals and the final was over as a contest, with Celtic, still a young side, looking stronger as the game went on. McNair showed his versatility by turning out at centre-half in place of Loney, and Celtic's left-winger was the famous Bobby Templeton, signed earlier in the season. He was a splendid player, a 'sand-dancer' whose play was described as "on the wing he danced like a sunbeam, glided here and there in mazy waltzes, or darted for goal as the notion seized him". He had the looks and charisma of a matinee idol and the story was told often of his encounter with the lion at Kilmarnock; for a wager of £10 he entered the lion's cage as cool as ever, apparently patting the beast and turning its tail to the applause of the spectators. It was a sign of Celtic's teamwork and effectiveness that the appearance of such a star as Templeton should be considered a luxury, and he was quietly transferred to Kilmarnock, to be replaced by Hamilton, happy to resume his customary berth on the left wing.

A year later, Celtic faced St. Mirren in the Scottish Cup final before 55,000 at Hampden. Celtic's side had evolved into an easily recognised formation: Adams, McNair, Weir, Young, Loney, Hay, Bennett, McMenemy, Quinn, Somers, Hamilton. St. Mirren offered little resistance in a most one-sided final as Celtic romped to a 5-1 triumph. The overawed Saints found the occasion too much for them and, irked by a couple of refereeing decisions in Celtic's favour, were no match for a rampant Celtic side. Bennett, who had been rumoured ready to sign for Rangers, gave his club a farewell present of two goals before joining the Ibrox club amid allegations of 'tapping'. St. Mirren's defence seemed to give up after Quinn scored Celtic's second goal from a suspiciously offside position shortly before half-time and when Bennett added the third immediately after the interval the match was over. So Celtic gained the second 'double' in Scottish football, and in consecutive years — an indication of their supremacy; in fact, Celtic won every tournament open to them that year, winning the Glasgow Cup by beating Rangers 2-1, the Charity Cup with a comfortable 3-0 win over Queen's Park, and of course the championship by a four-point margin over Falkirk.

However, the club's bid to achieve the double for the third year in a row failed by the narrowest of margins, even if the 'failure' was hardly the players' fault. The league was won by a herculean effort in the closing stages to overcome Dundee's challenge. After a replay in the Scottish Cup final against Rangers, Celtic were called upon to complete their schedule of eight league games within 12 days and garner 12 points from them. The champions made it, but it was nailbitingly close. Consider the situation on the last Saturday of the season. Celtic had dropped a crucial point in a drawn game at Parkhead against Airdrie and this meant that Celtic now had to gain six points from four fixtures, three of which were to be played away from home. They started off convincingly with Quinn netting three in a 4-0 win on the Monday at Parkhead over Motherwell, and followed that up with an equally satisfactory defeat of Queen's Park at Cathkin by 5-0 on the Wednesday night, with Quinn scoring another hat-trick; two hard games were due on the Thursday and the Friday, Hibernian at Easter Road and Hamilton at Douglas Park, and Celtic lost 1-0 at Edinburgh despite constant pressure in the second half, leaving the match at Hamilton to decide the championship. The game attracted a larger crowd than usual: "Never have I seen the Hamilton enclosure look so well, and probably never more mixed a crowd has lined that enclosure. A survey showed that not only were the collier and ironworker class present, but the city had sent its representation, nor were these same solely Celtic followers — far from it. There were present large numbers from the Barracks, and quite a goodly number of a class who rarely patronise football matches, but who were evidently attracted by the sensational and dramatic finish to the league contest" (*Glasgow Observer*: 8 May, 1909). Celtic pressed from the start and Davy Hamilton scored with a fierce drive to give them a 1-0 lead at half-time, but with Quinn limping on the right wing and with fatigue setting in the issue was still in doubt. McMenemy settled the match with a characteristic goal, gathering the ball cleverly, gaining some space and a little time before despatching a well-placed shot just inside the post from 12 yards. Although Hamilton Accies scored a late goal Celtic had won the championship for the fifth year in a row.

Fate decreed that the opportunity to gain the third consecutive double would be denied the team. Once again the 'Old Firm' faced each other in the Scottish Cup final as the teams lined up on 10 April, 1909.

> *Celtic*: Adams, McNair, Weir, Young, Dodds, Hay, Munro, McMenemy, Quinn, Somers, Hamilton.

Rangers: Rennie, Law, Craig, May, Stark, Galt, Bennett, Gilchrist, Campbell, McPherson, Smith.

It started off in typical Rangers-Celtic style with both teams playing all out to establish mastery, and the game swinging from end to end. Celtic drew first blood when Quinn escaped the close attentions of Stark to head a goal after 30 minutes, and at half-time the score was still 1-0. Celtic survived some early Rangers' pressure and looked to be in control until Gilchrist equalised in the 72nd minute, and were shocked when Bennett, the former Celtic player, broke away and scored a solo goal only three minutes later. Celtic were stung into immediate retaliation and stormed Rangers' goal for an equaliser . . . and gained it with a controversial counter with only ten minutes left. Celtic's new right-winger, Munro, tried a speculative cross-shot and Rennie, Rangers' perfectionist goalkeeper, gathered the ball cleanly enough but, trying to avoid the onrushing Quinn, he stepped backwards over his line; the referee, in good position to judge, awarded the goal immediately, despite the protests of some Rangers' defenders. The game ended in a 2-2 deadlock, a fair result after an enthralling final that had hugely entertained the 70,000 crowd, but trouble was in the air for the replay a week later.

The rules of the SFA were clear about any replay; if this game ended in another draw there had to be a third game. Any change in the rules could only be introduced in the proper forum and in the approved manner, but Willie Maley unwisely contacted Rangers about the possibility of playing extra time to decide the replay and passed his views on to a newspaper which printed them and seconded the idea. Rangers treated the brief contact by Maley as informal and did not raise the matter officially. Unfortunately, however, the newspaper the *Daily Record and Mail* did not retract its suggestion and many spectators turned up for the replay feeling they were entitled to see a result from a 'final'.

Both teams made changes from the first game, Celtic's being Kivlichan replacing Munro; thus, both sides had former players of the other club playing on their right wings. Rangers scored after twenty minutes to lead at half-time, but Quinn equalised in the second half. The game finished 1-1 and the trouble began.

Several players, most of them Celtic's, stayed on the field at the whistle as if expecting the referee to order extra time, and made for the pavilion only after a significant delay. The crowd was encouraged by this reaction from the players and called for the game to continue, but when nothing happened several spectators moved on to the field to protest; the police moved to stop the encroachment and the violence escalated quickly. Hundreds of spectators poured on to the pitch, Celtic and Rangers' supporters alike united in an orgy of destruction; the badly outnumbered police contingent was unable to cope with the invasion and had to send for reinforcements. The mob attacked the barricades, set a bonfire on the track and fuelled it, contemporary accounts agreed, with whisky, attempted to burn the pay-boxes, and fought the police with stones and cinders from the running track; they attacked the members of the fire brigade summoned to deal with the fires and made their task impossible by cutting the hoses. The violence continued for hours and it was the blackest day in Scottish football to that date.

The mood was sombre when directors of Celtic and Rangers met after the replay to discuss the situation. They agreed on a joint statement and a united course of action: "Although it was mooted during the week that extra time might be played in the event of a draw, it was found that the Cup Competition rules prevented this. On account of the regrettable occurrences of Saturday, both clubs agree to petition the Association that the final tie be abandoned." The clubs also declared that they would not play another game, and that one of them would scratch first. This co-operation between Rangers and Celtic was not a disinterested action; both clubs' supporters had disgraced the occasion, causing anxiety in the boardrooms as the SFA prepared to meet to ponder the consequences. Despite the new solidarity, Rangers emerged with slightly more credit from the affair, as it was Celtic's bungled approach in raising the matter of extra time that had drawn the public's attention to the situation, and most of the players who had remained on the field longer at the end of the match were Celtic's (eight to Rangers' two, judging by one photograph).

The SFA council met and after an acrimonious discussion carried the following motion by 15 votes to 11: "That to mark the Association's disapproval of the riotous conduct of a section of the spectators at Hampden Park, and to avoid a repetition, the Cup competition for this season be finished and the cup and medals be withheld." To compensate Queen's Park for the extensive damages to the ground, the most modern in the kingdom when it was opened only six years before, the SFA contributed £500 and the clubs were ordered to provide £150 each.

The newspapers and the general public condemned the hooliganism, but a selection from the letter printed in the *Evening Times* of 20 April, 1909, suggests a diversity of opinion in determining the blame: "After Saturday's riot I would suggest the withdrawal of all policemen from football matches and substitute a regiment of soldiers with fixed bayonets . . ."; "It is impossible not to deplore such a scene as occurred at Hampden but the ends of justice and truth are not served best by considering resistance to police brutality as necessarily wrong or by stigmatising all resisters as disorderly hooligans . . ."; "Few who follow the dealings of the magistrates with this class of savages are surprised at

the result of their grandmotherly methods of treating such rascals . . .";
"A cure would be for the Association to revert to the former practice of
charging a shilling admission to the final. This would exclude some
thousands of the hooligans who would then have the sixpence to spend
on buying soap to wash their faces and get their chins scraped; to cleanse
their mouths of filthy speech would require a miracle, but their
exclusion would prevent the pollution of the atmosphere and ears of the
ordinary man-in-the-street . . .".

Of course the scenes at the final of 1909 were a national disgrace, but
one has to wonder if an element of nemesis did not lurk in the situation.
In past seasons too many 'cup finals' had been played out as 'friendlies'
at the unknowing expense of the spectators, and their suspicions had
been aroused by the drawn Glasgow Cup-ties in the previous season
between the 'Old Firm'; on this occasion the 'fans' (and the word comes
originally from the more appropriate 'fanatics') took matters into their
own hands. As the first Ibrox Disaster in 1902 had its roots in the
tendency of the clubs to profit from the sport at the expense of adequate
organisation, so too did the Hampden Riot.

The next season (1909-10) marked the start of Celtic's inevitable
decline, but the team still managed to win the championship by two
points over Falkirk who might have won but for a loss of form as the
campaign drew to a close. Celtic's veterans nursed their resources and
did just enough to win. Surprisingly, Celtic's neighbours, Clyde,
defeated the favourites in the semi-final of the Scottish Cup at Shawfield
by 3-1, with the defence uncharacteristically shaky in front of the
Welsh goalkeeper, Roose, who was replacing, on loan, the injured
Adams.

Some changes had been made in the line-up. McNair was now the
regular right-back, from where he continued to demonstrate scientific
football by passing the ball from deep in defence, dribbling in his own
penalty area, and dispossessing opponents rather than tackling them;
'Sunny Jim' Young was the right-half in front of him, strong and totally
reliable; Joe Dodds, another capable defender, was fielded most often
at left-back, but filled in at centre-half and was equally impressive in
both positions. Neither Munro nor Kivlichan was the perfect replacement
for Alec Bennett who had joined Rangers, but nobody could fill that
gap satisfactorily. Peter Somers, an exceptional inside-forward had
gone, transferred to Hamilton Accies, a rare hint of trouble at a club
deemed to be the best run and organised in Britain.

However, the Celtic team from 1904 to 1910 was the best side in
Scotland, and probably in Britain, and its accomplishments deserve
comparison with those of the side managed by Jock Stein between 1965
and 1970. Every great team has to be judged by its complete record in
the tournaments it played, and Celtic's was an impressive one:

	League	Scottish Cup	Glasgow Cup	Charity Cup
1903-04	Third Lanark	Celtic	Third Lanark	Rangers
1904-05	Celtic	Third Lanark	Celtic	Celtic
1905-06	Celtic	Hearts	Celtic	Rangers
1906-07	Celtic	Celtic	Celtic	Rangers
1907-08	Celtic	Celtic	Celtic	Celtic
1908-09	Celtic	—	Third Lanark	Rangers
1909-10	Celtic	Dundee	Celtic	Clyde

The league record was a remarkable one, and the statistics show the consistency:

	P	W	D	L	F	A	Pts
1904-05	26	18	5	3	68	31	41
1905-06	30	24	1	5	76	19	49
1906-07	34	23	9	2	80	30	55
1907-08	34	24	7	3	86	27	55
1908-09	34	23	5	6	71	24	51
1909-10	34	24	6	4	63	22	54
TOTAL:	192	136	33	23	444	153	305

In honour of the feat the Scottish League later presented Celtic with a shield, confident that no other team could match it, and it was not until a more modern Celtic dominated its epoch that the record could be surpassed.

One Celtic partisan pointed out that the only tournament the club did not monopolise was the Charity Cup, and the reason was simple: this tournament came at the very end of the season and by then Celtic's players were feeling the strain more than most. The team was slightly less successful in cup play than in the league, largely due to its scientific, patient style of play which did not always pay off in sudden-death tournaments, but a glance at its overall record from 1904 to 1910 reveals considerable accomplishments by any standard. Over the period of six years the number of changes in personnel was minimal and the most famous line-up, to be recited for 40 years by every generation of boys in Celtic households, was as follows: Adams (247); McNair (583), Weir; Young (392), Loney (253), Hay (217); Bennett, McMenemy (453); Quinn (271); Somers, Hamilton (223). The numbers in parentheses indicate the number of appearances in league games for the club, and were compiled from a list of players who had made more than 200 appearances, considered a lengthy period of service. Of the 43 men listed in the publication[2] no fewer than eight were regular members of this side — a clear indication of the team's consistency and the club's stability.

Some supporters complained of the relative neglect of the players by the Scottish selectors and suggested bias against the club, but the *Dundee Post* put matters into perspective in May, 1908: "Take the

Celtic team from stem to stern and it will be found that there is a strange absence of the class of men who are usually associated with international work. This year places were grudgingly found for only two players, which was some advance certainly, but far short of what might be looked for from a team capable of such achievements . . . Yet, truth to tell, apart from McNair and Quinn, the players as individuals do not bulk largely. What then is the secret of success? It lies simply in the wisdom of the directors who, having got together a really good team, though not brilliant individualists, have kept them persistently together, and thus have brought them to a knowledge of each other's methods which make them of far more value than the so-called 'teams of all the talents'."

Willie Maley, the architect of Celtic's concept that a team should be built and not collected, could not have agreed more.

Notes
1 There had been speculation in the newspapers prior to the final that a young Celt would shortly join Rangers. This was clearly Bennett, whose fondness for Rangers since boyhood was well known. Indeed, when with Rutherglen Glencairn, he had only turned down the chance to go to Ibrox because of a "meagre offer". His absence in this final would thus appear to have been a diplomatic one.
2 *Celtic F.C. Facts and Figures 1888-1981:* P. Woods, 1981.

10

TRANSITION

THE Celtic team of the previous six years had been one of the game's greatest combinations up to that time, but it had played with so few changes in personnel for so long and with such poor cover in reserve that when decline set in the fall was bound to be a steep one. In 1910-11 the perennial league champions tumbled from first place to fifth, tied with Dundee.

The break-up of the side had started back in 1908 with the transfer of Alec Bennett to Rangers and continued with the transfer of Peter Somers, the fetch-and-carry man of the attack, to Hamilton in 1910; the captain, Jimmy Hay, had a dispute with the club over his terms and was transferred to Newcastle, as did Jamie Weir who went to Middlesbrough. Some players were showing signs of wear and tear. Orr had retired, Adams was feeling the strain in goal although he continued to play well, and even the great Quinn, at last being affected by his cumulative injuries, was starting to miss matches. The others were ageing at much the same rate and the signs of decay were showing.

In 1910-11 the defence was as solid as ever, but the forwards found it increasingly hard to score consistently; after 15 league games the defence had yielded only nine goals, the lowest goals against total in the league, but the forwards had scored a miserable 19, and 14 points had been lost in those games. The talk was of bad luck, but it was equally clear that the vital spark had gone. The tight matches that had been won in past seasons by a late effort were now slipping away despite the team's valiant endeavours; the experience that had enabled Celtic to hold off challenges from Falkirk and Dundee in the recent past was no longer enough, and nothing could halt the decline but changes in the line-up.

Into the side came a most remarkable inside-forward. Young Patsy Gallacher from Clydebank Juniors did not look the part, as he was stooped, painfully thin and short, but he established himself in the side immediately when he joined up in 1911 with his repertoire of dribbling skills and his willingness to take goalscoring chances. He posed a problem for Maley as he usually played at inside-right, and the manager solved it by switching McMenemy to inside-left. Bennett's departure had caused another problem on the right wing. Kivlichan, signed from Rangers, was a useful short-term solution and scored some memorable goals, but he was not the complete answer and was transferred to Bradford Park Avenue, whose manager was Tom Maley, Willie's brother. That particular problem was eventually solved by the signing of Andy McAtee from Mossend Hibs, a short but speedy winger with great strength in his legs that gave him a powerful shot. A new keeper, Mulrooney, was signed to replace the veteran Adams in 1911 and was highly promising until he was forced to retire with a serious illness after only two seasons, to be replaced in turn by Charlie Shaw, bought from Queens Park Rangers for £100. The task of replacing the dependable Loney was given in the end to Peter Johnstone, a strapping Fifer from Glencraig, who had filled a number of other positions satisfactorily when required. The search was on for a successor to Quinn and he was eventually found in Jimmy McColl from St Anthony's, a small, nippy centre with an eye for goals.

Celtic's problems were exacerbated by the policy of not running a reserve side. Justified on economic grounds, amid grumbling about declining patronage induced by complacency among the club's supporters, drawbacks were revealed with the loss of experienced players. The situation was brought into sharp focus with injuries to Davy Adams, the goalkeeper. Celtic had to borrow a reserve from Rangers at one stage in 1906 and had to replace Adams with L. R. Roose, a Welsh amateur internationalist, in a cup-tie in 1910 that was lost because of "defensive misunderstandings".

While the newcomers took time to find themselves at Parkhead, the supporters had to settle for a transitional period. It was a period that most clubs would have considered the highlight of their history as Celtic won consecutive Scottish Cups in 1911 and 1912, finished second in the league table behind Rangers twice, won the Charity Cup in 1912, 1913 and 1914 and emerged from the transition to establish another dynasty that dominated Scottish football starting in 1914.

In 1911 Celtic won the Scottish Cup to atone for the lapses in the league, and it was a victory earned by defensive strength. Throughout the cup campaign Celtic did not concede a goal, defeating St Mirren 2-0, Galston 1-0, Clyde 1-0, Aberdeen 1-0 in the semi-final, and all the ties, including the Aberdeen match, were played at Celtic Park. These teams lined up at Ibrox before 45,000 on 8 April:

> *Celtic*: Adams, McNair, Dodds, Young, McAteer, Hay, Kivlichan, McMenemy, Quinn, Hastie, Hamilton.

Hamilton Academicals: Watson J., Davie, Miller, Watson P., McLaughlin W., Eglinton, McLaughlin J. H., Waugh, Hunter, Hastie, McNeill.

Hamilton, in 16th place in the league and the outsiders, put up a splendid fight in the final, played on a hard patch; it was a defensive battle with the forwards failing to open up two stout defences, but Hamilton had the better of the second half and Celtic were glad to hear the whistle. Celtic made changes for the replay: Hay and Dodds switched positions to allow the more aggressive Dodds to join in the attack, Kivlichan took over Hastie's place at inside-left, his own place on the right wing being filled by McAtee. Celtic's greater resources showed in the replay that took place a week later, and two second-half goals, by Quinn in the 60th minute and McAteer near the end, brought the cup to Parkhead for the seventh time.

John Brown on the point of scoring his goal in the 1912 Scottish Cup semi-final victory over Hearts at Ibrox.

A year later Celtic, in second place in the league, faced the third-placed Clyde in the final, again at Ibrox, before a crowd of 50,000.

Celtic: Mulrooney, McNair, Dodds, Young, Loney, Johnstone, McAtee, Gallacher, Quinn, McMenemy, Brown.

Clyde: Grant, Gilligan, Blair, Walker, McAndrew, Collins, Hamilton, Jackson, Morrison, Carmichael, Stevens.

Celtic were obviously improving and on the threshold of attaining their traditional supremacy in the Scottish game, having reached the final by beating a strong Hearts team at Ibrox in the semi-final, the first time the SFA had insisted on neutral grounds for that stage of the tournament. In the earlier rounds Celtic had a stormy ride: Dunfermline faced Celtic in the first round via the hazardous route of winning the Qualifying Cup and held the holders to a narrow 1-0 result; at Aberdeen Celtic were down by 2-0 with 20 minutes left but rallied to get a replay at Parkhead. In the final Clyde put up a stout resistance; in fact, they had more of the play but could find no way past the Celtic rearguard that had introduced a new keeper who won a medal in his first season. Clyde's fate was sealed in 30 minutes when McMenemy took advantage of a defensive lapse to score the only goal of the half; Patsy Gallacher, also playing in his first final, punished a similar mistake in the second half and Celtic retained the cup. One unique feature of this final was that the competing teams were managed by brothers, Willie Maley of Celtic and Alec of Clyde.

Celtic were forced to take second place in the league to a powerful Rangers squad and it was apparent from the *Glasgow Observer* that resentment was clouding the issue in the continuing rivalry: "There was never much doubt about the matter after the first three months of the season, when the Light Blues were hardly ever off their own ground. I don't think we are ever likely to see any league club favoured in the way of home fixtures as Rangers were this season. Had Mr Wilton drawn up his club's fixtures he would hardly have made a better job of it!" (30 March, 1912); and ". . . win or lose, Rangers are always certain of good gates because, don't you see, they are the only city team on which the bigots can rely to take a fall out of the Celtic. . . . The Celts made Rangers or perhaps it would be putting it more fairly to say that Rangers made themselves at the Celtic's expense" (22 February, 1913).

But by 1914, a year better known for darker events, Celtic were once more the dominant team and club in Scottish football.

11

DOMINATION

THE undoubted promise of the emerging Celtic side was fulfilled in the last season before the Great War; in 1913-14 Celtic came within a hairsbreadth of winning every trophy in Scotland, and were unfortunate not to do so.

It was a relatively shaky start to the season, with Celtic losing to a fluke goal at Cathkin in a replayed Glasgow Cup tie against Third Lanark and showing signs of inconsistency in the league. After six matches the record was mediocre — three wins, two defeats, and one draw — and already the team trailed Rangers and Hearts. One problem seemed insoluble: who could replace Jimmy Quinn? It was clear that Quinn was going to make only a few appearances and the decision had to be made now. The problem was a two-fold one; the other regular forwards had relied so much on him to finish off their moves that they could be considered goal-shy, and it was difficult to find another leader in the same heroic mould as Quinn.

At the end of the previous season young Bernard Connolly had been given a chance to fill the role; he did well on the firm grounds in the Charity Cup, scoring once against Third Lanark in a 2-1 win at Cathkin and netting two goals against Rangers in the final, won 3-2 at Parkhead. But he was small and slightly built, a ball-worker rather than a spearhead, and a liability on the heavy winter pitches; his run lasted for nine matches and he scored a respectable four goals, but he was not a Quinn.

Young Jimmy McColl, a junior internationalist with St Anthony's, made his debut at outside-right against Dundee in a 1-0 win on 18 October, and Maley, noting his well-developed positional sense, astutely drafted him into the centre soon after. He was a success with his nimble play, and his subsequent seven goals from 17 league games indicates this, but he was still small, young, and inexperienced. Maley decided that it was time to buy a proven player and he settled on an Englishman, the oddly named Ebenezer Owers, then with Clyde;

85

Owers was an experienced forward, a bustler who could score goals, and he netted nine in his 14 games at centre, but he did not lead with authority. The supporters were given a taste of what was missing when Quinn himself made a rare appearance at Greenock and scored two goals in a 4-0 win.

The strength of the team lay in defence and it was a powerful aggregate: Shaw; McNair and Dodds; Young, Johnstone and McMaster. The goalkeeper, Charlie Shaw, had proved to be an outstanding capture; although quite small he was solidly built, but as agile as a cat. At full-back the phlegmatic Alec McNair complemented his more energetic partner Joe Dodds, a fierce competitor, quick in the tackle and eager to join in attack. Veteran right-half Jim Young still held his place; bought on a hunch more than a decade earlier from Bristol the giant Ayrshire man, fairheaded and solidly built, was a magnificent servant. With long legs that seemed to telescope for tackles, this often ungainly player was a difficult man to get round, and an inspiration to his colleagues with his enthusiasm. Peter Johnstone, originally a promising inside-left, developed into a solid centre-half, utterly dependable and strong on the ground and in the air, while Jimmy McMaster looked like solving the problem posed by the departure of Hay to Newcastle. Over the course of the league season of 38 games this defence conceded 14 goals, and gave up only seven in the last 32 games.

Celtic made up some ground on Rangers with a 2-0 win at Ibrox in October, despite the absence of McMenemy who had suffered a broken collar-bone three weeks earlier against Aberdeen; the goals were scored by McAtee and Whitehead, another trialist at centre-forward in Quinn's place, but Shaw had to excel, in the closing stages saving a penalty taken by Bennett as Rangers rallied. Rangers' effective challenge for the flag ended on New Year's Day when Celtic thrashed them 4-0 at Parkhead, and from then on it was clear that Celtic would finish as champions, the only defeat in the last 32 matches coming at Falkirk on a day when Dodds, McMenemy and Browning were playing for Scotland against Wales and McNair was off injured. In the end Celtic finished up a comfortable six points ahead of Rangers with this record: P38 W30 D5 L3 F81 Agst14 Pts65.

The forward line, although it contained some outstanding players, had not yet linked up as a cohesive unit, partly as a result of McMenemy missing 18 matches with injury and international appearances, but as soon as a centre was found it would set scoring records. McAtee and Gallacher formed a formidable wing; the winger was a speed-merchant, always keen to shoot for goal, while Gallacher was already indicating that he was an inside-forward of genius, finishing the season as the leading scorer with 21 goals, although spectators were more impressed with his dazzling array of dribbling skills. The left wing of McMenemy and Browning was equally effective; McMenemy, always referred to as 'Napoleon', was a master tactician, cunningly capable of changing the whole direction of the attack with one adroit move, while his partner had all the qualities of straightforwardness and was a deadly shot with his left foot. It needed only a centre-forward to complete the unit, and by the season's end one had emerged.

The Scottish Cup was noteworthy for a series of away fixtures for Celtic against Clyde (0-0), Forfar (5-0) and Motherwell (3-1) before facing Third Lanark (2-0) in the semi-final at Ibrox; only Clyde offered stiff resistance, forcing Celtic to a replay, won by 2-0 at Celtic Park. For the final at Ibrox on 11 April, 1914, the following teams faced each other:

> *Celtic*: Shaw, McNair, Dodds, Young, Johnstone, McMaster, McAtee, Gallacher, Owers, McMenemy, Browning.
> *Hibernian*: Allan, Girdwood, Templeton, Kerr, Paterson, Grossert, Wilson, Fleming, Hendren, Wood, Smith.

The match was disappointing as neither side mastered the difficult windy conditions; neither forward line settled and combined play was at a premium, but Owers at centre for Celtic had a miserable day and was replaced by McColl for the replay on the following Thursday on the same field. However, it was a vastly different game. Celtic started off brightly and young McColl scored two goals within a short spell, the goals coming at the 8th and 11th minute marks, to put the result beyond doubt. Browning, a highly effective winger capped against Wales that season, added two more and Celtic strolled home, winners by 4-1 before a crowd of 40,000.

At the end of the season Celtic won the Charity Cup again, for the third year in a row, by defeating Third Lanark 6-0 in the final after an easy 3-0 win over Queen's Park. McColl, now established as the centre and the successor to Quinn, troubled the great Jimmy Brownlie in the Thirds' goal with his sprightliness, and he was to bother many other keepers in the future.

The outbreak of war in 1914 changed the nature of football in Scotland; indeed there was some discussion about whether football should close down for the duration of the war, but eventually it was agreed that the sport should continue with modifications. No player was allowed to make a full-time living from football, wages being limited to a £1 minimum and £2 maximum, at the discretion of the club, and no close-season wages were permitted; all players who were not in the forces had to work at some war-related industry and were not permitted to play on Saturdays unless they had done their week's work beforehand. Matches were scheduled only for Saturdays and holidays to

CELTIC'S TRIUMPH.

"Sunny Jim" Shoulders Off the Trophy to Parkhead.

Celtic captain Jimmy Young with the spoils of the 1914 Scottish Cup victory over Hibs. Evening News, 17 April, 1914.

prevent midweek games from interfering with overtime work in the factories, and clubs were not allowed to have their players released early from work to travel to away games. The Football Associations of Scotland and England agreed to abandon international matches and the SFA decided to withhold the Scottish Cup during the hostilities, but fortunately the League felt it better to continue, although the guarantee of £50 for visiting teams was reduced to £30.

During the war Celtic dominated Scottish football, but grumbles were heard about the club's contribution to the war effort; like the complaints about Rangers' supremacy in the next war the rumours were ill-founded. Celtic's players, as did other footballers, served in the forces, worked in the yards, in the forges and down the mine-shafts: one ex-player, Willie Angus, was awarded the Victoria Cross for rescuing an officer in the trench warfare in France, sustaining severe wounds and losing the sight of an eye in the action; Peter Johnstone, the regular centre-half, was 'killed in action' in France in June 1917. Other players — like Patsy Gallacher who worked in the shipyards, Joe Dodds in munitions work at Beardmore's, Willie Loney at Barr and Stroud's the manufacturer of rangefinders, Andy McAtee in the mines — were engaged in vital war work.

The club itself did its part. Willie Maley sent footballs to the men in training and to the soldiers at the Front on behalf of the club, and the manager was thanked by the Scottish Fusiliers' Association for "the kindness you have shown to the wounded soldiers at Stobhill [Hospital]". Half-time appeals were made over the loudspeakers asking for recruits to enlist "before the fun is over" and the Celtic Sports in 1915 were used as a recruiting rally; the club offered Celtic Park free of charge for a 'boxing carnival' in aid of the Fund for Limbless Heroes; and since 1892 soldiers in uniform had been admitted free to the ground for games. Rejected for military service on age grounds, Willie Maley took to task the critics of wartime football: ". . . The reference to football managers putting football before the war is an unjust and cruel one. My family have not shirked their duty in this respect: my brother's second boy died fighting in France last year, his eldest boy is in the Navy, his fourth son is in the Flying Corps, and his third son forced to remain in war work. My eldest boy lies in a London hospital; he was seriously wounded recently in France; and my youngest son, aged eighteen the other day, is at Fort Matilda with eleven months' service already. John McCartney, of the Hearts, has a son fighting, as has Dan McMichael of the Hibs, and Jamie Phillips of Aberdeen. E. M. Tarbet, of Third Lanark, offered his services and was refused on account of his health, I believe. Willie Wilton, of Rangers, is doing good work in the Bellahouston Hospital. Several of the others are working in war work, whilst I personally have the greatest pride and pleasure in the general services I render to all and sundry, including prisoners of war in Germany, who have had reason to remember the name of the Celtic club and, incidentally, its secretary." (*Weekly Mail and Record*: 9 December, 1916.)

The letter was prompted in part by the appearance of Patsy Gallacher before the Glasgow Munitions Tribunal in November 1916. Gallacher was working in the shipyards, where he had started off as an apprentice shipwright, but had been reported for 'bad timekeeping'. Gallacher offered no excuse and was fined £3 by the tribunal, and the publicity was guaranteed to warn other footballers of their patriotic duties; however, Gallacher was later suspended by the League from 19 December till 27 January and Celtic fined £25. Controversy erupted, Celtic and the *Glasgow Observer* both contending that the club and player had been treated unfairly, and the familiar charges of prejudice against Celtic were raised.

It could not be claimed that the punishment was illegal. Gallacher was fined by the tribunal as a worker, and suspended by the League as a player, there being no question of a double punishment as the League had drawn up wartime regulations to govern the different conditions, but Celtic claimed that the punishment was excessive and geared to punish the club. It pointed out the length of the suspension and suggested a shorter term would have been appropriate; it indicated that the timing was finely calculated to hurt the team's chances of retaining the title; it suggested that the League had overstepped its mandate by suspending a player (for the first time in its 26-year history): "Some of us will take a lot of convincing before we believe that being a Celt was not Gallacher's biggest crime. And most of us arrive at that opinion because we know the club has been hit and hard hit, through the player. The League were good enough to put it in writing that the Celtic manager and his directors knew absolutely nothing about Gallacher's timekeeping. If it could have been shown that the player had been discovered training at Parkhead when he ought to have been working at Clydebank there would have been an excellent case against the club. Instead it was admitted and put on record that the Celtic officials knew nothing of their players' doings from Saturday afternoon to the following Saturday morning. Why then the £25 fine? Well, it seems that the club committed an error of judgement in not suspending Gallacher immediately he had been tried and fined by the tribunal. One could advance arguments against the Celts doing such a thing; they could reasonably say that a fine and a showing-up were sufficient punishment. . . . I contend that as a first offender he ought not to have been suspended at all. But he gets practically a couple of months' suspension; he will miss eight matches before turning out on the first Saturday of February. It is the irregular term of suspension that brings out the unusual spirit; from the 19th December to the 27th January, the latter date a Saturday, and therefore carefully included, is a variation from the usual one-month's suspension, and tells its own tale." (*Glasgow Observer*: 30 December, 1916.)

Students of propaganda would recognise immediately the characteristic style of its columnist, 'Man in the Know'. Again, it is the historian's task to examine the facts reasonably and objectively, in this case after a lapse of 70 years. The Celtic complaints are not justified. Gallacher was suspended shortly after the findings of the tribunal and could not surely have been dealt with prior to the ruling of that legal body, and thus the complaint regarding the timing of the suspension is unfounded; the League dealt with the matter instead of referring it to the SFA because the wartime conditions had given it a sanction to do so; the suspension may well have been a lengthy one, but it seems clear that the football authorities were anxious to set an example. Gallacher, as an outstanding player in an exceptional team and a weekly columnist for a popular newspaper, was an obvious target; the player, though, felt that the punishments were vindictive, pointing out that some players with other clubs had been leaving their work early to play for their teams "under assumed names" without being punished.

In 1914-15 Celtic encountered unexpected opposition from Hearts, as Rangers started off badly and were never in real contention; in January Celtic were still three points behind the Edinburgh side with Rangers struggling in fifth place a further 12 points behind Celtic. Confidence was still high at Parkhead, however, as Hearts had completed the easier part of their schedule while Celtic had finished the hard part of their programme, and so it turned out. Celtic finally regained first place on 10 April with a fine win over Aberdeen, on the same day that Hearts lost to Morton at Greenock, missing two penalties in the process. Celtic took three points from their two remaining games, 4-0 at Cathkin over Third Lanark and 1-1 at Fir Park against Motherwell, to win with relative ease at the end. Celtic managed to match their record of the previous season almost exactly, a remarkable feat of consistency. For the fourth year in a row the team won the Charity Cup by beating Rangers 3-2 at Ibrox in the final to end the season on another high note.

Consistency was the feature of this Celtic team, and it is worth examining how this was attained. It was a settled team, and was reaching full maturity just as the war broke out in 1914, the 'double' of the last pre-war season attesting to that; and it contained several outstanding players then at the height of their powers. McNair and Dodds were considered the best full-back combination in Britain, while it was difficult to find a better pair of inside-forwards than the young Patsy Gallacher and the veteran Jimmy McMenemy; and whether by accident or design Celtic had arrived at the concept of 'the all-purpose player'. In general Celtic used a remarkably small number of players in winning the four consecutive championships, but the club employed these players astutely. McNair was most often fielded at right-back but could serve equally well in any position; Dodds at left-back could cover at centre-half in an emergency and had been switched to left-half for the 1911 final replay against Hamilton; a versatile defender, Tommy McGregor, regularly filled in for anybody injured or unable to be released from work in time; 'Sunny Jim' Young would and did play in all three half-back positions; McMenemy had moved easily over to inside-left to make room for the talented Gallacher at inside-right; young Joe Cassidy could play almost any forward position. The great advantage was that if changes had to be made and a recruit brought in, other more experienced players could be switched to ensure that disruption could be kept to a minimum.

Maley was now at the height of his powers; during the war years he was in his mid-forties, and had served the club for more than 25 years as player, secretary, and manager. At the time of his silver anniversary with the club in 1913 he was given an honorarium of 300 guineas and the *Glasgow Observer* referred to his contribution: "I can only say of him, as was said of Sir Christopher Wren, the world-famous architect of St Paul's Cathedral, 'if you wish to see his monument, look around'." (24 May, 1913.) Maley had grown into the job; he had been the force behind the decision to change to a youth policy at the turn of the century, had influenced the play of the great side that won six championships in a row, and now after a short and successful period of transition he was in charge of another wonderful side. He had skill in picking out a potentially good player and the intuition for playing him when he was ready to take his place; he had a talent for tinkering, and the patience to experiment with the player until he had found the right position for him, or sometimes the right blend for the team. However, above all he was the epitome of the manager at that time; an imposing figure physically, erect and still fit, he was tireless in his efforts on behalf of the club and he exuded authority, imposing his will on young players, but he had a very human touch; at club functions he participated in all the songs and dances with gusto.

Some claim that he was the person responsible for fostering 'the Celtic spirit', that intangible enthusiasm which has permeated the club, its players and supporters for so much of its history. He worked hard, but with a missionary purpose that showed clearly he felt the club was more important than any individual; thus, he could appeal strongly and unselfconsciously to the players' emotions and motivate his teams to produce an extra effort at critical times. Even Rangers players were aware of this spirit, as their captain, James Gordon, noted: "The Celts appear to have the magic power of obtaining new players, some of them nothing special at the time, but in a few short months they become infected by the Celtic atmosphere and they form part of a very smoothly running machine, and proceed to do their bit in the way of creating more and greater club records." (*Weekly Record*: 22 April, 1916.)

In 1915-16 Celtic won the league and nobody offered any real opposition, Rangers coming a distant second; so far ahead were Celtic as the campaign entered its final stages that the club offered to play two outstanding fixtures on the same day in order to help complete the schedule in the agreed time. So Celtic lined up on Saturday 15 April at 3.15 against Raith Rovers at Parkhead, and immediately after the game travelled to Fir Park to face Motherwell; the most remarkable feature was that Celtic were expected to win both matches, and did so easily.

Willie Maley was most anxious to complete the matches, sensing that it was a historic occasion. Ayr United, scheduled to face Motherwell on the afternoon at Fir Park, envisaged the loss of revenue from a public faced with two matches on the same day at the same venue, and Motherwell offered them the bare league guarantee, an offer that Ayr were reluctant to take; so, Maley added on an extra £10 as a sweetener and the game was played, with Ayr winning. Meanwhile, at Celtic Park, the game with Raith Rovers was proceeding as planned. Maley had delivered a homily to the players, reminding them of the story of the dog who found itself with two bones and was unable to concentrate on one at a time. Such a tactics talk apparently was sufficient to motivate this Celtic side, and it won 6-0 with Patsy Gallacher scoring three times, though he did not get the credit for the important goals – O'Kane scored the second, the goal that meant a hundred league goals for Celtic, and Dodds, playing at centre-half scored the sixth, the goal that surpassed the previous record of 103 held by Falkirk. Upon arrival at Fir Park it was decided to replace O'Kane with the equally young Joe Cassidy, on leave from his regiment, and that was the only change as Celtic carried on to win comfortably by 3-1.

A few weeks later Celtic inevitably won the Charity Cup for the fifth year in succession, this time beating Partick Thistle 2-0 in a one-sided final, Jim Young celebrating his 13th anniversary as a Celtic player with a goal and Patsy Gallacher dribbling round several opponents for the other counter.

The following season continued the monopoly of the honours with Celtic winning every competition as in the previous season: the Glasgow Cup by 3-1 over Clyde and, of course, the Charity Cup by beating Queen's Park 1-0, the latter accomplishment for the sixth year in a row. In the process of winning the championship by ten points over Morton Celtic also established the record for the longest run without defeat in Scottish League football by remaining undefeated in 62 matches between 13 November, 1915, and 21 April, 1917.

The success in the Charity Cup seemed highly appropriate as the ravages of the war were badly affecting the poor in Glasgow and there were many cases of hardship. One newspaper felt moved to comment on the increasing demands: "As everyone knows, the Celtic Club was founded for charity's sake, and that object has never been lost sight of. But everyone does not know that the Celts are always giving, that never a week passes without an appeal coming before the directors from some of our local orphanages or others deserving institutions. The club, founded thirty years ago to provide dinners for hungry, little ones, still keeps up the good work; Smyllum, Nazareth House, St Joseph's Home have reason to know this. Broken men and jaded women know also that a Celtic 'line' has enabled them to get over a bad accident or a long illness, and secure a new lease of life in one or other of our convalescent homes." (*Glasgow Observer*: 26 May, 1917.) Celtic's participation in the Charity Cup tournament, and the traditional enthusiasm of the supporters for a good cause meant increased gates, especially at the finals; Celtic also played in other well-attended charity games including one against an all-star side selected from the other teams in the league, with the proceeds going to the Belgian Relief Fund.

The increased awareness of social responsibility was a welcome return to the older values which would have pleased the late Brother Walfrid. In June 1911, four years before his death, Walfrid had a final meeting with his old colleagues — Tom and Willie Maley, chairman James Kelly, and director Michael Dunbar — when he accompanied Celtic players and officials from Folkestone, near his home, to London on their way home from a continental tour. Tom Maley, then a football writer with the *Glasgow Observer*, recorded the affection that the old cleric still felt for Celtic, despite the misgivings he must have held about the direction the club had taken after his departure from Glasgow two decades earlier: "Well, well, time has brought changes; outside ourselves there are few left of the old brigade. I know none of the present lot [of players], but they are under the old colours and are quartered in the dear old quarters, and that suffices."

12

HEAD-TO-HEAD; TOE-TO-TOE

TWO different clubs; two different teams; two different approaches; two different styles; and two different philosophies, representing two different cultures. Some have summed up the rivalry between Celtic and Rangers in those terms.

During the 1917-18 season the differences became more pronounced; Rangers, fretting under Celtic's dominance, seemed to decide on an escalation of their traditional approach. The Ibrox club was now a rich one, the owner of a splendid and profitable stadium, sustained by a loyal and considerable body of supporters, and represented on the field by a succession of fine teams and players, but in most people's minds Celtic were still the dominant team in Scotland. Rangers were determined to wrest that supremacy away and in order to do so proceeded to gather players from other clubs. What they were doing was a normal practice, but Rangers were criticised for adopting it, not for the policy itself, but for the timing. During the war a normal situation did not exist and players were allowed to turn out for clubs other than their own at short notice; 'temporary transfers' were arranged between clubs as long as the players could show acceptable and patriotic reasons for moving from one location to another. Rangers made a concentrated and conscious effort to gather star players and soldiers stationed in Scotland, to replace their own missing men and to field a competitive team. The unfortunate aspect of the timing was that several clubs were deprived of good players at a time when they had already lost men to the forces; Hearts, for example, saw the whole first team volunteer for service shortly after the outbreak of war and could not afford to lose any more.

It remains a moot point. Predictably, the *Glasgow Observer* did not approve: "By the simple process of choosing an international team and importing it *en bloc* to Ibrox, Rangers hoped to deprive Celtic of the flag . . . down Govan way the new stars tumbled in such clusters that some of them were crowded out" (20 March, 1918) and the annual report of the Celtic secretary in the 1918-19 guide had much the same tone of offended sensibility: "What honour or credit pertains to honour won through other clubs' players is a matter that beats me! Also, Celtic's recruiting policy could be copied by some of our neighbours who, however, seem more inclined to poach from their neighbours or buying 'ready-mades'." Coming from the club that had hand-picked players from Scotland and England in order to adorn its own early teams, the statement lost some of its moral force.

In 1917-18 Rangers finally broke the Celtic stranglehold on the championship, winning the title by a single point with the issue remaining in doubt till the last game of the campaign. The *Glasgow Observer* was less than gracious in extending its congratulations: "For that reason a Clyde supporter has far more reason to be proud of his club, even if it be found at the bottom of the league table tonight, than an Ibrox enthusiast could possibly be of the mixed lot that gave Rangers first place last Saturday. 'Mixed' is hardly the name for the conglomeration of Queen's Park, Oldham Athletic, Hearts, Hibernian, Clyde, Dumbarton, Raith Rovers, Dundee, Morton and Sheffield Wednesday that masqueraded in Rangers' colours this season. Fancy a club that has played in the Scottish Cup for well over forty years having only one of its own rearing — Gordon — in the team that wins a Scottish League championship. Later on the saner Ibrox supporter will be ashamed of an honour that is claimed by the club and is shared by nearly a dozen others" (20 April, 1918).

Celtic could argue that the league was lost by the absence of players that the club had given to the forces. By that time the war had dragged on for more than three years, bogged down in the mud of Belgium and France at a horrendous cost in lives without much prospect of an end in the near future; as the war of attrition continued, the generals called for more and more soldiers and recruits. In the last year of the war Celtic players in uniform included Willie McStay, Andy McAtee, Joe Dodds, John McMaster, Michael Gilhooley, Joe Cassidy and Willie Ribchester. Despite the temporary absence of those players and the tragic loss of Peter Johnstone the side put up a determined struggle to retain the championship,

The situation was resolved on the very last day of the 1917-18 season; Celtic faced a strong Motherwell side at Parkhead and Rangers took on lowly Clyde at Ibrox. Rangers and Celtic were level in points and, had they finished equal, it would have meant another play-off match, as in 1905. Rangers won 2-1 over Clyde, however, and Motherwell held on for a 1-1 draw at Celtic Park despite fierce pressure on their goal for the last fifteen minutes as Celtic made desperate efforts to get the winner.

Certainly Rangers had improved over their form of recent seasons, but Celtic had slipped a little. Celtic's main problem was at wing-half where for much of the season the champions struggled without McMaster, now serving in the army, and the veteran Young, who damaged a knee so severely in 1917 that he never played again. Another recurring problem was at centre-forward where Jimmy McColl, proficient goalscorer though he was, appeared injury-prone and unable to deal with the harsh treatment meted out to centres; in November 1917 he had to undergo an operation for appendicitis and took a long time to regain his confidence and form. Others had shaded off a fraction and this was reflected in the number of points dropped at home in drawn games. The correspondent for the *Glasgow Observer* had a different view: "I am aware that it is an old story, but it is none the less true. Celts, pitted against any league side playing in its ordinary form, would simply win in a dawdle. But no league team plays ordinary football against the record-holders. A sort of super-football, mostly of the demoniac brand, is produced for Celts' benefit, so that our men are continually 'up against it'. It is simply marvellous that they can stand the never-ending strain." (20 April, 1918.) As far as football (and Celtic) was concerned 'Man in the Know' perceived matters with all the objectivity of a detached retina sufferer.

The only consolation for Celtic in this season was the lifting of the Charity Cup for the seventh time in a row, by beating Partick Thistle 2-0 in the final, but Rangers had picked up the other Glasgow trophy earlier in the season.

October was a miserable month for Celtic in the last wartime season: on the 5th Rangers defeated Celtic easily by 2-0 in the Glasgow Cup final to retain the trophy; on the 12th Kilmarnock surprisingly held Celtic to a 1-1 draw; and on the 19th Rangers came to Parkhead and administered a 3-0 thrashing to a disorganised Celtic side. The Celtic supporters were in a state of despair as Rangers moved out in front by three points, a lead that was increased to five by December. Celtic had dropped points in a drawn game with Hearts at Parkhead and a defeat at Motherwell while Rangers in losing their unbeaten record at Kilmarnock slipped only a little.

Celtic moved into contention in January, holding on for a hard-earned point at Ibrox in a 1-1 draw on New Year's Day and following that up with a 2-0 win over Clyde the next day, and victories over Third Lanark (3-2) and Clydebank (3-1). Rangers, struggling after the Ne'erday clash, lost 1-0 to Partick Thistle at Firhill and lost again on the 11th, this time to Morton at Cappielow by 1-0, and drew 2-2 with St. Mirren at Love Street and 1-1 with Ayr United at Somerset Park.

Celtic had settled to a consistent level of performance despite a rash of injuries and the unavailability of some players, and did not lose a league game from 7 December, 20 consecutive matches without defeat, in a sustained challenge for the flag, but once more the outcome was not decided until the closing days of the campaign. Leading by a single point, Celtic faced two difficult away matches: Hearts at Tynecastle and Ayr at Somerset Park.

On 28 April Celtic went to Tynecastle and managed a 3-2 win on a ground that had proved troublesome in the past; Andy McAtee on the right wing was in his unstoppable mood, leading the way with a spectacular goal and creating two others, but Hearts staged a comeback by scoring two late goals and caused anxiety among the Celtic rearguard. On 10 May Celtic faced 'the Honest Men' before a record crowd at Ayr and won comfortably 2-0; once more McAtee was in devastating form, scoring the first goal, a blazing shot from a pass by McLean, and creating the second for McLean with a long run and a lofted cross. The *Glasgow Observer* was delighted: "Fifteen times champions, and the 15th success the greatest of all! Looking back on the many fine achievements of past Celtic elevens, I cannot find anything to surpass the performance of the haphazard collection which brought the fifteenth championship flag to Parkhead. One has only to recall the circumstances: half of the team in khaki or engaged in munition work, the remainder knocked out one after the other by accident or illness, McColl off for months, Browning off for good, it is feared, Gallacher and McNair chipped now and then, only Shaw, Cringan, Brown and McLean able to come up smiling, week in week out." (17 May, 1919.)

The struggle for dominance in Scottish football was on in earnest, and there was little to chose between the teams:

1917-18	P	W	D	L	For	Agst	Pts
Rangers.............	34	25	6	3	66	24	56
Celtic.................	34	24	7	3	66	26	55
Kilmarnock..........	34	19	5	10	69	41	43

1918-19	P	W	D	L	For	Agst	Pts
Celtic.................	34	26	6	2	71	22	58
Rangers.............	34	26	5	3	86	16	57
Morton...............	34	18	11	5	76	38	47

The newspapers, aware of the struggle for supremacy between the clubs, were trying to analyse the situation: "A subject which is frequently discussed is how the Celts can come to the top so often against teams which, on paper at least, look superior. In defence they may be better than, say, the Rangers, although the goal figures don't say so, but a half-back line like Gordon, Dixon and Walls would probably bring more in the market than McStay, Cringan and Brown. Then with forwards of the reputation of Archibald, Bowie, McLean, Cunningham and Donnachie these are more fascinating 'star' lines than even McAtee, Gallacher, McColl, McMenemy and McLean; what then is the secret of Celtic's success? I was going to say because of the greater harmony at Parkhead compared with Ibrox; but I never heard that there was any discord in the Rangers camp. Still there must be something, an inspiration which brings the Celts up. I have always held that Willie Maley has had much, nearly all, to do with the success of the Celtic." (*Weekly Record*: 17 May, 1919.) The same edition of the paper made further comments on the rivalry: "At Ibrox they are for ever enthusiastically on the hunt for the best, the very best, they can provide for their patrons. They spend money, and they get the goods. No doubt about it! My conclusion as to the failure of the Light Blues to carry off supreme honours this season, as in some others, is 'the embarrassment of riches'. . . . There is a lesson in the fate of Rangers' aspirations this season which ought not to be forgotten. They ought to take a page from the Celtic copy-book. At Parkhead they believe in the exuberance of youth. They have a healthy appreciation of the valuable vitality of the aspirant to honours and therein, I think, the secret of Celtic's success lies."

Perhaps the difference between the clubs was shown in the first match of the next season. Celtic, although crowned as champions, introduced a newcomer at centre-forward — a nineteen-year-old from St. Anthony's, Tommy McInally. Against Clydebank at Parkhead the youngster scored all Celtic's goals in a 3-1 win and followed that performance by scoring two more against Dumbarton, the second after a vintage effort by Gallacher: "With a wonderful wriggle, two flips, two jumps, and a side-slip, Pat diddled five opponents, survived two trips, stumbled, recovered and stumbled again and fell, but in falling gave the ball to McInally, who took it sweetly first time and deftly piloted it past McTurk." (*Glasgow Observer*: 23 August, 1919.)

One wonders if Rangers would have introduced an inexperienced newcomer into a championship line-up and especially a recruit such as McInally. He was a prolific scorer, but inconsistent and prone to lapses in concentration; a likeable, exuberant lad he was liable to play to the gallery instead of applying himself to the immediate task: "Previous to being dropped, the Barrhead boy, though scoring regularly and sometimes — as in the Partick Thistle cup-tie — miraculously, was producing some of the most pitiful piffle imaginable. Dense stupidity appeared to dominate his movements, he kept continually doing the wrong things, and with monotonous regularity the best laid schemes of the brainy Celtic wingers led up to what seemed certain scoring chances only to find the whole thing wrecked and ruined by McInally's inexplicable weakness." (*Glasgow Observer*: 12 June, 1920.) The "inexplicable weakness" was, of course, the inexperience of youth. In general Celtic's problem throughout the season was the lack of goalscoring punch; after McInally's demotion the club tried several others in his place, including

McColl (but he had lost his confidence), the youngster Tom Craig who scored two goals on his league debut but faded away, and McLean who moved from his spot on the left wing. McInally, eventually, was restored to the team and ended up as leading scorer with a commendable 39 goals.

The league was effectively lost at Parkhead on Ne'erday when Rangers held on tenaciously to their six-point lead by virtue of a 1-1 draw. Celtic still had two games in hand, but points that should have been won were thrown away in drawn games, and a defeat was sustained at Clydebank, who had failed to qualify for the Scottish Cup competition, restored after the war.

Any hope of closing the gap with Rangers, now a comfortable three points ahead, was given up in drawn games at Parkhead late in April; St. Mirren managed a 2-2 draw to frustrate Celtic and some supporters who threw bottles near the end, and Dundee surprisingly held out for a 1-1 tie. The match with Dundee was never completed but the result was allowed to stand; the crowd were exasperated at Celtic's performance, suspicious that Dundee 'had lain down' at Ibrox two days earlier when they lost 6-1, and angered at the roughness of the Dundee tackling. Ten minutes from the end, following an incident between McLean and Rawlings in which the Celt seemed more at fault, many in the crowd invaded the field; two Dundee players, Raith and McIntosh, were assaulted and injured and the referee attacked. The absence of policemen on duty was considered to be a contributory factor in the hooliganism which was downplayed in the newspapers: "Since the iron railing disappeared, the small fry has become unpleasantly conspicuous at Parkhead. Not content with free admission — they burrow below the turnstiles — this vast army of ragamuffins has made a practice of dashing across the field and capturing the reserved terracing in front of the Grand Stand . . . and the whistle had sounded for a foul, when to everybody's astonishment the pitch was suddenly black with an army of small but amazingly impudent boys. A few adults of the hooligan class followed, and in an instant players and officials were surrounded by a surging mob. From the press-box, one could see how valiantly the Celtic players strove to defend the Dundonians. I saw McNair seize and throw aside a madman who was striking at the referee. The whole incident was causeless and meaningless, but to outsiders it can only appear in a sinister aspect. Thus is every club at the mercy of the slum element which revels in wild disorder and violence." (*Glasgow Observer*: 1 May, 1920.)

Rangers had won the league, but Celtic gained the minor consolations of lifting the Glasgow Cup and the Charity Cup. In the former tournament Celtic beat Partick Thistle in the final 1-0 through

McInally's goal, after scraping past Rangers by 1-0 and defeating Queen's Park by 3-1; and in the Charity Cup beat Queen's Park 1-0 at Hampden in the final after defeating Rangers 2-1 at Ibrox.

Neither Celtic nor Rangers, though, won the Scottish Cup; that honour went to Kilmarnock who defeated Albion Rovers 3-2 at Hampden. Rangers beat Celtic in the quarter-final at Ibrox 1-0, Celtic with a half-fit Gallacher at centre-forward failing to rise to the occasion in front of 80,500, but the Ibrox team fell to Albion Rovers in the semi-final after two replays.

The summer months of 1920, the traditional close season for football clubs, were filled with speculation and news about Celtic and Rangers — and for once the rumours and reports in the newspapers deserved to be described as "momentous". The developments accurately reflected the difference in approach between the two clubs and foreshadowed much of the inter-war period.

Early in May 1920 William Wilton, Rangers' secretary-manager and a highly respected official, was drowned near Gourock; he had been quietly efficient in helping Rangers to their high position in Scottish football. Wilton was replaced as manager by Bill Struth, the club's highly regarded trainer; the former had accepted victory graciously and defeat with equanimity, his frequent comment after losing being a philosophical "We'll live to fight another day", but his successor was vastly different. Struth was a most determined man, unwilling to accept defeat lightly and prepared to go to great lengths to ensure victory. On the field Rangers would be even more formidable, and physical. Wilton's responsibilities as the club's secretary were taken over by somebody else, leaving Struth free to concentrate on the team and players; Maley, on the other hand, was to continue as Celtic's secretary-manager until 1940, twenty years later, when Celtic followed Rangers' example in organisation by appointing McStay as manager and White as secretary.

In June a flurry of transfer activity took place and once more the difference in outlook was reflected in the developments. Rangers, after several years' wooing, landed Alan Morton of Queen's Park and at last solved a long-standing problem on the left wing by gaining one of the most exciting and dangerous players in the country; only a week later Celtic gave a free transfer to Jimmy McMenemy, a veteran at Parkhead and an outstanding inside-forward since 1903. Perhaps McMenemy was past his best, but he had a lot of football left as Partick Thistle found when he led them to their only Scottish Cup success a year later, and the release of the player heightened speculation that all was not well at Parkhead, especially in view of the contradictory reports: "In the succeeding year Jimmy McMenemy's career as a Celtic player came to a close. Young lads were pushing on for places. Jimmy had reached the veteran stage. But we did not want him to leave us. Jimmy, however, thought it time to go and off he went. With our full consent he joined Partick Thistle . . ." (*Weekly News*: 8 August, 1936). That excerpt came from a serialisation of Willie Maley's life story, written by Maley for the newspaper years later, and is at variance with a journalist's account at the time of the transfer: "I expected James to be able to tell me exactly the reason for what had happened. My expectations are not yet realised. Up to this moment he has no more knowledge as to why he is away from the club than you or I. Surprised a little at the delay in being offered terms, he didn't worry a great deal . . . but the day came when he was called before the directors. Naturally he felt that the time had now come when terms were to be discussed. But, what happened? I am telling you the story as he told it to me on Monday. On appearing before the Board he was calmly asked if he was retiring from the game. His answer was that he wasn't quite decided about that. Some jocular remarks passed between the parties, and then McMenemy was asked point-blank if he would be pleased were he granted a free transfer. His answer was in the affirmative. Little more transpired. The interview was over, and James McMenemy, after 18 years' service, had ceased to be a Celtic player. . . . Without asking one question he left the directors with whom he had been associated for so many years, and immediately began to lay his plans for the future. There had been no differences between the directors and himself so far as he was aware." (*Weekly Record*: 26 June, 1920.)

Earlier in June Jimmy McColl, scorer of 115 league goals in his five seasons with Celtic, was transferred to Stoke City for £2,250, a considerable sum in those days, but Celtic were rocked with the revelation that Patsy Gallacher was considering moving over a dispute about terms. Gallacher wanted better wages for himself and, when his request was turned down by Celtic, found that Dundee Hibs, a non-league side destined to become better known later as Dundee United, were prepared to meet his demands. Celtic moved quickly to grant his financial requests and the cynics pointed out that it was because no transfer fee would be forthcoming if he joined a non-league side. But yet another player left in a dispute over money. Joe Dodds signed on for Cowdenbeath at the start of the season. One has to wonder about the constant friction over wages and bonuses that characterised this era. Both Celtic and Rangers were financially secure. Rangers with an average home crowd of 30,000 and total income of £50,946 in 1919-20 declared a dividend of 15% while Celtic made a profit of £8,275 on the season and that was before the transfer of McColl to Stoke. In Gallacher's case the club made serious efforts to retain the player, but were less zealous with others.

The close season developments had given Rangers a considerable boost, and the Ibrox side took full advantage of the situation; under Struth Rangers, a strong physical side but with considerable skills, won the league with ease by ten points over Celtic. At Parkhead the Ibrox men ground out a controversial 2-1 victory: "The evil didn't take too long to show its venomous head: in the very first dash towards Robb [Rangers' keeper] McInally was badly kicked, and for a time was only able to hop about on one leg. McAtee got a boot in the face, Gilchrist was laid out with an elbow, I think, after McInally had been taken away for good. Little McLean, going down the middle for the equaliser, was mercilessly thrown from behind, and lay motionless on his face while the ball was wildly kicked into touch. The frantic kicking-out tactics of the Ibrox defence pained many but surprised none. As kickers the Rangers' rearguard could vie with the most competent of Army mules; as tacticians they could give the Black-and-Tans a long start and a whacking. If there were to be any extension of the liberty taken by the Blue defence on Saturday, the Rangers might as well arm their men with hatchets." (*Glasgow Observer*: 30 October, 1920.) Celtic did have the consolation of winning the return game at Ibrox in January by 2-0, both goals netted by Cassidy, a victory that prevented Rangers from going through the entire league campaign of 42 matches without defeat in retaining their title. Surprisingly, Rangers did not do too well in cup play, losing to Celtic in both Glasgow cups, by 2-1 in the Glasgow Cup at Parkhead in the semi-final and by 2-0 in the final of the Charity Cup. Celtic duplicated the limited success of the previous season by winning both trophies, beating Clyde 1-0 in the Glasgow Cup final, but the feeling was growing that these tournaments had declined in importance and prestige and that the real interest was now in the championship and in the Scottish Cup.

Rangers fought their way to the Scottish Cup final, Celtic being eliminated by Hearts 2-1 at Parkhead in the quarter-final; however, the Ibrox club was still struggling against a hoodoo and lost to Partick Thistle at Celtic Park 1-0 before a disappointing crowd of 28,294, thousands being deterred by an increase in the admission price to two shillings (10p) and what looked like a foregone conclusion. McMenemy declared himself fit to play, but Thistle were without their centre-half and the valuable left-half, McMullan, injured in Scotland's 3-0 win over England: "McMenemy's intelligence allowed him to extend his career. If the body was slower, less supple, less responsive, astuteness and experience might ensure that the player positioned himself more perceptively and had less need of haste. With McMenemy's appearance it was guaranteed that there could be no easy victory for Rangers." (*100 Cups*: Hugh Keevins and Kevin McCarra, 1985.)

A glance over the distribution of the silverware for 1920-21 — a duplication of the previous season's — would suggest that little change had occurred, but the momentum had been moving to Ibrox little by little, and the margin in the league between the two sides was significant.

Celtic prepared for 1921-22 with more confidence than the previous season's form merited; Joe Dodds had returned from Cowdenbeath after only a year there and hopes were high about the promise shown by John Gilchrist from St. Anthony's at right-half and another youngster, John 'Jean' McFarlane from Wellesley Juniors, at inside-left. It was felt that players such as McInally and Cassidy, with a couple of seasons behind them would have reached full maturity.

The hopes were realised in a desperately close race for the championship, although Celtic had fallen behind early to Rangers. In mid-October Rangers were in a strong position, four points ahead and undefeated in the league and already holders of the Glasgow Cup by beating Celtic 1-0 in the final; Celtic had visited Ibrox and shared the points in a 1-1 draw. By early December, though, Celtic had pulled level on points, Rangers having lost 2-0 to Hearts at Ibrox and 1-0 at Brockville to Falkirk; still, Rangers had the advantage of a game in hand.

Celtic had improved considerably in defence, and surrendered only four goals in 21 undefeated home matches throughout the campaign, but it seemed as if the opportunity had gone when Rangers held on at Parkhead on 2 January for a scoreless draw. The only other side to prevent Celtic from scoring at Parkhead was Falkirk, at that time a redoubtable team, and in that particular fixture which ended 0-0 Cassidy was ordered off along with Scott of Falkirk; into his place while he served his suspension came the promising newcomer, 'Jean' McFarlane. The youngster was a polished player even from the start, displaying deft footwork and immediately striking up a fine understanding with McLean to form a dangerous left wing.

Rangers dropped both points in a 1-0 upset at home to Raith Rovers on 14 January, and Celtic took over at the top by one point. Celtic's thrust to the leadership was due to defensive strength once the rearguard had settled into a familiar line-up of Shaw; McNair, Dodds; Gilchrist, Cringan and McMaster. It was a unit that had its critics, but it was effective. Shaw had resumed his understanding with the full-back pairing of McNair and Dodds and was highly dependable. McNair, although he had slowed a little, had no equal in steering a winger into harmless positions and easing the ball away from him, while Dodds was a hardy back, strong in the tackle and as enthusiastic as ever. Gilchrist was a fine attacking half-back, but at times was casual in his defensive duties and was often criticised for his lack of bite in tackling, and McMaster, the other wing-half, was a veteran intelligently using his experience to circumvent the subtle erosion of his athleticism, while Cringan, the centre-half, was usually sound and dependable in everything he did. Willie Cringan was one of the few buys that Celtic made at this time; he had played for Celtic in wartime when his own club, Sunderland, closed down, and was purchased for £600 in 1917.

The forwards were a mixture, on their day capable of brilliant play, but often inconsistent. McAtee and Gallacher comprised an excellent wing, but McAtee was prone to off-days and Gallacher was a marked man. Cassidy and Adam McLean were much younger and capable of inspired play, but neither was particularly strong physically. As always the problem was at centre-forward where some claimed that nobody had been found to replace Jimmy Quinn who had retired almost ten years previously. McInally was the most frequent choice for the position and had proved a prolific scorer but questions were being asked about his commitment to the game and his style was a far cry from Quinn's headlong rushes that took so much of the weight off the others.

However, this Celtic team settled to a combined game and showed remarkable consistency in the battle for the league. Rangers were still favourites for the title, but Celtic kept on winning. On the last day of the league programme Celtic led by a single point but faced a formidable task at Cappielow against a Morton side enjoying a splendid season, while Rangers had a less daunting task at Shawfield against Clyde. It was a tense day: Rangers outplayed Clyde for most of the game but were unable to score, the match ending 0-0, but hopes were still high at half-time when news came through that Morton were leading 1-0. There was trouble at Greenock: a crowd of 23,000 jammed into Cappielow, with thousands left outside when the gates were closed. The Celtic fans turned out in great numbers but Morton were equally well supported, and the Celtic 'brake-clubs', now motorised, poured into Greenock, blowing bugles, showing their colours and waving banners expressly forbidden by the local police. Fighting had broken out on the way to the ground near Port Glasgow where many Morton fans in the strongly Protestant district took violent objection to the Sinn Fein flags and banners and hurled rivets at the 'brakes'. During half-time more fighting broke out on the terracings and spilled on to the pitch; after the match, other visiting fans had to fight their way back to the special trains, *en route* surrendering some of their banners that were burned in the streets. Fortunately, it was a happy result on the field as Celtic fought back for McAtee to score the equaliser with a few minutes left, a goal that secured the championship.

Morton won the Scottish Cup that year, defeating Rangers in the final as the Ibrox jinx continued, when keeper Robb was penalised for handling the ball outside the area and Morton scored from the free kick; Celtic had been abruptly upset by Hamilton Accies 3-1 at home, a most disappointing result made all the more bitter by a league victory over the same team a week later by 4-0.

Let us consider the respective standings for Celtic and Rangers in the league for the past three seasons:

1919-20	P	W	D	L	For	Agst	Pts
Rangers..............	42	31	9	2	106	25	71
Celtic.................	42	29	10	3	89	31	68
1920-21							
Rangers..............	42	35	6	1	91	24	76
Celtic.................	42	30	6	6	86	35	66
1921-22							
Celtic.................	42	27	13	2	83	20	67
Rangers..............	42	28	10	4	83	26	66

The overall picture indicates a close struggle for supremacy in the period from 1917 to 1922. Rangers had won three championships to Celtic's two, Celtic had won three Charity Cups to Rangers' two and Rangers held a similar advantage in the Glasgow Cup; only three Scottish Cup competitions had been held since the war and, while neither of the 'Old Firm' had won it, Rangers had put up a much better performance, losing surprisingly in successive finals.

13

SECOND BEST

THE history of Scottish football has largely been the perennial struggle between Celtic and Rangers, and the 1920s marked a decisive turn in the rivalry. Celtic declined noticeably in importance as Rangers correspondingly assumed the dominant position. It was not only that Rangers produced a series of better teams, although that was true; rather, those teams represented both the superior organisation and deployment of the Ibrox club's resources and the lowering of Celtic's ambition. Frankly, Celtic lacked a sense of purpose worthy of the club's traditions.

It was a difference in outlook that separated the 'Old Firm' in this decade; Rangers emerged as the club of 'big business' and Celtic remained the club of 'small business'. As a limited liability company Celtic directors have a responsibility to the shareholders and to themselves. In a normal, everyday business such a concern seems legitimate and worthy. Shareholders have a right to expect returns on their investments and should complain or react if their expectations are not met. However, is a football club the same as a business? For one thing, astute businessmen can cover the risks inherent in any business in a variety of ways; a football club's financial future may turn on such intangibles as the bounce of a ball, the toss of a coin, or a referee's decision. Luck, rather than the forces of the market decides the outcome. Ultimately, it depends on the nature of the shareholders, who may fall into one of two categories: those whose shares are a source of income, and those whose holdings represent an emotional investment in the organisation or the sport. No less an authority than the late Desmond White, the club's secretary for more than 40 years and its chairman for 15, has stated that "No one in their right senses would invest in football as a commercial enterprise, to make money". Any shareholder agreeing with this view would be wise to unload his holdings and reinvest his money in more profitable areas, leaving only those of a more altruistic nature to pick up the burden. Such a group, of course, would be content with a minimal return on its investment and would be willing to plough any profits back into the club.

The answer to whether a football club is a business or not might be a compromise; a football club should combine the practice and methods of a high-principled business with the spirit of the sport. The club should organise itself to make the best use of its resources and employ consistently businesslike procedures to make practical decisions, both short and long term; the spirit of the game is best expressed in a healthy attitude towards rivals and in the play of the team which should be entertaining, sporting and, in the case of a club like Celtic, successful.

Rangers chose to expand in the manner of 'big business': a massive reorganisation took place within Ibrox, players were bought and sold, adequate reserve cover was arranged and a new outlook evolved consistent with a dynamic, positive organisation. Celtic drifted in the manner of 'small business', reacting to events rather than influencing them and concerned unduly with the avoidance of financial loss.

Celtic's approach had all the virtues and failings of small business; it was admirable to see the balanced budget and the squaring of accounts, but the club refused to take financial risks and practised the false economy of being thrifty in small matters. Nowhere was this better illustrated than in the treatment of the players: many Celts felt aggrieved at their terms and often held out for more money at re-signing times; they were particularly concerned about the bonus question and the matter of benefits. While wages were in the region of £8 a week, among the highest in Scotland but probably lower than Rangers', bonuses were granted by the club on an irregular basis. In September, 1923, the team captain appeared before the Board on behalf of the players to request the introduction of a regular system — £2 for a win and £1 for a draw, He met with a cool reception, as chairman Tom White indignantly told one journalist : " . . . it was an impossible request the players were making and could not be considered. It has been the custom of the Celtic Board to give a handsome bonus if they won the League or the Cup, but to give a bonus for a win or a draw was unthinkable, considering the wages they were getting. . . . And after all, what good would it be for us to finish, say third or fourth in the League? When it is seen that we cannot win the championship, interest in what we are doing falls off. What good would accrue to the club then by paying £50 per player for 50 points earned when that number of points would mean practically nothing to the club?" In reply to a query as to what he thought of the future of football and the wages question, Mr White stated he thought that a maximum wage of £6 per week should be fixed and that every player ought to be given an opportunity to work if he wished to and do his training in the evenings. (*Weekly Record*: 8 September, 1923.)

Within a month of his appearance before the directors Willie Cringan, the spokesman on the players' behalf, was transferred to Third Lanark; during this decade too many other players were transferred from Celtic and too often the motivation was profit. An unfortunate pattern had emerged at Celtic Park. Because of the club's unique traditions, Celtic were able to call upon the allegiance of a vast pool of talent. Many young players wanted to play for the club and could be signed from junior clubs for little outlay and be paid relatively low wages. Within a few years some of them developed into highly skilled players and as such felt entitled to better terms, but, as the club was often reluctant to grant that request, an impasse would be reached; the players, many perhaps saddled with financial responsibilities, usually sought a solution in a demand for a transfer that would be quickly granted, with the profits falling to the club. It was a policy that weakened the team and soured many of the supporters for some seasons between the wars.

Another decision by the directors yielded the initiative to Rangers for the next fifteen years. In 1922 Celtic decided to dispense with the reserve side on economic grounds. Willie Maley, the architect of the club's original youth policy, could not have been pleased with this move, the manifest folly of which became more apparent as the years passed. The consistent flow of young players into the first team was hampered and the traditional Celtic teamwork and spirit was weakened. It was a decision that made many among the support wonder if the club was prepared to make a full commitment to the sport in the future.

In striking contrast to Celtic, Rangers enjoyed their greatest era, a period in which they dominated Scottish football. The rivalry that had grown between the clubs and the teams had taken on new dimensions with the appointment of Bill Struth as Rangers' manager in 1920. Till that time Rangers were a successful side, less so than Celtic, but always considered a leading contender for the honours. A feeling persisted, however, that Rangers tended to 'crack' on the big occasion, that the will to win was not always there. That image was changed dramatically under Struth, a ruthless disciplinarian who ruled the club from the manager's office. Rangers soon assumed a new character, with self-discipline, determination and hardness stressed. Struth demanded physical fitness, strength and persistence, with a total effort from each player for the whole match. As a trainer with Clyde and Rangers, Struth knew about fitness; as a manager, he was to prove how much he knew about motivation and he was highly effective, imposing his will in an atmosphere of fear. However, he also stressed the pride in club that has characterised most Rangers players since. Singlehandedly, he changed Rangers' image.

Unfortunately, the start of his rule at Ibrox coincides with the hardening of religious lines between the 'Old Firm'. The rivalry had always been a harsh one, fought out bitterly for football supremacy and profits; by enforcing a 'no Catholics' policy at Ibrox, Rangers turned the rivalry into 'a holy war'. As the team most capable of beating Celtic, Rangers had always attracted an unwelcome element within its support that had little to do with football or sport. This element, always sizeable and bolstered by the work force of Harland and Wolff (the Belfast company that had expanded its shipyard at Govan), found a spiritual home at Ibrox. By adopting a policy of religious apartheid Rangers had given bigotry a seal of approval and tacitly endorsed the vicious sectarianism now manifesting itself on the terracings whenever the teams met.

The most unfortunate aspect was that Rangers became a more successful club and organisation. Many of their large support were attracted by the success and relished the football supremacy, but others saw the success as justifying the shameful policy of religious discrimination. The profits produced by large crowds ensured further success and Rangers grew in stature as an institution, but for many Scots the glory attained by the teams on the field has been shadowed by the bigotry behind the scenes. The escalation caused by Rangers' hard-line policy was doubly unfortunate; it encouraged the sectarianism that has always existed in Scottish society, and it did so at a time when Celtic had moved some distance away from it. The Ibrox policy, profitable as it was in terms of money, only increased the simmering hostility between the clubs, the teams and the supporters.

The Catholic press was not slow to react to any club challenging Celtic, but outdid itself in its rabid denunciations: "Rangers have probably the biggest club following in Britain, and the number doubtless contains many respectable, fairminded and well conducted people. But there are others. On the terracing at the Dalmarnock end on Saturday there was congregated a gang, thousands strong, including the dregs and scourings of filthy slumdom, unwashed yahoos, jailbirds, night hawks, won't-works, 'burroo barnacles', and pavement pirates, all, or nearly all, in the scarecrow stage of verminous trampdom. This ragged army of insanitary pests was lavishly provided with orange and blue remnants, and these were flaunted in challenge as the football tide flowed this way or that. Practically without cessation for ninety minutes or more, the vagabond scum kept up a strident howl of the 'Boyne Water' chorus. Nothing so designedly provoking, so maliciously insulting, or so bestially ignorant has ever been witnessed even in the wildest exhibitions of Glasgow Orange bigotry. . . . Blatantly filthy language of the lowest criminal type assailed the shocked ears of decent onlookers. There was no getting away from it, chanted as it was by thousands of voices in bedlamite yells. The stentorian use of filthy language is a crime against the law of the land. Policemen lined the track and listened to the hooligan uproar, yet nothing was done to stop it. The scandal was renewed with increased violence in London Road after the match. Is it possible the Blue mob can do just anything and get away with it? Prompt official steps were taken to suppress and prosecute the green brake-club lads who dared sing 'The Dear Little Shamrock' in Paisley Road. Yet thousands of foulmouthed and blasphemous Orange ruffians are free to run amok over the East End of Glasgow. How do you account for it?" (*Glasgow Observer*: 1 November, 1924.)

Predictably, the same columnist was a shade more sympathetic in describing the Celtic support: "There has been considerable outcry lately regarding the behaviour of certain brake-clubs, especially when visiting away fields. These complaints do not apply to the Celtic brake-clubs whose members, reasonable, sentient beings, are models of decorum and possess official testimonials to their blameless behaviour. They are out merely to enjoy themselves in their own way without infringing the law or interfering with anybody. They are fond of singing, and to this no one can reasonably object. On Saturday the boys sang to their hearts' content. They gave us so many rousing choruses — 'Hail, Glorious Saint Patrick', 'God Save Ireland', 'Slievenamon', 'The Soldiers' Song'. . . . When Cassidy's second goal made victory sure, it was fine to hear the massed thousands at the western end of the Ibrox oval chanting thunderously 'On Erin's Green Valleys'. But as I have remarked, the greatest scene of all was the homeward procession of the scores of beflagged brakes loaded with enthusiasts delirious with the heady vintage of victory. The most amazing and amusing ingenuity had been displayed in suitably inscribing the score on the sides of the various charabancs. No two brakes showed quite the same wording. The humourists got in much fine work and absolutely vetoed the simple legend — Celtic 2, Rangers 0. Cassidy figured largely in the chalked inscriptions. We had Cassidy 2, Undefeated Rangers 0 . . . then we had the semi-political allusions — Rebels 2, Black-and-Tans 0, and Sinn Fein 2, League of Nations 0, the latter a sly allusion to the cosmopolitan character of the Blue team. It was a delight to see the boys so thoroughly enjoying themselves. It was their turn and they made full use of it. Good luck to them, and to the team which gave them ample cause for rejoicing." (*Glasgow Observer*: 8 January, 1921.)

The battle-lines had been drawn up, and God was on the side of the big battalions. Under Struth's direction Rangers were to establish a clear, undeniable footballing supremacy and were to retain it for 15 years. As one perceptive commentator on British football observed: "It was a struggle between two virtues: those of improvisation and inspiration (Celtic), and those of organisation and method (Rangers)."

Immediately after World War I a generation starved of entertainment had flocked to football matches. With the boom, gates climbed sharply

JOS. WALKER (OUR CARTOONIST) CALLS ON THE CELTS

Celtic FC as viewed by the cartoonist of Sports Budget and Football Special, *10 February, 1923. Left to right: Cassidy, Cringan, McAtee, McStay (W), Shaw, Gilchrist, MacFarlane, McStay (J), Gallagher, McNair, McLean.*

and the crowd of 97,000 at the first post-war final between Kilmarnock and Albion Rovers attests to the popularity of the sport. Sadly, the growth was a short-lived phenomenon as economic forces took over once again and many fans were unable to afford the price of admission. The recession affected all clubs, but it hurt Celtic more than most; despite the gains made by Catholics in Glasgow and elsewhere in Scotland, as labourers and unskilled workers they were more vulnerable to lay-offs in bad times. Thus, Celtic's support was eroded during this decade since a large number of the fans could not afford the luxury of regular football. To Celtic's credit the club recognised the hardships that ordinary working men and the unemployed were having. When the Scottish League met to consider raising the price of admission from 8d (3½p) to one shilling (5p) for the 1919-20 season, Celtic instructed Willie Maley to propose a compromise figure of 9d (4p). The 'country' clubs' votes ensured the shilling rate, as Maley had gloomily predicted. In fact, Celtic decided to allow ex-servicemen now unemployed to enter at the 'boys' gate' for sixpence (2½p). Visiting clubs tacitly endorsed the practice until, a few seasons later, one club protested, and the admirable custom was discontinued at the request of the League.

A detailed examination of season 1922-23 indicated Celtic's comparative decline; it was a season marked by player unrest, managerial pessimism, inconsistency on the field, a mediocre, lacklustre performance in the league, but culminating in the capture of the Scottish Cup at the end.

The first player to express public dissatisfaction with the club was the flamboyant Tommy McInally and this was scarcely surprising. McInally was always too much of an individualist to fit into any predestined mould and had been in trouble with his manager frequently in the past for lapses in discipline. Maley, who had been remarkably patient with his temperamental star, finally decided it was time for a transfer and McInally moved for a substantial fee to Third Lanark in September 1922.

Later that month Celtic transferred Willie Crilly. This player, a scoring sensation in Alloa's promotion bid with 50 goals, had been signed at the end of season 1921-22 despite well-aired doubts about his physique. At only five feet, four inches, and of slight build, Crilly was expected to have a hard time in the higher division and the misgivings were fully justified in short order. Crilly himself requested the move, leaving Celtic to rue the deal that had cost them money and a useful player, Tom 'Tully' Craig, who joined Alloa as part of the deal because he was considered "injury-prone" (Craig later joined Rangers and became one of their most durable players in a lengthy career).

The most unfortunate aspect of these transfers was that Celtic were left without a recognised centre-forward, virtually at the start of the campaign, and lack of scoring punch was the major criticism of the team' performance from then on. Willie Maley was not in his most pleasant mood as the team struggled to find form. It seemed that he was still dubious about the Board's decision to carry on without a reserve side; always an advocate of young players, Maley saw that the flow of capable players into the first team was about to dry up and that the side would be normally 'carrying' a couple of players still learning the basics of their craft. In a most revealing interview with the reporter of the *Weekly Record* on 4 November, 1922, he declared that he would be "quite happy" if Celtic retained their First Division status so that the younger players would have a chance to mature and replace some of his ageing performers. Regardless of his motivation or mood, it was an unfortunate statement, scarcely calculated to inspire confidence among the players and supporters or to please his directors.

In the league Celtic continued to struggle. After a 3-1 defeat by Rangers at Celtic Park the consensus was "that the young ones are too young and the old ones are too old". The next week at Shawfield, Celtic made wholesale changes in position and managed a 1-0 win, but one writer in the *Weekly Record* wondered "If Celtic's next surprise selection will have Patsy Gallacher between the posts?"; a week later, on 11 November, Celtic lost surprisingly to Ayr United at Parkhead by a score of 4-1 and the same newspaper reported that one disgruntled supporter had commented that "the directors had to break away from the fallacy of getting players for nothing". Shortly after, Aberdeen, who had previously gained only one point at Parkhead, managed to record their first win at Celtic Park. Early in 1923 John Gilchrist was transferred to Preston North End after a series of incidents that indicated all was not well at Celtic Park: Gilchrist, a half-back of considerable talent and polish but frequently criticised for lack of 'bite', was suspended for missing training on two Mondays — Celtic had recently revised the training schedule in a bid to arrest the decline — and the explanation that he had been resting an injured ankle at home and had left the house only to get cigarettes was not accepted by the directors. The player was immediately given a *sine die* club suspension and quickly transferred south. Plagued by injuries and self-handicapped by lack of reserve power, Celtic hovered out of the running for the championship throughout the campaign and finished an undistinguished and distant third, nine points behind the winners, Rangers.

In typical Celtic fashion, however, the club managed to salvage something from a dismal season by winning the Scottish Cup; this was the tenth triumph in the tournament and equalled the record of Queen's Park. It was not a memorable campaign, although some of the names of the opponents might evoke nostalgia. The first round sent Celtic to Lochgelly where it was anticipated that the Glasgow side would exact retribution for generations of Scottish schoolboys on the town where straps were manufactured, but Celtic won through by only 3-2 — scarcely the thrashing expected. A home draw for Celtic meant the elimination of Hurlford by a more acceptable 4-0 margin and the advantage of another home game helped to dispose of East Fife by 2-1. Joe Cassidy, now playing at centre, was in splendid form, netting all of Celtic's goals in these ties; he was helped by two cunning inside-forwards, the inimitable Patsy Gallacher and the veteran Adam McLean now being fielded at inside-left. On the right wing the ageing McAtee had been brought back and provided admirable service for his centre, as did Paddy Connolly, a straightforward winger on the left who was introduced earlier in the season.

The progress, as always in cup play, got much harder at the quarter-final stage; again Celtic were fortunate in the draw with a fixture at Parkhead against the formidable Raith Rovers with Alex James at inside-forward. Celtic put the Fifers' goal under constant pressure, but their resolute defence put up a strong resistance; it made only one mistake, but when McLean scored after a mix-up it was enough to let Celtic through to the semi-final against Motherwell. This match was played at Ibrox before 75,000, and the hero was centre-half and captain, Willie Cringan, the man faced with the task of containing Hugh Ferguson, Motherwell's prolific scorer. Ferguson, who ended up with 283 league goals for the Lanarkshire side and who was to score Cardiff's goal against Arsenal in the 1927 FA final to bring that trophy to Wales

114

*Willie Cringan, followed by Adam McLean and Patsy Gallacher, leads out Celtic for the Scottish Cup semi-final vs Motherwell at Ibrox. Celtic won 2-0. (*Glasgow Observer: *17 March, 1923.)*

for the first time, could not shake off Cringan, a player often unfairly criticised by the Celtic supporters as lacking 'devil'. Cringan obeyed Maley's instructions to the letter and dogged Ferguson's footsteps throughout as Celtic went on to win 2-0.

The final was perhaps the dullest of all Scottish Cup finals, so tedious that one fan admitted to having had more interesting days watching his grass grow. As always, however, some features emerged. Once again the Maley brothers were in managerial opposition and, just as when he was in charge of Clyde back in 1912, Alec was on the losing side; the former Celtic player, Jimmy McColl, who had scored two of the goals that helped defeat Hibs in the 1914 replay, was now playing for the Edinburgh side, but he too was doomed to disappointment. The teams lined up before 80,000 at Hampden on 31 March, 1923.

> *Celtic*: Shaw, McNair, McStay W., McStay J., Cringan, McFarlane, McAtee, Gallacher, Cassidy, McLean, Connolly.
> *Hibernian*: Harper, McGinnigle, Dornan, Kerr, Miller, Shaw, Ritchie, Dunn, McColl, Halligan, Walker.

It turned out, as expected, to be a grim defensive battle. Hibs had not given up a goal on their progress to Hampden but it was a tragic mistake by their internationalist keeper, Harper, that decided the final. Ten minutes after half-time he completely misjudged a long lob from McFarlane and the alert Cassidy had a simple task in heading the ball into an empty net. One player's performance was worth noting. At the age of 39, Alec McNair had been restored to Celtic's team to calm down some of the more exuberant defenders; in this, his last final, he was the most complete footballer on the field, never putting a foot wrong, never out of position and, as always, attempting to be constructive from well back in defence.

The decline continued during the following season (1923-24); perhaps the surprising triumph in the Scottish Cup had fooled the Board that things were on the brink of improving but, if so, it was a wildly optimistic assumption. This was to be one of Celtic's most miserable seasons, with scarcely a flicker of relief.

Discontent was manifesting itself on the field and in the dressing room. The players were disappointed with the bonus system and Cringan, although not a leader in the revolt, as captain took the players' concerns to the directors where he met with a Dickensian reception. The request for a pound-per-point bonus for league play was summarily dismissed, and a dispirited Celtic team took the field at Parkhead to lose to Partick Thistle for the first time in the league after a period of 25 years, a result that 'Man in the Know' attributed to "the seeming mercenary spirit of the players, who were expected to respect the proud traditions and exalted spirit of the green-and-white brigade and wear the famous colours more for love than for money" (*Glasgow Observer*: 15 September, 1923).

Maley was still in a pessimistic mood, and in a radio interview on 28 September he astoundingly conceded the championship to Rangers; he remarked that Rangers looked like winning the title again, unless the brilliant, young Airdrie side added some tenacity to its undoubted sparkle. With less than a quarter of the programme completed, and by omitting any reference to his own club's hopes, he had discounted any challenge from Parkhead. It was a baffling performance by the manager and he was taken to task for it: "It seems queer to say the least that a club manager should prophesy that his team cannot win the competition in which they are every week engaged. Poor encouragement, surely, for the players! A word of praise, a pat on the back, a cheery slogan of hopefulness would work wonders with any team." (*Glasgow Eastern Standard*: 7 October, 1923.) It would appear that Maley was experiencing some difficulty with the Board at this stage, because the principal shareholder in the newspaper was Tom White, the club's chairman. Perhaps Maley was already privy to the knowledge that Willie Cringan was about to be transferred, as he was on 13 October, less than a month after his request for regular bonuses.

Rangers continued to dominate the league, establishing an early lead and maintaining it during the campaign, and the difference between the clubs was starkly revealed in a Glasgow Cup semi-final at Ibrox. Rangers won 1-0 and Celtic supporters attributed the defeat to the absence of Joe Cassidy, his replacement being McGee, an inexperienced youngster forced to play out of his regular position; it was observed that had Rangers' centre, Henderson, been forced to call off, his deputy would have been the Dane, Carl Hansen, considered by many to be a better player than the regular choice.

Celtic's policy appeared to be to retain a squad of twelve proven players backed up by some promising youngsters; because the club did not field a reserve team, the recruits made only intermittent appearances or were loaned to other clubs for experience, as was done for Jimmy McGrory with Clydebank in 1923-24 and John Thomson, briefly, with Ayr United in 1926-27. Rangers on the other hand, packed their reserve side with strong players who could have made the grade with most other teams. The clubs showed another revealing difference in their recruiting of players: Celtic continued the practice of picking up juniors and rearing them to maturity, while Rangers were prepared to buy established men from other clubs, notably Bob McPhail from Airdrie in 1927. Overall, it was a situation that was bound to favour Rangers, though Celtic could reasonably argue that the economic climate was hurting its supporters more than those of Rangers. Celtic had continued a policy of admitting ex-servicemen for 6d, but in 1925 Cowdenbeath lodged a claim for £70 alleged to have been lost on their last two visits to Parkhead; the League adjudged the loss at £16, ordering Celtic to pay that amount to the Fife club and ruling that Celtic cease charging the lower rate. Attendances were in decline from the mid-1920s, but the traditional enthusiasm of the supporters still flourished: "How often you and I have seen and pitied the forlorn groups hanging around outside Celtic Park gazing longingly and enviously at lucky fellows able to plank down their shillings at the turnstiles . . . the 'great excluded' shivering in the rain outwith the barricade, and trying to figure out what was happening within, reading a meaning into the crowd's cheers, yells, and groans, and visualising Gallacher, McLean, McGrory or McFarlane shining like demi-gods in the unseen fray." (*Glasgow Observer*: 5 December, 1925.)

Celtic made little impact in the league and the hopes were once more centred on the Scottish Cup. The holders of the trophy, Celtic were drawn to face Kilmarnock in Ayrshire and to the disappointment of the supporters the score was 2-0 in favour of the underdogs. Maley, writing in the club handbook for 1924-25, expressed his anger: ". . . a display unworthy of the great name of either the club or themselves at a vital match at Kilmarnock. The defeat practically was

117

the difference between a year which would clear itself and the tremendous loss which the club has been saddled with this past year." It had been the first occasion since the shock defeat at Arthurlie in 1897 that Celtic had been eliminated at the first stage, but the manager appeared more incensed at the loss of £3,285 sustained in the year.

Maley was in a most difficult position; he was the only person at Parkhead since the earliest days apart from James Kelly who was now a director. Not regarded as the most genial of men, he was growing more estranged from the directors and from some of his younger players. With the increasing concern at Celtic Park over money Maley had to work within the confines of a tight budget, and he was preoccupied with financial matters. The tone of the handbooks became more and more critical and players were blamed for performances that had led to a decline in form and subsequent loss of revenue. Unfortunately, it was a trend that was doomed to continue.

In 1925 Celtic once more salvaged a disappointing season by capturing the Scottish Cup, and again it was a surprise because at the start of the tournament Rangers, Hibernian, Airdrie and even Partick Thistle were more favoured to win. Rangers, league champions for six out of the previous eight years, were still having problems in the cup although they were often the favourites.

At Cathkin Celtic swept past Third Lanark by 5-1 with a new centre-forward scoring three of the goals. Jimmy McGrory, destined to be a legendary figure, had played only a few games back in 1923-24 before being loaned to Clydebank for experience, but when he scored against Celtic in an upset win at Parkhead he was recalled at the end of that season. He was a striker in the style of Jimmy Quinn; tireless in the single-minded pursuit of goals, courageous in the thick of battle, and blessed with a sunny disposition and modesty. He was the epitome of sportsmanship in a rough era. Because of his promise, Celtic had no qualms about transferring the talented Joe Cassidy to Bolton Wanderers early in the season for £5,000. By September the critics were recognising a new star: "So far he has given complete satisfaction, and it begins to look as if Quinn's mantle has at long last fallen on worthy shoulders. McGrory's style is reminiscent of the great Croy man, particularly in the fearless dash with which he bores into the opposing defences." (*Glasgow Observer*: 20 September, 1924.)

It took three fiercely contested matches to dispose of St. Mirren: a 0-0 draw at Love Street was followed by a 1-1 deadlock at Celtic Park and Celtic scraped through by a McGrory goal at Ibrox. This match ended on a controversial note. In the last minute a Saints' forward was fouled on the edge of the penalty area and the referee, the always colourful Peter Craigmyle from Aberdeen, made a theatrical production of examining the exact spot before awarding a free kick inches outside the box. The Paisley men wanted a penalty, continued to protest and refused to take the free kick from the position where the referee had placed the ball for them. The Celtic 'wall' was back in place, the 'Buddies' stood glaring at the official and the seconds ticked past. Wisely, Mr Craigmyle, the sole judge of the time, whistled for the end of the game.

More than 100,000 turned up at Hampden to see the 'Old Firm' in the semi-final. Before the match the Celtic players, under the leadership of Gallacher, held a tactics talk — a most infrequent occurrence. Gallacher felt that Rangers, despite starting as favourites and having beaten Celtic twice in the league, would be the more nervous team; he suggested that Celtic make a concentrated effort to avoid giving up an early goal that might soothe Ibrox nerves and that it could be done by pulling back the inside-forwards, Thomson and himself, into semi-defensive positions for the first 15 minutes and advising the wingers and young McGrory to be ready for the quick break. The result was an unexpectedly easy 5-0 rout of the Light Blues, with McGrory and McLean each scoring twice and Thomson adding another.

Celtic faced Dundee in the final, played on 11 April, 1925, before 75,137.

> *Celtic*: Shevlin, McStay W., Hilley, Wilson, McStay J., McFarlane, Connolly, Gallacher, McGrory, Thomson, McLean.
> *Dundee*: Britton, Brown, Thomson, Ross, Rankine W., Irving, Duncan, McLean, Halliday, Rankine J., Gilmour.

Dundee led 1-0 at half-time through a McLean goal after 30 minutes, netted from a rebound off the crossbar. In the second half Celtic pressed furiously, but Dundee looked like holding on till a most astonishing goal from the most remarkable player on the field decided the outcome. So varied are the accounts of the goal that one can see why it sometimes takes centuries for the Church to verify a miracle: ". . . the truth as recorded in contemporary accounts is remarkable enough. A Connolly free kick was flighted in to Gallacher in the thick of the dark blue jerseys. The little Irishman somehow twisted, tricked, and squeezed his way through, adding the final flourish of catapulting himself over the line with the ball wedged between his feet. Indeed, his boots were caught up in the netting and he lay there . . . until the other players freed him." (*100 Cups*: Hugh Keevins and Kevin McCarra, 1985.) Only Patsy could have scored that goal, and Dundee wilted visibly, with Britton's long delays at taking goalkicks a telling symbol of their anxiety. A few minutes from the end McGrory snatched the winner with a more orthodox counter by diving to head home a typical goal and Celtic, with eleven triumphs in the tournament, were now the record-holders. A new generation of players was establishing itself at Celtic

Park, and the goalscorers indicated the trend; for Gallacher it was his last final and for McGrory it was the first. As if sensing the mood of the times, Maley handed the cup over to young McGrory for him to hold up to the crowds as the team bus slowly made its way back into the city.

For once in the 1920s an air of optimism pervaded Celtic Park. A clever young team was being forged and the gradual replacement of the veterans was progressing at a suitable pace without too much disruption or on-the-job training. Already some youngsters, thrown in at the deep end, had established themselves as members of the side. Outstanding players such as Peter Wilson, a smooth right-half from Ayrshire, and Hugh Hilley, a most capable defender; Alec Thomson from Fife soon developed into a classic Scottish inside-forward; the McStay brothers, Willie, a few years older than Jimmy, added some strength and muscle to the defence; Connolly and McGrory belied their youth with their performances; young McLean was proving to be an outstanding left-winger, thriving on the abundant service from the veteran McFarlane. A lingering doubt had to exist about the fitness of Gallacher. After 14 years as one of the most exceptional inside-forwards in the country and as the inspiration of the team, injuries had started to exact a toll. To the vast delight of the supporters Celtic moved to buy a player in anticipation of replacing him, none other than the wayward Tommy McInally who had spent the previous three years with Third Lanark. It was a boost to the morale of the supporters to see Celtic spend money on a player, and it was an investment that paid immediate dividends.

There followed an exhilarating season, if not a completely successful one. The Glasgow Cup, with one replay against Thistle and two against Rangers, showed in microcosm the range of emotions experienced by the players and supporters, as this excerpt describing the match at Firhill indicates: "The crowd oscillated between breathless, soundless suspense and deafening, frenzied uproar. Celtic's anxiety deepened almost to despair as the minutes swiftly sped, and the equaliser would not come. Hope had nearly died when Wilson's delightful pass and Thomson's smashing drive restored equality. The scene that ensued baffles description. The scorer was nearly suffocated in the frantic embraces of his delighted comrades. The crowd went mad, men and youths, perfect strangers to each other, shook hands, embraced, danced, sang, shouted, and even wept for joy. Green and white waved in triumph everywhere on the terracing. It was a memorable moment!" (*Glasgow Observer*: 12 September, 1925.) The crowd at Firhill that day was a splendid 40,000 and a clear indication to Celtic's directors that a competitive side would always attract the crowds to compensate for any outlay in transfer fees. After defeating Thistle 5-1 in the replay, Celtic faced Rangers at Parkhead in the next round and the tie ended 2-2, two first-half goals by McGrory being matched by a pair from Cunningham. The replay at

Ibrox ended in a 1-1 draw and a third match was played, also at Ibrox, during which goals in extra time put Celtic through by a 2-0 score. McGrory scored the first and, as Rangers struggled to get back into the game, Gallacher decided the outcome with a characteristic effort, outwitting several opponents before netting. It was Gallacher's last goal for Celtic, his appearances becoming more infrequent as the season advanced. Again, the supporters celebrated noisily. Four brake-club charabancs were re-routed to the police station, where most of the 120 arrested spent the night singing choruses at the rival fans in the adjoining cells.

Celtic's side was still youthful and showed the typical inconsistency of inexperience only two days later when the joy of the victory over Rangers turned to gloom at Celtic Park where a determined Clyde, at that time in the Second Division, held on for a 2-1 win in the final, despite being outplayed for long spells.

Celtic's progress in the league was acceptable despite autumn setbacks at Dundee, Airdrie and Ibrox. The team made its first appearance at Tannadice to meet the newly promoted Dundee United and lost 1-0 to a long-range shot from Howieson, whose drive beat the smallish Shevlin high up; within the next four weeks Celtic were thrashed 5-1 by the often scintillating Airdrie and succumbed to the only goal in the 'Old Firm' encounter at Ibrox.

Still, the youthful Celtic, free from injury trouble with the exception of Gallacher, were settling and embarked on an extended run of 16 matches without defeat. Rangers experienced a rash of injuries and for once did not mount any challenge, finishing in sixth place, their lowest-ever standing. While Airdrie, Motherwell, St. Mirren and Hearts were in contention the competition was so keen among them that they succeeded only in trading points with each other. At the end Celtic finished up a comfortable eight points ahead of runners-up Airdrie, a side that fielded such players as Bob McPhail and Hughie Gallacher.

McInally had assumed Patsy Gallacher's role as general at inside-left, a position from which he established an immediate and profitable rapport with Adam McLean. Nourished by the service from McFarlane at left-half, it was a devastating partnership. McLean was a clever winger, a goalscorer who could cross a ball accurately from any angle for McGrory to finish; McInally, once a prolific scorer at centre-forward in his younger days, had developed into a superb tactician. His control and nerve was such that he could still cause bewilderment among defenders and amusement on the terracings with his patented mannerism of stopping suddenly, in order to look around with casual insolence, before re-directing the flow of the game. The most popular player in the side was the youthful Jimmy McGrory who had developed into a prolific scorer; he chased every ball with enthusiasm, he took on defences and he pursued goals with single-mindedness. He was remarkably successful and, for a relatively short centre, he was outstanding in the air. The most common tactic for Celtic's forwards was to provide crosses for McGrory's head and it was a thrilling spectacle to see McGrory in action either leaping high in the air or diving headlong to make contact with the ball.

If the annexation of the league championship for the 17th time, and the Charity Cup for the 20th by beating Queen's Park 2-1 at Ibrox, were causes of jubilation, the defeat in the Scottish Cup final was a disappointment. Celtic had gained three 'doubles', in 1907, 1908 and 1914, and hoped for another, but St. Mirren, who had put up a fight against Celtic the previous season had other ideas. Celtic were favoured because the team had played well against strong opposition in the earlier rounds. A 5-0 defeat of Kilmarnock at Rugby Park was followed by an equally impressive 4-0 win over Hamilton at Celtic Park, but the most formidable hurdle appeared to be the one at Tynecastle on 20 February against Hearts. Celtic were expected to be contenders for the 'double', but a feeling was growing in the east that Hearts, on current form and progress, had a chance too. 51,000 looked on: "Fully an hour before the kick-off the capacity of the Hearts' enclosure was fully taxed, and later the field was invaded. Hundreds were turned away, while hundreds more were compelled to view the game from the roofs of adjoining tenements, works, sheds, and even churches." (*Glasgow Observer*: 29 May, 1926.) The comparatively young Celtic side was not perturbed at the scenes and an early goal by McInally gave them confidence; McInally added a second shortly after the interval, while McGrory and Connolly increased the margin to four. After disposing of Dumbarton by 6-1 at Parkhead, and Aberdeen by 2-1 at Tynecastle, Celtic qualified to meet St. Mirren in the final on 10 April before 98,620.

> *Celtic*: Shevlin, McStay W., Hilley, Wilson, McStay J., McFarlane, Connolly, Thomson, McGrory, McInally, Leitch.
> *St. Mirren*: Bradford, Finlay, Newbiggin, Morrison, Summers, McDonald, Morgan, Gebbie, McCrae, Howieson, Thomson.

Celtic were handicapped by the absence of McLean. The winger was injured on 13 March, but had returned for league games against Partick Thistle and Kilmarnock at the beginning of April. He was then forced to call off with a recurrence. The traditional Parkhead policy of choosing from a limited squad backfired when the club had to field the inexperienced youngster Leitch; the replacement played well, but the side's teamwork was badly affected. St. Mirren established supremacy from the start and took the game to Celtic with determined attacks. Within three minutes they had scored when McCrae smartly headed in a corner that Shevlin could not reach. The keeper, clearly unsettled by his lapse, gave up another goal after 29 minutes when Howieson netted with a lobbed shot; earlier in the season the same player had scored from 35 yards when playing for Dundee United against Celtic. The rugged Saints' defenders gave nothing away after that, and Celtic's forwards rarely looked dangerous, and so the cup went deservedly to Paisley for the first time.

It seemed the Celtic did not have the playing resources to mount a successful challenge on two major fronts simultaneously. In 1925-26 a brave attempt had been made, but it was too largely dependent on freedom from injury.

The next season, 1926-27, was a continuation of the trend. Celtic, the league champions, made a fine start to the campaign until an ominously inconsistent spell in September when points were dropped to Clyde (2-2 at Shawfield), Hamilton Accies (2-2 at Celtic Park) and to Hibernian (2-3 at Easter Road).

In 1926, the year of the General Strike, football for many was a luxury and for the opening game of the season at Rugby Park many Celtic supporters walked to the ground from Glasgow, a distance of more than 20 miles; at the league match with Queen's Park two weeks later Celtic supporters barracked the opposition half-back who 'had done his bit' on a locomotive during the Strike.

Celtic's only consolation this season lay in the Glasgow Cup. In the semi-final played at Parkhead on 27 September they eliminated Thistle by 3-1 with the goals shared by McGrory, McLean and McInally; in the final on 9 October Celtic beat Rangers by 1-0 at Hampden, the goal being scored inevitably by McGrory.

McGrory was in devastating form early in the season. He netted four against Queen's Park in a 6-1 rout at Hampden on 28 August, five against Aberdeen in a 6-2 win at Parkhead on 23 October, four against Dunfermline at East End Park in a 6-0 canter on 20 November and a week later five more against Dundee United in a 7-2 win at Celtic Park: later in the season he was to score five against Clyde on 15 January, four against St. Mirren on 26 February, besides a more mundane hat-trick against Hamilton on 16 February and a clutch of doubles interspersed with numerous singles. He had assumed the mantle of Jimmy Quinn — and its burden.

The team's title hopes received a severe dent at Ne'erday with a defeat by 2-1 at Ibrox and a much more unacceptable reverse by 3-2 from Queen's Park at Parkhead only two days later. A partial recovery was halted abruptly by another defeat from Hibernian, this time at Celtic Park, and any chance for the championship was now contingent upon Rangers losing points. With the determined Struth in charge, still smarting from the previous year's eclipse, that was unlikely. Subconsciously, the players began to concentrate on the Scottish Cup as the more likely prospect and the draw for the first round sent the side to Palmerston to face Second Division Queen of the South; it was a tense battle on the rural, unfamiliar pitch and Celtic were held to a 0-0 draw. On the following Wednesday, Celtic quietly and methodically disposed of the Doonhamers' challenge by 4-1 and earned the right to travel to Brechin on 5 February. Again Celtic were unsettled by the surroundings, although managing to win by 6-3 with McGrory leading the way with four goals.

Maley was concerned about the defence, which had been conceding too many goals, and he determined to introduce a new keeper — young John Thomson, signed from Wellesley Juniors, and in the absence of a reserve team loaned out to Ayr United at one stage. The new goalkeeper made his debut on 12 February against Dundee at Dens Park, playing well although conceding a 'soft' goal in a 2-1 win. One of the club officials, attempting to console him for the mistake, was taken aback at the matter-of-fact way in which the youngster, only 18 years of age, assured him that it would not happen again. A week later Celtic returned to Dundee in the third round of the Cup, and Thomson retained his place. It was a tie that generated tremendous excitement and a number of Celtic supporters, presumably unemployed, set out on foot for Dundee on the Wednesday, arriving on the Friday night to be joined by thousands more on the Saturday morning. With a record 37,477 packed inside, Celtic managed a commendable 4-2 win and the new keeper impressed the crowd with his composure and his sure handling of awkward shots.

After disposing of Bo'ness United 5-2 in yet another away game, Celtic faced Falkirk in the semi-final at Ibrox. The 'Bairns' were pleased with the choice of ground, having defeated Rangers there in the last round. Falkirk were a strong side, forever threatening to make a serious bid for the honours but always falling just short through lack of resources. However, they had made a most interesting capture — Patsy Gallacher had joined them after another dispute with Celtic over his terms. Feeling that his best days were behind him, Celtic allowed him to leave, and Falkirk got another six years of useful service from the wily veteran who had already justified his transfer by creating the goal that eliminated Rangers. However, Celtic played well if cautiously and won 1-0 through an Adam McLean goal to qualify for the final against East Fife on 16 April, 1927.

> *Celtic*: Thomson J., McStay W., Hilley, Wilson, McStay J., McFarlane, Connolly, Thomson A., McInally, McMenemy, McLean.
> *East Fife*: Gilfillan, Robertson, Gillespie, Hope, Brown, Russell, Weir, Paterson, Wood, Barrett, Edgar.

East Fife, a mid-table Second Division side, had scrambled their way to the final although they had gained a worthy win in a replay at Pittodrie and had upset the favoured Partick Thistle in the semi-final at Tynecastle. Celtic were clear favourites, despite having to play without McGrory. The centre-forward had injured his ribs at Falkirk on 6 April, when Celtic's league aspirations ended in a 4-1 defeat, and he did not play again that season. Celtic moved McInally to centre, and took a chance on John McMenemy, the son of the famous 'Napoleon'. Within seven minutes Celtic fell behind when Wood, a prolific scorer in the lower division, rose to head Edgar's accurate cross behind Thomson. Less than a minute later the scores were level. Robertson fouled McLean and the Celtic winger made threatening gestures at the defender who retorted in kind; McFarlane slipped the free kick to Connolly who crossed low and hard for the doubly unfortunate Robertson to stab past his own keeper. Celtic moved ahead in 35 minutes when smart leading-up play gave McLean a chance from close range. Straight from the second-half kick-off Celtic scored a third goal, Connolly finishing off a lightning strike to put the final beyond the Fifers' reach.

The crowd of 80,500 settled down for more goals, but without McGrory Celtic were in an exasperating mood. The forwards indulged in clever dribbles and intricate passing that revealed the difference in class between the sides, but apparently decided to leave the finishing to McInally. The 'new' centre, rusty in the position after playing so long at inside-forward as a field general, missed several golden opportunities that the razor-sharp McGrory would have converted with ease and covered his lapses by clowning continually throughout the last 30 minutes.

The season, however, ended on a distinct note of anti-climax. On the Monday following the cup triumph Celtic entertained Rangers in a postponed league fixture at Parkhead and gave a lacklustre display in losing 1-0 to the new champions, and three weeks later were beaten again at Celtic Park by Rangers 4-1 in the Charity Cup.

Despite the Scottish Cup's presence at Parkhead, Celtic were still far behind Rangers in consistent performance. The chief consolation of the period for Celtic supporters was Rangers' continuing failure in the Scottish Cup, an astonishing length of 25 years having elapsed since Rangers had won the premier tourney. The inimitable 'Man in the Know' made frequent references to the situation: "Anonymous letters, abusive in tone, are a regular feature and to these I offer no objection so long as the topic is football and nothing else. But a letter, signed 'Ibrox Blue', reaching me this morning, is of a nature so scurrilous and ignorantly bigoted that I can only ascribe its origin to some scummy and slummy skulker of the underworld where bag-snatchers and razor-slashers foregather to devise midnight outrages and curse the Celtic.

. . . One has merely to glance at an Ibrox brake-club to see that most of them are only half-witted. So, let us forgive our anonymous assailant who is probably stung to raving madness by his favourites' annual Cup humiliation." (*Glasgow Observer*: 19 March, 1927.) The same journalist, noting that one Rangers fan had been carried out of the terracing at the Celtic-Rangers match at half-time as Celtic's recently won Scottish Cup was being paraded round the track, unkindly attributed the spectator's collapse to the unaccustomed sight of the silverware. He criticised the Rangers supporters for their behaviour at that match, and succeeded in outdoing himself: "The blue-bedecked crowd at the Dalmarnock end earned fame of a kind by actually pelting with stones and clinkers the collectors, ladies and young boys included, who were carrying round the sheets for the Dalbeth Convent collection. The Blue following have many dirty misdeeds to their credit, but surely this was the dirtiest. Let it never be forgotten that Rangers' supporters stoned women and children engaged in a work of charity. The Germans never did anything worse than this, and when the game and the players are merely a shadowy memory this shameful thing will be remembered." (*Glasgow Observer*: 23 April, 1927.)

In the 1928 final Rangers gained the sweetest retribution of all by winning the Cup, and by defeating Celtic 4-0 in the process. The following teams faced each other before a record crowd of 118,115 at Hampden Park on 14 April:

> *Rangers*: Hamilton T., Gray, Hamilton R., Buchanan, Meiklejohn, Craig, Archibald, Cunningham, Fleming, McPhail, Morton.
> *Celtic*: Thomson J., McStay W., Donohue, Wilson, McStay J., McFarlane, Connolly, Thomson A., McGrory, McInally, McLean.

All the ingredients of an 'Old Firm' needle-match were present. Rangers and Celtic had engaged in a thrilling battle for the league flag for months, but Celtic had lost their advantage in the past week and the momentum now favoured Rangers; against that was the memory of a quarter century's failure in the Cup and the prospect of facing the record-holders in the last stage.

It was a clash of two different approaches to the game. As a distinguished football historian indicated about the rivalry: ". . . it epitomised the ancient tribal animosities by now wrapped up in religious colours . . . it stood for the virtues of efficiency on the one hand and inspiration on the other. As outsiders we remain content with the stylistic contrasts maintained across the years by these two great foundations." (*A History of British Football*: Percy M. Young, 1968.) Four years earlier, in 1924, a newspaper had noticed the change in Rangers' attitude: "It has been instructive to watch Rangers playing this season. They have entered on almost every game with a vim and forcing power, maintained for a long period, which was almost new to Scottish football. They pursued the ball with relentless speed, they tackled with great dash and vigour, and smashed the ball goalwards with amazing directness and strength. They were ahead of the referee's whistle often at taking free kicks. They gave the observer the impression that no one but themselves had the right to kick the ball." (*Weekly Record*: 26 January, 1924.) To describe Rangers as a team of mere force was inadequate; no side that contained players like Meiklejohn at half-back or Morton on the left wing could be considered short of skill. Even the ranks of Tuscany had to join in the universal praise for such men; 'Man in the Know' frequently referred to Morton as "wee Alan", and on one memorable occasion when Meiklejohn had inspired Rangers to a comeback against Celtic he pondered long and hard before bestowing the supreme accolade on Rangers' captain: "Meiklejohn — great enough to be a Celt!"

Rangers' hopes were boosted considerably by the absence through injury of Celtic's left-back, Willie 'Peter' McGonagle, and Celtic's lack of reserve strength was to be ruthlessly exploited by the Ibrox side. Celtic won the toss and, taking the initial advantage of a strong wind, immediately put Rangers' goal under siege. Hamilton was in fine form and made some sparkling saves; one brilliant dive to divert a raging shot from Connolly was later to be regarded as a turning point in the game. Meiklejohn kept a tight grip on McGrory and Rangers held out till half-time.

With the wind behind them in the second half Rangers stormed into attack and Thomson had to be alert in dealing with dangerous crosses from Morton and Archibald, who had the beating of Celtic's replacement at left-back. Ten minutes into the half came a most dramatic moment. Rangers had been awarded a penalty kick when a Celtic hand cleared a scoring shot from the goal line. Meiklejohn, aware of the tension of the situation, squared up to his responsibilities as captain and elected to take the kick himself; faced with young John Thomson, already considered the best keeper in Scotland, and burdened with the knowledge of years of failure, he placed the ball carefully before driving a fierce shot into the Celtic net. From then on Rangers were unstoppable. In 68 minutes McPhail added a second and Archibald, running freely on the right wing, scored two more with glorious drives to end the hoodoo in the most decisive manner.

When the whistle went at the end, Rangers' supporters revelled in the joy of their greatest victory, and to the credit of Celtic's supporters both teams were cheered off the field sportingly.

14

DECLINE

THE season that ended so dismally with the crushing defeat at Hampden in the Scottish Cup final had started off deceptively brightly. Celtic remained undefeated in the league until mid-October and had recorded some notable results. Only two points were dropped in drawn matches with Hamilton and Dunfermline in away fixtures, and splendid progress was being made in the Glasgow Cup. Celtic defeated Queen's Park in the first round by 4-1 at Hampden with McGrory getting a hat-trick, and then thrashed Third Lanark at Celtic Park with McGrory netting five goals; in the final against Rangers on 8 August, 1927, on a windswept Hampden Celtic retained the trophy winning through by 2-1, and McGrory scored the decisive goal. Earlier in the same week, Celtic had entertained the English Cup winners, Cardiff City, at Parkhead and won by 4-1 with McGrory scoring all the goals.

Holders of the Scottish Cup after the win over East Fife, holders of the Glasgow Cup after the win over Rangers, winners of a challenge match against Cardiff City and leaders in the league . . . Celtic looked in fine shape for the remainder of the season, but the glory was to be short-lived. The squad was limited in numbers if not in skill; any injury was going to affect the team's performance considerably while an injury to McGrory would be catastrophic.

Only a week after losing to Celtic in the Glasgow Cup Rangers bounced back to beat Celtic in the league at Ibrox; the next fixture was at Pittodrie and Celtic lost 3-1 to Aberdeen. However, free from injury and approaching New Year, Celtic had regained form and recovered some ground on Rangers. The return fixture at Parkhead on 2 January between the clubs was widely anticipated as the league decider and in a typically hard-fought match Celtic won 1-0 through McGrory's goal. The next day McGrory scored all three goals against Queen's Park in a 3-1 win, and matched that performance with another hat-trick against Falkirk in a 3-1 win at Brockville on the Saturday; only a week later he led Celtic to a 9-0 defeat of Dunfermline with eight goals, still a record for a league match in the top Scottish division.

It was a neck-and-neck struggle with Rangers for the flag, but Rangers had the experience in winning championships; both clubs were making steady progress in the Cup. Hopes were rising in both camps that the double could be attained and each would have settled for a split of the honours. In such a situation the odds favour the better organised team and Rangers were superbly prepared to cope with injuries. As the season drew to an end they were considered fitter, thanks to Struth's regimen.

Celtic started to exhibit signs of the strain as they prepared at Seamill for a fourth-round cup tie at Fir Park against Motherwell. McInally was suspended and dropped from the line-up for not turning up for training sessions, the reason being that he was sulking because of a practical joke that had been pulled on him. Despite the absence of the side's most naturally talented player Celtic still eked out a 2-0 victory, but it was a disquieting incident, hinting at tensions in the squad. Later in the month, on 24 March, Celtic struggled to a 2-1 win over Queen's Park in the Scottish Cup semi-final at Ibrox; the amateurs outplayed Celtic for long spells, but their powerful forwards could not find a way past Thomson, already recognised despite his youth as one of the best keepers in Scotland.

One week before the Scottish Cup final against Rangers, and with the club's playing resources painfully extended, Celtic's bubble finally burst. Motherwell defeated Celtic 3-1 at Fir Park, but the worst aspect of the loss for Celtic was the injury to McGonagle, the regular left-back. This dependable and rugged defender was sidelined with a knee injury that later required a cartilage operation. The club did not have adequate reserve strength and was forced to call upon Donoghue, who was not considered a full-back. Two days after the defeat at Motherwell Celtic made the short trip to Airdrie and lost again by 3-1. The Celtic players had to reconcile themselves to the loss of the league to the perennial champions, Rangers. After mounting a real and sustained challenge, and leading in the stretch to be installed briefly as slight favourites, it was a difficult blow to overcome.

The psychological advantage had switched to the 'Light Blues', and for once in a Scottish Cup final the Ibrox men took full advantage of the situation; Archibald had a 'field-day' against the reserve whose performance was described as 'pitiful'. The inevitability of Rangers' success in the league had been extended now to the Scottish Cup and, like the other clubs in Scotland when facing Rangers, Celtic started to exhibit some of the symptoms of an inferiority complex.

Because of Celtic's chronic state of unreadiness, nemesis had been exacted. However, it was a cruel lesson and destined to be a long one. Wholesale changes were made at Celtic Park in the close season, the directors apparently deciding on a purge which started in May with the transfer of McInally to Sunderland to the real dismay of the fans who recognised him as a wayward genius — annoying, frustrating, immature at times, but an inside-forward of supreme intelligence and still capable of scoring goals with either foot. During the previous season he had been suspended by the club for breaches of training and had always posed problems for the management. Annoyed with his recurring problems in attitude, disappointed by a weak performance in the Scottish Cup against Rangers when he had been swept aside by Rangers' strong tackling, and eager to recoup financially, Celtic transferred him for the second time, on this occasion to Sunderland for £2,500. Maley, who always had a soft spot for the player, expressed his feelings thus: "McInally's transfer to Sunderland wipes out his connection with the team that made him, and to whom he has not been quite fair, and this last transaction through him was a business one which will square to a certain extent the club's financial dealings with him, and this part of the matter is at least satisfactory." (*Glasgow Observer*: 4 August, 1928.) Celtic apparently hoped to replace the star with either Doyle, a fringe player, or with Riley, a provisional signing from Maryhill Hibs, and the vagueness in planning was a depressing indication that the drift at Parkhead was continuing.

Within a few months McInally's partner, Adam McLean, had joined him at Sunderland; McLean, a 12-year veteran with the club and a winger that McGrory considered as superior to Alan Morton, was allowed to leave after a dispute over terms. The winger had been given one benefit after seven years, but considered with some justification that his length of service entitled him to another; when the club turned down his request he asked for a transfer that was granted promptly. Not surprisingly his position was difficult to fill and created a persistent problem for Celtic over the next few years.

Celtic went so far as to inform English clubs by means of a circular that other players were available for transfer; the list included Paddy Connolly, who also felt entitled to a benefit, and Frank Doyle, earlier earmarked as the successor to McInally. This sale of players was most distasteful, especially as no real need existed for the weakening of the club's personnel; after the cup run and the challenge for the flag the club made a profit of £2,070 on the season. However, plans were being made to re-design the Grant Stand whose safety was starting to cause concern, and it was clear that the directors felt the need to raise cash for the project.

In an incredibly shortsighted attempt to gain some of the required money, they tried to sell Jimmy McGrory. For years English clubs had been interested in the most prolific scorer in the game but McGrory, 'Celtic daft' from his earliest days, never considered a move. Maley was instructed to complete the transfer to Arsenal for what would have been a British record fee and the player, preparing for a holiday and pilgrimage to Lourdes with his manager and McInally (who called off the trip after his transfer), was totally unaware of the negotiations. When the pair arrived in London *en route* to France they were met by Arsenal's manager, Herbert Chapman; still unaware of the real situation, McGrory was increasingly puzzled at the turns in the conversation and avoided committing himself. Maley, throughout the holiday, made no reference to the incident, but once more in London, on the return journey, they were met by Chapman who tried every ploy to land McGrory, without success.

McGrory stayed at Celtic Park, but it was only his desire to do so that kept him there; the Board was eager to sell the centre-forward. Maley, as manager, had to comply with their demands and later, in trying to defend the club's behaviour, resorted to a most blatant deception. In an interview with 'Waverley', the noted journalist who was baffled by the attempt to sell the club's most outstanding performer, he lamely diverted attention away from the club's role with a transparent *non sequitur*: "If any player is not contented with his lot at Celtic Park, then we are willing to transfer him. . . .Our policy is that when one of our players is affected by the wanderlust he loses half of his value to Celtic." In this shameful episode the only person to emerge with credit was McGrory; the other parties had apparently forgotten their responsibility to the best traditions of the club and the supporters. McGrory, that most loyal, wholehearted and skilful of players, was signed on again for £1 a week less than most of his colleagues, a shabby and parsimonious reward for the man whose conduct and performances made him 'the heart of the club'. To this day it remains baffling that the Board could ever consider an offer for his transfer; it becomes utterly incredible to realise that they had initiated it.

During this most unsettling close season even Willie Maley's position was placed in jeopardy. In the latter stages of the 1927-28 campaign Maley's health suffered and, after 41 years at Celtic Park, rumours started to circulate about a possible successor. The name most frequently linked with the post was that of Paddy Travers of Aberdeen, a highly popular and respected manager and, of course, much younger than Maley, now in his sixties. The trip to Lourdes with McGrory was partly to recuperate and, when he returned in better health after the holiday, the rumours dwindled away.

Such upheaval behind the scenes could only have a detrimental effect on the team's performance during season 1928-29. Until injuries took their inevitable toll of the squad's resources the team did reasonably well. Early on Celtic won the Glasgow Cup again, beating Rangers deservedly if surprisingly at Ibrox in the first round by 2-1, eliminating Third Lanark 5-1 in a replayed semi-final, and in a memorable final defeating Queen's Park 2-0 at Hampden before 40,000. Queen's Park, after years of struggling, had settled on a strong formation and traditionally gave Celtic hard matches. In this final Queen's Park were decidedly unlucky. They outplayed Celtic throughout the first half and only an incredible display by John Thomson kept them from running up an insurmountable lead after an hour's play; as so often happens, Celtic broke out of defence to score twice for the win. At the end of the match the Hampden stand rose to a man to salute the performance of Celtic's goalkeeper, because of his youth still known as 'the boy keeper'.

As anticipated, the rest of the season was mediocre. Celtic did not have the resources on the field and no serious challenge came from Parkhead for the championship, which was won inevitably by Rangers; in the Cup Celtic made steady progress by eliminating Arthurlie (5-1), East Stirlingshire (3-0), Arbroath (4-1) and Motherwell (2-1) in a replay at Fir Park, until meeting Kilmarnock in the semi-final at Ibrox where the Ayrshire side, the eventual winners of the trophy won 1-0.

It was a side with weaknesses in key positions, and all the heroics of John Thomson in goal and the scoring of Jimmy McGrory could not bolster a challenge for the honours. When either was absent, the play of the whole team slumped. Thomson, a most gallant keeper, dived to save his goal at an opponent's feet in a league game against Airdrie in February 1930 and sustained a fractured jaw and rib injuries; McGrory was marked closely and tackled fiercely but, despite the covering, Celtic regularly looked to him to chase every ball, and often he was required to turn out when only half fit.

The major interest was developments off the field. In another attempt to raise money the club renovated the racing track around the pitch and held speedway meetings during the close season in 1928. The roof of the Grant Stand was damaged in a winter storm, and the stand itself was in the process of demolition on 28 March, 1929, when the pavilion opposite was destroyed by fire and many of the club's original records and photographs were lost in the blaze. Celtic, without dressing-room facilities, were forced to play 'home' games elsewhere: the team played Hibs at Easter Road (1-4), Thistle at Firhill (1-0), Third Lanark (3-1) and Falkirk at Shawfield (3-0), and Queen's Park at Hampden (1-2).

Once more a close-season clearance sale was in effect at Celtic Park. Willie McStay, the captain and a veteran defender, was transferred to Hearts and 'Jean' McFarlane, a stalwart at left-half, moved to Middlesbrough. In return the only player to arrive was Paddy Kavanagh from Dublin's Bohemians, touted before his arrival as 'a second Alan Morton' and hailed as the successor to Adam McLean; predictably he was neither and soon faded from memory. One wit described Celtic's policy as "the Serendipity Factor" and went on to explain: star players would be sold at great profit and replaced with no detriment to the team by unknown youngsters. Unfortunately, the process had about as much chance of success as ordering oysters in an expensive restaurant and confidently expecting to find in the last oyster a pearl with which to pay the bill.

The last season of the 20s (1929-30) started on a bright note with the opening of the new stand, a splendid structure that was to be in service intact until 1971; Hearts were the visitors that day and retired defeated by 2-1. However, in another disappointing season, the first 'bare cupboard' since 1901, Celtic finished a dismal fourth in the league, and went down weakly to St Mirren by 3-1 in the Scottish Cup at Paisley. In the Glasgow Cup Rangers defeated Celtic by a convincing 4-0 score in a replayed final, and in the Charity Cup final the match between Rangers and Celtic ended in a 2-2 draw. As each team had also gained the same number of corners, the outcome was decided by tossing a coin; Rangers won the toss, and the trophy.

This meant that the Ibrox club had won every honour in Scotland, both major and minor. The Celtic handbook was at pains to indicate that Rangers' feat could not compare with Celtic's accomplishment in 1907-08 when the club won all four outright, but the fact remained that Rangers had won everything and Celtic nothing. The pendulum had swung completely in Rangers' favour, and the mood in each camp reflected the change. Rangers were completely different in attitude and performance from pre-war seasons: "Bill Struth in his years as manager set out not only to make Rangers the best team in the land but always to think that they were. They were the best dressed. They had the best facilities. They were the best paid and the best treated. He instilled in them a tremendous conceit which eventually developed an arrogance in themselves and a sense of inferiority in most of the others. It was reckoned that Rangers' reputation could usually be depended upon as worth a goal start." (*One Hundred Years of Scottish Football*: John Rafferty, 1973.)

Celtic, it seemed, had not recovered from the tail-spin in form at the end of the 1927-28 season which had led to a crushing defeat in the cup final and a disappointing conclusion in the league campaign. They were in danger of becoming 'one of the other teams' and, until a basic reorganisation was effected at Parkhead, would remain in that condition.

15

TRIUMPH AND DISASTER

Celtic Party on board the liner 'Caledonia' at Yorkhill Quay, Glasgow, before departure for the USA in May 1931.

AT last the unfulfilled promise of recent seasons looked capable of realisation. It was a young side, but the talent was considerable. Several fine youngsters had 'arrived' and were delighting the support with their fine performances. Charlie Napier, known as 'Happy Feet', was inconsistent, but on form was difficult for any defence to contain, and Peter Scarff was an inside forward of real brilliance and potentially one of the greatest in the game. Willie Cook had established himself at right-back, satisfactorily filling the place of Willie McStay, and Bert Thomson was showing nice touches on the right wing. Even more encouraging, in the long term, was the decision to field a reserve side after a gap of eight years during which Celtic had paid a severe penalty for shortsightedness.

However, the club and its supporters were to experience a wide range of emotions in the next two seasons. Optimism for the future that seemed close at hand, joy at a cup triumph, satisfaction at a sustained challenge for the league, but much of it became irrelevant when real tragedy struck and as a consequence the team lost its collective will.

It was a three-way race for the flag, and Celtic were closely involved to the end, finishing up only two points behind Rangers and ahead of the perennial challengers of the Depression years, Motherwell. With a little more luck the flag might have been won. On 7 February, 1931, Celtic led by goal difference from Motherwell who had played two games more, and by two points from Rangers who had played one match more, but Celtic dropped both points on 18 February to Clyde at Parkhead, and a few weeks later a rare mistake by John Thomson contributed to a loss a Firhill when he attempted to punch away an awkward cross on a snow-bound surface and instead helped the ball into the net. The absence of Jimmy McGrory through injury was a major factor in the loss of another point to Dundee at Parkhead, and it was clear that reserve strength was still at a premium. Even into the '30s the Scottish Cup was considered the most important trophy and, as Celtic's title hopes started to fade, it seemed that the greater effort was being put into the cup. Three difficult away ties were completed successfully: a narrow 2-1 win to scrape past East Fife, another hard-fought struggle culminating in a 3-2 win over Dundee United, and a comfortable 4-1 canter against Morton. The team struck convincing form against Aberdeen to eliminate the northerners 4-0 at Celtic Park in the quarter-final, and were equally effective against Kilmarnock in the semi-final, winning 3-0 to qualify for another final, at Hampden on 11 April, 1931.

The Scottish Cup final was anticipated with a great deal of pleasure, and it turned out to be the most dramatic ever. Celtic, emerging from the doldrums, had produced a fine young team bolstered with veterans Jimmy McStay and Peter Wilson in defence, and Jimmy McGrory in the forward line, while Motherwell, frequent challengers to Rangers' dominance, were a classic side and deservedly most popular with the neutral followers of the game.

> *Celtic:* Thomson J., Cook, McGonagle, Wilson, McStay, Geatons, Thomson R., Thomson A., McGrory, Scarff, Napier.
> *Motherwell:* McClory, Johnman, Hunter, Wales, Craig, Telfer, Murdoch, McMenemy, McFadyen, Stevenson, Ferrier.

Motherwell were the sentimental favourites, never having won the cup and having gained respect for a 'no-transfer' policy, all the more commendable in a provincial club subject to declining gates in a town memorably described as "an industrial cemetery". Most fans admired their attractive football, and genuinely regretted that they seemed always fated to be 'the bridesmaid' in the league.

After 20 minutes Motherwell were two goals up and apparently in control. Both goals were a touch fortunate, although deserved on play, as the shots by Stevenson in the sixth minute and by McMenemy in the 20th were deflected slightly past Thomson in Celtic's goal. Predictably, Celtic fought back with spirit, but Motherwell's famous left wing of Stevenson and Ferrier were dangerous in their breakaways, and prolific scorer McFadyen had to be watched constantly. Celtic claimed a penalty when a defender handled near the goal-line, and chased the referee round the goal in protest, but Mr Craigmyle, a flamboyant character, claimed later that he was unaware of the pursuing players and was taking up position for the corner kick. At half-time, with the score unchanged, the Lanarkshire side's supporters started to celebrate; dozens of homing-pigeons were released to carry back the news that the cup was bound for Motherwell.

With only ten minutes left a Motherwell victory was a safe prediction. At least a sizeable group of Motherwell fans felt so, as they started to leave the stadium, eager to return home and take part in the celebrations already starting. One edition (soon recalled) of an evening newspaper was already proclaiming Motherwell's triumph, but Celtic still pressed forward and the 'Well defenders, earlier so composed, were conceding a number of free kicks to contain the Celtic forwards. With seven minutes left Craig stopped another promising raid by handling deliberately, and as Napier prepared to take it the defensive wall braced itself for another drive from Celtic's strongest shot. This time Napier lofted the ball over them and McGrory lunged forward to net from almost a sitting position. Shrugging off the congratulations of his colleagues, McGrory raced into the back of the net to retrieve the ball; running back to the centre circle with the ball, he spurned the handshakes, gesturing and pointing up to the clock, a feature of the main Hampden stand until 1945.

Responding to the goal and McGrory's show of spirit the Celtic supporters among the 104,803 crowd rallied noisily behind the team once more and the Celtic players flung themselves into frantic attacks. The Celtic pressure continued, minute after minute, but the final had reached its closing seconds before Motherwell's goal was endangered. The defenders had abandoned their studied calm of the first half and were happy to clear at all costs. Bert Thomson on the right wing, after gathering a loose ball, shook off Hunter near the corner flag and whipped over a swirling in-swinging cross into the crowded penalty area, hoping that McGrory somehow would get to it. Perhaps the same thought was bothering Alan Craig, Motherwell's pivot, who went for the cross intending to head the ball past for a corner that might never be taken. His head met the ball, and sent it spinning high into his own net past the helpless keeper. The raw emotions made it a moment to remember. The Celtic players, leaping and shouting for joy, raced over to Thomson, and the terracings exploded into green-and-white, to such an extent that severe crushing occurred at the King's Park end of the stadium, but one man was oblivious to the tumult around him. Craig lay on the turf, pounding it with clenched fists in frustration, and was still on the ground at the whistle a few seconds later. When the referee approached to ask him if he was all right, the player stared blankly at him, barely comprehending the question; all he could say in a shocked monotone was: "I've done it . . . I've done it." (Fifty years later Jimmy McGrory could still recall the sight of the anguished opponent with characteristic compassion.)

Indeed he had, for Motherwell were fated to wait another 21 years to capture their first cup, and were to lose in four more finals — three to Celtic, including the 1931 replay — before that date. On the Wednesday Celtic were more purposeful on the damp pitch, leading by 3-1 at half-time and running out convincing winners at the end by 4-2; the Celtic scorers were appropriately enough the heroes of the first game, Bert Thomson and Jimmy McGrory, each with two.

At the end of the game John Thomson sought out his counterpart, Alan McClory, and, in the manner of all goalkeepers, he commiserated with the Motherwell keeper who had had a shaky evening. The young Celt, only 23 but established as Scotland's goalkeeper, joined his mates in the pavilion to celebrate, although by all accounts he would be more of an observer than an active participant in the merriment. For a footballer, 'the aristocrats of the working-class', he seemed to have a glittering life ahead of him. Young, handsome and popular wherever he played; quiet, modest and unassuming despite his athletic skills; a young man from a humble Fife mining village, but now preparing for a summer tour of the United States and Canada; a sensible lad who had started to plan his future in gents' outfitting, and who had recently got engaged; despite his youth, acclaimed as the best keeper in the country, and attracting the attention of the wealthy Arsenal. Yet, within five months he would be dead and the saddest chapter in Celtic's story was to be written.

However, at the start of season 1931-32 optimism was the prevailing note at Parkhead; the euphoria of the Scottish Cup victory and the long-awaited, triumphant tour of the United States contributed to the mood. Recalling the closeness of the last league race and anticipating that the young team might be more experienced in coping with the stress, the management thought that the championship might be won (and thus Celtic's cherished record of six-in-a-row might not revert to a Rangers team that was threatening it). The initial displays fully justified the confidence as the team settled from the opening day, playing as one critic observed "the pure wine of soccer". The team was scoring almost at will; a 7-0 thrashing of Cowdenbeath was followed by a 6-1 defeat of Hamilton, but the vital test for the undefeated Celtic side was going to be the 'Old Firm' clash at Ibrox on 5 September.

Clearly Rangers were not about to yield their title without a stern fight, and more publicity than usual was generated in the newspapers. Waverley of the *Daily Record and Mail* commented that he could not recall such intense interest in the doings of the 'Old Firm' and hoped the match would be played in a more sporting spirit than last season's meetings.

The match at Ibrox was watched by an 80,000 crowd, absorbed by the tension of an encounter that both teams approached as if determined to avoid defeat. In Glasgow terms it was heading for "a draw, nae fitba", but five minutes after the interval came the moment that was to remain indelibly in the memory of every spectator. After breaking up a Celtic attack Rangers broke out of defence and Fleming released English completely in the clear. The young centre-forward gathered the ball and prepared to shoot from near the penalty spot, but the Celtic keeper with characteristic bravery dived headlong at his feet at the same split-second that the Ranger shot; the ball passed the right-hand post, but the players had clashed and one of them, John Thomson, lay still while the other, Sam English, in some pain from the collision, hobbled over to him. Frantically, forgetting his own injury, he waved for the trainers and ambulance men to attend the prone keeper whose blood was already seeping onto and staining the turf.

The Celtic supporters behind the far goal had started to cheer in relief at the narrow escape, but began to quieten in apprehension as the other players gathered round and the seriousness dawned on them. Behind Thomson's goal at a considerable distance from the group of players (and certainly far enough away to be unable to see the evidence of injury) the Rangers' supporters began to exult, but Meiklejohn, Rangers' captain and a most impressive figure, moved behind the goal and raised his arms to call for silence. The chorus gradually died down and the stricken player, his head now swathed in bandages, was borne off the field on a stretcher in a grim silence. As the party reached the running track the customary round of applause for an injured player briefly started up, but faded as quickly away. Willie Maley had already started to leave his seat in the stand and was heading towards the dressing room, and it has been said that John Thomson's fiancée screamed out in the sudden realisation of tragedy. In the dressing-room a doctor diagnosed a depressed fracture of the skull, and ordered the injured player be immediately transferred to the Victoria Infirmary where, despite the efforts of the hospital's staff, he did not regain consciousness, dying at 9.25 p.m. after an operation to relieve the pressure.

The match had continued without him, Geatons taking his place in goal, and petered out in a scoreless draw as neither team had much heart for the contest, although Scarff came close for Celtic in the closing minute with a solo effort.

The goalkeeper's death released an orgy of emotion. Twenty thousand watched at Queen St. Station as the coffin was placed on the train to carry it back to Fife; thousands more made the same sad journey by train to Cardenden for the funeral, and two coaches were filled with the wreaths and flowers; hundreds of others travelled there by bus or car, and many walked. Every current Celtic player was there and several from the past, and six members of Celtic's team carried the coffin the half mile from his home to the quiet graveyard. The road was lined many deep with mourners from beginning to end; the football world was united in grief, because a player had died at the height of his powers and the dead player was different.

"A great player who came to the game as a boy and left it still a boy; he had no predecessor, no successor. He was unique." (*Soccer: The Great Ones*: John Arlott, 1968.) This was John Rafferty's assessment of the young man who played all his football during the economic troubles of the late '20s and early '30s, and brightened those grim days for many, Celtic supporters and others, by his ability, grace and courage. Like every truly great keeper his talents were hereditary. Nobody can be taught how to clutch the hardest hit shot, or how to throw himself across a goalmouth to divert a drive with the merest touch and save a goal; keepers are born with those sharp eyes, strong hands, and lightning reflexes. He looked the part, too. A good-looking youngster, if a shade serious, a slim, graceful and athletic body, apparently vulnerable to fierce charges; but with a quickness on his feet and balance that a cat might have envied. He had courage to go with it. Football then was a contact sport; players wore heavy boots with reinforced toe caps, shoulder charging was allowed, and teams regularly assigned a forward to harry and charge the opposing goalkeeper, who was given no more protection than other players. Most keepers kept to the safety of their line, and the more brave ventured out to the six-yard line, but Thomson insisted that any ball out as far as the penalty spot was his; and he had been injured before, in February 1930 when a similarly brave save against Airdrie had cost him a fractured jaw.

He added an extra dimension to the game in Scotland, a touch of glamour to a sport that was already acting as a form of escapism to many caught in the economic struggle to survive. Moray McLaren in his book *The Scots* describes the background to which performers such as Thomson brought a touch of colour: "The grey skies of the Scottish winter, the grim industrial countryside with the great hills above and behind it, and the grey sea at its gates; those skies and that countryside which had once seemed to provide a sombre but suitable, almost

John Thomson in action at Ibrox, c. 1930.

majestic, background for Scotland's titantic struggle with the new age of industry now combined to make a huge amphitheatre in which was played a tragedy of poverty, squalor and creeping inanition."

How good was he? It would be almost impossible to give an objective opinion, given the circumstances of his death, but fairly conclusive evidence indicates that he was as good a keeper as his admirers claimed. He was the recognised goalkeeper for Scotland and the Scottish League, and had gained eight representative honours — a remarkably fast progress for a goalkeeper, given his youth and height (only five feet, nine inches). His team-mates thought predictably he was the best keeper of them all, but a number of opponents, sound judges of players, made the same assessment.[1]

A strange reply made by Willie Maley at the Fatal Accident Inquiry held on 15 October, 1931, served to identify John Thomson as a martyr for the cause and retain a place for him in Celtic folklore. In reply to the fiscal's routine question as to whether Maley believed it was an accident, his answer was: "I hope it was an accident." Maley was under emotional stress at the inquiry, but the statement should have been withdrawn or qualified immediately or shortly afterwards. English was entirely blameless in the incident as photographs and newsreel films clearly show, but Maley's answer — he was seated in the stand and according to

140

his own testimony did not have a clear view — helped to ensure that English would be haunted by the incident for the rest of his career. English, although summoned to the inquiry by the Crown, was surprisingly not called to give evidence despite his obvious value in resolving any doubts.

To this day John Thomson remains a legendary figure as the player who died for the club; paradoxically, he should have been remembered as one of the greatest keepers in the Scottish game. His death in action ensured a sporting immortality, unlike the majority of athletes who fade and decline with age. As the poet said:

> "Now, you will not swell the rout
> Of lads that wore their honours out;
> Runners whom renown outran,
> And the name died before the man."

The team never recovered from the blow, and it was scarcely surprising. After Thomson's death points were dropped prodigally, to such an extent that it appeared as if the heart had been taken from the side. Injuries played a part also. McGrory, as was happening more frequently now, was off for an extended period, Bert Thomson and Peter Wilson were sidelined for spells, and Peter Scarff, for whom a great career was once predicted, had to be rested with the first symptoms of the illness that was to remove him from the line-up before Christmas, and indeed was to lead to an untimely death the following year. The slump was a natural reaction to the loss of the young goalkeeper. A new keeper was signed to take Thomson's place, and he was a surprising choice. During the American tour Celtic had been defeated by Fall River, a local team inspired largely by the performance of their keeper to whom Celtic now turned. Joe Kennaway was a sound keeper, performing consistently till the outbreak of World War II and, in fact, gaining international recognition for three countries — the United States, Canada and Scotland.

That season the side finished a respectable third in the league, although far behind Rangers and Motherwell; the Lanarkshire club ended up as champions for the only time in their history, to the acclaim of most fans in Scotland.

The most obvious cause of Celtic's slump was the loss of the goalkeeper and its effect on morale, but a more prosaic reason existed for Celtic's travail. The more perceptive of the sports journalists could see it clearly enough, as this excerpt from a constructively critical article indicates:

"No one has more sympathy with the Parkhead board in its cruel experience this season than I have, but that does not blind me to the fact that they do not carry the number of first-class reserves that one would expect a club of their eminence to do.

"In most cases want of cash is the excuse, and quite a sound excuse it is, but this cannot apply to Celtic. Celtic can only be Celtic by representing all that is best in Scottish football, and it does seem strange that those responsible have failed so far in their obvious duty as to neglect that essential — reserve power. Lack of it probably lost them the Glasgow Cup, or perhaps I may put it that by reason of its possession Rangers were ultimately able to come out on top. They kept pushing in fresh players in each replay.

"The policy of rearing one's own players is a sound one, and is to be commended, but if incurable weaknesses crop up, a club of Celtic's standing ought not to have any hesitation in putting an end to the trouble by purchase.

"To have a dependable side is a duty a club owes to its supporters. In this case Celtic owe it also to their reputation, and likewise to Scottish football." (*Sunday Mail*: 21 February, 1932.)

Celtic's lack of reserves was shown most pitifully in the Scottish Cup match at Fir Park against Motherwell when McGrory was chosen to lead the attack although he was clearly not fit, and had to retire after 30 minutes. Simply, he was chosen because there was nobody else. After McGrory's forced withdrawal, Motherwell went on to win comfortably 2-0.

Some years would elapse before the youngsters in Celtic's reserves were fully ready for the task.

Notes

1 For example, J. B. McAlpine, noted Queen's Park forward of the 1920s and early 1930s, had no hesitation in nominating Thomson as the finest goalkeeper he had seen, when being interviewed by that club's historian Bob Crampsey. McAlpine had played against both Thomson and Jerry Dawson of Rangers and with Jack Harkness, all three Scottish international goalkeepers.

16

WAITING

CELTIC FOOTBALL CLUB, 1932-33.
Back row: C Geatons, W Cook, J Kennaway, W McGonagle, J Cameron, J Qusklay (Trainer). Front row: R Thomson, J McGrory, P Wilson, J McStay, A Thomson, C Napier.

WHILE the loss of John Thomson was a grievous blow to the club, it took too long for Celtic to recover its challenging position in the Scottish game. The next three seasons could well be described as semi-permanent transition as the club drifted through the Depression and waited for better days ahead.

Money, or the alleged lack of it, was a recurring theme at Parkhead, and it manifested itself in most aspects of the running of the club. Saddest to record was the continuing practice of selling established players and replacing them with promising youngsters. Once more the club reiterated its tiresome claim that any dissatisfied player was free to move elsewhere, but the situation was not as clear-cut as that. The wages at Celtic Park, as at most other grounds, were cut to correspond with the economic ravages of the period, but it seemed that Celtic could have met some of the demands made by the players. Peter Wilson, Alec

143

Thomson and Jimmy McStay had trouble in coming to financial terms with the club and were transferred, the latter two players on free transfers, while other men such as Joe Kennaway, Chic Geatons and 'Peter' McGonagle originally refused the terms offered by the club. The club might claim that it had little choice, but the players were in the more difficult position; they had to face the prospect of accepting reduced wages or refusing to sign, but the real dread always lurking in the background was unemployment and the 'dole'.

One critic, 'Jack o' Clubs', commented scathingly that "the Celts do not believe in paying high fees; they believe in getting them". (*Sunday Mail*: 29 January 1933.) Another anonymously suggested that the Celtic directors did not want to attract interest, but only to collect it. For the true supporters it was a demoralising practice. Many fans had watched the young players learn their trade, had encouraged their efforts, and then at a time when these men were close to their best had seen them depart for sums of money that did not seem to be used for adequate replacements. Willie Cook, a promising right-back and capped for Ireland, was one such player and he was transferred to Everton for a healthy fee in 1932; Bert Thomson, the regular right-winger and a hero in the 1931 cup final, was transferred to Blackpool for £2,000 in 1933 after serving a *sine die* suspension imposed by the club for breaches of training regulations.

In those cases the recently revived Alliance (reserve) team provided suitable replacements. Bobby Hogg, signed from Royal Albert, became the youngest regular professional in the country at the age of 17 when he took over from Cook at right-back; and Jimmy Delaney, signed from Stoneyburn in 1934, took over on the right wing the following season and made the position uniquely his own. Charlie Napier was another player transferred, to Derby County in June 1935 for £5,000.

Attendance had dropped significantly. The industrial recession of the early '30s had hit Glasgow hard and many could not afford football at all, while others showed what they felt about the club's attitude by staying away — a step that Celtic supporters did not take lightly. The management experimented with the players, the youngsters took time to settle, and like every team in transition Celtic got off to a series of bad starts in the league that put the title out of sight before New Year. Because of the aggravating inconsistency displayed by the experimental sides a feeling grew among the supporters that Celtic was only 'a cup-tie team' and the crowds dwindled accordingly.

The fears that the club was not really serious about mounting a challenge for the honours were increased with the speculation regarding the future of the reserve side. Only recently restored after a disastrous lapse, the team was not a money-making proposition, especially in away games, and the directors gave serious consideration in 1932 to disbanding it again, despite the detrimental effects of the previous decision. Willie Maley could not have been sanguine about that, as he was in the process of rebuilding with juniors who would establish themselves in the reserves and who showed promise in their occasional first-team appearances; youngsters such as the cultured half back-cum-forward Malcolm MacDonald, an outstanding prospect, and the lively Johnny Crum who impressed when he replaced the injury-prone McGrory during 1932-33, as did John Divers when he took over from Napier, out with damaged knees during 1933-34. The quick, direct, Jimmy Delaney, who was signed in 1934, typified the more purposeful style that Celtic were seeking from their new breed of young forwards. He made an immediate impression, as this report after a 5-1 win over Albion Rovers would indicate: "He is speedy, never shirks a tackle, can beat his man on the run and his crosses are invariably the acme of perfection. In addition he showed an intelligent sense of position; and that he is no mean shot is testified by the three goals he scored. Not every day does an extreme winger find the net on three occasions." (*Sunday Mail*: 3 February, 1935.)

It was a trying period while the club waited for the members of the reserve team to mature, but it was also a period of drift for the club; some claimed that the rigid adherence to a home-grown policy provided a ready-made excuse for not spending money on established players. Maley, becoming increasingly preoccupied with financial matters, argued on behalf of his directors that Celtic did not have the money to compete with English clubs for players, and questioned if suitable players were available; he complained bitterly that early dismissal from the cup had cost the club £5,000 in the 1933-34 season, and blamed the players for lack of spirit. The columnist for the *Glasgow Observer*, however, wondered if there was not something wrong with the scouting system as Celtic, in his view, had the first choice of the best talent in Scotland with hundreds of budding footballers having ambitions to wear the green and white.

Some observers thought the club was out of date in its methods or tactics: "Their form is far from reassuring, and supporters are wondering if the Celtic style of playing soccer is effete and useless in these days of hustle and bustle. Close passing in the traditional Celtic style is not bringing the old-time results. Hamilton Academicals recently and Falkirk on Saturday withstood all their weaving, replied with wide passing, and walked off with the points. No lover of good football will condemn the Celtic style of keeping the ball on the floor. It would be a severe blow to Scottish football if ever the club abandoned artistry and took to the cruder methods exploited by certain other clubs." (*Glasgow Observer*: 21 January, 1933.) During the inter-war period the game had undergone further development with the change in the offside rule[1] and the subsequent introduction of the 'stopper' centre-half. Rangers in particular had found the 'third-back game' to their liking and had been most effective in defence. Celtic had not found the proper players for the roles, nor had they come up yet with a new formation to circumvent formidable defences, and relied too much on Jimmy McGrory's foraging.

One has to wonder what Celtic would have done without this man. The greatest scorer in British football may not have been the most polished player in the game, but no Celtic player has so consistently lifted the spirits of the supporters with his tenacity and opportunism. All the more commendable when considering that, unlike Jimmy Quinn, he had to wait until his career was drawing to a close, in 1935-36, before playing in an outstanding Celtic side and receiving a proper service. Unquestionably, without McGrory, Celtic's record in the first half of the '30s would have been even more dismal.

The only major accomplishment was the winning of the Scottish Cup of 1933, and Celtic vindicated their reputation as cup-fighters in the campaign. Early in the New Year the team was mired in fourth place in the league table and doing badly. It was a relief, therefore, to be drawn against Dunfermline of the second division and to win 7-1 at East End Park. For the second year in succession Celtic knocked out Falkirk at Parkhead, this time 2-0, thanks to two McGrory goals memorable in their execution, one a leaping header and the other a lob over the keeper after dummying a bemused defender.

In the next round Celtic struggled at Parkhead to overcome Partick Thistle, who had beaten them home and away by 2-1 in the league that season. Celtic scraped a 2-1 win to face the stuffy Albion Rovers in the quarter-finals. It took two matches to get by the Lanarkshire side, a 1-1 draw at Coatbridge leading to a 3-1 victory at Parkhead, and yet another replay to get by Hearts at Hampden in the semi-final after a 0-0 draw watched by 90,000. In that replay Celtic's forwards struck form and the score of 2-1 was a poor reflection of the difference between the sides, Hearts' defence frequently being over-run by Celtic's lively forwards.

In the final on 15 April, 1933, these teams lined up:

> *Celtic*: Kennaway, Hogg, McGonagle, Wilson, McStay J., Geatons, Thomson R., Thomson A., McGrory, Napier, O'Donnell H.
> *Motherwell*: McClory, Crapnell, Ellis, Wales, Blair, McKenzie, Murdoch, McMenemy, McFadyen, Stevenson, Ferrier.

Again Motherwell were the popular choice and their team seemed marginally stronger than that of two years previously with both full-backs capped — Crapnell, signed from Airdrie, was the Scottish right-back and Ellis was a Welsh internationalist at left-back. However, a nagging doubt remained about their temperament in the hurly-burly of cup football.

Motherwell started off better in a scrappy match, but lost heart when they could not find a way past the resolute Celtic defence marshalled by McStay, who was faced with the task of containing the prolific

McFadyen, the scorer of 15 goals in Motherwell's triumphant progress to Hampden. The crowd of 102,339 was disappointed in the absence of combined play and bright attacking thrusts, but Celtic gradually asserted control of the midfield; the score at half-time was 0-0, a reflection of the grimness of the struggle.

McGrory nips in to score the only goal of the 1933 Scottish Cup final, watched by Bertie Thomson (left) and Alec Thomson (right). Motherwell fated to be runners-up to Celtic again.

Within three minutes of the restart Celtic took the lead with a scrambled goal. The Motherwell defenders failed to clear, the ball rebounding from Crapnell's back in the direction of McGrory, who alertly turned it into the net. Only two weeks before McGrory, in one of his infrequent appearances for Scotland, had scored both goals in his country's 2-1 victory over England and he considered Hampden his lucky ground in April of 1933. The more objective spectator might have questioned his 'luck' watching him hobbling through the closing stages of the match: "In the opening minute of the final one of his teeth had been knocked out and he played the first half hour in a dazed state. He left the pitch at full-time with his right thumb staved, his ankle swollen, and his knee painfully injured. He would have thought little of it. Jimmy McGrory," recalled a team-mate four decades later, "played as if he was Celtic." (*One Hundred Cups*: Hugh Keevins/Kevin McCarra, 1985.)

147

In 1934-35 Celtic had revived sufficiently to mount a sustained challenge for the league flag, despite the now customary miserable start to the campaign, with the forwards failing to score in four of the first five matches. On 8 September, Celtic managed to get one point from Rangers at Parkhead in a 1-1 draw: "Celtic have a bit to travel before they produce anything. Their youngsters were clever at times, but that cleverness was not properly applied; they need nursing a bit. It is some time since we were told that Celtic were at the transition stage; they still are!" (*Sunday Mail*: 9 September, 1934.) Rangers had a strong side, favourites for the championship again, but they were slipping, although, always pragmatic, could invariably scramble victories when off form, a talent that seemed beyond the young Celtic sides of the period.

By early October Celtic, after successive defeats by lowly Albion Rovers at Coatbridge and Queen of the South at Parkhead by scores of 2-1, were nine points behind Rangers and had played a game more. It seemed as if another mediocre season was in prospect for the long-suffering supporters, as a newspaper indicated: "Matters seem to be drifting too long out Parkhead way. A weak Celts team is a misfortune for football." (*Sunday Mail*: 7 October, 1934.)

It was at this stage that Celtic appointed Jimmy McMenemy as coach to bring on the youngsters, and a remarkable transformation came over the side. Before the end of the year Celtic lost only one more match, a 3-2 setback from Hibs at Easter Road, but any lingering title aspirations effectively ended at Ibrox in the Ne'erday clash. Celtic lost 2-1 but could be considered unlucky as Napier had to retire shortly before half-time, having overstretched himself straining for a pass. Later in the match McGonagle was ordered off, foolishly throwing the ball at Rangers' Bob McPhail in a moment of temper. Celtic paid heavily for McGonagle's lapse; he missed the critical match at Pittodrie against Aberdeen during his 14-day suspension and Celtic lost 2-0. At the end of the league programme Celtic finished second in the table, a respectable three points behind Rangers.

The gap was closing: in 1932-33, fourth place; in 1933-34, third place; and in 1934-35 second place. It would not require much more to challenge the supremacy of Rangers.

Notes

1 In 1925 the number of opponents needed between a player and the opposition goal-line to present offside (when the ball was last played) was reduced from three to two. Thus the tactic of a 'stopper' centre-half (or 'third back') to operate deep between his full-backs, its evolution being credited by the journalist W. G. Gallacher ('Waverley') to the Queen's Park internationalist Bob Gillespie.

17

REVIVAL

DURING the close season Celtic made an important signing, a clear indication that the directors were serious about fielding a first-class team. It was a surprise, as the player was Queen's Park centre-half Willie Lyon. Many found it difficult to recall the last time Celtic had signed a Queen's Parker because, in accordance with a long-standing practice, the club had left the amateur players severely alone, a policy greatly appreciated by Queen's Park and which had done much to improve the originally cool relations between the clubs. Lyon was a commanding figure, efficient and cool, and capable of exerting authority over his colleagues. The newspapers had little doubt about his value: ". . . having the height and weight besides the skill to adorn a position in the Parkhead team that has never been satisfactorily filled since Jamie McStay took his football kit to Hamilton. I predict for Lyon a career at Celtic Park as brilliant as most of his predecessors. He should impart strength to a position in the Celtic team that needed a man of his power and courage to support young forwards that required greater inspiration from behind than they were getting." (*Sunday Mail*: 19 May, 1935.)

Inevitably, some players left Parkhead; the most disquieting was the transfer of Napier (to Derby County for £5,000), who left expressing dissatisfaction about the club's reluctance to grant him a benefit after six years of service, and the double transfer of the O'Donnell brothers Frank and Hugh, to Preston North End; the brothers were inseparable and were unhappy at the barracking Frank had experienced from some supporters. To balance this the performances of the recruits, at last, were matching the reports of their promise. The practical value of restoring and reviving the Alliance team at the start of the 30s was being demonstrated as the youngsters, having worked through the system, took their places in the first eleven: Jimmy Delaney from Stoneyburn Juniors, Johnny Crum from Ashfield, John Divers from Renfrew, Malcolm MacDonald from St. Anthony's, Willie Buchan from Grange Rovers, George Paterson from Dunipace.

149

Perhaps one important factor had been the appointment of a former player, the famous Jimmy McMenemy, as 'coach' starting in October, 1934; McMenemy, one of the greatest of all inside-forwards and fully meriting the nickname 'Napoleon', was given much of the credit for developing the talents of his sons. It was a tentative relationship, however, a verbal and non-contractual arrangement lasting only till the end of the season when he was appointed as 'trainer', although his duties seem to have remained the same. "McMenemy's long experience as a player makes him capable of understanding the players' problems, temperamental and otherwise, for which he is certain to have the exact remedy: a word of advice to a youngster, a joke and a laugh with a player off-form, and an incitement to greater effort, spoken in the most diplomatic manner, is Jimmy's way — the way that is likely to put new life into the Celtic." (*Glasgow Observer*: 1 June, 1935.)

The supporters were heartened by the signs that the club was serious about wresting football supremacy from Rangers, and had started to rally round once more. The increase in season ticket sales would indicate this, as would the swelling attendances as it became clear that a fine team, entertaining and adventurous, was evolving at Parkhead. Or perhaps it was another sign of better economic times.

The season opened with a tough fixture, and a defeat at Pittodrie by 3-1, but the team settled quickly and some of the forward play was innovative and exciting; the forwards were young and sprightly, described after one match as playing "with the determination and quickness of terriers in a rat-hunt". Several outstanding forwards were delighting the supporters with captivating displays. On the right wing young Jimmy Delaney was a particular favourite, appealing with his speed, enthusiasm and goal-scoring talent; clever inside-forwards such as Malcolm MacDonald, already displaying his versatility and prodigious skills, and John Divers, a tall, well-built youngster with goalscoring punch, made appearances; Willie Buchan was another intelligent forward, blessed with the knack of scoring important goals; Johnny Crum impressed with his electric energy and sharpness. But one forward, by that time considered a veteran and the man who had carried the team for some years, had his greatest year, thriving on the unaccustomed service from his inside men and the support of other goal-hungry forwards — Jimmy McGrory scored 50 league goals, a club record for one season (and a feat that made one wonder what the greatest scorer in British football might have attained had he been given comparable support throughout his career). After the opening-day setback the side went 18 league matches without defeat, dropping only two points. McGrory, the club's leading scorer for so many lean seasons, was closing in on the world record for league goals held by Hugh Ferguson since 1930, surpassing it with a hat-trick against

Aberdeen at Parkhead on 21 December *en route* to his career total with Celtic of 397 league goals (also a British record for a single club). On 14 March he scored three goals against Motherwell, and by most estimates netted them within a three-minute span, to lead Celtic to a 5-0 win; and on 18 April, the day the team claimed the championship with a 6-0 victory over Ayr United, he scored yet another hat-trick, his seventh of the season — and still it was not to be a completely happy year for McGrory. Missing the last league game of the campaign against Thistle at Firhill (a 3-1 win), he lost his chance to pass or equal the Scottish League's First Division record total of 52 in one season held by McFadyen of Motherwell and ended up with 50. Despite his scoring touch, he was not chosen for the international against England at Wembley, a pitch he never played on; generally the selectors had preferred Hughie Gallacher at centre forward and, as the troubled Anglo-Scot was another player of genius, it was considered McGrory's misfortune to be a contemporary. However, this time they chose the relatively unknown McCulloch of Brentford and the newspapers reported that he "appeared often out of position, and never once got his head to a crossed ball".

While it was McGrory's year for scoring, Celtic's teamwork had tightened considerably and the improvement was noted in victories at

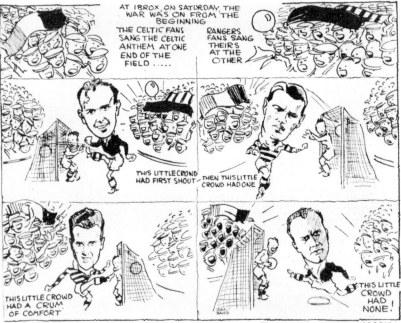

A cartoonist's view of Celtic's 2-1 victory over Rangers in season 1935/36. Murphy and Crum scored for Celtic. Scottish Daily Express, *23 September, 1935.*

'bogey' grounds. On 21 September, despite McGrory's absence but with his substitute Crum outstanding, Celtic triumphed 2-1 at Ibrox to record their first league win there since 1920-21; a similar 2-1 victory was attained at Fir Park on 26 October to overcome Motherwell for the first time at that ground since 1926-27; and later in the season the team defeated Dundee 2-0, the first win at Dens Park since 1928-29. Kennaway was a consistent keeper, capable and unruffled in dealing effectively with forwards who challenged him physically, perhaps as a result of playing ice-hockey in his youth; the highlight of his year was a splendid diving save from Meiklejohn's penalty kick in the closing minutes at Ibrox to preserve a 2-1 lead. At centre-half Lyon was a dominant figure both in the air and on the ground, and he was reaching a close understanding with Kennaway towards the end of the season. All the other players, of course, had been recruited from junior ranks, and displayed the teamwork and understanding attained by playing together for the Alliance side.

The speed of the forwards and their intelligent use of open space posed many problems for defences entrenched in a 'third-back' game that had been stifling creativity. Celtic's threat came from all quarters and special mention must be made of the wingers, Delaney and Murphy. Delaney was a Will-o'-the-wisp figure, always on the lookout for goals and popping up in dangerous positions in the penalty area to bother defences, while Frank Murphy was suggesting that he had solved a chronic problem for Celtic on the other wing with his unorthodox play, being ready to cut in and shoot for goal as the mood struck him.

Rangers put up a determined defence of their title, and won at Celtic Park on Ne'erday by 4-3 to keep in touch, but nothing could stop this Celtic side. The team showed its resolution in overcoming Clyde 4-0 at Shawfield on 29 February despite an injury to Lyon after 15 minutes; the pivot went to outside-right, Buchan to right-half, Delaney assumed a wandering role at inside-right, and the versatile Chic Geatons took over effectively at centre-half. Rangers, as always, were dour and grim, winning tight games although struggling, but the Ibrox challenge foundered at Hamilton late in March. It was Celtic's first flag in ten years, the longest interval between league titles up to that time, and the durable McGrory was the only survivor of the previous side. The fans celebrated the recovery, and felt the icing was put on the cake with a refreshing display in the Charity Cup final to beat Rangers 4-2, the hero Delaney leading the way with three goals and inevitably McGrory scoring the other; significantly, it was the first win also in that tournament for ten years.

In 1936-37 hopes were high that the championship could be retained, and the team made a good start, although the play was not as scintillating as the previous season's. In late December Celtic were only

The first goal of Jimmy Delaney's hat-trick in the Charity Cup final vs Rangers at Hampden, May 1936. Jerry Dawson is the goalkeeper left helpless as the scorer turns away.

one point behind the leaders Aberdeen and had the advantage of a game in hand. On the heavy grounds of a Scottish winter, however, the lightweight Celtic forwards were at a disadvantage, their combined play frequently bogging down in the mud. Queen of the South won surprisingly by 1-0 at Dumfries on 19 December, Rangers were too physical for Celtic at Ibrox and the champions were lucky to escape with only a 1-0 Ne'erday defeat. Later in January Aberdeen won 1-0 at Pittodrie to boost their own challenge and virtually end Celtic's. Losing interest in the league and concentrating on progress in the cup, Celtic fell further behind to finish in third place, nine points behind Rangers and two behind Aberdeen.

Celtic's campaign in the Scottish Cup almost ended at an early stage. Sent to face Stenhousemuir at Ochilview, Celtic approached the fixture with confidence, but the Warriors put up a tremendous struggle against the record-holders. Consider what that club's official history says of the match: "Stenhousemuir did not upset the Glasgow giants by shock tactics. On a playing field on which underfoot conditions were conducive to good football, Celtic were eventually outplayed by a better team. But after dominating almost all of the game, Stenhousemuir suffered a disastrous setback on the 70-minute mark . . . Carruth headed against the crossbar and the ever alert Jimmy McGrory was there to head the ball home. Only two minutes later and despair was turned to jubilation. Jimmy McNair slipped the ball forward and Charlie Howie took it in his stride to smash home an unsaveable 'daisy-cutter' which simply flew past the diving Celtic 'keeper, Kennaway. The Celtic defence was now reeling: 'Muir's Robert Murray was clean through when a visiting defender handled. 'Penalty' came the roar from the 3,000-strong Stenhousemuir crowd. Referee Craigmyle thought otherwise, but till their dying day you will never convince a 'Muir enthusiast (and others too) that it wasn't a valid claim." (*The Warriors*: Peter Moulds, 1984.)

Relieved at the narrow escape, Celtic won the replay at Parkhead comfortably by 2-0. Celtic had much less trouble with Albion Rovers at Coatbridge to win 5-2, and East Fife at Methil to record a 3-0 decision, before meeting Motherwell at Parkhead in the quarter-final. After only 20 minutes play in a thrilling cup-tie five goals had been scored. Motherwell were in front by 3-2 and retained that lead till half-time; Celtic came out for the second half determined-looking, to the roars of the expectant supporters. However, within a minute the composed Motherwell side had scored again, a goal netted by the elegant Stevenson, and Celtic faced elimination. Celtic exerted tremendous pressure on the Motherwell goal and were partially rewarded when Delaney, always a menace in cup-ties, was fouled in the box; Lyon took the penalty kick in the emphatic manner approved and laid down by his manager. The battle raged on with Celtic pressing, and ten minutes from the end Buchan equalised after a fine solo effort in which he beat two defenders cleanly and, as the others closed in, shot with great coolness past the Motherwell keeper, McArthur. Celtic's invincible reputation in replays was confirmed with a 2-1 win at Fir Park, Buchan again scoring a late goal to win the game.

If the cup-ties with Motherwell were thrillers, the semi-final against Clyde was a drab affair. Celtic won 2-0 in a match marked by poor finishing, but Jimmy McGrory showed a flash of his goal-snatching ability when he took full advantage of a momentary lapse in concentration by centre-half Robb, who had guarded him tightly till then. He gathered the ball quickly, closed in on keeper Brown and rammed the ball into the net to give Celtic the important first goal and settle nerves. It seemed, however, that at last the great McGrory was showing signs of slowing down after so many years; on heavy grounds he seemed to have lost that vital half-step, but he could still take chances as Clyde had found out to their cost.

On 24 April, 1937, Hampden Park was crammed with 146,433 spectators, still a record for a club match in Europe and a far cry from the 3,000 present at the near disaster at Stenhousemuir in the first round. More than 20,000 others were locked out and spent much of the game milling around, listening to the roars of the crowd following the exchanges between these teams:

Celtic: Kennaway, Hogg, Morrison, Geatons, Lyon, Paterson, Delaney, Buchan, McGrory, Crum, Murphy.
Aberdeen: Johnstone, Cooper, Temple, Dunlop, Falloon, Thomson, Beynon, MacKenzie, Armstrong, Mills, Lang.

Celtic's 1937 Scottish Cup triumph as viewed by the cartoonist of Daily Record
and Mail, *26 April, 1937.*

Both teams were eager to provide a spectacle for the huge crowd, and
the opening thrusts were bright and promising, with Celtic first to settle.
After 12 minutes Celtic scored when the Aberdeen keeper could not
hold a shot from Buchan and Crum, always an alert player, nipped in to
shoot home the loose ball. Celtic's lead lasted less than a minute; a cross
from Beynon was miscued by Lyon past his keeper for Armstrong to net
easily.

In the second half Celtic assumed control of the final, the clever and
unexpected moves of Crum and Buchan troubling the Aberdeen
defenders while Geatons was controlling midfield with a fine display of
sharp tackling, clever dribbling and accurate passing. The winning goal
came twenty minutes from the end. McGrory's neat slip left Buchan in
the clear and the inside-forward advanced on Johnstone's goal to release
a low drive that entered the net at the post. It was Celtic's cup, but
Aberdeen staged a thrilling late rally that had the supporters whistling
for the end in their anxiety.

The season ended on another happy note, with Celtic retaining the
Charity Cup; after beating Clyde 3-1 Celtic faced Queen's Park in the

final. It turned out to be a thriller as Queen's Park, having eliminated Rangers by 3-0, were eager to repeat the performance over the other half of the 'Old Firm'. With ten minutes left Queen's Park led by 3-2, centre-forward 'Mac' Dodds leading the way with a hat-trick against his former colleague Willie Lyon. After a long career Dodds, playing his last game at Hampden, had won no medals, but had gained the respect of his opponents, amateur and professional alike. As Celtic pressed for an equaliser Lyon congratulated him: "Well, that's it (a medal) this time," but Dodds replied cautiously: "Don't be too sure; you know these fellows you're with now!" McGrory equalised near the end, but Queen's Park still held a commanding lead on corners and the cup seemed bound for Hampden, and Dodds' first medal was virtually assured. In the last minute Lyon joined his forwards in a bid for the winner and, after a pass from Geatons, fired a long-range shot that completely beat the keeper for a 4-3 win.

Hopes were high that Celtic would land the championship again in 1937-38, a fitting manner to celebrate the jubilee season, but early mishaps in the campaign endangered the prospects. A draw against lowly Queen of the South and a loss by 2-1 at Kilmarnock promoted pessimism, and the mood was made worse by a lack-lustre performance at Ibrox in a 3-1 defeat in September. In a shock loss at Arbroath by 2-0 on 9 October both Lyon and Delaney were injured and the team was now four points behind Rangers in the league.

Perhaps the worst news was the transfer of Willie Buchan, the scoring hero of the Scottish Cup; the inside-right, regarded as the inspiration in attack, was transferred to Blackpool in mid-November for a handsome £10,000. Many supporters feared that the transfer heralded a return to the policy of selling the best players for what the market would bear, and anticipated the worst. The regular columnist in the *Glasgow Observer* claimed that the manager had weighed up all the factors involved before agreeing to the transfer, but this was hardly true. Malcolm MacDonald took Buchan's place and John Divers filled the other inside-forward position. Maley claimed much of the credit for the successful changes, conveniently forgetting that both forwards had been available for transfer earlier in the season while playing in the reserve side. Negotiations between Liverpool and Celtic for MacDonald had reached an advanced stage before the English club baulked at Celtic's valuation of £4,000 and withdrew.

Another significant change was at centre-forward where Jimmy McGrory retired after a magnificent career. Injury had hampered him in recent seasons but he was, as always, an inspirational leader. He played his last game against Queen's Park on 16 October and scored a goal, beating the Amateurs' keeper D. White, later to become known as Celtic's chairman. McGrory's place was taken by Johnny Crum, a nippy little player, who formed a celebrated inside trio with MacDonald and Divers. The three men established an immediate rapport and understanding, the main feature of their play being fast passing and rapid interchanging that invariably found one of them loose in front of goal.

On 27 November Celtic made inroads into Rangers' lead by beating Falkirk 2-0 comfortably at Parkhead and learning that Rangers had lost 3-0 at Ibrox to Hearts, a hat-trick by young Andy Black making the difference. On New Year's Day Celtic took over first place in the best way possible by thrashing Rangers 3-0 at Parkhead before a crowd of 83,500[1]. Rangers defenders were awkward and cumbersome against the pace of the Celtic forwards. A week later Celtic went to Tynecastle, and dimmed Hearts' hopes for the title with a 4-2 win, another match highlighted by glorious forward play that perplexed the opposing defence. Celtic had settled into a fixed formation and were playing inspired football, as a run of 13 successive league victories would indicate. Celtic clinched the title on 23 April with a 3-1 win at Paisley over St. Mirren, an appropriate present for Willie Maley's 70th birthday.

Three weeks later Celtic faced Rangers in the Charity Cup final in a bid to win the trophy for the third year in a row. Celtic turned on another co-ordinated display to win easily 2-0 — an excellent tune-up for the Empire Exhibition tournament in the summer, which was won in memorable style by beating the best teams in Scotland and England.[2]

The Jubilee was celebrated off the field as well. The club entertained officials of the SFA, and representatives of other Scottish league sides, members of Glasgow's town council and the Lord Provost; all current team members were present, as were as many of the past teams who were available to come to the Grosvenor Restaurant on 16 June, 1938, for the banquet. Proudly displayed were the symbols of football success — the Charity Cup of 1938, the Empire Exhibition Trophy 1938, the Glasgow Exhibition Cup of 1901, gained a year later,[3] and the Shield presented by the SFA to honour the six consecutive league titles won between 1904 and 1910. Almost as visible was the sense of pride and satisfaction derived from half a century of accomplishment that permeated the atmosphere, and the conviction that 'the good old days' had returned.

One of the highlights of the evening was a presentation to the manager, Willie Maley, to celebrate his own 50 year association with the club. The chairman presented the manager with a cheque for 2,500 guineas and Maley could reflect proudly on his contribution to the club and teams' successes, but rifts had already appeared in the lute and the relationship between manager and directors was uneasy.

In 1931 when Celtic finally toured America, a country that had figured prominently in Irish emigration, it was not an unqualified success. As manager and secretary Maley had to make all the arrangements for what was basically a missionary trip by the club; he had to confirm the reservations, check accommodations, finalise the details of fixtures, and act as 'major-domo' of the party. Several factors made it a less than pleasant experience. Local teams did not relish being used as doormats for the visitors, playing enthusiastically and sometimes roughly to inflict three defeats on Celtic; the heat or, more accurately, the humidity drained the energy of the whole party and taxed the patience of Maley, then 63 years of age. The journeys of a thousand miles or more across the United States were made by train and often induced boredom; the hotels were only partly air-conditioned and thus the members of the Celtic party did not enjoy comfortable rest at nights; but an incident at the start particularly rankled with the directors. Maley had angled for an invitation to be extended to his brother, Tom, a member of Celtic's first team back in 1888, but none was forthcoming. The manager, admittedly not the best of sailors, confined himself to his cabin for most of the voyage, and on arrival in New York took to his bed in the hotel pleading serious illness and asking that the directors send for his brother to take him home to Scotland. The directors swallowed their pride to send for the brother, and were not too surprised to see Willie recover almost immediately to greet Tom on the dock in New York.

Maley was reluctant to accept any of the blame for lack of success, preferring to blame a variety of reasons instead: injuries, bad luck, the bias of referees and often the attitude of his own players. Throughout the bad seasons in the 30s Maley was not an easy person to live with and his comments in the Celtic handbooks make very uncomfortable reading: "One cannot leave this game [a Scottish Cup-tie lost 2-0 against St. Mirren] without voicing the disappointment of all true followers at the careless, indifferent play shown by certain of our team, and one can see from the balance sheet of the Club what that cost us. Between cup ties and league games I am putting it mildly when I say it was a clear loss of £5,000 to the Club, not to speak of the loss of morale and public support which followed the ignominious defeat. . . . This carelessness of the Team has cost the Club much in recent years but the Board have decided that such will not be tolerated again and that the men privileged to wear Celtic jerseys must live and act up to the spirit which has made a name for the Club in football which they don't intend to see thrown away by lack of energy or enthusiasm . . ." (re 1933-34).

Despite the improvement shown in the later 30s some supporters felt the record could have been better, and these fans pointed to shock defeats in the Scottish Cup at the hands of little-fancied opponents. In 1935-36, when Celtic won the league, the team put up a weak display to lose 2-1 to St. Johnstone at Parkhead, and in 1937-38, again as league champions, Celtic took Kilmarnock, now managed by Jimmy McGrory, too lightly and were upset 2-1 in a match also played at Celtic Park. This latter match may have signalled a turning point in Maley's career; certainly, questions were being asked about his strange behaviour towards Jimmy McGrory. At least one Celtic director felt that McGrory, now nearing the end as a player, would make a suitable assistant to Maley, but the older man fought the suggestion vehemently, having survived earlier hints that Jimmy McMenemy, the club's trainer, would soon succeed him. When McGrory went to Kilmarnock in December, 1937, Maley delayed the move until he had ensured that Kilmarnock, although in relegation trouble, would not be allowed to field McGrory as a player. Shortly after the appointment, Kilmarnock visited Celtic Park on Christmas Day (!) 1937; Celtic were in rampant form against the hapless Killie and led by 6-0 at half-time, and McGrory was rightly perturbed to learn later that Maley had insisted then on Celtic not letting up — in effect 'rubbing it in'. At the start of the new season (1938-39) Celtic again thrashed Kilmarnock by 9-1 at Parkhead, but perhaps Jimmy McGrory and Kilmarnock had the best revenge by knocking Celtic out of the cup between those crushing defeats.

There was a deeply disturbing scene in Maley's office after the cup tie. Understandably elated with the result, McGrory waited discreetly for a few minutes before entering the office to thank Maley for a sporting match and to accept his congratulations, but Maley sat at his desk in silence ignoring McGrory's presence and with his eyes fixed on some papers. Such poor sportsmanship on Maley's part was not lost on directors who felt that a change might be in the club's best interest.

The next season afforded the best excuse. Celtic started off brightly, and many sportswriters felt that the team would win everything. They thrashed Kilmarnock 9-1 on the opening match of the season, and followed that performance with a 6-2 win over Rangers, both games played at Celtic Park. The team could score away from home too, with a 5-1 romp at Tynecastle over Hearts, an 8-1 win at Coatbridge against Albion Rovers, and two 6-1 victories over Raith Rovers and Third Lanark at Parkhead. However, points were being dropped carelessly in drawn games against lowly opposition and a disastrous slump in form at Christmas and New Year ended any hope of a successful defence of the championship.

On Christmas Eve Celtic once more failed at Pittodrie where the club had not won since 1925-26. Now an ominous five points behind Rangers, Celtic visited Ibrox and before a record crowd of 118,567[4] in a frenzied atmosphere went down by 2-1, Celtic's misery was compounded by further losses to Queen's Park at Parkhead by 1-0 and by 4-0 to Raith Rovers at Kirkcaldy within the week (teams which finished at the bottom of the league). Celtic's challenge had foundered, and the team finished a distant second in the league, eleven points behind Rangers.

Celtic manager Willie Maley and trainer Jimmy McMenemy, c. 1937.

There were still hopes that the Scottish Cup might be captured, and Celtic began the campaign with an away tie against Burntisland Shipyard; arriving only two minutes before the kick-off, but ready to play, Celtic at one stage were in a 3-3 position, but pulled away to win 8-3. After a 7-1 win at Montrose, Celtic eliminated Hearts 2-1 after extra time at Parkhead in a midweek replay before a crowd of 80,840; however, in the quarter-final at Motherwell Celtic slumped to a 3-1 defeat, having played "bereft of inspiration and co-operation".

It was a miserable season for Maley, who had to deal with a highly talented squad cursed with inconsistency. Morale was low throughout the season, and injuries to key players contributed to the atmosphere. George Paterson and Malcolm MacDonald were sidelined for several matches, and the popular Jimmy Delaney broke his arm on 1 April, 1939, against Arbroath, an injury that put him out of action for two seasons. Several players were dissatisfied with their terms, possibly a hangover from a feeling that the team had not been adequately rewarded for the Exhibition Cup triumph. At the end of the season Paterson and Geatons initially refused to re-sign, the former seeking a benefit after seven years' service and the latter wanting a rise in wages. Maley too had his problems, engaged in a prolonged squabble with the directors over the taxation of his honorarium of 2,500 guineas, amid signs that he was losing his grip. He was absent for a long spell through illness and discipline had lapsed to the extent that dressing room regulations had to be tightened up, with "only directors, manager and trainer being allowed into the players' quarters before and after a match." (*Glasgow Observer*: 13 January, 1939.) These matters, allied to unspecified "rumours of the kind one doesn't like to hear", forced that newspaper's football correspondent to deny that a wholesale reorganisation at Parkhead was imminent, but they were straws in the wind.

At the start of the next campaign, however, most people were not too concerned about football.

Notes

1 Celtic's record home attendance. Attendance is widely quoted in reference works as being 92,000, but this figure seems to refer more likely to the potential capacity. The *Bulletin* report of the match lists 83,500 as the attendance and the account has an authentic ring to it. In similar vein, it should be noted that the architect's measurements for Ibrox indicated a potential capacity of 136,940, yet 118,567 attended the 1939 'Old Firm' Ne'erday fixture there with the gates closed 15 minutes before the kick-off.

2 and 3 See chapter 'The trophy room'.

4 Celtic has featured in record crowds for most competitions the club has played in: Scottish League: 118,567 vs Rangers (Ibrox) 2 January, 1939. Also a British league match record.

Scottish Cup: 146,433 vs Aberdeen (Hampden) 24 April, 1937. Also a European club match record.

League Cup: 107,609 vs Rangers (Hampden) 23 October, 1966.

European Cup: 136,505 vs Leeds United (Hampden) 15 April, 1970.

Premier League: 69,594 vs Rangers (Ibrox) 30 August, 1975. Record set on first day of the new league.

18

FORGOTTEN MEN, FORGOTTEN DAYS

AFTER the declaration of war on 3 September, 1939, the Scottish League suspended its operations 'for the duration', but the clubs formed regional divisions to carry on some form of football, although necessarily artificial. Wartime restrictions on travel and petrol shortages made it impossible for Lanarkshire clubs to fulfil fixtures in places as far away as Aberdeen, and so Celtic played in the Western Regional Division for the first season. It was a confusing period, the World War entering that phase to be known as 'the Phoney War', and Scottish football reflected that uncertainty. When it became apparent that no immediate danger threatened, and that the continuation of some form of football might provide a boost in morale for the civilian population, things became more organised. The majority of the clubs were grouped into a Southern League that continued to the end of the war six years later, with some sides deciding to disband, such as Kilmarnock whose ground was used as a munitions dump. Most players, as healthy, young men, were expected to volunteer or to be 'called up' for the forces, while others might be exempt because of their trades or through work at the shipyards. Players' wages were fixed at £2 a week with some expenses allowed, and clubs could arrange temporary transfers of players unable to travel to their regular clubs' grounds. Fears were expressed about the dangers posed by large crowds attending football matches and offering a target for German bombers, and for a time crowds were limited depending on the location; at Ibrox, where 118,567 had watched the 1939 match between Rangers and Celtic, the maximum allowed was 15,000.

Celtic endured a great deal of internal strife during this first season and most concerned the deteriorating relationship between manager and Board. The only security that any manager has is success, and sometimes even that is not enough. Maley, now 71 years of age, had been Celtic's only manager, his association with the club extending back 52 years; he had led the club to its most glittering triumphs, but

163

these had become more sporadic in recent seasons, although a renaissance of sorts was apparent with substantial accomplishments in the late '30s.

The relationship between the manager and his directors had become progressively uneasy. The Board, despite its protestations in the mid '30s that Maley was secure in his position, noted the manager's age and that his health had started to fail (he had been absent for much of the disappointing 1938-39 season) and resented increasingly Maley's autocratic approach. An unfortunate dispute over money was an indication of the coolness that existed. Friction still lingered between the club and Maley over the honorarium presented at the Jubilee Dinner to "our wonderful manager" by the chairman. Maley, despite the munificence of the gift, was incensed at having to pay tax on it and wrangled with the Board for some time about the issue. The Board was bemused at the dispute, and perturbed at the team and officials continuing to dine at the Bank Restaurant, owned by Maley but described by Desmond White later, in the preface to the club's official history, as "hardly the place to feed a football team, as it was really a glorified public house frequented by bookmakers and others" . . . and having to pay the full rate for the privilege.

This attitude towards the Bank Restaurant betrayed a snobbery unworthy of the club's background and its Christian origins. The Bank may not have been the most acceptable of restaurants, but it was 'a fitba' howff' where men would gather for discussions about the game amid comfortable surroundings. The young would meet for advice, the old would gather for reminiscence, and retired players, down on their luck, would drop in for a meal and often enough a 'loan' of money from Maley. Sometimes these improvident ex-players would insist on leaving memorabilia as pledges with Maley to salve their pride, and the respected journalist John Macadam was once given a Cup medal, left by a famous internationalist, with these words from Maley: "You're fond of these things, and you'd better keep it; I don't know where he's got to, but I don't think he'll be back."

Maley was too proud to consider resignation, although he kept giving hints about the time "when my work will have to be handed over to younger hands". He felt that he still had a contribution to make to the club, but an opportunity for the Board to act arose with the shocking decline in the team's playing standards during the first wartime season. In 1938 Celtic had won the championship with the side that also gained the Empire Exhibition Trophy, but in December, 1939, Celtic were near the foot of the table although only two changes had occurred in the line-up, Kennaway having returned to the United States at the outbreak of the war and Delaney being still missing with his arm break. Around Christmas, 1939, Maley met with Tom White, the chairman, to discuss

164

the situation and it was a tense meeting, the upshot being Maley's retiral from his responsibilities as manager and secretary. The 'retiral' was not voluntary as Maley considered that he still had much to offer the club, perhaps as secretary, and he was understandably bitter about the turn of events, so much so that he did not attend a Celtic game at Parkhead until almost ten years later.

The brief announcement of the news, released on Ne'erday 1940 with little publicity in newspapers whose sporting coverage was understandably curtailed in wartime, was barely expanded upon officially a month later in the programme for the Celtic-Morton match at Parkhead on 10 February: "Since our last issue Mr. William Maley has retired after serving the club for fifty-two years. The parting cannot fail to cause widespread regret, and to Mr. Maley probably most of all, as the club and all it stands for has been his life's work. May his leisure be long and full of happiness is the prayer of every true Celt!" Sadly, Maley's leisure, while long, was not happy, as he lived another 18 years a bitter man, upset at what he considered scurvy treatment, though the parting was inevitable in the circumstances.

The post of manager was offered to Jimmy McStay, a former captain of the team who had recently completed a successful first season as manager of Alloa, while Desmond White, the chairman's son and a chartered accountant, assumed the role of secretary (a position he would hold, among other responsibilities until his death in 1985). Jimmy McStay did not have the chance to be a real manager. Despite the promise from the Celtic directors of a free hand in running the club such as he had enjoyed in guiding Alloa to promotion to the first division, he found himself hamstrung in his efforts to keep Celtic going as a force in wartime football. Robert Kelly admitted in his autobiography that McStay could be considered "a part-time manager" and that Celtic had already earmarked his successor. One has to consider this a disquieting confession, since the question arises as to whether McStay was informed about the caretaker nature of his appointment. If he was not told, it was an unworthy deception; if he was, it was a mystifying and morale-sapping decision. According to Kelly, Celtic were really interested in Jimmy McGrory, appointed manager of Kilmarnock in 1937. Presuming that he was available, it would have been much more fair to McStay for Celtic to have moved for McGrory in 1940, if that was their ultimate intention.

McStay's problems were not far to find. He inherited largely an Empire Exhibition team that was playing without spirit or motivation. The players, sensing that wartime football was unreal, that the wages were too low, that training was curtailed, that Maley was losing control, had become dispirited, but contrarily still compared McStay unfavourably with Maley at his best. They saw immediately that McStay was self-effacing, unlike Maley who could be dictatorial, and perceived that the newcomer was relatively ill-at-ease, following in the steps of a commanding figure steeped in the politics of Celtic Park. In contrast to Maley who had acted as both manager and secretary, McStay was appointed as manager only and remained an outsider whose only hope of survival was to achieve outstanding success under the most adverse of conditions.

Celtic's Board clearly decided not to take wartime football seriously, and that error in judgement affected the playing standards of the club for the six war years and for some seasons afterwards. The club that had raised the morale and spirit of a local community in its early years now neglected its primary mandate, in effect refusing to entertain its support. Other clubs availed themselves of the chance to field players normally based in England but stationed in Scotland for brief periods. Thus, unfashionable clubs like Morton used Stanley Matthews and Tommy Lawton, Hamilton Academicals obtained Frank Swift, Partick Thistle used Bill Shankly, Aberdeen got Stan Mortenson, while Hibernian profited by Matt Busby's influence. In particular, the opportunity to field Busby was squandered. The Manchester City wing-half, a Lanarkshire man, found himself stationed in Scotland and volunteered his services to Celtic. McStay was delighted, realising the beneficial effects that such a player and personality would have on his youngsters. He approached the directors for their permission to field him, but to his astonishment and disappointment he was turned down. Rumoured to be 'Celtic-daft', Busby trained a few times at Celtic Park hoping for a game, but eventually was persuaded by Hibs to guest for them. Many perceptive critics trace the Edinburgh side's fine showing after the war to the influence of Busby; Busby, by then, was with Manchester United and embarking on a glittering managerial career. One is left to speculate ruefully on the wasted opportunity that conceivably might have led to Busby's taking over a similar role at Parkhead instead.

Alex Dowdells, who was appointed Celtic's trainer in 1940 and retained the position until his move to Leicester in 1956, had little doubt that the seeds of the club's troubles after the war were sown when the decision to do without guest players was made: "Celtic had a vintage period before I went to Parkhead in 1940, but when the war came and players' wages were cut to £2 a week many boys thought it wasn't worth playing seriously and so the standard of the team went down. But one of the biggest factors in Celtic's decline was the decision not to have guest players during the war. Guest players did a good job in maintaining a standard of play as well as bringing on a nucleus of youngsters; but not at Parkhead. Not only were the new boys not being prepared, but the standards had slumped. So, when the war ended and football restarted in earnest, we were in a bad way."

Celtic arranged to employ some players from other clubs on a short-term basis such as Waddell (Aberdeen), a centre-half who had returned to Bishopbriggs to work as a plumber before joining up in the forces, as well as Johnstone, a goalkeeper from the same club, who also returned to Glasgow. McStay used his contacts with Alloa to sign up Ferguson and Gillan; McGrory may have used his influence at Kilmarnock to persuade Hunter and Dornan to report to Celtic Park. None of these players was of traditional Celtic class, unfortunately. Other players with stronger Celtic connections were ignored. Frank and Hugh O'Donnell wrote to McStay offering their services but were turned down by the Board, and Frank played for Hearts during the war. Willie Buchan, a prolific scorer, played for Stenhousemuir and Charlie Napier, another effective forward, signed on for Falkirk, as did John Fitzsimmons, a goalscoring outside-left destined to become better known as the Celtic team doctor in later years.

A typical Celtic side of the early war seasons would be this one (which played in Celtic's first Southern League Cup game at Airdrie on 1 March, 1941, and won 2-1): Johnstone (Aberdeen), Hogg, Milne, MacDonald, Waddell (Aberdeen), McLaughlin, Lynch, Divers, Crum, Gillan (Alloa), Murphy.

McStay had the authority to sign youngsters, juvenile players, juniors, Boys' Guild players and schoolboys, but had to have the approval of the directors for any approach to a top-notch performer. Permission was rarely granted. He was forced to field teams that were not ready, consisting of mere apprentices. R. E. Kingsley ('Rex') described the situation: "It used to be a big thrill to beat Celtic; now clubs consider it an indignity if they don't. It may be dire necessity which demands the fielding of so many youngsters who should in the ordinary way be in the reserve side, but it's a bit sad to watch just the same. These Celtic youngsters are all clever, but they're all at the same stage and need a Matt Busby to father them." (*Sunday Mail*: 7 February, 1943.)

He signed some lads at an early age and had the satisfaction of seeing them mature into fine players. Willie Miller (Maryhill Harp), an exceptional keeper signed in 1942 at 17, John McPhail (Strathclyde) also 17 years of age and only recently out of St. Mungo's Academy, signed in 1941 and Bobby Evans (St. Anthony's) signed on at 16 in 1944. Many others were engaged but, lacking the coaching and training, did not develop as might be expected. Too much depended on the veterans such as Delaney, who made a welcome return in 1941-42, Paterson, whose appearances were dependent on weekend passes from the RAF, Hogg, always steady at right-back, and Malcolm MacDonald, most gifted and temperamental of players.

However, it became clear that McStay was not in complete charge of selection and that his suggestions might be overruled at the last minute. Several prominent players, given leave by their commanding officers in order to play football, were allowed to watch from the sidelines despite the manager's frustration. Peculiar formations were fielded, such as the forward line given the task of beating England's keeper, Frank Swift, who was guesting for Hamilton Accies: McDonald P., McAuley, Rae, McGowan, Long — the sort of players that 'Rex' was to describe as "should have been sitting in the boys' chair at the barber's". For an important Summer Cup tie against Hibs in Edinburgh in 1945 — Jimmy McStay's last game as manager — the following inside-forwards were selected: McPhail ('Big John'), Gallacher ('Big Jackie'), McLaughlin ('Big Joe') — a trio that might well have qualified as the heaviest and most ponderous in the club's history. Malcolm MacDonald, "a football genius", was frequently fielded at full-back where his constructive talents were wasted. The truth was that McStay had got so discouraged that eventually he had given up selecting the team and left that to the directors. The consequence was that Celtic's line-up frequently did not make much sense and caused a supporter to recall the definition of a camel as "a horse designed by a committee". The youngsters did not have a chance to develop properly, as team selection varied wildly from week to week and the result was justifiable unrest among the players. Crum and Divers went to Morton in the close-season of 1942. Gillan and Long were allowed to leave despite the manager's legitimate protest that it left the team short of acceptable players. Other men such as Kelly, Young and Duncan left with no great effort being made to retain them. Celtic lost some valuable players this way. John Kelly, a clever winger on right and left, departed for Morton and later was transferred to Barnsley for whom he was playing when he gained caps against Wales and Ireland in 1949. Davie Duncan, a strong, straightforward outside-left went to East Fife and won three caps in 1948 against France, Switzerland and Belgium at a period Celtic were desperate to find a left-winger. Hugh Long, a useful half-back, was transferred to Clyde and was chosen for Scotland against Ireland in 1947. Andy Young later formed part of that fine Raith Rovers' half-back line of Young, Colville and Leigh, and Joe McLaughlin joined him at Kirkcaldy after gaining a Scottish Cup winners' medal with Aberdeen in the first post-war season.

For many Celtic supporters the most unacceptable aspect of this period, unofficial as it was, became the virtual yielding of football supremacy in Scotland to Rangers. Rangers had dominated the 20s, but Celtic were staging a revival in the 30s. Sadly, during the war Celtic made little effort to compete with the Ibrox club.

It was a sad contrast to the club's performance during the First World War and two commentaries illustrate the difference. In a five-part history of the club printed in 1927 in the *Glasgow Observer* the following statement appeared: "The fame of our great club is world-wide; during the War the trenches of Flanders and Gallipoli resounded with talk of the Celtic." But during the Second World War one supporter, serving in the Forces and expressing the dissatisfaction of many, wrote to a newspaper to suggest that the name 'Celtic' be dropped for the duration of the war or until a team worthy of the club's glorious past could be fielded.

" HE'S FED UP ABOUT CELTIC."
How the Celtic fans serving overseas must have felt about wartime results, as viewed by the Sunday Mail *cartoonist, 17 December, 1944.*

Consider the league standings:[1]

		P	W	D	L	F	A	Pts	Psn
Rangers	1939-40	30	22	4	4	72	36	48	1st
	1940-41	30	21	4	5	79	33	46	1st
	1941-42	30	22	4	4	97	35	48	1st
	1942-43	30	22	6	2	89	23	50	1st
	1943-44	30	23	4	3	90	27	50	1st
	1944-45	30	23	3	4	88	27	49	1st
Celtic	1939-40	30	9	6	15	55	61	24	13th
	1940-41	30	14	6	10	48	40	34	5th
	1941-42	30	15	9	6	69	50	39	3rd
	1942-43	30	10	8	12	61	76	28	10th
	1943-44	30	18	7	5	71	43	43	2nd
	1944-45	30	20	2	8	70	42	42	2nd

The totals were more depressing:

	P	W	D	L	F	A	Pts
Rangers	180	133	25	22	515	181	291
Celtic	180	86	38	56	374	312	210

What accounted for Rangers' supremacy? It was accomplished by greater effort and organisation, under the leadership of Bill Struth. The Rangers' manager saw that his priority was to provide entertainment for their supporters by turning out winning teams and he expended considerable energy in achieving his aim. He made it part of his job to find war work for his players as close to Ibrox as possible, and thus Rangers were a more settled team than most. He decided to field a reserve team that played in the North-Eastern League despite the travelling inconvenience, and provided adequate back-up strength with players like Rae and Little who could have won places in any other side; he retained the mystique of Rangers' superiority by making strenuous efforts to keep Ibrox Park a showplace throughout the war; he fielded guest players including Stanley Matthews, but more regularly Gillick and Caskie of Everton who were happy to return to Rangers on a full-time basis after the war. Above all he gave the impression that he was in complete charge of operations at Ibrox, unlike McStay at Parkhead.

Some Celtic supporters (and historians) have been critical of Rangers' success during the war, pointing out that the period is considered 'unofficial' and hinting that the Ibrox club had taken advantage of the wartime situation to strengthen its position in Scottish football; the charges are correct in both instances but Rangers can not be criticised on those grounds. Under the dynamic leadership of Struth Rangers continued as they had done between the wars, as the most consistent and successful Scottish club. Struth, as manager, was quite right in perceiving that his duty to his club and its support was to carry on as best he could to provide entertainment and success. The entertainment they provided was a contribution to the general morale of the civilian population; the success was a boost to the club's support. Any Celtic criticism must be regarded as sour grapes. An article in *The Celtic View* in 1984 suggested that Celtic were forced to field makeshift sides because so many of their players were in the Forces and that Rangers were able to field a regular side throughout the war. This is a false accusation: most changes in Celtic's line-up were caused by the lack of success and smacked of experimentation enforced by panic, and a number of the pre-war players were available for much of the war. Rangers did field a more settled team because it was a winning side and changes were unnecessary. The charge that those Rangers' players who were in the Forces were given preferential treatment was manifestly false, notably in the case of Willie Thornton, described as a member of the 'BEF', the abbreviation for the British Expeditionary Force sarcastically rendered in the article as 'Back Every Friday'. Thornton, a splendid centre-forward and a most sporting player, played only 17 games for Rangers during military service (at times overseas), a period in which he won the Military Medal for gallantry.[2]

Pointedly, Willie Maley, writing for a Glasgow paper, praised Rangers for their superior effort: "(Rangers) undoubtedly showed a splendid example to their neighbours in that they showed in all their work a zeal and energy which brought them the great success they have achieved in 1939-40."

In fairness to McStay, it should be noted that an improvement occurred in the last two seasons, 1943-44 and 1944-45, with Celtic finishing second each time in the Southern League and winning both games at Ibrox to atone for a lamentable display in 1943 when the Ne'erday fixture was lost by 8-1 (on that day Crum, playing for Morton against St. Mirren, scored six goals). The fine performances of Miller in goal delighted the supporters, but too much responsibility was being

Jimmy Delaney, Celtic's most prominent wartime player, evades Jock 'Tiger' Shaw of Rangers during a match in 1944/45 season.

placed on Jimmy Delaney. Delaney was a Will-o'-the-wisp figure darting everywhere, and playing well at outside-right or at centre; one letter-writer noted that he was Celtic's one real forward and that "the others may as well be in Janefield Cemetery". During 1943-44 Celtic kept in touch with Rangers in the league till New Year's Day when Rangers won 3-1 at Parkhead, and played consistently to finish second seven points behind. Despite the frustration felt by many at the frequent changes that made it difficult for the younger players to settle and develop, the supporters continued to turn up to encourage the team. They hoped for a breakthrough in the Southern League Cup that followed the league programme and the side performed excitingly in the sectional play with victories, home and away, over Partick Thistle, Falkirk and Hamilton; the match at Firhill was a thriller, 38,000 watching Celtic win 1-0 through a goal scored by McAloon, recently signed from Wolverhampton. However, in the semi-final Celtic faced the favourites, Rangers, and lost 4-2 before 87,000 at Hampden in a keenly contested game. It was much the same the following season with Celtic again finishing seven points behind Rangers in the league, the highlight of the campaign being the winning goal by George Paterson against Rangers on New Year's Day, 1945, from 35 yards.

However, McStay had become discouraged by his lack of authority and the directors were looking to replace him. While on holiday with his family at Ayr in July, 1945, McStay learned of the rumours about his impending dismissal via the newspapers and met the chairman, Tom White, upon his return. Seemingly, even as he alighted from the tramcar at Parkhead Cross, he noticed a newspaper billboard announcing that Jimmy McGrory was likely to take over at Celtic Park. The meeting was short, with White asking him to hand in his resignation.

Despite the obstacles placed in his path, under him Celtic won the Glasgow Cup in 1940-41, the Charity Cup in 1942-43, the Victory-in-Europe trophy in 1945, and managed respectable league finishes in his last two seasons in charge. Perhaps McStay had some justification for his contention that he was treated unfairly and judged harshly, but his self-confessed unassertiveness had surely undermined his position. It does, however, say a great deal for his loyalty that he soon offered his services to Jimmy McGrory as a scout.

The circumstances surrounding the dismissal of two managers within the space of five years forces an assessment of the Board. Clearly the directors exercised their rightful prerogative in the hiring and firing of managers, but the decisions did little for the stability of the club in such difficult times. More significantly, perhaps, the vacuum left by the departure of a strong manager in Willie Maley was to be filled for a quarter of a century by a Board (or rather, for the most part, a chairman) whose assumption of the control that Maley had latterly exercised in team selection would come repeatedly into question.

Notes
1 1939-40 in Western Regional League; other wartime seasons in Southern League.
2 Information from *Growing with glory*: Ian Peebles, 1973.

19

POST-WAR BLUES

THERE was an air of excitement as the supporters waited for the start of the first post-war season. In May 1945 Celtic had won the Victory-in-Europe Cup and that was considered an omen of better times. Really there should have been no grounds for optimism, because at Celtic Park the preparations for full-time football were inadequate. The stadium was in a dreadful state of disrepair after years of wartime shortages and pardonable neglect. On the terracing weeds had sprouted in places, while the wooden steps and barriers were rotting and dangerous; the roof of the covered enclosure was leaking in spots and flakes of rust floated down on spectators on match days. 'Paradise' had a hollow, mocking ring to it.

The supporters watched the flurry of off-field developments with general satisfaction; a wave of approval greeted the appointment of Jimmy McGrory as manager, although there were misgivings about the abrupt firing of Jimmy McStay. McGrory, modest and soft-spoken, returned to Celtic Park having gained valuable and successful experience at Kilmarnock. Another pre-war stalwart, Chic Geatons, returned as coach for the youngsters, while great hopes were expressed about the capture of Tommy Kiernan, a proven goalscorer bought from Albion Rovers for £4,000.

It was to prove a difficult season for the new manager in coping with his players, an uneasy blend of veterans and youngsters. Some members of the famous side that won the Empire Exhibition Trophy were still on the books, but all were in the veteran class and the new manager was realistic enough to ring the changes. It was felt that John Divers was too slow and he was given a free transfer to rejoin Morton. He inflicted a great deal of damage on Celtic in the next three seasons with his intelligent play. MacDonald lost form before being dropped, and immediately demanded a transfer which was granted with a move to Brentford. Hogg and Paterson continued to give good service and held their places, but in February 1946 the club and the supporters suffered the greatest blow with the loss of Jimmy Delaney to Manchester United. He was the last real link with the pre-war days, still capable of taking the half chance and above all a man who could lift the spirits of the team with his enthusiasm and example.

Delaney stressed that he had no quarrel with the club, indicating that his concern was financial security; at 31 and with lingering fears about his arm injury, he had reason to be worried. No footballer in Scotland was going to make a fortune from the game. The executive of the Players' Association, formed earlier in the year, approached the clubs on 18 October, 1945, with the following proposals: that the regular wage for a first-team player should be £6 a week; that bonuses of £2 be given for a win, and £1 for a draw. The clubs agreed to the bonus clause but rejected the basic wage, offering £4 instead, to which the players gave a very reluctant assent. Perhaps the clubs had no real choice, but the consequences were crippling for the Scottish game. Many players, including Delaney, were forced to move south for higher wages.

The younger players posed different problems for the harassed manager. Those still in the Forces or embarking on National Service had to rely on the good will of their commanding officers for weekend passes and often the manager had to wait till noon on Saturday to find out if they were available.

Celtic never really settled in that first, unofficial season and finished a distant fourth behind Rangers, Hibernian and Aberdeen; for Celtic it was a continuation of wartime woes, and it was these clubs who had made the greatest efforts to continue football during the war who were rewarded with success.

The hopes of a trophy rested on the Victory Cup, organised to celebrate the successful end of the war. Starting in late April it was an early experiment in summer football and crowds packed Muirton and Stark's Park to watch Celtic win with ease over St. Johnstone (8-2) and Raith Rovers (2-0) and so qualify for the semi-final against Rangers. On 1 June, 1946, at Hampden the sides battled to a 0-0 deadlock before 66,000 spectators. Rangers had much more of the play, but Celtic's defence was resolute and Miller, who had been considered doubtful before the game with a wrist injury, was superb in goal, particularly with a salmon-like leap to deflect a raging shot from Thornton.

The replay before 46,000 on the following Wednesday was a bitter experience for Celtic. Rangers won the toss to take advantage of a strong wind but led by only 1-0 at the interval, a score-line that left Celtic with a great chance to win. There were ominous scenes in the Celtic dressing-room at half-time as Paterson, the side's captain and usually the most even-tempered of players, complained bitterly to the club officials that the referee did not appear to be at his physical or

175

mental best; other players supported the complaint, some adding that they could smell liquor on his breath.

The second half was a fiasco. Sirrell, who had troubled Shaw in the first half with his clever play, received a further injury to his ankle and was rendered useless. A few minutes later Rangers were awarded a penalty kick, a decision by Mr Dale that appeared harsh as Thornton clearly 'dived'; Paterson, holding the ball, appealed strenuously against the award and was ordered off when he was reluctant to hand it over. Mallan had been dragging his feet over the penalty spot in disgust, and he was sent off too. Four spectators, enraged at the proceedings, aimed themselves in the direction of the referee but were stopped well short of their target by the police and removed. Young scored from the spot and Rangers advanced to the final, winners by 2-0 over a Celtic side eventually reduced to seven fit players, Gallacher having to retire with his injury and Sirrell limping.

The referee came in for a great deal of criticism for his handling of the match, and his particular actions during the penalty incident, but this public sympathy was of little consolation to Celtic. The subsequent punishments were even more difficult to accept: Mallan and Paterson were suspended for three months and, amazingly Matt Lynch, who had not received a caution and who had absented himself from the dispute over the penalty, was suspended for one month. Lynch was so incensed against this afterthought of the referee that he appealed against his suspension and was supported by the testimony of his immediate opponent, Duncanson, who cleared the Celt in writing of any wrongdoing; to this day Lynch has the letter which exonerates him completely, and adds jokingly that he intends to keep it "as it will help me get into Heaven". Despite this sporting gesture on the part of the Rangers player, the appeal was turned down, and on this note the first peacetime season ended with Celtic surprisingly not pursuing the matter, as they should have done to protect their players from unfair punishment.

Matters were to get worse in the next two seasons because the Celtic side of that time was poor, managing on good days to raise its game only to the mediocre; it offered neither satisfaction on the field, nor hope for the future. More and more the support was becoming agitated at the lack of success. Things reached crisis proportions early in September, 1946, after a mid-week game at Parkhead won 4-1 by Third Lanark. Crowds of supporters gathered outside the main entrance to the stand to call for the resignation of the chairman, Mr Tom White; police were called in to disperse the demonstrators, now swollen to two thousand, and to move them back from the club's property to London Road, a public thoroughfare, where the protest continued until after the chairman had left the premises. That same week the executive of the Celtic

Supporters Association met to consider a boycott of the forthcoming 'Old Firm' match, proposed by their Rangers' counterparts as a protest against Celtic's raising the stand price to 7/6d (37.5p). The executive rejected that proposal, but discussed at some length a questionnaire to be presented to the directors. Several key issues were raised: the signing of new players, the scouting system, the training and fitness programmes, wages and bonuses, the financial security of retired players and inevitably the responsibility for the team selection. The Supporters Association, inaugurated in September, 1944, had passed a most important test with credit and dignity; without resorting to the blackmail of a boycott they had made their position known — that of a reasonable and informed body of support, concerned enough to offer constructive criticism. Yet, in Glasgow, the football supporter suffers very often from a form of schizophrenia: on one side, a wide knowledge and a genuine love of the game; on the other, a fierce, partisan loyalty to one team. Is it this classic confrontation between reason and emotion that makes his reaction so volatile and unpredictable? During and after the match, in the company of his fellow-supporters, nobody can be more harshly critical of his team's performance, but back at work on Monday nobody is quicker to take offence at any criticism offered by an outsider.

Between a great club and its support there exists a rapport, enhanced by tradition and sustained by habit. The links that bind the supporter to his team have been forged in the heat of emotion, in the joy of victory or in the gloom of defeat; in the rage of a vital goal disallowed, or the delight of one scored late in the game; in the haze of anger at a Celtic player injured and unattended, or in the electricity of tension before a match with Rangers. The ties that bind him with the club are different in kind but just as lasting. Many of the thousands who throng the terracings at Celtic Park today are descended from those who were the beneficiaries of the original purpose of the club and for them the loyalty is a little more intense. In 1946 it had been too long since Celtic supporters had celebrated consistent success.

In the first seasons after the war money was a real problem at Celtic Park. The search was for a goalscorer and early in 1946-47 the veteran McAloon (Brentford) came in a straight swop for Paterson who was still depressed by his suspension; in February 1946 the money received for Delaney had been spent in purchasing Bogan from Hibernian.

The results showed a slight improvement and thoughts of relegation were cast aside for a while but, disturbingly, a coarseness had been allowed to creep into the play. At Ibrox on New Year's Day 1947, 50 free kicks marred the contest and 34 were awarded to Rangers, statistics which detracted from the 1-1 result; only ten days later Willie Gallacher was sent off when playing against Queen's Park; and in the last league game of the season Sirrell was ordered off along with Watson of Motherwell. Playing in such a hard, physical style Celtic had been expected to do well in the hurly-burly of the Scottish Cup and the first-round defeat at Dundee was a bitter disappointment. Despite having to play at Dens Park, Celtic started as clear favourites over the Division B side, but to the distress of many supporters in the all-ticket crowd it was the outsiders who played the attractive football to win deservedly by 2-1. Celtic had contributed little to the proceedings except muscle and it was only a defensive error with four minutes left that brought a consolation goal for Celtic.

On 4 March, 1947, Tom White died. The loss of the chairman was a severe blow, and it seemed doubly unfortunate that the man who had helped guide the club to some of its greatest triumphs should have died when its fortunes were at their lowest. Since the end of the war his health had been failing and White, a director since 1906 and chairman from 1914, had been unable to assume the dynamic role the times required. His place as chairman was taken over by Robert Kelly, but there was no immediate improvement; indeed things were to get even worse during the next season.

CELTIC FOOTBALL CLUB, 1946-47.
Back row: Lynch, McMillan, Hogg, Miller, McDonald, Milne. Front row: Jordan, Kiernan, Rae, McAloon, Hazlett.

The main problem lay among the forwards ('the Five Sorrowful Mysteries' as the more religious called them). Nine league games after New Year in 1948 produced only three goals, and two of them came from the penalty spot. Willie Corbett the centre-half was under considerable pressure, but he scored the winning goals against Aberdeen and Falkirk from penalties. At Brockville a tense, physical match had reached injury time when Celtic were awarded a soft penalty. The Falkirk players milled around the referee protesting in the hope that the rumpus and the delay would have its effect on Corbett's nerves; the Celt placed the ball on the spot, looked thoughtfully at Jerry Dawson, an ex-Ranger, in goal and hammered the ball low into the corner of the net at the right-hand post.

After Morton knocked Celtic out of the Scottish Cup at Ibrox in the semi-final, Celtic's league form went into a complete tailspin and there was increasing tension as the team slipped down the table into the relegation zone. On the Thursday night of 15 April, 1948, the regular board meeting at Celtic Park lasted much longer than usual as the directors discussed Saturday's game at Dens against Dundee. It was Celtic's last league game of the season, and it was shaping up as a critical one for the club; in recent seasons Celtic had flirted with the spectre of relegation but this time the threat seemed real. Another loss at Dundee, where they had been defeated soundly in the past, or even a draw, would mean an agonizing wait as the other threatened clubs fought grimly to pass Celtic's total; a win would preserve their status.

The stage was set for Dens Park, but rightly most sports writers were too concerned about the Rangers-Morton cup final, due to be played on the same day, to be unduly occupied with the grim struggle at Dundee, and Celtic received the appropriate reward for mediocrity — neglect. When the team was announced it contained a few surprises. For the first time Bobby Evans was picked at right-half, while behind him Bobby Hogg was selected for the last time as a final tribute to his experience; Jock Weir, signed from Blackburn Rovers three months previously, moved to the right wing, and John McPhail made a welcome re-appearance after injury as his partner.

A crowd of 31,000, many of whom had travelled from Glasgow with all their customary enthusiasm, saw Celtic take command early, hoping for a quick goal to calm relegation nerves. Play was bright and attractive, the only sign of tension being the occasional hurried pass, and the immediate aim of a goal was realised after 14 minutes when Weir netted amid scenes of jubilation on the terracing. Those same supporters were plunged into despair only an hour later when MacKay scored to give Dundee a 2-1 lead, and once again threaten Celtic's future. Dundee, free from anxiety, were playing cultured football and had assumed command of the game. Celtic, with a touch of desperation in their play, took a grip of the struggle and started to exert a pressure that became more intense as the minutes ticked away: Evans, a revelation at right-half, raced to take every throw-in, the normally plodding McAuley galloped to take free kicks; McPhail's searching passes probed for weaknesses, while Weir harried the left flank to trouble the keeper with his attentions. For once in that luckless season effort was rewarded, when Weir equalised and a bare two minutes from time scrambled home the winner — his own third goal.

The last blast of the referee's whistle was the prelude to Celtic's pent-up relief. The players hugged each other and danced with joy (and in 1948 players were less demonstrative than at present); the terracings were a swirling sea of green and white.

Still, victory in a relegation battle is at best a tarnished glory, and all the emotion generated by the win could not conceal the fact that it was a situation that never should have involved a club of Celtic's stature. Clearly, a strong case could have been presented in 1948 for replacing Jimmy McGrory as manager. By Celtic standards his record was deplorable: a three-year slide to the brink of relegation, annual dismissal from the League Cup at the early stages, a defeat in the first round of the Scottish Cup by a Division B side, not even the consolation of a Glasgow or Charity Cup. Of the players bought from other clubs (Kiernan, Bogan, McAloon and Weir) none was a complete success, although Weir repaid his transfer fee with his three goals at Dundee. Ironically, of the players released or transferred, Divers had helped Morton to the Scottish Cup final, and Delaney starred for Manchester United against Blackpool at Wembley a week after Weir performed his unexpected heroics.

McGrory admitted later how close he had come to leaving: "I had the worst experience I've ever had in football, the spectre of relegation haunting Celtic . . . It was with a heavy heart and a great deal of anxiety that we left Celtic Park for Dundee on 17 April that year. On the way north I discussed the situation with our new chairman, Bob Kelly. I knew inwardly that if Celtic lost I would have to resign after only a couple of years in the managerial chair." (*A Lifetime in Paradise*: Jimmy McGrory/Gerry McNee, 1975.) What saved him was the loyalty of the chairman, and his own character. Nobody in Scottish football, player or manager, has been more deservedly loved than Jimmy McGrory. He was totally genuine and sincere, he was quiet and modest, he was incapable of malice or nastiness; in short, he did not have the ruthless streak that successful managers seem to require.

When he became chairman, Bob Kelly was relatively young, filled with energy, and dedicated to the task of making Celtic great once again. He felt that a successful 'partnership' between himself as chairman and McGrory as manager could be established because they

180

had much in common: both were devout Catholics and men of principle, both were kindly and charitable men who would have been embarrassed to hear themselves described so, both were cautious and traditional in their approach to football. In general, both felt that Celtic teams and players should be reared at Parkhead, imbued with Celtic tradition and pride, and play clean, constructive football. Sad to relate, it was an arrangement that had little hope of success. No manager can feel equal to a chairman, and no manager can feel comfortable dealing with the chairman who determines his salary, who can withhold raises, and who has the power to dismiss him. Historically the roles differ: the chairman is concerned with the club, its policies and traditions, the manager involved with the team, its selections and performances. Too often, however, the roles overlap and in British football there have been frequent interventions from the board room to the detriment of the team. Discussions between Bob Kelly and Jimmy McGrory were often decided by the personality of the two men; both were fundamentally private men and disliked confrontation, although Bob Kelly adopted an austere, autocratic manner and an air of gruffness to compensate for this trait. Thus, his opinions were expressed in terms more forceful than required, and he could be intimidating, and his views on most football matters were clear and rigidly held. Jimmy McGrory was equally reserved but, unlike the chairman, often assumed a more diffident attitude which at times was mistaken for meekness. A personality as strong as Bob Kelly found it difficult to accept views differing from his own; a personality as modest as Jimmy McGrory was too willing to consider seriously others' opinions. Both could say in all honesty, and they did, that they rarely disagreed, but this was because the manager deferred too often to his chairman's wishes.

Bob Kelly was reluctant to consider releasing McGrory because he had a great personal liking and respect for "the finest man's man in football" as he described him; in a club that valued tradition and continuity, it was almost distasteful to contemplate another change in manager within such a short period. It has been said that discussions took place around the late 1940s among the directors about approaching Matt Busby; it would have been a futile attempt as Busby, now established as manager of Manchester United, was not available. Besides, Busby, who was known to have removed directors from the dressing-room before talking to his players, would not have tolerated any interference from the boardroom in the selection of the team. If such discussions ever did take place, the thought of a manager capable of acting so independently would have resolved the matter.

20

RESPECTABILITY

Celtic take the field for a friendly vs Lazio in Rome, May 1950. John McPhail leads out Celtic followed by goalkeeper John Bonnar. Score was 0-0.

CELTIC were determined to regain the respect of the football world, the directors rightly seeing that the escape from the disgrace of relegation was a matter for relief and not celebration. Under the leadership of Bob Kelly the directors and manager at last saw the need for positive action. They engaged a new coach, the vastly experienced Jimmy Hogan who was credited with influencing profoundly the development of the game in Austria and Hungary, but by 1948 he was almost 70 years of age. Celtic had tried for months to persuade Wilf Mannion (Middlesbrough), the England inside-forward, to move north, but his club was not serious about releasing him, and negotiations broke down. They captured Charlie Tully from Belfast Celtic for £8,000, but could not land his team mates, Currie and Vernon, signed John Bonnar from Arbroath as a back-up for Miller, and when the forward line still proved inconsistent they persuaded Leslie Johnston of Clyde to join them.

Over the course of the next three seasons Celtic were a respectable side, neither more nor less, often promising more than was achieved. Celtic teams produced memorable performances with outstanding victories or shock defeats, and so unpredictable was their form that the supporters felt a kinship with the long-suffering followers of Partick Thistle. The championship, to be dominated by a strong Rangers side with its 'Iron Curtain' defence and an attractive Hibernian team with its 'Famous Five' forward line, would always be out of reach for such an inconsistent side, but the occasional breakthrough in cup competition cheered up the supporters.

On 27 September, 1948, Celtic won their first trophy since the war in the Glasgow Cup against Third Lanark with a crowd of 87,000 looking on; earlier in the tournament Celtic had defeated Partick Thistle in a replay before 51,000 at Parkhead, and Queen's Park at Hampden before 39,000 — crowds that indicated clearly the enthusiasm, optimism and the hunger for success that permeated those days. In the final Thirds started off playing inspired football, fluent in attack with Jimmy Mason, an inside-man of the traditional Scottish school, orchestrating their forwards with a flow of precision passes, and Bobby Mitchell, a gangling unorthodox winger, bewildering Celtic defenders in a virtuoso performance. Several fine saves by Miller kept Celtic's hopes alive, as Thirds led by only 1-0 at half-time.

Five minutes into the second half the turning point came. Mitchell shot a penalty kick against the base of Miller's right-hand post and, conscious of a reprieve, Celtic bounced back into the game. Willie Gallacher, Patsy's son, scored one of his infrequent goals for the equaliser. Thirds held out until eight minutes from the end when a long, swerving shot from Jock Weir found the net high up with Petrie groping, dazzled by the sun and deceived by the infamous Hampden swirl. Just before the end, Weir added a third goal as insurance against a Third Lanark fight-back. Celtic's side: Miller, Milne, Mallan, Evans, Boden, McAuley, Weir, Gallacher W., Gallacher J., Tully, Paton.

For Celtic and their supporters the trophy was the tangible evidence that the side had finally matured, an optimistic assumption. The coach (and he probably was Celtic's first 'coach' as opposed to 'trainer') was exerting some influence over the style of the team: "Most of their players are now obviously following a pattern of thought which seems to lay down as a basic principle that constructive football will in the long run pay handsome dividends." (*Glasgow Herald*: 6 September, 1948.) Despite that observation, Hogan's coaching was only partially successful.

He was still a vibrant personality, but a generation gap existed between him and his players, and more than others Scottish footballers were reluctant to accept coaching and the self-discipline that goes with it. Significantly, the one Celt who claimed to have learned from Hogan was Tommy Docherty, mostly a reserve and the only player of those days to gain a substantial, if controversial, reputation later as a manager and coach.

It was not a team of acceptable Celtic class, having only three players of outstanding ability: Miller, Evans and Tully. In goal Miller had often been a graceful, gallant figure, risking injury with daring dives at opponents' feet and of all Celtic's keepers he was probably the busiest, an indication of the weakness in front of him. Evans had established himself quickly at right-half after a humdrum spell as a utility forward. His tackling was strong and scrupulously fair, his anticipation was uncanny and his distribution improved rapidly. Tully was a gifted, intelligent player and, although he was not a goalscorer, his dribbling and playmaking made chances for others; it was frustrating to see the chances he created wasted by leaden-footed and slow-thinking colleagues.

Pragmatic and successful teams have the discipline to produce workmanlike performances under adverse circumstances and can scramble wins when off form; this Celtic side did not have that gift, being more likely to snatch defeat from the jaws of victory. Too many matches were lost by a single goal, where points might have been gained by a more sustained or intelligent effort.

The greatest disappointment came in the Scottish Cup when the draw sent them once more to Dundee, this time to face lowly, unfashionable United of Division B at Tannadice. Shocked by the enthusiasm of the outsiders, Celtic never settled and United fully deserved their sensational 4-3 win. It had been a thriller, one of the unforgettable moments in cup football and an upset, but for Celtic there had been too many such upsets and the supporters were bitter.

A year later, at the end of 1949-50, Celtic landed another minor trophy by defeating Rangers in the final of the Charity Cup on 6 May, before a splendid crowd of 81,000 that had been put into a rare good humour by the antics of the American comedian, Danny Kaye, who was introduced to both teams prior to the kick-off. John McPhail led the attack well, distributing the ball accurately and causing unaccustomed panic throughout Rangers' defence; he scored two of the goals and his attentions forced Cox to deflect a clearance past Brown for the third. Shortly after half-time Celtic led by those three goals but a rally and two late goals by Rangers made the score respectable; the season ended as it had begun, with a 3-2 win over Rangers and a real promise for the future. Celtic's line-up showed changes from the previous year: Bonnar, Haughney, Milne, Evans, McGrory, Baillie, Collins, Fernie, McPhail, Peacock, Tully.

Several new players had broken into the side. Bonnar replaced Miller who had been inconsistent of late. Baillie won the left-half position from McAuley and formed a fine partnership with Evans. Collins made a memorable debut against Rangers and 'Tiger' Shaw on the opening day of the season and retained his position throughout. In the last month of the season Fernie and Peacock, two young inside-forwards of vastly contrasting style, had been given an extended run and were pleasing the fans with their play. On 4 March John McPhail was picked to play at centre-forward against Falkirk and, although he wandered out of position at times, scored three goals, and later in the month he scored four against East Fife. Celtic for the first time in a decade had a centre.

The promise was realised in 1951, with a long-awaited victory in the Scottish Cup, the first since 1937.

Anxiety was the prevailing mood at Celtic Park as the first round approached, because Celtic were scheduled to face the dour East Fife at Methil, and injuries continued to mount, forcing Celtic to field a make-shift side: Rollo replaced Milne at left-back, McGrory took over from Mallan at pivot, and Weir filled in for McPhail, out with a muscle strain sustained on New Year's Day when Celtic's challenge for the league foundered. It was a team out of form, without a win in 1951. Celtic's defence was shaky on the iron-hard pitch, and the tie entered the closing stages with East Fife leading 2-1. Evans and Baillie took the calculated risk of joining in attack, but Celtic met with no success until Collins moved to inside-right and immediately hit the post from 30 yards. The efforts were rewarded with a memorable goal in 82 minutes. Baillie sent Tully scampering down the left with a deft pass and the Irishman, after beating one defender, hesitated as if considering the gaining of yet another corner, but decided finally to cross the ball. The cross floated over a couple of yards too far out for the keeper and little Bobby Collins reached it first, outleaping everybody to head cleanly into the net.

Celtic made changes for the replay: though only half fit, McPhail led the attack, and Bonnar, who had allowed Black's corner to slip from his grasp for East Fife's first goal, was replaced by George Hunter making his debut. Celtic won convincingly 4-2, and McPhail scored twice. A remarkable first half decided the outcome of the Hearts-Celtic clash at Tynecastle on 24 February before a capacity crowd of 49,000. Shortly after the kick-off thousands spilled from the crowded terracing behind Celtic's goal where Hunter was playing in only his fifth game; a slim youth of 19, he seemed unaware of the commotion behind him and performed incredibly. He dived to hold two fierce drives from Wardhaugh at the post, he deflected a close-in header from Bauld over the bar with an instinctive leap, he parried a free kick from Laing and gallantly blocked Bauld's shot from the rebound. His astonishing coolness under pressure was shown in one incident near half-time, when he clashed with Sloan. The winger was being treated by the trainer, the referee was discussing the crowd situation with a police inspector, constables were easing the spectators back into the terracing and, in the midst of all this, Hunter was sitting calmly on the ball apparently lost in private thought. His astonishing performance inspired Celtic to a 2-1 win.

When Celtic met Aberdeen at Parkhead on 10 March, the gates had to be closed and hundreds of youngsters watched from the track as Celtic outplayed Aberdeen to win 3-0.

Three weeks later Celtic survived a hectic semi-final with Raith Rovers at Hampden in a match that the underrated Fifers were unlucky to lose. Twice Raith fought back to equalise, and nearing the end it seemed that Celtic would be glad to settle for a draw. But in the closing seconds Baillie hoisted a free kick towards the far post where McPhail, challenged by goalkeeper Johnstone and Colville, rose for it; when the three large men collided the ball broke to Tully who prodded it into the net. The suspicion remained that McPhail had impeded the defenders after the collision, but the goal stood. The only difference between the teams was Tully, playing at his superlative best to torment the right flank of Rovers' defence, taunting and teasing McClure before beating him in a variety of ways; his great day was crowned when he scored the winning goal.

John McPhail scores the only goal of the 1951 Scottish Cup final vs Motherwell.

186

Motherwell faced Celtic at Hampden on 21 April and the following teams lined up:

Celtic: Hunter, Fallon, Rollo, Evans, Boden, Baillie, Weir, Collins, McPhail, Peacock, Tully.

Motherwell: Johnstone, Kilmarnock, Shaw, McLeod, Paton, Redpath, Humphries, Watson, Kelly, Forrest, Aitkenhead.

It should have been an enthralling contest, but nerves and a fiery pitch produced a tense, over-anxious occasion marred by interruptions of the National Anthem before the game. One dramatic and unforgettable moment salvaged it. After 14 minutes Baillie halted a Motherwell attack and swung a long ball head-high down the middle; McPhail beat Paton to the ball, evaded the challenge of Shaw, and forced Johnstone out from his goal before lofting the ball over him.

In the heady, and unaccustomed, atmosphere of success the joy of the supporters was unrestrained. The contributions of individual players were praised: Collins at Methil, Hunter at Tynecastle, Tully at Hampden; the efforts of Fallon, Rollo, and Boden who played above themselves in the campaign; the impeccable performances of Evans and Baillie throughout and the heroics of John McPhail. Hampered by injury and listed as doubtful for all of the earlier ties, McPhail was an inspiring captain; nobody who was there could ever forget the collective intake of breath before his name was read out over the loudspeakers, nor the sustained roar of acclaim that greeted it, and how gallantly he responded to those cheers.

In the months that followed, it seemed that the old days had returned to Celtic Park. As had happened after the 1931 final, a Celtic party of players and officials toured the United States and Canada. The tour was limited mainly to the eastern cities of New York, Philadelphia, Toronto and Montreal with one game in Chicago. The exiles as always were enthusiastic, eager to see and touch the Scottish Cup brought along with permission of the SFA. The results were satisfactory, with victories over the New York All-Stars (5-1), the Philadelphia All-Stars (6-2), and the National League in Toronto (2-1); against Fulham (2-0), and Eintracht (3-1); and another permanent trophy was gained by beating the Polish White Eagles in Chicago (4-0). Upon their return to Glasgow and a hysterical reception, Celtic along with the other First Division sides participated in the St. Mungo Cup, and won it in fine style.[1]

With Celtic's twin triumphs in 1951 coming only four months apart, many supporters assumed that the club had regained its rightful position in Scottish football and some even anticipated the winning of the league championship in the near future. Celtic, however, had merely attained a level of competence and not pre-eminence. Critics could see the flaws inherent in the cup-winning sides and noted the lack of reserve strength to mount a sustained challenge. The team was barely adequate at full-back and centre-half. Opinion was still divided about the merits of George Hunter as keeper; his poise in the Scottish Cup was praised lavishly, but his lapses in the St. Mungo Cup were noted with misgiving.

No such doubts existed about the quality of one forward, Bobby Collins. Pitchforked into the team as a teenager, he had made an instant impression; small but stocky, he was a natural football player. With his abundant energy and confidence, he challenged for every ball but he had even more compelling gifts: speed, both physical and mental, close dribbling skills, a fierce shot, and accuracy in passing remarkable in one so young. Already he had been selected for Scotland, and was destined for a glittering career.

In the next two seasons, however, Celtic were reduced to ineffectuality once more, this time by a series of injuries. After a routine medical check-up revealed symptoms of serious illness, the club sent George Hunter to Switzerland to convalesce for several months; when he returned he never did become the complete keeper he had promised to be. John McPhail came back from the North American tour overweight and painfully slow, and eventually was dropped from the side. Bobby Collins broke an arm in a pre-season friendly game and was out of action until near Christmas; Sean Fallon fractured his arm at Falkirk and, although he finished the match, was later unavailable for five weeks; Joe Baillie tore knee ligaments at Airdrie and was unfit for a year, never regaining his place in the side. John Millsopp, a young player recently introduced, died in hospital after an appendicitis operation.

The resources of a truly strong club would have been taxed to cope with the situation, and Celtic was still far from that. No reservoir of talent or character existed to fall back on, and the predictable response was to resort to an increase in physical effort rather than skill to produce results; in both league and cup the results were disappointing, a 2-1 defeat at Cathkin by Third Lanark in the Scottish Cup — the club's first reverse in a replay in the competition for over 60 years — indicating the mediocrity.

It was sad to note the decline in McPhail's form; injury-prone, plagued with weight problems he was struggling to retain his place. His days as an effective centre were over because of his slowness — "as slow as treacle in January" one fan described him — but incredibly he was picked to play long after it was clear he could not produce his past form. An enthusiastic player frustrated by his lack of mobility, he felt compelled to assume the role of battering-ram and it was painful to witness a skilled performer so reduced.

During this most depressing season (1951-52) an SFA edict that threatened the future existence of the club diverted attention from the field,[2] and this may have been a factor in the general malaise, a depression that affected even Charlie Tully who, after showing welcome signs of restraint and maturity, revealed too much petulance and was often as irksome to Celtic as to the opposition.

Things could only improve, and the surprise signing of a veteran centre-half from a non-league team in Wales contributed to the change. Neither of the regular pivots was completely satisfactory (Tully described them ambiguously as 'passable'), and Celtic felt that Jock Stein, formerly a workmanlike defender for lowly Albion Rovers and Llanelli, might provide cheap cover as well as acting as a mentor while playing with the reserves. He was signed in late 1951 for £1,200, making his debut a few days later against St. Mirren when the other centre-halves failed fitness tests; he performed creditably, held his place in the team, was appointed captain and exerted a steadying influence on his colleagues. A year later, beside him at left-half, John McPhail was restored to the team, happily match-fit again with his customary whole-hearted approach to the game.

Despite a lowly standing in the league in 1952-53 and dismissal by Rangers in the quarter-final of the Scottish Cup, Celtic were due to participate in the Coronation Cup at the season's end. The pressing need was for a centre-forward who could score goals; in the last months of the season Celtic tried almost every forward on the books, before admitting the obvious and buying a player. The choice was Neil Mochan, a proven scorer with Morton and Middlesbrough, and self-admittedly "Celtic-daft", who signed in time to swell the gate at the Charity Cup final against Queen's Park. Typically, he scored twice, helping the team to a 3-1 win over the amateurs and provided a boost in morale for the game against Arsenal two days later.[3]

The stage was set for unexpected glory.

Notes
1 St. Mungo Cup — See chapter 'The trophy room'.
2 The abortive attempt by a faction of the SFA to forbid the flying of the Eire flag at Parkhead. Bob Kelly's firm stand on the matter eventually carried the day.
3 Coronation Cup — See chapter 'The trophy room'.

21

AMONG THE HONOURS

HAVING won the Coronation Cup against all the odds in 1953 Celtic's long-awaited revival continued, and the next season was to prove the most satisfying since the end of the war. At last Celtic won the championship and topped that by winning the Scottish Cup, the club's first double since 1913-1914.

There was a sickening start to the season: a miserable, out-of-form series in the League Cup, in the section with Aberdeen, East Fife and Airdrie, led to elimination; after a creditable 1-1 draw at Ibrox Celtic were thrashed 4-0 in a Glasgow Cup replay; and on the opening day of the league campaign came a humiliating defeat at the hands of newly promoted and subsequently inept Hamilton Accies.

Things improved gradually. On 19 September came a fine performance at Ibrox, a 1-1 draw fought out in drenching rain and marked by violent mob scenes at half-time after a policeman attempted to remove a Union Jack from the Rangers end, and mounted police had to gallop across the turf towards the disorder with batons raised; on 7 November an enthralling match with Hibernian at Celtic Park ended in a 2-2 draw, although Tully was carried off after only 10 minutes and Celtic had to fight back in a torrential downpour to equalise through a header by Jock Stein with only six minutes left; on 26 December came a memorable 7-1 win in the mud at Shawfield over Clyde on a day when many had to walk to the game because of a transportation strike. And, at last, a win over Rangers on New Year's Day by 1-0 before 53,000, Mochan scoring the goal after Rangers' defence got into a fankle. There was an intriguing moment before the kick-off when Rangers protested about the choice of ball and tried to substitute a leather one for the all-weather white ball introduced into Scottish football earlier that season; the referee vetoed that attempt amid cheers from the Celtic supporters, well aware that the lighter, more lively ball favoured ball-players like Fernie and Tully.

It seemed, however, that the championship had been decided at Tynecastle on 6 February, 1954, when Hearts faced Celtic before an all-ticket 49,000. Both sides were virtually tied for first place, Hearts being six points ahead, but Celtic had three games in hand. Hearts, after hanging on in the first half, opened strongly on the restart as Souness ripped apart the Celtic defence in a long run in the first minute to cross for Bauld to head cleanly into the net; only four minutes later Bauld repeated his goal in a breakaway raid. Hearts, scarcely in the game, now led by two goals, and the title seemed booked for Edinburgh. Celtic still attacked furiously and the hard-pressed Hearts' defence was forced to concede two penalties, both of which Haughney converted with characteristic full-blooded shots.

Disaster struck Celtic late in the game, almost three minutes into injury-time by most estimates, when Hunter rose to clutch cleanly a high ball only to be bundled over the line by Wardhaugh who collided with him in mid-air and had clearly used his elbow in the clash. Leaving Tynecastle after the match the players were visibly dispirited at the result, but on the bus back to Glasgow the talk switched to the remaining fixtures and they agreed that Hearts faced the more difficult task despite their advantage.

Two weeks later the first indication came that the tide had turned in Celtic's favour. Celtic were in rampant form, smashing Dundee 5-1 at Parkhead despite Bill Brown's spectacular saves, while at Tynecastle Rangers, luckily by all accounts, held Hearts to a 3-3 draw. On 6 March Celtic continued to apply the pressure by outplaying East Fife 4-1, and Hearts lost at Kirkcaldy by 4-2 to Raith Rovers. Celtic were now five points behind, but still had the advantage of those three games in hand. The feeling was that the Edinburgh side, despite its great talent, was suspect in temperament and might have difficulty in holding off a sustained challenge. Both sides won on 17 March; Celtic with Bonnar returning to goal and Fallon restored to centre-forward swept aside Airdrie 6-0, but Hearts won easily over Hamilton as expected.

The decisive match was at Firhill against Partick Thistle who had moved up to third place and still entertained outside hopes of the title themselves. Thistle attacked from the start to take an early lead from Willie Sharp's goal; after Walsh was injured in 15 minutes only Bonnar's fine saves kept Celtic in the game with a chance.

Firhill deserves its reputation for thrills. For the visit of Celtic the terracings are invariably packed, and in parts the spectators are close enough to see every grimace and to hear every grunt of effort as the players respond to the proximity of the crowd and give their all in a bid for victory. Still, no second half even at Firhill has matched that one. Celtic's cause seemed hopeless when Mochan also was hurt and limped on the other wing, but Celtic fought for every ball and contested every yard to force Thistle back into frantic defence; the terracings were in an uproar of encouragement and erupted into bedlam when news came through that Hearts were trailing at Aberdeen.

Celtic launched attack after attack, and with 20 minutes gone Fallon crashed in the equaliser from a goalmouth scramble; ten minutes later Fernie made his inimitable way along the by-line, swerving past two defenders to shoot fiercely against Ledgerwood and leaping high to head the rebound past the keeper; in the very last minute Fallon added a third goal, somehow surviving heavy tackling from Davidson in a thrilling forty-yard gallop. At the end the crowd left, exultant but drained of emotion.

Hearts could not respond to this sustained Celtic challenge, and before the season's end Celtic had increased the lead to a healthy five-point margin, eventually clinching the title with a 3-0 win over Hibs at Easter Road. It was a splendid achievement, reassuring in that it was accomplished not through brilliance, but by steadiness and efficiency. Stein as captain had established a sense of purpose in the team, and the consistency reflected the new attitude. Following the loss at Tynecastle that could have broken the spirit of a lesser team Celtic won nine successive league games, five away from home, scoring 34 goals while giving up only four.

Celtic and their supporters were jubilant, but even more dramatic joy was in store because the side had won its way through to the Scottish Cup final. Once more it was a reward for temperament. All the ties were away from home and against teams that had been giving Celtic trouble in the recent past: the first-round tie against Falkirk had to be postponed until 17 February because Brockville was waterlogged and Celtic, without impressing, deserved a narrow 2-1 win; Stirling was rightly considered a 'bogey' ground and the signs were ominous when the home side took an early two-goal lead, but Celtic rallied, the turning point being a magnificent free kick taken by Mochan 35 yards out that left the keeper motionless; Hamilton, destined for relegation, provided stern opposition in the quarter-final in a typical cup-tie characterised by fierce, uncompromising tackles, with Willie Fernie singled out for harsh treatment, but the quiet Fifer had the last laugh by scoring the winner in the 2-1 victory.

Motherwell, running away with the second division title, posed some problems for Celtic in the semi-final at Hampden in front of 102,000, where Charlie Aitken headed a free kick past Bonnar in the last minute to force a replay, but on 5 April a crowd of 92,662 saw Celtic dispose of the challenge. As in the first game, John Higgins confirmed his mastery over the veteran full-back, Archie Shaw, avoiding his bull-like rushes with the grace of a matador. Those who preferred the more direct Bobby Collins on the right wing were won over by this Higgins display that helped to fashion a 3-1 win. In the other semi-final Aberdeen had crushed Rangers by 6-0, and qualified to face Celtic in the final watched by 130,060 on 24 April, 1954.

Aberdeen: Martin, Mitchell, Caldwell, Allister, Young, Glen, Leggat, Hamilton, Buckley, Clunie, Hather.
Celtic: Bonnar, Haughney, Meechan, Evans, Stein, Peacock, Higgins, Fernie, Fallon, Tully, Mochan.

Celtic made a whirlwind start, hoping to take advantage of the nervous Dons. Aberdeen's defence gave away corner after corner but Martin, tall and confident in goal, steadied his hard-pressed mates and by half-time Aberdeen had regained their composure. Celtic went ahead in the 50th minute. Mochan recovered a loose ball on the right wing and considered the situation as he made some ground; at last he fired a venomous, swerving shot across the face of the goal hoping for a deflection, a gambit that had been successful a week earlier at Easter Road, and the ball was diverted past the helpless Martin by the centre-half Young, unable to avoid contact with the cross-shot. Aberdeen, to their credit, came back and equalised two minutes later when Buckley

Sean Fallon notches Celtic's winner in the 1954 Scottish Cup final vs Aberdeen.

scored from a neat, headed pass from Hamilton, and the battle raged on.

A goal characteristic of the season, gave Celtic the cup. Fernie received the ball from a throw-in and was edged closer to the goal-line by the defenders; as he had done so often, the inside-forward swerved and weaved his way along the line to roll the final pass back for Sean Fallon to prod into the net in the 63rd minute.

Hopes were high for the next season (1954-1955) because the double had been accomplished so competently and deservedly, although admittedly it had not been a vintage year. The defence was solid, and eventually the forwards were constructive and effective; in 1954-55 the side was marginally better and more confident, but Celtic got nothing out of the season, finishing second in the championship to Aberdeen and losing in a replayed cup final with Clyde.

Early in the league campaign Celtic moved out in front by defeating the major challengers, Rangers and Aberdeen, convincingly. On 18 September Rangers lined up at Celtic Park without Woodburn, the centre-half, suspended *sine die* earlier in the week by the SFA for repeated field indiscretions, and Celtic handled them comfortably to win 2-0 through second-half goals by Walsh and Higgins; on 9 October Celtic went to Pittodrie and won easily again by 2-0 with goals coming from Mochan and Haughney, who sent Martin the wrong way from the penalty spot (a relatively rare practice in 1954).

A poor November cost Celtic the championship. Two players, Fallon and the infinitely more valuable Higgins, were injured and sidelined for an extended period. Points were dropped carelessly in drawn games with St. Mirren (1-1), Motherwell (2-2), and East Fife (2-2) and, finally, on 20 November Celtic lost their unbeaten record in another epic battle at Firhill. Within four minutes Thistle led 2-0 through goals alertly snapped up by Smith and Howitt. Celtic swept into immediate counter-attack at a furious pace on the greasy surface and tied the score before half-time. Celtic dominated play at the start of the second half but Thistle, displaying rare coolness amid the fiery exchanges, scored twice with masterfully constructed goals. The abiding memory though was neither the goals nor the near misses, but the absorbing individual duels springing up spontaneously on the field like the pairing-off of knights in a medieval pitched battle. The speedy Smith jousting against the stolid Stein, the great-hearted McGowan containing the mercurial Collins, a graceful, elegant McKenzie surviving the attentions of the desperate Fallon, exuberant Evans rejoicing in the clamour and matching wits with the intelligent Sharp and in goal, defying all Celtic's efforts, was a splendid Ledgerwood.

Aberdeen were remarkably consistent at this stage and had built up a five-point lead over Celtic, but the supporters consoled themselves with

194

the thought that the standings were identical to the previous season's. Unlike Hearts, however, Aberdeen showed coolness under the strain, revealing no sign of nerves and losing ground only slightly to Celtic when the teams met at Parkhead on 16 April, but too late to affect the outcome. Aberdeen had clinched the title a week earlier, and the announcer at Celtic Park extended the club's congratulations publicly, inviting the crowd to give the Aberdeen players "a truly Celtic welcome". When Aberdeen took the field a minute or so later they were greeted in splendid fashion, with waves of applause breaking from every part of the ground in a sustained, generous and sincere recognition of their achievement and a belated acknowledgement of the northern side's sporting attitude in the previous year's Scottish Cup final. No other club, its team, or supporters had abdicated more gracefully. To the delight of the 45,000 basking in the April sunshine Celtic raised the quality of their game to match the occasion and defeated the newly crowned champions by 2-1, both goals being scored by John McPhail, recently and deservedly restored to centre-forward after a long absence.

Celtic eventually finished as runners-up, a performance all the more commendable because the team was only rarely in top form after the New Year. It was satisfying to record that under Jock Stein as captain a new trait had been developing in this Celtic team; the displays and results did not reflect merely the current mood of the team's members, but were based on determination, drive and even dourness. Often players were out of touch, or the ball was breaking badly for them; however, a spirit would assert itself not in confidence nor brilliance, but in earnestness and industry. Despite the consolation of the new consistency, the feeling at the season's end was one of distinct disappointment with the lack of tangible success. The legitimate complaint was that better use could have been made of the forwards available. The supporters were divided over the problem posed by the choice of Higgins or Collins for the right wing; Higgins, a slim, frail winger with an uncanny sense of position and deadly finishing, or Collins, a short, stocky bundle of energy. Higgins was preferred, and Collins became the victim of his own versatility, reduced to replacing the other forwards in turn. Out of favour was Mochan, the leading scorer of the previous season, and that was an unfortunate decision because he had a keen football intelligence and could always score goals. Celtic's mystifying reluctance to employ these goalscorers regularly was shown by a preference for unlikely and unproductive 'forwards' such as Sean Fallon, Alec Boden and Eric Smith.

At the end of the campaign only three points separated Celtic and Aberdeen; it could have been much closer.

Celtic's failure in the Scottish Cup final marked a turning point in the club's history. On the road to Hampden Celtic encountered unexpectedly stiff resistance from Alloa, Kilmarnock and Hamilton, as well as in a replayed semi-final with Airdrie. For that replay Celtic made an important change by recalling John McPhail as centre. McPhail had experienced injury problems, but was playing well for the reserves and enjoying his football again, having changed his style and now being noted as a distributor of the ball. Baillie, Airdrie's young giant at centre-half, was left stranded repeatedly by McPhail's astute passing and deceptive ambles into dangerous positions. Both Celtic's goals, the margin of victory, were scored by McPhail with intelligent shots, firmly hit and beautifully placed away from the keeper early in the second half. Clyde, always capable of clever football, had beaten Aberdeen after a replay in the other semi-final and the following teams faced each other on 23 April:

> *Clyde*: Hewkins, Murphy, Haddock, Granville, Anderson, Laing, Divers, Robertson, Hill, Brown, Ring.
> *Celtic*: Bonnar, Haughney, Meechan, Evans, Stein, Peacock, Collins, Fernie, McPhail, Walsh, Tully.

This was the first Scottish Cup final to be televised live and the BBC, possibly reluctant to entrust such an important event to a Scottish commentator, sent up Kenneth Wolstenholme to provide the expertise. Celtic were clearly more accustomed to Hampden Park and its atmosphere, seizing the initiative from the referee's whistle. The crowd of 106,234, smaller than anticipated because of the TV coverage, was soon roaring in anticipation of early goals as Evans and Peacock joined in attacks. Collins, clearly in form, had the beating of Haddock, and McPhail hit the post in seven minutes with a neat flick; it took 35 minutes for Clyde's goal to fall when Fernie passed inside Anderson for

Celtic defenders look on in consternation as Robertson's corner snatches a late equaliser for Clyde in the 1955 Scottish Cup final.

Walsh to race through and shoot home powerfully from the edge of the penalty area. At half-time it was agreed that Clyde had done well to keep the score down.

Early in the second half Celtic decided on a change of tactics: both inside-men, Fernie and Walsh, neither noted for defensive qualities, were pulled back with the result that Evans and Peacock retreated into strictly back-up roles behind them. Clyde slowly gained momentum and nearing the end had control of midfield, but were rarely getting close to Bonnar.

The spectators, earlier so noisy, had quietened to an apprehensive rumble . . . and Clyde forced a corner on the right with only two minutes left.

Surprisingly, the tallest of Clyde's forwards, Robertson, elected to take it, placing the ball with his customary deliberation before crossing it into the Celtic goalmouth. It was a high, straight cross, and at first sight directed too close to Celtic's goal because no Clyde forward was near to challenge for it. Bonnar rose for the ball completely alone, but a few feet away from him, its flight began to alter and it hung agonizingly for a moment above the keeper's straining reach to break limply from his fingertips and bounce over the line, with Haughney and Meechan immobile in their consternation at the posts. After the game Robertson was to admit that "it was a poor corner".

In their dressing-room ten minutes before the kick-off of the replay the Clyde players, in the varying final stages of readiness and unable to conceal the taut, frayed nerves of the situation, were told of the changes in Celtic's team. Collins had been dropped, Walsh moved to outside right, Fallon restored to centre, and McPhail switched to inside-left. Haddock, an urchin grin splitting his face, made a jubilant round of the dressing-room exhorting his colleagues. Among the 69,000 crowd, huddling miserably on the terracing against the showers and the gusting wind, speculation was rampant about the reason for the changes; the main controversy was over the omission of Collins, a player who never should have been left out of a cup-tie team in the opinion of most supporters, and it was recalled that he had been one of the better performers in the first game. The appearance of the teams cut short the debate, but the worst fears of the fans were realised as Clyde started with renewed confidence. A different team in outlook, Clyde played with a controlled eagerness and grilled Celtic's defence throughout the first half. That defence, organised by Stein and drilled into cohesion after two years of playing together, was fully extended to hold out. Bonnar earned several rounds of applause for his sure-handed manner in dealing with dangerous situations but, as feared on the terracing, the Celtic attack had not mounted a sustained offensive. Early in the second half Celtic established a territorial advantage, moving upfield in

197

transparent, leaden-footed attacks . . . and Clyde broke away for Tommy Ring to scramble in what proved the winning goal.[1] After Ring's goal, and with time running out, Celtic were galvanised into short-lived domination, gaining corner after corner and, from one taken by Tully, McPhail's powerful header was turned over the bar by Hewkins with a startled leap.

Later there was universal condemnation of Celtic's choice of forwards. Clyde's weakness in defence lay in a lack of speed among its veterans, but Celtic had played the hand exactly as Clyde would have wished. Fallon, not fully match-fit after a long absence, was an earnest plodder, McPhail could no longer do the work of an inside-forward, and Walsh was ill-at-ease on the wing. Most galling was the sight of two forwards with pace and shooting power, Bobby Collins and Neil Mochan, sitting on the sidelines.

Archie Robertson's "poor corner" marked the end of an era in the Scottish Cup for Celtic. Traditionally it was Celtic, the famed cup-fighters, who raised their game and performed brilliantly under the pressure but, in 1955, a keeper had erred and a forward line had flopped. It was to be another ten years till the Scottish Cup again adorned the board-room at Celtic Park; time after time Celtic teams would fight their way through to the closing stages, and time after time they would lose, often in bizarre circumstances.

Despite running into a spate of injuries in the League Cup in 1955-1956, Celtic made a good start by capturing the Glasgow Cup after an intriguing campaign. Clyde, fresh from the Scottish Cup triumph, were the first opponents and this time Celtic included the two forwards dropped from the replay, Collins and Mochan; both played well in a 4-0 rout as Mochan scored three times with Anderson, Clyde's captain and centre-half hero in the cup final, having no answer to his speed and thrust. After beating Thistle at Firhill in a match notable only for being played on a Friday night, Celtic advanced to the final against Rangers played on the September Bank Holiday before 53,000 who were vastly entertained in a 1-1 draw. The replay took place on 26 December, before 39,000 at Hampden:

> *Rangers*: Niven, Caldow, Little, McColl, Young, Rae, Scott, Simpson, Kichenbrand, Baird, Hubbard.
> *Celtic*: Beattie, Haughney, Fallon, Evans, Stein, Peacock, Smith, Fernie, Sharkey, Collins, Mochan.

Everybody was looking forward to the duels down the middle, a clash between the veteran pivots, Young and Stein, and two newcomers, Sharkey and Kichenbrand, greatly differing but equally promising centre-forwards. Kichenbrand, a powerfully built South African dubbed 'the Rhino', had absolutely no polish but he could panic defences with his headlong dashes; Sharkey, a slimly built youngster from Rutherglen

198

Glencairn and a former inside-left, whom Celtic were trying to convert to a centre, still retained the intellectual approach favoured by inside-forwards. In recent weeks both had been scoring memorable goals.

Celtic pulled ahead in the closing minutes to win the replay by 5-3. Sharkey's cleverness sorely troubled the ageing Young to gain him two fine goals. Each time he worked his way into perfect position and indulged in a characteristic caress of the ball before leaving Niven helpless with rising shots patented to scrape under the bar. While Stein was forced to treat Kichenbrand with respect, he ended up clearly the master. The South African, however, clearly bothered Dick Beattie who revealed hints of a suspect temperament in dealing with the situation. The young keeper was badly at fault for two goals, remaining rooted to his line when a cross from Baird floated over for Kichenbrand to head in at the far post, and later holding the centre-forward needlessly to give away a penalty which Hubbard inevitably converted. A year later both centres, about whom arguments had raged, had disappeared into the limbo of reserve football and were available for transfer.

Celtic had run into a spate of injuries in the League Cup at the sectional stage that proved an insurmountable handicap in the league campaign: Bonnar, recovering from a leg strain, was replaced by young Beattie and Stein's ankle injury, stubborn to heal despite prolonged treatment, forced the captain's retirement from the game by the end of the season.

The Scottish Cup final was anticipated with a great deal of relish, because after 50 years Hearts had at last survived the earlier rounds to appear at Hampden. The Edinburgh side had been playing inspired football in recent months, and were installed as favourites after thrashing Rangers 4-0. On paper Hearts were a formidable team: two splendid, hard-tackling wing halves in Dave MacKay and John Cumming backed up the famed forward unit of Conn, Bauld and Wardhaugh, popularly nicknamed 'the Terrible Trio' for their deadly shooting and sharp interchanging. The one unresolved question before the match was Hearts' temperament, especially when faced with a team of Celtic's tradition and enthusiasm, but Celtic had marched to another final without impressing and their plans for the final were disrupted by injury. Stein had broken down again with a recurrence of his ankle injury and Collins was unavailable through injury, having to miss also the international against England.

Changes had to be made: Evans took over from Stein as captain and centre-half, a reasonable choice as was Smith at right-half in Evans' place, but incredible selections were made in the forward line. A virtually unknown youngster, Billy Craig, was chosen at outside right in his cup-tie debut, and he was partnered by Haughney who moved up from his regular spot at right-back. Haughney's place at full-back was taken by Meechan, who switched from left-back to be replaced by Fallon. Two experienced forwards were available in Sharkey and Walsh but neither was chosen; and to add to the confusion the players were not informed of the line-up until the lunchtime of the match day.

> *Celtic*: Beattie, Meechan, Fallon, Smith, Evans, Peacock, Craig, Haughney, Mochan, Fernie, Tully.
> *Hearts*: Duff, Kirk, McKenzie, MacKay, Glidden, Cumming, Young, Conn, Bauld, Wardhaugh, Crawford.

A final generates its own sense of excitement with the realisation that a momentary lapse in concentration can be cruelly punished, that a split-second reaction can be rewarded so ultimately, and the certain knowledge that the match will be replayed in memory for years. This is what causes the adrenalin to surge, the nerves to fray and upsets to occur. On 21 April, 1956, all the trappings of ceremony combined: brilliant sunshine bathed the vast stadium in colour and warmth as almost 133,000 waited the kick-off, the pitch looked hard and fast, and there was the merest hint of the infamous Hampden swirl.

But this time there was no upset, no shock victory. Hearts fully deserved their 3-1 win, and perhaps their greatest victory was over themselves and the burden of their reputation. Crawford was the danger-man and scored twice; the first came after 21 minutes, a crisply hit shot from the edge of the penalty area, but the second only three minutes into the second half finished Celtic, a trundling, half-hit shot from close range after Bauld had been allowed to meander unchallenged down the left wing. John Cumming epitomised the spirit of Hearts and their new sense of purpose by playing on with blood seeping through a bandage that barely covered a head wound.

For once in a Scottish Cup final Celtic had been 'the other team'.

Notes
1 When Ring visited his mother's home for a meal the following day his brothers, who were keen Celtic supporters, refused to join him at the table and did not speak to him for several days.

22

LEAGUE CUP BREAKTHROUGH

CELTIC'S record in the League Cup had been deplorable, and by 1956 many supporters considered the tournament a jinx. Devised during World War II as the Southern League Cup, it was retained without change in format, although renamed the Scottish League Cup; its admirers called it "a cup-tie with a second chance" because of the home and away sectional play. Celtic's repeated failures were all the more astonishing, given the club's reputation as cup-fighters and the fact that the tournament traditionally opened the season, the team's pre-season training being widely considered much more strenuous than any of their rivals', including, as it did, runs up Ben Lomond. Still, Celtic had rarely survived the sectional play, often being victims of Rangers, grim, dogged adversaries as always. Celtic had provided wonderful moments in their victories: Paton's glorious goal in a 2-0 win at Parkhead in 1947, Tully's great display in a 3-1 victory in 1948, Collins' sparkling debut and Haughney's winner in a 3-2 upset in 1949, and a memorable 4-1 triumph at Ibrox in 1955 . . . but all these memories take on a bitter-sweet flavour with the realisation that Rangers had won the return match to advance to the quarter-finals at the expense of Celtic.

The barrier was crossed by the signing of a new centre-forward, Billy McPhail — a move felt to be a considerable gamble. Nobody disputed his intelligence or skill, but some withheld total recognition because of their belief that he lacked determination and drive. A weak ankle and a knee condition that required periodic draining had removed him from Clyde's line-up for long spells, giving him a reputation as a delicate player. A former Queen's Parker, fittingly imbued with the spirit of the amateur sportsman, McPhail represented a type of cavalier leader that has vanished from the scene. Some players, like Jimmy Quinn, never knew the meaning of fear, and their headlong style reflected this; Billy McPhail, however, had forced himself to examine his physical limitations in the cold light of logic. His courage was real, his skill considerable — and it was the deadliness of the rapier rather than the bludgeoning of the claymore.

In the 1956 League Cup Celtic were drawn in a most difficult section, having to meet Aberdeen, the holders, along with those redoubtable cup fighters East Fife and inevitably Rangers, so often the nemesis. It was to prove a grim, although successful, test of temperament as five of the six matches ended up in narrow victories and the other was drawn.

Naturally, tension filled the encounters with Rangers, the first at Parkhead on 15 August. After 34 minutes Celtic moved ahead with the type of goal that was to become increasingly familiar. Haughney intercepted a pass in his own half of the field then advanced about ten yards before driving a crisp, punched clearance towards McPhail; the centre diverted the ball the merest fraction with his head and Collins, on the move from the moment Haughney started his progress, raced through the middle to beat Niven cleanly from 12 yards out. Rangers equalised right on half-time, and Haughney squandered a chance to put Celtic ahead by missing a penalty. However, Tully gave Celtic the lead with 20 minutes left. A corner from the right was scrambled away and half cleared towards Tully, who gained possession about eight yards out, but with his back to the goal; the Irishman slowed down to control the awkward ball and then played it delicately over his head to the junction of the far post and crossbar where the lob dipped to elude the frantic efforts of Niven and Little. Celtic, for once, took full advantage of the situation by going to Ibrox two weeks later and refusing to be drawn into the rough-and-tumble of a cup-tie. A crowd of 84,000 saw Celtic play composed football with a sensible emphasis on defence to gain a 0-0 draw and almost ensure their passage into the quarter-finals, a feat that was accomplished on the Saturday with a 1-0 win at Methil over East Fife.

After eliminating Dunfermline Athletic Celtic faced Clyde in the semi-final, and McPhail scored both goals to dispose of his former club 2-0.

In the club's first League Cup final Celtic faced Partick Thistle on 27 October before a crowd of 58,000 at Hampden. It was a most disappointing match, with Celtic's forwards at their exasperating and frustrating worst. Thistle finished extra time with only nine men, Davidson and Smith being injured, but the 'Jags' came closer to scoring when McKenzie forced Beattie to make a fine save in the closing minute. Changes were made for the midweek replay:

Celtic: Beattie, Haughney, Fallon, Evans, Jack, Peacock, Tully, Collins, McPhail, Fernie, Mochan.

Partick Thistle: Ledgerwood, Kerr, Gibb, Collins, Crawford, Mathers, McKenzie, Wright, Hogan, McParland, Ewing.

Play was much brighter than in the first game, although the forwards continued to miss chances. Celtic decided the outcome with a burst of scoring, three goals coming within a six-minute period early in the second half. McPhail scored the first after 49 minutes, anticipating a pass back and gathering the ball neatly before hooking it cleverly over Ledgerwood's shoulder. Within a minute he had scored again after good work by Tully and Mochan. Collins finished the scoring a few minutes later, racing on to a pass from Evans, forced to play on the right wing in the second half through injury. Celtic's best player on the day was Tully: "Sooner or later, one felt, this mercurial player who was having one of his best days of dexterous ball control, astute passing, intelligent crossing and corner-kicking, would contrive a scoring chance as not even his finicky colleagues could squander." (*Glasgow Herald*: 1 November, 1956.)

After all the heartbreak of recent years the League Cup had been captured, but in a curious mood of anti-climax; one year later the mood was one of jubilation and triumph.

Celtic's first task in retaining the trophy was to qualify for the later stages, a mission made all the more difficult after a surprise 3-1 defeat at Easter Road by Hibernian. For the return match Celtic made some significant changes. Two youngsters made their debuts, John Donnelly appearing at right-back and Bertie Auld at outside-left. Sammy Wilson, picked up on a free transfer from St. Mirren lined up at inside-left to start a profitable partnership with McPhail, and Fernie was moved back to right-half. Celtic won the match convincingly by 2-0 with the twin-spearhead of McPhail and Wilson scoring the goals, but the revelation for the 50,000 crowd was the vigorous display of the often diffident Fernie at right-half, and he drew surprised murmurs from the crowd when instead of trying to dribble his way out of trouble he smashed one clearance on to the roof of the 'Jungle' — the only safe thing to do.

On 19 October, 1957, the following teams lined up for an unforgettable encounter in the final:

Celtic: Beattie, Donnelly, Fallon, Fernie, Evans, Peacock, Tully, Collins, McPhail, Wilson, Mochan.
Rangers: Niven, Shearer, Caldow, McColl, Valentine, Davis, Scott, Simpson, Murray, Baird, Hubbard.

With only a few minutes remaining to play one Celtic supporter, joyfully belligerent, threw out his challenge to the world, waving a couple of crumpled pound-notes in his fist: "Celtic'll get a penalty . . . Tully'll take it . . . he'll score . . . wi' a f--- scissors-kick!" There were no takers, and that reflected the extent of Celtic's superiority over Rangers in the final. In the last minute, as fate would have it, Celtic were awarded a penalty kick, but the Celt who stepped up to take it was Fernie, as cool and as immaculate as ever. He tucked the ball neatly into the right-hand corner and turned self-effacingly for the congratulations. Trotting back to the halfway line, had he looked up, he would have seen his own keeper standing on the edge of his area with both hands raised in salute, and seven fingers fully extended; behind Beattie's goal the packed Celtic end at Hampden were still rejoicing, convulsed in the happiest delirium of all and close to losing count of the number of Celtic goals.

It was a triumph for football and the architect of the victory was Fernie: "This wonderful footballer who achieves his purpose without the merest suggestion of relying on the physical, and who suffers the crude, unfair attempts to stop him without a thought of retaliation." (*Glasgow Herald*: 21 October, 1957.)

Two individual jousts determined the extent of the triumph. Mochan, surprisingly often left out of the side, was restored on the left wing, where his speed and direct dribbling confused Shearer, and when the full-back resorted to heavy tackling the stocky Mochan immediately sent him sprawling; McPhail from the opening whistle established a mastery over Valentine, Rangers' highly touted centre-half recently signed from Queen's Park, by beating him repeatedly on the ground in a variety of ways and demoralised his opponent by winning most balls in the air. Between them the pair scored five goals. Mochan netted twice, one of them particularly crucial, only a minute before the interval; and McPhail scored a second-half hat-trick against a defence that was becoming increasingly agitated with every passing minute.

During the opening 20 minutes of the match Celtic gained control, and both Tully and Collins had struck the woodwork with Niven hopelessly beaten. The suspicion was lurking in the minds of the supporters that the forwards might be heading for a frustratingly unlucky afternoon, until the 23rd minute. McPhail rose to a cross and headed the ball down and back towards Wilson, who connected on the drop from 12 yards' range; two minutes later Collins thundered a ferocious drive from a 30–yard free kick against the crossbar yet again, and it seemed with half-time approaching that a one-goal lead might be the meagre reward for all Celtic's domination. Mochan's goal decided the outcome; receiving a lofted pass from McPhail, the winger left Shearer and McColl sprawling helplessly in his wake before cutting in to blast his shot into the far corner of the net.

The second half, which developed rapidly into a rout, was a delight for Celtic supporters. Time after time Fernie would stride into attack, leaving Rangers' 'hard men', Baird and Davis, floundering behind him; Evans' anticipation made Rangers' infrequent attacks look much more foolish than they actually were; Collins supplied the other forwards with the bullets in a constant flow of accurate passes, long and short; Tully, now in the veteran stage, relied exclusively on his intelligence and ball control, and no player in Scotland had more of those qualities.

Rangers gained no consolation whatsoever. Any sympathy for Murray limping on the left wing in the second half was qualified by the memory that he had injured himself in fouling Evans from behind and

Billy McPhail slams Celtic's fourth goal past Rangers goalkeeper George Niven, League Cup final 1957.

had been penalised for it; Simpson's irrelevant goal was scored while Evans was being treated on the sidelines; and ten minutes from the end fighting broke out among those Rangers' supporters still in the ground and held up the game momentarily.

All too soon the final whistle sounded, and Celtic had retained the League Cup with a 7-1 win, a score that still stands as a record for a national final in Scotland. It was a day to remember and savour. For the fanatics, the most resounding victory over Rangers; for the admirers, the most convincing display for many years; and for the purists, the just reward for talent, skill and self-control overcoming power and force.

205

23

"SEVEN LEAN YEARS"

Pat Crerand coolly waits to pass back to Frank Haffey at Ibrox during a League Cup tie in 1960. Rangers' Ralph Brand and Sammy Baird wait to pounce.

A FOOTBALL club and its supporters share a complex relationship based on tacit agreements, and the continuance of this association is a matter of trust. The supporters have to believe that the directors will do their best with the club's resources and talent, and that profits at the gate or through transfer fees will effect improvements. The supporters of most Scottish teams have accepted deplorable and dangerously primitive conditions on the terracings for years; the situation at the match itself, antiquated and overcrowded transport systems, the thinly veiled hostility of local citizens . . . all can be tolerated if the trust is there — the shared perception that Board, management and players are doing their best, that policy and administrative decisions are understandable and acceptable, that the club is modern in its approach, training and performance.

True supporters care. They care enough to argue vehemently but often perceptively about the team, the players, the issues; they care enough to commit themselves to the cause of the club; they care enough to turn up week after week and support the team; they care enough to criticise among themselves their own players. The opposite of love, after all, is not hate, but indifference.

Celtic supporters have been renowned for their loyalty through the years, and in the '50s were often described as 'The Faithful' in the press. Like their Rangers' counterparts, they demand success and for the 'Old Firm' no excuse for failure or mediocrity is acceptable given their stature, resources and support.

Yet, during the seven years that followed the 7-1 triumph over Rangers in the League Cup of 1957, not one major trophy was won, and the rapport between the club and its supporters was endangered. What went wrong? The reason was two-fold. The successful side of 1957 consisted of veterans and within three years retirements, injuries and transfers had destroyed it; by 1960 the club had embarked on a 'youth policy', ill-conceived and badly handled, that lasted twice as long as anticipated.

Let us consider first the disintegration of the 1957 team. Having won the League Cup in October, the team was in first place in the league and undefeated after eleven games following crucial visits to Ibrox (3-2) and Easter Road (1-0). All the hopes for the season were shattered on 21 December when Partick Thistle won 3-2 at Parkhead, but much worse were the injuries to Fernie and McPhail which put them out of action for months, and revealed unreadiness in the reserve strength. In the next pre-season trial (1958), played at exhibition pace, McPhail broke down once more and was forced to retire permanently from the sport; in the same game Fallon was injured and after medical advice decided to retire also. A few weeks later Evans, consistently injury-free in his career, hurt his back against Clyde in the opening league game and was sidelined for four months. The subsequent changes apparently motivated unrest among some established players, and was a principal factor in causing Collins and Fernie to request transfers; significantly, both players, who had represented Scotland in the World Cup held in Sweden and had come into contact with Anglo-Scots, went to England, Collins to Everton in September and Fernie to Middlesbrough in December. At the season's end Tully retired, going back to Ireland to manage; a year later Evans asked for a transfer "for personal reasons" and moved to Chelsea.

Injuries may be unpredictable, but retirements are inevitable; a well-organised club has to prepare for both possibilities and Celtic was not ready. Even more distressing to the supporters was the departure of Collins and Fernie, both at the height of their powers. It seemed that little effort was made to keep them at Parkhead, and the club's often repeated statement that "no player who is dissatisfied at Celtic Park will be held there" sounded too self-righteous; a club has a responsibility to make strenuous efforts to retain its players, and an abdication of that responsibility is a disservice to the support. Some felt that the transfer fees, which totalled £40,000, served to defray the costs of the expensive floodlights that were installed shortly after.

Thus, circumstances rather than policy forced Celtic to field a team of youngsters, a side of promising apprentices. During the break-up of the 1957 team a period of transition was inevitable and the supporters accepted it as such. Reports about the progress of the reserves, now being coached by Jock Stein, were encouraging. The former captain, recently retired, was a natural coach despite his lack of formal qualifications. He was innovative but practical, cheerful but strict, and above all capable of motivating his charges, but much to the irritation of his young charges Stein was allowed to accept the vacant managerial post at Dunfermline Athletic. Stein, successful coach as he was, was seeking wider scope for talents that had bloomed relatively late in his playing career, and in the BBC TV series *MacLeod at Large* (1972) he stated that when the Dunfermline opportunity arose he discussed the situation with Bob Kelly in order to clarify his future prospects at Parkhead; it was Stein's belief that "then Sir Robert Kelly thought that I had gone as far as I would expect to go with a club like Celtic; I was a non-Catholic and maybe they felt that I wouldn't achieve the job as manager, but I moved out to try and prove that I could be a manager." In a reshuffle the coaching responsibilities for the first team were taken over by Sean Fallon who was being groomed by Kelly as McGrory's successor.

In 1960 Celtic's regular squad was the youngest in the country, and legitimate doubts about its readiness were being expressed. Celtic had drifted into a 'youth policy', hopeful that full maturity would be attained within a couple of years, but the outcome was that Celtic Park became a football backwater for the first half of the decade. Simply, Celtic persisted in fielding sides that were too young, that were still learning their trade. It appeared that the club was restoring, with obstinate pride, a policy introduced nearly sixty years earlier: ". . . and it should delight all who have Celtic's interests at heart that, unless there are unforeseen circumstances, we shall be fielding in the forthcoming season in the top class of football in Scotland a team who have joined us from no higher grade than the juniors." This excerpt from the *Celtic Football Guide* to 1961-62 was a rare article by the chairman, who continued "and we ask that young players on the threshold of their careers be not ruined by ill-advised attacks on them while they are doing their best . . . and I think if we all show a little patience in the months to come we shall have much to delight us."

The manager's comments in the same annual were, however, showing increasing signs of frustration: "With a year's experience behind a few of our younger players we could look forward to a reasonably good season, but it did not turn out that way" (1960-61); and ". . . there can be no doubt that our youth policy is finally reaching the stage where we can confidently expect dividends " (1961-62); and " 'So near and yet so far'; There is no doubt that we should have been in amongst the honours, but always failed at the critical moment" (1962-63).

The period of failure extended from the League Cup final in October, 1957, until the Scottish Cup final of April 1965, or slightly more than the Biblical 'seven lean years'. Was it such a period of failure? The criticism was two-fold: nothing was won, and the club was taking too long to become a modern football organisation. By most standards Celtic's record was a respectable one. Before breaking through in the Scottish Cup of 1965, Celtic lost twice in replayed finals (1961, 1963) and were defeated in three semi-finals (1959, 1960, 1962); there were narrow defeats in the League Cup in the semi-final (1958) and final (1964); Celtic did win the Charity Cup twice (1959, 1961) and the Glasgow Cup an equal number of times (1962, 1964). The club was never threatened with relegation and had its moments in the championship in latter years; in the first serious venture into Europe Celtic had won through to the semi-final of the Cup-Winners' Cup (1964).

Many times the players must have felt that fate had conspired against them, especially in the Scottish Cup. In the 1959 semi-final Celtic's legendary fame as cup fighters was pitted against Paisley folklore; it was asserted that the Cup would return to the burgh only after the tramlines were lifted, as they had just been, but in truth it was the Saints' superior tactics on the day that showed they were on the right tracks. Luck seemed to have turned in the 1960 campaign. Mochan, recently restored as centre after being out of favour, scored all five goals for Celtic in a replay against the holders, St. Mirren, at Parkhead and later in the same week the club came within six minutes of embarrassment at the hands of Highland League side Elgin City at a packed Boroughbriggs. Till that stage Celtic trailed by 1-0, but a frenzied rally forced two very late goals to scrape through; luck and form deserted Celtic in the semi-final replay against Rangers at Hampden when the team played weakly in the second half to succumb by 4-1 — and this was a Rangers' side heading for European humiliation against Eintracht Frankfurt. In the 1961 final and replay the youngsters had the misfortune to encounter inspired performances by Dunfermline's Connachan, whose initial desire to be a goalkeeper had, ironically, been stimulated by watching Celtic's Willie Miller.

The club's glaring inconsistency was most apparent in the league championship. In 1958-59, managing barely a point a game, Celtic finished in sixth place; in 1959-60, with less than a point a game, the side dropped to ninth position; in 1960-61 an improvement saw Celtic move up to fourth spot, and in the following season Celtic finished third behind Dundee and second-placed Rangers. Celtic had mounted a serious challenge for the flag till March 1962, when a 1-0 loss at Airdrie ended it; some Celtic defenders, furious at a lapse in concentration by Haffey that had gifted Airdrie the goal, converged upon the keeper to express their feelings in a welcome sign of increasing professionalism.

The League Cup continued to provide grief for Celtic. For five consecutive seasons Celtic failed to get past the sectional play and this spell was bridged by two disappointing defeats in 1958 by Partick Thistle and in 1964 by Rangers. In the 1958 semi-final an experienced Thistle intelligently exploited gaps in Celtic's defence with breakaways to win 2-1, and in the 1964 final Celtic, although favoured to win over an out-of-form Rangers, failed to cash in on early supremacy to lose again by 2-1.

Several Celtic teams of the post-war era had performed much less creditably, but had redeemed themselves by winning a major honour. This Celtic squad provided honest entertainment, with an emphasis on attacking football; as young teams they were at once the delight and despair of their followers. The see-saw fluctuations in form were best revealed in the 1962 Scottish Cup. Celtic won a thriller at Tynecastle against Hearts by 4-3 before an all-ticket crowd when Crerand scored from a twice-taken penalty, and came from 3-1 down against Third Lanark to force a 4-4 draw; in the replay Celtic won emphatically by 4-0 with superb goals from John Hughes and Alec Byrne, equally unpredictable wingers. In the semi-final at Ibrox Celtic faced St. Mirren, a side they had trounced by 5-0 only five days earlier at Love Street, but the strange decision to drop Carroll, who had tormented the Paisley side in the first game, in favour of the less nimble Hughes contributed to a shock 3-1 defeat.

Celtic's first important foray into Europe was an exhilarating run in the 1963-64 Cup-Winnners Cup, but it ended in characteristic disarray at Budapest. Playing with verve and grit, aided with lashings of raw talent, Celtic had fought through to the semi-final by eliminating Basle (Switzerland), the more formidable Dinamo Zagreb (Yugoslavia) and Slovan Bratislava (Czechoslovakia), beating the latter 1-0 at home and abroad. Indeed Celtic's youngsters performed so impressively that the Czech crowd rose to them at the end, captivated especially by the trickery of Jimmy Johnstone. In the first leg of the semi-final Celtic established control against the powerful MTK squad to win 3-0, but two weeks later slumped to a 4-0 defeat in Hungary when the team showed tactical immaturity by not adopting a more defensive posture.

Celtic, in the early 60s, had some admirable individual players: Billy

210

McNeill was a commanding pivot despite his youth, and many clubs envied the full-back partnership of the stylishly constructive Duncan McKay and the sturdy, reliable Jim Kennedy, the superb passing of wing-half Pat Crerand, the power and energy of inside-forward Bobby Murdoch, the impish skills of Jimmy Johnstone, and the exciting, if erratic, John Hughes. Celtic were "poised for greatness", but a justifiable fear existed that the potential might never be realised. The crying need was for experience and direction, as Cyril Horne, always an astute observer of Celtic, commented on Bobby Lennox's debut: "Lennox found the pace of his first Scottish League game overwhelming and none of his forward colleagues were capable of coaxing him into confidence." (*Glasgow Herald*: 5 March, 1962). Jock Stein, then Dunfermline's manager, was in the habit of heartening Celtic supporters of his acquaintance with the observation that the Celtic sides of these seasons were not as bad as results would indicate; his usual comment was "a good side".

The misery and frustration felt by the support was caused by three factors. During this time Rangers dominated Scottish football; Celtic were reluctant to exercise the option of buying proven players of talent and experience; and there was the growing conviction that, while the club was being steered firmly, it was headed in a wrong direction.

Time after time Rangers would collect the honours and the attendant glory, and the often-used rationalization that the trophies had been gained through brute strength was absurd because those Rangers teams displayed commendable skill, and never more convincingly than against Celtic in the replayed final of 1963 when even Celtic supporters had to admire with a numb despair the control, artistry and flair of McMillan and Baxter, the trickery and speed of Henderson and Wilson, the sudden menace of Millar and Brand. During these seasons Rangers were thoroughly ruthless in exploiting the inexperience of Celtic teams. Rangers demonstrated a clear lesson for Celtic: whenever necessary to bolster their perennial challenge, Rangers were prepared to buy established players: Millar (Dunfermline), Baillie and McMillan (Airdrie), Telfer and McLean (St. Mirren), Baxter (Raith Rovers). Waverley of the *Daily Record* wrote perceptively: "Rangers are at the top and aim to stay there. Their huge following would not tolerate the lack of success which, year in and year out, has made the Celtic faithful a sorely suffering fraternity."

Celtic concentrated on processing their own players, a policy that often ended in disappointment, in a recurring pattern of unfulfilled promise, a pattern reluctantly presented here as 'the Jim Conway syndrome'. Jim was signed as a boy, made his debut as a youth of 17, was encouraged by everybody because of his undoubted potential and to the end of his Celtic career Jim showed . . . promise. Too many young players, most of them forwards, could be placed in this sad category. Chic Geatons, a fine half-back in the 30s and a trainer-coach after the war, was sympathetic to the plight of the young players: "We didn't get any coaching, not in the form it's known today at any rate. But we were coached all right in the best manner possible — that is during an actual game by the older players. . . . The question I ask myself is: If Celtic are too much at the mercy of one man's whims and fancies, is there anybody around with the courage to stand up and insist on a new deal for the club? It is all wrong that the chairman should take over so much managerial direction; the chairman should be the chairman, the directors should be directors, and the manager should manage." (*Weekly News*: 8 October, 1960.)

Geatons had struck a raw nerve among the supporters, many of whom were convinced that Celtic's maladministration was an obstacle to the quest for honours. Few among the support blamed Jimmy McGrory or called for his resignation; the censure and criticism was reserved almost exclusively for the chairman.

During this period Robert Kelly was assisted by Jimmy McGrory as manager and Sean Fallon as coach; it was not a triumvirate that inspired confidence among the supporters. They sensed that the chairman was too actively involved in the day-to-day running of the club and encroached upon the manager's prerogatives in such matters as team selection and transfers; the manager, respected as he was, was not independent enough to stand up strongly for his views and his record since 1945 had been at best moderate; the coach, remembered as a wholehearted full-back and unlikely centre, laboured under the handicap of being compared unfavourably to Jock Stein by the youngsters.

Above all the chairman respected loyalty and integrity: the integrity of men who had played gallantly and well for Celtic, the loyalty of men who would have played for nothing. In his autobiography Jimmy McGrory admitted his reluctance to demand top wages as a player, although some of his colleagues were earning more: "I couldn't believe it as one by one they told me they were on £9 . . . there was me thinking all those years that I was among the big shots with £8. I had even turned down a British record fee to join Arsenal. But that was me with cash. I was hopeless when it came to asking for more, and I suppose that's why I got left behind. I didn't have the push when it came to negotiating and I was the type who would much rather have been offered money than ask for it. I was a little hurt after learning that, but at the end of the day I balanced it out by thinking of the many times I was allowed to pull that green-and-white jersey over my head and that was reward enough for me." (*A Lifetime In Paradise*: McGrory/McNee, 1975.)

Such old-fashioned virtues deserve success, but Celtic weren't successful, neither in organisation nor performance. Because of a stubborn adherence to a youth policy and the neglect of modern training or tactics, Celtic had handicapped themselves.

Mainly at Robert Kelly's insistence, Celtic displayed a healthy attitude towards the sport, stressing a constructive, attacking approach, and adhering to a strict code of conduct on the field. At times such a naïve attitude was punished severely: too often young Celtic teams when attacking furiously, would leave themselves exposed at the back, and experienced sides would wait patiently for the scoring opportunity to present itself. Celtic's recognition of the referee's authority also cost them dearly. Clearly, Celtic players had been instructed to avoid trouble on the field, to turn away when fouled, to accept decisions without question; however, too many referees, especially in Rangers-Celtic matches, where shows of dissension on the field could influence behaviour on the terracing, decided that discretion was the better part of valour and acted accordingly. The club's adherence to this code forced the transfer of two players who could have helped the team considerably, Auld and Crerand. Auld, an outside-left, was fearless, aggressive and fiercely independent, the sort of player who gets into trouble on the field until he matures (already he had been ordered off, while playing for Scotland against Holland in 1959). In May, 1961, despite the manager's objections, he was transferred to Birmingham City for whom he later appeared in a Fairs Cities' cup final. Crerand, a 'Celtic-daft' lad, had become an automatic choice for Scotland, but was increasingly frustrated at the continuing lack of success at club level. Like Auld he was in trouble with referees and was ordered off twice in 1961 (while playing for Scotland against Czechoslovakia, and surprisingly in a five-a-side tournament at Falkirk during the close-season). At half-time in the Ibrox dressing-room in January, 1963, he and Sean Fallon staged a violent confrontation when he was criticised by his coach. Immediately dropped from the side, he was soon transferred to Manchester United for £56,000, the details having been worked out over the phone by Robert Kelly and Matt Busby; the manager was not consulted, being called in only to formalise the transaction and to console the tearful player, who had first heard of his move from a reporter as he returned from Mass on the Sunday. Of course, these players posed discipline problems, but football is a young man's game and many players have been 'tearaways'; effective management can channel that energy into legitimate expression. Significantly, Matt Busby rushed to sign Crerand and did not have any fears about handling him, and Stein upon his return to Celtic Park was eager to utilise Auld, who had been re-signed for Celtic by Jimmy McGrory in January 1965.

To be frank, Celtic's practice during these years should not be dignified with the term 'youth policy'. Everybody in football had been fascinated by 'the Busby Babes', the ill-fated Manchester United side

213

tragically destroyed in an air crash at Munich, and in the burgeoning 'pop' culture of the late '50s and early '60s youth was elevated *per se*. In direct contrast with Celtic, Manchester United practised a calculated policy: youngsters made their way into the side when they were ready, physically and emotionally, and that was only after a systematic apprenticeship. That club provided admirable coaching and development within the several teams fielded each week; at Celtic Park, 'the Kelly Kids' were, for the most part, left to their own devices to develop as players and only the strongest survived. Jim Craig, in an interview for the *Scottish Football Historian* (May/June 1984), recalls the mindless lapping of the track and considered it "nonsensical — like training for snooker by boxing", adding that: "The university (Glasgow) team could have shown the pre-Stein Celtic a thing or two when it came to training." Nor was there a restoration of the practice that brought the club such glory in the first two decades of the century: the patient, methodical grooming and perseverance of Maley's programme was absent.

The policy was not practised consistently. Several players with a leaven of experience were purchased: after an unhappy stay in England Willie Fernie came back from Middlesbrough, but his studied approach became an outdated liability; Billy Price, a left-half, was signed from Falkirk in the summer of 1961 and added more repose to both defence and attack; Bobby Craig, once of Third Lanark and an inside-forward of vast experience, was obtained from Blackburn Rovers in October 1962, but never settled down at Parkhead; Paddy Turner, an Eire internationalist inside-forward was signed from Morton in the summer of 1963 for £10,000, but made only fourteen appearances before being transferred to Glentoran at the end of the season for £1,000; Ronnie Simpson, a veteran keeper, came from Hibernian in September, 1964, and proved a delightful surprise; Hugh Maxwell, another inside-forward, came from Falkirk with an obscure reputation in November 1964 and left anonymously for St. Johnstone in June 1965, and Auld returned in 1965 after four years in England. The purchases indicated concern on Celtic's part, but a disquieting feature should be noted: all were older players, if not veterans; all had been picked up in the bargain basement of the transfer market . . . and two of them (Fernie and Auld) were former favourites whose return served to renew the original annoyance that they had been allowed to leave.

Some of the transfers were induced through panic, and nowhere was this more apparent than in a fruitless scramble after Alfredo di Stefano in August 1964. The famed striker of Real Madrid had been released from his contract by the Spanish club, and Celtic embarked on a wild-goose chase to land the South American superstar. The club phoned Spain, but the player was on holiday and the calls were not returned; the club sent telegrams but these were ignored, until a belated reply rejecting the offer finally arrived at Celtic Park. Despite the player's manifest lack of interest and unavailability (he had recently agreed to a lucrative one-year contract with Espanol), the club ordered Jimmy McGrory to make a hurried, undignified trip to Spain, accompanied by John Cushley, the reserve centre-half and a graduate in languages from Glasgow University, in a futile bid to change his mind. It was fortunate for Celtic that di Stefano dismissed the overtures. Magnificent player that he was, di Stefano had an arrogant streak and ruled imperiously at Madrid for years. Well-substantiated rumours were disconcerting: he insisted that passes be made direct to his feet and ignored others; he forced Didi, Brazil's World Cup star, to quit Madrid because his vanity would not allow a newcomer to usurp his popularity; he accepted Puskas as a team mate only when the Hungarian wisely gave up a chance to score in order to lay on a goal for him, a goal that gained for di Stefano the Spanish leading scorer title.

At the age of 38 the proud Argentinian would not have welcomed the rigours of a Scottish winter to play alongside apprentices, even at the princely £30,000 that Celtic offered him for less than one season. Thoughtful supporters had to wonder about the club's sense of direction; for years the club had advocated a long-term policy based on young teams of traditional Celtic values. Surely the frantic chase after di Stefano contradicted this.

The supporters were caught in an age-old dilemma, continuing to cheer and encourage the team while disapproving of the stuttering policy. There were visible and increasing signs of their frustration. In the replay of the Scottish Cup final on 26 April, 1961, as the match slipped away in Dunfermline's direction thanks to an incredible display by their keeper, Connachan, the mood of the supporters took on a sullen, ugly note in the closing minutes; a year later, in the Scottish Cup semi-final at Ibrox, hundreds of Celtic supporters poured on to the pitch in a misguided bid to have the tie halted as St. Mirren led by 3-0; at another Scottish Cup final replay on 15 May, 1963, early in the second half tens of thousands of supporters left Hampden in an ominous quiet, unable to watch as the Ibrox men toyed with Celtic on their way to a 3-0 rout; after a drawn League Cup game at Parkhead against Queen of the South on 17 August, 1963, several arrests were made when hundreds demonstrated outside the ground, calling for the resignation of Robert Kelly; on 24 October, 1963, the directors and manager met with the executive of the Supporters' Association to consider the situation at a meeting described by the club as "leading to a lively discussion".

By 1965 the level of frustration was dangerously high, the main reason being that Celtic had come heartbreakingly close so often and had ended up with nothing. Resentment was prevalent because some of the wounds had been self-inflicted, especially in the Scottish Cup; in the 50s eccentric team selection had been a factor in successive final defeats by Clyde and Hearts, and it seemed that the practice was continuing into the 60s.

In 1961, due to play against a revitalised Dunfermline Athletic under Jock Stein, Celtic had to resolve a problem at left-half. Peacock had been replaced by Clark because of injury, but was fully recovered; the inexperienced Clark was chosen although Peacock was the side's captain and the regular penalty-taker, and Clark apparently was visibly upset at being picked to play instead of the popular Irishman. The final ended 0-0 although Dunfermline were forced to play the last 13 minutes a man short when their centre-half was injured. Clark was again preferred for the replay, the club giving permission for Peacock to represent Northern Ireland in a friendly international against Italy on the eve of the replay (Stein, with the singlemindedness of the professional, rejected a similar request for Cunningham's services for the same game). A dramatic development just prior to the replay made Celtic's decision questionable. Kennedy, the regular left-back, was rushed to hospital with appendicitis and had to be replaced by O'Neill, a youngster making his debut. The calming influence of Peacock's experience could have made a difference in those tense matches; and significantly, at the end of the season, Peacock, the longest-serving player on the club's books, returned to Ireland to act as player-manager of Coleraine "on the best of terms with the club".

Two years later Celtic faced a strong Rangers' side in the first 'Old Firm' final since 1928, and gained a creditable 1-1 draw, mainly due to

Bobby Murdoch scores Celtic's goal in the 1-1 drawn match of 1963 Scottish Cup final vs Rangers, following up a Bobby Shearer goal-line clearance after a shot by John Hughes (no. 9).

Frank Haffey's heroics in goal. Changes were made for the replay; both wingers were dropped although they had played well in the first game, young Johnstone in particular bothering Rangers' defence with his confident dribbling and netting a goal that was disallowed. The recast forward line, with players switched around for no apparent reason and including the apparently unfit veteran Bobby Craig, was a predictable flop. As Rangers humiliated their disorganised team in the second half Celtic supporters left in droves long before the end, rightly bitter at the chopping and changing; one newspaper pointed out that during the season Celtic had fielded eight outside-rights, seven inside-rights, six centre-forwards, seven inside-lefts, and six outside-lefts.

In January, 1965, a depressingly familiar scenario was unfolding at Celtic Park. Earlier that season the team had lost in the League Cup final to an out-of-form Rangers despite starting favourites; it had been outclassed by the experienced Barcelona in the Fairs Cities Cup; the team was nowhere near contention in the league championship (eventually finishing eighth), and the Scottish Cup remained as the only opportunity to salvage yet another disappointing season. The supporters (and the players) were far from optimistic, fearing that a jinx of sorts had settled over Parkhead and that, despite the club's natural assets, fate allied to poor judgement would conspire to deprive Celtic of a place among the honours. Billy McNeill would later admit that he intended it to be his last season at Parkhead, Bobby Lennox was apparently destined for Falkirk, and Jimmy Johnstone's career as a club and international player was in a trough.

It was a depressing time, the mid-winter of 1964-65, when a member of Celtic's backroom staff could lament in private that "Celtic are finished" and the journalist John Fairgrieve would highlight the club's mediocrity: "They are being left behind by provincial clubs with a fraction of their resources. They are being left so far behind by Rangers that is no longer a race." (*Scottish Daily Mail*: 12 January, 1965.) The almost inevitable defeat at Ibrox on Ne'erday, where the collective frustration of fans and players came to a boil with the ordering-off of Johnstone and a missed penalty by Murdoch, heralded the start of a further slump in form which aroused genuine alarm that, at long last, 'The Faithful' had had enough as attendance figures started to decline ominously. Shortly Celtic had to travel to Love Street to take on St Mirren in the Scottish Cup, and the 'Saints' had inflicted two crushing defeats on Celtic in that competition in recent seasons. The slide was halted on 30 January with a dazzling display on an icy Celtic Park when the players, visibly uplifted (as if sensing a wind of change), routed Aberdeen by 8-0.

Less than 24 hours later the situation, with its gloom and fears, was to experience a transformation which began with the bustle of a press conference and was completed, a few weeks later, by Bob Kelly's firm handshake and the words: "It's all yours now".[1]

Notes
1 Although Stein's appointment was announced on 31 January, he stayed on at Easter Road until Hibs installed a new manager (Bob Shankly) before taking over at Celtic Park on 9 March.

24

PARADISE REGAINED

OVER the years Jock Stein had kept in close contact with Bob Kelly, and went to him at different times for advice: immediately prior to his appointment as manager of Dunfermline, when Hibernian had approached him to take over at Easter Road, and now most recently about an offer made by Wolverhampton Wanderers. He met with Kelly for lunch in Glasgow's North British Hotel to discuss the offer: Wolverhampton had recently sacked the revered Stan Cullis after a lifetime with the club, to universal condemnation, and Stein thus considered their blandishments cautiously. He had made sure that Celtic would remember him through his meetings with Kelly over the years, but it was only at this late stage that the chairman finally, suddenly, asked him if he was interested in coming back to Celtic Park as manager; of course Stein was interested.

The chairman's power may be gauged by the fact that he made the offer before consulting the other members of the Board, but they did not hesitate in endorsing it. They were aware of the work Stein had done at Dunfermline in saving the club from relegation and in winning the Scottish Cup, and admired Dunfermline's stirring adventures in Europe; they recognised his achievement in Edinburgh in restoring the morale of a club in the doldrums by winning the Summer Cup, and they noted Hibs' current challenge for the league. If changes were to be made, Jock Stein was their man.

The major reorganisation within Celtic Park caused by Stein's return as manager was, understandably, not as smooth as it appeared. Bob Kelly had to tell Jimmy McGrory that after twenty years he was to be replaced as manager, and he did so with characteristic speed and bluntness; a reliable account indicates that he went into McGrory's office to interrupt the manager while he was making up the wages for the players and staff to break the news. The blow was softened by offering him a newly created position as Public Relations Officer at much the same salary, and with the assurance that it was a lifetime appointment.

Kelly was most reluctant to abandon his long-term plans for Sean Fallon. As a player the Irishman had been a regular member of Celtic teams as full-back or centre, and often to the disapproval of the supporters; after injury forced his retirement in 1958, he had progressed to become chief coach, and throughout the youth-policy period was the team's mentor; the chairman had been grooming him as McGrory's successor, and when he met Stein to discuss the details of the takeover he astonished him with the proposal that Fallon and Stein share the responsibilities in a dual managership. Stein asked for more time to consider the suggestion, and, using the Wolves offer in a game of bluff and after consulting Desmond White, the club's secretary-director (as much to discover another director's views as for advice), rejected it rightly as unworkable. Stein had longed for the chance to be Celtic's manager; the challenge of running one of Britain's great clubs and the significance of being the club's first Protestant manager had their historic appeal to a man very conscious of the importance of football in the social life of Scotland. Kelly was forced to back down, though Fallon was appointed the assistant manager.

The changes were announced at a press conference held on 31 January, 1965. Journalists, quick to sense that power was slipping away from the chairman, put him on the defensive. Kelly tried to rationalise the appointments as part of a planned, orderly progression, but the reporters knew that the reorganisation was a tacit admission of failure.

In answer to their questions he stated that Stein would be staying at Easter Road for a few weeks until Hibs had found a replacement. He conceded that "the times are changing" and that Stein would have complete control over team matters, that the new man would be making coaching and scouting appointments, that he would be freed from the routine office work that took up so much of a manager's time; the chairman, at his most self-righteous, seemed unaware that by endorsing the new order he was condemning the practices that had hampered the club for at least a decade.

The newspapers were quick to stress the new manager's religion, and tried to fan a controversy about how the supporters would accept a non-Catholic as manager. It was a waste of time. The news was greeted with approval and unqualified delight: approval at the treatment and settlement accorded McGrory, delight at Stein's appointment and his religion was a non-issue with them. The fans were familiar with the outline of his career. Signed for Albion Rovers from Blantyre Victoria as a left-half during wartime by Webber Lees, he had switched to centre-half in an emergency, making his debut against Celtic in a 4-4 draw. A dispute over wages led to his leaving Coatbridge and moving to Wales and non-league Llanelli "for £12 a week and no future". Celtic signed him 18 months later as a reserve centre-half for £1,200, and

Stein, whose home in Lanarkshire had been burgled twice and whose wife, Jean, missed Scotland, was glad to return, though such was the sectarian divide within the country's industrial heartland that his decision to join Celtic did not find favour within Stein's family associations described by sportswriter Hugh McIlvanney, as "vehemently Protestant"[1]. Only four days later, on 8 December, 1951, he made his debut and retained his place; soon he was appointed captain, exerting a considerable influence on the men around him, an influence out of proportion to his talent, but more in line with his character and football intelligence; he gained one representative honour, a League 'cap' against England, but a serious ankle injury that left him with a permanent limp ended his playing career in 1956, leaving him free to assume the coaching responsibilities that Celtic first envisioned for him when he was brought back from Wales.

Jock Stein's own personality assured a successful transition when he took over on 9 March, 1965. He was confident, cheerful and authoritative; he assembled the players and introduced himself, and one recalls him saying: "I promise to do my best for you, but in return you have to do your best for me." He was aware that Jimmy McGrory was in a difficult position and eased it by calling him 'Boss', thus assuring that the former manager would be treated with continuing respect as well as affection, and at any celebrations in the future he made sure that McGrory was always given a prominent place.

Even before he took over at Celtic Park his influence had been felt; a new spirit was coursing through the club and a sense of excitement was prevalent. Celtic made excellent progress in the Scottish Cup after the news of the appointment, beating St. Mirren 3-0 at Paisley, Queen's Park 1-0 at Hampden, and Kilmarnock 3-2 at Celtic Park on 6 March, the same day that Hibernian, playing under Stein for the last time, knocked out Rangers at Easter Road. With Stein now in charge at Parkhead Celtic still needed a replay in the semi-final following a 2-2 draw with Motherwell, but ousted the Lanarkshire team comfortably by 3-0 in the replay to face Dunfermline at Hampden.

A couple of days before the final Stein showed Bob Kelly the team he had selected for the match, a side that had Bobby Murdoch at right-half. Kelly, who had first spotted Murdoch as a 12-year-old playing in a park game, bristled and pointed out that he was a forward and not a half-back. This sort of situation would have resulted in Jimmy McGrory changing the line-up, but Stein was made of sterner stuff, ending the skirmish with the polite but firm statement: "Well, you'll see on Saturday that he is."

On 24 April before 108,800 the following teams lined up:

Celtic: Fallon, Young, Gemmell, Murdoch, McNeill, Clark, Chalmers, Gallagher, Hughes, Lennox, Auld.

221

Celtic players acknowledge the cheers of their fans after the 1965 Scottish Cup triumph.

Dunfermline: Herriot, Callaghan W., Lunn, Thomson, McLean, Callaghan T., Edwards, Smith, McLaughlin, Melrose, Sinclair.

Celtic booked the assistance of a strong wind for the first half, but Dunfermline stunned them in 15 minutes when Melrose lobbed the ball into an empty net after a mix-up in Celtic's defence. Auld equalised after 31 minutes, bravely stationing himself a yard from the line to await a rebound from the crossbar, a ball that soared tenement-high above the goal, and heading it into the net despite the attentions of Dunfermline defenders. Gloom and silence descended on the Celtic support only a minute from the interval when McLaughlin crashed home a shot from 20 yards after a free kick, and the Fifers trooped off satisfied: they had weathered Celtic's opening onslaught, had just struck a psychological blow, and now were to have the wind behind them.

Celtic roared into attack on the resumption, and Auld again equalised in six minutes, after a quick one-two with Lennox had carved the defence leaving Auld free to shoot crisply past Herriot's outstretched foot. Both teams scorned cautious, defensive play and the battle raged on with see-saw variations; although Clark had to scrape one effort off the line, the momentum was gradually passing to Celtic and Dunfermline reluctantly admitted the trend by pulling their inside-forwards back to help in defence.

The minutes slipping past were filled with increasing tension, Celtic's confidence was growing, and a roar from the terracing desperate in its yearning swelled in accompaniment; the feeling was growing that history was on Celtic's side. The youngsters, reviving Celtic's proud traditions as cup-fighters, had twice fought back to level terms and despite the wind against them were pushing Dunfermline into frantic defence; it was now or never as Celtic forced corner after corner.

Another corner, this time on the left, to be taken by Gallagher, hurrying over to place the ball. Across it comes, a high, floating ball and too far out for the keeper, but he has left his goal . . . somebody is there — McNeill . . . and his header rages into the net.

For two seconds Hampden's vast bowl was still, stunned with the sudden shock of decision, and then erupted into bedlam; the roar continued, minute after minute, and its prevailing note changed; it was not merely the burst of joy that a goal produces, rather it was a tumultuous welcome to the future and the instinctive realisation by all Celtic's support that the young men had grown up and that nothing, now nor in the years to come, would withstand their collective spirit. McNeill, the young captain, had emerged from nowhere to score the goal that history demanded. As a member of the team in the past he had delighted in the joy of victory and been despondent in the misery of defeat, but now in full maturity he stood revelling in the moment of triumph.

The manager was quick to realise the significance of the result, and the authors of a modern history of Dunfermline Athletic, his former club, revealed his good fortune. Jock Stein, who had got off to the kind of start that convinced players and fans of his messianic status, would reflect later that "It wouldn't have gone as well for Celtic had they not won this game." (*Black and White Magic*: J. Paterson/D. Scott, 1984.)

As if to emphasise the point, for years afterwards the largest-framed photograph in his office at Celtic Park showed Billy McNeill borne aloft at the end of the match on the shoulders of his jubilant colleagues. The glory days had dawned.

Notes

1 The rumour of a tattoo of 'King Billy' etched on Stein's chest was never fully dispelled, despite clear evidence that it was a myth.

25

"I CAN DIE HAPPY, SON!"

ON 7 May, 1966, Celtic supporters packed Motherwell's trim Fir Park, ready to celebrate a league championship, the first since 1954; for the fans, already assured that the flag was won, it was a green-and-white festival and their joyful day was complete when Bobby Lennox scrambled in the only goal in the last minute. For 20 minutes afterwards they stayed in their places, chanting each player's name, cheering and singing, and insisting that Jock Stein join his men on the field.

After Celtic's struggling win over Dunfermline three days previously, two telegrams had arrived at Celtic Park from Ibrox; although Celtic still had to visit Motherwell and collect one point for an outright win, Rangers had conceded the championship graciously. John Wilson, their vice-chairman, and Scot Symon, the manager, could scarcely have realised that they were acknowledging the start of a new era in Scottish football, destined to be dominated by Celtic whose prestige would reverberate around Europe. "The chase is over . . ."; so read one of the sentences, and it was a chase with the lead changing hands more than once, a chase heightened by the inevitable, grim pursuit of Rangers, as always tenacious and stubborn, reluctant to admit defeat. Rejoicing would have been understandable at the flag's coming to Celtic Park after an absence of 12 years, but the mood was mingled with relief because, over the course of the campaign, Rangers provided the stuff of high drama: a fierce, unrelenting conflict, the squaring-off of 'mighty opposites', a challenge that taxed Celtic's resources to the limit and left the supporters limp with the unbearable dread of last-minute failure.

By October Celtic were being recognised as legitimate challengers for the title when beating Rangers 2-1 in the final of the League Cup. It had been a nail-biting progress to the final, with two ties lost in the first week of the campaign (1-2 away to Dundee United, 0-2 at home to Dundee), but Celtic qualified for the next stage through wins against the Dundee sides and Motherwell. A memorable semi-final with Hibernian at Ibrox ended 2-2 after extra time with 47,000 soaking-wet spectators applauding both teams from the pitch. Lennox crashed in the equaliser well into injury time to force the extra 30 minutes' play. Celtic won the replay 4-0, but a bitter squabble about the venue marred the occasion. Players and officials from both clubs were unanimous in condemning the quality of the Ibrox floodlights, a feeling shared by many spectators; the clubs approached the Management Committee of the league suggesting a switch to Hampden Park for the replay, but the committee upheld the original decision to hold the game at Ibrox despite added protests from both Supporters' Associations. The objections were valid: the calibre of the Ibrox lights had been questioned before, fans travelling from Edinburgh would have to face an extra hour's journey through city traffic, and the winners of the other semi-final would have the advantage of a recent game at Hampden behind them. More galling was the realisation that Celtic and Hibernian supporters were subsidising one of their keenest rivals (a considerable percentage of the gate receipts at games played on neutral ground is awarded to the hosts); one critic noted acidly that at any rate Rangers seemed ready to welcome money in any denomination.

On 23 October Celtic fielded the same side against Rangers in the final: Simpson, Young, Gemmell, Murdoch, McNeill, Clark, Johnstone, Gallagher, McBride, Lennox, Hughes.

Within seconds of the kick-off Ian Young served notice to the record crowd of 107,609 that Rangers were about to experience Celtic's new-found determination when he sent Johnstone crashing with a crunching tackle. Celtic were going to fight for every ball, to contest every yard, and it was Rangers who cracked first. Hughes was having one of his glorious days, roasting Johansen and troubling the rest of Rangers' defence with his dangerous runs; with no danger apparent, McKinnon surprisingly handled the ball inside the penalty area and Hughes scored from the spot by sending Ritchie the wrong way. Shortly afterwards Provan tripped Johnstone, and Hughes netted again, although this time the keeper got a hand to his drive. Celtic revealed a shade more finesse than Rangers, managing to weather a late flurry of pressure that reduced the lead to 2-1.

After the presentation Celtic went back on to the field to exhibit the cup to supporters in a half-lap of honour, but the celebrations were cut short when hundreds of Rangers' supporters invaded the field to halt the proceedings and to inflict harm on Celtic players. The police were quick to clear a path to the dressing-room for the players and to restore order, but it was a frightening scene that could have been disastrous had the Celtic support still massed on the terracings joined in the disturbances. The official upshot was that laps of honour were banned for some years, a decision that was probably wise, but which deprived Celtic supporters of additional celebrations in the future.

Celtic achieved an important result a few days later, travelling to Dens Park and winning the postponed league game 2-1; it was significant because it followed the cup final, and it was the sort of fixture that Celtic had treated too casually in the recent past, but it was clear that Stein was not going to allow lapses in concentration.

The flag was won in direct confrontations between the challengers, and Celtic's first such trial came at East End Park against Dunfermline Athletic on 18 December. Celtic survived the tension to win 2-0, and accomplished the victory through planning. Celtic restored Chalmers to cash in on the fast breakaway, and opted for a semi-defensive struggle; Dunfermline had a clear territorial advantage but Celtic were much more dangerous, springing Chalmers loose twice to score against an out-manoeuvred defence. Recognising the hand behind the tactics the Celtic followers on the terracings introduced a new chant: "Jock Stein! Jock Stein!"

A week later, on Christmas Day, Celtic thrashed Morton at Celtic Park 8-1, and Dunfermline edged out Rangers at Ibrox. Due to meet at Parkhead on January 3, Celtic and Rangers were now level in points. Before the kick-off the Celtic fans among the 66,000 crowd were in full song, but they were silenced abruptly in the first minute when Wilson took full advantage of the treacherous footing to give Rangers the lead. Despite constant pressure Celtic were still behind at the interval, but it was different in the second half. After five minutes Celtic drew level as Gemmell, joining in attack, was re-routed to the by-line, but he crossed low into the goalmouth towards McBride, who fooled the defenders by stepping over the ball to leave Chalmers alone in front of Ritchie. Celtic were rampant now, fluent and imaginative in attack while Rangers were ponderous and predictable. Celtic continued to press, romping to a 5-1 win as three Rangers were booked in the second half. Chalmers in particular thrived, scoring three goals.

Having humbled the closest challengers, Celtic seemed certain to win the championship with ease. It did not look possible for Rangers to re-group and rally to mount another challenge, but that has been an Ibrox trademark — the ability to plug away with determination, to impose a collective will on events, and to rewrite the history of the Scottish game with dourness.

Only two months later, Rangers were firmly installed as favourites, leading Celtic by two points; Celtic had lost three away matches in a row (against Aberdeen, Hearts and Stirling Albion) and, while it was scarcely surprising to lose at Pittodrie and Tynecastle, Celtic could offer a reasonable excuse this time. Celtic had begun to pay the price for success, and those defeats followed the European Cup-Winners Cup ties with Dynamo Kiev.

Because winter in Russia ruled out Kiev as a venue in January, Celtic agreed to play at Tbilisi although the switch involved a much longer journey; the Russians placed further obstacles in their path, objecting to Celtic's choice of airline (Aer Lingus) and insisting that any flight be routed through Moscow. After the match, a satisfactory 1-1 draw, the return was plagued with problems. At Tbilisi a catering mixup caused a delay of two hours; at Moscow trouble in the instrument panel forced a further delay of five hours, during which the entire party had to stay on board in some discomfort; 'freezing rain' forced an unscheduled stopover at Stockholm where the team stayed the night; the discovery of a burst valve just prior to departure ruled out that particular airliner, and Aer Lingus had to divert a regular flight to the Swedish capital to return the players and officials to Prestwick on the Friday night. Surprisingly, Celtic did not request a postponement of the fixture with Hearts and after the party had landed the players dashed to Parkhead for an 11 p.m. loosening-up session after the trying 48-hour return trip in order to prepare for the match at Tynecastle. How much the rigours of travel, the changes in routine, the adjustment to time-zones and the enforced boredom affected Celtic's performance cannot be calculated, but the two points surrendered that day could have cost the championship and would have been a scurvy reward for a splendid performance in Russia that enhanced Scotland's reputation as a football nation. It was not typical of Celtic's new-found consistency to lose (2-3) to a side reduced to ten men after five minutes.

After the upset at Stirling the mood was one of unrelieved gloom. Celtic were now two points behind Rangers and had an inferior goal average; progress in the Scottish Cup and in Europe had caused a pile-up in fixtures and, although eleven games remained, the momentum had passed to Rangers, who had the edge in experience.

Jock Stein expressed private anxiety about his team's relative inexperience, but coaxed methodical football from the side as it applied renewed pressure on Rangers. It was not the sparkling vintage of the early season, but it was effective as Celtic did not lose again during that league campaign, and Rangers showed the strain more. A crowd of 72,000 left Parkhead singing after a convincing cup win on 9 March over Hearts by 3-1, delighted by the news that Rangers had lost surprisingly 3-2 at Falkirk. Rangers continued to drop points in drawn games with Kilmarnock and Hearts and losing to Dundee United but Celtic too struggled to a 2-2 draw at Firhill against Partick Thistle. Indeed, the young Celtic team needed all Stein's enthusiasm and leadership in the closing stages. On 14 April when Celtic defeated Liverpool in the first leg of the Cup-Winners Cup semi-final by 1-0 at Parkhead, Rangers were three points behind, but the gap was reduced to two with Celtic's 0-0 draw at Easter Road two days later; in the return match at Anfield on 19 April Celtic were controversially knocked out of European competition when a goal by Lennox in the last minute was disallowed and, by winning 2-1 against Motherwell, Rangers drew level in points; on the Saturday (23 April) Celtic and Rangers battled to a 0-0 deadlock in the Scottish Cup final, and in the replay Celtic lost 1-0. Although still enjoying the advantage of a game in hand and a superior goal average, Celtic had failed to score in four successive matches and had been defeated in major cup competitions. It was going to be a test of nerve and at Greenock on 30 April Celtic were edgy, surviving a missed penalty by Morton in the first half before settling to a 2-0 win; Rangers kept up the pressure by winning 2-1 at Dunfermline; at Parkhead against Dunfermline on 4 May the team came from behind to register a 2-1 victory while Rangers, still hoping for a slip, crushed Clyde 4-0 at Ibrox . . . and so the celebrations at Fir Park had a touch of relief about them.

The Central Station echoed and resounded with the cheers as the 'specials' returned from Motherwell and the fans poured down the platforms. One observer, later a noted sports writer, caught the mood with this cameo: "An elderly gentleman walking down the platform beside me turned, tears welling in his eyes, and said proudly, 'I've waited a long time to see this again; I can die happy now, son'." (*And You'll Never Walk Alone*: Gerald McNee, 1972.)

Apart from the performances of the team, a youthful side still inexperienced in the pursuit of honours, what gave Celtic supporters most satisfaction was the professionalism shown by the new manager, Jock Stein. It was a textbook illustration, an insight into the modern

Jock Stein gives a tactics talk, March 1967, during the filming of 'The Celtic Story'.

game. He sensed the value in keeping the supporters informed and aware of the issues, he perceived the need to change tactics for particular matches, and he was adept at the handling of a pool of first-team players.

The club had decided in 1965 to publish its own newspaper, *The Celtic View*; the driving force behind it was Jack McGinn, the first editor and later a director of the club, and Stein made astute use of the opportunities it offered to 'educate' the fans. He took the time to explain why changes had been made, and the fans appreciated it; he encouraged good behaviour among the supporters, and they responded to his appeals.

He revealed his increasing mastery of tactics by changing the style of the team for successive matches: caution at East End Park against Dunfermline, and all-out attack against Morton at Celtic Park a week later. He chose 'horses for courses'; a prime example was the selection of the inconsistent John Hughes against Dundee's internationalist Hamilton, who was often troubled by the winger's rushes.

He exerted an easy control over the members of the first-team squad, and imposed it by personally supervising and taking part in the practice games. One youngster was confused about what to call him when he wanted a pass, shouting out amid smiles and hoots of laughter: "Mr Stein! Mr Stein!" The manager quietly took him aside and explained: "Don't call me 'Mr Stein.' They call me 'Boss'. You do the same, son."

He was fully aware of the spur of competition and encouraged his fringe players to fight for places, writing in *The Celtic View* of 3 November, 1965: "Celtic have several players who cannot gain a regular place in the first team, although they are of the top class in Scotland . . . their presence assures that the first-eleven men concentrate on doing well in every single game."

The players soon realised that he meant exactly what he said and to the alarm of some members of the 1965 cup-winning side there was genuine competition for places. Simpson replaced Fallon in goal, although when he was a Hibs' keeper he had several squabbles with Stein had been allowed to leave; Jim Craig, a signing from the unlikely Glasgow University, challenged Young for the right-back position and the berth was his by the end of the season; John Cushley replaced McNeill after the captain sustained an injury and retained the position for a further month after McNeill's full recovery; Charlie Gallagher started the season as the inside-forward and later alternated with Auld (in general Gallagher was preferred till February, when Auld was recalled to engineer Celtic's run-in for the championship).

Other players were finally given extended runs in a settled position and established themselves: Murdoch, as Stein had forecast, emerged as an outstanding half-back, a position where he welcomed facing the ball and thus gaining an extra split second; Johnstone was encouraged to express himself on the right wing after languishing in the reserves, and Hughes, the manager sensed, needed the space of the left wing to operate at maximum efficiency.

Stein felt that Celtic needed another goalscorer to help take some of the load off Lennox and Chalmers, so Joe McBride had come from Motherwell for £22,000 in June 1965. McBride, a cheerful extrovert, had played for several clubs without really establishing himself as a 'star' (Celtic had expressed interest often in the past but had always drawn back). Stein did not hesitate, signing him in the close season and Celtic had a potent strike force at last.

The players respected the new manager immediately, sensing that he was 'a players' man'. They noted his independence from Bob Kelly, and admired his rapport with Jimmy McGrory; they were won over by the new training regimen that stressed ballwork, and physical fitness that concentrated on pace and alertness; they came to respect his assessment of opposing teams, and welcomed his straightforward directions; they appreciated his handling of the media, knowing that no newspaper would publish unfair criticism of them with the redoubtable Stein ready to act as their defender.

The supporters, players, and directors were ecstatic about the triumph in the championship, but the manager remained calm amid the euphoria and was already planning for an even brighter future. He had decided that the forthcoming North American tour might be the opportunity to test those plans.

26

THOSE GLORY, GLORY DAYS

MUCH of the planning that led to Celtic's greatest year in Scotland and Europe was conceived, practised and perfected on a comprehensive tour of North America, a tour that started off casually in Bermuda, then moved north to criss-cross Canada and the United States. Because it followed an arduous season in which the championship and the League Cup were won and bids for the Scottish Cup and the European Cup-Winners' Cup came agonizingly close, some critics had misgivings about it, but the manager had a few things up his sleeve: he insisted on first-class travel arrangements with direct jet-connections and air-conditioned hotels to combat the heat and humidity; he approved of the opposition with three games lined up against Tottenham Hotspur and fixtures with Bayern Munich (West Germany) and Atlas (Mexico) as well as warm-up sessions against local teams; he suggested to the players that while they were champions of Scotland they could still improve, and that a new formation might be tried.

Stein was never fully satisfied and had studied his players, noting their virtues and flaws. He was, as always, prepared to make changes and experiment: he gave Auld a new role by pulling him back into midfield to dictate play alongside Murdoch; he encouraged Tommy Gemmell to overlap even more and join in the attack; he gave O'Neill, a steady defender, an opportunity to replace Jim Craig when the regular full-back had to miss the tour because of his work as a dental student. It was a splendid tour; the team went through it undefeated and returned refreshed in spirit and ready to try out their innovations in competition.

Celtic got off to a high-powered start in the League Cup, and stormed their way to the final on 29 October, when these teams lined up:

Rangers: Martin, Johansen, Provan, Greig, McKinnon, Smith D, Henderson, Watson, McLean, Smith A., Johnston (Wilson).
Celtic: Simpson, Gemmell, O'Neill, Murdoch, McNeill, Clark, Johnstone, Lennox, McBride, Auld, Hughes (Chalmers).

Rangers, desperate for a win, aware that their long-standing

231

supremacy in Scottish football was passing to Celtic, and still smarting from two recent defeats (a 4-0 rout in the Glasgow Cup and a 2-0 defeat in the league at Parkhead), hoped for great things from two expensive close-season signings, Alec Smith (Dunfermline) and Dave Smith (Aberdeen).

The match was hard and uncompromising. Rangers made it a physical confrontation, fighting with more determination than skill. They had more of the play but, hard as they tried, they could not produce the type of move that led to Celtic's goal in the 18th minute. Auld gathered the ball 40 yards out, holding it as he calculated the possibilities, and slung over a high cross beyond the far post where McBride headed the ball back intelligently for Lennox to connect perfectly. The contrast in style between the teams was apparent. Rangers had the strength to pin Celtic back in defence for sustained periods, but Celtic had the skill and speed to slice open Rangers' defence. Still retaining his position after the tour, Willie O'Neill was outstanding as full-back, mastering the tricky Henderson and clearing the ball off the line with Simpson stranded.

The 'Old Firm' encounters decided the championship. In the first, at Parkhead on 17 September, Celtic attacked from the opening whistle, scoring twice through Auld and Murdoch within three minutes and then playing a 'cat-and-mouse' game with the Ibrox team for the rest of the game, content to give up space to Rangers but closing down all the important zones. Celtic's autumn visit to Edinburgh ended in a defeat for the previously unbeaten Hibernian by 5-3 in an entertaining game enjoyed by the large crowd which saw McBride, a last-minute choice at inside-right, score four goals. On 19 November Celtic scraped past Dunfermline at East End Park by 5-4 after an old-fashioned thriller; three times Celtic were behind by two goals (0-2, 1-3, 2-4), but McBride's penalty late in the game proved the winner. Previously, the team's play had been marked with a sense of excitement; now there was an aura of invincibility. The supporters started to realise that it might just be possible to win everything, the Glasgow Cup and the League Cup having been captured; by New Year the team was leading the league by a healthy four points, in the European Cup they had reached the quarter-finals, and were favoured to win the Scottish Cup. The surprising Dundee United inflicted two of Celtic's three competitive defeats that season (Vojvodina's 1-0 win in Yugoslavia was the other), and that remarkable double in the league, by the same score of 3-2, set up Rangers' last chance of a title upset; however, Celtic's disciplined performance on a muddy Ibrox on 6 May earned the required point in a 2-2 draw, with both Celtic's goals coming from Johnstone.

Another important signing helped: Hearts' striker, Willie Wallace, became available in December 1966 and Stein moved quickly to bid for him, knowing of Rangers' interest. In sport, where a common saying is that the good managers are lucky, Stein derived an extra bonus from this signing because McBride, the leading scorer in the country, began to experience twinges in his knees and had to be sidelined shortly afterwards for a cartilage operation.

In the Scottish Cup Rangers looked to be the greatest threat to Celtic, but while Celtic were sweeping past Arbroath 4-0 at Parkhead many in the large crowd were listening to transistor radios with delighted disbelief as Berwick Rangers knocked out the Ibrox side in one of the most incredible upsets in cup football. Aberdeen were confident approaching the final against Celtic, having drawn both league games and hinting that Celtic might be jaded after a mid-week European semi-final in Prague; however, it turned out to be no contest on 29 April when the following sides faced each other:

> *Celtic*: Simpson, Craig, Gemmell, Murdoch, McNeill, Clark, Johnstone, Wallace, Chalmers, Auld, Lennox.
> *Aberdeen*: Clark, Whyte, Shewan, Munro, McMillan, Petersen, Wilson, Smith, Storrie, Melrose, Johnston.

Aberdeen, forced to leave manager Eddie Turnbull behind in the hotel with a stomach disorder, opted to concentrate on defence. Stein had anticipated those tactics, and at this late stage in the season came up with yet another gambit; he asked Chalmers, always an intelligent runner off the ball, to play wide on the right wing and thus take the full back with him, leaving Johnstone free to roam at will. Both goals were scored by Wallace, and with cruel timing for the Dons, one coming three minutes before half-time and the other only four minutes after the break. Celtic's was a team performance but outstanding was Jim Craig, restored to the side at right-back and performing with authority; years later in an interview Craig was to say that he felt O'Neill was unlucky to be the regular reserve because he had been playing more steadily than Gemmell or himself, but that Stein decided to gamble on pace and flair in attack.

As Celtic made progress in the European Cup, it was becoming clear that an exceptional team was being forged at Parkhead; it was a side without a weakness and with outstanding individual strengths but, above all, it was a team. One journalist, based in England, enjoyed coming to Glasgow and described it: ". . . an exhilarating team that sought to blend athletic speed and combativeness with imagination, delicacy of touch at close quarters, and surges of virtuosity." Seemingly an impossible ideal to attain, Celtic in 1967 under Stein had the men to realise it.

In goal Simpson, always considered a 'lucky' keeper and happy to clear shots with elbows, knees or feet, was a model of concentration in keeping 'a clean sheet' in half of his games with Celtic and relished a new nickname, 'Faither'; at full-back Craig and Gemmell, both tall, strapping and athletic, were noted for their overlapping but capable in defence where they could match any winger for pace; the heart of the defence was solid and McNeill, an admirable captain, dominated there, unbeatable in the air, competent on the ground and assisted by the sweeper, Clark, who always seemed unhurried in his tackles, interceptions or clearances; the midfield pair afforded a contrast in appearance, Murdoch, powerfully built and exuding strength whereas Auld, a hard, little man, radiated cunning; up front much depended on Johnstone, a tiny figure who would have looked at home in racing silks, but a man of courage and skill enough to turn any defence inside out; Lennox, another small man, blessed with an incredible burst of speed, could run all day and still be sharp enough to seize the half-chance; Chalmers, now being considered a veteran, had lost little of his natural speed and remained dangerous near goal with both head and foot; Wallace prowled restlessly and his stocky frame commanded respect from defenders. The reserve strength was impressive too: Fallon, although prone to lapses in concentration, was a capable keeper and Cushley had proved an efficient stand-in for McNeill; on his day Hughes could be the best forward in Scotland either in the middle or on the wing while, whenever he was fielded, Gallagher made vital contributions with astute passing and crosses; missing from the line-up for the second half of the season was McBride, and he still finished the leading scorer in Scotland.

The nerve centre of the team was in midfield with Murdoch and Auld; they appeared to be a direct contrast with Murdoch's strength and Auld's cunning, but each complemented the other superbly. Auld, a foxy player, had a hardness about him and was more than capable of holding his own in any rough-house; and Murdoch, for all his muscle and stamina, had the most delicate touch in passing. They had other qualities in common: maturity and style, a hunger for goals, and competitive steel; they hated to lose and exerted tremendous efforts to avoid defeat. It was said that Murdoch blazed in through the front door, while Auld stole round the back.

And yet the team was more than the sum of its parts, and that was due to Stein's influence; perhaps the manager's greatest gift was that he could make men do for him more than they would have been able to do for themselves. The players trusted and respected him, and had gained confidence in themselves, their assignments and their team-mates. Stein never asked a player to do more than he was capable of, but he expected total effort and concentration.

Sometimes the team had to be convinced. In the first round of the European Cup the Swiss champions Zurich packed their goal and defended grimly at Parkhead to hold Celtic to a 2-0 win; the Celtic players were certain that in Switzerland their opponents would come at them, but Stein had sensed that they did not have the attacking flair to pose that type of threat. Before the second leg the players and Stein held spirited discussions, but Stein was insistent and his prediction was entirely borne out, leading to a convincing 3-0 win. The quarter-final with Vojvodina of Yugoslavia was critical. Celtic had returned to Glasgow 1-0 down to a late goal, and knew it was going to be hard. Because of his knee operation McBride was ruled out, and Wallace, a recent signing, was not eligible. The Yugoslavs were organised and disciplined in defence, and dangerous on the break; one sensed that in a mediocre year they could have won the European Cup. At half-time Celtic had still not broken through although the pressure on the visitors' goal was increasing. After 60 minutes Celtic got the vital break when the giant keeper, Pantelic, fumbled a cross for Chalmers to sweep alertly into the net; despite constant and fierce pressure the Yugoslavs held on, intent on getting a play-off in neutral Rotterdam. In the last minute Celtic gained another corner and Gallacher moved over to the right to take it; as he was about to cross the ball, two Celtic forwards darted out from the packed goalmouth, taking defenders with them; Gallagher's cross was flighted perfectly into the penalty area and McNeill had a clear and unimpeded run to head the ball strongly into the net.

Perhaps no other set of supporters celebrate as noisily as Celtic's, but they surpassed themselves, celebrating long after the whistle, unheard among the joy; by this stage in the season the English journalists were taking an interest in the football activities north of Hadrian's Wall and one recalled sitting in the press-box musing on the drama still unfolding on the terracings and overhearing a Scottish colleague solemnly commenting as he passed him: "Aye, Jock cut the margin fine tonight."

The struggle with Dukla Prague in the semi-final revealed yet another aspect of the team's tactical resourcefulness. Celtic had struggled to build up a 3-1 lead from the first leg in Glasgow through Wallace's two fine goals, but were apprehensive about the return. Recalling another occasion when Celtic had foolishly squandered a three-goal lead behind the Iron Curtain (against MTK of Budapest in the 1964 Cup-Winners Cup), Stein determined that it would not happen again and he decided to defend in depth. A photograph of Celtic's team taken just before the kick-off is most revealing; standing in the back row the defenders look resolute, more so than normally but the forwards, crouching in front, betray the tension, looking ill-at-ease with strained expressions and clenched fists. Obeying Stein's orders to defend, Celtic closed every avenue to goal, with the midfield pair in ultra-defensive positions and the other forwards pulled back to help out, leaving Steve Chalmers as a brave but lonely runner up front; the Czechs rarely looked like scoring and Celtic's tactics earned a goalless scoreline that put them into the final. Still, Stein was unhappy about the tactics employed and in later years always felt a shade uncomfortable in discussing them.

The preparation for the final bore a more characteristic Stein imprint. Knowing that the supporters planned to be there in large numbers, having saved for months although the match was to be televised live, he took pains in *The Celtic View* and in every interview to discuss the historic importance of the occasion and the need for exemplary behaviour (and when one considers the scenes at later European finals he was totally successful in his appeal). Interviewed on TV in Portugal he stressed Celtic's usual emphasis on attack, deliberately contrasting it with Inter Milan's defensive outlook and knowing that the Italians, even while playing at home in a previous final against Lisbon's beloved Benfica, had employed sterile, negative tactics in a 1-0 win over a side reduced to ten men (and the local fans got the message). He had seen Inter play and every Celtic practice, either at Barrowfield or in Lisbon, was designed to stress ways of prising open that defence; he warned the players about the Portuguese sun, recalling painful sunburns suffered by some Scottish players before an international fixture in 1950, but he took his players along to train in the stadium at 5.30 p.m., the scheduled kick-off time; he kept up a good-natured banter in the days before the match and, observing the conduct of the supporters as they started to arrive in a predominantly Catholic country, found a rich vein of humour in the situation, commenting at breakfast, "I hear they've made the ten o'clock Mass all-ticket . . .". When the team, dressed in blazers and grey flannels, examined the pitch an hour before the match to be greeted tumultuously by thousands of supporters, he mused just loudly enough to be heard by his players, "I wonder how many months of overtime those lads have put in to be here tonight?" In the long, shaded tunnel as the teams lined up side by side on 25 May, 1967, the relatively inexperienced and all-Scottish team alongside the sophisticated, disciplined Italian champions, and started towards the sunlit pitch, he may have been the one who started off his men singing their supporters' songs, a move that visibly shocked their opponents; and, when he made his way with the substitutes and assistants to the bench, his work was almost over . . . it was, as always, up to the players.

> *Celtic*: Simpson, Craig, Gemmell, Murdoch, McNeill, Clark, Johnstone, Wallace, Chalmers, Auld, Lennox.
> *Inter Milan*: Sarti, Burgnich, Facchetti, Bedin, Guarneri, Picchi, Domenghini, Bicicli, Mazzola, Cappellini, Corso.

After only seven minutes' play the worst fears of every Scot were realised; both teams had made a nervous start, but Celtic looked to be settling when Milan broke away for Craig to pull down Cappellini from behind. Mazzola coolly scored from the spot, and the most renowned defensive team in Europe pulled back its players, with a sweeper playing behind four rugged defenders and with four midfielders closing down on any attempt at penetration. Celtic attacked and came close several times before the interval, but found Sarti in top form behind that resolute defence. Jim Craig recalls the mood in the dressing-room at half-time; despite the pressure on the Italians' goal, Celtic players felt a shade downcast thinking they had not really performed that well, because few of the moves aimed at opening up the game had been executed as planned in training. Some players anticipated a spirited pep-talk, but were surprised at Stein's calm; he encouraged them, assuring them things were going well, that the Italians would tire more than they would, that they had been a shade too direct in their methods, and he reminded them that the way to beat the packed defence was by turning it.

In 62 minutes, after sustained pressure, Inter's goal fell. Craig, the man who had given away the penalty, moved up with his forwards and started towards the penalty area; he rolled the ball back for Gemmell

Tommy Gemmell's piledriver brings Celtic the equaliser in Lisbon, European Cup final 1967. Bobby Lennox is in the foreground.

and the other full-back hit one of his celebrated 'specials' from 25 yards for a glorious goal. The supporters went mad with delight in Lisbon; in Glasgow chairs toppled over, beer was spilt, and the celebrations started, but it was not till five minutes from the end that Chalmers diverted a shot from Murdoch past the Italian keeper, the man who had kept his team's hopes alive for so long.

Inter, outplayed for the entire game, could not summon up anything for a comeback, but the minutes passed slowly. Showing signs of the tension, Jock Stein started away from the bench and along the touchline in the direction of the dressing-room; even as he did so the whistle went, and he limped happily towards his goalkeeper to congratulate him; he reached Simpson at the same moment as McNeill and one of the first fans to scale the moat; and one photograph published later caught the moment when the manager, the young captain, the veteran keeper, and a kilted supporter met in a spontaneous and moving embrace.

From the point of accomplishment alone it was Celtic's finest hour, but more appropriately it symbolised the club's traditional enthusiasm and skill in a characteristic display of vigorous, attacking play for a vast and enthralled European TV audience. The performance revitalised a competition in the grip of defensive and cynical football in much the same way as the club's founding eighty years earlier had breathed fresh life into the native game. The continental press rightly saw this as a more significant achievement than the important breakthrough that Celtic had made in becoming the first British club to win the most prestigious trophy in club football. Bill Shankly, the only other British manager present on this historic evening, pushed through the crowds outside the Celtic dressing-room, and made his way towards his colleague, like himself a former miner, to congratulate him; unselfconsciously he proclaimed: "John, you'll be immortal now . . .".

After the *annus mirabilis* of 1967 came the 'letdown' of the following year, but so high were the standards that the team retained the championship, the League Cup, and the Glasgow Cup — a vintage year normally.

Celtic faced a difficult challenge in the League Cup section. Dundee United and Aberdeen had spent the summer doing missionary work in the United States and from the start were match-fit. The other team in the grouping was Rangers, whose flurry of deals in the close season indicated their anxiety to catch up to Celtic. David White resigned as Clyde's manager and went to Ibrox as assistant to Scot Symon; Morton's stylish Danish keeper, Sorensen, joined his compatriot, Johansen; Ferguson, a dangerous striker from Dunfermline, was reunited with a former team-mate Alec Smith; Penman was lured from Dens Park and Persson, a Swedish winger, left Tannadice for Ibrox. In a desperate attempt to catch up with Celtic Rangers had spent a fortune, and appeared willing to waive their traditional claim as representatives of Scotland.

For the first 'Old Firm' clash 94,168 packed Ibrox, and the gates were closed before the kick-off with thousands still outside. Gemmell gave Celtic an early lead from a penalty, but Penman equalised late on, cleverly fooling Celtic's defence with a free kick. For Celtic it was a satisfactory result, preserving a one-point lead. Tension was high for the return at Celtic Park, with everybody recognising that the match would decide the section and probably the destination of the League Cup. Rangers' team selection indicated they had opted for power rather than finesse, and Celtic supporters were anxious, having detected a slight falling-off from the magnificence of the previous season.

Rangers took an early lead against the run of play when Henderson broke away to draw Simpson from his goal before netting. Celtic's defenders appealed for offside, supported by a linesman's flag that the referee chose to ignore. Celtic increased the tempo, but Rangers survived to half-time, although Lennox had a goal disallowed. The battle raged on until, with thirteen minutes to play, Parkhead offered the spectacle that only this most bitter of all rivalries can produce: from the jam-packed Celtic end not a sound, not a movement as they stood stunned into disbelief and from the Rangers' end wave after wave of frenzied cheering. Henderson had broken away again to be fouled by Craig within the box. Rangers' players, sagging under the constant Celtic pressure seconds before, were jubilant as they moved upfield to watch Johansen put the result beyond doubt. Johansen strode forward confidently, but his shot crashed against the crossbar to the delight of the Celtic players and supporters; the Dane was so flustered at the outcome that he attempted to score by heading the rebound (had he netted, the goal wouldn't have counted).

The effect was instantaneous. Celtic swarmed round Rangers' goalmouth with recharged energy and nothing could withstand the surge; a corner from the left swerved in the wind, as Sorenson and Murdoch collided in mid-air, and towards Wallace who alertly headed in the goal that shattered Rangers. On the terracing the scene was one of unadulterated joy, a bedlam of delight made all the more sweet by Rangers' bitter show of dispute and the sight of some Rangers' defenders throwing themselves to the turf in the realisation of failure. Rangers wilted visibly, and Celtic pressed home the advantage; Murdoch made ground, striding forward with majestic force to unleash a fierce drive high into the net past Sorenson from twenty yards. The pressure continued, and Lennox darted through a dispirited defence to add a third goal for a famous victory.

Delighted with the result, the manager claimed in the next issue of *The Celtic View* that it was the greatest success under his command and, as Stein was often at pains to downplay the importance of matches against Rangers, it is worth considering his statement in full. Stein felt that Celtic's task in recent encounters with Rangers had been made more difficult by the attitude of the referees; in this particular match a doubtful goal for Rangers had stood, and an apparently more valid one by Celtic had been disallowed, but the most disturbing feature was the tolerant approach adopted by the referee towards the crude tackling by Rangers.

Previous Celtic teams, especially those of the 'youth-policy era', could not have coped, but Celtic under Stein was a side with a vastly different outlook. Nobody could doubt the desire to win and the will to succeed, but no criticism appeared anywhere of ruthlessness on Celtic's part in the drive for victory; indeed the success gained by the team was welcomed and praised as much for its flair and attitude as for the feeling of pride engendered by the European and domestic triumphs. The fixtures with Rangers became even more critical, the matches that decided championships and won cups. Celtic had the more skilful side, and Rangers approached the matches with their customary determination hardened into a desperate resolve to win or at worst to avoid a humiliating defeat; conceding Celtic's superiority in skill they relied on physique and power to intimidate or ruffle the Parkhead side. Frequently, Celtic were knocked off-stride, but no longer were the players intimidated; with Stein as their manager they could take care of themselves. While the purist might quibble at the retaliation, the realist had to agree with it. Reporters did not help the situation; so eager were they to prove their papers' impartiality, and thus ensure continuing patronage, that the blame for the coarseness in the matches was invariably shared — a moral stance that condemns retaliation as much as the initial provocation, and rarely discriminates between the degrees of offences. More than ever the 'Old Firm' was engaged in psychological and physical warfare.

On 18 October, 1967, Celtic and Dundee lined up at Hampden for the final:

> *Celtic*: Simpson, Craig, Gemmell, Murdoch, McNeill, Clark, Chalmers, Lennox, Wallace, Auld (O'Neill), Hughes.
> *Dundee*: Arrol, Wilson R., Houston, Murray, Stewart, Stuart, Campbell, McLean J., Wilson S., McLean G., Bryce.

Stein had to resolve one crisis before the game; Johnstone was ineligible due to suspension, having been ordered off against St. Johnstone, and Stein chose Chalmers as the replacement. It was a controversial decision on his part because the veteran had scored only one goal since the memorable counter at Lisbon; any latent criticism was stilled in the opening minutes when a long-range header from

Steve Chalmers nods Celtic's first goal in League Cup final victory over Dundee, 1967.

McNeill, drifting wide of the goal, was neatly turned into the net by Chalmers. It was a typical goal from Chalmers, unspectacular but scored by a man in perfect position. Whenever Dundee threatened to narrow the gap, Celtic stepped up the pace to win comfortably by 5-3.

The strain of keeping up the impossibly high standards of the previous season showed early in the pursuit of a third championship in a row. Celtic opened with a home win against Clyde (3-0), but lost to Rangers at Ibrox (0-1), and dropped another vital point to St. Johnstone at home (1-1). Despite the shock of an early dismissal in the European Cup by Dynamo Kiev (USSR) and the lingering trauma of the fiasco with Racing Club of Argentina (when three Celtic and two Racing players were sent off in a play-off for the 'World Club Championship' in Montevideo, won 1-0 by Racing Club after unsavoury incidents had marred the home and away ties and foreshadowed the events in Uruguay).

Celtic settled down to closing the gap; without being inspired the team was consistent and solid, and by the New Year had pulled to within two points of Rangers. The Ibrox club, unhappy at the developments in the Scottish scene, had made further changes. Scot Symon, at the time

241

the most consistently successful manager in Scotland over a period of years, was fired although Rangers were leading the league. But their great rivals, Celtic, were in South America preparing to do battle for the 'World Club Championship'. Symon was replaced by his relatively youthful assistant, David White, and the side continued undefeated prior to the clash at Parkhead. Celtic had to win and made a fine start, playing with pace and imagination on a lifeless mid-winter pitch before 75,000 to lead 1-0 at half-time. Rangers revived shortly after the interval when Fallon allowed a moderately hit shot to trickle between his legs for a soft equaliser, but Murdoch restored the lead with a memorable goal. He controlled the ball in mid-air, with his back to Rangers' goal, to pivot and smash a ferocious shot past Sorensen; still Fallon's miserable luck continued when, two minutes from the end, he contrived to dive over a half-hit shot from twenty-five yards from Johansen. Celtic, despite outplaying their rivals, had been checked and held to a draw, remaining two points behind.

Stein was rightly worried about the situation, realising that no other teams were in contention; he sensed that Rangers would not drop too many points in the latter half of the season. He called a meeting of his first-team pool to discuss matters; he welcomed suggestions, and even offered to change the training schedule; he indicated that it would be a close race, and that goal average might be a factor; he asked for a shade more effort and improvement.

Throughout January and February Celtic won consistently, but Rangers matched that point for point; by late March a few hints had appeared that the Ibrox club was becoming edgy although it had dropped only one point to Celtic. Celtic had to face up to an ominous cluster of away fixtures, but the side was playing with flair and sparkle to win them all: St. Johnstone (6-1), Dundee United (5-0), Hearts (2-0) and Aberdeen (1-0).

As Rangers struggled the momentum was switching to Celtic, who received a psychological boost from the Ibrox boardroom after the 'Old Firm' had been paired in the semi-final of the Glasgow Cup and Celtic, relatively free from other commitments, pressed for a date. Rangers were in an awkward position; although they still led in the league race by one point and were through to the quarter-finals of the Scottish Cup and the Fairs Cup, their recent form had been shaky. Perhaps another match might have jeopardised their chances, but they made one of the more publicly shameful decisions in their history; citing "a congestion of fixtures" — a feeble excuse — they withdrew from the tournament rather than face Celtic and risk a humiliating defeat. Nobody was fooled by the official reason, least of all the Rangers' supporters who had to undergo a merciless ribbing as they were taunted with accusations of cowardice. More demoralising than that was the fact that the ploy failed miserably: in the Scottish Cup Hearts beat them at Tynecastle in a replay, in the Fairs Cup Leeds United eliminated them at Elland Road amid violent scenes and, on the night that Celtic defeated Clyde 8-0 in the Glasgow Cup final, Morton held them to a 3-3 draw in the league at Greenock.

Three days later the same Morton side gave Celtic a fright. Welcomed on to Celtic Park with murmurs of grateful appreciation by a large crowd, they held Celtic to a 1-1 tie with only 30 seconds left. Rangers, now level in points with Celtic, were leading 2-1 at Kilmarnock and news of that score was spreading round the terracings amid growing despair, when in the dying seconds Bobby Lennox scrambled in the winning goal.

Yet another decision by Rangers backfired miserably. Knowing that Celtic's last league game at Dunfermline had to be postponed because of Dunfermline's appearance in the Scottish Cup final against Hearts, they went ahead with their home fixture against Aberdeen in the hope of keeping up the pressure on Celtic, while the Scottish Cup final was being played a few miles away before its lowest post-war attendance. Stein had already decided that a Celtic party would be at Hampden, and encouraged Celtic supporters to turn up and enjoy the occasion. A few minutes after the whistle at Hampden, an incredulous Jock Stein nearly broke a leg as he jumped off the steps of the Hampden entrance upon hearing the news that Aberdeen had beaten Rangers 3-2 to inflict on the Ibrox side their first league defeat of the season (and in their last game).

Three days later Celtic claimed the championship at East End Park by defeating the newly crowned cup holders 2-1 before a record crowd. By the end of the season Celtic were back to their best; since the defeat at Ibrox in September, Celtic had played 32 league matches without a loss and since New Year (and Stein's pep-talk) had won 16 in a row.

Two players made a significant contribution: Bobby Lennox was in splendid form latterly, scoring in 13 consecutive games if the Glasgow Cup is included, and Charlie Gallagher, brought into the side to replace the injured Auld, preserved the rhythm in Celtic's play with his intelligent distribution and long passing that the front runners relished.

Some critics feel that the Celtic team of 1968-69 was even better than the 'Lisbon Lions' and can supply compelling arguments for their claim. They gained the domestic treble of championship, Scottish Cup and League Cup; they were strengthened by two important signings in Tom Callaghan (Dunfermline Athletic) and Harry Hood (Clyde); George Connelly and Jim Brogan established themselves in the playing pool; and another two players, previously undervalued because of inconsistency, John Hughes and John Fallon, made a dramatic improvement and won regular places; and the members of the Lisbon team were more mature, capable of further changes in tactics.

Celtic made a confident start to retaining the League Cup by winning 2-0 at Ibrox, taking ruthless advantage of a flustered John Greig's misjudgement, and a fortnight later won the return match at Parkhead by 1-0. The other two teams in the section, Partick Thistle and Morton, served as sparring-partners and were unable to cope with the threat from Celtic's forwards. Wallace and Lennox had developed a fine understanding and never could be covered fully — one might be contained but the other could break loose for several goals, helped by the intelligent running of his partner. Against Thistle at Parkhead Wallace scored four times, and Lennox surpassed that with five at Firhill. Jimmy Johnstone bewildered defenders with tanner-ba' dribbling on the right, while John Hughes overpowered them with forceful runs down the left.

A fire at Hampden Park that damaged the pavilion and many seats in the stand forced a delay in holding the final, and it was not until 5 April, 1969, that Celtic claimed the trophy again by beating Hibernian 6-2 before 72,420 spectators. Some changes had been effected in Celtic's line-up. Simpson had injured his shoulder in a Scottish Cup tie against Clyde and it was slow to heal; Fallon, as he was doing more frequently of late, replaced him. Clark was the first member of the Lisbon Lions to lose his place permanently as Jim Brogan, a young, speedy defender with a bite in his tackles, moved up. John Hughes, annoyed with himself for not earning a place in the Lisbon team, had worked hard since then and was playing the best, and most consistent, football of his career, but he was unlucky to injure an ankle badly at Perth only a few days before the final. Celtic gave a superb display to win in style; three goals up at half-time, the cupholders came out looking for more in the second half. Concentrating on attack, they left gaps in defence, but Fallon earned an ovation for spectacular saves near the end, an indication that his lapses of the previous season had been forgiven if not forgotten. Even the ranks of Tuscany joined in the praise: "But all credit to Celtic for a wonderful display of attacking football . . . and the huge crowd was entertained to football at its brilliant best. Celtic in this mood are among the best in the world, and Hibs were toiling most of the afternoon." (*Evening News* (Edinburgh): 5 April, 1969.)

The Scottish Cup final provided another memorable day for Celtic, as the team fully avenged the 4-0 defeat inflicted by Rangers in the 1928 final; it turned out to be agony for Rangers, so desperate to win the cup and salvage an otherwise barren season. Approaching the final, Rangers were confident because of a league double over Celtic and were more encouraged when Celtic had to play without their regular wingers: Johnstone was ineligible through suspension, and Hughes was still unfit.

George Connelly takes advantage of a defensive mix-up to net Celtic's third goal vs Rangers in the 1969 Scottish Cup final.

Although Johnstone was replaced by young George Connelly, Stein had decided that the Fifer would play mainly in midfield. Before a crowd of 132,000 these teams lined up on 26 April:

> *Rangers*: Martin, Johansen, Mathieson, Greig, McKinnon, Smith, Henderson, Penman, Ferguson, Johnston, Persson.
> *Celtic*: Fallon, Craig, Gemmell, Murdoch, McNeill, Brogan (Clark), Connelly, Chalmers, Wallace, Lennox, Auld.

In only two minutes Celtic scored after incredible defensive lapses by Rangers. McNeill came up for a Lennox corner free of attentions and headed the ball for goal; it was not a particularly hard header, but no Ranger was standing at the post and the ball bounced into the net at the base of the unguarded upright with the Rangers' defenders staring in disbelief. Worse was to come for the Ibrox side, praised so often for dour, defensive heroics. Connelly intercepted a short pass in

245

midfield and prodded the ball forward past Mathieson for Lennox to accelerate clear of the other defenders before slowing down to steady himself as he shot past Martin into the far corner; less than a minute later Connelly settled the game by dispossessing Greig at a short goal-kick, walking up to Martin to send him diving the wrong way, and, after carefully avoiding the keeper's flailing legs, ran the ball into the empty net. Both goals, the second and third, had come within the last minute of the first half and left the Celtic end celebrating all through the interval as the Rangers' supporters started to make their way towards the exits. Despite the score the match was a fierce, savage affair and Celtic's counter-attacks tortured Rangers' defence as Auld, Murdoch and Connelly waited to gain possession before releasing long, accurate passes. The inevitable happened in 75 minutes when Chalmers raced away from the centre circle and used the intelligent running of Lennox as a decoy for twenty yards before scoring at the near post. It was all too much for the remaining Rangers' supporters; over the retaining wall they poured in their thousands and trudged towards the gates with only a few having enough spirit left to attempt damaging the nets to hold up play.

The 'treble' had been achieved within a three-week span in April; the championship was settled at Kilmarnock when a late goal by Gemmell gained a 2-2 draw, after the side had shrugged off an uncharacteristic slump in December marked by successive draws against Falkirk (0-0), Kilmarnock (1-1), and Airdrie (0-0) that were followed by a second league defeat from Rangers by 1-0 at Ibrox. This latter result would normally have ensured the title for Ibrox, but Rangers continued to drop points in unexpected places to allow Celtic to win the flag with a degree of comfort. Never permitting himself to becoming satisfied with his squad, Stein had purchased two valuable players in Tommy Callaghan (Dunfermline), a midfielder, for £30,000 and Harry Hood (Clyde), a striker, for £40,000; the relatively modest fees for the pair indicated Stein's customary shrewdness in the vagaries of the transfer market.

Celtic hoped to gain the most elusive trophy of all, the European Cup, and the hopes were realistic. The team negotiated the difficult hurdles of St. Etienne (France) and Red Star (Yugoslavia) in exciting manner: an exhilarating performance at Parkhead helped, said the French, by some sympathetic refereeing decisions, resulted in a 4-0 win over 'Les Verts' that redeemed a two-goal first-leg deficit and a magical display from Jimmy Johnstone helped to rout the powerful Yugoslavs 5-1 at Celtic Park. In the first leg of the quarter-final at the San Siro Stadium Celtic defended in depth to hold A.C. Milan to a goalless draw which boded well for the return, but one moment's carelessness in defence at Parkhead let in Prati after 13 minutes, and all Celtic's subsequent pressure, without the services of the razor-sharp Lennox (out through injury), could not retrieve the situation.

In 1969-70 fate was still unkind to Rangers. Faced with the likelihood of another barren season the club made further changes and spent another fortune. Halfway through the previous season £100,000 had been spent to get Colin Stein from Hibs and £50,000 for Alex MacDonald from St. Johnstone; Willie Thornton, manager of Partick Thistle, had returned to Ibrox in September 1968 as White's assistant; now Gerhardt Neef, a German goalkeeper, was signed on to replace Martin and, in a futile bid to turn back the clock, manager White brought back Jim Baxter from England. Being drawn in the same League Cup section as Celtic was not the recommended therapy for restoring dented morale.

In the first 'Old Firm' clash at Ibrox Celtic started confidently and scored through Hood in eight minutes; for the rest of the half Celtic played in continental fashion to avoid physical contact with flustered opponents. It was vastly different in the second half when Rangers equalised quickly and then dominated play to win 2-1. The other clubs provided practice matches before the next confrontation of the giants on 20 August, 1969, at Celtic Park. In a gripping match, with the score still tied 0-0 shortly after the interval, a linesman's flag seemed to have decided the outcome: as play continued elsewhere Hughes had felled Rangers' Johnston in retaliation, and the immediate rage from the Rangers' end swelled to an exultant clamour as the referee halted play to consult his linesman; for some time Mr. Callaghan discussed the situation with his assistant and eventually called Hughes towards him. The Celtic winger, who had been cautioned in the first half, approached in some dread, but to his manifest relief the referee confined his action to warning the Celt again; in an 'Old Firm' match an obvious break had been given to Celtic! Rangers' goal fell in 68 minutes as Celtic stepped up the pace; Neef fumbled a free kick from Murdoch and Gemmell, up with his forwards, dived full length to head the ball into the net for the winning goal.

Rangers, understandably furious at the referee's decision, refused to accept the dismissal with grace. Shortly afterwards the Ibrox club levelled an official complaint about the refereeing, and at the inquiry Mr. Callaghan, generally recognised as a top referee, was suspended from duty for two months. In suspending the referee the SFA had weakened the position of all referees, as had Rangers in complaining about a specific match and incident; every sport has to uphold the convention that referees' decisions are invariably correct, and field discipline on the players' part is contingent on the authority of referees; and every club has to accept that referees, while prone to human error, are generally fair and impartial in their decisions. Certainly this referee had made a serious mistake that had influenced the result of the tie, but the recognised procedure for demoting a referee would have been adequate in this case; normally all reports about a referee's competence and performances are studied at the end of the season and a consensus reached, while decisions based on an isolated attack on a referee's integrity or competence can result only in harm for the sport.

Celtic were not moving with their customary fluency as they advanced through the tournament, meeting with unexpectedly stiff resistance from Aberdeen and Ayr United. The problem lay with Murdoch's fitness: one of Stein's first decisions as manager had been to play Murdoch in midfield where he had always been willing to do the work of two men but, hampered by a recurring ankle injury, he had put on weight and was labouring in training and on the field. Stein finally ordered him to a health farm in England where he was able to shed sixteen pounds in ten days and returned with renewed energy and vitality.

On 25 October, 1969, these teams lined up at Hampden before 73,067:

> *St. Johnstone:* Donaldson, Lambie, Coburn, Gordon, Rooney, McPhee, Aird, Hall, McCarry (Whitelaw), Connolly, Aitken.
>
> *Celtic:* Fallon, Craig, Hay, Murdoch, McNeill, Brogan, Callaghan, Hood, Hughes, Chalmers (Johnstone), Auld.

The usually unfashionable Perth side had been the talk of Scottish football, scoring plentifully and playing with a free-flowing confidence; some weeks previously they had managed a deserved 2-2 draw at Celtic Park. Although Murdoch was approaching full fitness and top form, Celtic still had problems. Simpson had re-injured his shoulder in the semi-final against Ayr United, and Lennox was ruled out with an ankle injury. Wallace was under suspension after being ordered off at Dunfermline. In addition Stein had decided to leave out two of his regulars. Johnstone and Gemmell had played in a gruelling match for Scotland at Hamburg against West Germany during which the latter had been ordered off. The manager decided to drop them, replacing them with Tom Callaghan and young David Hay, though listing Johnstone as substitute. Gemmell had clearly been disciplined for his sending-off (a repetition of a highly publicised incident in South America) but only learned of his demotion in the dressing-room shortly before the kick-off.[1]

Auld scored the only goal in the second minute to give Celtic the lead, netting from close range after a Chalmers' header had been parried by Donaldson on to the bar, but the outsiders fought back well in a refreshingly open and attacking game and only a splendid Fallon save from a blistering Rooney shot in the dying seconds prevented an equaliser.

The prospects of duplicating the feat of the 1967 team were growing better with each week as the league championship seemed destined for Parkhead to join the League Cup;[2] simultaneously Celtic were advancing in the Scottish Cup and the European Cup, despite facing formidable opposition in both tournaments. In the Scottish Cup the only luck Celtic enjoyed was in getting home advantage, a characteristic of the Stein years: Celtic defeated Dunfermline 2-1, a last-minute goal from Hood avoiding a tricky replay at East End Park, and romped past Dundee United by 4-0. The draw for the quarter-final sent Rangers to Parkhead, and in a torrid match Celtic won 3-1 after Rangers opened the scoring. One player (Alex MacDonald of Rangers) was sent off, and several players of both sides could have had little complaint had they been asked to join him; the trouble escalated after Rangers' early goal, when a jubilant Ibrox player provocatively 'congratulated' Jim Craig when he headed a cross into his own goal. Feelings were as high on the terracing as on the field at this incident, and before the day was over several arrests had been made among both sets of supporters. The Glasgow magistrates wrote to the SFA expressing their concern, and put some of the blame on the behaviour of the teams, naming the captains, Billy McNeill and John Greig, for promoting "conduct calculated to be inflammatory". In response the SFA called the players, the managers, and the chairmen of both clubs to a meeting to discuss the situation, but it was clearly a sop to public concern rather than a serious attempt to solve the problems. After disposing of Dundee's challenge in the semi-final at Hampden by 2-1, Celtic qualified to face Aberdeen in the final on 11 April, 1970, before 108,434:

> *Celtic*: Williams, Hay, Gemmell, Murdoch, McNeill, Brogan, Johnstone, Wallace, Connelly, Lennox, Hughes (Auld).
> *Aberdeen*: Clark, Boel, Murray, Hermiston, McMillan, Buchan M., McKay, Robb, Forrest, Harper, Graham.

Many Celtic supporters down the years have voiced suspicions that referees have been biased against Celtic and if 'evidence' were to be gathered to support such a contention this Scottish Cup final would have to be cited. Bluntly put, the referee, Mr. R. H. Davidson (Airdrie), had a poor match; unfortunately, it was not the only time this particular official had controversial charge of games involving Celtic. The trouble started mid-way through the first half. Within a ten-minute period Mr. Davidson had affected the outcome of the final, and rendered his handling of it as indelibly controversial. In 26 minutes Murdoch was unable to avoid contact with a cross-shot from the right; no Aberdeen player appealed, but the referee awarded a penalty, indicating that the Celt had handled deliberately. Before Harper had converted the gift into a goal, two Celtic players had been booked for their protests. Worse was to follow. Celtic had been stung into immediate ascendancy and, as Clark (a markedly one-footed keeper) prepared to clear, Lennox stood directly in his path to un-nerve him. The ploy worked because the Dons' goalkeeper dropped the ball for the Celtic striker to net what seemed a valid, if inelegant equaliser, but the goal was disallowed. Within another ten minutes the fury of the Celtic supporters had reached boiling point and the mood of the players revealed visible frustration when Lennox, in full flight for goal, was clearly tripped within the penalty area and no penalty was awarded.

It seems a pity that Aberdeen's triumph should have been achieved under such questionable circumstances; they were a well-organised outfit, emerging under Eddie Turnbull's control as worthy challengers to the 'Old Firm'. The second half was a grim and nervous affair. Celtic, obviously unsettled at the officiating, openly challenged several decisions, while Aberdeen defended soundly but irritated the spectators by a reliance on the offside trap. With eight minutes left McKay, a scorer in every round for Aberdeen, broke away and scored a decisive goal; although Lennox netted with two minutes left, young McKay again raced through an over-extended Celtic defence in the last minute to end the scoring.

The bitterness did not end with the whistle: "Jock Stein's denunciation of the match official started at the top of the stairs inside Hampden's crowded foyer and did not stop until he had reached the bottom, where he hinted to waiting pressmen that there ought to be an investigation into Davidson's handing of the match." (*100 Cups*: Keevins/McCarra, 1985.) The manager was fined, but the paltry amount (£10) was a clear indication that some SFA members felt there were extenuating circumstances for his outburst.

The European Cup campaign of 1969-70 recalls the start of Dickens' novel *A Tale of Two Cities*: "It was the best of times; it was the worst of times . . .".

It was a drama of fluctuating emotions, and the conclusion will be remembered as long as there are Celtic supporters to replay it in memory. The first round pitted Celtic against the Swiss club, Basle, and it proved an ideal tune-up for the stiffer competition later. Basle played above themselves in Switzerland, and Celtic settled for a 0-0 draw, but in the second leg at Parkhead an early goal by Hood (in the first minute) settled the outcome, and Gemmell added a second. The fabled Benfica, perennial champions of Portugal, were the next visitors to Parkhead and were swept aside as Celtic's pace and invention was too much. Gemmell established Celtic's supremacy in the second minute when he crashed in an awesome shot from thirty-five yards out and Celtic were a shade unlucky to build up only a 3-0 lead. In Lisbon Celtic needed the full advantage of that lead; the 'Eagles' stormed into attack, scoring twice just before the interval, including a goal from Eusebio. The Portuguese attacked constantly in the second half, but Celtic looked to have survived when the ninety-minute mark was reached. However, the referee added on some time for injuries and other delays; play continued for almost two more minutes, and Benfica scored again. The odds were now against Celtic in the extra time, but McNeill marshalled his defence to hold out. The outcome was settled in the referee's room where the captains met with the official to decide who should advance ... by tossing a coin! McNeill had a reputation for not guessing correctly, but that night he chose correctly and Celtic qualified by a most unsatisfactory method.[3]

By the time the draw for the quarter-finals had arrived all the possible opponents looked formidable, and Celtic drew Fiorentina; however, Auld's masterly direction in midfield hoisted Celtic to another 3-0 win at Parkhead. In the return match at Florence Celtic played a containing game to confine Fiorentina's superiority to the unimportant areas of the field; with Johnstone given a roving commission to hold the ball as much as possible, the Italians could not take too many chances in defence and gained only the slight consolation of a 1-0 win.

The draw for the semi-final resulted in the pairing that most fans would have preferred as the final — Leeds United vs Celtic. It was the first time that the reigning champions of Scotland and England had met in a fully competitive match under European jurisdiction, and such was the power and efficiency of Leeds that Celtic were considered the underdogs. Jock Stein spoke candidly to the reporters in Celtic's headquarters at Harrogate: "Usually, we're favourites; we won't be favourites tomorrow and that, gentlemen, does not bother us at all. Even people well disposed towards us think Leeds will beat us. Well, we'll soon see, won't we?"

Controversy was in the air before the match. Don Revie, a master of gamesmanship, suggested that his team was tired and jaded in its pursuit of the honours, and fielded his reserve side against Derby County in a league game two days before the European match with Celtic "on medical advice". Jock Stein countered, scoffing at the ploy: "I've never heard of a team in the semi-final of the European Cup being 'jaded'." As Alan Hardaker, the secretary of the Football League, later testified, Revie had earlier rejected any number of convenient dates to clear off Leeds' backlog in fixtures; so, any chaos was of their own making. Revie tried one more ploy. In the dressing room before the kickoff, as 45,000 packed into Elland Road, and the songs and chants of supporters filled the April evening, Celtic received a minor shock; because both teams normally wore white stockings, the visitors had to change and Revie blandly supplied an interesting choice — blue stockings or orange?

Within a minute of the start Celtic, on the offensive immediately, had scored. George Connelly controlled a through ball to shoot powerfully from twenty yards and a defender deflected it past the startled Sprake. For the rest of the half Celtic, with Johnstone at his best, dominated and Leeds were forced to defend grimly; it was different in the second half as Leeds swept into attack and the Celtic defenders under McNeill's leadership hung on, while Lennox and Johnstone waited for the breakaway. The match, a memorable and enthralling clash, ended 1-0 for Celtic.

The return was scheduled for Hampden, on 15 April, and Stein warned against complacency. The crowd was limited to 134,000 and all tickets had been snapped up weeks before, but some became available unexpectedly when Leeds supporters returned a substantial proportion of theirs.[4] Wallace had to withdraw from Celtic's side and Stein, with his gift of total recall, remembering John Hughes' performance against Jackie Charlton in a League international five years before, decided to move the winger into the middle. In 13 minutes Bremner, working like a Trojan in midfield, picked up a loose ball to score from long range with a viciously swerving shot and the teams were level again. The issue was decided in midfield where Murdoch and Auld squared off against Bremner and Giles; it was a struggle between three Scots and an Irishman, fought out with passion and cunning, with skill and force, and gradually the tide turned the way of the Celtic pair. Another Celt was in devastating form: Jimmy Johnstone, singled out beforehand by Stein in all the team talks as the pivotal man, was running riot on the right and forcing both Hunter and Cooper back into desperate defence in increasingly vain attempts to contain him. Two minutes into the second half Celtic equalised. Auld picked up a short corner on the right and whipped over a curving cross for Hughes to head past Sprake. Only three minutes later the Welsh internationalist, diving to defend his goal, was injured in a collision and replaced by Harvey, later to play for Scotland; the first touch Harvey had of the ball was to pick it out of the net. Johnstone in the middle of a mazy run turned the ball back into the path of the thundering Murdoch who unleashed a ferocious shot into the net. It was all over bar the singing; the immense crowd celebrated with every song in the repertoire, and afterwards stayed for an emotional lap of honour.

The final was played in the San Siro stadium in Milan on 6 May, 1970, against Feyenoord of Rotterdam, and it proved to be a sad night in Celtic's history. After the humiliation of Leeds home and away Celtic were the favourites, the critics ignoring the dramatic improvement in Dutch football culminating later in Ajax's triumphs; one journalist considered Feyenoord's chances "as slender as a stick of spaghetti". Such was Stein's air of confidence that he struck some as paying only lip-service to the Dutch threat, as if the final was a tiresome chore after the Everest-like triumph of the Leeds' matches. Although Stein made a

John Hughes heads Celtic's first goal against Leeds United at Hampden in the 1970 European Cup semi-final. Jack Charlton and Terry Cooper (no. 3) are the Leeds defenders.

point of warning his squad not to take Feyenoord too lightly, the impression remained among officials, players and supporters that a second European Cup was booked for Parkhead. The party was accommodated in quarters some thirty miles out of Milan and, while they afforded ideal training facilities, the players missed some of the atmosphere building up for a European Cup final. Jim Craig, by then displaced by David Hay, sensed the difference between the preparations for Lisbon and those for Milan: "Everyone's main aim was to play in the European Cup final (1967), but there's a story which illustrates how naïve we were: If you go left from the hotel there's a road that takes you into the country; anyway, we went along this road to a man called Brodie Lennox's house to watch an international match that was live on TV. I think Jock thought we should get out of the hotel for a while. We saw the game and were coming back down the road when Neillie Mochan looked across and saw the hotel's sign and said: 'Let's cut down this hill and take a shortcut.' Down the hill we went in pitch darkness and across a back lot. We all ran down this hill in pitch darkness on the eve of a European Cup final, and anyone could have broken a leg! Three years later in Milan (before we played Feyenoord) training was a question of 'After you, Claude'. Our innocence was our great strength in 1967." (*Scottish Football Historian*: May/June, 1984.)

> *Celtic*: Williams, Hay, Gemmell, Murdoch, McNeill, Brogan, Johnstone, Wallace, Hughes, Auld (Connelly), Lennox.
>
> *Feyenoord*: Graafland, Romeyn (Haak), Israel, Laseroms, Van Duivenbode, Jansen, Van Hanegem, Hasil, Wery, Kindvall, Moulijin.

When Celtic and Feyenoord trooped on to the pitch the omens were against Celtic as the supporters of both sides greeted their teams: "[Celtic supporters] on the day were seen but not heard. The flushed, straining faces mouthed all the splendid martial songs but only a Glaswegian lip-reader could have deciphered their message. They might have been singing behind a 2-ft thickness of glass rather than across the wide rims of Italian beer goblets. "It's no' fair," said a small man wearing an Irish tricolour over his head like a shawl. "Those bloody horns have got us beat. There must be as many of us as there are of them, but you could burst your lungs and never be heard against that lot." If the Celtic supporters lost, what chance did mere players have? And the Celtic players have, so to speak, never been merer than they were on Wednesday." (*Observer*: 10 May, 1970.)

After only a few minutes' play it was clear that Celtic were not striking the form that had destroyed Leeds; the side was attacking but the normal urgency and flow was missing. The momentum of the game had already started to turn in Feyenoord's direction when Celtic scored in 30 minutes. Murdoch teed up a free kick for Gemmell and the full-back's drive baffled the keeper, partly screened by the referee. Feyenoord equalised within a few minutes when Israel scored with a long, drooping header after a series of partial clearances by a slack Celtic defence, and at half-time the score was still level.

The second half belonged to Feyenoord as the better prepared Dutch side exploited Celtic's uncharacteristic sluggishness. Their coach had been thorough, having analysed Celtic's game and provided his players with individual instructions about possible weaknesses in Celtic's approach. Kindvall, the Swedish centre-forward, was asked to run directly at McNeill on the ground with the ball and Celtic's captain had an uncomfortable night; Moulijn, an experienced winger, stayed well upfield, forcing Hay to stick close to him in a purely defensive role; lastly, Feyenoord knew the importance of playing the match at their own pace as they moved the ball around expertly in midfield and rarely allowed Celtic to mount a sustained offensive. The wonder was that Celtic held out for the ninety minutes, and agitation was clearly visible on the Celtic bench. Some players felt that Celtic should have opted for a more defensive policy and settled for a draw by bringing on Craig in Hay's place at full-back, moving Hay to midfield where his tenacity might have made a difference in the flow of the match; some felt that Brogan, limping from an early injury, and Johnstone, shaken by heavy tackling, should have been replaced . . . but Stein made only one change, taking off Auld and substituting Connelly without much effect.

In extra time Feyenoord pressed after Hughes had come close for Celtic from the opening kick-off, but Celtic held out until three minutes from the end; a quickly taken free kick was too high for McNeill and the

Celt used his hand, prepared to concede a penalty, but the ball went on to Kindvall who scored, the capable Italian referee (Lo Bello) allowing the advantage rule.

The post-mortems by the supporters in the following days were bitter: the players, whose agent had unwisely scheduled a press conference the following day to announce various commercial ventures, had been distracted by their financial interests; Stein had been too confident and had allowed his players to take things too much for granted.

Anybody close to the scenes at the end would refute the claim that the players were playing only for money: the numbness was real, the pain was heartfelt, and the tears flowed; the coach ride back to Varese was funereal, each player wrapped in his own misery.

As the players and Stein were prepared to admit, it was self-evident that the underrated Feyenoord were much better than most people recognised, and a team that played its own game regardless of the opposition. In the following season, playing in South America for the World Club Championship that had eluded Celtic, they found themselves two goals down early in the match but came back to draw, and won the return match 4-2 in Holland.

The trouble with Celtic that night in Milan was a Scottish (and a human) trait; the adulation heaped on the players after the Leeds games was just too much. No matter that Stein publicly said his players should treat Feyenoord with respect, the players felt in their hearts that the European Cup had already been won — at Hampden against the English champions.

The serpent of complacency had crept into 'Paradise'.

Notes

1 Gemmell was so upset that he requested a transfer and, although the breach was apparently soon healed, it came as no surprise that, following another disciplinary problem (in a tour of the United States seven months later), he was transferred to Nottingham Forest in December 1971.

2 The Glasgow Cup final was delayed until the start of the next season, and Celtic won it by beating Rangers 3-1.

3 Bob Kelly was so opposed to the method that he sought alternative solutions; the system adopted as a result was the penalties decider, although Kelly preferred to count the number of corner kicks (as a better indicator of the way the match had been played).

4 The official attendance was given as 136,505, and several thousands more gained admission when a gate was rushed.

27

STRUGGLING AT THE TOP

IT may seem strange that a defeat in a European Cup final, and only by
a single goal after extra time, should be considered a disaster, but so
absolute was the faith of the supporters in Jock Stein's Celtic that the
loss in Milan was felt paradoxically to be a low point in the club's
history. It was a major accomplishment in the first place to qualify for
the competition, and to fight through to the final by eliminating such
sides as Fiorentina, Benfica and Leeds United; it was certainly a bitter
disappointment to lose, and by the team's own standards to have played
badly, but it was not a disaster.

The European Cup final of 1970, however, should be regarded as a
turning point; it marked the end of the most glorious period of
accomplishment in Celtic's history, a five-year epoch marked as much
by style and flair, colour and excitement as by competitive success . . . it
signalled the end of Celtic's apparent invincibility, and Stein's own aura
of infallibility. The words to be applied to Celtic and their manager in
the future would have to be selected from a more narrow range,
encompassing the merely human. The team and the players would have
to be considered outstanding by most standards, and the manager an
exceptional one . . . but from now on the hyperbole of the reporters
would be more restrained and the expectations of the supporters more
realistic. In a sense, Celtic's relative decline after Milan symbolised the
change in mood in Britain, from the heady '60s to the greyer, more
utilitarian present.

Stein's most immediate problem was to keep his club at the top
during the oncoming period of transition, the most difficult task for any
manager, while age, injury, and events were taking an inevitable toll of
the quality pool of players (including fourteen internationalists) which
he had recently enjoyed.

The final at Milan was to be followed by another tour of the United
States and Canada, but this venture was a failure; it was not the morale-
building venture, nor an opportunity to work out new tactics, as was the

The loneliness of defeat–Jock Stein at the end of the 1970 European Cup final.

tour of 1966. Celtic were involved in a tournament with Manchester United and an Italian side, Bari, a competition that had started while Celtic were in Milan. The players were still demoralised when they left Prestwick for Toronto, and a rough landing at Montreal caused by a burst tyre did not soothe nerves. The weather throughout the short tour was humid, almost unbearably so, and Celtic's plans had not allowed much time for preparation nor recovery from jet-lag; only a day after landing in Toronto Celtic were playing against the better-acclimatised Manchester United, who defeated the Scots easily by 2-0. The next match, by then a virtually meaningless encounter, was against Bari in New York on 13 July and the undistinguished Italian side held Celtic to a 1-1 draw in sauna-like conditions. Four days later Celtic again faced

Bari, this time back in Toronto, and the match had to be postponed from the Saturday night when a thunderstorm struck the city. The game was played on the Sunday, in late afternoon eventually; scheduled to start at 2 p.m. the kick-off time was delayed frequently until 3.25 as the Canadian organisers scrambled to attract more customers. The attendance was a miserable 4,000, lost in Exhibition Stadium and a stark contrast in mood and numbers to the record crowd of 32,000 in the same stadium two years previously that had seen Celtic defeat AC Milan, and the match was abandoned near the end after the Italian side walked off in protest at refereeing decisions (2-2).

Off-field, matters were little better. The players resented playing in a pointless tournament in unfamiliar surroundings, and were still reacting to Milan; Jock Stein, not amused by the attitude of his players and the organisation of the tournament left shortly after the Bari game in Toronto for Scotland, apparently without consulting other members of the party. He suggested at Toronto airport that he was returning to have his ankle treated, to catch up on paperwork, and to deal with a contract ultimatum from Jimmy Johnstone who had been permitted to miss the tour because of his fear of flying and the fatigue of a long season. It was an unconvincing explanation and the rumours started: some saw his abrupt departure as symptomatic of his exasperation at the events of Milan and afterwards, while others felt he had left to ponder his future at Celtic Park.

His responsibilities on the tour were assumed by Sean Fallon, but Desmond White had to fly out from Scotland to take overall control of the party; before he arrived in North America, however, two players had been sent home by Fallon for breaches of discipline. Gemmell and Auld, never easy men to control at the best of times, were, like the others, still disappointed at the loss in Milan, resentful that Johnstone had been allowed to stay home, and becoming more and more frustrated at the boredom of this tour.

It was not going to be an easy task for the manager to regain full control of his squad, and to retain its absolute confidence; some might argue that he never did.

The Glasgow Cup, sadly reduced in status and held over from the previous season, afforded Stein an opportunity to tinker before the start of the season; in the final against a full-strength Rangers at Hampden on 10 August, 1970, he fielded a youthful side, containing six players generally recognised as reserves, and Celtic won the match easily by 3-1. It was an early indication to the squad that changes could be made.

By October, however, Celtic were showing alarming signs of inconsistency and decline; the team had advanced to another League Cup final but its progress had been less than triumphant. At Dundee in the first leg of the quarter-final Johnstone had put Celtic two up at half-time, but the Dens Park side fought back to gain a 2-2 draw; in the second leg Celtic swept aside the challenge by 5-1 before 41,000 at Parkhead. In the semi-final Dumbarton from the Second Division held Celtic to a 0-0 draw even after extra time, and took the replay to extra time again before yielding 4-3, unluckily it was felt. Celtic's opponents in the final were Rangers, and the Parkhead side was the odds-on favourite as Rangers had to line up without John Greig, a wholehearted and often inspiring captain. To the dismay of the supporters in the crowd of 106,263 on 24 October at Hampden Celtic gave another disappointing display, and did not get involved in the match until near the end; before half-time Rangers' new centre, Derek Johnstone, a youngster of only 16, scored with a fine header. Rangers fully deserved their victory, for their first major trophy since 1966; to the credit of *The Celtic View* the club newspaper agreed and its generous headline read: "This was the right result!"

Stein had to review the situation: this was the third major final within six months in which Celtic had slumped in form to lose despite starting as favourites. He had to start wondering about his side's attitude and its air of over-confidence; he had to consider if some of his players were past their best. The thought occurred to him that his team, although still relatively young, was starting to suffer from 'burn-out', a type of staleness that affects performance subtly but perceptibly.

As usual he reached the right conclusions: he could no longer hold on to his older players for sentimental reasons while the youngsters clamoured for places. Milan had been such a traumatic blow to his own and to the players' pride that full recovery would take time. Typically, he speeded up the process of rejuvenation by calculated moves. His first tactic was to freshen the team by allowing some of his youthful players to make appearances. Many of his experienced players at Dunfermline and Hibernian appreciated that he never asked them to do more than they were capable of and that his approach was always practical; in a similar manner he was protective of the novices' welfare. He fielded them for short, but extended, periods and the youngsters quickly gained in confidence and experience, while their more experienced colleagues were forced to keep a watchful eye on them. Back in the reserves after their introductory spell was over, young players like McGrain, Macari and Quinn, brimming with confidence and eager to return to 'the big-time', served as examples to the others.

Already some youngsters had established themselves as regulars in the first team pool, and Stein made it clear that membership of the 'Lisbon Lions' alone would not guarantee a first-team place. Simpson was the first member of the famous side to retire, and his position was taken for a time by Fallon and later by Evan Williams, signed from Wolverhampton Wanderers; Clark had been replaced by Jim Brogan and only made two appearances throughout the season while Auld, in the veteran stage, could no longer withstand the challenge from George Connelly and was limited to eight appearances.

Although he was renowned for his loyalty to his players, like all effective managers Stein did not shrink from the difficult decisions; shortly after a home defeat by Aberdeen in December he dropped both Jimmy Johnstone and Billy McNeill for the visit to Cappielow (and was gratified with a 3-0 win over Morton). He was faced with an unusual problem in defence. Stein had largely pioneered the tactic of the aggressive, overlapping full-back to circumvent the highly organised defences of the European sides and in the Lisbon pair of Craig and Gemmell he had two superb exponents of the art; however, the role placed tremendous physical demands on both of them as they were expected to join in attacks with lung-bursting dashes, and yet be back in a defensive stance for any counter-attack. The basic tactic was imaginative and highly effective, but it did have disadvantages; both Celtic full-backs were to retire from the game relatively young, and a contributory factor might have been the physical strain of their role. Sensing a shading-off in their effectiveness Stein was able to introduce younger players, but he was faced with a plethora of riches. Danny McGrain made an impressive debut in the opening league game against Morton, Jimmy Quinn was equally effective against Rangers in the Glasgow Cup, and David Hay played superbly at full-back whenever he was fielded there. At the same time, neither Craig nor Gemmell was significantly past his best.

If Stein was concerned about the inconsistent form of his regulars, he did not allow it to affect the team's results too much; at the end of the season the supporters could look back on another league and cup double. In the league campaign which ended with Celtic's equalling the 'six-in-a-row' accomplishment of an earlier side, the main competition came from a confident Aberdeen. The northerners, who had won the Scottish Cup the previous season by beating Celtic 3-1, had no inferiority complex and shortly after New Year led by four points; at one stage Aberdeen posted 15 league wins in a row, including a 1-0 victory at Celtic Park. Aberdeen's challenge was built around the soundness of Bobby Clark in goal and the defensive skills of their young captain, Martin Buchan, as sweeper, with Steve Murray acting most effectively as the link man in midfield.

Rangers had got off to a slow start, and were mounting only a distant challenge when they played Celtic at Ibrox on 2 January, 1971. Celtic took the lead near the end through Johnstone, and hundreds of Rangers' supporters started to drift away in disappointment; with only seconds left in the match Colin Stein grabbed an unexpected equaliser and indirectly caused the second Ibrox disaster. Hearing the roar of joy that greeted the goal, many Rangers' fans rushed back up the giant stairway but, before they reached the top, the referee had blown for time-up and thousands, still excited and delighted at the dramatic reprieve, poured towards the same exit; in the rush and in the unexpected collision with their fellow fans, many tripped and fell to the ground, literally crushed in the ensuing melee by the crowds of spectators leaving the ground, unaware until too late of the developing tragedy and, because of the crush from behind, unable to stop. Most of the crowd who had left by the other exits were totally ignorant of the disaster until they switched on their radios or television sets at home, assuming that the ambulances and police cars they had seen racing towards Ibrox after the match were in response to outbreaks of hooliganism.

However, at the end of the saddest day in Scottish football, when an 'Old Firm' match and its result was irrelevant, sixty-six fans lay dead and many more were injured. The only consolation in the tragedy lay in the fact that even the most rabid of supporters could sense its real significance and could share the mourning; players and officials of both clubs attended memorial services in St. Andrew's Cathedral (Roman Catholic) and Glasgow Cathedral (Presbyterian); Celtic expressed sympathy with Rangers and the victims by volunteering future assistance, and showed it in the most tangible way by sending a cheque for £10,000 immediately.

On 16 January Celtic gained the psychological advantage over Aberdeen: the Dons lost a goal after twelve successive clean sheets and, more importantly, two points at Easter Road to Hibs, while Celtic travelled to a tricky fixture at Dens Park and ran riot to defeat Dundee by 8-1. The most important match in the league campaign took place at Aberdeen on 17 April; Celtic led by a point, but whoever won this match at such a late stage in the season would have to be favourites for the title. After only four minutes Hood put Celtic ahead when he coolly glided home a cross from close range, and although Aberdeen fought back to gain a draw Celtic were securely in the driving seat.

On 29 April, Celtic clinched the title with a 2-0 win over Ayr United in a match played at Hampden because the stand at Celtic Park was being renovated.

However, for the last league match of the season against Clyde two days later, Celtic played at Parkhead. Approaching this fixture, a meaningless game after the flag had been won, Stein urged all Celtic supporters to be there: "You'll be able to tell your grandchildren about this game," he promised, and with a fine sense of the theatrical he revealed his intentions to field the 'Lisbon Lions', Celtic's pride, for the very last time. Before an emotionally charged crowd of 35,000 the European Cup winners of 1967 took the field, led out by the non-playing

Ronnie Simpson, who had retired a year previously. Clyde, aware of their supporting role, added to the occasion by providing a sporting, positive opposition as Celtic won by 6-1. Stein, of course, knew it was the last opportunity to see that team because he had arranged for the transfers of two of them; Auld, who left the field on the shoulders of his colleagues, was transferred to Hibs shortly afterwards, and Clark, unobtrusive as sweeper until required, joined Morton in the close season.

Shortly afterwards, the Scottish Cup was back in Paradise. On the way to the final Celtic coped with largely moderate opposition. In the first hurdle Celtic handled Queen of the South (from the Second Division) with ease at Parkhead by 5-1, but at the next stage stuttered to a 1-1 draw against Dunfermline. Stein was so incensed at the displays of some senior players that he was on the verge of bringing in his youngsters for the replay at Dunfermline; however, the weather conditions were so bad that he felt it would be unfair to do so, and he fielded much the same team, which again struggled but eked out a 1-0 win in the club's first Scottish Cup match outside Glasgow in almost five years.

Raith Rovers, another lower division side, provided no competition at Parkhead as Celtic ran up a 7-1 score to advance to the semi-final against Airdrie; once more Celtic were uneasy, even after leading by 3-1, and allowed Airdrie to salvage a 3-3 draw. In the replay Celtic, competent if not inspired, deserved a 2-0 win, and thus qualified for the final against Rangers. Rangers, in fourth place in the table, had their hopes for the season now fixed on the Scottish Cup, and in depriving Celtic of a double:

Celtic: Williams, Craig, Brogan, Connelly, McNeill, Hay, Johnstone, Lennox, Wallace, Callaghan, Hood.
Rangers: McCloy, Miller, Mathieson, Greig, McKinnon, Jackson, Henderson, Penman (Johnstone), Stein, MacDonald, Johnston.

A crowd of 120,092 witnessed a nervous affair. Celtic led deservedly at half-time through an opportunistic goal by Lennox in 40 minutes, but Rangers pressed in the second half. Celtic appeared to have weathered their frantic attempts to equalise, but with only four minutes left Derek Johnstone, the substitute, took full advantage of a moment's hesitation between Williams and Connelly to force a replay. Both sides made changes for the replay, held on the Wednesday (12 May, 1971) before 103,332. Rangers' young right-back, Miller, had played on gallantly in the first game ignoring the pain of a broken jaw, but he could not turn out for the replay, and Rangers decided to take a chance on a debutant, Denny, to replace him. Stein had not been happy at the effort shown by the forwards and regrouped the front line with Wallace dropping into the role of substitute and being replaced by Macari.

Within a few minutes it was clear that Celtic were going to test the youthful debutant at right-back. Callaghan, a strong and direct runner, was forceful down the left where he was joined repeatedly by Johnstone, who had been given a roving commission by Stein. Rangers' defence, under constant pressure, was hard pressed to survive. Macari was a threatening presence in the penalty area, and after 24 minutes he snapped up a chance following a corner. A minute later the final seemed over as a contest when McKinnon, troubled by Johnstone's elusive dribbling, hauled down the winger, and Hood converted the penalty. For the remainder of the half Celtic toyed with Rangers, with Johnstone in his inimitable form, but no more scoring resulted.

Rangers made earnest efforts to get back into the game after the interval, and were partially rewarded when Craig diverted the ball into his own net after 58 minutes. Celtic resisted further attempts with relative ease and held on to win 2-1. While it was refreshing to see the Rangers' fans still on the terracing at the presentation rather than on the field, Jock Stein could not resist the comment: "A good result for Rangers."

Apart from the League Cup final the major disappointment was in Europe. Celtic advanced comfortably to the quarter-finals against Ajax Amsterdam after disposing of Kokkola (Finland) by a 14-0 aggregate and Waterford (Eire) by 10-2. The Dutch champions, on the threshold of their great European days, were different class and in Amsterdam an ultra-defensive Celtic gave up three goals in the last half hour after soaking up an hour's pressure, with some critics feeling that Celtic had not yet fully appreciated the technical advantage of grabbing an away goal. In the second leg, held at Hampden because of ground renovations at Parkhead, Ajax played within themselves, refusing to panic when yielding a goal to Johnstone after 28 minutes of frantic, unsophisticated Celtic pressure.

A "disappointing" year consisted of winning the championship, gaining the Scottish Cup, losing in the final of the League Cup, and reaching the quarter-final of the European Cup, but Stein's stan- dards were such that a feeling of disappointment persisted. It had been a difficult season for the manager, starting with the events of Milan and the frustrations of a tour nobody wanted. He had been puzzled at times by the eccentric form of some senior players, but pleased at the displays of his youngsters; and privately Stein had spent considerable time thinking about his own future. During the season Stein pondered the advisability of a move to Manchester United who were anxious to land him; it was a tempting prospect with the security of a lucrative contract and the prospect of a fresh challenge. In the end, perhaps for family reasons or out of a deep sense of loyalty to Celtic and Bob Kelly (now Sir Robert Kelly), who was in failing health, he decided to stay; to end the rumours and the speculation he made his decision known to the players shortly before the important league match at Pittodrie that decided the championship. It was not the first approach to engage Stein's mind. An even more intriguing possibility had emerged briefly in the late '60s. At some point then Stein was approached informally but unmistakably by "somebody from Ibrox" (almost certainly Willie Allison, the Rangers' PRO and a former journalist), to sound out the possibility of Stein's moving to take charge of Rangers. At first glance it seemed a ridiculous notion, but it was not too far-fetched. Stein, a Lanarkshire man, came from a background that would have permitted him to fit in at Ibrox; the position of Rangers' manager is a prestigious one, and Stein, a man aware of football history and his own place in it, might have relished the opportunity to restore Rangers' fortunes as he had done Celtic's; and Rangers have always had the reputation of trying to buy themselves out of trouble. But for one reason or another the "negotiations" came to nothing.

Despite these private concerns Jock Stein carried on at Celtic Park with his customary enthusiasm and dedication. John Rafferty described part of the workload: "He took the training every morning, stayed on for special coaching of individuals, was interminably on the telephone at the ground and in his home, talking to football people, to managers, to contacts, becoming satiated with the current news in the game. He was ever available to the press, providing the routine news of the team, arguing, trying to influence opinion, putting the club's case and at times winning press friends by helping with a story on a dull day."

The following season (1971-72) was a highly successful one, but one result in the League Cup was to remain in everybody's memory. Celtic had started off in spectacular fashion by beating Rangers twice at Ibrox in the sectional play. On the opening day Celtic won convincingly by 2-0, and the promising newcomer Dalglish scored from the penalty spot to clinch the win; forced to play again at Rangers' ground because of continuing reconstruction at Parkhead only a few days after being upset by Morton, Celtic thrashed their traditional rivals by 3-0. The mature play of Dalglish was a revelation; he scored the important first goal by taking his chance coolly, and set up Callaghan's volley for the second by fighting for the ball and retaining it despite fierce challenges before crossing to the tall Fifer. A new star had entered the Parkhead firmament!

Celtic handled the challenge of Clydebank easily in the quarter-final, advancing by an 11-2 aggregate, and coped with St. Mirren effectively by 3-0 in the semi-final. However, the final produced one of the greatest upsets in Scottish football history, and appropriately it involved Partick Thistle. A crowd of 62,740 turned up at Hampden on 23 October, 1971, expecting to see Celtic win with ease, despite the absence through injury of McNeill, but the captain's authority and leadership were sorely missed. To the astonishment of the spectators Thistle, attacking from the whistle, led deservedly by four goals after only 37 minutes. It was reported that many Rangers' fans left Ibrox when they heard the news of Thistle's goals and rushed over to Hampden to witness the discomfiture of their rivals. In the second half Celtic pressed but found young Alan Rough in superb form in Thistle's goal, and were able to score only once through Dalglish.

The Celtic supporters stayed till the end and sportingly cheered the Thistle players as they received their medals, the first such major presentation to 'the Jags' in fifty years. Stein also acknowledged publicly that Celtic had no complaint about the result, but privately he was furious at a lacklustre performance.

He acted quickly: two days after the final he signed Denis Connaghan, St. Mirren's keeper, and within a week he surprised the football world by signing John 'Dixie' Deans, Motherwell's striker. Deans, a short, chunky forward, had been a chronic disciplinary problem, and was serving a suspension when Stein signed him, but Stein, confident he could handle him, had few worries on that score. Both signings were timely and inexpensive (they cost a total of only £37,500) but more importantly they were successful. Connaghan provided much needed competition for Williams, and Deans finished the season as top scorer with 27 goals.

The signings indicated that Celtic was a side in transition, and the departures offered the clearest proof. Auld and Clark had already left, and in September Chalmers joined Morton as player-coach; by December Gemmell had been transferred to Nottingham Forest, while Wallace and Hughes had joined Crystal Palace. Still, Celtic ruled the roost in Scotland as newcomers like Dalglish and Macari could not be denied their places in the side. Other relative newcomers such as Connelly, Hood and Callaghan were fitting into the picture, and Stein was delighted with McNeill's continued enthusiasm and competitiveness. Indeed, the captain was the only ever-present in the league programme with 34 appearances.

Although Celtic ended up with their easiest league title in the great run of nine in a row, the campaign was not without drama. Celtic gained an early advantage over Rangers by winning 9-1 against Clyde on the opening day while Rangers were losing 3-2 at Firhill, and added to it by repeating the two League Cup wins at Ibrox with another victory, this time by 3-2. A critical match was at Dunfermline on 27 October, four days after the debacle in the League Cup final. Celtic fielded the new keeper, Connaghan, but lost an early goal to the Fifers and saw Murdoch limp off the field after 25 minutes. McNeill, back in the team after his recovery from injury, rallied his men and equalised in 60 minutes following a free kick; only ten minutes from the end a neat move involving Brogan and Macari created a chance for Lennox to snatch the winner.

Aberdeen made a strong early challenge and earned a draw at Parkhead on 6 November, but two impressive away victories for Celtic against Thistle and Dundee United, both by 5-1, helped the club into first place. In the New Year clash at Parkhead a last-minute goal by Jim Brogan earned Celtic a 2-1 win (the first league double over Rangers for 58 years) and when Celtic won 3-0 over St. Johnstone at Perth on 22 January, 1972, while Aberdeen were losing 1-0 at Dunfermline, Celtic moved out a comfortable four points ahead of the 'Dons'. Aberdeen's fading hopes disappeared with the transfer of their captain Martin Buchan to Manchester United in March; while Aberdeen had method they lacked Celtic's flair. The only question that remained was where and when Celtic would clinch the title. Celtic accomplished this (gaining a seventh championship in succession to beat their own record) by winning 3-0 at Methil against East Fife with the prolific Deans getting two of the goals. Aberdeen finished a distant second, ten points behind.

After the shock of the League Cup Celtic had settled to a splendid consistency, and were making fine progress in the European and Scottish cups as well as leading in the league. Stein was surprised at Celtic's fine showing in Europe, having felt that it would take two years before Celtic would be ready for another assault on the major trophy. In the first round Celtic were upset by Boldklub Copenhagen 1903 by 2-1 in Denmark, but recovered to win 3-0 at Parkhead, and followed that with the trouncing of another European minnow, Sliema Wanderers (Malta), by 7-1 on aggregate.

In the quarter-final Celtic faced the redoubtable Ujpest Dozsa, a squad that some felt was emerging as Hungary's best port-war club side. Jimmy Johnstone had to withdraw from the first leg at Budapest through illness, and Danny McGrain made his European debut, but Celtic's youngsters rose magnificently to the challenge and pulled off a 2-1 win. Stein opted for a 4-4-2 formation, with Murdoch, Hay, Dalglish and Hood faced with the task of gaining control of midfield and Lennox and Macari given the assignment of harrying the Hungarian defence with their nippiness. Celtic got an early break when Horvath deflected a shot past his own keeper, but the same player redeemed himself with the equaliser, a ferociously struck drive from thirty yards; five minutes from time young Macari lobbed the ball over the keeper's head to give Celtic victory. The return leg at Parkhead was not a formality. Dunai took advantage of hesitancy in Celtic's defence to give Ujpest Dozsa a lead after five minutes, and it was only in the second half that Celtic, lifted by Johnstone's appearance as substitute, equalised through Macari who latched on to a short passback to put Celtic through to face Inter Milan in what was to be a memorable semi-final. The Italians had reached that stage after a controversial series with Borussia Moenchengladbach (West Germany) in the second round. Inter, thrashed 7-1 in Munich, had been successful in an appeal based on an alleged injury to a forward caused by a bottle-throwing incident. The Italians won the return leg 4-2 in Milan, and achieved a scoreless draw in the replay of the first leg held in Berlin.

The first leg of the semi-final was played at the San Siro Stadium where Celtic played a defensive game, marked by clever possession play that frustrated the Italians, but it was felt by many of the travelling support that Inter were vulnerable to breakaway attacks. Perhaps Celtic were reluctant to risk too much in attack, especially when extra men were deployed in defence to help cover young Pat McCluskey who had to replace Brogan in the second half. Warned by Stein, everybody sensed that Inter would come to Parkhead prepared to defend in depth through 120 minutes' play and take their chances on the penalty decider . . . and that was exactly how it turned out. Mazzola slotted home the first in the same efficient manner as he had done in Lisbon five years earlier. Celtic's first penalty was taken by Deans and he appeared to become unnerved by the hushed silence that had fallen over the 75,000 crowd already fearing the worst and by the sudden movement of the Italian keeper just before he shot, Deans, who had been crashing home the practice penalties at Seamill in the days prior to the match, seemed to change his mind in the split second before he shot and his attempt ballooned over the bar. The whoops of the Italian players could be heard over the murmurs of the numbed crowd, and an experienced squad that contained such as Facchetti, Boninsegna, Burgnich and Jair was not going to give up the unexpected advantage. Stein had already dismissed the procedure as "funfair soccer", but ironically the method of deciding tied games had stemmed largely from Bob Kelly's campaign to end the farcical 'toss-of-the-coin' method previously employed, and which had got Celtic past Benfica in 1969. It was a crushing disappointment to lose under such circumstances and Stein, who six months previously would have been pleasantly surprised to reach the semi-final, expressed his disappointment: "[Celtic] came within a whisker of reaching the final and possibly winning the trophy. We may have a better Celtic team in the seasons ahead, but who can say with certainty that we will ever have a better chance of winning Europe's supreme trophy?" (*The Celtic View*: June, 1972.)

Some of the air of disappointment was dispelled on 6 May, in the Scottish Cup final, and John Rafferty, football journalist with *The Scotsman* and an astute observer of Stein and his methods, traced the origins of the triumph to a confrontation between the manager and Bobby Murdoch some weeks before. Stein was becoming frustrated with the frequent injuries and continuing weight problems of his midfield star, at the time described by Rafferty as "too heavy and sluggish to do himself justice". Stein ended the conversation with the threat, "Get it off, or get out!" Stung by the criticism Murdoch worked even harder to lose the excess weight, and as the season drew to a close his form was improving with every outing. It was fortunate that he was at his best because Celtic were without two of their brightest stars, out through injury: the invaluable David Hay was sidelined and Danny McGrain, a most promising full-back, had fractured his skull at Falkirk. Kenny Dalglish had enjoyed a splendid season, but was showing signs of fatigue at the end.

Celtic: Williams, Craig, Brogan, Murdoch, McNeill, Connelly, Johnstone, Deans, Macari, Dalglish, Callaghan.
Hibernian: Herriot, Brownlie, Schaedler, Stanton, Black, Blackley, Edwards, Hazel, Gordon, O'Rourke, Duncan (Auld).

For another Celtic player it was a chance for redemption. Deans was a swashbuckling striker, and he soon shrugged off his costly penalty miss, but detractors suggested his goals were against run-of-the-mill opposition. In this Scottish Cup final he had something to prove, and luckless Hibs suffered as a consequence. In only two minutes McNeill, up with his forwards for a Callaghan free kick, found the ball dropping at his feet instead of his head, but managed to place the ball neatly past the goalkeeper from six yards; Hibs, who had earned their way to Hampden with a convincing semi-final win over Rangers, fought back pluckily and equalised in 12 minutes through Gordon. Deans restored Celtic's lead in 23 minutes, clamouring for Murdoch to hoist another free kick in his direction and then outleaping the Hibs defenders despite his shortness to head powerfully into the net.

At half-time Celtic led by 2-1, and the final was still in some doubt until Deans settled the issue with one of the most remarkable goals in Scottish Cup history. He gathered a misdirected clearance before rounding the goalkeeper to advance on goal along the by-line; he sidestepped Brownlie and the keeper, Herriot, once more, and then shot into the empty net before finishing off his spectacular feat by somersaulting in his happiness to acknowledge the cheers of the Celtic supporters in the crowd of 106,102. Hibs were shattered by the goal and in the 74th minute Deans completed his hat trick by cleverly running on to a through ball from Callaghan. In the last seven minutes Macari wrapped things up with two goals, with both moves originating from Jim Craig, playing in his last game for the club before leaving for South Africa.

Celtic had been in irresistible form, and most of the danger started with Bobby Murdoch, who directed the play with long, accurate passes that tortured the Edinburgh defence with their subtlety, and with short,

'Dixie' Deans heads Celtic's second goal in the 1972 Scottish Cup final versus Hibs.

neat passes that linked the midfield with the attackers. Most of the obvious glory went to Deans with his three goals as it was only the second hat trick in a Scottish Cup final (the other was by Jimmy Quinn in 1904), and Celtic's 6-1 victory equalled the previous record established by Renton in 1888.

In the next season (1972-73) it was Celtic's experience that just retained the league championship; at one stage, however, it appeared that the Parkhead men were going to have an easy time in gaining the eighth title in succession. Rangers had got off to their now customary dreadful start, and so contemptuous were some Celtic supporters of the Ibrox challenge that when John Greig scored a consolation goal for Rangers in Celtic's 3-1 win at Hampden on September 16 he was cheered ironically. Despite that, the championship was not decided until the last match of the season, and it was the same Rangers, under Jock Wallace's direction, who challenged till the very end. From 2 December, when they lost 1-0 to Hearts at Ibrox, Rangers did not lose another league game and dropped only two points in drawn matches with Aberdeen.

Celtic's difficulties started around Christmas when several players came down with an influenza virus that forced the postponement of two games; even more alarming, and in view of later events ominous, was the illness of Jock Stein. The manager was confined to hospital — and in the coronary ward — for observation until released in mid-January.

With hindsight it is obvious that Celtic's manager was working himself into exhaustion for the club. Both John Rafferty and Bill Shankly commented on the restlessness within Stein. Rafferty wrote: ". . . travelling to keep himself abreast of what was happening in football, imparting what he had learned to his players, worrying and scheming and planning; Stein worked extraordinary hours for the club. This total involvement in the affairs of the club inevitably placed a heavy strain on the man. He never did sleep well; on trips abroad it was noticed that he was always last in bed, and nobody was ever down before him in the morning. There was the strain of long, fast journeys to watch football. If there was a mid-week match in England when Celtic were not playing, in Manchester, Liverpool or Leeds, he would motor down after the afternoon's work was done at Celtic Park, talk a bit, watch the football, then motor back immediately afterwards and be the first man at Celtic Park in the morning. Such exertions were more than any man could bear." Shankly noted Stein's impatience to get out of the Celtic car park: "Jock thinks he should just be able to climb in and drive away. I've seen him twisting his steering-wheel and I've said, 'You're not trying to take it off, are you, Jock? You won't manage that.' If he's hemmed in by other cars he'll say, 'Who the hell put those bloody cars there?'"

Such was his concern for the fans, whom he labelled "the most important people in football", that on one wintry Saturday during the previous season he had stationed himself at a main road junction outside Glasgow to flag down supporters' buses with the news that a game at Dundee had been cancelled. His stay in hospital was not free from tension as Celtic lost 2-1 at Ibrox on 6 January, 1973, falling to a last-minute goal by Conn. Shortly afterwards Lou Macari was transferred to Manchester United for £200,000. Macari had previously requested a transfer, in 1971, during a contractual dispute, and had been restless since joining the Scottish squad under Tommy Docherty; at Manchester he linked up again with Docherty, the recently appointed manager, who had quit the national post to take over at Old Trafford.

Macari's move symbolised the difference between the Lisbon squad and the new Celtic that was replacing it. The 'Lisbon Lions' had a collective pride, and an exuberance that was retained even with the passing of time, imbued with a sense of joy and excitement that made the spectators aware that this was a team enjoying itself; the transitional team that followed was less exuberant, a team with some outstanding individuals forged into a formidable unit by the force of the manager's personality. Both were highly successful sides, but one represented the more cynical reality of the contemporary game and its players. Macari was the new breed of professional footballer — talented, eager to prove himself, unashamedly ambitious for glory, status and money. He was the equivalent of a soldier of fortune or a mercenary; unlike many others at Parkhead, he was not 'a jersey player' and his skills would take him wherever his personal needs were met. Stein insisted that he would not have gone had Celtic not the replacements for him, but for a time it looked as if the manager had miscalculated as Celtic dropped vital points.

On 27 January Celtic suffered another last-minute defeat, a shock 2-1 loss to relegation-bound Airdrie at Broomfield when a new keeper, Alistair Hunter from Kilmarnock, was making his debut and Murdoch missed a penalty. Nerves (or carelessness) was a factor a week later when Dalglish missed from the spot against Kilmarnock, although Celtic coasted to a comfortable 4-0 win, but the side slipped a little with two draws in succession (1-1 against Thistle at Parkhead, and 2-2 away to East Fife). This latter fixture was a frustrating match as Celtic missed three penalties in the second half, if one includes a re-take; the sinners, Murdoch, Hood and Dalglish, were reprieved by a scrambled goal in the last minute by the tireless Deans that salvaged a draw.

At that stage in the campaign Stein felt privately that Celtic were going to lose the championship to the challenging Rangers; after a 2-2 draw at Tannadice on 10 March, Celtic's advantage lay in goal difference only, and the side's morale had been dented. For some time goalkeeping had been a problem at Parkhead. After Simpson's retirement a number of replacements had been tried with varying degrees of success — Fallon, Williams, Connaghan — but now Hunter's consistency promised to end the search for a successor. With seven league matches left Celtic steadied admirably to prove their championship pedigree, and remained unbeaten to the end of the campaign, taking the maximum points (Hunter conceding only one goal) and on the penultimate Saturday of the league season Rangers finally dropped a point in a 2-2 draw at Pittodrie. Celtic, now needing only a single point for the title, travelled to Easter Road on 28 April, 1973, and won 3-0 in a highly professional manner with the leading scorers, Deans and Dalglish, both netting.

The eighth championship in a row had been won, but clear signs of struggle had appeared; the strain showed just as clearly in the cup competitions, none of which Celtic won.

The League Cup format was altered this season, the start of a period of regular changes, and Celtic had no difficulty in qualifying, along with East Fife, from a section that included Arbroath and Stirling Albion. The First Division sides had been seeded with weaker Second Division outfits, as much for the financial benefit of lesser clubs as to ensure quality ties later. After disposing of Stranraer by 7-3 on aggregate Celtic faced Dundee and lost the first leg 1-0 at Dens Park, but won the second by 3-2 at Parkhead. Before the start of extra time Stein, clearly angered with the controversial refereeing of Mr. Davidson, emerged from the dugout to have words with the official in an exchange that cost him a severe censure from the SFA and a fine of £100. The extra thirty minutes were scoreless, but Celtic had little difficulty in winning a play-off at neutral Hampden Park by 4-1 to advance to a semi-final with Aberdeen where twice the side came from behind to win 3-2.

A crowd of 71,696 saw the final on 9 December against Hibernian at Hampden, and it turned out to be another League Cup letdown. As the Edinburgh side had done in the pre-season Drybrough Cup, their forwards exploited Celtic's defensive uncertainties, this time on a rainswept, windy field. In 60 minutes Edwards lobbed the ball over the Celtic 'wall' for Stanton to shoot past Williams; only five minutes later, as the Celtic defenders were concerned about the dangerous Gordon at the far post, Stanton cleverly crossed for the flying O'Rourke to head home at the near post. Despite a rally by Celtic and a goal from Dalglish in 76 minutes, Hibernian held on to win their first national trophy in seventy years. For Celtic it was the third successive League Cup final defeat . . . and grounds for concern.

Europe offered little in the way of consolation. Celtic making their seventh appearance in the competition (against Rangers' six and Manchester United's five), were now Britain's leading representative, but it was scarcely a good year. The team struggled against Rosenborg Trondheim (Norway) in the first round, although managing to win both legs — an unimpressive 2-1 win at Hampden, and a 3-1 victory in Norway. The draw pitted the club against Ujpest Dozsa again, and this time the Hungarian side was better prepared than seven months previously when their season had just resumed after the mid-winter break. At Parkhead Ujpest held Celtic to a narrow 2-1 win, and were confident of their chances in the second leg. The confidence was justified as the Hungarians, inspired by Bene and Dunai, shredded Celtic's defence in the opening twenty minutes; by that stage Celtic had conceded three goals and, in the end, lost the tie by a 4-2 aggregate. For only the second time in seven years' participation in the tournament Celtic had failed to reach the last eight.

The 1973 Scottish Cup final was graced with royalty in the person of Princess Alexandra, and featured the 'Old Firm'. Celtic had played well in the closing stages of the league and in the cup, first ousting East Fife 4-1 at Parkhead and then Motherwell 4-0 at Fir Park where Hunter saved an early penalty in brilliant fashion.

Controversy marred the quarter-final against Aberdeen at Celtic Park. In the opening minute a goal by Jimmy Johnstone was disallowed on the testimony of a linesman's flag, and in 60 minutes the little winger was ordered off after an incident with full-back Hermiston. At the conclusion of the scoreless draw the referee, inevitably Mr. R. H. Davidson, required a police escort from the ground. Another headed goal by Billy McNeill decided the replay at Pittodrie in the dying minutes, and Celtic advanced to the semi-final. Celtic's feeling that Johnstone had been dealt with harshly at Parkhead was vindicated by an SFA enquiry that exonerated him.

On 5 May, 1973, the following teams lined up at Hampden before 122,714 spectators in an emotionally charged atmosphere:

> *Celtic*: Hunter, McGrain, Brogan (Lennox), Murdoch, McNeill, Connelly, Johnstone, Deans, Dalglish, Hay, Callaghan.
> *Rangers*: McCloy, Jardine, Mathieson, Greig, Johnstone, MacDonald, McLean, Forsyth, Parlane, Conn, Young.

Celtic started brightly, playing attractive football, but ominously the defenders appeared to be risking interceptions with a series of short passes in their own half. Rangers, characteristic of their method in the 70s under Wallace, opted for power and chased every ball with determination, and even after Dalglish had given Celtic a deserved lead in 25 minutes forced back the Parkhead side in search of the equaliser. Only ten minutes later MacDonald brushed aside a tentative tackle by Connelly to cross for Parlane to head powerfully into the net.

Within thirty seconds of the second half Rangers shocked Celtic with another goal, Conn outpacing Celtic defenders for a long ball to score. Celtic soon recovered and swarmed round Rangers' goal, and in 52 minutes Greig had little option in clearing a Deans' shot from the line with his hand. George Connelly was given the task of taking the penalty and, faced with the pressure of beating McCloy backed with the massed Rangers' end behind him (and knowing Celtic's recent trouble from the spot), the tall Fifer efficiently slotted a low drive past the keeper. The momentum had switched to Celtic again, and Johnstone scored what appeared a valid goal when he latched on to a Dalglish pass to lob the ball over the keeper's head and place it in the net, but the counter was disallowed.

The hectic pace, however, favoured Rangers. Celtic still tried to maintain a more composed approach but the defence, uneasy since the goal immediately after half-time, was showing signs of strain. On the hour Rangers grabbed the winner. McLean took a free kick perfectly for Johnstone to head and the ball beat Hunter to strike a post; it rebounded along the line to strike the other post tantalisingly and, as everybody else stood as if turned to stone, Forsyth, scarcely the most mobile of attackers, was allowed to advance and prod the ball over the line. Just before the free kick was taken Celtic's left-back, Brogan, was helped from the field and his normal defensive duties would have involved covering that post, but fatally Celtic had not reorganised in time after the injury, having substituted Lennox for the injured player. In the closing stages, as Celtic pressed furiously for the equaliser, Rangers came closer to increasing their lead in frequent breakaways.

Celtic had paid a heavy price for a lack of urgency when on top, and for their failure to match Rangers' aerial power.

The signs of decline were more perceptible throughout the next season (1973-74) despite the gloss of an outwardly successful campaign and Stein's usual masterly projection of Celtic's image.

Unlike the glory years several players were unhappy at Parkhead and sought transfers: from now on trouble with discontented players was to be a constant factor at Celtic Park. George Connelly, a most gifted sweeper or midfield player, was a sad example. The quiet Fifer had been signed as a teenager, and had soon entranced the large crowd at a European tie at half-time with his 'keepie-uppy' skills; behind the calm façade of a young player who had scored in two Scottish Cup finals against Rangers, all was not well. Connelly, an intensely private individual, had little of the extroversion characteristic of the modern professional footballer and was seldom a participant in the dressing-room banter. The first public awareness of his difficulties surfaced in June, 1973, when he abruptly left the Scottish international party at Glasgow Airport in the hour before departure for Switzerland; in November he walked out of Celtic Park equally surprisingly, but Stein was able to effect a healing of the breach. Unfortunately, the cure was shortlived and the player requested a transfer in February, 1974, but no other club made a satisfactory offer when he was listed; for the rest of his career at Parkhead this most distinguished player performed under a shadow, and sadly didn't attain his full potential in terms of honours.

Connelly's closest friend at Parkhead, David Hay, a tigerish defender and an outstanding player for Scotland in the World Cup of 1974 in Germany, was also embroiled in a lengthy financial dispute with the club arising from an injury in a cup-tie two years earlier; because of the injury he was not considered eligible for bonus payments and became so upset that he too requested a transfer. Alistair Hunter had played so well in his first season for Celtic that he had become Scotland's regular keeper, but in September, 1973, against Czechoslovakia in a World Cup qualifying match he conceded a 'soft' goal, and his confidence and form eroded so much that he lost his place in Celtic's team to Connaghan.

Bobby Murdoch was transferred to Middlesbrough in September. Murdoch, one of the stalwarts of the outstanding teams of the past ten years, had become 'expendable' as Stein tinkered with the line-up, hoping to find the elusive blend. In the close season Stein had moved quickly to sign Aberdeen's gifted midfielder, Steve Murray. Murray, an all-purpose player, was described as "always busy and thoughtful", and Murdoch, after twelve years at Parkhead, felt that the purchase signalled a change of tactics on his manager's part: "The boss decided he wanted runners in midfield, and that is just not my style. Some men can run all day, but I have always tried to make the ball do the work instead." During the season he played an outstanding role in helping Middlesbrough gain promotion to the First Division.

As always, Stein had his problems with Jimmy Johnstone; however, this time so poor was the winger's form in the first half of the season that it did appear that Johnstone had lost his appetite for the game.

In the league campaign that earned for Celtic the distinction of a world record for successive championships[1] it was Celtic's sheer professionalism and experience that eventually told, only two points being dropped in their meetings with their closest rivals, namely Hibs, Rangers and Aberdeen.

Seemingly inevitable was the clinching of the title away from home, this time at Falkirk, and so none of the titles in this record sequence was finally decided at Celtic Park.

On 15 September at Ibrox Jimmy Johnstone, as he had done before at that ground, shocked Rangers' defence with a headed goal, giving Celtic a 1-0 win; in the New Year clash at Parkhead Bobby Lennox ended Rangers' challenge for the title with a sliding goal in another 1-0 win. Hibernian emerged as the only threat to Celtic, and the champions took the decisive step towards retaining the title by winning 4-2 at Easter Road on 23 February, 1974.

For Celtic it was an incredible ninth championship in a row, and a whole generation of Scots had grown up knowing no other side as champions, but unfortunately their dominance was so complete that the impression was created that the Scottish First Division was a walkover for Celtic. Jock Stein was only half joking when he claimed later that the League was reorganised to bring an end to the monopoly. One critic (Basil Easterbrook) felt that Celtic should withdraw from the Scottish League and apply for a place in the top English division: "What possible sense of achievement can remain for an outfit equipped at world club level to keep visiting places of less than 50,000 population like Dunfermline and wiping the floor with the local sides?" Billy McNeill conceded that one of the regrets in his career was that Celtic had not played in a more competitive environment, believing that the team could have attained an even greater degree of excellence. However, nobody could deny Celtic's accomplishment nor the admirable consistency that had come to be taken for granted. In the crucial match at Easter Road Deans scored the clincher with another superb header from near the by-line but, apart from his exploits against Hibs, he made other headlines in the season. He scored six goals against Partick Thistle on 17 November, 1973, seriously threatening Jimmy McGrory's record of eight against Dunfermline back in January, 1928. In a Scottish Cup tie against Clydebank on 27 January before 28,000 when he scored Celtic's first goal in a 6-1 win, it was the first scored in Sunday football in

Scotland. During the miners' dispute of 1973/74 the government had banned the use of floodlighting as an energy-saving measure and the SFA had sanctioned football on the Sabbath.

Celtic continued with the practice, beating Albion Rovers by the same convincing score before finding Motherwell more difficult Sunday visitors in the quarter-final. Celtic twice found themselves a goal down, but fought back to force a draw before 56,000 spectators, and in the replay at Fir Park another Deans' header brought a 1-0 win.

In the semi-final Tommy Gemmell, now with Dundee, made a tactical error by questioning Jimmy Johnstone's current value to Celtic. Johnstone, after a difficult spell, was coming back into form and gave the best possible answer to his former colleague's taunt of "Jimmy who?" by scoring the only goal of the game.

Dundee United, playing in their first final, provided the opposition for Celtic on 4 May before a crowd of 75,959 but were unnerved by the tension of the occasion.

> *Celtic*: Connaghan, McGrain (Callaghan), Brogan, Murray, McNeill, McCluskey, Johnstone, Hood, Deans, Hay, Dalglish.
> *Dundee United*: Davie, Gardner, Kopel, Copland, Smith D. (Traynor), Smith W., Payne (Rolland), Knox, Gray, Fleming, Houston.

Celtic played competently, if not brilliantly, and settled the outcome with two goals midway through the first half. Hood nipped in after 20 minutes to head a bouncing through-ball from Deans over the advancing Davie, and Murray scored in 25 minutes after neat work by Johnstone and Hood. United made an effort to get back into the match after the interval but lost heart after a marvellous, if reflex, save by Connaghan from a header by the dangerous Andy Gray. In the last minute of a latterly tedious final Deans took a pass from Dalglish to add a third goal and seal Celtic's victory.

The League Cup, that season played under an experimental offside rule — with no offside being called in the area of the field enclosed by extended eighteen-yard lines — was another disappointment for Celtic. Once more two teams qualified from each section and, not surprisingly both Celtic and Rangers advanced to the knock-out stages at the expense of Arbroath and Falkirk, having shared the points between themselves with a victory on the other's ground. It took Celtic a 'decider' to get past Motherwell: Celtic won 2-1 at Fir Park, but lost 1-0 at Parkhead and in the play-off, again at Celtic Park, managed a 3-2 win. In the quarter-final Aberdeen put up a stout resistance, holding Celtic to a 3-2 decision at Celtic Park, but in the second leg Celtic defended dourly to hold on for a 0-0 draw and qualified to face Rangers in the semi-final. The sharpness of Harry Hood, scorer of a hat trick, was a measure of the difference in class between the old rivals in Celtic's 3-1 win on a rain-soaked Hampden.

The final was scheduled for 15 December, 1973 (scarcely the most appropriate month for the final of a national tournament) and it was played in an unreal atmosphere. Both clubs were unwilling to play on the treacherous pitch, hastily cleared of the snow that had covered it and still icy in places, but the referee passed it as "playable"; only 27,974 braved the rain and sleet to attend and others stayed away because of the inconvenience of the 1.30 start caused by the power crisis. Celtic's performance matched the dreich surroundings, their only tactical ploy being to release long balls from out of defence for the front runners to take advantage of the experimental offside rule. However, Dundee's defence was tight and Celtic's forwards (Dalglish, Hood and Wilson) were never able to break free. Dundee's strikers looked more dangerous, and after 75 minutes Gordon Wallace breasted down a free kick with his back to the goal to swivel and drive the ball past Hunter for the only goal of the match.

Celtic's European campaign, destined to end in controversy seven months later, started off with an easy fixture against the Finnish side TPS Turku, and Celtic advanced on a 9-1 aggregate — 6-1 in Finland, and 3-0 at home. Celtic then made ominously heavy weather of getting past the little-considered Danes, Vejle BK. At Celtic Park the first leg finished up 0-0, a performance that underlined the growing feeling that Celtic were no longer a genuine European force, and in Denmark a single goal by Bobby Lennox eked out the narrowest victory; along with Johnstone, McNeill and Lennox were the only survivors of the Lisbon team.

The draw once more favoured Celtic, bringing a quarter-final pairing with Basle of Switzerland, but the Swiss team surprised Celtic with a 3-2 win at Basle after Wilson had given Celtic an early lead. Celtic stormed into attack from the start of the second leg at Parkhead and had the fans singing with two quick goals from Deans and Dalglish, but Basle fought back with two goals before half-time. Tom Callaghan gave Celtic a 3-2 lead, and a tie on aggregate, ten minutes after the interval, but despite Celtic's pressure the Swiss held out to extend the match into extra time. Celtic's winner came from a headed goal by Steve Murray ten minutes into the extra half hour, to give Celtic a 6-5 aggregate win. The pessimists noted that 11 years previously Celtic had eliminated the same club 10-1 on aggregate in the Cup-Winners' Cup.

The semi-final first leg against Atletico Madrid of Spain was staged at Celtic Park on 10 April, 1974. It was a night of football from which Celtic's supporters emerged with glowing praise, the team with credit, and the Spaniards with universal censure. From the opening whistle Atletico's players kicked and hacked their way through ninety disgraceful minutes; before the end seven of them had been booked by the Turkish referee, Mr. Babacan, and three sent off. Celtic pressed throughout the match, but were unable to capitalise on the numerical advantage. After the game, some criticism was levelled at the players for this failure, but amid the flying boots, the hacking and the tripping it was physically dangerous to play a normal game and it became impossible to build up any rhythm with the frequent and prolonged stoppages; that only two Celtic players were booked despite the provocation was in itself commendable. The supporters, massed in a 73,000 crowd, deserved the lavish praise bestowed on them. They cheered on the team from the start, booed the foul play of the visitors, and despite the happenings on the field remained on the terracings without fighting or throwing missiles. What prompted the tactics employed by the Spanish side? For one thing, they were managed by Juan Carlos Lorenzo who had been in charge of the Argentine national side in the 1966 World Cup — a team described by the normally taciturn Alf Ramsay as "animals", and he refused to allow his players to swop jerseys with them after the 1-0 win at Wembley. Sadly, the cynical approach adopted by Atletico reflected the worse aspects of the modern game. Atletico knew that an outbreak of crowd trouble at Celtic Park would be severly punished by UEFA, and it seemed that Lorenzo, aware of the riots in Barcelona at the conclusion of the 1972 Rangers-Moscow Dynamo match, hoped to provoke similar scenes in Glasgow. He underestimated the long-term education of the Celtic supporters by Jock Stein in frequent columns published in *The Celtic View*; the behaviour of the supporters delighted the manager, and justified his faith in them.

UEFA displayed its customary ambivalent attitude towards the behaviour of Latin clubs, refusing to expel the club from the competition, nor responding to the suggestion that the second leg be played on a neutral ground. Instead the authorities contented themselves with, later, levying a fine that the Madrid club considered laughable, and automatically banning the three players sent off from the second leg. It was noted that Atletico had fielded a strange team at Parkhead. Of the players barred, only Ayala was a recognised regular. Celtic, fearing reprisals from UEFA if the club refused to complete the engagement, decided to travel to Madrid two weeks later. Confined to the hotel under police escort amid a tense atmosphere, and aware that the Spanish press had stirred up a hate campaign, the players were unable to relax or train effectively, especially after Johnstone had received a death threat over the hotel phone. In the match Celtic eventually went down to two late goals. The only consolation was that Bayern Munich defeated Atletico in a replayed final, restoring a sense of justice to the competition. The last word came in the best history of the competition: "Their persistent disregard for the laws mocked the spirit of international competition. In the city where Real Madrid lit a torch for the European Cup, Atletico did their best to extinguish it."

(*The European Cup 1955-1980*: John Motson/John Rowlinson, 1980.)

The next season marked not only the first cup 'double' of the decade, but also the disappointment of not achieving ten successive titles and of a first round European exit at the hands of Greece's Olympiakos.

Celtic advanced to the knock-out stages of the League Cup by topping a section that included Ayr United, Dundee United and Motherwell. The side stuttered a little against Hamilton, but won both legs of the quarter-final, by 2-0 at Parkhead and 4-2 at Douglas Park. Airdrie put up a fight in the semi-final before going down 1-0.

Hibernian were the opposition for the final, sensibly held on 26 October, 1974, but still under the experimental offside rule. In the 70s, when Celtic and Hibs clashed, invariably a starring role was assigned to 'Dixie' Deans. Only a week earlier he had led Celtic to a 5-0 rout over the Edinburgh side with a hat-trick and in the final he repeated the performance, this time in a 6-3 win. Johnstone was at his impish best and his dribbling disturbed Hibs' plans as he swept past defenders before cutting the ball back from the line; Dalglish, by now a complete player, orchestrated the midfield; and Deans revelled in the service to harass the Edinburgh defence. Johnstone scored the first goal in only six minutes, racing clear of his markers to net a Dalglish pass. In 40 minutes Deans was the first to react to a McCluskey through ball and fired it past McArthur but Harper reduced the margin two minutes later. Wilson added a third only two minutes into the second half but Harper pulled one back when he took advantage of a mix-up between McNeill and Hunter. Deans scored his second to give Celtic a 4-2 lead with a low shot, and then completed the hat-trick with the type of goal that he seemed to reserve for Hibs: a Hood corner landed at Johnstone's feet for the winger to fire the ball at goal, and Deans launched himself at the drive to head the ball into the net before the stunned opponents, team-mates and 53,848 crowd could believe it. Murray completed Celtic's scoring fifteen minutes from the end and Harper scored a consolation goal for Hibs in 83 minutes, gaining a hat-trick for himself in Celtic's 6-3 triumph.

Celtic: Hunter, McGrain, Brogan, Murray, McNeill, McCluskey, Johnstone, Dalglish, Deans, Hood, Wilson.
Hibernian: McArthur, Brownlie (Smith), Bremner, Stanton, Spalding, Blackley, Edwards, Cropley, Harper, Munro, Duncan (Murray).

Both sides met again in the Scottish Cup at Easter Road in January, and Celtic opted for a semi-defensive strategy in view of weaknesses that were becoming apparent in the faltering league campaign. Celtic won comfortably 2-0, and Deans scored yet again. For the next round against Clydebank at Parkhead Jock Stein, still troubled by problems in defence, dropped Billy McNeill and Ally Hunter, replacing them with

Roddy MacDonald and Graham Barclay, and Celtic won 4-1. The league form was disheartening, but the team was surviving in the Cup. At Dumbarton, always a potentially tricky venue, Celtic managed a 2-1 win with goals from Wilson and a new powerfully built midfielder, Ronnie Glavin from Partick Thistle, to qualify for a third successive semi-final against Dundee, winning through 1-0 by another Glavin goal. In the final, played on 3 May, 1975, the unfashionable Airdrieonians lined up against Celtic before a crowd of 75,457.

Airdrie: McWilliams, Jonquin, Cowan, Menzies, Black, Whiteford, McCann, Walker, McCulloch (March), Lapsley (Reynolds), Wilson.

Celtic: Latchford, McGrain, Lynch, Murray, McNeill, McCluskey, Hood, Glavin, Dalglish, Lennox, Wilson.

Celtic pressed from the start on a sun-drenched Hampden, and Airdrie's hopes of containing Celtic's early surge were dashed in 14 minutes when Wilson headed a cross from Dalglish past McWilliams. Surprisingly, Airdrie did not collapse, but instead fought back to equalise three minutes from the interval. Straight from the kick-off Celtic attacked to gain a corner and Wilson, again unmarked, headed home Lennox's cross to restore the lead. Paul Wilson, the team's leading scorer that season, deserved special credit for his performance in the final, the unpredictable forward having played the match under the shadow of a family bereavement. Shortly after the interval, when the speedy Lennox was tripped, Pat McCluskey settled the outcome by converting the penalty, and both teams played out the last half hour quietly. At the whistle, and after the presentation of the medals, the Celtic players made a fuss over Billy McNeill and later hoisted him on to their shoulders to the acclaim of supporters instinctively aware that the most successful career in football was over.

Despite the glory of cup play, the season marked the end of Celtic's dominance in the championship. The new champions, Rangers, signalled the conclusion of the reign with an eventually emphatic 3-0 win at Ibrox on 4 January, 1975.

Celtic had started off well in defence of the title, and went into the Ibrox fixture in first place, buoyed up with a recent, devastating 6-0 victory against Dundee at Dens Park. In the 'Old Firm' clash, however, Celtic paid the full penalty for missed chances early on, and carelessness in defence later. On the heavy pitch Rangers' more direct methods paid off and the Ibrox club, which had avoided its recent slow start to the campaign, joined Celtic at the top of the table.

A week later two more points were lost in a 3-2 defeat at home to Motherwell, and Celtic's hold on the championship was slipping. In the next few matches more points were squandered as Celtic continued to struggle, and hope for a 'ten in a row' disappeared at Easter Road on 22 February, 1975. Ian Archer captured the mood in his column: "The

Paul Wilson heads Celtic's first goal in 1975 Scottish Cup final.

crown lies shakily on Celtic's head. One little nudge and it will roll in one huge clatter, rolling down the steps of the throne from which they have ruled this Scottish Kingdom for the past nine years. There should be much sadness abroad in the land.

"Coming back from the capital by train, looking into the deep-set eyes of Celtic supporters who seemed to have fought a long campaign in the desert rather than attended a football match, you were in touch with grief.

"Those of us who have tugged at their coat-tails for so long and felt proud to be with them when the plane touched down at some remote foreign capital to find their fame had preceded them found no joy at all in desperate, possibly ruinous, defeat at Easter Road.

"This last decade has established Celtic as one of the great clubs in the world. Not as lastingly famous as the unique Real Madrid, not as individually talented nor explosive as Ajax of Amsterdam. But more friendly and better loved than Inter, more attractive than any English club since the last revival of Tottenham Hotspur. They trod more new paths than any Scotsman since Dr Livingstone left Blantyre.

"So, when the lights were turned up and the part finished, when it was seen that under the makeup was a tired face, when all that happened on Saturday, it was difficult not to cry a little, for if Celtic made their own players rich and famous, their own supporters a few inches taller, and mere observers a little happier, they made Scotland a good bit better.

"These were Saturday's thoughts, morose and made worse by the historical probability that we shall not see their like again. A part of everyone who likes his football had disappeared from his soul as, in these last few weeks, the glory of nine years has vanished in the confusion of the tenth." (*Glasgow Herald*: 24 February, 1975.)

The league title slipped further and further away, and Celtic finished a distant third, four points behind Hibernian and eleven behind Rangers.

After the Scottish Cup victory over Airdrie, Stein had to consider his rebuilding plans. Three more stalwarts had ended their days at Celtic Park: Billy McNeill had announced his retirement immediately following the final, Jimmy Johnstone was allowed to leave for the unlikely pastures of San José (USA), and Jim Brogan, no longer guaranteed a first-team spot, left for Coventry City. George Connelly, unable to cope with the spotlight pressures of a modern professional footballer, had walked out in September, 1974, and, sadly, thereafter played only briefly for Celtic. David Hay, after his World Cup heroics for Scotland in West Germany, had departed for Chelsea in 1974 and his ball-winning skills in midfield were missed. Goalkeeping woes, assumed to be solved finally with the capture of Hunter, reappeared when he lost form as did his deputy, Connaghan and in mid-season Celtic had signed Peter Latchford from West Bromwich Albion in a bid to solve them.

Jock Stein, always the man to relish a different challenge, was driving back to Glasgow from Manchester Airport in the summer of 1975 at his usual high speed when his Mercedes was involved in a head-on collision with another car coming the wrong way on the notorious A74. Unconscious, Stein was rushed to hospital with injuries so severe that it was feared he would never assume his duties again. For 1975-76 at least Celtic would have to struggle without 'the Big Man'.

Notes
1 An honour shared with MTK Budapest, between 1917 and 1922, and CDNA Sofia, between 1954 and 1962, with nine successive titles.

28

FADING GLORY

IN Jock Stein's absence Sean Fallon, his assistant since 1965, took over the management role. The earnest deputy found it a difficult year for a variety of reasons, the most important being simply that he was not Jock Stein.

Loyally Stein stated that he would have found it a difficult season himself, and Sean Fallon was unlucky to experience the absence of regular players. George Connelly once more walked out, prompting an indefinite suspension by an exasperated management, while Steve Murray, a player around whom a new Celtic could have been built, missed most of the season after a toe injury. Others were unable to produce their best form. Hood and Lennox struggled for most of the season, while Glavin, noted for his ferocious shot, scored in only one of his nineteen competitive matches and Deans, whose irrepressible spirit had been channelled cunningly by Stein, scored only 17 in a lacklustre campaign and was transferred to Luton Town at the end of the season.

The highlight was the scintillating form of Kenny Dalglish and Danny McGrain; both were now approaching their best and played splendidly throughout. Fallon could not recall McGrain having a poor game and Dalglish, appointed captain in August, scored 32 goals although he was not technically a striker, playing slightly behind the front runners. Another encouraging feature was the promise revealed by youngsters such as Roy Aitken, Tommy Burns and George McCluskey when they were blooded during the season.

Fallon had mixed results from his forays into the transfer market. Johannes Evaldsson, an Icelandic internationalist defender immediately dubbed as 'Shuggie' by the supporters, was signed in the close season and proved a fine investment, but winger John Doyle, signed in March 1976 for £90,000 from Ayr United to bolster a challenge for the league title, was injured in his debut against Dundee and struggled to regain full fitness.

This was the first season of the Premier League, the Scottish League having reorganised into three divisions consisting of the Premier (10 clubs), the First (14), and the Second (14), but once more the championship was dominated by the 'Old Firm'.[1] Celtic made the early running despite a 2-1 loss on the opening day at Ibrox before a record crowd for the Premier Division of 69,594. After another defeat at Ibrox on Ne'erday by 1-0 and a 3-3 draw at Parkhead against Dundee two days later, Celtic strung together nine successive wins to keep ahead of Rangers, who also were in the middle of an undefeated run. On 2 April, 1976, Celtic's run was halted with a 3-2 loss at Tannadice, and the side started to show signs of edginess under the strain of Rangers' challenge; in the next three matches Celtic dropped five points with a home draw against Aberdeen (1-1), a loss at Easter Road to Hibs (0-2), and a shock defeat at Parkhead by Ayr United (1-2).

Rangers had the advantage of fielding a settled side and, without ever being considered an outstanding side, kept on steadily to win the title by a margin of six points. Celtic's main problem in the campaign was a failure to cope directly with Rangers, earning only two points in drawn games at Parkhead and losing both games at Ibrox. A curious statement by Sean Fallon prior to the Ne'erday defeat at Ibrox betrayed Celtic's lack of conviction even though three points clear at the top: "We go into the game with the advantage that, even if we lose, we will still be a point ahead." (*Daily Record*: 31 December, 1975.)

In the League Cup Rangers once more proved a nemesis to Celtic in the final. Celtic's progress to Hampden was relatively trouble-free, eliminating Aberdeen, Hearts and Dumbarton in the sectional play, winning home and away against Stenhousemuir in the quarter-final, and sidelining Thistle in the semi-final with a first-half goal from Edvaldsson.

The final, played on 25 October, 1975, with a 1 p.m. kick-off in an attempt to combat the threat of hooliganism, attracted only 58,806, and was undoubtedly the worst 'Old Firm' League Cup final to date. It was a dour struggle, the flair of the ball-workers and the creativity of the midfielders being stifled and snuffed out by close marking and physical challenges. Celtic officials were incensed at the latitude extended by the referee, W. Anderson (East Kilbride), to some Rangers' defenders, most notably Forsyth, significantly nicknamed "Jaws" by his admirers. The only goal came midway through the second half, a typically opportunistic diving header from Alex MacDonald, and Celtic could produce no effective counter.

Disappointing displays ended Celtic's interest in the other two cups. In the Scottish Cup Celtic moved into a 2-0 lead against Motherwell at Fir Park, but overall complacency and defensive carelessness contributed to a shock 3-2 defeat at the first hurdle. A promising run in the European Cup-Winners' Cup, the club's first venture in this tournament in a decade, was ended at the quarter-final stage by a merely competent

East German side, Sachsenring Zwickau. In the first leg at Parkhead Celtic missed chances, including a penalty from Bobby Lennox, before Dalglish scored. The Germans broke away in the last minute and Blank equalised, taking advantage of an overexposed defence. In the second leg the same player scored in only five minutes, and Celtic rarely looked like coming back, although Roddy MacDonald's header from a corner near the end appeared a valid equaliser.

For the first time since 1963-64 Celtic had gained none of the major trophies. Certainly the absence of Stein and the doubts about his being able to resume his career were major factors in contributing to the malaise. Fallon tried hard and worked conscientiously, but his earnestness could not make up for the leadership that only Stein could provide. Throughout the season Celtic were too often a pedestrian side, frequently unable to raise their game, and in the closing stages, when every match was important, revealed too many ragged edges.

Jock Stein's return in time for 1976-77 required further changes: Dave McParland, formerly Thistle's manager, came to Celtic Park as assistant manager and Sean Fallon was placed in charge of a reorganised scouting system. McParland took over the tracksuit aspects of management while Stein watched from the touchline having not fully recovered from his injuries. Stein expressed complete satisfaction with the work of McParland, suggesting in an interview with Ken Gallagher of the *Daily Record* in February, 1977, that he had Stein's endorsement as Celtic's next manager.

Stein saw clearly that Celtic had developed weaknesses down the middle and moved with characteristic speed and acumen to remedy the situation. Early in September he persuaded Hibernian to part with Pat Stanton, their 32-year-old captain, in exchange for young Jackie McNamara, and later in the month bought Joe Craig, a forceful and direct leader-cum-striker from Partick Thistle for £60,000. Stanton was employed as a sweeper behind young MacDonald, where his skill in reading situations helped to restore stability to the heart of the defence. Craig could score goals, took much of the weight off Dalglish, and made more space for Glavin to drive through from midfield.

Celtic, playing under a management duo that radiated confidence, enjoyed a resurgence. On 20 October, 1976, Celtic swept aside the title challenge of the recently impressive Dundee United by 5-1 at Parkhead, with Glavin scoring three goals. A month later, against Hearts at Tynecastle Celtic fought back from a 1-3 deficit for a dramatic victory — Lennox pulled one back before McGrain and Dalglish, as they had done in midweek against Wales in a World Cup tie, combined superbly for the equaliser, and with only three minutes left Glavin crashed home the winner. In the following midweek Celtic went to Ibrox and Joe Craig swivelled to rifle home a 20-yarder which brought the first league win over Rangers (1-0) since January 1974. Celtic had embarked on an impressive run of 14 Premier Division matches without defeat, with 13 wins and only one point yielded. On 11 January, 1977, Celtic again beat Rangers, this time at Parkhead on a pitch rendered barely playable through frost, and took over first place in the league. Playing consistent and at times inspired football, Celtic kept control of the situation and ended the hopes of Dundee United with a 2-0 win at Parkhead on 26 March when Latchford's deputy, the experienced and capable Roy Baines, saved a penalty taken by his opposite number, Hamish McAlpine. Due to a petty ban on TV coverage imposed by Tom Hart, Hibernian's temperamental chairman, viewers were denied the pleasure of seeing Joe Craig's volley that clinched the title on 16 April.[2]

Joe Craig's volley clinches the title at Easter Road, 1977.

Stein, concentrating on rebuilding the team, did not expect to make much impression in Europe, and his prediction was borne out with an early exit in the UEFA Cup. Celtic's chance was lost in a 2-2 draw at home to Wisla Krakow, because the workmanlike Polish team scored twice

without reply from Celtic behind the 'Iron Curtain' in the return leg.
Once more the League Cup proved a disappointment for Celtic. Celtic
dropped only two points in draws with Dumbarton and Dundee United
in the sectional play to qualify for an easy assignment against Albion
Rovers that ended in a 6-0 aggregate score. Hearts put up a strong
resistance in the semi-final at Hampden, going down bitterly after a
hotly disputed penalty that Dalglish converted in a 2-1 win. Aberdeen,
impressive conquerors of Rangers by 5-1 in the other semi-final,
provided the opposition at Hampden on 6 November before 69,707; the
final, Celtic's thirteenth in succession, thoroughly deserved the 'unlucky'
tag associated with that number. Celtic pressed from the start, and went
ahead after 15 minutes from another Dalglish penalty, but Aberdeen
stayed cool and fought back to equalise ten minutes later. Celtic
resumed the pressure on the Dons' goal, but missed numerous chances
on the rain-soaked turf after excellent leading-up work. The experience
of Stanton and Craig was missed, the newcomers having to drop out
because of being 'cup-tied' with their previous clubs. The misery of the
Celtic supporters, huddled on the exposed King's Park terracing in the
rain, was compounded when Robb snatched a hardly deserved winner
for Aberdeen in extra time. Even Jock Stein, almost outraged at
previous League Cup reverses, was philosophic about this defeat.

Celtic's progress in the Scottish Cup was threatened at Airdrie when
the First Division side took the lead, but a late equaliser by Johnny
Doyle saved the day; at Parkhead Celtic thrashed the 'Waysiders' by 5-0.
In the next round, played on a Sunday before 40,000, Celtic were
shocked by a last-minute equaliser for a stuffy Ayr United, but managed
to win the replay convincingly at Ayr by 3-1.

Celtic's luck in the draw continued. Queen of the South visited Celtic
Park and left defeated by 5-1, and in the semi-final Dundee succumbed
to two goals from Joe Craig. Celtic had reached the final for the 40th
time having had to face only one side from the highest division (Ayr
United) in their latest progress to Hampden.

On 7 May, 1977, the following teams lined up in the rain before a
disappointing crowd of 54,252, reduced by bad weather and live TV
coverage[3]:

> *Celtic*: Latchford, McGrain, Lynch, Stanton, MacDonald, Aitken, Dalglish,
> Edvaldsson, Craig, Wilson, Conn.
> *Rangers*: Kennedy, Jardine, Greig, Forsyth, Jackson, Watson (Robertson),
> McLean, Hamilton, Parlane, MacDonald, Johnstone.

One of the most intriguing features of this final was the appearance of
Alfie Conn for Celtic. This player, a son of the Hearts man of the 50s,
had played for Rangers before moving south to Tottenham Hotspur. He
had always been a flamboyant forward and Jock Stein, who could have a
mischievous streak in him at times, moved to sign him for £65,000 in

March 1977, when he became the twelfth, and so far last, player to have played for both 'Old Firm' clubs. Stein had no qualms about signing the former Ranger, a man who had always played well against Celtic and who had scored a goal for Rangers against Celtic in the 1973 final.

It was not a memorable final. Celtic, without the drive of the injured Glavin, opted for containment, and Rangers had little success at breaching their defence. Rangers' predictable threat of aerial power was met capably by the height of MacDonald and Edvaldsson, with Stanton standing by to mop up any looseness. An Andy Lynch penalty kick in the 20th minute was enough to separate the teams, despite Rangers' frantic appeals to referee Valentine (Dundee) that Johnstone had not handled a MacDonald header on the line.

Jock Stein's last season in charge of Celtic was a disappointing one for the club and disastrous by his standards, but it was doomed from the outset with various factors wrecking the optimism surrounding the squad's potential.

During the close season Celtic had embarked on a Far East tour, and did well to win an international tournament with a £20,000 first prize in competition with Arsenal, Red Star (Belgrade), and the Australian national team. However, Stein was concerned about the continuing unhappiness of Kenny Dalglish, who had renewed his request for a transfer and had not travelled with the Celtic party. Upon returning to Scotland, Stein made strenuous efforts to persuade the player to remain at Parkhead, but reluctantly had to phone Bob Paisley at Liverpool to tell him of Dalglish's impending availability, as he had promised to do. A few days before the start of season 1977-78 Dalglish was transferred to Liverpool, the English champions, for a record fee between British clubs of £440,000; the current odds of 4/7 on Celtic for the Premier League title immediately lengthened.

Celtic opened the defence of the championship with a home match against Dundee United at Parkhead and dropped a point in a scoreless draw but, more significantly, lost two key players. Both Pat Stanton and Alfie Conn were carried off suffering from knee injuries, Conn's being scheduled for an immediate operation and, after exhaustive tests, Stanton's also required surgery. The players, unfortunately, never did make full recoveries although the younger Conn made thirteen appearances later in the season (failing to score in any) while the veteran Stanton decided to retire at the end of the season.

The loss of two such players, when coupled with the transfer of Dalglish, proved too much, but Stein's choice of men to replace them or to boost morale was singularly unconvincing.[4] Roy Kay, a full-back, had come from Hearts on a free transfer in the close season; John Dowie, a midfielder, from Fulham for £25,000; Joe Filippi, another defender, from Ayr United for £15,000 plus a young Celtic player, and Frank

Munro, a central defender, from Wolverhampton. The latter's fortunes with Celtic summed up the tenor of the season. Munro, who was hesitant about joining Celtic (initially on loan) and whose fitness was questionable, was surprisingly appointed team captain in the absence of McGrain and in his first match for Celtic, against St. Mirren, had the misfortune to slice a clearance past his own keeper. When his loan period was over, he baulked at Celtic's subsequent offer and had to be coaxed into playing for the club; at the end of the season he was given a free transfer.

Nothing seemed to go right for Stein as player after player came down with injury. Danny McGrain's was the most serious (a mysterious ankle injury that sidelined him for over a year and threatened his career) but others suffered as well. Burns and Aitken, both promising young players, were out with routine injuries but Doyle had to undergo a cartilage operation and Lynch was hospitalised with appendicitis. The team's discipline suffered as the ill-luck continued. At Ayr Johnny Doyle was sent off unluckily when his shot for goal, struck after an unheard whistle, hit the referee in the face; young Roy Aitken was ordered off in a Scottish Cup replay at Kilmarnock; at Ibrox it seemed as if the whole Celtic team was on the verge of walking off the pitch after the referee allowed a disputed goal for Rangers to stand in a 3-1 defeat in January 1978.

It was a most uneasy time. The new players were not settling in as well as expected and Stein's almost legendary skill in the transfer market was being openly questioned; the younger players, such as Tommy Burns and George McCluskey, were becoming discouraged at the lack of support on the field from their experienced colleagues. Some wondered if a jinx had settled over Parkhead. Certainly, the lack of spirit and poor morale would not have been tolerated by Stein in his normal frame of mind. Too many stories attest to the strong discipline ordinarily exercised by the manager to doubt this.

Stein was preoccupied for much of the season. It was recognised in football circles that the relationship between the manager and the chairman, Desmond White, was strained at times. Little empathy existed between the two, unlike the association that had evolved between Stein and Kelly. The manager's frustration erupted with the publication of the club's official history, written by journalist, Gerry McNee. Suspicious of the timing of its publication (almost a decade before the club's centenary) and noting the author's acknowledgement of the help provided by the chairman and three directors, Stein resented the criticism of his preparation for the European Cup final in 1970 and other reservations apparently held in private till then by the Board. The manager commented angrily: "I refused to contribute to the book. That is why they are making a stab at me. Everyone from the chairman down seems to have read the book except me!"

Back in 1969, Stein had indicated that he would consider retiring at the age of 55 (in 1978), but the chairman's justification of the changes made in May 1978 suggested that implementing the decision had not been unilateral on Stein's part and that the process "had not been painless."

Desmond White continued: "It is a truism that, no matter how talented and successful the manager, there comes a time when the pressures and strains start to take their toll. As well as knowing better than most just what these pressures entail for a man at the top, Jock Stein suffered serious physical injury as an innocent victim of a major road accident. These factors combined to bring home to him several months ago that the time was now opportune for the directors to consider seriously the appointment of a successor. Football is more than ever a young man's game these days and this dictum applies, relatively speaking, just as much to managers and coaches as to players." (*The Celtic View*: Summer Issue, 1978.)[5]

The Celtic Board clearly — and on the evidence justifiably — believed that Stein's best days were behind him, and others felt that after the horrific accident in 1975 Stein was never again the same man: "Certainly the edge of his managerial style, the abrasive sharpness which cut through the record books to give his Celtic nine league championships in a row, was suddenly lost. Stein up to then had been an obsessive manager, first at Celtic Park every morning, last out every evening. Chance visitors were as liable to find him cutting the grass as giving a team talk. Suddenly, all that changed. He became more distant, detached. And in his three remaining seasons at Parkhead the club won the league just once, the Cup just once, and the League Cup not at all; that was, by his earlier superlative standards, a paltry, even pitiful, record." (*Sunday Standard*: June 6, 1982.)[6]

Danny McGrain, out with injury for most of the season, was incensed at the attitude of some players and, given Stein's reputation as a disciplinarian, added fuel to the argument that the manager had lost his urge to succeed: "It would be easy to point to the injuries . . . as the reason, but it wouldn't be right . . . It was bad enough having to sit in the stand and watch the team struggle to defeat against teams they should hammer week in week out. What made it worse for me was the fact that after bad defeats certain players were swanning around, smiling to friends, signing autographs, and obviously not over-worried at pushing the club to its lowest ebb in thirteen years." (*Celtic: My Team*: Danny McGrain, 1978.)

Perhaps the last and most significant word should be left to Tony Queen, a fellow-passenger in the car: "Nobody ever really recovered from that crash; the scars were always there."

The account of the season's performance makes dismal reading. In the league a fifth-place finish, with as many losses (15) as wins, the first Scottish Cup defeat for 29 years at the hands of a lower division side when losing a replay 1-0 at Kilmarnock, a loss to Rangers in the League Cup final after extra time to another disputed goal, and elimination from the European Cup in the second round after an abysmal display in Austria against SW Innsbruck. After this latter defeat Stein felt so discouraged that he went to bed early, declining to stay up to see the match highlights on TV — and he was a man who always had trouble sleeping at night.

The shake-up at Parkhead at the end of the season involved the appointment of a new manager, Billy McNeill, and an assistant, John Clark. In the reshuffle Sean Fallon's connection with the club was severed after twenty-eight years and Dave McParland, who had played a major role as coach in 1976-77 and been touted as the next manager, was released, an inevitable victim of the disastrous season experienced by his illustrious superior. Jock Stein was offered, and initially accepted, a seat on the Board of directors effective later that year. Perhaps to the relief of the Board, who probably preferred a clean break with the past and who may have harboured qualms about the influence of such a strong personality on policy decisions, Stein did not take up the appointment, being lured back into football management with Leeds United and later with Scotland. It was a temptation he found easy to yield to, as he was not ecstatic about the role envisioned for him at Celtic Park; apparently, he was viewed as the ideal choice to revive the stagnant Celtic Pools and thus pump more money into the club, a demeaning method of utilising the knowledge and experience of the most significant figure in the history of Scottish football. In one conversation with the chairman Stein reminded White he was "a football man, not a ticket salesman". Another factor that affected his decision not to take up the director's seat was his concern that he should not be intruding upon any of the new manager's responsibilities. Stein was aware of the difficulties that had emerged at Old Trafford when Matt Busby moved up. However, the circumstances surrounding Stein's departure inevitably fuelled speculation that the Board's offer, which would have made Stein the club's first non-Catholic director, was not a serious one.

What did he accomplish in his years at Parkhead?

Strictly from Celtic's point of view he must be considered, along with Maley, as the most important influence on the club's development. He restored the club to a domestic eminence it had not held consistently since prior to World War 1; the success since the early 20s had been sporadic and nothing like the exploits consistently achieved since 1965. It had become difficult to remember the mediocrity of the Celtic teams prior to Stein's appointment and the despair of long-suffering supporters, raised on tales of a distant past and consoled by fading legends. In his twelve years in charge at Celtic Park (excluding 1975-76) the club won ten Scottish League championships, eight Scottish Cups, six League Cups and the European Cup of 1967 — an unparalleled record. For the first time he made the name of Celtic respected and feared on the Continent. Scotland's (and Celtic's) reputation in Europe for some years became a notable one, making up in part for the humiliations suffered by Rangers at the highest level by clubs such as Eintracht Frankfurt, Real Madrid, AC Milan, and Tottenham Hotspur. Defeat in Europe for Celtic in his heyday, even when inflicted by the truly great teams, came as something of a surprise and a disappointment; the horizons and expectations of the club and its supporters were broadened to a remarkable extent.

At home he helped to change the structure of Scottish football; with the rise in Celtic's fortunes and the relative decline in Rangers', journalists belatedly took a long, hard look at the Ibrox club's policies. Rangers, in desperate attempts to emulate Celtic's success, spent fortunes in the transfer market, but failed to surpass Celtic; their directors demanded success and changed managers ruthlessly, as in the case of Scot Symon and David White. The impression of Ibrox as a bastion of stability was destroyed by the success attained by Celtic under Stein.

Almost single-handedly he changed the image of the manager in Scotland, elevating the position from its former derogatory description as "a secretary with some practical knowledge of the game" to its present stature: ". . . a very 'big' man indeed, courted by many people in varying walks of life, his opinions valued, his views on tactics and strategy held up as gospel, his services sought by several leading clubs in England and Europe, all prepared to pay him huge salaries . . . he has towered over Scottish football like no manager before him — no, not even Struth nor Maley could compare." (*The Team Makers*: Peter Morris, 1971.) Fortunately for football, his methods were not esoteric. He combined the traditional virtues of dedication with attention to the smallest detail, the motivation of players to perform always professionally and occasionally superbly, and the ability to get across his point so that it seemed the most logical solution to a problem; his common sense raised almost to an intellectual force made him a revolutionary figure in Scotland. Like most revolutionaries, at least the successful ones, he was widely imitated. Today managers such as Alex Ferguson and Jim McLean take for granted the methods that he pioneered or promoted — the track-suit coaching, the scouting of the opposition, the management of a pool of players. His accomplishments have to remain as unique within football.

Notes

1 In view of the achievements of the 'New Firm' it is interesting to note that both Aberdeen and Dundee United required points from their last match to avoid relegation. Re the new league set-up, the number of clubs in the Premier League requires that the teams meet each other four times in a season.

2 Surprisingly not one of the ten league titles won by Celtic under Stein was clinched at Celtic Park.

3 It was the first such live coverage of the event in twenty years, and the attendance at this and subsequent finals makes one question the wisdom of the policy.

4 The only successful 'buy' was that of Tom McAdam for £60,000 from Dundee United. Originally signed as a striker McAdam later achieved more success as a central defender.

5 Mr. White at the time of his death in July 1985 was 74 years old, and still Celtic's chairman.

6 The journalist (Harry Reid) should have said 'two', as Sean Fallon was in charge for 1975-76.

29

RESTORATION . . .

WHEN Billy McNeill returned to Celtic Park it was to the acclaim of the supporters who remembered him as the most successful player in the club's history and noted his growing maturity as a manager with Aberdeen. McNeill was delighted to be offered the Celtic post, but he had doubts about leaving Aberdeen. The 'Dons' had come so close the previous season in both League and Cup and were giving clear hints of the powerhouse they were about to become in the Scottish game. On a more personal level McNeill and his young family had regrets about leaving the north-east city where they had settled comfortably, and he was enjoying life as a celebrity in a less frenzied football atmosphere than in Glasgow.

His first impression after his return to Parkhead from the exhilaration of Aberdeen had to be disappointing. He inherited a team that within one season had slid into the apathy of a middle-of-the-table side; he viewed the ageing facilities with increasing dismay, feeling that the ground development had not matched the club's recent stature. McNeill also knew that some players were self-satisfied and no longer motivated. Characteristically, he recognised the opportunity that the situation afforded him and he welcomed it as a challenge. Described as "a young man in a hurry", he felt that pride was the key, and he saw it as his first and principal task to restore that pride and confidence in every level of the club: the administration, the players and the supporters. Like Stein he was instinctively aware of Celtic as "a family", and made strenuous efforts to foster that image. After one early season defeat by Hearts, already earmarked for relegation, he angrily expounded on the side's responsibilities: "It has become obvious that some of these players do not deserve to be wearing Celtic jerseys. Too few of them seem to realise what playing for a club like ours means: that you have to be prepared to work and sacrifice and play till you drop. We are an extraordinary club, and we demand extraordinary standards." Every word conveying the pride in being a Celt. "An extraordinary club," he claimed, and he meant it; it was his first priority to remind those players who had forgotten.

He looked to players who personified the Celtic spirit to raise the morale of the others and to inspire the youngsters. Even as McGrain was recovering full fitness during his long lie-off he appointed him club captain, a popular decision with players and supporters. As an unwilling spectator McGrain had suffered during the previous season's setbacks, describing the attitude of some of his colleagues in typically blunt terms: "There is an inherent attribute in every player with a true feeling for the club — fighting spirit. By tradition when the chips are down then Celtic are always at their most dangerous. Too many players last season seemed to have never heard of that tradition, and that made me sick . . . I find that unforgiveable." (*Celtic: My Team*: Danny McGrain, 1978.)

McNeill saw clearly that the team needed an infusion of new blood as much to restore confidence as to strengthen the squad, and proved his reputation as a sound judge of a player by two early signings — winger Davie Provan from Kilmarnock for £120,000 and midfielder Murdo MacLeod from Dumbarton for £100,000. Both players were to play an important role in the bid for the championship, and established an immediate rapport with the supporters. From the psychological viewpoint the signings were astute. It was a clear indication to the supporters that the club was serious again about going after the honours after the deterioration of the previous season when Stein sought to boost his injury-hit squad with fringe players of doubtful calibre.

Much later in the season the new manager made another signing — a surprise one. He persuaded Bobby Lennox that he could still do a job for the team after his return from Houston Hurricane in the United States, and the cheerful Lennox, despite his years, was an inspirational presence on the field.

The League Cup was the first test of the new boss's calibre. It was a commendable effort, although for the first time in fourteen years the club did not reach the final. Celtic had to face both Dundee sides home and away in the new cup-tie format that had been adopted the previous season and won convincingly. Dundee were eliminated by scores of 3-1 at Celtic Park and 3-0 at Dens, while Dundee United lost 3-2 at Tannadice and 1-0 at Parkhead. Motherwell caused a stir by winning the first-leg 1-0 at Parkhead, but Celtic won comfortably by 4-1 at Fir Park to advance to the quarter-finals where Montrose were removed on a 4-2 aggregate after an honourable 1-1 draw at home.

Celtic's luck ran out in a controversial semi-final against Rangers on an appropriate date, 13 December, 1978. Celtic led early through a goal scored by Doyle after a fine pass from Burns, but after 25 minutes Rangers equalised from a doubtful and hotly disputed penalty. Rangers' winger Cooper had already overrun the ball when he stumbled stretching for it and to the astonishment of the Celtic defenders the referee awarded Rangers a penalty kick. Tommy Burns, the young red-headed forward of great promise, was too insistent in his protests to the linesman and was ordered off.

The match boiled up immediately into a physical struggle, and early in the second half Miller, Rangers' midfielder, was sent off for persistent fouling. Tom McAdam restored Celtic's lead in 65 minutes and, with Celtic leading by 2-1 and both teams now reduced to ten men, it looked as if Celtic were going to scrape through. Rangers exerted pressure on the Celtic goal and with only ten minutes left their centre-half Jackson tried a shot that was deflected past the committed Latchford to send the semi-final into extra time.

The odds had switched now in Rangers' favour, as Celtic had played short-handed for thirty minutes more than their opponents. Still the match continued evenly until the 23rd minute of extra time when a seemingly harmless cross was deflected off the leg of a hapless Celtic defender past Latchford to let Rangers advance to the final.

In the league campaign Celtic made respectable progress, an improvement over the previous season, but were struggling to find the scoring touch to finish off fine approach work. Approaching Christmas with a slump in form it seemed as if Celtic's challenge had foundered, but the team got help from an unexpected source. The winter of 1978-79 was a most bitter one, and more than most clubs Celtic's fixture list fell into arrears. It was a blessing in disguise as the team, in the midst of its miserable patch, welcomed the chance to regroup. Celtic were not able to resume a regular schedule of league games until 3 March, 1979, at which date the team was languishing near the bottom of the table — a false position because of the number of games postponed. With the renewal of the programme Celtic's fortunes soon began to improve. Restored to the team after an absence of eighteen months came Danny McGrain, a steadying influence in defence and as captain a positive effect on every member of the side.

No club had yet established a clear supremacy in the league, an indication that the Premier Division had produced the desired levelling effect, and at the end of April three teams were still in the running for the title. Dundee United led the table, with Celtic a point ahead of Rangers in second place, but the Glasgow clubs had games in hand over their new rival. Celtic faced the leaders at Parkhead on 28 April and in the second half outplayed United to win more convincingly than the 2-1 score would suggest; an interested observer was Jock Stein who was struck by the stamina, fitness and pace of the Celtic team so late in the season.

However, only a week later it appeared as if the race was over when

The evergreen Bobby Lennox nets Celtic's clincher against St. Mirren at Ibrox,
May 1979.

the 'Old Firm' met at Hampden Park in Rangers' home game, Ibrox
undergoing a massive reconstruction. Rangers won deservedly 1-0,
having put more into the game and, now leading by one point with only
four games left, were in the driver's seat.

Celtic did have one considerable advantage in the stretch. Rangers
had reached the final of the Scottish Cup and were to face Hibernian in
a long-drawn-out affair before winning the trophy in a third match.
Always pragmatic, McNeill, feeling that the championship was beyond
Celtic, expressed confidence that the team would qualify for European
competition by finishing high up in the table.

As Stein had astutely observed, however, Celtic's fitness and spirit
was now becoming a major factor. Only two days after the setback at
Hampden Celtic went to Firhill and, although falling behind to an early
goal, fought back spiritedly to win 2-1 over Partick Thistle. Later in the
same week Celtic faced St. Mirren at Ibrox as the Paisley side's ground
was undergoing renovations and won 2-0, the decisive goal coming from
Bobby Lennox at a stage when the 'Buddies' were threatening to
equalise. On the following Monday night Celtic won another nerve-
testing encounter with the doomed Hearts by 1-0 at Parkhead. Celtic
now had one match left, the postponed clash with Rangers at Celtic

Park. The situation was crystal-clear; a Celtic win brought them the league title, but a draw would suit Rangers who had two games in hand despite trailing Celtic by three points.

Celtic pressed from the start but at half-time Rangers, although opting wisely for a semi-defensive strategy, led by a 1-0 margin. After ten more minutes of fierce Celtic pressure in the second half Rangers supporters must have thought the flag was bound for Ibrox. Doyle, incensed after a series of crushing tackles by Rangers' defenders, aimed a kick at Alex MacDonald, another fiery competitor, and was promptly sent off. As the teams adjusted themselves to the changing situation Celtic made a substitution, replacing defender Mike Conroy with forward Bobby Lennox in what appeared little more than a gallant gesture. The pace was unrelenting, the tackles fierce, every yard was contested, every ball fought over. Despite their advantage in manpower, the confidence brought by the one-goal lead, and the psychological cushion of needing only a draw, Rangers found themselves struggling to hold on as Celtic surged forward. In the 67th minute Roy Aitken, up with his forwards, headed the equaliser, but the player and fans knew that this goal alone would be useless, and so Celtic continued the onslaught to a swelling bedlam of encouragement from the terracing. After 75 minutes George McCluskey put Celtic ahead by 2-1 to the now incredulous joy of the supporters, but within two minutes the same supporters were abruptly silenced in full song; Bobby Russell scored a fine if unexpected equaliser.

Stilled momentarily, the more pessimistic on the Celtic terracings murmured darkly of 'a moral victory', but the Celtic players once more drew upon reserves of energy and strength, and bombarded Rangers' goal. With only seven minutes left Celtic took the lead again at 3-2; a spinning cross from George McCluskey was desperately pushed out by the goalkeeper, but skidded off Jackson for an own goal. By now pandemonium was erupting on three-quarters of the ground, as Celtic, despite the precarious nature of the lead, continued to press. In the last minute of this memorable 'Old Firm' struggle Murdo MacLeod burst through an Ibrox defence reeling from the constant pressure and fired in a stupendous drive from twenty yards that left McCloy helpless. Seconds later the whistle went, unheard amidst scenes unmatched since the European Cup glory of a decade previously. Delirious with joy the supporters struggled to comprehend the magnitude of the accomplishment: a goal down in a match they had to win, a man short with thirty-five minutes to play, and to outscore by four goals to two a full-strength Rangers' team going for the 'treble', it was a night to remember. The headline in the *Evening Times* caught the drama: "The night passion and courage created a legend"! Earlier in the season, after that disappointing defeat at Tynecastle, the manager, a man imbued with Celtic's pride and tradition, had reminded his players of their collective responsibility, echoing the sentiments expressed by Jock Stein at his testimonial dinner when he asserted that the real Celtic fans were the salt of the earth, supporters who would always get behind a Celtic side striving to provide the club's renowned entertaining brand of football and trying to give value for money. By the season's end the traditional enthusiasm and spirit had been restored in full on the field and terracing.

For many supporters it seemed as if the days of glory had returned, but McNeill was not fooled by the euphoria of 21 May, 1979; more than most he knew that the league was won by spirit rather than skill, and he was determined to restore Celtic to the heights attained under Stein's command. He was pleased with the progress of the reserve team and he was anxious for some of its promising youngsters to break through and win a regular place on merit in the first eleven, but that prospect was still a year away at least. During the 1979-80 season he was to make two more incursions into the transfer market, buying Dom Sullivan, a midfielder from Aberdeen, for £80,000 and in March 1980 he purchased forward Frank McGarvey from Liverpool for a Scottish record fee of £250,000.

Celtic led the league from an early stage, the only defeat in the first ten matches coming at Cappielow — a 1-0 loss to Morton, surprisingly making a bid for the championship. After New Year the team slipped a little by dropping points in drawn games, some of which should have been won: Partick Thistle and Dundee salvaged draws with late goals and St. Mirren fought back to get a 2-2 draw after trailing by 2-0 at Parkhead. It was not overconfidence that caused the loss of points; rather it was the difference between reaching for the top and in holding on at the top. In winning the championship Celtic had accomplished much by honest effort and spirit, aided perhaps by the awareness that they were rated outsiders; now the team was expected to produce results and to win major honours. As McNeill knew, his squad did not have the depth to challenge for a 'treble' of championship, Scottish Cup and European Cup.

In the European Cup Celtic had made unsteady progress to the quarter-finals. The draw had sent the team to Albania, the most repressive of Communist countries, so much so that the Balkan authorities had refused visas for reporters to cover the match and supporters to accompany the party. It was an unreal atmosphere with Celtic the better side, but going down to a 1-0 defeat; in the second leg, despite losing an early goal when Sneddon headed past his own keeper, Celtic moved ahead to win comfortably 4-1 as the mysterious Albanians, watched by a curious 50,000, had no answer to the clever dribbling of Provan. Celtic appeared to have an easy passage into the next round with a match against Dundalk of Eire. The Irish part-timers were said to be casual in their approach to the fixture, the coach seemingly giving them time off and permission to enjoy themselves on the day before. This 'method' seemed to work as Dundalk came back from a 2-0 deficit to make Celtic work for a narrow and precarious 3-2 lead. With away goals counting double in the case of a tie, Celtic did not look forward to the visit to a packed Oriel Park — an engagement that had once seemed little more than a pleasant jaunt. McNeill opted for defence, and Celtic got the required result, a 0-0 draw, to advance into the quarter-finals and a meeting with one of the great teams of Europe — Real Madrid.

On 5 March Celtic took on the Spanish champions before a capacity crowd of 67,000 at Celtic Park. For much of the first half Real played the more composed football and frequently threatened Celtic's goal with dangerous raids. Celtic's traditional enthusiasm could make little headway against a solid, organised defence. In the second half, urged on by the roars of the crowd and with full-back Sneddon finding lots of room on the right, Celtic took the game to Real Madrid and hammered at their goal; before the whistle Celtic had scored twice, through McCluskey and a glorious header from Doyle. Two weeks later at the famed Bernabeu Stadium a crowd of just under 120,000 saw Celtic start brightly and make chances that were squandered. They started to fade before half-time, becoming intimidated as the indulgent referee ignored some crude tackling by the home team, particularly two vicious fouls on Doyle and Lennox that were allowed to go unpunished. In the last minute of the first half, with McNeill praying for the whistle, Latchford was penalised for 'timewasting', and the referee permitted a dubious goal by Santillana to stand although it appeared that the Spaniard had impeded the Celtic keeper in the subsequent melee. In the dressing-room at the interval McNeill and the veterans of the squad tried in vain to assure the youngsters that they could hold on to their lead, but the ordeal of facing a legendary team in the most prestigious tournament of all before a partisan crowd and a weak referee was too much. Perhaps a more methodical side might have survived but Celtic, too dependent on inspiration to raise their game, could not consolidate the position. More and more Real dominated the second half, boosted by their captain Pirri who had missed the first leg at Parkhead. When the equaliser came it was only a matter of time before Real got the winner, a goal which came with five minutes remaining. It was a disappointing end to the quarter-final, and an almost mortal blow to Celtic's season, as it turned out.

Celtic still led the league by a healthy eight points, and were making steady progress in the Scottish Cup, but understandably after Madrid the team's morale dropped. However, on 2 April the championship seemed won when Celtic beat Rangers 1-0 at Parkhead with a header four minutes from the end by newcomer Frank McGarvey.

Aberdeen, who had ousted Celtic from the League Cup in the quarter-final earlier in the season, were keeping in touch in the championship, and played the leaders at Parkhead on the following Saturday. In the first half Celtic pressed but did not look likely to pierce the Aberdeen defence, starting to establish its reputation as Scotland's most resolute. Aberdeen, prompted by Strachan, moved intelligently into attack and scored first through Jarvie. Shortly afterwards Doyle headed the equaliser past Clark, and the Celtic fans relaxed again, but right on half-time Tom McAdam, now playing well as a central defender, was concussed and had to retire from the match. After McGhee exploited defensive errors to give Aberdeen an early second-half lead, Bobby Lennox missed a splendid opportunity of an equaliser when his weakly hit penalty was easily anticipated by his old adversary, Clark.

The clash showed the basic difference between the sides. Aberdeen were admirably organised, especially in defence, and were prepared to wait for the right opportunity to strike; Celtic seemed disorganised in defence after McAdam's withdrawal, and were impetuous in attack. Method and patient discipline on Aberdeen's part had won over inspiration and hasty improvisation on Celtic's and, for those perceptive enough to realise it, it was the dawning of a new age in Scottish football.

The title was effectively lost in two visits to Dundee within a fortnight. In the first encounter United struck top form and inflicted a crushing 3-0 defeat on a jittery Celtic team, and eleven days later Dundee, lingering in the relegation zone, pulled off an astonishing 5-1 win. The latter match was ludicrous at times with Celtic's defence non-existent and the forwards managing to squander gilt-edged changes. As the players trooped off the field in a state of shock it was apparent that McNeill's task was to restore badly eroded confidence if Celtic were to accomplish the 'double' that seemed likely only a month before.

Aberdeen had the momentum, confident as Celtic sagged and in form as Celtic floundered. The teams met at Parkhead shortly afterwards, in midweek, and Aberdeen gave an assured performance to win 3-1 against a drained Celtic. The champions rallied in the remaining matches though out of form, pressing Aberdeen till the end and finishing only one point behind the northern side who ended a fifteen-year 'Old Firm' monopoly of the championship and, as Dundee United had earlier won the League Cup by beating Aberdeen in the final, the feeling was growing that a 'New Firm' was being established on the north-east coast, but in the Scottish Cup a more typical situation presented itself as Celtic faced Rangers in the final.

Celtic had won their way through to the final in characteristically adventurous fashion, notably in an epic replay at Love Street against St. Mirren. The replay was earned only by a late equaliser by MacLeod from

Provan's cross and Celtic's travails continued in the replay. For most of the tie Celtic were behind in manpower and on the scoreline. Doyle was the hero of the hour, netting an equaliser after thirty minutes when Celtic had been reduced to ten men following McAdam's ordering off. In the second half he was fouled in the box and gained the penalty from which Lennox again equalised to force extra time, and in the first few minutes of extra time he embarked on a spectacular run, finishing by blasting a shot from a near-impossible angle into the net off the goalkeeper. Celtic beat Morton with relative ease in the quarter-final 2-0 at Parkhead, and walked over Hibernian by 5-0 in the semi-final, despite the presence of George Best in Hibs' team, and so qualified to face Rangers in the final on 10 May, 1980, before 70,303.

> *Rangers*: McCloy, Jardine, Dawson, Forsyth (Miller), Jackson, Stevens, Cooper, Russell, Johnstone, Smith, MacDonald J. (McLean).
> *Celtic:* Latchford, Sneddon, McGrain, Aitken, Conroy, MacLeod, Provan, Doyle (Lennox), McCluskey, Burns, McGarvey.

McNeill had to face an important decision about his line-up in the days prior to the match. The two regular central defenders, McAdam and MacDonald, were under suspension and a possible substitute, Casey, was injured. The manager sensed that Rangers would use the tactic of lobbing high balls into Celtic's penalty area to take advantage of the prowess of Johnstone and Smith in the air. Accordingly he chose Roy Aitken and Mike Conroy as the central defenders, the latter being a surprise choice as a relatively inexperienced player and not regarded as built to withstand the physical challenges of the Rangers' strikers. It was an exciting final with both teams taking turns to dominate, but no goals were scored in the regulation ninety minutes, although Latchford had to produce a fine save in the closing minute. Celtic's defence grew in confidence as the match went on, with young Conroy coping with the aerial threat of Johnstone while alongside him Aitken was a pillar of strength. In midfield Provan and MacLeod toiled manfully, helping in both defence and attack. The main source of bother to Rangers' defence was McGarvey, a constant thorn in their side with his clever holding and shielding of the ball.

Almost midway through extra time Celtic scored the winning goal, deservedly so on the play. McGrain moved upfield looking for an opportunity and fired a shot that McCloy seemed to have covered, but George McCluskey neatly deflected the ball past the stranded keeper.

It was a pity that such a meritorious performance should have been marred indelibly with scenes of hooliganism on the field at the end. Following the whistle the Celtic players moved towards the King's Park end of the ground to salute their supporters, some of whom in the absence of the usual considerable police presence jumped the fence to congratulate their team. Enraged at the distant celebration many

Rangers' supporters poured over the fence at the other end of the ground and within a few minutes the second Hampden Riot was on. The official SFA report clearly discriminated between the motives of the two sets of supporters: ". . . [the Celtic supporters] invaded the track and goal area for the purpose of cavorting around and generally celebrating with the Celtic players who had chosen to run to that end of the stadium, on the final whistle, to demonstrate to their supporters their exuberance at victory. At that stage of events there was nothing violent in the exchanges between players and fans. Rather it was a spontaneous, if misguided, expression of joy." The report went on to comment on the Rangers' supporters: "There was no question of celebration in the minds of the fans who invaded from the West end of the ground. They had violence in mind . . .".

A pitched battle was inevitable given the circumstances: "At the Rangers end of the field the presence of the green-and-white celebrants of victory was insult added to yet another setback, and hundreds of Rangers supporters swarmed across the field to vent their spite on the jubilant enemy at the other end. Celtic supporters were later condemned for their part in the brawls, and certainly they stood fist to fist, boot to boot, and bottle to bottle with the enemy, but what would have been thought of them if, at the sight of the charging Rangers supporters, they had turned and fled? There is no way they could have stood their ground and patiently explained to the advancing blue brigade that all they were doing was saluting their team and no insult was intended to worthy opponents. They were Glaswegians and Scottish, and they were being challenged: honour dictated only one course of action." (*The Old Firm*: Bill Murray, 1984.)

Who or what was to blame? One major error was made by the police just prior to the hooliganism, and that was to withdraw many of their number from the track and the stadium before the end of extra time. Experience has shown that two potential flash points for trouble are in the stadium at the final whistle and in the confrontation between pockets of rival fans outside in the streets. The police chose to deploy their main forces outside the stadium, although common sense might suggest that most Celtic supporters would elect to remain inside the ground to watch the presentation of the cup to their team after an 'Old Firm' victory, thus allowing Rangers supporters to disperse quietly. However, at the moment when the rival fans were swarming on to the field and starting to clash in a 'Donnybrook', scarcely enough police were inside the ground to deal with the ugly situation. Predictably the police blamed the Celtic players for rushing towards their supporters at the conclusion of the final and suggested it was a matter of provocation. It is not an argument that stands up well. Had Celtic players rushed to the Rangers' end to demonstrate their joy, that could be considered provocation and the only legal defence would have been temporary insanity; the police argument might as well have blamed McCluskey's goal for the outbreaks of hooliganism.

Both Rangers and Celtic were fined £20,000, a sum that the press felt was relatively light in view of the horrendous scenes that had disgraced the country's image. However, many newspapers started to examine once more the sectarian background that disfigures this rivalry and Rangers' policy came under particular scrutiny.

In 1980-81 Celtic won the championship again, this time comfortably and in the process establishing some Premier League records; at the end of the campaign the margin between Celtic and the runners-up Aberdeen was seven points, although earlier Celtic appeared to be struggling.

Both Rangers and Aberdeen, considered to be the main challengers along with Celtic for the title, inflicted home and away defeats on Celtic in the first half of the season. Aberdeen won handily by 2-0 at Parkhead, and administered a comprehensive 4-1 thrashing at Pittodrie — the latter so convincing a win that when Aberdeen manager Alex Ferguson warned his players about complacency over the title race after the match it was assumed by most that he was being merely diplomatic; Rangers eked out a fortunate 2-1 win with a last-minute goal from full-back Miller's speculative lash at the ball for a rare Premier League win at Celtic Park, but despatched Celtic with ease at Ibrox on November 1 to win 3-0. Three weeks later St. Mirren snatched another last-minute winner at Parkhead in an upset 2-1 victory, and at the turn of the year Celtic were apparently out of contention for the championship, three points behind Aberdeen, the titleholders, who had a game in hand.

McNeill, as every good manager does, made the required adjustments. He changed the training schedule to emphasise speed and sharpness, he spoke sharply to his squad about its responsibilities to the support that he later described unashamedly as "the best in the world; they want to demonstrate just how much they care about this club". He made changes in the team selection, linking the promising Charlie Nicholas with the more crafty Frank McGarvey to form a potent strike-force. An indication of the improvement in morale came with a gritty Ne'erday performance at Kilmarnock when the team, described after the Pittodrie defeat as "a bunch of timid, undisciplined, unco-ordinated players", picked itself up after yielding an early goal to win through by 2-1. By the time Celtic next faced Aberdeen the situation had changed dramatically; Aberdeen, hard-hit by injuries and a slump in Mark McGhee's goalscoring form, were shipping water while Celtic, helped by Frank McGarvey's opportunism in a season in which he ended up as Scotland's leading scorer, had strung together nine successive victories to take over first place. At Parkhead Aberdeen's last chance to retain their title faded as the teams fought out a 1-1 draw on 28 March, a fact that the disappointed Alex Ferguson was forced to admit after the match.

On 18 April Celtic won 1-0 at Ibrox against Rangers, whose challenge had faded in February with a 3-1 defeat at Parkhead. The Ibrox result meant the side had lost only one point in a run of thirteen matches. On the following Wednesday Celtic went to Tannadice and won 3-2 over Dundee United, Tommy Burns clinching the title in style by turning two defenders then hitting a drive into the roof of the net. It had been a highly satisfactory campaign in most aspects. An admirable consistency had been attained later in the season and reserve players had broken into the side. The team established three records in the Premier League with the most points in a season (56), the most wins (26) and the most goals scored (84). Pat Bonner, a young goalkeeper from Ireland, replaced Latchford when the Englishman was injured and retained the position with a series of fine performances which suggested that Celtic had at last found its finest young keeper since Willie Miller; a precociously talented Charlie Nicholas had burst into instant prominence, scoring memorable goals with audacious moves, and the tousle-haired youngster immediately became an idol of pop-star proportions to many supporters.

Still, McNeill was not completely satisfied, sensing that the squad was not deep enough in experience and skill to mount a sustained campaign on more than one front at the same time. Celtic's relatively disappointing performance in cup competition was to bear out his apprehensions.

In the League Cup Celtic were on the verge of a shock elimination in the first round. Stirling Albion, whose Annfield Park was once considered a 'bogey' ground, won 1-0 there in the first leg, and in the return at Celtic Park led 2-1 on aggregate with only three minutes left, but Tommy Burns equalised and in extra time Celtic, inspired by young Nicholas, just off the bench, piled on four goals against the tiring First Division representatives. Later in the competition Celtic again ran into difficulties when Partick Thistle forced the second leg into extra time before Celtic scored two unanswered goals to get through 3-1 on aggregate. The crowd at Parkhead for the second leg of the semi-final with Dundee United on 19 November, 1980, was given an indication that the balance of power had switched in the Scottish game. United, after holding Celtic to a 1-1 draw at Tannadice, were expected to put up a struggle before going down to honourable defeat, but the Dundee side produced a dazzling display of football, laced with resolve, to sweep aside Celtic's challenge with an emphatic 3-0 victory, their first win at Celtic Park since 1974-75. By that display the Tannadice side had served notice that they had 'arrived', a feeling borne out by the subsequent victory in their final.

In the Scottish Cup semi-final Celtic again fell victims to Dundee United, losing 3-2 at Hampden in a replay forced by a 0-0 draw. It seemed that Celtic, after a series of ties against inferior opposition in Berwick Rangers (2-0), Stirling Albion (3-0), and East Stirlingshire (2-0), were not geared for a side of the calibre of Dundee United. In the European Cup-Winners Cup Celtic were eliminated on the away goals rule after losing 1-0 in Rumania, the only highlights of the competition for Celtic being a 6-0 home victory over Hungarian opposition and the attempts of Glaswegian tongues to cope with the opponents' names — Diosgyoeri Miskolc and Politechnica Timisoara.

It was a similar situation throughout the next season (1981-82), a campaign that the manager was to describe as his most stressful. The saddest moment occurred on October with the accidental death of Johnny Doyle, tragically electrocuted at home. Doyle, a whole-hearted player, was a particular favourite among supporters who have traditionally put a premium on commitment.

Aberdeen were the most obvious and strongest contenders for Celtic's championship throne, but the 'Dons' got off to a slow start while Celtic led early, dropping only one point out of the first sixteen to set a torrid pace. At one stage in the early going Aberdeen were close to the bottom of the table, but started to revive; Celtic gained a considerable advantage by halting their recovery programme with a 2-1 win at Parkhead on 7 November. The champions consolidated their position two weeks later by drawing 3-3 with Rangers in an enthralling contest at Celtic Park, five goals coming in the opening twenty-three minutes; the crowd left the ground utterly drained and with the raw emotion of the clash and the high level of skill shown by both teams in a memorable match. It seemed as if the destination of the flag had been decided when Celtic went to Pittodrie on 30 January and defeated Aberdeen in what was already viewed as the decider. Despite being shocked by the loss of a first-minute goal Celtic rallied to win comfortably 3-1. Aberdeen, however, were now reaching a new level of attainment and embarked on an extended run in which they lost only one of their remaining twenty league matches, a sequence which included eight successive wins at the tail end of the campaign. Celtic were jolted out of any possible complacency when Aberdeen visited Parkhead and left with both points in a 1-0 win on 27 March. McNeill, sensing the surge of the Aberdeen challenge, demanded that his squad show all its professionalism in preserving a once substantial lead now starting to shrink. With injuries affecting Celtic's performance (McGrain, Burns, Sullivan, Nicholas and McGarvey were out of the line-up at various times) he called upon his reserves. Young Danny Crainie made a substantial contribution, scoring all the goals in a 3-0 win over Partick Thistle at Firhill, totalling seven goals from the same number of appearances in the closing stages of the league campaign. Two other youngsters were impressive. David Moyes, a tall, red-headed centre-half, seemed remarkably composed when asked to take over in the heart of defence, and young Paul McStay did everything asked of him when introduced, many supporters seeing in his control and bearing a successor to Kenny Dalglish. The joy at a 6-0 win over Hibs at Celtic Park on 1 May, atoning for two losses to the Edinburgh side earlier in the programme, was muted with the news that Aberdeen had won 5-0 at Dundee, and Celtic showed signs of nerves in a scoreless home draw with St. Mirren watched by an expectant 30,500 crowd on the 3 May public holiday. Later in the week Celtic went to Tannadice and crashed by 3-0, while Aberdeen turned the screw by trouncing St. Mirren 5-1.

Celtic's lapses and Aberdeen's resurgence made for an exciting finale to the season on 15 May, 1982. Aberdeen were to face Rangers at Pittodrie, and Celtic to meet St. Mirren at Parkhead; a Celtic loss by 1-0 and an Aberdeen win by 5-0 would give the title to the latter. Over 40,000 turned up at Celtic Park to watch the closing bid for the championship and as St. Mirren, with keeper Thomson outstanding, continued to hold out, many in the crowd followed by transistor radio the disturbing news from Aberdeen where the Dons had built up a 4-0 lead by half-time. The tension was reminiscent of the final league match against Morton on the same ground fourteen years earlier when Lennox scored a dramatic winner in the dying seconds to decide the championship and many had started to pray for such a happy conclusion. In the 63rd minute all the pent-up tension and frustration was released by a goal for Celtic. MacLeod passed forward to Burns who cleverly flicked the ball into the path of McCluskey and the striker went through to beat Thomson conclusively. Rampant now, Celtic struck again a few minutes later when McAdam headed Provan's corner down towards the goal and despite the Paisley protests the referee decided the ball had crossed the line. Before the end Burns created another chance for McCluskey to beat Thomson for a third goal.

It was a day of celebration for the supporters and journalist Ian Archer commented on the evident rapport at Celtic Park: "What was remarkable yesterday was the extraordinary performance by the Celtic fans, who supported the side throughout a hard patch in the game and who wouldn't go away afterwards. They commemorated the championship in their chants to the late Johnny Doyle and while that may read rather morbidly, it was strangely moving and sensitive. At the end Tommy Burns went over to where the invalid carriages are parked and shook hands with all those supporters — the act of a fine player and a proper gent. Maybe such actions, proving the affinity between those who play and those who watch, explain why this club has succeeded where others have failed. There is nothing wrong with passion in

football, and somehow Celtic have more of that commodity than most."
(*Sunday Standard*: 16 May, 1982.)

Once more Celtic had been a disappointment in the cups. For the first
time in eighteen years Celtic did not make the last eight in the League
Cup. They were eliminated in the sectional play, the organisers having
restored the initial format of the tournament in a vain bid to attract the
crowds. McNeill's close-season capture, defender Willie Garner (a
£40,000 buy from Aberdeen), made a luckless debut by deflecting a St.
Mirren shot past Bonner and later heading past his own keeper to
contribute to a 3-1 defeat. In midweek the whole defence was shaky in a
surprising loss to St. Johnstone by 2-0 and, despite winning the
remaining four matches, Celtic could not make up the lost ground
although they thrashed the sectional winners, St. Mirren, 5-1 at Paisley.
Celtic were unlucky in the draw for both Scottish and European Cups.
In an early round of the Scottish Cup Celtic had to go to Pittodrie to face
Aberdeen, who won through 1-0 by a Hewitt header; in the European
Cup Celtic faced Juventus and before 60,000 at Parkhead gained a
commendable 1-0 lead through MacLeod's goal, but it was not enough
to offset McGrain's absence in the Stadio Communale where Juventus
ran out 2-0 winners. The deplorable scenes in the European Cup final of
1985 came as no great surprise to the Celtic supporters at Turin who had
to endure violence to their persons and buses in an episode strangely
overlooked in the saturation coverage of the Brussels tragedy nearly
four years later.

On 4 December, 1982, Billy McNeill must have been the happiest
manager in British football after Celtic defeated Rangers 2-1 in the final
of the League Cup to win the trophy for the first time since 1974.

Celtic's progress to the final had been a triumphant procession as the
opposition from the more lowly divisions were routed. Dunfermline
Athletic, Alloa, and Arbroath were defeated with such ease that Celtic
ran up an aggregate score of 29-3 in the six games, with Charlie Nicholas
in glorious form. Partick Thistle were supposed to supply more stern
resistance in the quarter-final but Celtic swept aside their challenge to
win 7-0 on aggregate. However, recalling past experience with Dundee
United many supporters were anxious about the two-legged semi-final
against the Taysiders. In the first match Celtic played well to inflict a 2-0
defeat on United at Parkhead, Nicholas and McGarvey scoring first-half
goals. Dundee United at Tannadice were a different proposition,
attacking from the start, and with two minutes left led by two goals from
Sturrock, both scored in a stirring second half. Thirty minutes of extra
time at Tannadice against a rampant United was not a pleasant
prospect, and the Celtic supporters were delighted when Nicholas
swooped on to a Burns' pass and fired the ball past McAlpine to put
Celtic through 3-2 on aggregate to the final on 4 December.

Charlie Nicholas brandishes the League Cup, December 1982. Frank McGarvey on left, admires the silverware.

Rangers: Stewart, MacKinnon, Redford, McClelland, Paterson, Bett, Cooper, Prytz (Dawson), Johnstone, Russell (MacDonald), Smith.
Celtic: Bonner, McGrain, Sinclair, Aitken, McAdam, MacLeod, Provan, McStay (Reid), McGarvey, Burns, Nicholas.

Rangers made a move born of desperation almost on the eve of the final by acquiring on loan their former striker Gordon Smith from Brighton, but it made little difference as Celtic pressed from the start. With the wind and rain behind them, Celtic roared into attack in fluid, confident style to put Rangers' defence under immediate and continuous pressure. After 22 minutes, following a combined move by McStay and Provan, Nicholas boldly held the ball and delayed until a gap appeared in the defence before firing home an unexpected shot. Only eight minutes later MacLeod seized a loose clearance from the hard-pressed Rangers' defence and hit a typical pile-driver past the helpless keeper. Celtic continued to press till half-time but, to the disappointment of their supporters, were unable to add to the score. Rangers' anticipated revival started early in the second half, and the talented Bett fired in a free kick to reduce the gap to one goal. The last thirty minutes were a long, tense wait for the whistle as Celtic concentrated on defence, a decision marked by the substitution of Reid for McStay, and managed to hold on against a ponderous Rangers' attack.

Earlier in the season Celtic's performances in the European Cup had raised hopes that the team at last was on the brink of restoring the former stature of the club throughout the continent. Celtic faced the star-studded Ajax of Amsterdam at Parkhead and within four minutes were a goal down, a magnificent run on the left by Olsen being rounded off with clinical precision. Ten minutes later, after a period of sustained Celtic pressure, Cruyff pulled down Burns and Nicholas converted the penalty to tie the match. In 18 minutes Lerby netted a second for Ajax after a neat move by Olsen and Cruyff had carved open Celtic's defence, but only nine minutes later McGarvey equalised. It was a magnificent match played before 56,000 appreciative spectators, but the persistent feeling was that Celtic had little chance of winning in Amsterdam. On 29 September Celtic produced one of their great nights in Europe. In 34 minutes the elusive, darting Nicholas beat two men and picked up a neat return pass from McGarvey to chip the ball past keeper Schrijvers. Stunned only briefly, Ajax stormed into attack. Bonner made several fine saves to keep Celtic's hopes alive and the new defensive signing, Graeme Sinclair, stuck doggedly to the famous Cruyff, but it appeared to be in vain when Vanenburg equalised in 65 minutes. Urged on by a large travelling support Celtic attacked, realising that a 1-1 draw meant elimination. To the groans of the thousands of supporters McGarvey's header struck the bar with two minutes left, but Celtic pressed on and, in a dream-like finish, McCluskey left-footed the winning goal in the dying seconds of another thrilling match.

In the next round Celtic faced Real Sociedad of Spain, and managed to hold on fairly comfortably in San Sebastian before letting down their guard in the last fifteen minutes to concede two goals, both of them deflected by defenders past Bonner. Realising that Celtic had never ousted Spanish opponents in European competition, the party made a subdued flight home to Glasgow. The 2-1 win at Celtic Park was of little consolation, as the prospect of advancing was made remote by defensive slackness after 25 minutes and MacLeod's pair of goals was of academic interest. Despite that disappointment Celtic supporters could feel that with the maturing skills of a striker like Nicholas there was hope of a breakthrough in the near future at the highest level.

Celtic were the favourites for the championship, and in the first half of the season appeared certain to make it three in a row; however, some niggling doubts remained about the team's lack of a killer instinct when in front. Two weeks after a glorious display at Motherwell featuring a Nicholas hat-trick in a 7-0 rout, and only a few days after the result at Amsterdam, Celtic were leading impressively by 2-0 at Tannadice but allowed United to fight back to salvage a draw. In a similar pattern, after a historic 2-1 win at Ibrox on New Year's Day, Celtic's first win there in this Ne'erday fixture in 62 years. Celtic were hauled back by Dundee at Parkhead after being two goals up.[1]

Too often Celtic loosened their grip on the game. At relegation-threatened Motherwell Celtic, after leading 1-0, lost 2-1 to goals from Brian McClair; once more at Tannadice Dundee United came back to gain a 1-1 draw after Celtic had scored in five minutes; at Parkhead Aberdeen roared back into the game after Celtic scored to notch their second 3-1 win on the ground that season. It was a three-team race for the title but Celtic, still hoping for a domestic treble, were struggling to hold on as Aberdeen and Dundee United stepped up the pace. Aberdeen took over first place in mid-February, but Celtic had steadied by the start of April with three successive victories and had apparently dealt an over-cautious Dundee United a fatal blow with a 2-0 win at Parkhead on 6 April.

The hopes for the season were dashed in the space of one week which suggested truth in the poet's observation that "April is the cruellest month".

On 16 April Aberdeen defeated Celtic 1-0 in a tousy Scottish Cup semi-final at Hampden in which Celtic missed McGrain, under suspension, and Nicholas, a surprising absentee through 'injury'. A few days later, and only two weeks after the victory over United, Celtic once more faced the Dundee side at Celtic Park — and lost, unexpectedly and carelessly. Twice United took the lead, and twice Celtic fought back

311

tenaciously; the United defender Gough was ordered off in 58 minutes after tangling with Provan and Celtic looked in control of the situation. Perhaps unwisely, Celtic continued to storm into attack trying to get a winner, and the methodical United slipped away for Milne to lob the ball over Bonner's head. The team had to regroup and face the daunting prospect of a trip to Pittodrie on the Saturday. Celtic were dealt a third body blow in a week to their 'treble' hopes, Aberdeen winning 1-0. By now Celtic had to depend on a slip by the Tayside club, but under Jim McLean's guidance United were playing superbly. In the wake of that Parkhead win they beat Kilmarnock by 4-0, thrashed Morton at Greenock by a similar score on a Saturday when the club judiciously subsidised their supporters' trip, and Motherwell by the same margin.

The season was due for a spectacular finale on the last Saturday, 14 May. Dundee United had to visit Dens Park to play neighbours Dundee. Aberdeen had a home fixture with Hibernian, and Celtic had to visit Ibrox. It was an intriguing situation: Dundee United led by a point from both challengers who were ready to pounce on any slip but Celtic had a better goal difference than Aberdeen.

At half-time the situation appeared to have resolved itself in favour of the north-east. Aberdeen had raced into a 2-0 lead over Hibs and looked set to increase it; Dundee United quickly led by 2-0 against Dundee, but were pulled back to 2-1; and to the despair of the Celtic fans Rangers had gone ahead by 2-0 against the run of the play. The drama continued after the interval. Dundee started to apply pressure to United's goal as they took advantage of the slope at Dens Park, and the United fans began to worry as the news started to filter through by radio from Pittodrie and Ibrox, Aberdeen, newly crowned holders of the European Cup-Winners' Cup, continued to dominate and scored three more; but at Ibrox things had changed with shocking suddenness.

Two goals down at half-time, Celtic came out for the second half looking determined and before the end the rampant Celtic forwards, led by Nicholas, scored four unanswered goals for an astonishing comeback win. Delirious with joy and still hoping for an equaliser at Dens Park Celtic supporters shouted themselves hoarse, and when the news came through that United had held on for their first championship they shrugged off the disappointment and stayed behind in their seats long after the whistle to salute their team in a moving display of loyalty.

Many of them, sensing that Nicholas would soon be moving to England, having been the cynosure of envious eyes since mid-season, still sang and chanted with a defiant joy; but as they streamed from Ibrox few among them could have thought that Billy McNeill had been in charge of the team for the last time in a competitive match.[2]

Notes

1 Celtic's 1-0 win at Ibrox on Ne'erday 1945 was in the unofficial wartime Southern League.

2 Billy McNeill's last match in charge was the friendly in Ireland against Finn Harps in the following mid-week.

30

. . . AND ABDICATION

IF Jock Stein's return to Parkhead in 1965 was the source of widespread jubilation, then the abrupt departure of Billy McNeill in 1983 was the cause of universal gloom among the supporters. In the last weeks before leaving, McNeill carried out his duties in his normal business-like manner. In the wake of Charlie Nicholas's transfer to Arsenal for £750,000 — and after the months of speculation and rumour his move south was inevitable — McNeill moved quickly to sign Brian McClair, Motherwell's young striker, for £70,000, a shrewd bargain given the fact that the player would become the club's top scorer in the next three seasons; he ended intriguing speculation by re-signing the popular Murdo MacLeod, whom the newspapers were linking with Rangers, and he persuaded full-back Mark Reid to sign on again after both Reid and MacLeod had initially baulked at the terms in their contracts.

Even as he worked on consolidating Celtic's squad for the coming season, events backstage were unfolding with a tragic inexorability. Billy McNeill had been one of the genuine success stories in Scottish football, on and off the field. After a glittering career at Celtic Park, eighteen years of outstanding play and sterling service with his only senior club, McNeill had retired in 1975 to devote his time to business interests which were expanding rapidly. However, Clyde persuaded him to accept the position of manager two years later, but he was in charge at Shawfield for less than three months before the post at Aberdeen became available, and he soon had the northern side challenging for the honours. After Stein's retirement in 1978 and the invitation from Celtic, McNeill had to think carefully about accepting the manager's job at Parkhead, but his loyalty to Celtic overcame any practical considerations.

Ambitious, restlessly hardworking, articulate and a natural leader, McNeill was the embodiment of the successful young executive in private and public life. However, a major setback occurred in the early 80s with the collapse of a business venture. For McNeill, known to be "a careful man with money", it was a traumatic experience. Still, with commendable resilience he put the losses behind him, made adjustments to accord with his changed financial status, and continued to cope successfully with the pressures of being Celtic's manager. But, increasingly worried about the need for financial security, he felt that a contract, preferably a long-term one representing a rise in salary commensurate with his managerial success and the stature of the club, was a reasonable request to make of his directors given his record of a major trophy won in each of his five seasons.

The directors, however, recoiled with distaste to the manager's suggestion that his terms of employment be formalised. They would have reminded McNeill that no previous Celtic manager had a contract and that 'a gentleman's agreement' was more appropriate. A married man with a young family, McNeill as a player had seen Jimmy McGrory arrive at Celtic Park in the morning as manager and leave as public relations officer in the afternoon, grateful to be retained in the new role.

McNeill had a further grievance about his salary. It was to be revealed shortly afterwards, when the affair become public, that Celtic's manager was being paid at a lower rate than those of Rangers, Aberdeen and Dundee United. Few would dispute the fact that throughout his five-year tenure at Celtic Park Billy McNeill was more successful than John Greig, Alec Ferguson or Jim McLean. For some months McNeill had been negotiating in private with the club, but was making little headway against a Board not traditionally noted for generosity in financial transactions — so much so that one of its most famous and loyal players had described the directors some years earlier as "the Catholic Jews". On the eve of the pre-season tournament staged by Feyenoord in Rotterdam an "intense" McNeill told a pressman that he wanted the Board to make money available for an injection of experienced players. Sounding like a challenge, his statement hinted at the rift which widened as the season progressed: "I am looking to the Chairman, and the Board in general, to back me in my bid to strengthen and improve Celtic Football Club." (*Daily Record*: 6 August, 1982.)

Collectively, the Board was content to retain the status quo which denied the manager real power and authority within the club, and to modern minds such an approach has a distastefully semi-feudal tone to it. In fairness to the directors it should be noted that they did have some reservations about McNeill's performance. Concern had been expressed about two championships (1980 and 1983) lost in the closing stages after Celtic had enjoyed what appeared to be comfortable leads and some observers felt that McNeill's style was too emotional, his approach lacking the tactical awareness of a Ferguson or McLean; there was an undignified scuffle with a reporter on a European trip in 1980, the journalist ending up with a black eye; there was a shouting match on the touchline with a referee, Mr. Andrew Waddell, during a match with Aberdeen in October, 1982. The Board was not sympathetic to the defence that these were the lapses of a young man, still relatively inexperienced as a manager; within a four-week period in 1980 the directors twice reprimanded McNeill, and made a point of making it known. For the punch-up with the journalist that followed a heated discussion about the merits of a disallowed goal in a recent match with Rangers, McNeill was censured. Relations between the manager and the reporter, ironically Gerry McNee,[1] remained chilly and a month later McNeill was once more rebuked, this time for ignoring the journalist's questions at a press conference after a match. Subsequently, the chairman, Desmond White, read out a statement to the assembled press, while McNeill reportedly sat impassively in front of his directors: "You can rest assured that Mr. McNee will be accorded all the normal press facilities in future."

Unfortunately, little warmth and rapport existed between the manager and the chairman. Basically, it was a clash of outlooks. McNeill was young, ambitious and progressive, and White was old, cautious and reactionary. In the eyes of the supporters McNeill was more popular but, in the struggle between the employer and the employee, only one outcome could be anticipated. There was little of the rapport that evolved in the relationship between Bob Kelly and Jock Stein. McNeill was brisk, fuelled by a nervous energy, outgoing and cheerful in conversation, while White always remained distant, although genial in manner, and seemed ponderous in speech and appearance. Like his predecessor, Desmond White was a difficult man to approach; indeed, after knowing the chairman for more than forty years, a noted journalist had to admit that he had never come closer to understanding him.

At this point Manchester City, smarting under the disgrace of relegation to the Second Division, started to show an interest in McNeill, and Celtic's manager revealed his frustrations. In an interview with the *Sunday Mail* McNeill was quoted as saying "I find it disappointing that I've never been offered a contract by my present employers." This marked an escalation in the politics of negotiation, a raising of the ante in the bluff characteristic of all salary disputes. McNeill, as a successful manager, had a right to assume that he was playing with a strong hand, but he had miscalculated the nature of the game. Other Celtic managers, such as Willie Maley with an offer from Sheffield United in 1894 and Jock Stein with an open invitation from Manchester United in the 70s, had reportedly used the threat of leaving in order to gain better terms or more acceptable conditions and had stayed — to the satisfaction of the supporters, the benefit of the team, and the reputation of the club.

Billy McNeill in happier times, holding aloft the European Cup in Lisbon, 1967.

But this group of directors under Desmond White was not prepared to yield an inch. Choosing to ignore McNeill's statement as the negotiating ploy it manifestly was, and opting instead to regard it as a threat of blackmail, the chairman issued a terse communiqué on the following day: "Mr. McNeill's requests for a contract and wages increase have been unanimously rejected by the Celtic board of directors."

For Billy McNeill, known in his European Cup days as 'Caesar', it was "the most unkindest cut of all"; a proud man, he could no longer stay at Celtic Park to accept the humiliation of a comedown nor could he be expected to exert the same authority over his players. McNeill was stunned to learn of the release of the statement: "I am absolutely shattered; when I left the meeting there was no hint that a statement was being given out to the press."

Public opinion was on the manager's side. A sports editorial in the *Evening Times* of 28 June, 1983, termed the club's release as "insulting" and continued: "It doesn't really matter if the Celtic directors think they have been put under pressure by reports that Manchester City are interested in McNeill. Loyalty cuts both ways and Billy McNeill has every right to expect his employers to play the game with him instead of humiliating him publicly. Let the Celtic directors make no mistake. They must understand that the sympathy of the fans and the wider Scottish public is entirely with the manager." The team captain, Danny McGrain, interviewed by the *Daily Record*, spoke with typical bluntness: "For a start Billy McNeill has brought success to the club, and from the players' point of view he has been a great manager. When you consider most of the players got what they wanted in terms of contracts, it seems astonishing that the manager, the man at the helm, can't get what the players think he's worth." The fact that the players were under contract to the club, while the manager was not, did not escape the attention of the critics.

Within a few days McNeill was on his way to Manchester, but the controversy raged on. The club unwisely chose to reveal confidential financial matters, disclosing that the manager had been the recipient of a substantial loan from the club, and that the loan had still not been repaid. Such a petty and hasty action served only to create more sympathy for McNeill and opprobrium for the directors.

Ian Archer saw the affair in a wider context: "What became apparent as the events unfolded was that the septuagenarian (Mr White) was out of touch with what Celtic supporters wanted — and the way the game stands, warts and all, in the present day.

"The relationship between the elderly chairman and the most successful player in the club's history was never cosy. At the heart of it, one suspects, was the collision between two strong wills as to who was *the* man at Parkhead.

"At the basis was a row about money. For some time McNeill had been asking privately for a rise. He was not exactly getting satisfaction and it must have been galling that, at the same time, he was offering players somewhat larger increases to stay at the club. What started out as a private dispute became public when it was known that he was earning just £21,000 and that Manchester City wanted him as manager.[2]

"What became evident, though not to the Board, was that Celtic's supporters agreed with him. This was in a sense remarkable because many of those fans are out of work and find it difficult to put together £1.50 to stand on the terraces. That they, to a man, did not respond to McNeill's wishes with that well-known cry 'Greedy bastard!' shows the affection in which they held the first 'Brit' ever to hold the European Cup.

"With events taking an inevitable course, Celtic's decision to then release further details of his bonuses and the fact that he had £11,000 outstanding on an interest-free loan from the club was at least the act of desperate men, or at worst completely offensive. Having refused to respond to such questions earlier on the grounds of bad taste, they issued them when it suited to defend their corner.

" 'I never thought I would see the day when a Celtic Board acted like a Rangers Board,' said one of their friends. Quite amazingly, that statement was only issued to 'selected' newspapers, the country's largest-selling tabloid not receiving it, presumably on the grounds that its comments had upset the board.

"What is at stake is the style and future of Celtic Football Club. Founded honourably for the poor of Glasgow's East End, consistent subscribers to charity and, on a personal level, mostly people with big hearts and a friendly welcome, they stand for a great tradition. They may now be standing out of their time.

"Their stadium, soon to be the poor relation of the city's three great grounds, is no longer the centrepiece — and place of hope — for one of Europe's poorest parishes. . . . Yet the Celtic chairman still maintains that his supporters want to stand rather than sit.

"McNeill had a vision which extended beyond Scotland and Glasgow into Europe. He must have known how close after a win in 1967, then a loss in 1970, Celtic were to breaking out of those haunting visions of feudal rivalry into a place of worldwide fame. . . . That chance is now irrevocably gone." (*Sunday Standard*: 3 July, 1983.)

It was a bad time for the club, and tarnished most of all was the particular feeling that most Celtic supporters have for the team and the club, that sharing of feelings and experiences, that unique — among professional clubs — sense of 'family' summed up by one anguished supporter in a letter to a newspaper: ". . . deep sense of outrage that the name of our great club has been sullied in such an offensively public manner . . ..

319

"One cannot help but feel that these events so ill-befit Celtic and are so unseemly that they could never have been envisaged as happening at our club. This gutter behaviour, it had always been assumed, happened elsewhere but not within the portals of Celtic F.C. Such have been our traditions and our deeply felt sense of family (a family to which Mr. McNeill belonged for twenty-five years) that our anger cannot fully be expressed. The atmosphere of family has been destroyed, loyalty has been discarded, and our spirit of charity and tolerance has been dissipated into a meanness of spirit and servility to money that is deeply abhorrent.

"This cordiality, this special relationship between club and supporters, what is left of it? Old and dedicated supporters, who have weathered all storms and stood by the club during the long, lean years because it was their club, have had their emotions so corrupted by recent events that they may very well desert the club that they can no longer identify as theirs.

"In the eyes of many of the support our once great club is now merely mediocre, the same as all the rest, since what has separated us from them has now been so callously discarded. No doubt success will come the way of Celtic F.C. again, success in the playing sense that is, for one has the feeling that though there may well be a return to a degree of normality, the awareness is that, as with any soured relationship, things may achieve a plateau of tolerance but they will never be quite the same again. This is the legacy bequeathed to us by Mr. White and the directors of Celtic F.C. (*Glasgow Herald*: 7 July, 1983.)

Four months before his untimely death in September 1985, Jock Stein, whose former club's welfare was never far from his thoughts despite a lingering sense of grievance over his own departure, expressed his concern to one of the authors that the estrangement between McNeill and the Celtic directors showed no sign of being healed.

And so Celtic had to prepare for the future without its manager, and with no outstanding candidate in sight for the post. The way back from the debacle was not going to be easy.

Notes
1 The reporter (Gerry McNee) was the author of the club's official history published in 1978.
2 The chairman claimed that the manager had grossed £26,960 in his last year with the club. McNeill indicated that his basic salary was £22,000 plus bonuses (that had to be earned) and that he had been offered a raise to £25,000 when he informed Celtic of Manchester City's interest. Celtic's financial statement for the next year suggests sensitivity to the adverse publicity, revealing an increase in 'wages and salaries' of about 30%.

31

THE LATEST CHAPTER

WITH the close season upheavals dominating the headlines, Celtic had to move quickly in a bid to reassure supporters that the club was not in danger of becoming a high-grade nursery for the top English clubs (as had been suspected in the late 20s). The tradition of appointing a former player as manager was continued in the person of David Hay. Hay, a splendidly aggressive player in his Celtic days, had been transferred to Chelsea in 1974, but his playing career in England was cut short by an eye injury. He had only one year's experience as a manager in Scotland, having led Motherwell to promotion in 1981-82 but, despite his success at Fir Park, he had already resigned to take up a position in the United States which had not materialised by the time he was approached by Celtic. Hay, a quiet, serious man, considered the offer for a long time, admitting with typical candour later that he still had not made up his mind while on the way to Parkhead to meet the Board to give his final decision. The directors appointed Frank Connor as assistant manager and coach, feeling perhaps that Connor's brusque, if not abrasive, style might complement Hay's more subdued manner. Connor, briefly a Celtic goalkeeper in the 60s, had been manager of Second Division clubs and a coach of Celtic's reserve side. The appointments were not greeted with any great enthusiasm by a Celtic support still reeling in despair from the resignation of McNeill, the firing of his assistant Clark, and the transfers of Nicholas to Arsenal and McCluskey to Leeds United. The new manager made early excursions into the transfer market, buying Brian Whittaker, a full-back from Partick Thistle, for £50,000 and Jim Melrose, a striker from Coventry, for £100,000; however, neither Whittaker nor Melrose made much impact in his brief career at Celtic Park . . . nor did John Colquhoun, a winger signed from Stirling Albion for £60,000 later in the season.

Hay's first season was a most disappointing one. Celtic, for the first time since 1977-78, did not win a single trophy and, to make it even more frustrating, finished runners-up in every domestic competition. The League Cup had reached a stage of annual renovation in an attempt to bring back the crowds, and what emerged was a protracted, unsatisfactory affair that started in August and ended in March. The format was confusing: a knock-out round involving clubs from the lower divisions was followed by a home-and-away round with the previously seeded Premier teams competing, the survivors going on to sectional play which led to another home-and-away semi-final. One wag was reminded of the definition of a camel as "a horse, as designed by a committee."

Celtic's first fixture was a home-and-away tie against Brechin City, and a late goal from Celtic was the only difference between the sides at Glebe Park; to the annoyance of the crowd at Parkhead the expected goal feast did not materialise, and the second leg ended up 0-0. A sectional round followed with Celtic being matched up with Airdrie, Hibernian and Kilmarnock; after a couple of goal sprees (6-1 at Airdrie, and 5-1 over Hibs at Parkhead), Celtic slumped with three consecutive draws and had a tough match at Rugby Park against Kilmarnock to qualify for the later stages of the competition. Another narrow victory (1-0) ensured Celtic's progress.

The semi-final draw pitted Celtic against Aberdeen, with the first leg at Pittodrie where a gritty performance earned a 0-0 draw, setting the stage for the return match at Parkhead. Celtic were more aggressive than the Dons and advanced to the final through a penalty taken by Mark Reid after Burns had been pushed inside the area. The final was played on 25 March, 1984 against Rangers, and the crowd was a disappointing 66,369; a larger crowd might have been anticipated as the final was scheduled for a Sunday with no competition from other matches, but the game was telecast live.

Celtic: Bonner, McGrain, Reid, Aitken, McAdam, MacLeod, Provan (Sinclair), McStay, McGarvey (Melrose), Burns, McClair.

Rangers: McCloy, Nicholl, Dawson, McClelland, Paterson, McPherson, Russell, McCoist, Clark (McAdam), MacDonald (Burns), Cooper.

Celtic were favourites after the breakthrough against Aberdeen and because Rangers were experiencing a rocky spell, but it was another dissappointment in a League Cup final for the supporters. In a ragged match fought out mainly in midfield, four players from each side were booked and three penalties were awarded by the referee, Mr. Valentine (Dundee). The first penalty came when MacLeod tripped Russell needlessly in the corner of the box just before the interval and McCoist sent Bonner the wrong way. The result seemed beyond doubt in the 62nd minute when Celtic's central defenders were put into disarray by a long bouncing clearance from Rangers' keeper, McCloy, and McCoist took full advantage of the confusion to score his second goal. Celtic finally asserted themselves and five minutes later McClair netted with a volley after Burns had cunningly flighted a short free kick over Rangers' 'wall'. Celtic's pressure continued, but it was only in the last seconds of injury time that MacLeod was upended near goal. Reid, given the task of taking the penalty, blasted the ball past McCloy to put the final into extra time. After clawing their way back into the match, Celtic should have retained the initiative, but Rangers dominated the extra thirty minutes; their winning goal came from another McCoist penalty after Aitken had pushed the Rangers' striker with little danger apparent. Bonner saved the original attempt, but McCoist alertly netted the rebound for his hat trick to give Rangers the cup.

In midweek Celtic had the doubtful consolation of winning an unimportant league game at Parkhead against Rangers by 3-0 — the result they might have been expected to get in the final.

By this time Celtic's challenge for the league had faded as Aberdeen marched impressively to the title. The Dons established a new Premier League record with 57 points, conceding a meagre 21 goals, and finished up an impressive seven points ahead of Celtic. After a bright start to the campaign with five successive wins, Celtic slumped in October; two 1-1 home draws against St. Mirren and Hearts, with losses at Tannadice (1-2) and Pittodrie (1-3), and a solitary victory over Hibs at Parkhead (5-1) was scarcely championship form. Celtic seemed incapable of capitalising on early breakthroughs: against Hearts at Parkhead on 15 October, after MacLeod had missed a first-minute penalty and McGarvey had scored a spectacular goal on the stroke of half-time, Celtic allowed Hearts back into the match to equalise; on 19 November after going two goals up against St. Mirren in the first 20 minutes, Celtic's concentration wavered and the Paisley side won 4-2; on 27 December Celtic dominated the first half against Dundee United at Parkhead and went into the lead after 44 minutes, but dropped another point in a second-half letdown; on 7 January a relegation-bound Motherwell side snatched a 2-2 draw with a late goal at Fir Park; and on 23 March, after leading at half-time, Celtic succumbed to a rally from Dundee to lose 3-2 at Dens Park, and surrender any realistic hopes of the championship.

With such a recurring pattern one had to wonder about the tactics adopted by the team, and the doubts about the side at the higher levels were cruelly revealed in the UEFA Cup. In the first round of this competition Celtic struggled at Parkhead against Aarhus (Denmark) but managed a 1-0 win through a late header from Aitken that was fumbled by the keeper; the return leg was much easier, and Celtic controlled the tempo throughout to win 4-1. Things looked bleak after the first leg against Sporting Lisbon in Portugal, where Celtic barely managed to limit the Portuguese to a 2-0 score. Celtic had tradition on their side for the return, never having been eliminated by a Portuguese side in Europe. Aware of Sporting's weak away record, Celtic went for the jugular, scoring through a Burns header in 17 minutes and adding two more goals right on the interval. Against a team that appeared punchdrunk, Celtic finished the tie with a double on the hour for a 5-0 victory.

The third round draw produced a plum — Nottingham Forest against Celtic, with the first match scheduled for the City Ground in late November. It was an impressive display of support as 12,000 from Scotland headed south, and several thousand resident in England made their way to Nottingham; on a bitterly cold night Forest pulled in their largest crowd of the season, although the match was to be telecast live throughout Scotland. Noting the enthusiasm, Hugh McIlvanney raised once more the concept of a British Cup as one solution for football's economic ills: ". . . being drawn against Celtic in a European competition is the kind of privilege that can help English First Division clubs out of the hands of the bailiffs." (*Observer*: 4 December, 1983.) On a more sombre note, had those supporters not behaved with good humour and massive sense in the face of appalling stewarding and police control, the congestion at the end reserved for Celtic fans could have led to the type of fatalities witnessed at the Heysel Stadium in Brussels 18 months later. On the frozen pitch both teams attempted to provide an entertaining match, and Brian Clough, the Nottingham manager, admitted freely that his team was lucky to escape defeat, a result that would have been certain had Paul McStay not shot over the bar from relatively close range near the end. The second leg was another disappointment for the expectant fans packed into Celtic Park on 7 December: "the most committed crowd still available in British football" saw Celtic unable to penetrate a superbly disciplined defence, and struggle with the threats of well constructed breakaways. It was clear that Nottingham Forest had learned more about Celtic from the first match than Celtic had about them. Ten minutes after the interval Hodge netted after a long run down the right wing by Wigley, and fifteen minutes later Davenport raced down the left to lay on the decisive goal from Walsh; Celtic's suspect flanks had been outwitted, and MacLeod's late goal was little consolation for the all-ticket 67,000 who witnessed the end of a run of 34 European ties at home without defeat.

Celtic's best hope for a trophy rested in the Scottish Cup, a tournament that favours their inspirational type of approach. The early rounds renewed optimism among the supporters with a competent 4-0 win at Berwick, and two emphatic victories by 6-0 at East Fife and Motherwell. A potentially attractive semi-final against St. Mirren at Hampden was spoiled by chilly, blustery conditions. The Paisley side, struggling to overcome a semi-final jinx and under the pressure to prove themselves one of the Premier League elite, looked edgy in the first half despite the advantage of the wind and seemed to have lost their chance with the interval score tied at 1-1. Eight minutes from the end Paul McStay's half-hit shot rose in an arc over Thomson's head into the net to allow Celtic to advance to the final against Aberdeen.

> *Celtic*: Bonner, McGrain, Reid (Melrose), Aitken, McStay W, MacLeod, Provan, McStay P, McGarvey, Burns, McClair (Sinclair)
> *Aberdeen*: Leighton, McKimmie, Rougvie (Stark), Cooper, McLeish, Miller, Strachan, Simpson, McGhee, Black, Weir (Bell).

A disappointing crowd of 58,900 attended the televised finale on 19 May, 1984, but they witnessed one of the more controversial Scottish Cup finals. Celtic opened brightly and dominated the early play. Three first half opportunities fell to MacLeod: one sped a foot past Leighton's left-hand post, one was blocked, and the third was headed off the line by a defender. Celtic paid the penalty when Aberdeen scored in 24 minutes. It seemed to many in the crowd that McGrain had been impeded in his challenge on McGhee and the ball went to Black, who netted from what appeared an offside position. Celtic's protests to the linesman were abruptly terminated by the referee, Mr. Valentine (Dundee), and it was no surprise, given the feeling between the sides, that tempers began to rise on the field. Fifteen minutes later Roy Aitken was ordered off amid controversial circumstances. As McGhee sped down the right wing towards Celtic's goal, Aitken moved out to intercept his progress and his crunching tackle felled the Aberdeen striker. After a delay, while McGhee was being treated and some Aberdeen players, most noticeably Strachan, appeared to be advising the referee vociferously, Mr. Valentine raised the red card. Celtic's depleted squad, hastily reorganised with MacLeod acting as sweeper and McClair pulled back into midfield, buckled down to their uphill task with traditional spirit. The tempo picked up, and the tackling became even more ferocious as six players, three from each side, were booked. Five minutes from the end Celtic gained a deserved equaliser with a right-foot drive from Paul McStay to send the final into extra time. In the further thirty minutes Aberdeen understandably, had much more of the play as Celtic tired, and McGhee scored the winner from a Strachan cross in the 98th minute.

All of Celtic's pent-up frustration erupted after the match; Celtic claimed that the referee had been under undue pressure from the SFA to control the game firmly in order to avoid the scenes that had marred previous Celtic-Aberdeen matches in recent seasons. Apparently, the referee, in speaking to the players beforehand, had mentioned the official concern about rough play; the SFA secretary, Ernie Walker, was the target of much of Celtic's criticism for his alleged 'interference'. In a letter to one of the authors Mr. Walker commented rather cryptically on the matter: "One person who did speak to Mr. Valentine prior to the match was Mr. Jack Mowat, chairman of the referee supervisors' committee, as he had done with every cup final referee over the years, to wish him well for the game. There is surely no harm in this being done, nor is there any hint of interference with the referee's duties in this."

The furore at the conclusion of the final helped to obscure a general lowering in Celtic's level of performance, a feeling reinforced by a corresponding decline of almost 5000 spectators on average per league game at Parkhead.

In the close season Celtic came in for more criticism in the media, and from their friends. One newspaper, the *Sunday Post* of July 22, 1984, suggested that Celtic, having made an estimated profit of £445,000 in transfer dealing over the past five years, had got their priorities wrong by buying bargain players in exchange for stars. A well-known Glasgow lawyer and Celtic follower, Joseph Beltrami, wrote to the *Daily Record* complaining that Celtic's attitude was creating "an idle atmosphere of acceptance of a fringe position in the game well short of even second best."

The criticism seemed justified, as Celtic's only signing was Alan McInally from Ayr United for £95,000 in May, and Tommy Burns was moved to request a transfer in June, claiming a lack of ambition at the club: "I feel I have been too long at Parkhead, and there is a vast difference in the ability of the players who have left and those who have come. I am not prepared to go through it all again next season, and I had hoped there would be plans to make the type of signing which will make a difference in challenging in Europe." Burns' request for a transfer was turned down, and Celtic responded to the increasing anguish from the support by expressing interest in several players, none of whom seemed likely to move; the putative list included Narey, Dodds and Sturrock (Dundee United), Cooper (Aberdeen), and Jordan (Verona).

A lucrative sponsorship deal, completed in September 1984 in combination with Rangers, netted £250,000 for each club spread over three years. In return, a Scottish double-glazing firm, C.R. Smith, had its name advertised on the shirts of the Old Firm. For some reason both Rangers and Celtic had been actively seeking sponsors, but had found that business was unwilling to settle on one rather than the other for fear of incurring ill will. The only solution was to find a commercial sponsor rich enough to accommodate both at the same time. Inevitably, the more tradition-conscious fans expressed unhappiness with the arrangement, suggesting that the logo on the Celtic jerseys, in addition to the Umbro trademark and the club's own badge, has disfigured the famous hoops.

Celtic's challenge for the league was boosted by the transfer activity at

Pittodrie. In a mini-exodus the following players left: Strachan to Manchester United, Rougvie to Chelsea, and McGhee to Hamburg. But Celtic did not make any further moves to strengthen their squad until October when they signed the exciting Maurice ('Mo') Johnston, a striker from Watford, for a Scottish record fee of £400,000. By that time, however, the signing smacked more of Celtic's desperation to placate an increasingly disenchanted support and to stem the continuing haemorrhage at the turnstiles rather than a serious attempt at team-building; critics pointed out that Johnston could have been picked up a year earlier for little more than £100,000 when he was with Partick Thistle, but had been passed over in favour of Melrose.

Throughout the season Celtic had a welcome edge over Aberdeen, winning both fixtures at Parkhead and gaining one draw at Pittodrie, but the champions were a much more efficient side and went on to defend the title in convincing style, ending up seven points ahead of Celtic. Despite the loss of three internationalists, Aberdeen maintained an admirable consistency to establish another new record for the Premier League with 59 points; simply put, Aberdeen were a team whose members were in tune with the methods and tactics adopted, opting for a patient build-up behind a solid defence with intelligent, penetrating breaks into attack.

Celtic's challenge faded with the revelation of an Achilles' heel in dropping points to lesser lights. On 8 September Celtic needlessly conceded a late penalty equaliser to relegation-bound Dumbarton at Boghead; on 3 November, after Johnston had given Celtic an early lead at Cappielow, Morton, also doomed to relegation, scored twice for an upset win; on 9 February Celtic lost by 2-0 at Dundee, a 'bogey' ground in recent seasons, but the apathetic manner in which the defeat was sustained caused such irritation and disgust that scarves were thrown on to the track in protest.

Carelessness cost valuable points against Dundee United: at Celtic Park on 29 December Johnston missed a penalty in a 2-1 defeat, and at Tannadice on 2 March Grant missed a penalty in a 2-1 defeat, and Dundee United also eliminated Celtic from the League Cup in the quarter-final, winning 2-1 after extra time at Tannadice, where the gates had to be closed before the kick-off. It was the third successive cup-tie that Celtic had lost after a period of extra time, and it again raised questions about the team's ability to adjust to the changing circumstances.

In the European Cup-Winners' Cup Celtic faced new opposition in Ghent (Belgium), recovering from a 1-0 deficit incurred in the first leg to run out 3-0 winners at Parkhead, where they had never lost in this competition.

The next round sent Celtic to Vienna to face the famous Rapid, and it proved to be one of the most controversial ties in which Celtic have been involved. Austria, boasting a distinguished football history, has long acknowledged its debt to Scotland, but at the international level relations between the countries have been strained; one can recall an abandoned 'friendly' at Hampden in 1963, and the dismissal of Billy Steel in a 4-0 rout at Vienna in 1951.

In the first leg Celtic went down 3-1, but McClair scored a valuable away goal. The events at Parkhead were foreshadowed in Vienna, McInally being sent off in his European debut and three other Celts being booked, while Kienast almost crippled McGarvey with a vicious tackle. In the return leg, Rapid tried to slow the game down with possession football, offside tactics, and blatant time-wasting. McClair opened the scoring on the half hour and MacLeod's goal just before the interval handed Celtic the technical initiative (given their away goal). Their form was a revelation, some onlookers feeling it was the most convincing display in a European competition since the early Stein years, and the Austrians, under sustained pressure throughout, completely lost their composure after the break. Burns took full advantage of a fumble by a nervous keeper to give Celtic a third goal midway through the second half, although the Austrians protested unavailingly that Burns had fouled the keeper. Later, Kienast, the villain of the first leg in Celtic's eyes, was ordered off after punching Burns inside the penalty area but, astonishingly, amid the confusion, no penalty was awarded; and shortly afterwards the flustered goalkeeper, Ehn, clearly aimed a kick at Burns. This incident, coming about ten minutes from the end with Celtic leading 3-0 and Rapid already a man short, initiated a tempestuous 15 minute hold-up in play. The referee, linesman, and players congregated on the touchline, staging a heated dispute about the episode — in the event, unwisely and for too long, for despite the referee's eventual decision to rightly award a penalty kick, Rapid's Weinhofer left the field to claim that he had been injured by a bottle thrown from the 'Jungle'. Finally, when some semblance of order had been restored, Grant took the penalty, but missed, and Celtic ran out convincing winners by 3-0 to take the tie on aggregate. Nevertheless, the crowd left Parkhead in a subdued mood, anxious about the outcome of the bottle-throwing.

Although the TV highlights indicated that Weinhofer had not been struck by any of the bottles, and an experienced Red Cross official saw no sign of injury, the Austrian player left the ground with his head bandaged. It came as no surprise, therefore, when Rapid protested to UEFA, citing the infamous Inter Milan-Borussia Munchengladbach affair of thirteen years earlier as a precedent and demanding either Celtic's expulsion from the competition or, failing that, a replay of the second leg in a neutral country. The UEFA disciplinary committee met in Switzerland and, basing their findings on the report of the Swedish referee and the West German observer, found in Celtic's favour on every count bar one (Celtic were fined £4,000 for the bottle-throwing). Rapid were fined £5,000 for their on-field conduct, their coach was banned from the touchline for three European matches for his behaviour, Kienast was suspended for four European ties for being sent off, and, most importantly, Weinhofer's claim that he had been struck by a bottle was dismissed.

Celtic breathed more easily after the hearing, but the Austrian club had not exhausted its efforts. Encouraged by a split in the committee over the decision and, in the words of one writer, "having knocked on a few doors", Rapid lodged an appeal. This time Weinhofer and the Rapid team doctor appeared before the committee; and Celtic, who regarded it as "inconceivable" that the verdict would be overturned, were represented by Desmond White and another director, accompanied by Ernie Walker, the SFA secretary.

The appeal hearing was attended by only three out of a 21-strong committee (the Irish member, for one, not knowing about the meeting), and the findings were equally unusual. Although it was never established how Weinhofer had been hit, and although Rapid changed their testimony three times, UEFA accepted the Austrian contention that the player had been struck by "a small object" — not visible on TV replays — and that, since the Austrian club had to complete the tie with only nine men, the match had not been "regular".[1] UEFA ordered the fixture to be replayed at a venue at least one hundred miles from Parkhead and, in accordance with the Kafkaesque procedures of the hearing, doubled the fine originally imposed on Rapid.

Interestingly, when the Inter Milan defender Bergomi was injured by an object thrown in a UEFA cup-tie in Madrid five months later, the testimony of the Italians' doctor was rejected by the appeal committee.

If Celtic had been 'outmanoeuvred' at the hearing, even more disconcerting was the club's response to UEFA's latest folly. A few hours after the meeting in Switzerland the chairman, upon arrival at Glasgow Airport, stated to the waiting press corps that the only matter to be determined was the replay venue. The chairman seemed content to vent his anger on Rapid's successful deviation from the grounds of the original protest. Disquietingly, there was no suggestion of any internal debate about a possible withdrawal from the competition in protest, although the Scottish press overwelmingly condemned UEFA's somersault, nor would any approach be made to play the match behind closed doors to avert the danger of crowd trouble. Some wondered about the haste with which the club, or its representatives, accepted UEFA's order, despite the fairly recent, sad experience of Racing Club (Argentina) in 1967 and Atletico Madrid (Spain) in 1974. The decision to accept the ruling was questioned by reputable newspapers; one editorial, while recognising the unfairness of UEFA's decision and the cynicism of Rapid, hinted at a long-rooted problem: ". . . has at times been an air of collective paranoia about the club which has not been conducive to calm, rational conduct off the pitch — or indeed to calm, rational play." (*Glasgow Herald:* 14 December, 1984). Earlier, Hugh Keevins had expressed his doubts about the wisdom of Celtic's acceptance: "It is unlikely that any replay could be held anywhere without a feeling of deep resentment on the part of the Celtic supporters who will see it. . . . Wherever the game takes place, it will obviously be a highly charged occasion in which the forebearance of the Celtic players and their following will never be more necessary." (*The Scotsman*: 24 November, 1984.)

More than 40,000 followers poured over the border in a mood of fevered anticipation undeniably stimulated by a persecution complex and this helped fuel the ugly atmosphere inside Old Trafford on 12 December, although the overwhelming majority of the 51,500 crowd behaved in an exemplary manner. The occasion was too much for Celtic, again faced with the prospect of overhauling Rapid's 3-1 lead under disheartening circumstances. Rapid, better organised, sharper and more composed than in Glasgow, took full advantage of Celtic's frantic approach. In 15 minutes a shot from Aitken rebounded from the Austrian post, with most of Celtic's players stranded upfield; Rapid broke away and the speedy Pacult was released to evade McGrain's despairing lunge before rounding Bonner to net the only goal — and eliminate Celtic, who for the first time in European competition lost both legs of a tie. The overall situation was hard to accept gracefully, and the nagging fear that any precautions taken in Manchester might not be enough to restrain the frustrations among the wilder sections of the club's support turned into nightmarish reality in the second half. Sickening assaults were committed on two Rapid players (the goalkeeper and the goalscorer), but in such circumstances that it appeared the policing on the perimeter of the pitch was inadequate. The hooligans, both of whom were fans domiciled in England, were allowed to approach the Austrian players without much interference from the police who might have anticipated trouble.

Only the most hard-hearted supporter could fail to sympathise with the Celtic players who, burdened with a poor record in crunch matches in recent seasons, collapsed under the weight of public expectation amid such extraordinary circumstances.

In the team's hotel after the match one Celtic player vented his personal frustrations, exclaiming that Celtic were in danger of becoming "the nearly men" — a memorable phrase for a side that has neither realised fully its potential nor been blessed with much good fortune. However, the sports adage that a team creates its own luck may have a certain truth, because in recent seasons Celtic have not matched inspiration and skill to organisation and leadership (on and off the field).

The club had to wait for an agonizing five weeks for UEFA to rule on the disgraceful scenes at Old Trafford. In view of the hardening attitude of the continentals about the behaviour of British fans, the punishment was surprisingly lenient — a £17,000 fine and an order to play the next home leg in European competition behind closed doors. When many feared a lengthy ban from Europe, what accounted for the relatively light punishment? It emerged that a reservoir of official goodwill existed towards Celtic, based on a fine playing record in Europe and a recognition that the fans over the years had behaved well. Nobody within UEFA, including the Austrian delegate, pressed for a ban; and probably it was the organisation's belated recognition that their own mishandling of the affair had contributed heavily to the ultimate debacle at Manchester.

It took some time for the team to recover from the trauma of the Cup-Winners' Cup, notably in the league, but improvement was made in time for the Scottish Cup. In this, the hundredth competition for the Cup, Celtic were jolted early in the match at Douglas Park when Hamilton Accies took a first-half lead. Apparently still rusty from inactivity during the freeze-up, Celtic were slow to respond and had to thank Frank McGarvey's opportunism for two goals, the winner coming only five minutes from the end. After eliminating Inverness Thistle by 6-0 at Parkhead, with a rare Paul McStay hat-trick leading the way, Celtic faced a tough hurdle in the quarter-final against Dundee at Dens Park. The home side, having eliminated Rangers at Ibrox, was eager to complete an Old Firm double, but Celtic's competitive urge in a frenetic atmosphere (1-1) merited the replay at Parkhead which Celtic won 2-1 to advance to the semi-final against Motherwell of the First Division. Celtic's relief at facing Motherwell instead of Aberdeen or Dundee United, the other semi-finalists, vanished when the Lanarkshire side, drawing on an honourable cup tradition, forced another replay by holding Celtic to a 1-1 tie; indeed, Celtic were considered fortunate that in the dying minutes Forbes' header went flashing inches past when a goal seemed certain. However, Celtic asserted themselves in the replay, although the result was in doubt till three late goals from the favourites settled the match.

Celtic fans, desperate for success, accounted for at least three-quarters of the 60,436 crowd that watched the final against Dundee United on 18 May, 1985:

> *Celtic*: Bonner, McStay W., McGrain, Aitken, McAdam, MacLeod, Provan, McStay P. (O'Leary), Johnston, Burns (McClair), McGarvey.
> *Dundee United*: McAlpine, Malpas, Beedie (Holt), Gough, Hegarty, Narey, Bannon, Milne, Kirkwood, Sturrock, Dodds.

Throughout a pedestrian first half, when the action was largely confined to midfield, neither keeper was seriously troubled. The action heated up shortly after the interval. Dodds advanced down the left, rounded Aitken, and created an opening for Beedie to score in the 54th minute. Dundee United, confident about landing their first Scottish Cup, settled down to contain Celtic with neat possession play and sound defence. Celtic countered by reorganising their line-up. After substituting Pierce O'Leary for a lacklustre Paul McStay and bringing on McClair for Burns, the crucial move was that of Roy Aitken into midfield. Aitken, almost a year to the day when he was ordered off against Aberdeen, was an inspiring figure as he urged on Celtic and almost singlehandedly turned the final round.

After 76 minutes Bannon upended MacLeod just outside the penalty area when no danger seemed imminent; Provan took the free kick, and curled the ball high inside the left-hand post of United's keeper, McAlpine, to spark off joyous scenes on the terracing. United, earlier so assured and in command of the game, could not cope with the onslaught of a team summoning up reserves of energy, calling on an unequalled cup tradition and uplifted by the frenzied roars of a massive support sensing a quintessential Celtic victory. McAlpine had to rush from his goal to foil McGarvey, but shortly afterwards Aitken surged down the right wing and crossed to the unmarked McGarvey who headed powerfully past the bemused keeper in 84 minutes. McGarvey had noticed twinges of cramp only seconds before, but he forgot his discomfort in the joy of the goal; he was not alone, because on the packed King's Park terracing the supporters, frustrated for so long, were celebrating noisily. Long after the whistle they stood there, unwilling to leave still almost disbelieving the outcome.

It was fitting that the most successful and colourful club in the history of the competition should win the hundredth final in such a dramatic manner — eventually a triumph of the will over a technically superior side.

Amid the euphoria, many supporters felt that Celtic were still not a complete side. The optimists hoped that the breakthrough would result in increased confidence and further success in the future, but the realists had their doubts . . .

Hugh Keevins, writing in *The Scotsman* at the end of the 1985-86 campaign was to note that "the unusual comes at no extra cost with this club (Celtic)". Indeed, the last season to be covered in this volume almost defies analysis, as the supporters, after being in despair for much of the year, rejoiced mightily in a memorable finale.

The 1985 close season was an anxious time despite the lingering euphoria of the Scottish Cup triumph. Frank McGarvey, bought from Liverpool for an estimated £250,000 five years earlier, was transferred

332

Congratulation and jubilation . . . Celtic players Bonner, O'Leary, Provan, Aitken and McGarvey (holding the Scottish cup), join in the celebrations of the massed ranks of fans at Hampden, May 1985.

to St. Mirren for a meagre £70,000; McGarvey, a most unselfish player although the leading scorer in the Premier League at the time of his move, had netted a glorious winning goal in the closing minutes of the final against Dundee United, but rejected "an insulting offer" to re-sign. The player viewed the offer as a device for dispensing with his services, and left in unhappy circumstances for Paisley amid growing disquiet from the supporters.

Only a month after the triumph at Hampden the club lost the services of Desmond White, who died suddenly on holiday in Crete. The 73-year-old chairman had not enjoyed good health for a year, and the aggravation provoked by the Rapid Vienna affair had imposed such a strain on him that speculation about an early retirement was widespread. Like his predecessor, Sir Robert Kelly, Mr. White projected an austere image, a brusque, forthright manner concealing a most enigmatic individual. In private he could be a genial host, and a generous man as displayed, for example, in his providing for the dependants of Johnny Doyle. However, his aloofness distanced him from reporters and his unsympathetic handling of Billy McNeill's dismissal in 1983 was to shadow his latter years at Parkhead and tarnish his undoubted commitment to the club. While criticised by many for "having the soul of an accountant", Mr. White's fiscal caution had helped Celtic to avoid

333

the plight of such famous clubs as Wolves, virtually ruined by commercial recklessness in the modern soccer world. An editorial in *The Celt*, a respectable albeit underground magazine, commented: "A club of Celtic's stature needs a strong man at the top; otherwise, it is prey for the charlatans and fly-by-nights who buy English clubs and then treat them as playthings." (August, 1985.)

Tom Devlin, the senior director with 36 years' service at Celtic Park, was an unexpected choice for chairman in view of his indifferent health and his age, but an early declaration of intent seemed to indicate a change in the style of handling the club's affairs: "I want Celtic supporters to know that we now have a team behind the team. By that, I mean that everything will be discussed at Board level." (*Daily Record*: 1 July, 1985.)

At the beginning of the season it seemed clear that David Hay's ability in the job still was being assessed, if not by the Board then certainly by the supporters. The manager's 'laid-back' approach puzzled many in the support, so much was it at variance with his aggressive play in the late 60s and early 70s when his combative displays had earned him the nickname of "the quiet assassin". Accustomed to the celebrity status of previous managers, Jock Stein and Billy McNeill, the supporters found it difficult to return to the image projected by a Jimmy McGrory; used to the success gained since 1965, they dreaded a return to the famine of the 50s.

Hay preferred to leave the dugout histrionics to his assistant, Frank Connor. Following a splendid draw in Madrid against Atletico in the first round of the Cup-Winners' Cup one journalist commented: ". . . the only flashes of aggro could be seen in their training sessions, supervised by their abrasive coach Frank Connor. During a stint on Monday night Connor had an argument with Provan and Murdo MacLeod and there was a particularly explosive clash between him and Pierce O'Leary when the Irishman took exception to one of his refereeing decisions. 'I know my players,' Connor explained with a smile. 'The best way to bring the best out of some of them is to make them angry.' O'Leary, one of Celtic's substitutes against Atletico, took the point: 'When I joined Celtic, the first thing Frank said to me was, 'I'll soon sort you out!' " (*Sunday Times*: 22 September, 1985.)

The difficulty lay in realising the potential within the squad, arguably the best in the country. It seemed that Celtic suffered from a lack of will in the crunch games, and the evidence was starting to accumulate.

In the return leg against Atletico Madrid on 2 October, needing only a 0-0 draw to advance following 'Mo' Johnston's thrilling equaliser and Pat Bonner's penalty save in the Vicente Calderon Stadium, Celtic never struck form in a deserted Parkhead and were eliminated 2-1. In the League Cup, once again as in the immediate post-war years becoming a 'bogey' tournament for Celtic, the team advanced comfortably against Queen of the South (4-1) and Brechin City (7-0) before facing Hibs at Easter Road. Defensive uncertainty nullified sparkling forward play, and it seemed inevitable that Hibernian would equalise a spectacular solo goal from Roy Aitken which should have settled the tie in Celtic's favour; level 4-4 after extra-time, the match was decided on penalty shots and Hibs advanced.

The more perceptive fans noted that the defeat marked the fourth successive time Celtic had lost cup-ties after extra time; a 1-2 loss in the League Cup quarter-final in 1984-85 to Dundee United at Tannadice, a 2-3 defeat from Rangers in the 1984 League Cup final at Hampden, a heartbreaking loss by 1-2 to Aberdeen in the 1984 Scottish Cup final after Aitken's dismissal. The point was made that in each of those games Celtic had forced extra time with a late equaliser; the initiative, accordingly, should have passed to Celtic, but the matches were lost (pardonably so against Aberdeen, when down to ten men). In Europe a similar pattern was emerging. Splendid displays away from home against Nottingham Forest and Atletico Madrid were negated by moderate performances at home in the return leg. The logical conclusion to be drawn from all this should have been obvious; Celtic appeared unable to adjust tactically to the unfolding situation on the field in the closing stages.

Celtic, however, had made an impressive start to the league campaign, dropping only two points in their first eight games. A lethargic display on the opening day against Hearts at Tynecastle was redeemed by a last-minute equaliser in off the post by Paul McStay, and a solo effort by the same player in the first 'Old Firm' clash at Parkhead gained another point in a match that Celtic dominated throughout. On 14 September Celtic faced Aberdeen, the defending champions, before a crowd of 39,000 that observed a minute's silence for Jock Stein who had died shortly after Scotland's World Cup match in Wales earlier in the week. Celtic dominated, only to be shocked by a late equaliser from McDougall, but McClair notched the winner with a header from Provan's corner two minutes from the end.

Celtic's real problems started on 12 October with a shock defeat from Hearts at Parkhead where the Edinburgh side defended grimly to hold on for a 1-0 win, keeper Smith distinguishing himself with a splendid save from Aitken's header in the closing minutes. This encouraging performance started Hearts off on a remarkable run in which they were to remain undefeated for 27 league matches, and join in the race for the title along with the more fancied Aberdeen, Dundee United, Rangers and Celtic. The Parkhead challenge seemed to have foundered with a miserable sequence of games in late October and early November. Dundee United administered a football lesson to Celtic with a 3-0 victory, the largest home defeat for Celtic in five years; a week later Aberdeen thrashed Celtic 4-1 at Pittodrie after being outplayed for much of the first half; and worst of all, Rangers, already being revealed as a mediocre outfit in this campaign, beat Celtic 3-0 at Ibrox.

It was a bad time for Celtic, and David Hay. The newspapers speculated about the need for change, and suggested that the manager's job was on the line. Humiliated by all the leading contenders for the title, Celtic supporters had to consider the implications — either the players were not good enough or the coaching staff was not providing the appropriate tactics and motivation. One newspaper referred to the 'Old Firm' meeting, although attended by the second-largest crowd in Britain, as "the temporary championship of Glasgow" and pointed out the decline of the giants: "Both have toppled out of the League Cup at the hands of Hibs. Both have been put to the sword by Spanish opposition in the first round of European competition. And between them, they have had hardly a domestic victory in more than a month." (*Scottish Daily Express*: 11 November, 1985.) The writer, along with most followers of football, conceded that the 'New Firm' of Aberdeen and Dundee United were now the standard bearers at home and abroad. David Hay was under attack, and supporters pointed out the manager's failure to establish a rapport with the fans. He remained an enigma to the club's followers who recalled his understandable hesitation about accepting the job after McNeill's departure. Those who felt that the greatest honour in the game was being conferred upon him questioned his commitment, a feeling strengthened by his manner. Hay's phlegmatic approach served to conceal the manager's increasing sensitivity to a frustrating period in the club's history; he practised admirable self-discipline, trying not to get too carried away by an outstanding performance nor upset by a devastating setback. To many, however, Hay was "a stranger in Paradise", returning as manager after a decade of being virtually out of touch with the set-up to meet the challenge of a more egalitarian and competitive Scottish environment than existed in his playing days, and perhaps suffering under the handicap of only limited managerial experience with Motherwell. The greatest drawback to full acceptance by the club's followers was a psychological one — the burden of having to follow such charismatic managers as Stein and McNeill, and having to be judged by the impossibly high standards of the former.

In the midst of the decline David Hay was invited to perform the opening ceremony in November, 1985, to mark the 500th flat modernised by the Parkhead Housing Association. It seemed appropriate that the manager of Celtic should be involved in this worthwhile local project, and Hay was at ease as he spoke with charm and manifest sincerity. He commented appreciatively on the renovation work being carried out in an area of the city indelibly associated with the club, and recalled his own early days as a boy being raised in a tenement. His appeared a genuine success story, and the slim, boyish-looking and personable Hay made a favourable impact, giving the impression that his interests extended beyond football, and one wondered if the treatment for the series of injuries that curtailed his playing career had not matured him as a human being and given him a more balanced outlook on life. Certainly he had a basic honesty about him that was refreshing. After the humiliation at Ibrox he again contemplated resignation and hinted at a general malaise: "Everyone at Parkhead, and I mean everyone associated with the club, has to take a long, hard look at themselves after the defeat from Rangers, and none more so than myself." (*The Scotsman*: 11 November, 1985.)

Celtic's results showed some improvement in the aftermath of the slump. Mark McGhee, recently signed from Hamburg for £150,000, had made his debut against Rangers although not looking match-fit, and impressed against Clydebank in his home debut to score Celtic's goals in a 2-0 win. The side rallied to pick up points steadily. In the matches against the immediate challengers that would decide the championship Celtic's gradual improvement continued. At Tynecastle against Hearts, surprisingly making a title bid after a shaky start to the campaign, Celtic snatched another 1-1 draw, with McGhee scoring; on New Year's Day Celtic beat Rangers 2-0 at Parkhead with headed goals from defender Paul McGugan and striker Brian McClair, and on 11 January at Parkhead Celtic fought back to equalise against Aberdeen through a Peter Grant goal in a 1-1 draw. However, the critics were unimpressed and pointed to two defeats by Dundee United at Tannadice. On 23 December Celtic lost narrowly 1-0 to a Bannon penalty, but on 4 January were taken apart by a rampant United in a 4-2 loss.

David Hay, still under pressure from the supporters and from the Board, took a drastic measure. In a scene reminiscent of a Western movie, he summoned his assistant, Frank Connor, to a deserted Celtic Park on a Sunday afternoon in February, 1986, and fired him. Typically Hay had insisted on carrying out the unpleasant task himself. Connor left the ground after the ten-minute meeting "shattered" by the development, but although it was a surprise to the general public, relations between the two men had been strained for some time and some directors harboured reservations about the coach's conduct on the touchline. Nobody could deny, however, that the partnership had failed to instil the organisation and discipline, especially in defence, that was required of a first-class side and which had been so passionately advocated by Connor upon his appointment.

The dramatic step was viewed as an act of self-assertion by the manager who, as he did not immediately seek a replacement for

Connor, seemed intent on taking full control of the playing side of his responsibilities. Nobody knew better than Hay that his job now depended on results, and on 8 March it seemed that the manager's days were numbered.

After an unimpressive 2-0 win over St. Johnstone at Celtic Park and a struggle to overtake a spirited Queen's Park side by 2-1 on the same ground, Celtic faced the prospect of taking on Hibernian at Easter Road in the Scottish Cup quarter-finals — and gaining revenge for their dismissal from the League Cup. Celtic appeared in control and led at half-time through a McClair goal in 42 minutes, but in a tempestuous second half Hibs fought back to edge in front after falling behind 2-1 to a McGhee counter in the 60th minute; although McClair regained equality from the penalty spot with only four minutes left, another error allowed Hibs to snatch a last-minute victory when a modicum of organisation in defence should have ensured a replay. One reporter commented scathingly that the defence's vulnerability to the cross ball had "turned charity into a way of life."

It was widely assumed that Hay would be released from his responsibilities at the end of the season, and the speculation was growing that Billy McNeill might be approached to resume at Celtic Park. Hay was candid about the prospects of salvaging anything from the season: "We still have a slender chance of winning the championship and that is what we now have to concentrate all our energies on. Some of our players will be playing for their futures over the remaining weeks of the season. A lot of them could be doing more for the club than they are." At that stage Celtic's prospects looked remote. Aberdeen and Dundee United were tucked behind Hearts, but had games in hand as well as the experience in tight finishes. As Hearts' lengthy unbeaten run continued, the conviction grew that this was to be their year, the first championship flag for Tynecastle in 26 years. A fine team spirit, a formidable work rate, a defence admirably organised by ex-Ranger Sandy Jardine, and the ability of ex-Celt John Colquhoun and young John Robertson to snatch goals at crucial moments had kept the challenge going.

Hay's immediate task was to restore morale after the Easter Road defeat, and to prepare for the same series of fixtures that had resulted in humiliating losses earlier in the season.

Dundee United came to Parkhead on 15 March, supremely confident from three victories over Celtic in the Premier League, and led at half-time with a Dodds' goal against the run of play. With time running out for Celtic, substitute MacLeod netted from 15 yards to equalise. On 22 March Celtic went to Ibrox and, in a thrilling encounter, young Owen Archdeacon helped set up two first half goals for Johnston and McClair, but Willie McStay was ordered off for his second 'bookable' offence in 31 minutes and Rangers pulled back one goal three minutes later. Although a man short, Celtic scored a third goal two minutes after the restart when Burns accepted a perfect pass from Johnston, but Rangers stormed into attack to score three times within 11 minutes. Celtic's task seemed hopeless: a man short, a goal down at 3-4, playing against a stiff breeze and gusts of rain. From somewhere the Celtic spirit manifested itself yet again . . . and with 20 minutes to play MacLeod scored with a thunderous shot from nearly 30 yards to gain a merited draw.

The point dropped at Ibrox, however, meant that Celtic would probably have to win all the remaining fixtures, including one at Pittodrie, to have any chance of the title. An incisive second-half display against Clydebank at Kilbowie Park brought a 5-0 win, and sent the team to Aberdeen on 12 April with hopes high. A Johnston goal in the 49th minute gained both points for Celtic, their first victory there since December, 1982. The gap between Celtic and Hearts was shrinking, but the Edinburgh side held a seemingly impregnable lead, particularly after a 3-0 rout of Dundee United at Tannadice. Both Aberdeen and Dundee United, the 'New Firm' in Scottish football, had started to fade in the final stretch. However, as Celtic started to show a return to the form that had characterised their play earlier in the season, boosted by an exciting new find in teenage defender Derek Whyte, Hearts began to reveal signs of nervousness. In a tense encounter with Aberdeen they were saved by a late equaliser, and on the following Saturday struggled to an unconvincing 1-0 home win over lowly Clydebank. One writer noted that Hearts and their fans "were acting like they have a feeling they were going to get mugged." Sensing the possibility of Hearts collapsing, Celtic continued to exert pressure. On 19 April two late goals at Parkhead by Archdeacon and McClair earned them a 2-0 win over Hibs; on 26 April another two second-half goals, by McClair and Johnston, gave them a 2-0 victory against Dundee; and on 30 April, a midweek fixture at Motherwell, a pair by McClair brought yet another 2-0 result.

The Premier League campaign had come down to the last game of the season on 3 May, 1986. Hearts were clear favourites, needing only a point at Dundee to win the championship; Celtic headed to Paisley to meet St. Mirren as 6-1 outsiders, needing to win by three goals (and Hearts to lose). Celtic's hopes rested on Dundee who still had a chance of qualifying for Europe, if Motherwell drew at Ibrox. Celtic, urged on by their supporters, swept into attack at Love Street and McClair, the side's leading scorer for the third successive season, headed in Archdeacon's corner after only six minutes. Johnston scored in 32 minutes, and a minute later added the goal that gave Celtic the required three-goal margin with a wonderful counter. The ball was eased out of

Brian McClair's sixth minute header at Paisley sets Celtic on the road to the title, May 1986.

Celtic's penalty area and worked in clinical but thrilling fashion down the right in a manoeuvre involving McGrain, MacLeod, Paul McStay, Aitken, McGrain once more and McClair, who hoodwinked a Saints' defender before slipping the ball to Johnston and the striker beat the advancing keeper cleanly. Before the interval Paul McStay scored a fourth goal as insurance. At Dens Park Hearts had started off nervously although they had the noisy encouragement of a huge travelling support to help them, and after half-time had started to flood the midfield in a conscious effort to hold on for a 0-0 draw.

The crowds at the three grounds were linked by radio broadcasts. Given the instantaneous communication that radio provides, surprisingly erroneous information was to play a part in the unfolding drama. The Celtic players, comfortably ahead 4-0, were told in the dressing room at half-time that Dundee were leading 1-0; at Dens Park Hearts were aware of Celtic's commanding lead, but during the second half Dundee were boosted with the 'news' that Motherwell were holding Rangers to a draw.

It was an eerie atmosphere at Love Street as the Celtic fans watched their team continue to dominate, applauding Bonner for two fine saves and noting with approval McClair's second goal in 53 minutes. Their attention was concentrated on events at Dens Park, where Dundee had started to control the match and were exerting greater pressure on Hearts. The Edinburgh side, having conceded the initiative, pulled men back into defence and left only Colquhoun and Robertson up front.

With only seven minutes left Dundee's substitute Albert Kidd scored the most notable goal of his career. The Hearts' followers slumped in disbelief, stunned that their dreams of glory had been shattered; at Love Street the terracings erupted and burst into song as Celtic fans started to claim the championship; even at Ibrox celebrations broke out among the Rangers' supporters who, hearing amid the static of their radios that Kidd had scored, assumed that it was Walter Kidd, the Hearts captain. A minute or so later the same Dundee player added a second goal, to break Hearts' completely and give Celtic their 34th championship.

It was a memorable finale to the season, a typically spirited Celtic comeback, marked by eight wins in a row (and sixteen successive matches in the Premier League without defeat), gaining another championship. If not a vintage Celtic team, they have revived the traditional enthusiasm in a highly dramatic manner.

And what an appropriate way to end this account, with yet another reminder of what the authors claimed in Chapter 1: "The history of one of the world's great football clubs needs no embellishment from fiction."

Notes
1 The Austrians had already used their two allotted substitutes, and Kienast had been sent off, before Wienhofer's 'injury'.

THE STUFF OF LEGEND

IN the following pages we have attempted to give more detailed pen-pictures of twenty outstanding figures in Celtic's history. The reasoning is as follows; after completing some chapters of the volume, we felt that a vital ingredient was missing and would continue to be absent until we changed the approach. The missing factor was, of course, the human touch; when football followers gather, the talk is about the personalities and the incidents — for example, Celtic supporters will always talk about Charlie Tully and his twice-taken corner at Falkirk in 1953, but a detailed account would be out of place within the main text of this history because it was one of the few highlights of an otherwise miserable season. And so we had to devise this format in order to include the celebrated anecdotes. The men chosen were selected to represent the various decades of Celtic's history, and they are not meant to be considered the 'best' players in the club's history — although most of them would have graced any team with their presence. Rather, they represent aspects of the club's ambience, and symbolise a particular period in its history.

One last word. We sat down one night in 1983 at opposite ends of a kitchen table to write the names of the men we felt should be included; after quarter of an hour our lists were complete and, of the twenty eventually written about, we had agreed on seventeen. Two famous names are missing — Willie Maley and Jock Stein; as on Sir Christopher Wren's epitaph, the monument to those men is found elsewhere — on almost every page of this volume.

*James Kelly, Celtic's first captain, seated in middle of front row (ball at his feet).
Also worth noting in this photograph of an early Celtic side are: Back Row, (2nd
from right) John Glass, President. Middle Row, (2nd from left) Tom Maley, (2nd
from right) Willie Maley. Bottom Row, (2nd from right) Neil McCallum, scorer
of the club's first goal.*

JAMES KELLY

YOUNG Bob Kelly could scarcely believe what he was hearing, but he listened carefully with growing dismay as his father, James Kelly, JP, and former chairman of Celtic FC, outlined his argument. He conceded that his son had a genuine enthusiasm for football, he admitted that he was an acceptable centre-half for his junior club, Blantyre Victoria; he allowed that he might have a future in the game as a senior player . . . but there were some issues that had to be resolved first. Was it fair that he, coming as he did from a comfortable home, should compete for a berth on a football team against a working-class lad who needed the money? And did his withered arm not give him an unfair advantage over players who were reluctant to challenge him too vigorously for fear of injuring him? Bitterly disappointed as he was, Bob Kelly saw the merits in his father's views and was aware of the idealism lying behind them; shortly afterwards he gave up the game as a player.

This cameo reveals a great deal about James Kelly. The reader can recognise the material and social success it implies; it is a considerable progress from a humble start as an apprentice joiner in Renton to respectability and status as a JP and chairman of a famous football club. The reader can see immediately the strict code of honour that motivated his actions; it is a just man who would deny his son the opportunity to play football because of his privileged position. If he appears old-fashioned it is simply that James Kelly was a product of his times in attitude. He represented a recurring Victorian dream: a working-class lad gifted with athletic prowess being given an opportunity and, because of an innate maturity and propriety, taking advantage of the chance to become a financial, commercial and social success. He was a commendable example of upward mobility, moving smoothly from the working class into the middle class without giving up the virtues of ordinary people.

He was a man of his times, and he was the epitome of the Victorian athlete: he participated in athletics as well as football, and was renowned for his high and long jumping. As a footballer he was noted for a sporting attitude towards opponents and an infectious enthusiasm for the game; he was an industrious, hard-working player, earnest in application and concentration, and he rarely allowed himself to be provoked into retaliation by unfair tactics. Despite his fame as a member of Renton's 'world

345

championship' team, a reputation that made boys boast they had got close enough to him to touch his clothing, he was the most modest of men.

John Glass, often considered the person behind Celtic's immediate success, thought that convincing Kelly to join Celtic was his greatest accomplishment. He sensed that the new club needed instant credibility and that Kelly's signing would achieve that; he learned that other players would follow Kelly's example and move where he moved. It became imperative that Kelly sign on for Celtic, but it was not going to be easy. Only 22 years old, Kelly was well established as a player in a highly successful team; already he had played for Renton in three Scottish Cup finals, twice on the winning side — in 1885 against Vale of Leven by 3-1 and against Cambuslang in 1888 by a record 6-1 margin — and in those finals he showed his versatility by playing in three different positions — at outside-right, outside-left and centre-half.

However, Renton was doomed as a club because it was situated in a rural backwater and was to be badly affected by the legalisation of professionalism in England in 1885 and the illegal payments paid by Scottish clubs, especially in the cities; the break-up of the famous Renton team was inevitable and Kelly was coming to recognise the reality of the situation. While he was available, Celtic had keen competition. Hibs had some claims on his sympathies, being then both an Irish Catholic club (Kelly was a devout Catholic of Irish stock) and an established successful outfit, having won the Scottish Cup in 1887. Hibs' secretary, John McFadden, used these arguments in coaxing him into turning out against their arch-rivals Hearts and he contributed to a notable victory; a few weeks later he was persuaded to play for Celtic in their very first game, the friendly against Rangers, and playing centre-half he scored a goal in a 5-2 win. Hibs were eager to land him, Celtic were desperate to capture him, and his native club, Renton, still had hopes of retaining him.

John Glass, in the words of a contemporary, "camped on his doorstep" and used all his persuasive powers to convince him that his future lay with Celtic. He pointed out the advantages of staying in the West of Scotland, he stressed the idealistic nature of the new club's origins and these claims made an impression on Kelly . . . but, even more importantly, it now seems clear it was made worth his while to join Celtic; the young apprentice joiner from Renton, earning wages of perhaps 30/- (£1.50) a week, would soon purchase a public house for £650.

The importance of Kelly as a force in Scottish football can be seen by considering the dramatic effects on the three clubs bidding for him when he finally made his decision. Renton could not retain an eminent position and slipped into a gradual decline, to disappear from the league by 1898; Hibs could not sustain the mass defection of its players to Celtic after Kelly's signing and withdrew from football for a couple of seasons before emerging as the present-day club with no religious affiliations. With Kelly as captain Celtic, of course, went from strength to strength.

For a centre-half he was relatively small at five feet eight inches, but on a sturdy, stocky build. Despite his lack of height he was seldom beaten in the air, having a natural gift in timing allied to outstanding leaping powers probably developed from his days as a jumper. He had great speed, and was noted for his ability to pursue and recover the ball in helping out his colleagues; his tackling was incisive but universally recognised as being scrupulously fair. In his autobiography Sir Robert Kelly came close to suggesting that he was the player who initiated Celtic's traditional emphasis on attacking play. Two excerpts from newspapers support this claim; following Scotland's humiliation by England (5-0) in March, 1888, the *Athletic News* noted: "Kelly was the only success on the Scottish side. His play was a revelation; in fact he was the best half-back on the field. It was saddening to see his efforts so much retarded by the incompetence and inability of the forwards to make proper use of them." That last sentence would suggest that centre-halves still supported the forwards and provided passes for them in 1888, but a year later there was a hint that teams had tightened up in defence: "There are many people who believe that when Scotland adopted the centre-half-back position she sacrificed much of her power in the game, but we do not share altogether that opinion and if the players who fill this position in other clubs were men of Mr Kelly's calibre then there would be no difference of opinion on the matter nor would we have cause to regret having followed England in adding to the defensive parts of our elevens." (*Scottish Referee*: 21 January, 1889.) Kelly was the perfect exponent of the attacking centre-half because of his desire to be always in the thick of things; he was a dynamo, tireless both in defence and attack, his long 'drop' shots were a speciality. Celtic seem to have modelled their original style on the famous Preston North End side of the 1880s; that team, with a number of 'Scotch professors' prominent, was attack-minded and introduced a close-passing game that was revolutionary, and Celtic had in Kelly an ideal pivot for such a system.

With Celtic Kelly was to merit further honours; he played seven times for the Scottish League, and gained eight 'caps' in full internationals, five of which were the prestigious matches against England. He was to play in four more Scottish Cup finals (seven if we were to count the three 'friendly' games perpetrated on the unknowing spectators) and he played at centre-half in Celtic's first final, the famous 'snow final' of 1889, and also in Celtic's first cup triumph, a resounding 5-1 win over Queen's Park in 1892. He was the key member of the Celtic teams that won three league championships in four years between 1892 and 1896.

As a player in the emerging days of professionalism, the period of the paid amateur and afterwards, he did well financially, and quite rightly, out of his association with Celtic. Celtic, the most open of all Scottish clubs in paying players and in advocating the legalisation of professionalism, accordingly rewarded star players lucratively. Apart from his handsome signing-on incentive, Kelly received top wages at about £2 a week; in 1894 at the November meeting he was voted an honorarium of £100 'for past services'; in 1895 he got a bonus of £10 and a gold badge valued at £2 for helping to win the championship and in the same year, rather belatedly, he was given another £100 for having become 'a professional player'.

The early photographs capture a hint of the man: a serious, earnest expression, and an air of quiet confidence, an obvious impatience at being still, and a desire to be involved in action. These qualities were reflected in his contribution to Celtic on the field as captain, and in the pavilion as a member of the club. Off the field his industry was rewarded. In 1897, retired as a player, he became one of Celtic's first directorate after the change to a limited liability company, and was well established in Lanarkshire as a businessman and the owner of three pubs; in his adopted country he became a JP, and was a trustee of the Blantyre School Board for many years as well as a Lanarkshire county councillor; at Celtic Park he was elected chairman of the board in 1909 and served in that capacity until 1914, after which he continued as director until his death in February 1932.

SANDY McMAHON

THE month of August 1892 was a most trying one for Celtic's committee. In the early 1890s Scottish players, technically amateurs, were free to move almost at will and several of Celtic's best men were being wooed by English clubs. Apparently Madden and Brady had defected to Sheffield already, and even worse news had arrived by letter for John Glass; he read it and reread it with increasing gloom: "We beg to inform you that we have left the Celtic club and have signed for Notts Forest on a legal agreement. We have left to improve our position." The letter was signed by both Neil McCallum and Sandy McMahon.

The situation was now developing into a major crisis and Glass immediately took steps to contact his fellow committee members. In the previous season Celtic had achieved spectacular success by winning the three cups (the Scottish, the Glasgow, and the Charity Cups) and finishing second in the league; it was widely held that the key element was a highly effective forward line consisting of McCallum, Brady, Madden, McMahon and Campbell. Now it seemed that almost all had gone, but under John Glass this was a Celtic committee noted for determination and pragmatism. They decided to make a real effort to recover their players by despatching members south by train to contact them.

Reports vary as to the composition of the recovery party, but it appears that Glass and an unnamed member went to Sheffield where they were successful in persuading Madden to return with them; it is likely that Michael Dunbar and David Meikleham were the two delegates to travel to Nottingham looking for their players. They did not have high hopes of regaining Brady, but they were anxious to contact young Sandy McMahon, already being described as a prodigy and whose loss was considered irreplaceable. They discovered somehow that the player was being 'held' outside the city until he played his first game for Forest, and also that he was due to pay a brief visit to Nottingham, but he would be accompanied by some 'escorts'. The Celtic men haunted the train station until they saw McMahon arrive and they followed him to a hotel. Managing to strike up a conversation without arousing the suspicions of the escorts, they joined the group at a table; during the conversation McMahon was able to hint that he would be happy to return to Glasgow and that was enough. To the astonishment of his companions and the alarm of the other guests in

Drawing of Celtic stars Johnny Campbell, Sandy McMahon and Johnny Reynolds in Scottish Referee, *11 April, 1892 (heading refers to Scottish Cup triumph).*

the lobby of the hotel, the three Celts made a dash for the exit, scrambling over tables in their haste; they leaped on a cab and raced to the station where they boarded a moving train without knowing its destination. After an hour's journey they left the train, found the nearest main line station, and eventually made their way back to Glasgow for a rapturous welcome, Willie Maley having leaked the news to the newspapers after being informed by telegram of the successful coup.

Many felt that Sandy McMahon was well worth the trouble; one newspaper claimed "that he was the finest inside-left in Britain, and the mainspring of both Campbell and Madden's effectiveness". (*Scottish Sport*: 9 August, 1892.) He deserved the nickname 'the prince of dribblers', as another contemporary account indicates: ". . . so deft was he in manipulation of the ball. He patted and pirouetted with it in the manner of a premier danseuse", but he had more substantial qualities also. He was a prolific goalscorer with 119 goals in 173 league games and Willie Maley, who was Celtic's manager up to 1940 and who played alongside McMahon in the 1890s, thought that he was the greatest header of the ball the game had known, and he did not exclude Jimmy McGrory in making his choice. At corner kicks he was literally a marked man as he took up position with defenders elbowing, jostling, holding and obstructing in attempts to stop him. It took raw courage to play the game in those days and for McMahon to display his talents required real bravery, perhaps cultivated in the rugby-playing stronghold of Selkirk where he was born. He held the ball, thus inviting fierce tackles or 'charges' as they were called then and referees were inclined to interfere less than in today's game. "Those were no days of penalty kicks; a player tripped up from behind contenting himself with a demonstration of the rights of man on his opponent's front teeth," recalled one writer. He deserves a mention in the overall history of the sport because he was one of those innovative players who changed the nature of the game, rising above its early hurly-burly to be recognised as an artist. In the 1880s there was little combined play, the usual tactic being a long punt downfield followed by a cavalry charge with the hope that, in the ensuing scramble, a goal might be scored; an alternative method involved some brave player with ball control to dribble on his own as far as possible before being felled and allowing the ball to run loose to a team-mate. The resemblance between early football and rugby was clear.

Celtic from their first days were famous for their combined play and their attempts to raise the standard of the emerging sport as a team game, following the admirable example of Preston North End. Sandy McMahon formed the most famous left wing in football with John Campbell and that combination was one of the sporting glories of the times. The pair were first linked together in the last fifteen minutes of a league match at Cambuslang, and it was an immediate success: "With machine-like accuracy Sandy passed the ball to Campbell, darted forward for the return, skipped to the rear for a cute back-heel touch, danced dances with the sphere at his toe and generally indulged in such mazy gyrations that the opposing half-back was prepared to say that McMahon was in three places at once." Each was a skilled dribbler and a regular goalscorer with foot and head; each was a playmaker, a fine and accurate passer of the ball; and most importantly each brought out the best in the other, driving opponents frantic with their telepathic understanding of the other's intentions and whereabouts. Their finest hour might well have been the Scottish Cup final of 1892 when Celtic won the trophy for the first time by defeating Queen's Park 5-1 after being a goal down at the interval; in the second-half both McMahon and Campbell scored twice against a bewildered Spiders' defence, admittedly weakened through the absence of its regular full-backs. The goals were typical: Campbell's came from neat shots that finished off bouts of passing with his partner that had sliced open the defence, McMahon's pair consisted of a long dribble through the heart of the defence, and the inevitable header from a corner kick in the last minute.

His talents were recognised with six full caps, three against England, and with eight appearances for the Scottish League; he played in four league championship teams with Celtic between 1893 and 1898, and on three Scottish Cup winning sides.

Yet he was an unlikely looking player; his greatest admirer, Willie Maley, described him as "big and ungainly". He was over six feet in height with stooped shoulders and an awkward, shambling gait . . . until he got the ball. Then, hunched over it with arms outspread, he could weave his way past desperate defenders "with eel-like grace". In looks too he was scarcely a matinee idol, with a receding hairline and a thick, drooping moustache that partly concealed the absence of his front teeth, and the photographs invariably show a serious expression (perhaps Victorian footballers did not choose to smile for the camera). But he did have a natural dignity, as suggested by his nickname 'The Duke', and, although a most modest and retiring personality, he could be persuaded at the club concerts and sing-songs to entertain.

Surprisingly his party-piece consisted of lengthy excerpts from Shakespeare's plays recited with gusto in the approved manner of the famous actor-managers and to an appreciative audience of fellow-players and club officials.

Sadly, football, unlike cricket and golf, does not yet have a body of literature to commemorate the great players of the past, but McMahon's memory lingered on, as this memoir in the *Daily Record and Mail* of September, 1935, indicates: "You who did not see Sandy McMahon play know nothing about the weaving artistry of our football game; all ease and grace, as if born to make a football answer his will."

ALEC McNAIR

ALEC McNAIR rarely played to the gallery during his twenty years at Celtic Park, but he often provoked gales of laughter with his magisterial air of gravity and dignity. The winger would prance down the wing, dazzling with his control and skill, quietening the Celtic fans with his threat to their goal; he would slow down a little as if sensing that McNair was waiting for him; quickly he would twist and turn to evade him, but no matter how many or complicated his moves McNair was always placed between him and the goal. The fans could see the confidence oozing out of him as McNair gently steered him to the by-line and safety or almost apologetically, if clinically, dispossessed him; perhaps it was the incongruity that caused the fans to laugh — the contrast between the dashing forward and the stolid defender, the classic confrontation between youth and experience, or perhaps it was the age-old fascination of the duel between spider and fly, with the spectators wise enough this time to put their money on the spider.

Before Willie Maley signed him for Celtic he had heard about this player's versatility with Stenhousemuir and asked an official at Larbert to sound out McNair about joining Celtic for a close-season tour of the Highlands. McNair was contacted near midnight at home, and gave a characteristically deliberate answer: he would think it over and give a reply the next day, having slept on it. He did join up with Celtic for that tour and impressed Maley with his play and his poise. As Maley put it later: "He had an obvious sincerity and the straight look."

McNair had the instinctive virtuosity of the natural footballer, and was used by Celtic as a handyman for some time, although he usually played at right-half; he became an important member of Celtic's team that won the league championship six years in a row, and some would argue that he was the key player in the side. Throughout the first two seasons of that remarkable run he was the regular right-half, but in 1907 he took over in an emergency at right-back and became associated with that position ever afterwards; in fact Maley used him to cover several other positions as well and claimed that McNair had played every position for Celtic except goalkeeper. Not too surprisingly, he had started his career with the Warriors as an inside man, and had scored the winning goal in the Qualifying Cup for them with a header against Motherwell in 1901. No matter where he played, he retained the inside-forward's

A. M^cNAIR, CELTIC F.C.

Alec McNair, Glasgow Observer, 1910 portrait.

traditional mastery of the ball and the situation. He became recognised as a full-back although he was not an orthodox defender; most full-backs of that era played 'with fire and dash' which meant they tackled like terriors and cleared the ball with little regard for direction but with spectacular height and length. McNair was not in that category; he gave the impression of being slow, but he had little need of speed because of his exceptional positional sense and an uncanny ability to anticipate what his opponent would attempt; his tackling was surgical in execution because he sensed the exact moment the winger was losing control or confidence to deprive him of the ball painlessly; it was said that he seldom kicked the ball, preferring instead to sidefoot the clearance to a well-placed colleague or to pass into the open space for his inside-forwards. He was simply years ahead of his time in being 'the total footballer'; he was a player who never appeared young, "an old head on young shoulders" being a frequent description.

He controlled and influenced an area of the field as much by force of his personality as skill. Opposing inside men would despair of finding him a yard out of position and were unable to release their passes down the left; wingers would surrender the ball weakly after a token resistance; many Celtic counter-attacks would start from a McNair interception or, more accurately, intervention and precise pass.

He was the player as craftsman; an artisan definite and exact in all his movements, economical in words, gestures, and effort and the consequences of his every action were predictable and close to being inevitable. His pride in his ability and confidence in his control was such that he would choose to dribble the ball clear from his own penalty area rather than kick out wildly, a gambit that would cause much consternation on the terracings. However, there is nothing more soul-destroying for a forward to realise that the defender has more basic skills than himself; his coolness under pressure was proverbial, gaining him the lasting nickname of 'The Icicle'.

Throughout their history Celtic have evolved a characteristic style; they have been considered the team of inspiration, employing an 'off-the-cuff' methodology and relying on individual brilliance and heroics to pull them through, and traditionally they have been lauded as a team dedicated to attack. But during the time that McNair was at Celtic Park (and he played for twenty years) Celtic had the best organised defence in the land, and with Joe Dodds as partner the last lines were particularly strong. Dodds was a welcome relief to McNair's academic approach, favouring as he did a swashbuckling style. The goalkeeper with whom they were to develop an exceptional understanding was Charlie Shaw; McNair perfected the dubious and risky art of the pass back, often to the sounds of disapproval from the terracing. He ignored the complaints and continued his art of controlled football even from far back in defence. Only once was he known to have been affected by the crowd's reaction and it was not on a football pitch; he was playing in a golf tournament with other footballers and ended up in a fairway bunker. He surveyed the situation with typical calm, calculating that he was too close to the lip of the bunker to try for the green and estimating the chances of staying on the fairway if he played out sideways, when a quiet voice from the gallery disturbed him: "Pass it back tae Charlie." Smiling but perhaps a little rattled, McNair required two shots to get out.

The press description of his play and personality were universally consistent and a sample would read as follows: "cool and calm", "prosaic and practical", "effective and methodical", and "dignified and judicious". If at times he appeared to take risks, the chances were that he had calculated them to the exact percentage.

During his years at Parkhead McNair was a member of two different Celtic dynasties: the side that won the championship for six successive seasons between 1904 and 1910, and the side that won the championship a further four years in a row between 1914 and 1917, as well as two more flags in 1919 and 1922. Celtic were noted then as now for their cup-winning prowess: they won the Scottish Cup in 1907, 1908, 1911, 1912, 1914 and in 1923 — McNair played in all those finals and might have won a few more medals if the cup had not been withheld in 1909 because of the Hampden riot and not competed for during the five years of World War I when he was in his prime. He was honoured with 18 full Scottish 'caps', including three Victory internationals in 1919, and appeared in three different positions for his country: right-back, right-half and left-half.

He played in his last final in 1923, a 1-0 win over Hibernian, at the age of 39, and still was considered one of the outstanding performers on the field. Celtic had been shaky at the season's end and McNair was no longer a regular in the side because of recurring injuries, but in the emergency he was recalled to steady the defence. His performance that day, composed and efficient as always, was compared to that of a veteran actor summoning up reserves of strength and character responding to the demands of the audience, relying on his craft, experience and authority to compensate for any physical shortcomings. He could have chosen no more fitting finale to a magnificent career.

Following his retirement he became secretary-manager of Dundee, but he was never completely happy in a manager's office, leaving the post after a couple of years to settle as an accountant — a profession that seemed ideally suited to his temperament.

JIMMY QUINN

HE was the very stuff of legend; it seemed that ordinary language fell short in capturing the primal force that was Quinn. The sports writers in describing him reached out for Homeric terms, and predictably the essential epithets of the reporters became the conversational currency of the supporters; thus men, ordinarily unexpressive, could speak of him unselfconsciously as 'the man from Croy', or 'the iron man', or 'the man of a hundred injuries', or most commonly as 'the one and only Jimmy Quinn'. Even Celtic's most distinguished historian could not resist hyperbole in describing him: "With the deep chest and muscular shoulders of a charging bison he shed festoons of clinging opponents as he hurtled goalwards." (*The Celtic Story*: James E. Handley 1960.)

Willie Maley recounts how he travelled to Falkirk by train to see him play for Smithston Albion at Stenhousemuir, but on the platform he met William Wilton, the manager of Rangers. Afraid that Rangers were interested in him too and relieved that his rival was going to Bainsford Park to see a junior game, he accompanied Wilton to that game without revealing his own plans; feigning boredom he left at half-time and raced over to Stenhousemuir where he arrived in time to see Quinn leaving the field limping badly. He followed the player to the Plough Inn where the dressing room was located and offered his services to treat the injury, a sprained knee. He appraised the prospect: "Quinn I saw was a young man of fine physique, strong on his legs, broad shouldered, and deep chested." After introducing himself he offered Quinn the chance to sign for Celtic, but was astonished when Quinn turned him down by insisting: "I'm to stop in the juniors; that's my class." Despite his shock and disappointment Maley persisted and coaxed the youngster to sign a registration form, promising not to send it to the SFA without Quinn's permission. The next step was to get Quinn to meet with the other Celtic players and Maley accomplished this by inviting him to come along for some training sessions at Rothesay in January 1901; wisely Maley had already spoken to several players about being kind to the bashful recruit.

At the time Maley was in the process of changing Celtic's image from that of free-spenders to one of rearing their own players. He had confidence in Quinn's ability although he required patience as the recruit struggled to find his form and confidence, mainly on the

Drawing of Quinn's goal in first match of 1909 Scottish Cup final, Glasgow News, *12 April, 1909.*

left wing. The directors were not impressed by Quinn's progress, but Maley insisted that the player had the ability and character to succeed. The breakthrough came for Quinn and Celtic in the Glasgow Exhibition Trophy of 1902; Rangers had won this splendid trophy the year before, but put it up for competition to raise money for the victims of the first Ibrox disaster. After eliminating Sunderland, the English champions, Celtic faced Rangers in the final and won 3-2 after extra time. Quinn harried the Rangers' defence throughout the game with his strong running and scored all Celtic's goals from the centre-forward position.

He had the goal-scoring touch, and his goals were unmistakable; near goal he was a decisive finisher, never relying merely on the well-placed shot. He preferred the fierce blast "to mak' siccar" and keepers rarely had a chance; if they were unlucky enough to get a hand on the ball the force of the shot was sufficient for it to reach the net. He was a brave header of the ball, willing to risk injury by diving to make contact with optimistic crosses, and often ending up in the net alongside the ball. But the prevailing memory is of outstanding individual runs: a thrilling dash through the middle of a defence with opponents falling like ninepins in vain efforts to stop him, and the run ending with a venomous shot delivered just as he crashed to the ground. Nobody in the game had a greater hold on the public's imagination; there is a factor in greatness that demands recognition; in ballet, Nureyev; in opera, Pavarotti; in tennis, McEnroe; in golf, Nicklaus — all have a confidence and an assurance bordering at times on arrogance and a sense of physical presence that compels attention. Nobody is indifferent to the great performer, and Quinn had charisma.

He was not universally liked. While Celtic supporters adored him, the followers of other teams dreaded and hated him equally; his style increased the intensity of the emotions generated by his effectiveness. No defence could ignore his presence, nor could any opponent treat him with studied indifference as he chased every ball and harried every goalkeeper; there were memorable physical clashes with defenders resenting his rampaging style and attempting to stop him with jarring tackles, but Quinn, though only five feet, eight inches in height, was unstoppable when in full flight. At times it seemed that Quinn relished their physical challenge, and it was only later that he developed the cunning to dodge the charges. Throughout his career he symbolised the physical approach to the game, and the Scottish selectors recognised this by choosing him as outside-left against England in 1908; the reason for the controversial switch in position was to bring Quinn into direct confrontation with Bob Crompton of Blackburn Rovers, a feared English full-back capable of terrorising wingers. By all accounts it produced a memorable physical clash with the honours even at the end of the day. It could be argued too that his intimidating presence led indirectly to the replay and the 'Hampden riot' in 1909.

Quinn endeared himself within the Celtic litany by his performances against Rangers, who were then emerging as the greatest rivals to Celtic's dominance; and at that time the rivalry was intense but confined generally to football. His personal breakthrough came in the Exhibition Cup with a hat-trick against the 'Light Blues' in a 3-2 win in extra-time; in the 1904 final Maley again switched him to centre-forward to replace Bennett and the manager's faith in him was rewarded when he scored three goals to lead Celtic to another 3-2 win after being two goals down early in the game. Maley claimed that one of the most memorable and thrilling goals he had ever seen was Quinn's third when he dashed through the heart of the Ibrox defence brushing off stout challenges from Nick Smith and Jock Drummond, two redoubtable tacklers. He added to the legend by getting himself ordered off twice in games against Rangers, a clear indication to the supporters that he was trying with every nerve and sinew. Maley, always an apologist for his swashbuckling leader, suggested that Quinn's indiscretions were exaggerated: "All the men that Quinn killed are still alive."

After the second ordering-off and suspension the *Glasgow Star*, owned in part by Celtic's director Tom White, organised a subscription fund to compensate the player and the donations poured in: from the Celtic Brake Clubs — Springburn, Parkhead, Benburb and All Saints', Sacred Heart, St Mary's, St Anne's, St Patrick's, St Mungo's, St Saviour's, St John's, St Luke's; from the branches of The League of the Cross; $5 from Philadelphia that exchanged for £1, and contributions from New York and County Down; from Lanarkshire with tributes from Motherwell, Hamilton, Wishaw, Airdrie and Coatbridge; from the Clyde coast with offerings from Kirkcudbright, Saltcoats, Greenock, Port Glasgow and Paisley; and from Partick, Clydebank, Alexandria and Dumbarton; from collections at works with £5/8s/6d (£5.43) from the Dead Meat Market and £8/17s/6d (£8.88) from the Lanarkshire Steel Works; from the Scots contributing under such names as Stewart, Ross, Craig, Campbell and MacDonald; and from the Irish, a longer list rejoicing under the names of Brogan and Brennan, O'Brien and Doyle, McCloskey and Lynch; from the club's directors each of whom gave two guineas, and the players who contributed £8/10s/- (£8.50); from anonymous donors such as 'The Tailor's Gang' and 'The Undaunted Youth'; from the eminent Bailie M. J. Connell, BA, LLB, who gave another two guineas and the modestly obscure 'Boys of Parkhead Reformatory', the contributors of 12s/9d (64p). At the end the total came to a splendid £277/16s/1d (£277.80) which was presented to the player at a concert the proceeds of which went to charity; the great Quinn, too shy to speak in public, promised that he would give his thanks properly on the field upon his return the following Saturday. He came back in triumph, as he had done after his previous suspension: "When he scored his second goal after tearing through the opposition, some men wept for joy, others embraced their neighbours, while a few danced deliriously on the cinder track." (*Glasgow Observer*: 6 May, 1905.)

The splendid side that won the 1904 Scottish Cup and which dominated Scottish football for several years cost, by Maley's estimation, no more than £200. Possibly no other Celtic front line has been so balanced, effective and skilful: two outstanding wings with fast wingers, fine crossers of the ball, supplied by two intelligent inside-forwards, excellent in distribution; they gloried in combined play but all the patient build-up was calculated to spring Quinn loose with crosses from the wing or with probing through balls. Quinn added the basic element of muscle to the craft of the others; he added heart to their intelligence. He played in the traditional, heroic position — the spearhead and goalscorer, taking the heat off the others and bearing the brunt of the defenders' challenges . . . and rightly gathering the glory.

James E. Handley describes his charismatic effect even in his last season when repeated injury had hampered him: "Young men came to gaze on one of whom their elders could speak only in superlatives but the memory of him was to continue undimmed so long as any of the generation who knew him in his glory remained alive."

On a personal note one of the authors can attest to this claim. A very young boy, he visited Glasgow with his grandfather and was walking down Queen Street when an older man smoking a pipe passed them. The effect on his grandfather was electric, and he was normally a taciturn, unemotional man. He raced back along the street dragging a bewildered boy with him until he caught up: "Mr Quinn, Mr Quinn? Could I ask you to shake my grandson's hand?" Half an hour later, sitting on a bench in George Square and still partly overcome, he spoke in his most solemn voice: "Never forget that you have shaken hands with the greatest centre-forward that ever kicked a ba'."

PATSY GALLACHER

ABOUT forty years ago when one of the authors was a very junior member of the Penilee and Cardonald Celtic Supporters' Club, he enjoyed sitting back in the semi-darkness listening to his elders re-living 'the good old days'. Sooner or later the oldest would be prompted into reminiscence and invariably he would start: "Aye . . . but you should have seen Patsy . . .".

'Patsy' — even today he remains the one Celtic player identified, clearly and instantly, by his Christian name alone. For those few remaining who saw him play, he was the greatest inside-forward of them all. Robert Kelly, a man not noted for verbal extravagance, was unequivocal in his praise: ". . . the best player I ever saw. He was unexcelled as a dribbler and ball-worker, was always direct in his approach to goal, had a most uncanny gift of being able to change speed in a single stride, and no one then or since has had such perfect balance." Kelly normally presented a severe front in public but, speaking of Gallacher, he would become visibly animated, especially when describing Patsy's goal in the 1925 final against Dundee, a goal that he loved to demonstrate. Jock Stein was once moved to comment gently: "Every time the chairman describes that goal, he adds on another defender and gives Patsy a new way of beating him."

A shrimp of a man at five feet six inches and weighing only seven stones on his debut, he was a most unlikely athlete. His pale, thin face with its brooding expression increased the impression of vulnerability, and his characteristic style of dribbling, hunched over the ball apparently oblivious of onrushing defenders, made supporters cringe in dread. That was a false impression; able to anticipate the moves of every player on the field, he could gauge intentions in a flash and was prepared for anything, fair or foul. Football was rougher then, and he felt that at times referees failed to give him due protection under the rules, and so he would fight his own battles; a friend who questioned the wisdom of taking on bigger and heavier opponents was answered: "I've seldom failed." This combination of skill and hardiness produced in him the confidence to take on defences, sometimes with a courage that edged towards recklessness.

By tracing the outline of his career one could examine the structure of football in those days. He used to recall with pride his first team (Holy Redeemer Primary School) and his first award (an

A young Patsy Gallacher challenges Third Lanark's Thompson at Celtic Park in season 1911/12.

ironclad watch won in the Yoker Athletic Schools' Tournament). Patsy had to organise the team, acting as captain and secretary, because every teacher in the school was female; and Holy Redeemer were little fancied to win the competition. The organising committee was reluctant to hand over the cup to a team without an adult as manager and whose oldest member had just turned twelve, but the two Yoker Athletic players who had acted as linesmen for the tournament signed a guarantee that the boys would return the trophy in time for next year's competition, and so the trophy was borne in triumph back to the school.

Patsy joined Benvue, a team that played in 'the Clean Speech League', where players were threatened with ordering off for swearing. He then moved up to a juvenile side, Renfrew St James, with whom he won two representative honours: for Renfrewshire against Paisley at Love Street and for the Rest of Scotland against Lanarkshire at Fir Park. He signed on for Clydebank Juniors and an early appearance for them cost him a month's lay-off with poisoned toes, a consequence of playing a complete match in badly fitting boots borrowed from a friend. Senior scouts were attracted by his performances, but shook their heads at his puny build. However, he received invitations from both Celtic and Clyde to play in a tournament at Dumfries. Patsy was undecided and it was fortunate for Celtic that their scout was informed of Clyde's interest; he turned up at the Gallacher home at 6 a.m. to escort the player to the railway station. Although he played well and scored twice in the 6-1 defeat of a Dumfries Select, Celtic still had doubts about him; two weeks later he was given another trial against an Army Eleven and scored three goals in a 5-0 win. Despite misgivings Maley recognised that the youngster could score goals, and signed him.

He was so convincing at training, where the other players could not win the ball from him, that he was promoted quickly to the first team, making his debut against St Mirren at Celtic Park in November 1911, and his appearance invited ridicule. He was painfully thin, his frailty accentuated by the standard outfit of those days: long, baggy shorts, heavy shinguards and boots with reinforced toes. As soon as the game started it was clear that he had the quality that made the most previously sceptical aware they were in the presence of a genius. His first touches of the ball won over the crowd, his control and intelligence earning him instant admiration and respect, but when he picked himself up to carry on after a heavy tackle his spirit won their hearts. Heroes are created thus; skill and spirit promoting feelings of admiration and affection.

Within a month he had established himself as a regular in the side, and only six months later he was the owner of a Scottish Cup medal, having scored one of the goals that beat Clyde 2-0 in the final. Ball control gave him that extra split second to survey the scene and wreak havoc on defences; and he was not slow in movement or thought. Jimmy McGrory, who played alongside him, thought he was the fastest player over ten yards that he ever saw. Small and nimble, he could brake on a sixpence while defenders, reduced to ox-like clumsiness, lumbered on past him. He had the deadly repertoire of the complete inside-forward: elusive dribbles, cunning passes and dangerous shooting. Added to that was his spirit; 'defeat' was not a word found in his vocabulary, and when his side fell behind he became more than himself, urging on his team to greater efforts. It was then that he frequently produced his legendary feats; normally he subdued some of his individuality for the sake of teamwork, but when the overall plans were being checked Celtic turned to Patsy for inspiration.

He scored the most extraordinary goal in Scottish Cup history in 1925 (the one that so delighted Bob Kelly). Dundee were holding on to a 1-0 lead as the game entered the closing stages and looked capable of surviving despite Celtic's pressure. Gallacher picked up the ball and manoeuvred his way through the opposing defence until he found himself trapped a few feet short of Dundee's goal and was tackled heavily; reeling and stumbling from the collision, he fell to the ground but somehow kept the ball lodged between his feet . . . and somersaulted into the net, from which he had to be untangled.

He could be impatient with other players' failings, not realising that his own gifts were unique, and some dreaded his sharp tongue. At the same time he could relieve the tension in the dressing-room before an important match with his quips, and now and again he would regale his mates with an impromptu song or lead them in a chorus.

To the delight or disbelief of his colleagues he would sometimes match wits with his manager, Willie Maley, a most authoritative figure. The team had been taken to a quiet hotel in Dunbar for a break, but Gallacher was chafing a little under the restrictions and decided he would get round the curfew. He came to an arrangement with a chambermaid to borrow clothes and hid his own in a garden shed during the day; that night, dressed in the maid's clothes and wearing a black veil, he made his way through the lobby of the hotel only to see the manager and some directors seated strategically near the front door. Gallacher was unable to resist the temptation, and wished Maley a pleasant good-evening in a high-pitched voice as he passed. Mr Maley, always the gentleman, rose to answer and escorted the 'lady' to the door which he opened with a gallant bow. When the manager found out later about the caper, he gave Patsy a 'roasting', but Patsy always refused to reveal how Maley had learned the truth.

Quickly Celtic realised that Gallacher was the key to success and treated him accordingly. Football has always been a chancy living and, even as a teenager, Gallacher was shrewd enough to cover the risks; before signing for Celtic he insisted on being allowed to finish his apprenticeship as a shipwright in the yards at Clydebank. Later in his career, as an established player, he had Maley's permission to train alone in the afternoons so that he could devote his mornings to the running of his two public houses and, as Celtic's most valuable star, his wages were higher than the others'.

His colleagues, aware of his worth, did not resent the situation: football was played off the cuff and training was designed for general fitness. Gallacher was naturally fit, never troubled by weight problems, and knew how to keep in shape. Certainly the original doubts about his physique and stamina had been dispelled: Gallacher played fifteen years for Celtic and a further six years for Falkirk. Once he was injured after 30 minutes at Boghead against Dumbarton, but finished the game unaware till later that he had broken a bone in his leg.

He revitalised Celtic's team as the side that had created a record by winning six successive league titles slipped down to fifth place in 1910-11. With Gallacher in the team Celtic re-established its supremacy, gaining a further four championships in a row. His individual honours accumulated quickly with 13 caps for Ireland and Eire, and a couple of appearances for the Scottish League; seven championship badges, four Scottish Cup medals (and the competition was suspended during the five years of World War I), four Glasgow Cup medals and eleven Charity Cup medals.

Despite his reputation, a modern fan might ask the same questions that the senior scouts did in 1910, and the answers would be the same. Jimmy McGrory, echoing Robert Kelly's praise, had no doubts: "He was the greatest player I ever saw." Another man who knows a thing or two about greatness, Jack Nicklaus, has often championed the players from the past: "We can't blame them for beating the men they beat, and winning the tournaments they won. That's all you can do, beat the other guys who turn up. Would they win today? Sure . . . they would emerge from the field and end up on top — they would find a way to win."

TOMMY McINALLY

HIS manager surely described his own frustration best: "I have worried over Tommy, but when all is said and done, all his faults and foibles weighed up, I could never overcome a personal regard for this big, laughter-making boy from Barrhead who was out-and-out a Celt . . . and I am sure of this — that Tommy McInally in his pondering periods regrets very sincerely his premature departure from Parkhead." This statement came from Willie Maley following McInally's transfer to Third Lanark in 1922, and significantly McInally did return to Celtic later for the largest transfer fee the club had ever paid up to that time.

He was above all a personality and embodied all the virtues and flaws of the type. Stories abounded about his ready wit: at Cathkin in his Third Lanark days, as the players clustered around a board with draughtsmen to represent positions for a tactics talk, he upset the board, sending the counters flying, and shrugged his shoulders to point out in explanation: "Ach, that's jist the other team takin' the field." As he headed to the dressing-room at Tynecastle at half-time he was taunted by his immediate opponent, a defender noted for his aggressive physical approach: "Think you're a great player, eh? Well, I could eat you." McInally's quick reply: "Well, that's the only way to get some fitba' intae you." It was claimed that when he was sent off for tripping a referee and the official uttered the dreaded sentence "To the pavilion!", McInally responded: "Ref, could you no' make it the Empire? Ah've been tae the Pavilion this week already." Anecdotes such as these, even if not literally true, do reveal the player's personality and the impact he made on the public. McInally had the magnetism that invited the creation and spreading of stories about him.

"An out-and-out Celt" . . . for a Celtic player his background was impeccable. A "Celtic-daft" lad, he played as a teenager with the juvenile Croy Celtic before moving to the junior St Anthony's and from there to Celtic. In his first season (1919-20) the eighteen-year-old McInally made a favourable impression, scoring 39 goals, and capped that feat by netting 43 the next year. He had the attributes of the goalscorer: a tall, slim youngster who could shoot with both feet, a fine turn of speed, and a lad who welcomed the attention and the limelight.

There was, of course, a fatal flaw in his temperament: for him football was simply a game to be enjoyed, and Celtic Park was

Tommy McInally in action during the 1927 Scottish Cup final.

often a theatre for entertainers like himself to perform for his friends whom he numbered in the thousands. He could never remain serious for long, despite the best efforts of his manager, the autocratic Maley, then at the height of his powers and authority. McInally tested the patience of Maley sorely, but surprisingly Maley tolerated his player's foibles. Maley, practical, severe and self-disciplined, saw in the immature youngster perhaps some of the qualities that he lacked himself: irreverence, a sense of fun and a happy-go-lucky approach. No matter what the reason, Maley adopted the attitude of the permissive father to the prodigal and was reluctant to be severe with him; and the other players accepted the fact that McInally was the favoured son. It was rumoured that once Maley, furious at a poor performance by the team, was storming at his players and turned on McInally to accuse him: "You, McInally . . . you were seen coming out of a public house at half past nine last night! Is that true? And McInally confessed: "That's right, Boss. I couldn't stay any longer; they were closing." Maley had great difficulty in hiding his laughter, and cut short the tongue-lashing to regain his composure. No other player would have risked answering this manager in such a flippant tone. Even after his retirement as a player, McInally, in much the same way that formerly troublesome students relate to strict schoolmasters whom they like, still kept in touch with his manager, and became a regular and welcome *habitué* of the Bank Restaurant; football men would throng there to enjoy the discussions about the sport and the cheerful patter of McInally. His favourite story at the expense of Maley was the manager's reaction to the club's record defeat sustained in a holiday mood immediately after winning the Scottish Cup in 1937. Inevitably some customer at the restaurant would ask Maley: "I suppose you don't remember the time Motherwell beat Celtic 8-0 in . . ." and Maley would interrupt, bristling at the recollection: "How can I ever forget, when there are b------s like you to remind me?"

A character and a goalscorer, a skilled player and an exciting one. McInally was the type of personality to attract the crowds during the Depression; they would not be going to see dull, defensive play and were attracted by the colour and antics of Tommy McInally. His capers could pall at times, when he overdid his clowning at the expense of the occasion. At Ibrox Park during the final of a five-a-side tournament McInally, finding that nobody wanted to challenge him for the ball, sat down on it and waited for several minutes amid a crowd reaction that must have become increasingly impatient; in the 1927 Scottish Cup final against an outclassed East Fife team he 'entertained' the 80,000 crowd by shooting for goal from outrageous distances and angles and laughed off the missing of 'certs'. However, like many practical jokers he did not relish being the butt of others and, when one such prank at Seamill against him succeeded, he sulked for days and eventually was suspended by the club for missing the training sessions, thus being left out of the side for an important cup-tie at Motherwell.

Twice he was transferred from Celtic: in 1922 to Third Lanark and again in 1928 to Sunderland. In 1922 he could not agree to the terms offered by the club and was allowed to depart, but three years later, when Gallacher was showing signs of wear and tear, he returned to act as a field general. Maley had kept himself informed of the player's mood and described it: "He was pining for Celtic Park although he did not show this." Newspaper reports had linked McInally with an approach from Rangers, a surprising development considering the religious hard-line being adopted under Struth; at the time, however, Rangers' record in the Scottish Cup had become a laughing matter and they were becoming desperate to remedy the situation. Shortly after this development Celtic moved quickly to sign him again.

Upon his return he assumed the mantle of Patsy Gallacher, switching from scorer to goalmaker and he became an excellent playmaker, the sort of player described as characteristic of Scottish football: "To him flair was all: the shrug of the shoulders, the flick of the hip, the dummy, the careful precision pass, the body swerve; usually an inside-forward, although not always so, he was a specialist in altruism. His job was to make goals, not to score them, to hold the ball for the fraction of a second needed for his younger and more virile colleagues to take up position, then slide the ball to the man most likely to be able to shoot without distraction." (*Great Masters of Scottish Football*: Hugh Taylor, 1967.) It is interesting to speculate as to why such an artistic bent should flourish in a generally drab background of tenement backcourts or cobbled streets of mining villages in Scotland; similarly depressed backgrounds in England did not produce such a flowering. Perhaps it is the deep respect that Scots hold for sheer craftsmanship, but more likely it is a symbol of the greater scope the Scottish game has always provided for its artists, allied to a Scottish love of virtuosity and spectacle (an attitude that goes far to explain the reverence for the Wembley Wizards of 1928, the appreciation for the superb Real Madrid side at Hampden in 1960, and the pride in the 'Lisbon Lions' in 1967).

McInally was capable of being a masterly inside-forward; he had the football intelligence to plot moves out far ahead of his opponents, the control to fool defenders by stopping suddenly to open up new possibilities, and always the threat of his scoring power posed problems for any defence. A rare and original talent, he could have been a better player had he concentrated and taken the game more seriously. Perhaps it was his capacity for mischief that led many followers of the game to disregard his warnings about the prowess of the South Americans. In the 1920s he had gone on tour in that continent with Third Lanark and had observed at first hand their burgeoning skills, and in a newspaper article published prior to the 1954 World Cup he warned the insular Scots against false confidence; in that tournament Scotland, whose defenders "stood around like Highland cattle", were humiliated 7-0 by Uruguay.

Precociously talented, intelligent in football tactics, Tommy McInally often squandered his gifts for the popularity of the comedian and he has to be considered as a man who never realised his full potential . . . but Scottish football would have been grimmer without him, and surely he filled a more urgent human need for laughter and entertainment in those hard times.

PETER WILSON

IT has usually been Celtic's policy to raise their own players, finding them among the juvenile and junior teams and rearing them to full maturity; and very often it became a Celtic tradition to throw them in early at the deep end. Perhaps no cameo illustrates this recurring *motif* better than Peter Wilson's debut; a man many consider to be the best right-half in the club's history, and for a club with players of the calibre of 'Sunny Jim' Young, Bobby Evans, Pat Crerand and Bobby Murdoch filling that position through the years no higher praise could be offered.

Wilson, a native of Beith in Ayrshire, had been playing for his village amateur team when he was approached by a Celtic scout to sign a registration form; he played in a friendly against Third Lanark on 9 February, 1924, and was instructed to turn up at the Bank Restaurant for the following match. Wilson, a teenager and still wearing short knickerbocker trousers, arrived at St Enoch's railway station and like any country lad asked the nearest policeman the way to the restaurant; the policeman, perhaps realising that the boy might get lost, walked him over to the 'howff', one of the most famous meeting places for football men in Scotland. Maley met him outside and invited him in for a light lunch where he was brusquely introduced to the Celtic team, players that he recognised only from pictures in the newspapers. After lunch the players made their way to a waiting bus and the party, including the quiet Wilson, took off for the match. In Wilson's own words: "I didn't know where I was going; I was too shy to ask. The bus stopped at the football ground. While the rest of the players went into the dressing-room, I hung about the corridors. There I met a middle-aged man. 'Where am I?' I queried; he looked at me in a strange way, concluded I wasn't trying to pull his leg and answered, 'Fir Park'. I was in Motherwell. Mr Maley reappeared. You're playing right-half, sonny, he intimated. 'Motherwell have an outside-left called Ferrier; he has a good left foot — possibly you've heard of him?'"

And that was Peter Wilson's introduction to senior football, to mark the most feared outside-left in the Scottish game!

He turned out such a success that perhaps the club tempted fate too often in later years by introducing untried youngsters in much the same way; for one debut as satisfactory as Bobby Collins' in 1949 the fans can recall several that did not work out at all.

374

Peter Wilson jousts with Alan Morton of Rangers during the 1925 Scottish Cup semi-final at Hampden.

It would be unkind to categorise Wilson as 'a country bumpkin', but an element of truth exists in the description. He came from a small village in Ayrshire and had never been in Glasgow until he played for Celtic; his mother could not believe that anybody would pay her son £20 as a bonus to sign to play football and she put the money in a vase on the mantlepiece to await a claimant. In the 1920s, with the economical realities of Scotland as a harsh backdrop, life was more pedestrian and few working-class people moved about with the freedom enjoyed today. Stories abound of his fascination with the large department stores such as Woolworth's where he would spend hours, if not money, looking at the displays and watching the shoppers, and his friends complained of his getting lost. His unfamiliarity with city life and Glasgow was not uncommon. Jimmy Delaney, who joined Celtic in 1934 and who came from nearby Cleland in Lanarkshire, admitted that he had never been to Celtic Park before he played there. Jimmy McGrory indicated the 'innocence' of John Thomson when confronted with life outside his native mining village by recalling the goalkeeper's bewilderment at his colleagues' enthusiasm for a trip to Dublin to play Bohemians in a friendly in 1928. Thomson knew where Ireland was, but apparently was under the impression that it lay beyond the pale of civilisation, as he asked McGrory: "What kind of place is Dublin? Has it got houses like here?"

Like the other country lads above, however, Wilson was a true sophisticate on the field. In common with every great player, everything he did seemed exactly appropriate, his exquisite control creating time for himself. On dry, bumpy fields, on wet, heavy pitches he was a master, a quiet man who came to life with a ball at his feet. Never showy, nevertheless his feel for the game lent him grace and artistry, proving the validity of the saying, "True art lies in concealing the effort behind it". One journalist described the player of the 1920s admirably: "Our fondness for the suavity and grace of the men of arts and parts — which contrasted so bizarrely with their embarrassingly cumbersome equipment of iron-toed boots, laces that would have tied a liner securely to dock, long-john pants, shinguards that turned legs into supports for a billiards table and jerseys as old-fashioned as grannie's bathing costume — may be laughed to scorn by the 'mod' athletes of today in footwear as supple as an Indian's hunting moccasin and a strip as superbly designed for the job as the holster for a Colt revolver." (*Great Masters of Scottish Football*: Hugh Taylor, 1967.) Wilson was the finest passer of the ball in his day and his colleagues claimed that he stroked the ball towards them. For such a smooth, apparently effortless, player he had an explosive quality, often joining in attack to unleash a venomous shot. Comparisons are inevitable, if ultimately inconclusive, but he embodied the virtues of other noted Celtic right-halves: the build, smoothness and control of Willie Fernie, the passing of Pat Crerand, and the shooting of Bobby Murdoch.

He was not without his faults, the supporters often criticising him for his weakness in tackling and a reluctance 'to get stuck in'. An attacking wing-half, he used to recount the time he ran afoul of Patsy Gallacher, never slow to tell off his colleagues when he felt the situation demanded it. Still a teenager, Wilson moved upfield and, when he was unable to find a player open, carried on to beat a couple of opponents before crashing home a spectacular shot; jubilant, he turned to Patsy for congratulations but Gallacher shocked the youngster by snarling, "Get back to your kennel and make sure you stay there! It's us yins up front that dae the scorin'." Even from deep defence he could be constructive and the goal credited with starting 'the Hampden Roar' in the 1933 international against England illustrates this: with England pressing Wilson intercepted a pass on the edge of his own penalty area but, instead of clearing it wildly, he slipped a neat pass to Marshall (Rangers) who found McPhail and the inside-forward released McGrory for the famous goal.

He played eleven years for Celtic, earning a league championship badge in 1926, and four Scottish Cup medals in 1925, 1927, 1931 and 1933; he made four appearances for the Scottish League and gained another four full 'caps' against Northern Ireland (1926 and 1931), France (1930) and England (1933).

When he was a veteran he was transferred to Hibernian after a dispute about re-signing terms. Wilson observed the negotiations with Maley mildly: "The Boss expects you to play like a genius on Saturdays, and to think like a half-wit on pay-days."

The pictures show an old-fashioned look: his Celtic jersey without the collar, a serious expression on his face, arms folded in the conventional, awkward manner, hair wetted down and combed back . . . an anonymous, quiet player of the Depression years but, for Celtic supporters of an older generation, Peter Wilson of Beith.

JIMMY McGRORY

AS I waited in a classroom in Ottawa for the next parent to come in to discuss his son's progress,[1] I was looking forward to the interview, because the boy was doing well; his father, an Inspector in the Royal Canadian Mounted Police, was born in Glasgow but had lived in Canada for forty years. He turned up right on time, shook hands and we finished the discussion about the report-card in less than a minute. He paused to reach into his pocket and draw out a newspaper clipping and said: "My brother sent me this from Glasgow the other day." It was from the sports pages of the *Daily Record*, dated 21 October, 1982, and reviewed the career of Jimmy McGrory who had died the day before at the age of 78. We spent the remaining time of the interview talking about Celtic's best-loved player, not from what we had seen personally but from what our fathers had told us about him.

For many followers he was the greatest Celt of all, and not just for the goals he scored; his inspirational value was such that no game could be considered lost while McGrory was on the field foraging tirelessly, and chasing every ball with determination and enthusiasm. Successive Scottish Cup ties in 1933-34 illustrated his spirit. At Ayr "he did the work of a dozen men, leading the forwards in their onslaughts, helping the defenders when hard-pressed, and generally keeping the entire team at concert pitch" (*Glasgow Observer*: 10 February, 1934) and at Parkhead in the next round against Falkirk he roused the crowd with a spectacular goal: "McGrory charged after the ball with a fire, and zeal, and enthusiasm that made Hamill look a statue; the despair of Thomson as he left his goal to try and narrow the angle, and McGrory's shot, like a cannon ball tearing into the net, had all to be seen to be believed." (*Glasgow Observer*: 24 February, 1934.)

He was brought up in Garngad, a rough district in Glasgow, and, like most footballers, came from a poor family; there were four sisters and three brothers to be cared for and his mother died when he was 12. After a year in Boys' Guild football he joined the newly formed St Roch's Juniors where he described his £2 weekly wage as "a godsend to our family". He was so modest and genuinely amazed that Celtic would sign him that he could not bring himself to tell his family about it for three weeks. His first press clipping described him "as plucky as the usual Garngad product", but he was more than that; he had all the toughness and

378

McGrory sweeps the ball past Dawson for Celtic's first goal against Rangers at Ibrox, September 1933.

resilience required, but he had none of the coarseness so often assumed in such an environment.

Signed after the Junior Charity Cup final at Cathkin in June 1922, McGrory made his debut for Celtic on the same ground seven months later at inside-right in place of the injured Gallacher. For 1923-24 he was loaned to Clydebank to gain more experience, though the youngster believed it was a gentle hint that Celtic were thinking of getting rid of him. Clydebank, recently promoted and managed by a former Celt in Jimmy Hay, were virtually a Celtic nursery and McGrory did well, finishing the team's leading scorer with 13 goals from outside left, almost a third of Clydebank's league total — a feat which prompted the club's chairman to tell pressmen "I hope Celtic forget all about this laddie". The most significant goal, however, came at Parkhead and helped Clydebank to a shock 2-1 win, but could not save them from relegation. He was recalled to Celtic Park at the end of the season to replace Joe Cassidy at centre, but he failed to score in his first three matches of the 1924-25 season. His scoring touch returned under unusual circumstances; his father was buried on a Saturday morning, and McGrory reported to Willie Maley, expecting to be listed as the travelling reserve, but the manager took him aside twenty minutes before the start to say: "Look, I want you to play today; for ninety minutes, anyway, you'll get a chance to forget your bereavement." McGrory played that day against Falkirk, scored once and then a month later netted successive hat-tricks; the greatest scorer in the history of British football was on his way.

For most of his career McGrory played under the shadow of financial insecurity; typically he had assumed on his father's death a large share of the responsibility for the family. It was a miserable time for ordinary people: layoffs, low wages, the General Strike, and the chronic unemployment. His popularity was such that nobody grudged him his chance to make some money: "He did more than score goals; he converted countless numbers of supporters to the belief that football was all there was worth living for — and in the '30s that might not have been an unhealthy supposition." (Archie MacPherson's tribute on BBC TV: 20 October, 1982.) Despite his record and reputation McGrory never felt secure, and was always relieved when he was retained for another season; throughout his career he was underpaid, but he was always ready to lend a helping hand to anybody down on his luck.

He scored so many goals with headers, about a third of his tally at least, that it tended to overshadow his footwork, causing him to be dubbed 'The Mermaid' in his early years at Parkhead. One journalist (Hugh Taylor) described his speciality: ". . . the most tingling sensation I have experienced in a lifetime of watching the beloved game was seeing McGrory leap high, hover hawk-like, then twist that powerful neck, and flick the ball as fiercely as most players could kick it." His incredible ability to hang in the air till the cross reached him defied nature and at times he seemed to have repealed the law of gravity completely. Celtic's general, Patsy Gallacher, recognising the value of such a gift, instructed a new winger how to utilize it: "Son, you are only in this team because you can run fast and cross a ball; all you have to do is aim at that head (pointing to McGrory) and he'll do the rest. Now, one more thing — he likes the ball with the lace away from his head; so, away and practise that." And to back McGrory's claim as the greatest scorer of them all, it should be remembered that all those goals, 550 of them in first-class football, were scored with the traditional leather ball that soaked up the rain and the mud, becoming heavier as the game went on.

He claimed with characteristic modesty: "I was often in the right place at the right time. Goalscoring is in the mind, and I used to go looking for goals." And the goals came: five against each of Aberdeen, Dundee United and Clyde in 1926-27; eight against Dunfermline Athletic in 1928; nine hat-tricks in 1935-36, including three goals in three minutes against Motherwell . . . in a career described as "a goal a game for fifteen years." "In the right place at the right time . . ." — his positional sense was undervalued, probably because of his heading skill, but he was dangerous anywhere within the penalty area. He had all the centre-forward's gifts but perhaps his greatest was physical courage. Broad-shouldered, though not tall, he was fearless and threw himself at crosses that others would have considered out of reach. Jack Harkness, Scotland's keeper and a friend, saved him from serious injury once when he pushed the diving McGrory round his post to avoid a collision; the Celtic supporters howled for a penalty and booed the Hearts' keeper for the rest of the game, but McGrory made a point of letting the fans know that he was appreciative of the goalkeeper's action. Next season the same supporters gave Harkness a prolonged ovation when he took up his position, a gesture that the Hearts' man, later a respected journalist with the *Sunday Post*, recalled for many years.

He was Celtic's inspiration and led forward lines that contained some of the most brilliant, and unpredictable, inside men in Britain: Patsy Gallacher, Tommy McInally, Willie Buchan and Peter Scarff. When so many other players were dissatisfied with their wages or were restless in the late '20s and early '30s, McGrory wanted only to play for Celtic and fought strenuously against a shameful and ill-advised attempt to transfer him to Arsenal for a record fee. If you look through the scrapbooks or newspapers of the time, it is easy to spot McGrory — the player with the broad grin, happy to be playing football in a grim world and even getting paid for it. When the 'McGrory Club', reputed to be the first fan club named after a Celtic player, was formed around 1930 in Mossend, Lanarkshire, the members wore a lapel badge with "a white background and one green bar with the head and shoulders of the famous Celt, smiling as usual".

Many fans, not all of them Celtic supporters, felt that he deserved more than the meagre seven caps that he was given for Scotland, and in the hyperbole of football talk it was considered tragic that he played at the same time as Hughie Gallacher, whom the selectors generally preferred. In the broad sense McGrory was the much more fortunate. Gallacher, beset by personal and financial woes, committed suicide the day before he was due to appear in court to answer an assault charge laid by his daughter; McGrory to his last days remained 'the finest gentleman in the game'.

He scored six goals for Scotland in those seven games, and one of them is credited with starting 'the Hampden Roar' when he scored the winning goal against England in 1933. Bob McPhail of Rangers beat two men and cut into the centre, while McGrory took up position on the left to receive a perfect pass; McGrory rounded the English full-back and fired a fierce shot past Harry Hibbs. The crowd of 134,170 went wild with delight, and the Roar was born. The same Bob McPhail, himself Rangers' all-time highest scorer, visited him in hospital and said at the news of his death: "I like to think I was a good friend, and I am privileged to say so; I had a tremendous regard for him and found him a great man to have on my side."

He embodied the sport's finest philosophy, the game played vigorously, skilfully and competitively, but above all in the best traditions of sportsmanship. He did not have an enemy in the game nor in the world; his colleagues loved him and his rivals greeted him with affection and respect. This most modest of men was a figure from the far-off days when hard, simple and honest men played the game; his talents and heroic character become the raw material for legend transcending the decades and oceans; and thus two men who never saw him play could sit and talk in a distant classroom about a man who was truly great.

Notes
1 Tom Campbell, one of the co-authors, writes here of this experience.

JIMMY DELANEY

IN the early 50s Aberdeen sides were popular visitors to Celtic Park, but an added air of excitement pervaded the terracings on 13 January, 1951, before the teams took the field. Press photographers jostled for position on the track as the minutes ticked away, and when Aberdeen did appear they were greeted with delighted cheers because leading them out, as captain for the day, was Jimmy Delaney, trim and athletic as ever and reassuringly familiar even in a red jersey. The cheers continued for several minutes from all parts of the packed ground, to be renewed when he trotted up for the toss of the coin; as he made his way over to the right wing, the fans in the 'Jungle' roared their welcome, and later in the first half when he was tackled heavily from behind by Alec Rollo they growled in disapproval. Halfway through the second half, with the match poised at 2-2 before an absorbed crowd of 50,000, he slipped quietly into the middle to collect a pass from George Hamilton and net Aberdeen's third goal in their 4-3 win; after a momentary hesitation the fans cheered again and later, at the whistle, applauded him from the field. Perhaps no other player could have evoked such affection, or more accurately the love, that the Celtic supporters have always felt for Jimmy Delaney.

Although he came from Cleland in Lanarkshire, he played his junior football in the East of Scotland with Stoneyburn Juniors and Hibs made him the offer of a trial game. Celtic became interested at the same time and fortunately the date chosen for a similar trial was a week earlier. He turned up at Parkhead, the first time he had visited the ground, and after giving an impressive display was signed on for a bonus of £20. A year later, in 1935-36, as a first-team player his wages were between £3 and £4 a week, and he was thankful: "[the wages] put us higher than the working man, but there weren't very many men working at the time. Many of us had to keep the whole family going; there might be seven or eight in the family and none of them would be working. We simply couldn't save, everything had to go for the upkeep of the family." In Scotland between the Wars there was little respite from economic woes and the early 30s was the worst time.[1] Those young men, idolized by thousands for their athletic skills and clad in the bright jerseys of famous clubs, playing the national sport and apparently enjoying themselves, were often the only breadwinners in large and extended families. It was a precarious and often short

Jimmy Delaney as seen by the Glasgow Observer *cartoonist, 16 May, 1936.*

career, many players fearing the power of the manager, the man who could make the recommendations to his directors about dropping or transferring them. Although Delaney generally considered Willie Maley a benevolent father-figure, he recalled that after he scored a hat-trick against Rangers in the 1936 Charity Cup final in a 4-2 win he was met by Maley in the tunnel, congratulated briefly, and warned: "Don't let that go to your head." His long-time partner in a famous Celtic right wing, Malcolm MacDonald, was also advised: "You do what I tell you, Malcolm, or you won't be here very long."

Delaney was an old-fashioned winger, a member of an endangered species in today's often stereotyped game, and he was an exciting player. Blessed with a great burst of speed, unusually allied to excellent control, he was always dangerous on the break. He was a restless, courageous player and challenged for every ball, never giving defenders a moment's relief; in the most crowded of penalty areas he could find dangerous positions and occupy them to pose a constant threat to goalkeepers' peace of mind. The Celtic supporters loved him, recognising immediately a great heart. He epitomised 'the Celtic spirit'. fighting till the final whistle and never prepapred to admit defeat. He has an interesting view about problems with crowd behaviour: "In our day the crowds looked for thrills on the park; it kept them from fighting each other because there was so much excitement. Both teams went for goals and, honestly, how often do you see that today?"

With Delaney as a leader in the club's revival Celtic regained consistency in the late 30s, winning the championship in 1936 and 1938, and the Scottish Cup in 1937, and in the opinion of many topped those accomplishments by gaining the Empire Exhibition Trophy in 1938 when they beat the best teams in Britain in what could be termed an unofficial British championship. It took a replay to get by Sunderland by 3-1 after Delaney was injured in the first game; it was a struggle to scrape past Hearts 1-0 without Delaney; and with Delaney back on the wing for the final against Everton Celtic won 1-0 through Crum's goal in extra time.

Older fans still claim that Celtic side was the best the club ever fielded, and recall the glory of the forward line: Delaney, MacDonald, Crum, Divers and Murphy. All of them were brilliant individually and capable of winning any match on their own, but they combined beautifully, with quick passing and rapid interchanging bewildering defences; their understanding was so complete that it seemed they found each other by telepathy.

This was a team approaching its best, but it was fated to be broken up by the outbreak of World War II.

For Jimmy Delaney, however, it was a break of a different sort that affected his career. Playing at Celtic Park against Arbroath on 1 April, 1939, he was nudged by a defender and landed awkwardly on his arm. He suffered a horrendous fracture. "It was like a jigsaw puzzle to fit together the pieces," the surgeon was reported to have said, and he later confided that had his patient not been a professional footballer he would have considered amputation. In the months that followed there was more than one operation, including a bone-graft, and fears were expressed that he would never play again. It was more than two years before he returned to duty, in August, 1941; that day he played for Celtic's five-a-side team that won the event at Rangers' Sports and after a taxi-ride across the city turned out at Celtic's public trial match to a rapturous welcome.

Delaney was one of those players unfortunate to have their careers interrupted at their peak by the larger tragedy of World War II. Apart from the honours won with Celtic, he had established himself in Scotland's international team, gaining nine pre-war 'caps' at a time when the national side rarely played more than four games a season. His fractured arm changed that. When he was restored to Celtic's side he regained match fitness quickly and was soon considered the most dangerous winger in the country, but the selectors ignored him for two whole seasons of war-time internationals. Some Celtic supporters claimed bias was the reason, but this does not appear to be the case; the SFA was worried about his arm, and feared liability for further injury sustained in any match played under its auspices. The fans in Scotland, however, were smarting under frequent humiliations from a powerful English squad and kept demanding his selection. One Glasgow business man even volunteered to pay for the private insurance-policy at Lloyds to cover the risk. With his fitness being proved for Celtic every week he was eventually chosen for three internationals around the end of the war, including the famous Victory International against England at Hampden Park in April, 1946, when his dash and enthusiasm at centre-forward inspired an injury-weakened Scottish side and sorely troubled the English defence, disconcerting the normally unflappable Frank Swift in goal, and in the last minute he nipped in to score the only goal of the game, a goal that sent 134,000 Scots home delirious with joy.

During those war years Delaney was often the one Celtic

forward of real class, appearing frequently at centre-forward to solve that chronic problem. At one Southern League match at Coatbridge against humble Albion Rovers, after Delaney was injured and taken off, Celtic barely survived despite enjoying a three-goal lead — a clear indication of his influence; the game on 14 November, 1942, which ended in a 4-4 draw, was also noted for the debut of Albion Rovers' trialist centre-half, young Jock Stein from Blantyre Victoria, listed in the newspapers as 'Junior'.

When he scored that memorable goal against England, sadly he was no longer a Celt having been transferred a couple of months previously to Manchester United. Matt Busby often claimed that Delaney, his first signing, was his most important buy. Delaney had always been an inspirational player, capable of lifting the spirits of men around him, and was a bargain at £4,000; and in 1948 Manchester United, having staged a miraculous recovery under Busby's leadership from the ravages of the war, won the FA cup in a memorable final by 4-2 over Blackpool and Stanley Matthews. Delaney was to play almost five years for United, before returning to Scotland with Aberdeen for a fee of £3,000. Before retiring in 1956 he played for several other clubs. A short stay with Falkirk was followed with a move to Derry City for an Irish League record fee of £1,500 and a stint with Cork Athletic in the Republic as player-manager before finishing with Elgin City in the Highland League. He played wholeheartedly for each of his clubs, and had the rare distinction of winning cup medals in four countries: winners' medals with Celtic in 1937, Manchester United in 1948, Derry City in 1954 and a runners-up with Cork Athletic in 1956.

However, he would wish to be remembered as Jimmy Delaney of Celtic. In an interview for *The Celtic View* published in 1984 he recalled Tom Maley's funeral in 1935 at which somebody placed a Celtic jersey on the coffin as it was lowered into the ground: "I hope they do that for me."

Notes

1 In an interview with Bob Crampsey, Delaney stated that he had left school at 14 and worked a short time in the pits. However, he had been idle "a good while" when Celtic signed him in 1934. His wages as a provisional signing were £2 per week (*The Scottish footballer*: Bob Crampsey, 1978). It is worth noting that in 1935, when Delaney was earning around £4 as a fully signed player, the dole payment for a man was 17/– (85p) per week, plus 9/– (45p) for each adult dependant and 2/–(10p) for each dependent child.

WILLIE MILLER

IN 1963 Bob Crampsey wrote an article about keepers and gave an honourable mention to Willie Miller: "The greatest display of goalkeeping I've ever seen? . . . the greatest, and certainly the most courageous, was in 1947 . . . the occasion was the Scottish League-English League match at Hampden when England had their great team. The Scottish side was very weak, and it was confidently expected that we would be thrashed; that we weren't was due entirely to Willie Miller. Time and time again the white shirts sliced through the Scots' defence; time and time again Miller hurled himself at their feet with reckless gallantry. Eventually and inevitably he went down and didn't get up; he was taken off, had stitches put in his forehead, and returned — not to go on the wing, but back into goal where his first act was to dive headlong at the feet of Westcott of Wolves the English centre who was clean through. We lost 3-1, but the Hampden stand knew enough about courage to rise to the bandaged Miller at the end as he came wearily off."

Everybody who saw him play had to comment on his courage, most spectacularly demonstrated in dives at opponents' feet in brave attempts to save his goal. Celtic supporters held their breath often as their keeper lay still, dazed with the collision; clearly it was instinctive, physical courage of a high order, but it was much more than that. When Miller joined Celtic in May, 1942, from Maryhill Harp, less than eleven years had passed since another Celtic goalkeeper had died as a direct result of similar bravery; inside the foyer at Celtic Park, and only a few feet away from the home dressing-room, stands a memorial to John Thomson, dead at 23 years of age due to 'a depressed fracture of the skull' in saving a goal at Ibrox. Each day at training and on match days, as he headed to the pitch, Miller passed that memorial. The thought that he too might be injured some day must have flashed across his mind or may have been forced into his subconscious, but no keeper was more brave so often, or risked injury so much, as Willie Miller.

His early years at Parkhead seem to have been shaped by a slightly ambiguous Chinese saying: "May you live in exciting times." Arriving in 1942 as a teenager, he was fated to be a gallant fighter in a losing cause. Celtic's dazzling team that won the Empire Exhibition Trophy in 1938 had been broken up by the war,

A typically graceful dive by Willie Miller at Ibrox, 1949 (even if in vain).

and the club often fielded makeshift sides that revealed little skill and enthusiasm, as the directors made the strange decision to do without the services of guest players. Less famous clubs entertained their supporters with guest appearances by celebrated players who were stationed in the vicinity, but Celtic stubbornly included players from the previous year's Boys' Guild league. For Miller it was a mixed blessing. Although still a youngster, he won a place in one of the country's most famous teams, but at a period when its playing standards were at their lowest and when other sides were keen to exact retribution for years of Celtic's supremacy and fame. As an apprentice learning the most difficult position of all under war-time conditions, he had to do it without regular practice and coaching from more experienced players — and he played as the last line of defence in a club traditionally dedicated to attack.

Miller made his debut on 22 August, 1942, in a Southern League match at Parkhead against Hamilton Academicals; he had no chance with the two shots that beat him in the 2-2 draw and impressed with his clean and confident handling. Two weeks later he gave a memorable performance in a Glasgow Cup tie against Rangers at Ibrox which Celtic lost 2-1 after extra-time. The *Sunday Post* reporter described him as "daring and magnificent" and one incident summed up his play. Thornton teed up the ball for Alec Venters, a short and stocky inside-forward with the hardest shot in the game. Only twelve yards out and with the goal at his mercy, Venters took his time, putting all his weight behind it, but Miller clutched the ball and went down completely knocked out but still holding on to the ball.

It was scarcely surprising that he soon earned the epithet 'Celtic's busiest keeper', and he thrived on the situation with a series of splendid displays. Lithe and graceful, he cut a handsome figure, dealing stylishly with any type of shot on the ground or in the air; he was particularly effective in coping with the cross-ball, normally a source of anxiety for keepers. His handling was immaculate, his anticipation remarkable, and his bravery beyond dispute. The supporters recognised his talents instantly; at times he appeared to be the only player of genuine Celtic class on the field. By the end of the war he was being acclaimed as the best keeper in the country and a splendid performance in the semi-final of the Victory Cup against Rangers endorsed this view in the public's mind. The selectors were to recognise his ability with seven appearances for the Scottish League and six 'caps' for Scotland but it was not a vintage time for Scottish football and Miller's six appearances for the national team contained only one victory (over Luxembourg), although there was a commendable 1-1 draw with England in 1947 at Wembley.

After Charlie Tully signed for Celtic in 1948 Celtic's form and fortunes began to improve but, ironically, Miller's own standards began to decline. The man who had saved his team from humiliation so often was starting to reveal signs of inconsistency and his colleagues seemed aware of it. In a league game at Coatbridge against Albion Rovers he clearly misjudged a free kick hoisted into the penalty area from the centre line; at Easter Road he tried a short goal kick to Mallan only for Gordon Smith to dispossess the defender and shoot into an empty net; and at Ibrox there was a bizarre goal when Boden, preparing to pass back to the advancing Miller, suddenly turned and attempted to clear but a Rangers' forward blocked his clearance and the ball rose in a curving arc over Miller's head as the keeper, stranded near the penalty spot, made frantic efforts to regain his line.

At the time these isolated instances were dismissed as bad luck, but in retrospect it is clear that the goalkeeper had already started the inevitable decline that all athletes are heir to: the subtle deterioration in hair-trigger reflexes, the momentary lapses in absolute concentration, the subsequent twinges of doubt eroding self-confidence. Keepers are the most vulnerable of players; the tiniest error in judgement, the slightest hesitation is obvious to everybody in the stadium and, unlike the mistakes made by outfield players, the end result is often fatal. For a time the erosion of instinctive reactions can be hidden by technique or experience, but sooner or later it becomes apparent.

Miller had been an impeccable stylist, preferring to clutch cleanly even the hardest shot, and thus the slightest shading-off was obvious; contemporary goalkeepers like Ronnie Simpson were happy to scramble at times, but not Miller. He lost his place to Bonnar in 1949, and with that keeper consistent for the next season or two, Miller was quietly transferred to Clyde in 1950. He had played so regularly for Celtic since 1942 that it was surprising to realise that he was still only 26 at the time of his transfer.

What accounted for his decline at such a relatively young age? Perhaps the years of 'battle-fatigue' and injuries had taken their toll; perhaps the years of playing in miserable Celtic sides and weak Scottish teams had dulled his enthusiasm; perhaps finally it was a matter of confidence. Goalkeepers have to be supremely confident, even arrogantly so at times, and as Miller's youth slipped past so did "the first fine careless rapture" and nothing could compensate for the subtle loss.

He was an unlucky keeper; unfortunate that his best years were during the war, and that his best efforts were made in losing causes.

JOCK WEIR

AMONG the crowds milling around outside Ibrox an hour before the League international against England in March, 1949, a young boy hovered near a group of men chatting and laughing as they passed the time. He hesitated several times before plucking up enough nerve to approach the one person he recognised to ask for his autograph. Jock Weir ignored him for a while, but when the youngster persisted, he tried to end the exchange with the words: "No, you don't want my autograph, son; I'm no' a football player at all." Another fan, rushing past to join the queues at the turnstiles, paused just long enough to add his own observations: "Well, that's true, Jocky!"

However, on the Saturday of Celtic's last league game of 1947-48 Jock Weir had played himself into the club's folklore by scoring three goals at Dens Park against Dundee, goals that had won the relegation battle by 3-2. Signed in late February from Blackburn Rovers because Celtic desperately needed a scorer, he made his debut a few days later against Motherwell in the Scottish Cup before a crowd of 55,231, an indication of the loyalty of the support during that most depressing season.

Only a few weeks before his heroics at Dundee he had a wretched day in the cup semi-final against Morton at Ibrox as he struggled to elude their veteran centre-half, Millar; early in the extra time he was put through by McPhail but, faced only by Jimmy Cowan in Morton's net, he stubbed the ball weakly past the keeper's right-post to the groans of the great majority of 81,000 spectators.[1] The Greenock side recovered quickly from its one defensive lapse to score a late goal and qualify for a lucrative final with Rangers.

With Celtic's win at Dens Park ensuring Division A status, Weir became an overnight hero in the sport's tradition of hyperbole and a figure in Celtic's own mythology. The match at Dens Park was to assume epic proportions and it was to be regarded as a battle for survival. Later Celtic histories spoke of "shrieking headlines" in the newspapers and noted "the largely hostile crowd of 31,000" that packed the ground, eager to take ghoulish delight in "the funeral of a once great club"; sour comments were made about three 'goals' that the referee disallowed, and allegations that Dundee players were offered a special bonus to win the match surfaced some years later. The result was seen as a characteristic Celtic triumph over adversity, and some suggested that Weir's return from England and his move to outside-right for this particular game were inspired decisions.

For historians to whom facts are sacred, such myths have to be examined carefully and close scrutiny reveals often more about current attitudes than anything else. The events of 17 April, 1948, or more precisely the reports of the events, do merit such study and a reconstruction is called for. Celtic were threatened only remotely with relegation, and a loss at Dundee would still have required herculean efforts from Morton, Queen of the South and Airdrie to pass Celtic's total of points, Queen's Park being already doomed. A search through the sports pages of the more popular papers fails to find any great interest in the fixture, and it is not even mentioned in a recently published account of football in Dundee (*Across the Great Divide*: Jim Wilkie, 1984); the crowd of 31,000 that "packed" Dens Park was much smaller than the record 43,214 that watched Rangers play in the cup five years later, and must have included a considerable travelling support for Celtic. Few protests were made by the players on the field, nor were there outcries on the terracing at the disallowed goals, the general feeling being that the referee was correct in his decisions. The assertion that Dundee's players had been offered "the biggest bonus in the history of the club to beat Celtic" is an accusation impossible to prove. Of course, it was a relief to win and against the odds, but scarcely a matter for excessive jubilation. Weir had been purchased to score goals, and his switch to the right wing where he could utilise his speed was a routine change of position rather than an example of divine intervention. His three goals although valuable, were not memorable for their execution, all being scrambled home from a few yards out.

Still, Jock Weir filled a human need for heroic action that the times demanded. Stockily built and with a face reddened by exertion, he was a cheerful, exuberant character apparently untroubled by adversity; playing with enthusiasm and enjoyment he was a welcome contrast to his colleagues (one of the most plodding and colourless aggregations in Celtic's history). The supporters considered him a talisman, a good-luck charm, and identified with him instantly. He was a barometer of Celtic's fortunes. When he scored he rejoiced doubly and the fans celebrated with him; when he missed he would droop momentarily and the supporters slumped with him.

It was easy to understand this identification. For many among the support he was an *alter ego*, a projection of their unstated

Jock Weir (on left) welcomed to Celtic Park by Chic Geatons in February 1948.

desires. Out there on the pitch was the jaunty strut of Clydeside apprentices, the same immediate display of emotions close to the surface, a fellow who showed what he was thinking and feeling. While everybody recognised his obvious failings, nobody minded too much; the supporters tolerated his air of likeable incompetence and envied him the chance to wear the green-and-white and to retain a place in the team . . . and they always recalled that once his efforts had possibly saved the club from relegation. If enthusiasm and zest could do that for Jock Weir, it was just possible that other Glasgow dreams could come true; his mistakes were readily forgiven with the magnanimity that is usually reserved for one's own errors.

Only rarely could he outwit defenders cleanly; more often he would scramble past them, relying on a burst of speed to break clear. Signed as a scorer and playing for about four full seasons at Parkhead, he managed 45 goals, a respectable total. He was at best a stop-gap solution and, throughout his career with all his clubs, he was replaced when a more complete player came along. At Easter Road he had little chance of a regular place with centres like Johnny Cuthbertson and Alex Linwood available; at Parkhead he could not challenge a winger like Bobby Collins nor a centre like John McPhail. Thus, he was always a prospect for transfer and, like Barkis in the novel *David Copperfield*, was 'willin' ' to play for several clubs. He was transferred from Hibs to Blackburn Rovers for £10,000 as part of the exodus of Scottish players to England at the end of the war; only a year later he returned to Scotland when Celtic signed him for £7,000, a record fee for Celtic back in 1948; he moved on to Falkirk later for a modest sum, and played usefully at Brockville for a couple of seasons (and, in fact, scored one of Falkirk's goals against Celtic in the famous cup-tie when Tully netted his twice-taken corner kick in 1953).

Unlike many players who have to toil hard for years to gain the affection and respect of the fans, Jock Weir achieved fame in that one match in April, 1948; he deserves a place in the mythology of the club if not its history.

Notes
1 On the same day, at Hampden Park, Rangers and Hibernian played their semi-final before a crowd of 143,570, and the aggregate indicates Glasgow's enthusiasm for football in the immediate post-war period.

BOBBY EVANS

RED-HEADED, stockily built, and imbued with boundless energy, he personified the attacking wing-half urging on his forwards and eagerly joining in attack. He seemed totally committed to attack but he was rarely caught out, having an instinctive sense in knowing when to attack and when to defend. The risks that he took in moving upfield were finely calculated, a cautious abandon as it were; in the best sense of both words he was an 'amateur' in attack and a 'professional' in defence. He remained an enigma: his flaming red hair and energy suggested flamboyance but his tackling and industry indicated earnestness. He was a Roundhead masquerading as a Cavalier.

Evans should have been an automatic choice for Scotland, but for a time journalists pressed the claims of inferior, although adequate, right-halves such as McColl (Rangers), Scoular (Portsmouth), and Docherty (Preston); he was once incensed enough to write to the SFA asking that he not be considered for future honours. It was a hasty and unwise move on his part, and one that was fortunately ignored by the selectors eventually. Off the field he could be introspective, reacting too quickly to criticism that he felt unfair. There was some substance to his feeling of being badly treated as this excerpt from *The Scotsman* in 1960 indicates: ". . . a rash of vicious criticism of Bobby Evans breaks out just as the Scottish selectors prepare to pick a team. The general theme is that Evans, Celtic's centre half and Scotland's captain, must go. He is too old; he is slow on the turn; and never was a great player anyway. . . . It is amusing to remember that except when the selectors are about to gather Evans is wonderful." By then Evans had mellowed enough to tell that journalist, John Rafferty: "I don't mind now what is written. Unkind words just make me play harder."

Still, Evans always remained sensitive to criticism, even touchy. One spectator at a St. Mirren vs Celtic cup-tie in 1960 wrote to a Glasgow paper complaining that Evans was "unsporting" in halting a St. Mirren attack by deliberately handling the ball. That night the letter-writer, answering a knock on his door, faced Bobby Evans, earnestly prepared to defend his honour. Evans told him: "You have every right to your opinion about my fitness to play for Scotland, but I object to you calling me unsporting. Would you have preferred me to let Baker get the ball and then kick the feet from under him?" The conversation lasted for some

Bobby Evans beats Rangers' Johnny Hubbard to the ball, League Cup final 1957.

time, and when the discussion ended amicably one football fan knew about Evans' feelings regarding his reputation.

Another disagreement within Parkhead ended in a more violent manner, a physical scuffle between Evans and Tully. The two stars, one the heart and the other the intelligence of the team, had never been close, with Evans sensing that Tully's dedication and work-rate at times was less than total. Feelings reached the boiling point after Tully, in a newspaper article, had criticised a Scottish team's performance (and indirectly Evans') in a recent international. The two players taunted each other, and the situation soon degenerated into a fist-fight, halted only by the mass intervention of their team-mates; relations between them were strained, and matters did not look promising for Celtic, who were due to meet Rangers two days later in a League Cup final. Perhaps tension in the dressing-room is an appropriate preparation for a match, because Celtic beat Rangers 7-1 in that final.

Obviously capable of being riled and ultra-sensitive about criticism, Evans was trouble-free where it counted — on the field. In match after match he was never pulled up for fouling; his opponent would be tackled firmly but fairly, and on the rare occasion he rounded Evans he could count on not being pulled down from behind. In a long career with Celtic he was cautioned only twice, each time by J. A. Mowat, a strict referee, and one of those times was for resuming a protest to the referee on the way to the pavilion after the match. For a player as involved in each game as Evans, and as physically strong, his record was remarkable and a tribute to his sportsmanship; his forte was a highly developed sense of anticipation that enabled him to intercept passes and start counter-attacks.

Allied to his football gifts was an indomitable spirit that helped him play wholeheartedly every minute of every match regardless of the score; time after time he would rally his team and an early international appearance against Ireland in 1948 illustrated this quality. After a few minutes Scotland had fallen behind 2-0. The Hampden crowd, and some of the Scottish players, were stunned by developments, but Evans singlehandedly for a time turned the tide. He blunted further dangerous Irish raids and mastered his immediate opponent, the legendary Peter Doherty, and rallied the Scots with a stream of precision passes to his right wing of Waddell (Rangers) and Mason (Third Lanark). His performance, remarkable considering his youth and inexperience at this level of football, was the major factor in Scotland's 3-2 victory.

Perhaps the greatest tribute Celtic supporters paid him was their automatic assumption that he would perform impeccably game after game, season after season. In the poor Celtic teams immediately after the war he was clearly the best player; in better teams he was still the best; in the Coronation Cup against the best sides in Britain he was probably the most complete player on view and nobody did more to bring that trophy to Celtic Park. Cyril Horne of the *Glasgow Herald* praised his attitude as his greatest quality: "When he became a Celtic player there were few opportunities for a youngster to learn from his clubmates, struggling as they were, how to become a first-class player. Evans is, however, a first-class player and has been for several seasons and his wonderful spirit and willingness to subject self to team have made him so."

Evans started his career as an enthusiastic inside-left for St. Anthony's, but he was never completely comfortable as a forward although Celtic persisted in fielding him there for a couple of seasons. When injury dictated changes during a game he played well as a half-back, and he had one memorable afternoon at Hampden at right-half when, caked with mud, he covered every yard of the heavy pitch to thwart Queen's Park's bid to beat a ten-man Celtic. The first time he actually was selected to play at right-half was an important match for Celtic — the last league game of 1947-48 when Celtic travelled to Dens Park threatened with relegation; in that tension-packed game he gave hints of becoming a splendid wing-half, thriving in the midst of battle: "To see this fighting red-head storm into attacking action, drumming on relentlessly his colleagues in front, was like watching a tournament at an ancient court, with Evans the scarlet knight, the hero of the joust. He reminded me of a clan chief, a spectacular attacker who could rally faltering comrades with his clarion call." (*Great Masters of Scottish Football*: Hugh Taylor, 1967.) He improved rapidly at the start of the next season under the coaching of Jimmy Hogan and with the benefit of an extended run at right-half; within a few months he was capped for Scotland and established himself as a world-class player almost immediately. He gained 48 caps for Scotland in all, and deserved more. Later in his career he took over as centre-half for Celtic, but surprisingly he played as pivot for Scotland before he did for Celtic, in 1955 replacing an injured George Young against Austria in Vienna and the feared Hungarians in Budapest, and played magnificently. Although short for a centre-half at 5 feet 8 inches, his positional sense, concentration, and anticipation made him a difficult man to beat.

Despite being a wonderful servant to Celtic, Evans left Parkhead in 1960 under a cloud. Some had suggested moving him to full-back to introduce a promising newcomer in the person of Billy McNeill at centre-half, but Evans resented the proposal, with its veiled criticism of his play; off the field he was concerned about a business venture that was not proving as profitable as hoped and was causing only problems. Evans felt that the best solution might be a transfer to England, and he was allowed to go to Chelsea. However, he never settled in London and, after a short spell as player-manager of Newport County, moved back to Scotland where he played stoutly for Morton and as player-manager again for Third Lanark before ending his career with Raith Rovers at the age of forty. He will not be remembered for his days with other clubs, but as Bobby Evans of Celtic and Scotland and as one of the greatest half-backs in the game.

No Celtic player was more popular than Bobby Evans, and no player was more worthy of that popularity. He was an embodiment of Celtic's tradition: superb physical fitness, sound technical skills, and a wholehearted sporting attitude to his opponents and the game.

CHARLIE TULLY

THE news of his death at the early age of 47 in July, 1971, shocked the Celtic supporters, and it was a subdued crowd at Parkhead a few days later, on the opening day of the season, that watched Celtic face Dumbarton in the Drybrough Cup; although a youngster named Kenny Dalglish scored four goals in one of his early appearances, the talk later in the pubs was of Charlie Tully and his deeds.

Charlie Tully, the supreme individualist, was what the Americans like to label 'a clutch player'; in moments of crisis he was expected to rise to greatness and to produce under pressure. In this history he has been so chronicled, in flashes of genius that transformed games. Always intelligent, he was seldom consistent; his essence was an ability to upset defences by one way or another. In 1948 he arrived in Glasgow after an £8,000 transfer from Belfast Celtic, and his audacious dribbling caught the eye immediately; later, when age had slowed him down, his forte was astute distribution. At his best he could combine both gifts, but being supremely himself he invariably embroidered his performance with mannerisms.

His idiosyncracies were a direct result of his intelligence, because increasingly it became clear that they were calculated to madden, to tease, or to goad his immediate opponent into losing his composure and rush into reckless, precipitate action, and no forward in Scotland could better exploit that split second when a defender's annoyance overruled his judgement. How else could his questionable actions be explained? . . . the most blatant shove in the opening seconds of a match; the chesting of awkward balls with arms so close that he always gave the impression of handling; the obvious stealing of yards at throw-ins, and irritating delays in putting the ball into play; the practice of placing the ball for a corner kick the barest inch inside the arc; the disconcerting good manners in retrieving the ball and placing it for an opponent whom he had fouled seconds before; the infuriating chatter throughout the course of a match. Joe Mercer, Arsenal's captain and later manager of Manchester City, played against him in the Coronation Cup of 1953 and wrote: "Who could forget Charlie? Marking him was an education." When he realised the effect his streak of rebellion had on opponents, Tully elevated it into an art form; if gamesmanship is the art of winning questionably without actually cheating, Tully was its most successful practitioner and most ardent devotee.

Charlie Tully, an early 1950s portrait.

In the late 40s — the 'Age of Austerity' — Tully was the newspapers' delight on and off the field; he had colour and sparkle, with a sharp Irish wit softened by a disarming brogue. He did not look like an athlete: his hair was thinning even in his early twenties, there was the suspicion of a pot belly, and his rear-end jutted out; he was never fast, his top speed being described charitably as an ungainly gallop. The prevailing impression of Tully was of an air of mischief coupled with a cheeky grin, but it is easy to recall specifics: an awkward ball killed and under instant control, a scissor-kick along the ground to a colleague, a dummy or a swerve leaving an opponent so stranded that years later you still chuckled at the recollection. Nobody who was there could ever forget that display against Rangers in the League Cup of 1948 when he single-handedly ran the famous 'Iron Curtain' defence ragged with glorious dribbling and accurate passing: "Look at Charlie Tully. Rangers went in for strength, like granite. Charlie Tully had bowly legs and was bald and didn't look strong enough to beat carpets, yet he had more personality in his little finger than Rangers had in their whole team. Charlie would jink towards the Rangers' defence — you'd need guts to take on big Geordie Young and Willie Woodburn and Sammy Cox and Jock 'Tiger' Shaw — and when they came at him, ready to hammer him to the ground, he'd bamboozle them, pointing the way he pretended to pass the ball, sending them chasing in the wrong direction, or running on without the ball but still pretending to dribble so cleverly they'd follow him, trying to make a tackle." (*From Scenes Like These*: G. Williams, 1968.)

At least once the reality surpassed the legend. In the 1953 Scottish Cup Celtic were two goals down to Falkirk at Brockville shortly after half-time; Tully took a corner from the left, placing the ball a few inches outside the arc, and his swerving cross deceived the unsighted keeper to finish in the net. The referee, however, well aware of Tully's mannerism, spotted the lapse and ordered the kick retaken. The scene was a memorable one: Tully, hands on his hips, listening to the referee with feigned politeness, the spectators who had spilled on to the pitch being ushered back to the terracing, Tully now complaining that he had no room for a run at the ball, and finally handing it to the linesman in exasperation for him to place; at last the corner being taken . . . and unbelievably ending up in the net again untouched by any other player. At the time the feat was dismissed as a fluke by many, but a few months earlier, in October 1952, when playing for

Ireland against England in Belfast, Tully had completely deceived Merrick with another corner to help gain Ireland a surprising 2-2 draw; in fact, Tully, although not noted as a scorer, netted both goals for Ireland that day.

With the publicity and the attention came the controversy, and Tully was often petulant in his reactions to harsh tackling, but in the worst incident of all he was blameless. It happened at Ibrox in 1949 when Cox of Rangers, normally a left-half but switched to right-half for this match, and Tully chased a loose ball to the line; Cox turned and committed the most blatant foul by kicking over the ball and felling Tully inside the penalty area in full view of the packed Celtic end. When the referee waved play on, the immediate clamour for a penalty kick and punishment for Cox turned into an outraged anger; bottles were thrown, spectators sought the relative safety of the track, and several arrests were made.

The Celtic directors, confident in the merits of their case, asked the SFA to hold an inquiry into the causes of the disturbances, and on 8 September the Referee Committee reported that "they were satisfied that the rowdyism on the terracing was incited by the actions of two players — S. Cox (Rangers) and C. Tully (Celtic) — and an error on the part of the referee, R. B. Gebbie." Both players were reprimanded and the report of this was put on their records. It was an incredible outcome. The referee's error was clear, as he should have awarded a penalty and ordered Cox off; Cox's part was equally clear as he admitted candidly later, but it was difficult to see where Tully had committed any offence.

Celtic renewed their request for an inquiry, and when the secretary of the Players' Association asked for a transcript of the meeting he was informed curtly that one was not available. At the subsequent SFA Council meeting Bob Kelly moved that the report from the committee not be approved; in the discussion that followed the chairman of that committee stated that "Tully had simulated any slight injury he may have received" and pressed the Council to approve the report, and it did so by a vote of 25 to 5.

Worse was to follow for Tully. On 13 September Celtic met Rangers at Parkhead in the Glasgow Cup and it was a sporting, although keenly contested, match until two minutes from the end with the score 1-1. Rangers were awarded a free kick on the edge of the area that Celtic disputed fiercely, with reason; while the referee was handling the arguments the kick was taken behind his back, with no signal from him, for Rangers to score. To the utter disbelief of the crowd the goal was allowed to stand, and there was a considerable delay in restarting the game as the Celtic players, led by Tully, continued to discuss the situation among themselves and it was obvious that they were thinking about leaving the field as a protest. Later several players appeared before the Board to be questioned about the scenes, and Tully in particular was interrogated at length about the delay; the referee afterwards reported the Irishman to the Glasgow FA "for inciting his team to leave the field" and he was subsequently reprimanded by that organisation. Two weeks later the same teams met in the league at Ibrox in an unreal atmosphere, with Celtic having suggested that the game be postponed till later in the season and the Supporters' Association staging an effective boycott that left the Celtic end strangely deserted. Tully did not play because he had returned to Ireland for a short break "as his muscle strain needs rest, and his wife is ill", but rumours of a club suspension circulated widely. Defenders recognised quickly that the only way to stifle Tully was to mark him closely every moment; this close marking was part and parcel of the game and was accepted by Tully as such. Celtic Park resounded to the delighted cheers when his dazzling dribbling confused his shadow or murmured with appreciation at his clever passing. The vicious foul by Cox, however, was a new development and the unsympathetic attitude of officialdom complicated matters to a frustrating extent; Tully had been subjected to unduly harsh treatment on and off the field. Physically hurt, publicly criticised, and officially censured . . . and his offence lay in being fouled by another player. Tully became another instant martyr for many in Celtic's support, and was fated to remain a controversial figure for the rest of his career.

What is the last word about Charlie Tully? Appropriately enough it comes from show-business; every comedian wants to be taken seriously by playing the tragic role of Hamlet and perhaps Tully was, as always, the contrary — the prince of players who preferred at times to be the jester.

SIR ROBERT KELLY

HE was a man who took his pleasures seriously. For many years it was a familiar sight to see the tall, spare figure hunched in his seat in the Directors' Box and intent on every move on the field, his concentration inhibiting small-talk or conversation even during stoppages in play. One of the authors remembers sitting immediately behind him at the opening league game of 1970-71 and seeing Bobby Lennox settle the result with a glorious, brave header after a series of short, penetrating passes had split the Morton defence; the terracings and stand were buzzing for minutes afterwards, but Bob Kelly's only visible reaction was a momentary relaxing of the shoulders and an almost imperceptible nod of approval.

During his long tenure as Celtic's chairman, public opinion divided sharply on the value of his contribution to the club; throughout his rule he was ridiculed and praised, abused and revered, hated and, if not loved, respected. He was never popular, but before his death in 1971 the passing years, and latter success of the team under Stein, had blurred the edge of the criticism; his enemies had come to respect the integrity and consistency that sustained him, and his friends could admit his flaws and excuse them as the by-products of his enthusiasm.

The supporters recognised instinctively that he was the ultimate authority at Parkhead, and that very few decisions, no matter how small, were made without his prior knowledge and approval. Autocratic in manner and severe in appearance, he was a benevolent despot exercising strict control with the best interests of the club, as he saw them, at heart and, like most despots, imbued with a philosophy that was conservative and traditional.

Robert Kelly had an idealistic vision of the sport, a Corinthian approach inherited from his father whom he venerated. It was a simple outlook, uncluttered with artifice or sophistication: to play the game hard and fair, to respect but not fear opponents, to offer handshakes at the end regardless of the result. It was a philosophy that he never abandoned. In 1970 when the European Cup final between Celtic and Feyenoord was beset with problems, including transportation strikes, some discussion took place about the possibility of the game's being postponed or the venue switched, but Robert Kelly's response was characteristic: "We

A Celtic supporters club function in Bathgate, 1965, attended by Celtic officials. In the front row: Jimmy McGrory, Sean Fallon, Bob Kelly and Jock Stein.

have a field here and a ball; there's a referee and two teams waiting. We don't need anything else." It was a refreshingly old-fashioned approach to the occasion. He saw other issues in equally black-and-white tones and actions as right or wrong. Strong-willed and stubbornly honest, he courted unpopularity with a bluntness that verged on rudeness. Following a disappointing defeat at Budapest in the Cup-Winners' Cup in 1964 in a bruising match with MTK, he spoke at the official banquet: "If I have heard correctly, you claim that you learned the game from us early this century; let me assure you that no Celtic side I have ever seen has used such methods nor played in the manner you played tonight." (Celtic's officials suspected the referee of having been influenced by the hospitality of the host club.)

His black-and-white view of world politics helped to force the redrawing of the 1968-69 European Cup and the subsequent withdrawal of the Iron Curtain teams from the competition. Celtic were due to face the Hungarian team, Ferencvaros, and had almost completed the arrangements for the ties when troops from the Soviet Union and its Warsaw Pact allies invaded Czechoslovakia. The Celtic directors, at Kelly's bidding, sent a telegram to UEFA headquarters expressing revulsion at the military action and indicating concern that any team from Western Europe should be forced to play in countries behind the Iron Curtain. UEFA made the Solomon-like decision to redraw the first round to keep the East and West representatives apart until the political crisis had resolved itself; predictably, the teams from the Soviet Union, Bulgaria, East Germany, Hungary and Poland withdrew from the competition in protest. While Celtic's stand was controversial and a matter for debate, nobody doubted where Robert Kelly stood on the issue; he could not understand the pointed criticism that Celtic were willing to tour the United States while that country was involved in Vietnam.

He came from a football family, and the clubs, players, and the politics of the sport were discussed at the kitchen table late into the night. His father was James Kelly, a member of the famous Renton side of the 1880s and the stalwart around whom the original Celtic team was built; one brother played for Celtic and Motherwell as an amateur, and three others played for Queen's Park elevens. Bob Kelly himself played as a junior in Blantyre but gave up the game at the request of his father who was concerned about his son's arm disability and its unsettling effect upon opponents.

After his father's death he took his place on the Celtic Board in 1932, and following the death of Tom White in March 1947 he was appointed chairman, a position he occupied until shortly before his own death when he was acclaimed as president — a tribute to his leadership of the club over the years.

His value as a legislator was recognised quickly. In 1950 he was elected as president of the Scottish League and served in that capacity for six years being re-elected for a second term. This signal honour was calculated to give the League solid leadership in its power struggle with the SFA, a task that he completed to the satisfaction of the League. In May 1960 he was elected as president of that same SFA, and his term of office coincided with a revival in Scotland's football fortunes.

In the New Year's Honours List of 1969 the Queen made him Sir Robert Kelly, and few in football deserved the honour more. Typically, he felt that it was an honour for the club and not himself, asking that the proceeds from a fund set up to commemorate the knighthood be sent to Rosewell House, a charity in which he had become actively interested.

As Celtic's chairman he attended supporters' functions up and down Scotland faithfully, and not only during periods when Celtic were doing well. White-haired and stern in appearance, he inspired respect rather than affection; his occupation as stockbroker and sometime JP confirmed his air of rectitude. Blunt and outspoken, he rarely seemed relaxed at social gatherings, and scorned small-talk. Some attributed the aloofness to his withered right arm, the result of a childhood accident; he always felt at a slight disadvantage when required to shake hands with people upon introduction. John S. Thomson, a small, cheerful extrovert and Morton's chairman during the '60s, was able to ease that first awkward moment: "Whenever I met him at Celtic Park or Greenock, I just stuck out my left hand instead of the right; the first time I had to explain that I used to be in the Boy Scouts; once he accepted that he wasn't being initiated into the Masons, we got on really well."

The press dubbed him 'Mr. Celtic' and he took a certain pride in the epithet which was an entirely apt one. He lived for Celtic, and he served the club with an idealistic dedication. Caring passionately for Celtic's image, he was at pains to preserve the best of its traditions: he valued Celtic's reputation as an attacking side, offering entertainment and constructive football; he imposed a code of conduct on his teams, with an insistence on clean play and strict adherence to referees' authority. At a time when other clubs' directors paid lip service to clean, disciplined attacking play Bob Kelly's Celtic sides provided it, although it was not until Stein's management that the policy reached fruition. He was often a traditionalist in the best sense; Celtic was the last club in Britain to provide numbers to identify the players and it was significant that the numbers were on the shorts and not on the jerseys that he considered as the most distinctive in football. The new look made its debut to general satisfaction in a friendly against Sparta of Rotterdam on 14 May, 1960, and one can only speculate on what he would think of the present commercialism that has disfigured the green-and-white.

There was always a place in his team for the talented ball player and he favoured men like Tully, Fernie, Collins and Higgins in his line-ups. This preference was a factor in his advocating the all-weather white ball in the early '50s. Till then the brown leather one was the standard and a poor norm, as it got progressively heavier as the game went on, and on murky, pre-floodlight, afternoons almost impossible for spectators to follow. Kelly ordered the ground staff to fill baskets with balls for the referee to make the choice before the match, and made sure the vast majority were white. Referees, once they had satisfied themselves about the weight and circumference, usually opted for the white ball and the sport benefited. It seems almost incredible now, but a considerable outcry erupted in some papers about the 'new' ball and "its detrimental effect upon football."

His most celebrated defence of Celtic's traditions was his passionate fight in 1952 to preserve Celtic's right to fly the Eire flag at Parkhead. It was a defence of tradition, an attempt to honour the club's founders, but at times he was virtually isolated in the SFA chambers; however, his determination and moral courage prevailed and he was successful. A comment that he made in private at the time, though, was disquieting. He suggested that if Celtic were expelled he would start Gaelic Games at Celtic Park in the place of football — a move that would not have proved successful in any way.

He was not a mere traditionalist. Apart from the introduction of the all-weather ball that improved things for everybody, he took Celtic's squad to Wembley to see England play Hungary in 1953, and in the following year he led a Celtic party to Switzerland to watch the World Cup. Such missions were considered unusual in the '50s, but an immediate improvement was noticed in Celtic's performance culminating in the 'double' of 1954. Another benefit that could not be anticipated was the effect on the team's captain, Jock Stein, who often claimed that his initial awareness of tactics and coaching stemmed from watching the talented Hungarians destroy England's undefeated home record against foreigners (Eire in 1949 excepted).

His personality was so domineering that he interfered with Jimmy McGrory's running of the team, and involved himself with selecting the team. He fancied himself as a judge of players and persuaded the manager to agree with choices that could be described charitably as eccentric. Those selections reflected a penchant for the long-shot, a lifetime habit that comforted bookies; perhaps a romantic streak lurked there, an echo of Peter Wilson's debut back in the '20s. Two famous Celts recall that before one league game in the '60s the players on the coach spotted one of the reserves at a bus-stop going to the game. The youngster was given a lift and, impressed with the lad's enthusiasm and the Celtic scarf round his neck, Kelly prevailed upon McGrory to change the line-up to include the 'hitch-hiker'. Unfortunately, Celtic lost the game and the debutant was not an outstanding success. He persisted in his odd selections despite supporters' protests. Kelly, one journalist recalled, was "The sort of person who was inclined to listen to other opinions without having much intention of changing his own. With a strong voice and a dedication to Celtic and football, he wasn't a man people opposed. Not liking his ideas was one thing, telling him so was another". Inevitably, he dominated the legislative chambers of football as he did his club.

Within Celtic Park he continued the club's tradition of tolerance, and supervised its logical evolution. Critics, while forced to admit that the club fielded players of different religions, continued to snipe that the administrative positions were always filled with Catholics. Over the years Kelly demolished that argument by appointing the men he felt best suited for the job. Thus, a succession of non-Catholic captains were chosen: Stein (1952-56), Evans (1956-60), and Peacock (1960-61). Of course this was not a new policy as Celtic had always selected its captains on merit, most notably Willie Lyon in the immediate pre-war seasons and George Paterson during the war. Under Kelly, the club appointed full-time coaches and at least two were Protestants, namely George Paterson and Jock Stein.

In 1965 he appointed Jock Stein as Celtic's manager perhaps tardily,[1] but with more power than any previous manager. And Bob Kelly could joke wryly that 25% of Celtic's managers had been Protestant.

He was so protective of Celtic's good reputation that it has been suggested he preferred an honourable failure to a tarnished success; in this regard he was a victim of a ghetto mentality. Although he came from a fine family and became a leading figure of the Catholic community in the West of Scotland, he never was able to liberate himself fully from the legacy of persecution that was so prevalent in his youth. His reaction to the bigotry was an understandable and laudable one — a determination to rise above the circumstances, and gain psychological immunity through exemplary behaviour. This helps to explain the puritanical zeal with which he imposed an unrealistic code on Celtic teams, and his visceral response to any breaches of it. He was unable to forgive Pat Crerand for his on-field indiscretions, by contemporary standards not excessive, and Bertie Auld was transferred because of a questionable attitude.

That same ghetto mentality accounted for a basic distrust of change, and a corresponding distrust of strangers and their motives. The individual fines of £250 levied on the players (all of them, including the goalkeeper) responsible for the shambles against Racing Club in 1967 were aimed as much at warding off unlikely punishment from the SFA as for bringing discredit on the club's name. He was opposed, rightly as it turned out, to live coverage of matches by TV, realising that any money gained by the fees could not compensate for the loss in atmosphere inside the ground. Kelly did not share Jock Stein's enthusiasm for European competition, objecting to the two-leg format that he felt contributed to defensive play, and as far back as 1964 he was advocating a British Cup tournament. As president of the SFA he took a parochial view of the World Cup: "I can see no sense in playing the tournament in Chile, a remote country in which I understand it takes one year to become acclimatised." (*Observer*: 8 May, 1960.)

He remained cool towards the press, and some journalists pursuing legitimate lines of inquiry found him often brusque and distant. When he gave up the pressures of running Celtic on his own, he mellowed considerably to become much more approachable although he still remained an outspoken elder statesman.

His upbringing also produced a fierce loyalty towards those whom he trusted. He valued the integrity of men like Jimmy McGrory and Sean Fallon, retaining them as manager and coach when results suggested it was time for changes. Significantly, at the time of Stein's appointment as manager, he reorganised the structure of the club to find room for McGrory as Public Relations officer for life, and for Fallon as Assistant Manager.

Stockbrokers, Justices of the Peace, club chairmen, and Presidents of the SFA are not generally recognised as people afflicted with self-doubt, and Robert Kelly was no exception. During the prolonged period of failure prior to Stein's tenure he infuriated many Celtic supporters with his self-righteous attitude, refusing to admit that the youth policy was badly conceived and organised or that a problem existed: "Come back in two years, and you'll see a good Celtic team," he once suggested coldly to the critics.

Early in 1965, however, he came to realise that changes had to be made for the sake of the club. When he finally offered Jock Stein the position of manager he knew he was abdicating the role he had assumed in the day-to-day running of the club. For Robert Kelly to hand that trust over to another, no matter how well qualified, was a real sacrifice; it took courage to admit that the

Corinthian days were over, and that the age of the consummate professional had arrived. When he took that most unselfish action, he earned the epithet "Mr. Celtic".

Notes
1 Kelly felt a residual loyalty to Jimmy McGrory (and Sean Fallon), and in 1960 had intimated to Jock Stein that the time was not yet ripe for a non-Catholic manager of Celtic (see chapter "Seven Lean Years").

BILLY McNEILL

THE image of Celtic's captain, Billy McNeill, was a recurring one in the late '60s and early '70s as the photographs, now yellowing in the scrapbooks, have captured him in all aspects of his role: serious and determined, leading out his men to do battle; with hair neatly brushed and immaculate, shaking hands or exchanging pennants with the opposing captain; surviving the jostling and elbowing from defenders to connect with the ball at a corner kick; proudly holding aloft a cup won minutes before on the field; and the other side of the coin, surprisingly often at the end of a gruelling match, repeated glimpses of eyes slightly glazed and a face drained with emotion and exhaustion, having given everything in the previous 90 minutes.

Throughout the club's most successful era he was Celtic's captain, and nobody ever looked more the part. Tall, fair-headed, handsome in an athletic way, his air of brisk confidence exuded authority. From his earliest days he had been described as 'officer material', an appropriate evaluation as his father served in the army. McNeill looked different from the traditional pivots ('the men with blue jowls, centre partings, and broken noses') but he shared with every other capable centre-half the one essential of the role — authority. He was tall enough to be unbeatable in the air, and mobile enough to cover a wide area; he had the determination, allied with physical strength, to challenge for the ball confidently; from his first match he had a competitive edge, hating to lose, and as a consequence his concentration was unwavering throughout a game.

McNeill's attitude towards his football career was highly professional in the best sense. He had been encouraged by his parents to complete his leaving certificate at school, and he spent some time in the offices of an insurance broker to prepare for his future; as a player he served a useful apprenticeship with junior Blantyre Victoria, as had Jock Stein before him, before embarking on a full-time career with Celtic. He emerged as one of the few unqualified successes of the youth policy, establishing himself at centre-half after the departure of Evans to Chelsea; before that he had extended runs at right-back and right-half. His consistent play soon earned him a place in Scotland's side, but he was unlucky in making his debut against England at Wembley in the 9-3 debacle; his was one of the acceptable performances that day and he went

413

Billy McNeill's dramatic winner vs Dunfermline in 1965 Scottish Cup final.

on to make a further 28 appearances for Scotland. including two victories over England at Hampden in 1962 and 1964.

Playing for Celtic in those seasons was a frustrating experience for such a consistent and rightly ambitious player, apparently destined for a career of honourable oblivion, and he chafed under the strain. When Celtic lost the opening match of 1963 by 3-0 to Rangers at Parkhead, McNeill was at fault for one of the goals with a short pass-back and Celtic's next programme described it as "a stupid mistake". McNeill was so incensed that he sought a meeting with Jimmy McGrory, insisting that the comment be withdrawn. Throughout the season there was talk of a transfer to Tottenham Hotspur and the speculation ended only with the return of Jock Stein as manager. McNeill and Stein were to form the most formidable captain-manager partnership in British football and the two men had a great deal in common: both were articulate and thoughtful in football matters, leaders on and off the field and ambitious, both accepted responsibility naturally and both played at centre-half, became captains of Celtic, and later managers of the club.

As coach during McNeill's formative years, Stein had a profound effect, but as manager he enforced the painfully at times lesson. In the championship season of 1965-66 McNeill was injured early, to be replaced by Cushley for almost three months. Cushley played well and helped Celtic move into first place, starring in a 5-1 rout of Rangers, but McNeill assumed, as did everybody else,

414

that the captain would be restored to the side when he recovered. But Stein continued to field Cushley, and within earshot of McNeill the manager praised his deputy: "I like the way John's been playing; I know he can be relied upon to carry out instructions exactly." The lesson was not lost upon McNeill when he did regain his place a few weeks later, and the captain also set a good example by accepting graciously the strict regimen set down for him by the manager and trainers. As a big man he was a member of what Stein sometimes called his 'heavy squad'; along with players like Murdoch, Gemmell, Wallace and Hughes he had to submit to a more rigorous schedule, and the extra work he accepted as the dues to be paid by a complete professional.

He was a most consistent player, and his record shows the rewards for consistency. In a career that stetched from 1958 to 1975 he made 486 league appearances for Celtic (and only Alec McNair made more); he gained nine championship medals, and seven Scottish Cup medals from his twelve final appearances; he earned six League Cup medals from nine final appearances; and led Celtic in nine European Cup campaigns to appear in two finals, winning in 1967; he was capped 29 times for Scotland and nine times for the Scottish League.

Like every defender he enjoyed moving into attack for set pieces, and some of the goals he scored have been etched into Celtic's history — goals against Dunfermline, Vojvodina, Racing Club and Rangers.

When he scored against Dunfermline Athletic at Hampden on 24 April, 1965, he ended Celtic's long years of exile and ushered in the glory of the next decade. Celtic had fought back twice to tie the score, and were exerting great pressure on the Fifers' goal; Gallagher took a corner on the left, and placed it too far out for the keeper; McNeill's head met the cross perfectly and the ball raged into the net amid tumultuous scenes in the crowd of 108,880 Against Vojvodina in the 1967 European Cup quarter-final he scored even more dramatically in the closing seconds; the grim Yugoslavs were barely hanging on, hoping for a play-off in Holland but Celtic gained another corner on the right; inevitably Gallagher took it, flighting it accurately into the heart of the penalty area for McNeill to rise above everybody else and crash it into the net. In the ill-fated series against Racing Club of Argentina, McNeill scored another gallant and memorable goal to give Celtic the victory in the opening match at Hampden; jostled and elbowed as he fought his way into the penalty area, he stopped as if to complain to the referee but then resumed his run and his header flew into the net. On 26 April, 1969, he shocked Rangers in the cup final with a goal in the second minute; McNeill had taken a knock in Rangers' opening attack, and when he came downfield for Lennox's corner he was left completely unmarked to rise alone and head a simple goal that devastated Rangers.[1]

In Europe he has experienced both triumph and disaster; at Lisbon against Inter Milan he gave an impeccable display to lead his side to its most famous victory, but at Milan against Feyenoord he was uncharacteristically ill-at-ease and vulnerable. His most traumatic moment came in the referee's room at the Estadio de Luz in Lisbon at 12.20 a.m. after an epic tie with Benfica had ended in a stalemate. Benfica had recovered magnificently from a three-goal deficit to equalise with a goal scored late in injury time but McNeill had rallied his troops enough to hold out in the extra thirty minutes. Now he was called upon to decide the outcome in the most arbitrary manner — by the toss of a coin; he guessed correctly and Celtic advanced to the quarter-finals.

He was an inspiring captain, and a commanding presence as his nickname 'Caesar' might indicate. It was not an easy task to be captain of a Celtic team that was feared across Europe; the swashbuckling Gemmell, the phlegmatic Murdoch, the unpredictable Johnstone, the lion-hearted Lennox, the pawky Auld, the moody Hughes . . . all had to surrender a part of their individuality for the team effort, and McNeill's was the steadying influence on the field. When he was not there, he was badly missed; the astonishing defeat by 4-1 from Partick Thistle in the League Cup final of 1971-72 could be attributed largely to his absence.

His air of confidence was shown in France during Celtic's first attempt at the European Cup; when he was called upon to make a speech as the captain, a task not relished by footballers, he delighted the host club Nantes by responding in French, perhaps not in the most polished of accents but with an effort appreciated by the Frenchmen.[2] After his venture into French, on the way to the stadium in Nantes, the players were in a buoyant mood, singing their supporters' songs. When the bus reached the ground, and as the directors were leaving at the front, McNeill held back his players for a minute; he motioned for silence and waited till he got it, and said quietly: "Right lads, we have a job to do tonight."

His decision to retire from the game while still at the top reflected his whole attitude as a player. Aware that he had lost half a step in speed and beginning to feel the aches and pains more each season, he sensed it was time to step down; a lesser man would have carried on, but not McNeill. He told his team just before the Scottish Cup final against Airdrie in 1975 of his decision, and they responded with an impressive 3-1 win; and so the last memory of Billy McNeill as a player was an appropriate one, borne aloft on the shoulders of his team and showing the Scottish Cup for the supporters to cheer.

Notes
1 McNeill also scored in the 1972 final against Hibernian in a 6-1 win, making it the third final in which he had scored.
2 Several years later as Celtic's manager he impressed Spanish journalists by answering some of their questions at a press conference in their native tongue.

JIMMY JOHNSTONE

HE was the most easily recognised Celtic player of them all: a diminutive, slight figure whose apparent frailty aroused immediate sympathy, and who covered the ground at speed with an odd, scuttling motion that earned him the nickname of 'The Flying Flea' from a French newspaper. His skill was prodigious, and he performed magic with the ball, 'dummying' some backs so conclusively that they almost had to pay to get back into the ground; his manager would order him in the tense opening minutes of European ties on the continent to take on defenders and win over the crowd with his tricks; his greatest games were played on the big occasion and against the most formidable opposition.

An original talent, the tiny winger with the flaming red hair fought a career-long battle against a suspect temperament. Despite his fame and talent, he was a troubled, insecure player who compelled the fierce, protective devotion of so many Celtic supporters because he was one of them; he was idolised by those supporters who identified with him completely, responding to him and accepting him totally, faults as well as virtues. As a Lowland Scot and a wee man with red hair perhaps he had a natural affinity with trouble, and this self-destructive trait endeared him even more to his public. "He is not a bad boy with regard to being against authority. It is just that if there is trouble, or a problem, Jimmy seems to be in the thick of it," — that was Jock Stein's assessment of his wayward star.

He was suspended on two occasions by his own club: against Dundee United in 1968 Stein substituted him in the second half when he persisted in going his own way tactically, but heading towards the dressing room the aggrieved Johnstone shouted at his manager in the dugout, causing an irate Stein to race up the tunnel after him and the sequel was a week's suspension; in 1967 against Queen's Park in a Scottish Cup tie he became so frustrated at the enthusiastic attentions of a Spiders' defender that he made as if to butt him, and although the referee missed the incident Jock Stein did not, and again Johnstone was suspended for a week.

Jock Stein tried a variety of approaches in dealing with the player. He tried encouragement, building up his confidence with praise; he tried patience and gentle persuasion; he tried treating him exactly like the others; he tried intimidation and threats,

The courage of Jimmy Johnstone, evading the swipe of a Dukla Prague defender in the European Cup tie vs Dukla Prague at Parkhead, April 1967.

veiled and explicit; he tried indirect approaches through journalists, his colleagues, and the team doctor. In a sense, all of them worked, because in his later years Johnstone's behaviour did show a marked improvement and it was clear that he was making heroic efforts to curb his temper by resisting the crude attempts of some defenders to goad him into retaliation, but one always waited in

419

dread of a violent explosion. In fact Stein once stated, and he was not joking, that his own greatest claim to fame might be that he was the man who kept Jimmy Johnstone in the game for half a dozen years longer than believed possible. Theirs was a running feud that had elements of classic farce. Stein, suspecting that his star was going off the rails, would phone Johnstone's favourite haunts until he found him; not identifying himself, he would get him to accept the phone call, and when he did so Stein would roar at him to get himself out of there and straight home.

His controversial career as a Scotland player stemmed from that same insecurity which was worse in his early days. He dreaded meeting the Scottish squad, being in literal awe of the worldly, self-confident men like Baxter and Law, and for a time he was convinced that the Rangers' players in the side were reluctant to pass to him, clearly preferring their own man, Henderson, whom Johnstone had replaced; he resented fiercely the partisan attitude of some Rangers' supporters towards him in a Scottish jersey. The newspapers speculated about squabbles between him and Bobby Brown, the Scottish manager, but Johnstone denied this and claimed the highest regard for Brown. However, there was a violent and predictable personality clash between Johnstone and the squad's trainer, Walter McCrae, who had a reputation as a martinet. Brown had chosen the side to meet England in February, 1968, and left out Johnstone. The manager arranged a practice game at Largs between his Scottish team and Celtic. Unwisely, and unknown to Brown, McCrae sought out Johnstone in the hotel and asked him to act as a linesman, but Johnstone was still smarting at not being picked and refused, with the result that McCrae ordered him to run the line, only for Johnstone to refuse more emphatically. During a practice game Gilzean (Tottenham Hotspur) was injured and had to withdraw from the team to face England; later that night Brown came to Johnstone's room and during a long conversation impressed the Celt with his patience and sincerity. He left the decision about replacing Gilzean and playing in the match to Johnstone; by then, however, Johnstone's nerves were frazzled and he declined, thinking that he would be of little use to the team. To Johnstone's admiration and relief Brown accepted his decision with good grace. Johnstone enjoyed the last laugh over McCrae; shortly afterwards the winger had 'one of his days' and helped Celtic to a 6-0 win over Kilmarnock at Rugby Park. Passing close to the home side's dugout at the whistle, he could not resist shouting over to McCrae: "Not bad for a linesman!"

Months later, after signing a new contract with Celtic and still feeling unsettled about being abused by Rangers' fans while playing for Scotland, he went to Jock Stein to announce that he no longer wanted to represent his country and that he would devote all his energies into playing for his club. It was an immature decision, and the papers exploited the situation fully, placing both Johnstone and Brown in an awkward position. The manager manoeuvred his way out of the impasse perfectly: having left Johnstone out of an unimportant international against Denmark, he phoned the player about ten days before the vital match against Austria in the World Cup at Hampden. He had little trouble in persuading Johnstone to accept an invitation to play, the winger feeling he owed Brown something for his faith in him. He played a vital part in Scotland's 2-1 win, and Johnstone felt that his international career started in that match.

He was not free, however, from further controversy as a Scotland player. In May, 1969, he was forced to withdraw from the Scottish party to travel to Wembley because of illness and to end the rumours his doctor had to issue a medical bulletin; and five years later came the incident that made every front page. During the British Championship Scotland regained form against Wales and the squad, now under Willie Ormond, relaxed at their Largs hotel after the win. Following a few drinks and a midnight walk along the beach with some other players, Johnstone ended up alone in a rowboat equipped with one oar — apparently two might have hindered him; he was singing happily, unaware that he was drifting out to sea and there was considerable anxiety (at least on shore) before the coastal authorities rescued him. The ensuing publicity was overdone; as one critic pointed out, nobody would have noticed had it been a rugby team involved. A few days later the little winger shrugged off the fuss, giving a vintage performance in a 2-0 win over England.

From his first game for Celtic his courage was never in doubt, but it seemed to have a self-destructive edge to it, in that he sought and welcomed the challenges of opponents invariably bigger than himself. Many defenders realised quickly that the only way to stop him was through vicious tackling, and too often he was felled brutally in full flight. His apologists claimed that his troubles stemmed from hair-trigger reactions to such assaults, but this was not true of his early days when he seemed anxious to prove his manhood by taking on opponents such as Cowan (Partick Thistle) and Aird (St. Johnstone), equally small wingers.

His great games stretched belief to the limits, magnificent

displays against Inter Milan, Red Star (Belgrade), and Leeds United. In the European Cup final at Lisbon in 1967 his jinking helped to stretch the famed Italian defence and delighted the millions of TV watchers across Europe. In Glasgow there was the shock of recognition: surely this was the intricate virtuosity of street football with a tanner ba', but elevated to a superlative degree and presented on a world stage. Like an acrobat or a juggler Johnstone constantly risked absurdity with his moves, but there was nothing funny about the wee man; he was a serious artist performing by instinct, and employing skills honed by hours of solitary practice.

In 1968 Jock Stein utilized his morbid terror of flying to dramatic effect; he made a deal with Johnstone that he would not be required to travel to Belgrade if Celtic had established a four-goal lead against Red Star, one of Europe's most formidable sides. "Herr Ott's refereeing showed to what heights modern football can rise if the players are made to play the ball. Little Jimmy Johnstone, often controversial and fiery but always potentially great, relished being relieved of worry over life and limb . . . some of the things he did in stirring the Yugoslav defence into confusion were more appropriate to a circus juggler. If he could take a referee like Herr Ott around with him to give just the protection that the laws of the game entitle him to, then he could be the greatest player of all time. As Johnstone cavorted and jinked it was apparent that the only way to stop him in that mood was to kick him into subjection. On any other night that would have been done; those runs would have been brought to an end with Johnstone writhing on the turf, and an opponent with outspread hands explaining that it had been an accident. The worry about him in the long run is that he is particularly susceptible to the football destroyer because of his temperament and the nature of his play. He plays on his nerves and, unlike the others, will turn into a ruck of defenders and beat them with the cheekiness of his move; he plays so near to defenders that he is near enough for kicking. He is so highly strung in reaching for the peak of performance, as against Red Star, that all his good resolutions about field behaviour are pushed from his mind and only instinctive reaction is left . . .". (*Observer*: 21 November, 1968.)

In 1970, before a record attendance for a European Cup tie of 136,505, Johnstone destroyed Leeds United despite being marked by Terry Cooper the highly respected England full-back: ". . . although the demolition of Leeds United had been a closely integrated team operation, Johnstone's contribution was vital.

Johnstone lanced Leeds' morale in the first couple of minutes and set the tone; two lightning, sinuous runs had Cooper stretching and struggling, and Hunter backing up with instant desperation. There was to be none of Cooper's surges down the left wing this time; he was nailed deep in his own territory, occupied with the insoluble problem of containing a man who could outrun anyone and take the ball past on either side with magical ease. In a close dribble Johnstone is always prepared to buy an early tackle by making it appear that he has knocked the ball further forward than he had intended; the bait swallowed, the defender moves to intercept only for Johnstone with a lightning change of pace to sneak the ball away. Jock Stein was unequivocal in his admiration of the little winger. As soon as the final whistle blew, seen but unheard with the Niagaras of sound cascading down the terracing, he rushed on to the field to hug him like a great, happy bear." (*Sunday Times*: 19 April, 1970.)

There was yet another reason for the Celtic supporters' adulation: he always played his heart out against Rangers despite close physical marking, and was a frequent scorer against them, with a surprising number coming from headers. His bitterness at his treatment while representing Scotland was sublimated into a desire to beat Rangers, and he was often successful.

His last appearance at Celtic Park was his joint benefit game with Bobby Lennox, a memorable 4-0 win over Manchester United before 50,000 rain-soaked fans in May, 1976. Long after the whistle the two little men trotted round the track wiping their tears while the crowd paid them an emotionally charged tribute. As they finally headed towards the pavilion, Jimmy stopped in his tracks and turned back in the direction of the 'Jungle'. He raised his arm as if in one final salute to the most loyal of his fans; but instead he drew it back and threw his boots, no longer needed, into the depths of the 'Jungle'. No gesture dreamed up by Public Relations men could have been more effective.

DANNY McGRAIN

IN the mid-1970s many claimed that Danny McGrain was one of the best full-backs in the world, and not only in the ultra-chauvinist Scottish press were these claims made. Everybody who saw him play made the assertion, with raw emotion by the fan in 'the Jungle' and with more clinical analysis by the critic in the press box. It was an accolade deserved thoroughly, and worn modestly.

In 1967, at the time of his signing, Celtic had one of the most respected sides in Europe, current holders of the European Cup and threatening to monopolise the honours in Scotland. It was an exhilarating time to be a Celtic youngster, and Danny established himself in a reserve side soon to be known as 'the Quality Street Kids'. Among his new mates were Kenny Dalglish and Lou Macari in the forward line, and David Hay and George Connelly in the midfield. At first McGrain was considered a midfield player, but in keeping with a Celtic tradition he was tried elsewhere, often playing as a central defender in this youthful side that appeared certain to replace the 'Lisbon Lions'. Sadly, only McGrain of the players mentioned was to spend his entire career at Parkhead, the others leaving for a variety of reasons.

Along with Dalglish he made the decision to go full-time at an early age. As it was Stein's policy that all his full-time players train together, McGrain made steady progress, dramatically accelerated when the manager persuaded him that his best position was full-back, but still allowed him to express his natural attacking bent by overlapping. McGrain was surprised to find how much more time he had further back in defence, and thrived in his new role. Stein chose him as right-back in the first team for the opening league game against Morton at Celtic Park in August, 1970, and he played well in the few games that the manager permitted him as a taste of the big time.[1] When he was restored later to the side as a more complete player, his consistent, skilful displays soon established him as a regular.

In 1972 his career was threatened by a serious injury sustained at Brockville on 25 March; he went for a high ball along with Doug Somner, and a clash of heads occurred. McGrain carried on after treatment from the trainer but complained of dizziness at half-time to a colleague and, as he lined up in the tunnel for the second half, he fainted. He regained consciousness in a Falkirk hospital where his injury had been diagnosed as a fractured skull, the type of

424

injury most dreaded by players. McGrain had to undergo a slow recovery and a considerable delay before the specialist gave him permission to resume training. He had to build up his confidence again, especially in heading, but McGrain has always been a determined character, revealing lots of courage in overcoming this major setback to a promising career. When he returned at the start of the next season, his play soon caught the eye. Perfectly fit and with renewed confidence, he developed into the epitome of the modern overlapping defender. Besides that adventurous streak he had other talents; a burst of speed could get him to the line and he had control enough to cut the ball back and create havoc among defenders. In defence he was equally skilled; ever watchful and a model of concentration, he was a master at turning defence into attack through his anticipation. When it was required his tackling was keen with all the weight of a sturdy frame behind it. He was a man to be reckoned with.

McGrain made his Scottish debut against Wales at Wrexham in 1973 and retained his place when fit in the national team for an impressive span of nine years which extended to the World Cup of 1982. Although McGrain was more accustomed to playing on the right, in his early Scottish appearances he was often chosen on the left to accommodate the talented Sandy Jardine of Rangers; but no matter where he played McGrain handled his opponents with ease, and his own sorties into attack posed more difficult questions for the other side. Composed and cool he kept his natural streak of aggression under control, but at times he revealed hints of a highly competitive edge. Against Wales McGrain had played impeccably to master the highly touted Leighton James, and after the whistle the Welshman accidentally bumped into him in the poorly lit tunnel. McGrain turned quickly and commented to a Scottish journalist: "See that? He still can't get round me!"

Many observers felt that Scotland's tragi-comic performance in the 1978 World Cup in Argentina owed a fair amount to McGrain's absence, when the Celt missed the final stages because of a serious ankle injury. In a routine tackle with a Hibs' player, ironically a close friend of his, McGrain got a simple knock, and finished the game comfortably enough. A couple of days later the pain flared up, as it was to do so throughout the season and cause real fears that his career was over even at its height. The injury was a frustrating one that defied exact diagnosis and treatment, leaving McGrain close to despair at times. Frequent examinations by different specialists failed to uncover the specific cause of the pain, and McGrain was at his wits' end as he endured the suggested and

Danny McGrain in the mid-1970s.

often contradictory treatment: hot and cold compresses, complete rest and rigorous exercise; X-rays were taken *ad nauseam*, his lower leg was encased in plaster, a biopsy was performed, even acupuncture was tried. It was clear to the despairing athlete that the doctors were puzzled by the injury, and could not suggest with real conviction any sustained course of therapy. Mainly for his peace of mind, the club sent him finally on an extended holiday to Majorca, and during his weeks there he was forced to ponder the prospect of a future without football. Even as he was doing so he started to become aware, at first vaguely and then with increasing hope and conviction, that the recurring pain had stopped as mysteriously as it had started. Tentatively he restarted exercising, and found that the pain had gone; he resumed full training without ill-effect and was restored eventually to the side, having been out of action for over a year.

Upon his return a noticeable change had occurred in his style; he was no longer the daring, darting full-back, but a more restrained player, aware that his extra speed had gone, either with the erosion of the years or the effects of his injury. He was still basically an attacking defender, but now a more selective exponent of the art, and he evolved into an 'elder statesman' type with highly honed skills in anticipation and distribution.

His reaction to both injuries indicates a resilient character, and a determination to fight back and overcome any obstacle. This admirable trait was to be tested when he was informed that he had contracted diabetes. Some athletes are able to deal with injuries as part and parcel of their work, but few can accept illness or disease. Diabetes, a chronic condition causing losses in energy and sudden drops in weight, requires daily injections of insulin, and as no cure exists it has a particular stigma for athletes. In facing up squarely to the condition as a permanent one, McGrain showed typical courage and a considerable maturity. It was first diagnosed after the 1974 World Cup in Germany, and McGrain was shocked to discover that another match in that competition might have killed him. In a later interview McGrain was to state that he felt he was of some benefit to other sufferers who could more readily accept their condition knowing that it was shared by a top athlete.

He has always been mature, a thorough professional from his earliest days, and he deserves an added credit in that his accomplishments — as Celtic's captain in league and cup triumphs, as one of its most long-serving players with over 600 appearances, and as Celtic's most honoured player, with 62 caps for Scotland — were achieved while Celtic had been in relative decline.

Cheerfulness, loyalty and common sense — he has the good qualities of decent, ordinary folk in Glasgow in such abundance that his virtues as an exceptional player come as a surprise. The model of a one-club professional, he is a throwback to an earlier and simpler time; and, lest anybody construe that as a condescending description, let it be said unequivocally that for a number of years he was one of the best defenders in the world.

Jock Stein could watch his growth as a player and man with a great deal of personal satisfaction. The manager, who started off himself in humble circumstances, once remarked that it gave him pleasure to see what some players got out of the game deservedly: "A nice house, money in the bank, a good wife and children . . ." and he would have also noted approvingly the player's expressed concern about the plight of the unemployed.

However, one man may have suffered agonies at his accomplishments and fortunately he is unknown. When McGrain was a teenager beginning to attract attention with his play for Queen's Park Victoria XI, one scout from Ibrox watched him and was impressed enough to ask him his name; hearing "Daniel Fergus McGrain" with its misleading associations, and attuned to Glasgow nuances, the Rangers' scout lost interest, assuming that the boy was a Catholic. It was a monumental blunder. Of course, the youngster was a promising player, but he was a Protestant and, like most of his family, a Rangers' supporter. When Sean Fallon saw him some weeks later and was equally impressed, he had no hesitation in signing him for Celtic, and his subsequent popularity with the supporters at Parkhead makes a most compelling argument for increased tolerance in Scottish football.

Notes
1 McGrain made his debut as a substitute in the League Cup match with Dundee United at Tannadice on 26 August, 1970.

KENNY DALGLISH

CELTIC'S triumph in winning the European Cup in 1967 changed the nature of the club's place in Scottish football; the remarkable success itself, combined with the style and flair with which it was accomplished, impressed everybody, foreigners and Scots alike. Celtic had become a talking point and the focus of the football world. Additional thousands poured in to see this team, the players became household names and were begged for personal appearances, the manager was besieged for interviews and his comments repeated as gospel — the club was basking in the glory.

One local spin-off was that several lads who normally might not have given serious thought to joining Celtic were forced to evaluate the situation in a new light. Celtic were the best side in Europe, perhaps in the world. They played with a refreshing sense of adventure and joy. You could almost see the *esprit de corps* about the whole organisation, Protestants and Catholics alike united as a football team producing glorious, attacking play and successful beyond belief. Kenny Dalglish was such a boy, and it is almost comical to consider the scene in the Dalglish household one evening in 1967 a few minutes before Sean Fallon was due to arrive for a visit. Mrs Dalglish bustled around the flat, situated in a multi-storey overlooking Rangers' training ground at the Albion, as she tidied up a living room already neat as a pin, all the while worrying about the reactions of her husband; Mr Dalglish sat in his chair only half reading the paper, caught in a Glasgow dilemma — here he was, a passionate and life-long Rangers' supporter, waiting for the arrival of Celtic's assistant manager, a man "with a face like a map of Ireland" and a brogue that twenty years in Glasgow had not changed, a former Celtic full-back noted for a whole-hearted physical approach, especially in matches against Rangers, and here he was, the father of a promising player now to be interviewed by the best club in Scotland, a club with which his son was already training. The traditional claims of warm, friendly Glasgow hospitality conflicted with a suspicion generated and fuelled by tribal loyalty. Young Kenny was in a panic of his own, having noticed almost too late that he had forgotten to take down the photographs of his favourite team and players in the living room; even as he raced around to remove his Rangers' pictures the bell rang . . .

Any anxiety was unnecessary: Celtic were keen to land a

Kenny Dalglish in action in the early 1970s.

youngster in the hope that he might develop into a player, and Fallon was there to visit the home, to answer the concerns of the parents and to assure them that their son's interests would be kept in mind at all times; and he wanted to have a look at the lad in his own home with his parents.

It was a successful meeting. The Dalglish family were impressed with the Celtic assurances, and the down-to-earth presentation of them. Sean Fallon was satisfied with what he saw — a respectable working-class family with mutual pride and affection between parents and son.

By rights Kenny Dalglish should have been a Rangers' player. His father had taken him to Rangers' home games from an early age, and he idolised their players, a favourite surprisingly being Don Kichenbrand, a battering-ram centre. He played for his school team in the morning, and his Boys' Brigade unit in the afternoon; the schoolboy selectors recognised his ability with two 'caps' against England and Ireland; he progressed to Possil Y.M. and later Glasgow United. The ironic fact was that Rangers knew all about him, and their chief scout was confident that he would end up at Ibrox when they chose to make their move.

When Celtic showed interest, however, they appeared not as Rangers' traditional rivals but as the champions of Europe, and it was a symbol of Celtic's new stature that Dalglish would sign on with no misgivings. Celtic's first move was the conventional one of finding a suitable junior side for the youngster, and they settled on Cumbernauld United where Dalglish played well throughout his season there. To whet his appetite he was allowed to continue training at Celtic Park once a week with the other recruits. Knowing by then that he wanted a career in football, he sought a meeting with Jock Stein after a training session to ask if he could go full time. Stein was well aware of the lad's potential, but he advised caution, suggesting another season at Cumbernauld, the continuation of his apprenticeship as a joiner, and a review of the situation in the future. But young Dalglish was determined and knew his worth. He returned for another meeting this time with the moral support of his father, and they persuaded Stein to agree with the request.

So Dalglish reported to Celtic Park in 1968 as a full-time professional at only 17 years of age, but he was in good hands. Sean Fallon was in charge of the reserves and he was a model of fitness for any athlete; Jock Stein insisted that all his full-timers train together as a unit, and Dalglish made rapid progress. On the one hand, the members of the first team pool comprised one of the best sides in Europe but, on the other, they remained typically Scottish, unpretentious, cheerful and always ready to help out. Stein supervised the training personally, and one story illustrates the spirit of the club. A vigorous session had just ended but while the players made their way to the showers Stein noticed his two youngest professionals, McGrain and Dalglish, still on the field practising an overlapping set-piece. He limped over to them and watched in silence for a few minutes; abruptly he took up a defensive position and asked "How does this affect that move?" and he forced his youngsters to think about ways of dealing with that defender. At the end of the extra period they had worked out a solution, a joint undertaking by two unknown lads and the most famous manager in Europe.

Dalglish quickly established himself in the reserve side, a team that many felt could have held its own in the First Division. As with all gifted players there was a discussion about his best position. Celtic, recognising the potential of the complete player that he promised to be, gave him the scope to express himself. Often he played in the midfield and usually in the more attacking role; more frequently he played as a striker but wherever he was fielded he impressed with his developing skills and his attitude. Years later, when asked in an interview about his best position, Stein had to ponder before replying: "With a player like Kenny you don't talk about positions; you just give him a jersey."

The other full-timers paid him their ultimate compliment. Recognising an exceptional talent, they accepted him immediately. There were no cliques among that Lisbon squad, and everybody pitched in to help the newcomers. Although Stein rarely rushed his youngsters, Dalglish made an early debut on 25 September, 1968, when he made a second-half appearance against Hamilton Accies in a League Cup tie. A year later, on 4 October, 1969, he was chosen to start against Raith Rovers at Parkhead when he replaced the injured Bobby Murdoch who sat beside young Dalglish in the dressing-room and asked if he was nervous. Dalglish assured him he was not, but Murdoch with mock seriousness suggested to the youngster that he try putting his boots on the correct feet; almost before he realised he was being kidded, it was time to take the field.

After this introduction it was back to the obscurity of the reserves to finish his apprenticeship. When he returned to first-team duty he was ready. He played at Kilmarnock in a testimonial match for Frank Beattie and scored six goals in a 7-2 win; at the start of the next season, and still playing as a striker, he scored four of Celtic's five goals against Dumbarton in the Drybrough Cup, and followed that performance with three goals against St. Johnstone in the next round. In his first real match, a League Cup tie against Rangers at Ibrox, when Celtic were awarded a penalty his captain chose him to take it, despite the white-hot atmosphere of an 'Old Firm' battle. One can only speculate on his father's feelings at that moment when his son scored, sending the Rangers' keeper the wrong way.

From the start he was outstanding. He seemed to have played for years as a striker: his reflexes were razor-sharp, his finishing deadly, his positional sense instinctive, and there was an intelligence about him immediately apparent and remarkable in such a young player. As a forward he had other gifts. Deceptively strong, he was rarely brushed aside and could hold the ball, cleverly shielding it from opponents until support arrived, and he could pass the ball accurately when he sensed colleagues in a better scoring position. Like all great forwards he was courageous. Whenever Stein detected any shading-off in sharpness, physical or mental, he was quick to move him back to midfield for a change to refresh him. Dalglish was a complete player, and always adapted immediately although the roles and skills were different: his fitness and stamina allowed him to endure the physical challenge of the position, his control enabled him to gain and retain possession, his passing posed a threat to the best-organised defence, and his talent for dribbling through on his own to shoot for goal could never be discounted.

In the years after the bitter disappointment of the 1970 European Cup final Dalglish was expected to be a leader in Celtic's bid to regain supremacy in the game, and he played superbly — as mid-field general, as striker, and as the team's captain. In Scotland Celtic never relinquished control and Dalglish had the medal collection to prove it, with four championship badges, four Scottish Cup medals and a League Cup medal, after his seven years in the first team. But Celtic would never aspire to the European summit again and that forced Dalglish to consider a move to England. Dalglish realised that Celtic were falling short of the highest class.

It was his legitimate ambition as a player to express his talents in the best company, the same aspiration that brought him to Celtic Park as a boy, that caused him to request a transfer in 1975. It was a genuine professionalism and loyalty to Celtic that made him withdraw the request. Stein had been seriously hurt in a car accident, Fallon had taken over in the emergency, the captain,

Billy McNeill, had recently retired, the team was in a transitional phase and Dalglish, although basically unhappy, decided to stay on to help the club. Shortly before the Scottish Cup final with Rangers in May 1977 he showed the same loyalty and ethical sense. Anxious to leave but aware that the news of his not renewing his contract with Celtic was bound to surface before the match, and would certainly affect the play of his mates, he signed on but told the manager that he still wanted away, then led his side to a 1-0 win over their greatest rivals.

Despite Stein's persistent attempts to keep him, despite the offer of a better contract, despite the lure of a testimonial game at the end of his career, Kenny Dalglish went to England and Liverpool, where his talent would reap the professional and financial rewards of the bigger stage. With his attitude and sportsmanship, with his skills and performances he has been a credit to the game wherever he has played. It was sad to hear the abusive treatment that he received from many Celtic followers when he returned to Parkhead to play for Liverpool in the testimonial game for Jock Stein. True Celtic supporters couldn't fail to appreciate the contribution he made in his ten years at Celtic Park, nor could they grudge him the personal fulfilment that he sought, attained and earned. How pleasant, then, to record the marvellous reception that Celtic fans accorded to Kenny Dalglish during the parade of Scottish Cup-winning captains before the 100th final in 1985.

ROY AITKEN

ON the night of 19 May, 1984 the talk in the pub centred on that day's controversial Scottish Cup final between Celtic and Aberdeen and time after time the discussion returned to the topic of Roy Aitken's ordering-off after 39 minutes' play. While the participants were Celtic supporters to a man, the comments and arguments did not reflect any degree of unanimity. Like the beverages, the conversation was free-flowing and spirited: inevitably, some held that Aitken had been dismissed unjustly, and invoked 'the conspiracy theory' to explain the background, motives, and actions of the referee; others, more charitably, felt that Mr Valentine had a most difficult assignment and that his decision was a courageous one, if a bit harsh; several complained bitterly about the conduct of Aberdeen players, indicating that the forward tackled by Aitken had tumbled theatrically to the ground apparently at death's door (but in extra time scored the winning goal, and was later voted 'the Man of the Match'), and remembering that other players, especially the unpopular Strachan, seemed to be exhorting the referee and to send Aitken off for the foul; one blamed the bad feeling throughout on the pre-match hysteria in the media to the effect that Celtic were 'desperate' to win the cup and so salvage a frustrating season; all agreed candidly that recent matches between Celtic and Aberdeen had become pitched-battles, and significantly the prevailing impression was that Celtic had been more often at fault in the rough play and intimidation. Indeed the point was raised more than once in the course of the evening that Celtic were now 'a physical side' and at times excessively so. The tone was more subdued when the discussion focused on Aitken himself. Nobody questioned the man's commitment nor his talent, but most expressed genuine regret that Aitken, after nine years as a regular, had still not fully realised his potential and that his composure remained suspect despite his experience; as one expressed it, "If I had told you this morning that a player was going to be booked or sent off today, everybody in this pub would have considered Roy Aitken as the most likely choice." Nobody disputed his point and when another voice suggested that Aitken, recognised as a wholehearted Celt, would be shattered at his ejection and the Celtic defeat, nobody demurred. However, that same night Roy Aitken, as he had promised to do, attended a supporters' club function at

Roy Aitken, stalwart Celt of the 1980s.

Coatbridge to pick up a presentation as "Player of the Year" and gamely socialised with the members. In 1984 the game had changed and the cynics would say for the worse but, whatever his private turmoil, Aitken as a professional footballer had to carry on as usual. It must have been a soul-searching time for the player, long touted as Celtic's next captain, as already that season he had been suspended twice, having accumulated ten cautions, and it was obvious that he would start the next season on the sidelines with yet another suspension (and the dubious distinction of being only the second player to be sent off in a Scottish Cup final). Named in the Scottish squad for the match against England, he decided prudently to withdraw and devote more time to his family; his wife, expecting their second child, was not too well and his older girl, a lively toddler of three, required a lot of attention.

A career that had seemed so glittering when he made his debut against Stenhousemuir in a League Cup tie at the age of 16 now seemed in jeopardy. An Ayrshire lad, he was attending St. Andrew's, Salcoats, when Celtic signed him on an 'S' form at only 13 on the advice of a scout whose son taught at the school. It could scarcely have been on the basis of his football prowess, because at that time the youngster was not attached to any organised team, although he was an outstanding athlete and was showing signs of becoming a first-class sprinter. Celtic placed him in their Boys' Club where he made rapid progress, and at the age of 16 he signed as a profesional; he fully expected to be farmed out to a junior club for experience, but Celtic called him up to Parkhead almost immediately.

The 1975-76 season was a memorable one for him. Still a student in Ayrshire, he completed his high-school education, combining that with part-time training at Parkhead, and before the end of the season he made his debut in the Premier League in a 1-0 win at Aberdeen. Sean Fallon, in charge of the first-team pool, was impressed with the youngster's bearing and, having consulted with Jock Stein (now making a slow recovery from his car accident), decided to give him an extended run in the demanding position of centre-half. Aitken played spendidly and consistently — remarkable for one so young — and justified the confidence of his mentors; it seemed that Aitken was destined to fill the place of Billy McNeill, who had retired at the end of the previous season, as neither MacDonald nor Edvaldsson had satisfied completely. Physically imposing, Aitken never shirked a tackle and, at the merest shade under six foot, he was capable in the air, while his obvious enthusiasm and youth made him an immediate favourite with the supporters. His age caused some unusual complications for his football club. When Celtic were installed at Seamill, the customary retreat for special training, Aitken joined his team-mates in the hotel after his days at school, and had to leave early in the mornings to be in time for his classes at Saltcoats; chosen for the important European game against Sachsenring Zwickau in East Germany, and experiencing bureaucratic delays over his passport and visa, he had to be 'adopted' by a Celtic official in order to gain admittance and play behind the Iron Curtain.

A year later he was firmly established as a regular member of the side, and played impressively to help Cetlic win the 'double'. By now he had developed ancillary skills and he could be fielded in a variety of roles — at centre-half, or alongside MacDonald as sweeper, or in midfield. In the league match at Ibrox in March 1977 that had such a vital bearing on the championship, Aitken scored both Celtic goals in a 2-2 draw; the first, a neat side-footer after a combined move gave Celtic the lead and the other, a full-blooded volley, equalised near the end.

Since that time Aitken has been an indispensable Celtic player, generating an air of intensity that is infectious. While he has been a most consistent performer (and if he avoids serious injury, he will almost certainly end up in the top five Celtic players in the number of appearances) his enthusiasm and determination can affect the outcome of important matches. Many fans would consider that his greatest game was the league decider against Rangers at Parkhead in 1978-79 when Celtic, down 1-0 with thirty minutes left and playing a man short after Doyle had been sent off, fought back in a white-hot atmosphere to win by 4-2 and gain the championship; Aitken (and MacLeod) covered every yard of the Parkhead pitch that night, urging Celtic on to equality and victory.

Still, with success has come a recurring difficulty with officials; Aitken tackles hard and, as a player who refuses to hide, is involved in every minute of every match. Besides a disturbingly high total of cautions, Aitken has been ordered off three times: in the 1978 Scottish Cup defeat at Kilmarnock, in the August 1979 2-2 league match with Rangers at Ibrox and, of course, against Aberdeen in that 1984 final. Significantly, all of these matches were physical encounters, and none was played at Celtic Park. Aitken is not a player easily intimidated by his opponents or surroundings, and he insists that he is not a dirty player: "I object when people call me a hard man of football. To me that means someone who goes out to hurt or injure an opponent, and that's something I've never done. I don't mind being called a hard player. Mostly I operate as a defender, and it's an area where you have to take care of yourself."

The pressures on central defenders are perhaps greater now than previously. When a goal lost can mean elimination from the rich European tournaments, the temptation is to be ruthless rather than half-hearted; when TV critics and cameras relentlessly probe for the mistake that caused a goal and, having found it, play and replay the sequence, the tendency is to be cautious rather than cavalier; when a forward, tackled even fairly, indulges in theatrics and feigns injury to gain a cheap foul, or get the opponent into trouble with the referee, the outcome can be to make defenders cynical. The central defender, often the last outfield player, has to develop an air of authority, if not intimidation, and frequently has to reinforce it with a show of aggression to survive. At moments of crisis in a match he can find himself isolated against opponents with all the advantages in speed, possession and control and, as the only defender with any chance of a successful intervention, he is often compelled to end the threat with a tactical or professional foul. The psychological strain of such a pattern is reminiscent of an airline pilot's description of his role: "Hours of boredom, punctuated with seconds of terror." Aitken, as a defender for almost ten years, often finds that his role in a match, although vital, has been confined to a negative one; he has to terminate attacks rather than initiate them and he has to prevent goals rather than create them. One has to wonder if his frequent breaches of discipline on the field are not the result of frustration, and if his admitted excesses in tackling are the manifestations of the tensions that create them. One has to wonder if his frequent chafing at the tactical role laid down for him. Off the field, apparently, he does not fit the pattern of 'the hard man'; rather, he is a quiet person leading a private life and raising a family away from the spotlight. His interests and hobbies indicate a creative bent: a good student in school despite the distractions of playing in the Premier League at 17, a talented pianist with a diploma to prove his prowess, a fine athlete in such diverse sports as basketball and sprinting. These are creative activities, and an outlet for self-expression.

In the last 15 minutes of the 1985 Scottish Cup final he was allowed to express that creative surge. A most competent Dundee United side had taken the lead shortly after half-time and survived the critical ten minutes after scoring; no team in Scotland was more capable of slowing down the play, or dampening the fires of opponents, and it seemed that the cup was bound for Tannadice for the first time. With both Celtic substitutes on, the signal was sent in for the team to regroup, and the upshot was Roy Aitken loose in the midfield, liberated from his defensive shackles. Alan Rough, the Hibernian and Scotland goalkeeper, once described the spectacle: "You can hear the trumpets blowing as he charges on!" Almost singlehandedly he turned that final round: he urged on his colleagues with voice and example, he won the ball outright from his midfield opponents or harried them into passing it hurriedly, he spread the play around and joined in every attack, unsettling the United defence, and in true story-book fashion his efforts were rewarded with two late goals for Celtic, and the winner came from a spectacular header by McGarvey from Aitken's cross. A year after his public disgrace Aitken was vindicated, but it was not a sudden transformation as Celtic supporters had seen the improvement in his composure over the season. He would never be accused of daintiness, but the days when he was rumoured to eat barbed-wire sandwiches for lunch seemed over. He confirmed his growing maturity a week later when he played a solid part in Scotland's 1-0 victory over England at Hampden. One cameo summed up his new-found attitude. After initiating a Scottish raid, and being unlucky to find the final cross coming a yard out of his reach, he had to rush back to help thwart the counter-attack; as an English forward was put through clear of the Scottish defenders, Aitken chased him for 30 yards, and the crowd tensed as they anticipated the possibilities. If Aitken could not catch him, it would be a goal for England; if Aitken hauled him down unceremoniously within the area, the penalty would bring the equaliser, and probably Aitken's own dismissal. As the pair raced on with Aitken gaining little by little, the Celtic defender did the right thing (by contemporary standards), he made his tackle from behind to concede the foul six yards outside the penalty area, but tackled as fairly as he could and within seconds of the whistle he had lifted himself from the ground to advance on the referee with hands outstretched, not in appeal against the decision, but with the contrition shown by one man of the world to another. The referee spoke to him briefly, but took no further action.

Since the 1984 cup final Aitken has been relatively trouble-free, but in the 80's every defender looks on cautions and suspensions as occupational hazards (and he has had his share), but the legitimate doubts being expressed about his career have receded. His international career has flourished lately; some Celtic supporters had felt that with his talents and enthusiasm Aitken should have been recognised more frequently by Scotland, but the Celt had found himself in direct competition with the Aberdeen pair of Miller and McLeish playing in front of Leighton in goal and, besides, the question of his temperament had not been fully answered. In 1985-86 Aitken finally and deservedly made an impact with the Scottish squad; he was a strong man in the World Cup cauldron at Cardiff on 10 September, and was a key figure in the play-off matches against Australia and in the finals in Mexico. The authors, in compiling this selection of Celtic players as representatives of the club in the past hundred years, originally considered Roy Aitken as a candidate three years ago, but felt they had to reject him because of his over-robust play. Nothing has given them more pleasure than to recognise the improvement of this most enthusiastic Celt.

EXTRA TIME

THIS section consists of aspects of Celtic's history; we felt it would have been awkward to include the material presented here within the main body of the text. And so, rather than insert the information in a piece-meal fashion, we made the decision to embody it within the framework of essays. As with the profiles, a conscious effort was made to avoid repetition.

THE SUPPORTERS

ONE of the people asked to read this manuscript prior to publication felt compelled to note that he felt the supporters had been mentioned too much in accounts of the matches described. The authors accepted the criticism as valid, but pointed out in defence that the Celtic supporters have rarely played a merely passive role . . . that they were participating with a passionate involvement, and that their vociferous encouragement during the games, and their loyal support during lean times, have had a significant part in shaping the unique character of the club, the team and the individual players. Most observers of Scottish football have commented on the legendary 'Celtic spirit'; that almost tangible enthusiasm may have its wellspring on the terracings, emanating from the mass of supporters often known collectively, especially in the 1950s as 'the faithful'.

Celtic supporters, in general, could be described as a raffish crew, certainly the type out of place at a garden-party at Holyrood Palace. Their instinctive choice of favourites reflects this characteristic. Jimmy Johnstone would be more popular than Charlie Gallagher, as would Charlie Tully in preference to Willie Fernie. The identification is with the troubled, temperamental player of genius often in trouble with the authorities rather than with the gifted and gentlemanly. Passionately involved with Celtic, they have reacted to in a variety of ways: proletarian delight at Jimmy Johnstone's 'tanner-ba' virtuosity, talismanic faith in the wholehearted efforts of Jimmy McGrory, approval and pride in Billy McNeill's air of authority, appreciation of Bobby Evans' heroics season after season. The players who meet with their disapproval are those felt not to be trying too hard, and, as a consequence, it is hard to recall any Celtic team that did not try with every nerve and sinew. With supporters of the type who would walk from Glasgow to Kilmarnock or Dundee during the Depression to see a football game it is not surprising that Celtic teams are known for their passion and intensity. Their followers' enthusiasm for Celtic is such that they cannot accept the fact that a player at the height of his powers might want to leave to play elsewhere, and while the abuse showered on Kenny Dalglish and Charlie Nicholas upon returning to Parkhead with their English teams is

445

entirely understandable it is regrettable to an extreme. They have a fundamental sense of recognition about a man's worth: Jack Harkness recalls being greeted with applause upon taking the field with Hearts in the 30s, because the previous season he had thrown Jimmy McGrory round the post to prevent the Celtic leader from colliding with it; at the time he was booed for his action, but McGrory made the motive known to the fans, who responded admirably later. Some players always receive a respectful welcome — men such as Jimmy McGowan of Partick Thistle, an enthusiastic, hard-tackling right-back of the 50s, and Willie McNaught of Raith Rovers, an elegant, under-capped left-back of the same era. One Rangers' player in particular, Willie Thornton, was admired for his skill and flair as well as for his gallantry during World War II in which he won the Military Cross; when he returned Celtic Park as manager of Dundee in the 50s he was greeted with a splendid and unsolicited ovation from the fans.

There have been many other moments of grace. In 1953 Celtic visited tiny Eyemouth in the Scottish Cup and won 4-0, but at the end many supporters vaulted over the primitive railing and invaded the field to carry off shoulder-high Eyemouth's young goalkeeper who had performed heroically; as recently as 1985 another teenager keeper, Fridge of Inverness Thistle, was given a sporting ovation for his play at Celtic Park in the Cup, as indeed were the other members of his outclassed team.

The behaviour of some Celtic supporters has, indeed, at times been disreputable and the only 'defence' that could be offered sometimes was that the misbehaviour had been related to some perceived injustice on the field — in effect, enthusiasm turned sour or bitter. Enough of that type of behaviour has been recorded elsewhere in this volume, but the authors note with regret that Celtic supporters are much the same as those of other clubs in the matter of chanting and singing vulgar or mindless doggerel. At one time it was only the 'Old Firm' supporters who sang, the Celtic fans drawing upon an extensive repertoire of Irish (or rebel) songs. With the 'copycat' effect of television coverage and a subsequent lowering of the standard of behaviour at matches, some younger supporters endanger the good reputation the club's supporters built up in the late 60s and early 70s.

The media, forgetting that the origin of the word 'fan' lies in 'fantastic', have criticised the conduct of football followers, and Celtic supporters have come in for their share of the censure. Nobody who loves the game of football can object to criticism of violence or hooliganism, whatever the provocation, but sometimes the avarice or negligence of the clubs are more to blame than the spectator. Recently, in the 1983 UEFA Cup game at Nottingham, the home club did not make adequate preparation for admitting the visiting spectators into the ground, not having enough turnstiles open for the 12,000 Celtic supporters allowed tickets; the authors can remember waiting for more than an hour in an ill-organised queue and advancing only a few yards before the police, acting on their own initiative, opened the large exit-doors to let the fans in. Unfortunately, most of the supporters who entered this way, unfamiliar with the City Ground, found themselves packed into a smallish enclosure near the corner flag when other parts of the ground were comparatively comfortable. Almost immediately after the kick-off the overcrowding became intolerable and several hundreds had to climb over the retaining wall for safety and waited to be re-directed to another part of the ground. The match was held up for several minutes till this was done, and the next day's headlines, at least in some English newspapers, mentioned 'field invasions'. Few of the reporters cared to mention the massive common sense of football followers in a criminally overcrowded situation that might have led to fatalities had the supporters not acted unilaterally. As two of the spectators in that particular enclosure who still retain the unchecked match ticket, the authors can vouch for the practical behaviour and exemplary conduct displayed by those followers.

Their forbearance in times of almost intolerable temptation should be recognised. One of the most shameful nights in European football was the Celtic-Atletico Madrid fiasco in Glasgow in April, 1974; that night the 73,000 spectators who turned up for the first leg of a European Cup semi-final were magnificent in their behaviour despite provocation that seemed cynically calculated to cause crowd troubles and possibly an invasion of the pitch. And at Milan in 1970 during and after a numbing defeat by Feyenoord in the European Cup final, the grief was profound but generally dignified; Danny McGrain, as a Celtic youngster, recalls sitting in the Celtic coach beside Kenny Dalglish, both staring in silence out of the window and seeing two supporters walking along the street back into the city with tears streaming down their faces. In fact, the interaction among the thousands of Dutch and Scottish supporters was most friendly before, during and after the match; and from the point-of-view of crowd behaviour in the 80s the final of 1970 could be regarded with nostalgia.

During his first five years as Celtic's manager Jock Stein took pains to indicate to the supporters that he expected good behaviour from them; and more frequently he got it, even when it might be unexpected. The reaction from the supporters was not only because Celtic did well on the field; the supporters felt that for the first time somebody in authority actually cared about their welfare and conduct.

Their joy has been unconfined when the occasion merited it. At Lisbon those supporters who had started to save and scrape to get there long before Celtic qualified for the final had the most climactic day of their lives; it may also have been one of the most chaotic and one journalist who enjoys observing Celtic supporters described the scenes at the airport as "a Dunkirk with happiness." Another commented on their appearance: "You've seen them arrive in Edinburgh looking dishevelled after an hour's train journey from Glasgow; well, imagine them after three or four days in Lisbon, and after the final whistle! They didn't care one hoot!" The leaping over the moat and the invasion of the field at the end was neither malicious nor mischievous; it was unadulterated joy; similarly, nobody present could ever forget the raw emotion of the 1970 semi-final at Hampden when Celtic beat Leeds United 2-1, to reinforce the 1-0 victory at Elland Road two weeks previously. More than 136,000 had roared and cheered themselves hoarse, but in the last half hour, with the issue beyond doubt, sang their hearts out; "it was some night".

The authors feel that most decent Celtic supporters have been blessed with the characteristics of ordinary working people; the ability to put things into some sort of perspective, a fundamental sense of honesty about football, and above all the saving grace of humour, a trait noted from the earliest days. In 1908, for example, a large group of supporters from Coatbridge rented a carriage on the 'special' to Aberdeen for a Scottish Cup tie, and emerged at the other end "dressed in the garb of 'darkie minstrels', some with whiskers and all with musical instruments ranging from tin whistles to drums." Many other anecdotes are familiar through countless repetition, and to the list the authors will offer a couple from first-hand experience.

In 1968-69 Celtic faced Rangers in the League Cup sectional play, and won 2-0 at Ibrox in the first game. For the return match at Parkhead a small van containing seven or eight Celtic supporters was travelling along Paisley Road West towards the ground. The driver, noticing the crowds waiting at bus stops, felt that room might be made for a few more. The van came to a halt just past a bus stop underneath a huge railway bridge and four men rushed over in answer to the invitation, climbed in awkwardly, and the van lumbered on to emerge into the bright sunshine at the end of the bridge. In the front, squeezed in between the driver and his twin brother, was a Rangers' supporter sporting a red-white-and blue scarf. He sat for a few seconds more, still happy at getting to the match on time, until he turned to glance at the driver, a burly man with a map of Ireland for a face and an Eire flag in his lapel. The wee Rangers' man, who might have been a jockey so slight was he, gulped and turned hopefully to his left to see the twin brother nodding reflectively to him. Almost despairingly he looked into the mirror, only to see Celtic supporters bedecked in various shades of green in the back. Quietly, and almost with resignation, he reached into his mouth and removed his false teeth, wrapping them inside his handkerchief and then putting them into his pocket.

The conversation was strained:

"Were ye at the Ibrox game, then, Jimmy?" asked the driver.

"Aye."

"Did ye enjoy it, Jimmy?"

A momentary hesitation was ended with another "Aye."

"I thought Celtic were a wee bit lucky. How aboot you?"

The answer when it emerged came with a rush and the reassurance:

"Naw, naw! Celtic played smashin'. They deserved tae win a'right."

After a pause and a glance at his brother the driver continued, "Dae ye really think so, Jimmy?"

"Oh aye, definitely. It should have been mair than two-nothin'."

The conversation lapsed after this exchange, a thoughful silence falling upon the members of the group. At last the van reached the Gallowgate, and made a slight detour to allow the Rangers' fan to leave and make his way to the stadium unscathed. There was one further diplomatic exchange:

"Jimmy?"

"Aye?"

"If ye like, we can gie ye a run hame. Wid ye like tae meet us here, efter the gemme?"

The wee Rangers' man stared in disbelief for several seconds before answering.

"Well, I have tae meet some pals . . . but, thanks a loat."

When he left a few seconds later, the crowd in the back of the van finally erupted into laughter.

And, lastly, to end on a note that seems to capture the optimism and spirit of 'the faithful': in the 1984 Scottish Cup final Roy Aitken was on his way to the dressing-room, ordered off by the referee after 40 minutes; Celtic were already a goal down to Aberdeen, the Scottish Cup holders, just crowned as league champions, recent holders of the European Cup-Winners Cup, and of course at full strength. Amid the silence from our spot on the King's Park end of the terracing, one Celtic supporter mused aloud: "Does that mean big Roy will miss the replay?"

THE STADIUM

THE development of Celtic Park has mirrored the growth of organised football in this country. Over the years improvements have been made certainly, but seldom has the opportunity been taken to alter the total concept for the benefit of the spectators in terms of comfort or convenience. As the club approaches its centenary, the ground remains an impressive monument, but to the game's exciting past. Celtic Park, now the second-largest club ground in Britain in capacity, is a lifeless and soulless place without people and has a dismal air with a small crowd, but when 60,000 pack it for an important match 'Paradise' revives and we know few other grounds that can generate the same sense of atmosphere. Unfortunately, those days are few and far between nowadays.

It remains, despite recent improvements, essentially a ground from the past. Designed to accommodate the vast crowds that flocked to watch football in times when the game was the only acceptable form of entertainment available for working men, it can have a dated, forlorn look, especially from the terracings behind the goals. The visitor is struck immediately by the disproportionate ratio of standing accommodation to seating, a disconcerting feature in a club that often has claimed an identity with the best interests of the mass of its support; as one of the authors has heard in 'the Jungle' at a recent match: "Ye cannae invite yur brother in, an' then jist let him staun an' don't gie him a seat, right?" The defensive posture that the club has adopted when the matter is raised in public suggests that change might be long in coming. Claiming to have investigated the views of the fans, the club newspaper has recently suggested that the great majority of them prefer the present old-fashioned, standards rather than pay an increase in admission for a seat.

Because the game has declined in spectator appeal and capacities have been reduced to meet safety requirements, never again will 146,433 crowd into Hampden Park for a Scottish Cup final as in 1937 to see Celtic play Aberdeen, nor will 118,567 ever throng Ibrox Park for a league game between Rangers and Celtic as in 1939 and, sadly, no crowds of 80,000 and over will ever be reported from Celtic Park again.

450

One has to conclude that the present trend in reduced ground capacity with seating for all, as evidenced in Ibrox with 45,000 and Pittodrie with 24,000, is the correct policy; on very few occasions is the capacity of football grounds reached, and the subdued atmosphere in a half-filled ground is too often depressing. The clubs must accept some of the responsibility for the decline in attendance because, in general, they have neglected comfort and, in an earlier age, the safety of the spectators: ". . . clubs treated their captive audience with something close to contempt. The notion grew up in boardrooms that crowds would always come in the numbers in which they flocked to grounds in the 1950s, and that it was not in the least necessary to improve spectator conditions. During the first sixty years of this century, Glasgow could make a very plausible claim to be regarded as the football capital of the world. For almost all of that period, the city could boast six First Division clubs, two grounds that would and did accommodate more than 100,000 spectators, another that would hold upwards of 80,000, and a fourth with a capacity of 50,000. These hordes would stand on railway sleepers, perilously linked to ash banks, and they would endure the Scottish climate in all its rigorous variety. They provided their own food or feasted upon cold mutton pies of doubtful vintage and pedigree. (A long-standing joke at the ground of Partick Thistle, where for a while the pies were of a brand known as V.C., was that you really should have won it before eating one.) Indifferent tea or Bovril was provided at highly inadequate refreshment huts often located in the least accessible parts of the ground. The toilet facilities would have caused comment even among the less fastidious Indian tribes of the Amazon. Lavatories were noxious and few, as the inhabitants of neighbouring streets knew to their cost." (*The Scottish Footballer*: Bob Crampsey, 1978.)

Celtic's first ground was a neat, compact enclosure built largely by volunteer labour within six months and by modern standards was primitive: "There was nothing very remarkable about Celtic Park I: it was certainly not an advance upon anything that existed — merely a good-sized level pitch surrounded by a narrow and almost unbanked cinder track, and flanked on the east by a somewhat provincial looking stand . . . By and by, a second stand was run up on the western side, and the gaps round the field were filled in by a modest attempt at molehill terracing." (*Evening Times*: 9 April, 1904.) Before 1891 Celtic had outgrown the facilities, and when the owner of the land, a gentleman with whom the club had several disputes, attempted to raise the rent from £50 a year to £450 the committee decided to move elsewhere (see also Chapter 3 re site, including map).

The surprising choice was only yards away across Janefield Street, and remains the site of the present ground. It was a bold decision: "An old brickfield, half filled with water to a depth of forty feet or more is

451

the last place on earth where one would have expected any organisation to construct a modern athletic enclosure in every respect." (*Scottish Sport*: 22 July, 1892.) The first job was to fill in the hole, a herculean task accomplished by unloading more than 100,000 carts of earth; much of the labour was volunteered from the Irish community that had adopted Celtic as a symbol of success. The ground was ready for the start of the 1892-93 season, and for the time it was a splendid ground. The playing field was perfectly level and covered with a lush surface; two tracks, one for running and the other for cycling, surrounded the pitch and provided a suitable barrier between the spectators and the players; one stand had already been constructed on the north side, parallel with Janefield Street, and it started 15 feet east of the pavilion which was located on the north-west side and extended for 320 feet with 15 tiers of seats, providing seating for 1,000 more than the Ibrox of that period; the pavilion, a separate structure in the style of Airdrie's present Broomfield Park, rose to a height of 30 feet and contained apartments for the teams, lavatories with hot and cold baths, a club office and a hall above the dressing-rooms where the teams and officials could meet for hospitality afterwards, in much the way as at club rugby games today. Plans called for the erection of another stand to be built at the London Road side, but this had to be delayed until the soil had settled completely.

Because of the banking required for the cycling track the closest spectators on the lowest level were raised six feet above the pitch, and had an excellent view of the proceedings and the newspaper article cited above went on to add ". . . the new Celtic Park was one of the best, if not actually the finest, grounds in the kingdom".

Of course, the track was improved for the World Cycling Championships held at the ground in 1897, and during this decade the quality of the facilities was recognised by the frequent selection of the ground for international fixtures. Other attractions were staged at the ground: cycling 'meets', motor-bike racing, speedway in 1928, a Coronation parade in 1911, boxing matches, the annual Celtic Sports — the latter being two-day affairs held in August that, under the guidance of Willie Maley and J.H. McLaughlin, became recognised as one of the premier athletic meetings in Britain, and during the Great War soldiers demonstrated on the pitch the techniques of trench-warfare with the aid of 'bombs', explosions and smoke-screens.

One of the new directors, James Grant, came to a private arrangement with the club in 1898 that he should construct a stand on the London Road, south side of the ground and operate it as a private venture: ". . . a two-storey building, lavishly equipped with padded tip-up seats and large, sliding windows which could be shut when it rained. Unfortunately, Grant had not allowed for condensation and the windows had to be

THE SCENE OF THE INTERNATIONAL MATCH BETWEEN SCOTLAND AND ENGLAND.

Sketch of Celtic Park by, the Special Artist of the "Evening Times."

Celtic Park viewed from the south side (London Road) by the artist of Glasgow's Evening Times, 8 April 1904. In the foreground is the Grant Stand, opposite which (at the top of the drawing), is the pavilion (on left), and stand damaged by fire only a month after this drawing was published.

removed to allow clear sight of the pitch. In addition the stand was set away from the pavilion and had four flights of stairs leading up to the seats." (*Football Grounds of England and Wales*: Simon Inglis, 1983.) It did not prove a popular facility, the main objection being the distance from the pavilion. Thus, Grant was relieved to sell it to the club at a loss shortly after a fire had destroyed the stand and the pavilion on the opposite side in May, 1904. Fortunately, the fire broke out on a Monday evening at 10.30 p.m. but it gutted the stand and damaged the pavilion; the stand, a mainly wooden structure that could seat 3,500 was completely razed, but the pavilion was able to be repaired.

After the repairs and renovations, alterations that replaced the original stand with the covered enclosure later to be immortalised as 'the Jungle', Celtic Park remained much the same for the next quarter of a century, until another fire destroyed the pavilion in March, 1929; as demolition work was in process on the 'Grant' Stand, Celtic were forced to play remaining fixtures elsewhere. This stand, once regarded with pride, was showing signs of wear-and-tear: the upper section had been damaged in a winter storm, and the Press Box, located on the roof, had a disconcerting sway on windy days. The new stand was ready for the first game of the 1929-30 season, a 2-1 victory over Hearts. The newspapers expressed satisfaction with the new look: "Celtic Park can now boast of the best equipped and most finely situated grandstand in the land. The inconvenience of having to pass through two entrances is experienced at Hampden and Ibrox, but it is not at Celtic Park. You enter direct from London Road to your seat . . . your vision commands a magnificent view of a steep, sloping stand enclosure, a banked track, and the finest playing field in Britain. Half of the enclosure is under cover, and the pavilion which is under the stand is the last word in efficiency." (*Glasgow Observer*: 17 August, 1929.) The article failed to mention, however, that the seating capacity of 5,000 was about half of the grounds of Rangers and Queen's Park. Even before the stand was opened in August 1929, Colonel Shaughnessy, a Celtic director, was quoted as saying that the Celtic Board was unanimous on having overhead cover for all at Celtic Park "when humanely possible" — an ambition that would not be realised until 1986.

Further improvements were slow in coming, because apart from essential maintenance work and cosmetic repairs, little was done to the ground until 1952 when three passageways were constructed on the East terracing (the Rangers end) in response to a request from the city magistrates. The only other innovation was the construction of the half-time scoreboard at the back of that terracing, a wooden structure with an unfortunate resemblance to a gallows and of value only to those who had purchased a match programme.

However, a dramatic change occured in the mid 50s when the serious work of covering the West terracing was undertaken, the project being completed in 1957 at a cost of £77,000; it was only a partial realisation of the plan, however, because the concrete arc did not cover the whole 'Celtic end', as was once envisioned.

The club was appreciably late in installing floodlights, but the delay had the advantage of ensuring that Celtic got the best available at that time. The system, known as 'Drenchlite', was installed by the Edinburgh company of Millar and Stables Ltd. for a cost of £40,000 in 1959, and the towers, the tops of which were 208 feet above the playing surface, were believed to be the highest such pylons in the world. The lights were first turned on for a friendly on 12 October, 1959 against Wolverhampton Wanderers the English champions, who won 2-0; however, Celtic historians have rightly noted that Celtic did experiment with a primitive lighting system back in the 1890s for a short period.

In 1964 the chairman revealed a major change in Celtic's thinking when he announced at a supporters' rally that Celtic intended to start a pool to raise money primarily for the development of the ground: " 'I have an important announcement to make,' Mr. Kelly said "Many considered this, but our great rivals Rangers are running one of these schemes. They are having help from outside the club, but our organiser will be one of our former players . . ." Mr. Kelly added: "We don't know yet when the Celtic pools will start but it will be as soon as possible. It is up to the organiser to decide what form it will take. One thing I can say definitely — it will be the biggest pool in Scotland.'" (*Scottish Daily Mail*: 2 March, 1964.) As might be gathered from the announcement, Celtic's approach to the concept was initially amateurish compared to Rangers'; the returns have never been fully realised, as they continue in the 70s and 80s to be outstripped by Rangers in business-like professionalism and profits, although, in fairness, the greater potential support for Rangers, given Scotland's socio-religious divide, must be acknowledged.

With the success of the side under Jock Stein, the subsequent increase at the turnstiles, and some returns from the pools, Celtic stepped up the pace of alterations starting in the late 60s. 'The Jungle', essentially a large open-air barn structure, was torn down and replaced in 1966 by the present, modern covered enclosure with a paved, concrete terracing underfoot, and two years later the East terracing (the Rangers end) was covered and the steps concreted.[1]

In 1971 came a most dramatic development: ". . . the club removed the roof of the stand and replaced it with a most unusual, angular white roof between April and August 1971. Costing £250,000, the work was done in such a way as not to disturb the facilities below. A huge girder, measuring 97.5 metres long and 5.3 metres deep, was transported to Parkhead all the way from Chichester, and hoisted up on two supporting posts on either side of the stand, to create a goalpost-like frame on which to rest the roof. It was a quite revolutionary way of redeveloping a stand, although not very economical, and it transformed . . . the existing base, which was converted to an all-seater stand with room for 8,686, but has it been a success? In purely aesthetic terms there is no doubt it enhances the dramatic quality of Parkhead, especially at evening matches when the lights underneath the roof give it an awesome appearance, exaggerated by the suspended 100-seater press box hung from the roof girder. But as a means of protecting people from the elements it fails somewhat, especially in the front." (*Football Grounds of England and Wales*: Simon Inglis, 1983.) The new stand was officially opened on 1 September, 1971 when Celtic defeated Nacional of Uruguay by 3-0.

Despite the reservations of the above writer the new stand altered the whole ambience of the ground for the better. Every seat in the stand has a complete, uninterrupted view of the field with no possible obstruction from pillars; the enclosure in front of the former stand was scrapped and the seating extended down almost to pitch-level; at the same time the floodlights were improved to bring them up to the most modern standards, the approaches to the ground from London Road were paved, and the training-ground at Barrowfield modernised.

After the tragic happenings at Ibrox on Ne'erday 1971 the government started to take a closer look at football grounds, and the result was the Safety of Sports Grounds Act which had the effect of ultimately reducing the capacity of Celtic Park by around a quarter to 60,000, the second-largest club ground in Britain; much of the subsequent renovations have been in the practical areas of crowd control at exits and entrances. Indeed, Celtic Park has an enviable safety record, unlike the always more modern Ibrox Park that has been the location of two disasters in this century.

Certainly changes have been made and each change has meant an improvement, but the ground leaves a lot to be desired as the alterations have been effected in a piece-meal form. Celtic Park remains an old-fashioned ground kept in reasonably good condition through costly modifications and repairs. The 'improvements' have been expensive but unimaginative; the view from the terracings behind the goals remains a distant one and has only the advantage now of a more solid footing and, depending on the direction of the wind, protection from rain.

Cynics have carped that Celtic have held back on ground improvements by a reluctance to go into debt, and that the major renovations in the past were largely financed by the sale of players. As circumstantial evidence they cite the exodus of established players in the late 20s and the attempted sale of Jimmy McGrory to Arsenal, suggesting that this was the method of paying off the financial burden of the new stand; similarly, they point to the sale of Collins and Fernie as being instrumental for the introduction of floodlights in 1959.

It is clear that the original expansion of the ground in the 1890s was linked with the profits to be made from special events: internationals, sports meetings, and the choice of the ground as a neutral venue. Once Celtic Park lost out to Hampden and Ibrox the interest in expansion waned, and very few improvements purely for the benefit of spectators were carried out for a number of years. Unfortunately, recent developments seem to have lacked an overall sense of direction and the effect is of patchwork repairs, renovations and modifications rather than an architectural statement.

Nowhere has the club's reluctance been more clearly expressed than in the matter of seating. Desmond White, while chairman in 1984, stated emphatically: "However, we won't be installing any more seating. We feel with so much unemployment, and the fact that football is a very much working-class sport, it has to be kept as cheap as possible for the fans. It can cost our fans £1 more to watch an 'Old Firm' game at Ibrox than at Celtic Park. But our fans have illustrated they don't want our stadium to be all-seated." (*Sunday Post*: 28 October, 1984.) His argument was roundly answered by a supporter's letter in the *Glasgow*

Herald of 5 November: ". . . Mr. White, a CA, should admit that his argument about seating is based on economic consideration rather than the wishes of his club's 'working-class' supporters. It reminds me of an attitude of 30s Tories, that council tenants should not be given baths as they would only keep their coal in them." At the moment the issue is a contentious one, but as time passes the club's viewpoint can only become more and more outdated.

In 1985 more improvements were carried out, the club benefiting from grant assistance by the Football Grounds Improvement Trust. Extra turnstiles and safer exits were installed at the north-west corner of the ground at Janefield Street, the busiest point of entry to the ground as it allows access to the 'Celtic end' and 'the Jungle'; on the East terracing a permanent barrier was erected to help segregate rival fans, a screen-type barrier that can be removed for matches against European clubs, and under-soil heating was installed.[2]

Unfortunately, surveys revealed the presence of old mine-working shafts under the 'Celtic end' which delayed the total cover of this West terracing (a project costing £1 million) until August 1986, when the completion of the undertaking meant cover now for 60,000 fans.

To end on a more optimistic note, negotiations are proceeding with the Scottish Development Agency and with GEAR to make significant changes in the over-all use of the ground. Provisional plans include a first-class training establishment, with a sports complex and office block, but with the massive infusion of aid the club can no longer claim exclusive use. It is not an unpleasing prospect, because at last, almost a hundred years later, one of Brother Walfrid's original aims for the club might be realised — the utilisation of the ground for the recreation and training of members of the community. Along with Celtic itself, that 'community' has now grown to include people of all religions and races.

Notes
1 The new covered enclosure retained the appellation 'the Jungle'.
2 Costs as follows: turnstiles and exits, together with new toilet facilities and new retaining walls (£½ million), barrier (£80,000), undersoil heating (£100,000). Encouragingly, more seating accommodation may be in the pipeline. The *Sunday Post* of 6 July, 1986, reported that discussions have taken place about building a stand on top of the enclosure opposite the main stand: "Regular residents of 'the Jungle', however, can breathe easy. Their stance will stay as long as they want it. But fans could be sitting on their roof!" Perhaps it is no longer far-fetched to envisage an all-seated Celtic Park within a decade or two?

THE TROPHY ROOM[1]

CELTIC'S claim to be the greatest Scottish football club has a substantial basis. It lies in almost a century of accomplishment in domestic competition, in later performances in Europe, and in an unparalleled record in prestigious invitational tournaments.

The tangible evidence is found in the trophy room at Celtic Park, where the visitor should linger and examine the silverware. He should concentrate on the permanent collection, trophies won outright on 'distant fields': the beautiful Glasgow Exhibition Trophy of 1901, the distinctive outline of the Empire Exhibition Trophy of 1938, the elegance of the Victory-in-Europe Cup of 1945, the late-Victorian elaboration of the St. Mungo Cup of 1951, the classic simplicity of the Coronation Cup of 1953, and dominating by its presence, if not size, a replica of the European Cup of 1967. Three of those invitational tournaments — those in 1902, 1938, and 1953 — were in effect British championships, and Celtic by winning all three established a remarkable record that no other club can match. Still, football is about matches played, goals scored, and men who performed, not about silver in cabinets polished once a month. It is the Celtic historian's pleasant task to recreate as far as possible the events behind these one-off trophies.

Surprisingly, Celtic were not the original winners of the Glasgow Exhibition Trophy, Rangers defeating them in the 1901 final, a controversial match marred by allegations of rough play and incompetent refereeing. The Ibrox side was so pleased with the handsome appearance of the trophy that it was immediately insured for £100, a considerable amount for the time. In April, 1902, one of the most horrible moments in British sport occurred at Ibox Park when part of the new wooden terracing, built in haste for the Scotland-England international, collapsed killing 25 people and injuring another 512, many of them seriously. In order to raise money to help compensate the victims Rangers decided to put up the trophy in competition with a select field; Rangers and Sunderland were the league champions, while Celtic and Everton were the runners-up. There was a feeling that the trophy should be renamed the British League Cup, and certainly the

458

Scottish press felt that the tournament was of the highest importance, the *Glasgow Herald* indicating its prestige by headlining the report of the last game, "British Championship Final Tie". The winning club was to receive the magnificent trophy, and the players were to receive gold badges, a gift from Bovril Limited (an indication that sponsorship is nothing new in football).

The tournament got underway on 30 April, 1902, when Celtic faced the English champions, Sunderland, at Celtic Park. Sunderland with one exception, fielded their regular team that included nine Scots, but Celtic were unimpressed, winning easily by 5-1. On the next day Rangers confronted Everton at Liverpool and the match finished 1-1 after extra time. The replay took place two days later at Celtic Park and Rangers won 3-2, a splendid result as four of the Ibrox side were absent on international duty for Scotland.

The final between Celtic and Rangers was held at Cathkin Park on 17 June before a crowd estimated at 7,000.

> *Celtic*: McPherson, Watson, Battles, Loney, Marshall, Orr, Crawford, Campbell, Quinn, McDermott, Hamilton.
> *Rangers*: Dickie, Smith N., Crawford, Gibson, Stark, Robertson, Lennie, Walker, Hamilton, Speedie, Smith A.

Rangers, back to full strength, had a formidable side, taking the field as clear favourites. Celtic were still in a transitional stage, and made one change from the team that beat Sunderland, Quinn moving into centre forward from his more regular spot on the left wing.

It turned into a typical 'Old Firm' match, neither side yielding an inch and the score at the end of 90 minutes was a 2-2 deadlock. Both Celtic's goals had been scored by young Quinn who troubled Rangers' defence with his powerful running and boundless energy; only two minutes from the end of the extra time he netted the winner, a close-in shot after a corner from Crawford that had been forced by Loney.[2]

Celtic placed the trophy in the Parkhead boardroom, apparently to the surprise and chagrin of Rangers who for some reason had expected it to be returned to Ibrox at the conclusion of the tournament. Several times in the next few years, up to the outbreak of World War I in 1914, the Rangers' directors approached Celtic asking that the trophy be put up for competition again, and Celtic's refusal was the source of some friction between the clubs.

Throughout the summer of 1938 the Empire Exhibition was held in Glasgow at the Bellahouston Park, and the authorities decided that a knock-out tournament featuring the best Scottish and English sides would be a fine attraction. Celtic, Rangers, Aberdeen and Hearts were invited from Scotland; Everton, Brentford, Chelsea and Sunderland came from England. All the ties were to be played at Ibrox Stadium, the closest ground to the site of the Exhibition, and the trophy was to be a replica in silver of the tower that symbolised the Exhibition.

Celtic, the Scottish champions, and star-filled Everton were the favourites on current form, but the other teams were formidable opposition. Aberdeen had a solid defence, and young George Hamilton up front; Hearts had six 'caps', four of whom were in defence and two at inside-forward, Tommy Walker and Andy Black; Rangers, playing at home, were bound to be eager to make up for a disappointing season. Brentford fielded Joe Crozier who was to play for Scotland in wartime and Gerry McAloon, later transferred to Celtic; Sunderland had the most feared inside forward in England, Horatio Carter, so often Stanley Matthews' partner; Chelsea provided interest with their Anglo-Scots, Jackson, formerly Thistle's keeper, and Craig, Motherwell's unlucky defender in 1931, but it was the powerful Everton squad that intrigued the fans. The Liverpool side had such depth that it fielded internationalists from all four home countries: Sagar, Mercer, Cunliffe, Lawton, Boyes and Geldard for England; Cook and Stevenson for Ireland; Jones for Wales, and Gillick for Scotland.

More than 55,000 saw the opening game on 25 May between Celtic and Sunderland which finished in a 0-0 draw, Celtic being a shade fortunate to hang on against a side that improved in the second half and dominated the last 15 minutes against a Celtic team weakened by injury. Only steady defensive work by Lyon, helped by reliable goalkeeping from Kennaway, kept the English side from advancing.

Celtic had to make changes for the replay the following night. Matt Lynch replaced Delaney while Malcolm MacDonald came in for Carruth, the regular right wing having been hurt in the first game. Despite the driving rain that quickly made the turf treacherous, Sunderland started where they had left off and Kennaway had to turn a glorious drive from Carter over the bar and to save at point-blank range from Burbank before Saunders gave Sunderland a deserved lead after 30 minutes. Celtic were stung into action and rallied immediately; eight minutes later Crum shot quickly on the turn to surprise the English defence and equalise. Early in the second half Divers scored twice within a few minutes, the first after patented, rapid interchanging with Crum and MacDonald had left him in the clear ten yards out, and the second after he coolly evaded Sunderland's offside trap to chip the ball over Mapson's head and into the net off the far post.

In the other ties Aberdeen thrashed Chelsea 4-0, Hearts edged Brentford 1-0 although outplayed for the whole second half, and Everton lived up to their reputation by winning easily by 2-0 against Rangers and playing delightful football after Lawton scored the second goal.

In the semi-finals Celtic lined up against Hearts, and Everton faced

Aberdeen. Once more the favourites scraped through, but both could consider themselves a little fortunate to survive. For more than an hour Hearts held the advantage over Celtic, but could not find a way past a resolute defence inspired by Kennaway who fielded the ball impeccably; after 65 minutes Celtic broke away and Crum, always an opportunist, snapped up a half-chance to the vast relief of Celtic's support among the 48,000 crowd. In the Everton-Aberdeen clash both sides staged a see-saw battle from the opening minute when Gillick put Everton ahead until the last when Lawton, a magnificent header of the ball, rose to a cross from Mercer to flick the winner past Johnstone for a 3-2 victory.

And so the final that everybody had wanted was played on 10 June, 1938, between two teams of equal ability and similar styles; both Celtic and Everton kept the ball on the ground, were constructive at wing-half, played solidly at the back and when on the attack were capable of inspired improvisation.

The crowd awaited the outcome of off-field developments with interest. The referee was selected by the toss of a coin, Mr. T. Thomson (Northumberland) being the choice over P. Craigmyle (Aberdeen) and he was later universally praised for his performance. The reserve strength of the English side was shown when Gillick had to withdraw, his place being taken by Geldard, another recent 'cap'. Celtic's hopes were raised by the return of Delaney on the right wing, to the disappointment of Lynch, whose name had already been printed on the programme.

Everton: Sagar, Cook, Greenhalgh, Mercer, Jones, Thomson, Geldard, Cunliffe, Lawton, Stevenson, Boyes.

Celtic: Kennaway, Hogg, Morrison, Geatons, Lyon, Paterson, Delaney, MacDonald, Crum, Divers, Murphy.

The final, watched by a crowd of 82,000, was a fitting climax to the series: "a game of sustained interest, played at a tremendous pace . . . and at times intense excitement." (*Glasgow Herald*: 11 June, 1938.) Celtic's attacks were direct and sharp, the inside forwards interchanging rapidly and shooting often; Delaney and Murphy chased every ball . . . but each attack was thwarted by the constructive Mercer and solid Welshman Jones, a most reliable centre-half. Everton were equally direct, with Lawton the chief menace on the ground and in the air; although Lyon was steady and resolute in marking him, Kennaway had to make one daring save at the centre's feet to avert a certain goal.

Despite the end-to-end pressure on them, the defences remained intact and the final moved into extra time, during which Everton were handicapped by an injury to Cunliffe, who moved out to the wing. Celtic pressed home the advantage. Jones had to clear one shot from the line with Sagar stranded far from the goal, but a goal had to come. Once again it was the alert Crum who netted the winner from a cute Divers'

461

flick after seven minutes of extra time, a powerful drive from 15 yards that the gallant Sagar touched but could not hold. In a rare display of public emotion of its type for 1938 Crum raced behind the goal to acknowledge the cheers of the supporters with a victory dance.

The Glasgow Charity Cup committee made hasty arrangements to join in the celebrations that marked the end of World War II in Europe. Celtic and Rangers were invited to participate in a challenge match for a trophy, the Victory-in-Europe Cup, with the proceeds going to charity. Rangers turned down the invitation, seemingly unwilling to jeopardise their chances in a Southern League Cup final later in the same week against Motherwell. At very short notice, and in the best spirit of their tradition, a youthful Queen's Park side replaced them and on 9 May, 1945 faced this Celtic team: Miller, Hogg, McDonald P., Lynch, Mallan, McPhail, Paton, MacDonald M., Gallacher, Evans, McLaughlin. The weather was fine, a large crowd turned up, the charities benefited, and the game was a spirited contest, described in the *Evening Times* as "a breath of fresh air." Celtic finally won, but only by the narrowest of margins, one goal and three corners to one goal and two corners, with Celtic's goal scored by Paton.

Upon the triumphant return from a North American tour that followed the Scottish Cup win of 1951, the club took part in a unique tournament initiated by Glasgow Corporation as a contribution to the Festival of Britain. Arranged along cup lines the tourney involved all the Division A teams (the Division B sides participated in the Quaich, which was won by Dumbarton) and the first round was scheduled for 14 July, the Saturday of the Glasgow Fair. On the date chosen the weather throughout Scotland was glorious and more than 172,000 watched the eight ties, the visit of Hearts to Celtic Park attracting 51,000 while 35,000 watched Rangers at Pittodrie against Aberdeen. Celtic, match-fit after the tour, were too fast and well-conditioned for Hearts, the score of 2-1 flattering the Edinburgh side. Celtic's goals were scored by McPhail and Jimmy Walsh, a red-haired youngster from Bo'ness United making his debut at inside-right; Aberdeen, helped by ex-Celt Jimmy Delaney, eliminated Rangers by the same score. An interesting feature of the second round was that the games were played on neutral grounds, and Celtic played Clyde at Firhill in a thriller that ended in a 4-4 draw, leaving 29,000 spectators utterly drained. Clyde, recently relegated to Division B, barely survived Celtic's opening flurry of attacks, but after only 15 minutes led by 2-0; both goals were scored by Linwood, a deadly scorer when he played for St. Mirren and Hibs, one a neat header in a breakaway and the other a long-range shot that deceived Hunter in Celtic's goal.

Until half-time Miller, Celtic's former keeper, defied his erstwhile mates with a gallant display that was helped by post and crossbar. Within nine minutes of the restart Celtic had pulled level; a fierce drive from Walsh was diverted past Miller by Haddock, and Collins rammed home a penalty two minutes later. Clyde, however, refused to wilt and took the game to Celtic with clever forward play; in 18 minutes young Tommy Ring restored Clyde's lead, and Robertson added to the lead shortly afterwards. Celtic appeared a beaten side, but Evans and Baillie urged on their forwards again and again, forcing Clyde to concede corner after corner. With eight minutes left to play, McPhail headed in a cross from Baillie, colliding at the same time with Miller, who required prolonged attention from the trainer. Celtic, upon the resumption, intensified the pressure. Shots rained in on Miller, still obviously semi-dazed, and with only one minute left Collins equalised in a goalmouth scramble.

Celtic made several changes for the replay, but one was significant: Sean Fallon moved up to centre-forward from full-back to replace McPhail, who had returned from the tour overweight and slow. The Irishman proved to be a difficult forward to contain, his odd, clever touches unsettling defences as much as his customary rampaging style; he netted twice in the replay with firmly hit shots from the edge of the area to lead the side to a convincing 4-1 win.

Raith Rovers were the opponents in the semi-final at Hampden and Celtic ran out comfortable winners by 3-1, Jimmy Walsh scoring all three goals. Tully, as he had done in the previous March's Scottish Cup semi-final, tormented the Fifers' defenders in a vintage performance to set up the chances for Walsh. In the other semi-final at Celtic Park Aberdeen and Hibernian fought out a 1-1 draw in a bad-tempered game; Aberdeen won the toss for the replay and used home ground advantage to eke out a 2-1 win. The final was played at Hampden on 1 August, 1951, before a crowd of 81,000 spectators:

> *Aberdeen*: Martin, Emery, Shaw, Harris, Thomson, Lowrie, Bogan, Yorston, Hamilton, Baird, Hather.
> *Celtic*: Hunter, Haughney, Rollo, Evans, Mallan, Baillie, Collins, Walsh, Fallon, Peacock, Tully.

Aberdeen quickly established control, pressing from the opening whistle. After 14 minutes Celtic suffered a double blow when Hunter, scrambling along his line to deal with a George Hamilton header, crashed into the post, leaving Yorston free to hook the ball into the unguarded net; the keeper was forced to retire for treatment and his place was taken by Evans. Following the return of Hunter to goal with head bandaged and of Evans to right-half, Celtic raged into attack, but Aberdeen broke away after 35 minutes for Bogan, himself an ex-Celt, to score with a spectacular shot on the run.

For the third time in the tournament Celtic found themselves two goals down, and for the third time rallied. With one minute left in the first half, Tully wandered over to the right in search of the ball and gained a throw in near the corner flag. He promptly converted it into a corner by cheekily playing the ball off Shaw's back as the defender retreated. Shaw was ruffled at the tactic and protested, but the referee, J.A. Mowat, generally considered Scotland's strictest, saw nothing wrong and awarded the corner; Tully took the corner, placing it accurately for Fallon to score an important goal.

The second half belonged to Celtic. Evans and Baillie, with their jerseys flapping outside their shorts in a mannerism picked up on the American tour to combat the heat, directed the one-way traffic with a stream of telling passes. Tully, visibly elated with the success of his throw-in gambit, caused all sorts of bother for Aberdeen's defence.

Early in the half Fallon broke through to equalise, and Celtic set out for the winner. That goal came 20 minutes from the end and it was engineered by Tully; he picked up a neat pass from Baillie, slipped past the hard-tackling Emery, released the ball to Peacock and, catching the return pass right on the by-line, crossed for Walsh to score. Aberdeen defenders protested mildly that Tully had allowed the ball to cross the line first, but referee and linesman, both in perfect position, disagreed with them. Celtic continued to press until the end, several times coming close to increasing the lead.

A dispute arose over the St. Mungo Cup itself, a row that in retrospect has its comical side. The Lord Provost presented the trophy to Celtic at a ceremony at the Kelvin Hall, and the late-Victorian silver cup, replete with the traditional symbols of Glasgow's patron saint, the bell, the bird, the tree and the salmon, was admired by all. After a Celtic director was mortified to find one of the salmon, doubling as a handle, coming away in his hand, some doubts were expressed about the exact pedigree of the trophy; the doubts were confirmed by a silversmith's inspection that revealed it to be second-hand. Originally crafted in 1894 for a yachting competition, it had been altered in 1912 for presentation to Provan Gas Works after defeating Glasgow Police at football. At first, Celtic wanted a new and more fitting trophy, offering to pay for one out of the club's share of the proceeds. A chilly exchange of letters between Celtic's chairman and the Lord Provost surfaced in the *Glasgow Herald*, and the matter was never fully resolved, but to this day the St. Mungo Cup remains at Celtic Park as a tangible memory of splendid football in the summer of 1951.

Two years later football joined in the celebrations for the coronation of Queen Elizabeth II when eight clubs, representing Scotland and England, were invited to play in another knock-out tournament in Glasgow: Rangers, Aberdeen, Hibernian and Celtic from Scotland, while Arsenal, Tottenham Hotspur, Manchester United and Newcastle United from England were invited to participate.

Celtic were ill-prepared for the Coronation Cup, having just completed a disastrous season, and clearly the invitation owed more to crowd-pulling power and a fine record in past tournaments of this type than to current form (indeed, there were suggestions that the club withdraw to avoid humiliation). There were problems in both defence and attack: Hunter had struggled to regain his confidence after a long illness and was replaced in goal by Bonnar, who had never been noted for consistency. McPhail was still the team's best centre-forward despite his lack of pace, but he had established himself as a very capable left-half and his successors did not inspire confidence — John McGrory chased every ball, and scored some goals, but he was cumbersome in the extreme, Sean Fallon was effective until his shock value wore off rapidly, and Jimmy Walsh, despite his promise, was more valuable at inside-right. The obvious solution was to buy a centre of proven worth, and the club eventually signed Neil Mochan from Middlesbrough in time to play in the final of the Charity Cup against Queen's Park; ironically, this prolific scorer and favourite with the fans was never fully recognised as a player by Bob Kelly and in later seasons was frequently dropped from the side.

465

Off the field financial problems had to be ironed out. Under the terms of the tournament the participating players were to receive £10 per game, a scurvy reward for competitive matches in the close season. Out of the gate receipts the competing clubs were to receive 25%, and the remaining 50% was to go to selected charities: the King George VI Memorial Fund, the National Playing Fields Association, and the Central Council of Physical Recreation. The English and Scottish Players Unions eventually petitioned the Ministry of Labour for better terms, and since the total attendance for the eight ties came to 440,526 they had a legitimate case. As with the other clubs, Celtic's players met to discuss the situation, but when the directors heard of the meeting the chairman took the unprecedented step of interviewing each recognised first-team player personally to satisfy himself that the man was ready and willing to play. Years later a story surfaced about the financial arrangements. Apparently when the organising committee was holding a last-minute meeting to iron out the remaining details, a communication was received by them to the effect that the final would not be played unless some readjustment of the players' remuneration was made; needless to say the match was played, the subsequent agreement remaining secret.

However, the other teams in the Coronation Cup had earned their invitations through merit: Rangers had just won the 'double', Hibernian had finished a close second in the league, while Aberdeen had taken Rangers to a replay in the cup final; Arsenal were the current English league champions, Manchester United and Tottenham Hotspur had won the title in the two previous seasons, while Newcastle United was the most feared side, having won the FA cup in 1951 and 1952.

Because of an English tour of South America there were some prominent absentees, but enough stars appeared to make it an intriguing competition. The Scottish fans expected great things from the Anglo-Scots in their club colours, players such as Ronnie Simpson, Frank Brennan and Bobby Mitchell of Newcastle United, and stormy Alec Forbes of Arsenal . . . and they looked forward to seeing famed English internationalists, Joe Mercer of Arsenal, Eddy Baily of Tottenham Hotspur, John Aston, Roger Byrne, Allenby Chilton and Stan Pearson of Manchester United, the near-legendary centre forwards Jackie Milburn of Newcastle and Jack Rowley of Manchester United . . . but perhaps the most intriguing of all was Manchester United's skipper, Johnny Carey, who had been selected to captain the Rest of Europe side at Hampden in 1947, an honour probably bestowed in recognition of his diplomatic skills honed in representing both Northern Ireland and the Republic.

In the opening round Hibernian and Tottenham Hotspur needed a replay before the Scots won 2-1, with Reilly netting the decisive goal in the dying seconds as he had done against England at Wembley a fortnight previously; Newcastle toyed with Aberdeen to win 4-0; Rangers scored early against Manchester United, but ran out of ideas to be outplayed in the second half, losing 2-1 . . . but the biggest shock was at Hampden on 11 May when Celtic played Arsenal.

Against Queen's Park in the Charity Cup Neil Mochan scored twice in a 3-1 win, but the Arsenal players who had watched the match left Hampden unworried about the forthcoming clash with Celtic. They were unwise to express their confidence to reporters, and Celtic's manager was astute enough to read the comments to his players before the match.

For the opening minute or so the 'Gunners' moved forward with a leisurely grace and precision that revealed total confidence bordering on arrogance. It was Bobby Evans who stepped in to halt this advance; he intercepted a pass, rounded an opponent, and swept a long, searching ball down the middle for Walsh whose shot hurtled just wide of the post. Celtic and all their supporters immediately realised that the Englishmen had been caught flat-footed and, to the roars of 59,000, Celtic moved into attack, playing with unaccustomed flair and with confidence increasing by the minute. In 24 minutes Bobby Collins scored directly from a corner, his swerving cross deceiving George Swindin, Arsenal's veteran keeper, and Celtic kept up the pressure on the Londoners' goal.

In the second half Arsenal rarely mounted a counter attack as Celtic hemmed them back into frantic defence for long periods. Evans and McPhail used the ball and the field superbly with crossfield passes, and probed the flanks for weaknesses. Mochan and Walsh troubled the Arsenal defence with their speed and readiness to shoot and indeed only superb goalkeeping by Swindin kept the score down to 1-0, having at one stage to dive gallantly at the feet of Celtic's full-back Alec Rollo to prevent another goal — and in 1953 full-backs did not overlap, and were conditioned not to cross the halfway line.

On Saturday, 16 May, the semi-finals were contested. At Ibrox Hibernian, with their famous forward line at its best, swamped Newcastle United, Turnbull scoring twice and Johnstone and Reilly once. At Hampden Celtic and Manchester United lined up before a crowd of 73,000.

> *Celtic*: Bonnar, Haughney, Rollo, Evans, Stein, McPhail, Collins, Walsh, Mochan, Peacock, Tully.
> *Manchester United*: Crompton, McNulty, Aston, Carey, Chilton, Gibson, Viollet, Downie, Rowley, Pearson, Byrne.

Helped by the stiff breeze, Celtic stormed United's goal for 20 minutes non-stop, gaining corner after corner. At last the opening goal came when Tully nimbly skipped past McNulty, then clipped the ball back to Peacock, racing in on the edge of the penalty area and the

Neil Mochan scoring against Manchester United in the semi-final of the Coronation Cup.

inside-man met the ball in full stride to find the net high up with a glorious shot. At half-time, though, the feeling was that a one-goal lead might not be enough against a strengthening wind and a team of United's reputation. Almost before the Englishmen had adjusted to the changeover, Mochan scored the decisive counter, but again it was Tully's skill that created the chance. Rollo sent a long clearance out of defence towards Tully who trapped and controlled the awkwardly bouncing and lively ball in one deft movement before lofting it over Chilton's head for the alert Mochan to race through from midfield and slip it past Crompton advancing from his goal.

A determined, late rally staged by United halted the premature celebrations, and Rowley snatched an opportunist goal near the end; in the dying moments Celtic barely held on and survived a claim for a penalty when Rollo armed the ball. The final was held on 20 May, 1953, with 108,000 packed into Hampden to see an all-Scottish final; shortly before the kick-off, gates were closed with an estimated 6,000 fans locked out because the Celtic end of the stadium was already dangerously overcrowded. Those unfortunates missed one of the most exciting matches in Celtic's history. Celtic had to make one change from the team that had eliminated the English sides, Tully being forced to withdraw after pulling a muscle in the semi-final and Fernie replaced him. Hibernian sent out the following: Younger, Govan, Paterson, Buchanan, Howie, Combe, Smith, Johnstone, Reilly, Turnbull, Ormond.

Urged on by the frantic roars from the crowd massed behind the goal at the King's Park end, Celtic pressed from the kick-off and Fernie repeatedly raced past Govan and other defenders in thrilling runs to panic the Edinburgh side; twice in the first ten minutes Younger had to dive daringly at his feet to save certain goals. A goal had to come, and after 28 minutes a well-directed clearance from Stein was flicked on by Fernie into Mochan's tracks; the centre chose the quickest way to goal and, as the Hibs' defenders closed in on him, he struck the most magnificent shot, a drive from fully 30 yards that Younger, already facing the evening sun, probably never saw. The Celtic following celebrated in typical fashion, exuberantly, noisily and long, but a minute from the interval Gordon Smith chilled them into silence when he carved the defence to create a chance for Reilly, with Bonnar producing a fine, diving save from the centre's header. It was a foretaste of the second half, the most enthralling, but almost certainly the longest and most agonizing, that Celtic supporters have ever had to endure. Hibs, with skilful wing-halves Buchanan and Combe moving forward to augment that magnificent forward line, threw everything into attack. It scarcely seemed possible that Celtic's defence could survive that onslaught, but the rearguard that night included several outstanding players and a much-maligned goalkeeper who was positively inspired.

Many supporters considered John Bonnar too small to be a dominating keeper and he was often criticised for his treatment of the cross ball, but in this second half he gave perhaps the finest performance ever given by a Celtic goalkeeper. His anticipation and daring averted certain goals when the Hibernian attackers broke through. Turnbull, a consistent scorer from dead-ball situations, fired in one free kick that the keeper did well to parry and by the time he had gathered the rebound a split-second later he found the keeper smothering the attempt at his feet; Johnstone and Reilly, so deadly from close range, could only watch in wonder as the goalkeeper seemed to change direction in mid-air to thwart their headers; Smith, playing on the keeper's lack of height, sent over dangerous crosses to see Bonnar pick them cleanly out of the air or scrape them away to safety with his fingertips. Packed behind the goal the Celtic supporters roared their approval time after time. Only once was he beaten, by a cunning shot from Johnstone, but McPhail had stationed himself alertly on the line to head it out. McPhail at left-half had played splendidly throughout the tournament, his clever distribution leading to many dangerous attacks. Beside him Stein was as solid as a rock, giving Reilly no opportunity for last-minute heroics; but the one Celt who put the seal of greatness on a splendid career was Bobby Evans, for so many seasons the outstanding player in Celtic teams. During the three ties Evans dominated his area of the field defensively, helped elsewhere when needed, and joined in attack enthusiastically. Three minutes from the end of the final, as Hibs still pressed furiously for the equaliser, once more it was Evans who intercepted a pass and moved upfield to release Fernie in the attack that led to Walsh scoring the second goal. In the Coronation Cup of 1953, when some Celts had their finest hour and when the best teams and players in Britain were gathered to compete, Bobby Evans was the most complete footballer in view — as always.

Notes

1 The trophy room at Celtic Park is designated the Presidential Room.
2 This match has sometimes been confused with the later match for the disaster fund played at Hampden Park on 20 August, 1902, in which Celtic trounced Rangers by 7-2, Quinn again scoring a hat trick.

EPILOGUE

IN a year's time, on 6 November, 1987, Celtic should celebrate their centenary. It will have been a century filled with drama and colour, with glorious victories and honourable defeats, with magnificent teams and memorable individuals; it will have been a century permeated with an indomitable spirit, allied to rare skills, and for followers of the sport and the club's supporters a source of satisfaction and pride. In an age of general apathy the passion of Celtic supporters shines like a beacon.

It will mark a record of accomplishment in Scottish football second to none, and an unrivalled reputation for entertaining play. It will be a time for congratulation and for reflection on a glorious contribution to the British game, but it must be seen also as an opportune moment to consider the future with a view to ensuring that the club moves into the second century with the same boldness, vigour and enterprise that animated the founders back in 1887; no room exists for complacency in the uncertain world of modern football. Today, it is imperative to satisfy heightened expectations in playing standards and spectator comfort. Football clubs require positive leadership and a sense of purpose to prosper and to survive.

So, what does the future hold for Celtic? The accomplishments of the past will be matched only if the club has learned from the past. Celtic would be wise to retain those traditions that have enhanced the club, and helped to make it a force in Scottish football; it must jettison those outdated and parochial attitudes which have hindered it — that lingering sense of insecurity in relationships with the Press and the football authorities, and a generally conservative approach to ground development, organisation and public relations.

If the immediate task is to re-establish the club as a genuine European force, and at the same time cope with the domestic ambitions of the 'New Firm' and the perennial challenge of Rangers, anticipating a revitalisation with the recent appointment of Graeme Souness as player-manager, Celtic supporters will expect a dynamic outlook and forceful direction on the part of the club to gear itself up for an even greater challenge in the coming decades should one vision of "Football 2000" prove to be accurate: ". . . a 16-strong British Football League,

471

including the top teams from Scotland, dealing directly with BBC and ITV and the new cable and satellite networks, at the top of a vast thriving pyramid of feeder leagues. This, at least, really is a Super League — a concept fully familiar to the United States, where the National Football League has a sports package geared to the age of family audiences, television, video, and advertising." (*Sunday Times*: 17 November, 1985.) The proposed British Cup competition, whose advocates envisage coming to fruition in 1987-88, may be the harbinger of this new age.

Will Celtic, the most renowned cup team in British football, be ready?

Index